Oxford Archaeological Guides
General Editor: Barry Cunliffe

Greece

Christopher Mee was formerly Assistant Director of the British School at Athens, and is now Professor of Classical Archaeology at the University of Liverpool. He specializes in the prehistory of Greece and has directed field projects in Laconia and on the Methana peninsula.

Antony Spawforth was formerly Assistant Director of the British School at Athens, and is now Professor of Ancient History and Greek Archaeology at Newcastle University and Curator of the Shefton Museum of Greek Art there. His publications include the new edition of the *Oxford Classical Dictionary* (1996) which he co-edited, and *The Oxford Companion to Classical Civilization* (1998); he also co-authored *Hellenistic and Roman Sparta: A Tale of Two Cities* (1989). He is a well-known presenter of television programmes in the BBC series 'Ancient Voices'.

Barry Cunliffe is Professor of European Archaeology at the University of Oxford. The author of over forty books, including *The Oxford Illustrated Prehistory of Europe* and *The Ancient Celts*, he has served as President of the Council for British Archaeology and the Society of Antiquaries, and is currently a member of the Ancient Monuments Board of English Heritage.

Oxford Archaeological Guides

Rome	Amanda Claridge
Scotland	Anna and Graham Ritchie
The Holy Land	Jerome Murphy-O'Connor
Spain	Roger Collins
Southern France	Henry Cleere
Greece	Christopher Mee and Antony Spawforth

FORTHCOMING

England	Timothy Darvill, Jane Timby, and Paul Stamper
Western Turkey	Hazel Dodge
Ireland	Conor Newman and Andy Halpin
Crete	Colin MacDonald and Sara Paton

Greece

An Oxford Archaeological Guide

Christopher Mee & Antony Spawforth

UNIVERSITY PRESS

OXFORD
UNIVERSITY PRESS

Great Clarendon Street, Oxford OX2 6DP

Oxford University Press is a department of the University of Oxford.
It furthers the University's objective of excellence in research, scholarship,
and education by publishing worldwide in
Oxford New York

Athens Auckland Bangkok Bogotá Buenos Aires Cape Town
Chennai Dar es Salaam Delhi Florence Hong Kong Istanbul Karachi
Kolkata Kuala Lumpur Madrid Melbourne Mexico City Mumbai Nairobi
Paris São Paulo Shanghai Singapore Taipei Tokyo Toronto Warsaw
with associated companies in Berlin Ibadan

Oxford is a registered trade mark of Oxford University Press
in the UK and in certain other countries

Published in the United States
by Oxford University Press Inc., New York

© Christopher Mee and Antony Spawforth 2001

All rights reserved. No part of this publication may be reproduced,
stored in a retrieval system, or transmitted, in any form or by any means,
without the prior permission in writing of Oxford University Press,
or as expressly permitted by law, or under terms agreed with the appropriate
reprographics rights organizations. Enquiries concerning reproduction
outside the scope of the above should be sent to the Rights Department,
Oxford University Press, at the address above

You must not circulate this book in any other binding or cover
and you must impose this same condition on any acquirer

British Library Cataloguing in Publication Data
Data available

Library of Congress Cataloging in Publication Data
Data available

ISBN 0-19-288058-6

1 3 5 7 9 10 8 6 4 2

Typeset by RefineCatch Limited, Bungay, Suffolk
Printed by Book Print S.L., Barcelona, Spain

Contents

Acknowledgements	xi
How to use this Guide	xii
Introduction	1
Environment and Ecology	1
Geology	1
Communications	2
Resources	3
Climate	4
Traditional Agriculture	5
The Countryside in Antiquity	5
The Impact of Agriculture on the Landscape	7
Historical Overview	8
The Palaeolithic, Neolithic, and Bronze Ages	8
The Geometric and Archaic Periods	10
The Classical Period	11
The Hellenistic Period	13
The Late Roman Republic and the Pax Romana	14
Greece in Late Antiquity	16
Warfare and Defence	17
Residential Space	20
Waterworks	23
The Agora and Gymnasium	25
Gods and their Sanctuaries	28
Competitions	34
The Greek Way of Death	36
Ancient Travellers and Tourists	42
Athens, Attika, and the Saronic	45
Athens	46
Akropolis	47
West of the Akropolis	58

Contents

    South Slope of the Akropolis — 61
    Agora — 65
    Roman Agora and Library of Hadrian — 73
    Olympieion — 76
    Kerameikos — 79
    National Museum — 84
    Epigraphic Museum — 90
    Numismatic Museum — 91
Piraeus — 91
Sounion — 96
Thorikos — 101
Laurion — 104
Brauron — 110
Marathon — 114
Rhamnous — 119
Amphiareion — 123
Phyle — 127
Eleutherai — 131
Aigosthena — 133
Eleusis — 136
Aigina — 142

Corinth and Environs — 149
Corinth — 149
Acrocorinth — 157
Isthmia — 159
Kenchreai — 163
Lechaion — 165
Diolkos — 166
Perachora — 167
Sikyon — 171

Argolid — 174
Nemea — 174
Mycenae — 178
Argos — 187

Argive Heraion	194
Nafplion	197
Tiryns	199
Dendra and Midea	202
Epidauros	205
Troizen	212
Lerna	214
Astros and Loukou	217
Lakonia	219
Sparta	220
Menelaion	225
Pellana	229
Amyklai and Vapheio	230
Epidauros Limera	231
Gytheion	233
Diros	233
Tainaron	234
Messenia	237
Kalamata	238
Pylos	238
Koryphasion and Voidokoilia	240
Pylos Palace and Chora Museum	241
Peristeria	245
Messene	246
Arkadia	253
Tripolis	253
Tegea	254
Mantineia	258
Orchomenos	261
Lousoi	263
Megalopolis	265
Lykosoura	268
Bassai and Phigaleia	270

Contents

    Lepreon   274
    Alipheira   277
    Gortys   280

Achaia and Elis   284
    Olympia   284
    Elis   294
    Patras   296
    Aigeira   298

Central Greece and Euboia   301
    Delphi   302
    Thebes   315
    Plataia   317
    Chaironeia   319
    Orchomenos   321
    Gla   323
    Ptoion   326
    Thermopylai   329
    Chalkis   330
    Eretria   331
    Lefkandi   337

Akarnania and Aitolia   342
    Stratos   343
    Oiniadai   345
    Pleuron   347
    Kalydon   350
    Thermon   353

Thessaly and Environs   358
    Volos   359
    Dimini   362
    Sesklo   365
    Velestino   367
    Demetrias   369

Nea Anchialos	372
Lamia	373
Epeiros	375
Ioannina	375
Dodona	376
Nekyomanteion	382
Kassope	384
Nikopolis	389
Macedonia	394
Thessaloniki	395
Olynthos	400
Torone	404
Amphipolis	407
Kavala	412
Philippi	413
Thasos	419
Aliki	425
Pella	428
Lefkadia	431
Veroia	434
Vergina	434
Dion	439
Chronology	446
Glossary	448
Select Bibliography	451
Index	455

Acknowledgements

We owe a great debt to the British School at Athens, where we first met and collaborated as students in the 1970s. The then Director, Hector Catling, put us to work in the same trench in his excavations at the Menelaion, a site fondly included in this Guide, and we first came to grips with many of the other sites as lecturers in the 1970s and 1980s on courses run by the School. The project has been supported by our employers, the Universities of Liverpool and Newcastle respectively, who helped to facilitate our research trips to Greece (in 1997, 1998, and 1999). Tony Spawforth would like to thank the staff of the Hellenic and Roman Societies Library in Bloomsbury for creating such congenial conditions for research. At the Press we thank Shelley Cox and George Miller, Nancy-Jane Rucker, who edited the Guide, and Simon Pressey for the illustrations. We deeply appreciate help of various kinds from Bill Cavanagh, Jim Crow, John Davies, John Gowlett, Sally Waite, Susan Walker, Geoffrey Waywell, Penny Wilson-Zarganis, and C. K. Williams II. Special thanks go to Christa Mee and Lee Stannard for moral support and practical advice. Our greatest debt of all is to the legions of dedicated scholars, alive and dead, whose indispensable studies of Greece's archaeological sites have made this book both possible and a pleasure to write.

Chris Mee

Tony Spawforth

How to use this Guide

SCOPE

The focus of this Guide is ancient Greece, from the Palaeolithic period to the end of antiquity (C7 AD). This coverage reflects our combined knowledge of the prehistory and classical history and archaeology of Greece. We omit medieval and later Greece, because these equally fascinating periods require an expertise which we do not claim to have.

Within our chosen time-span the aim is to cover all sites of major archaeological interest in any one region of Greece, as well as those where the historical importance may outweigh the rather unimpressive archaeological remains, and some smaller sites which are easily accessible. We have excluded sites where we felt that the reward would not justify the journey involved except to a professional archaeologist. We cover the mainland only, except for offshore islands which are either extensions of the mainland (Euboia) or can be reached by short sea-crossings and are, in effect, day trips (Thasos and Aigina). With major sites, we have not aimed at exhaustive coverage, but offer a selective tour prejudiced by personal interests. At all times, we focus on what you can actually see. The Guide divides the sites regionally. A star indicates a site of exceptional importance which should not be missed.

'PARTNER' FACTOR

From personal experience we are both very conscious of the tedium which travelling companions can experience who do not share our love of ruins ('piles of stones'). We have done our best to counter this by constantly having in mind whether a site has additional attractions, such as a nice beach or seaside location, an agreeable walk to get there, or spectacular views. Sites satisfying one or more of these criteria (as many do in Greece) are flagged with a ★ symbol.

MUSEUMS

We have included archaeological museums of major importance and those which are readily accessible. We have omitted museums which require a long detour. Where a museum has adequate captions in English, we have simply commented on those items of outstanding interest. It should be pointed out that some of the museums which were closed for renovation when we visited Greece have now reopened, and conversely that some of the museums which we saw have been shut temporarily.

OPENING HOURS

Although we made a note of when museums and those sites which are fenced and have restricted access were open, we have decided not to include this information because the times frequently change, on a seasonal basis and for other reasons. You can expect that the sites and museums will be open from 0830–1500 every day except Monday, when they are likely to be closed. Some large sites and museums close later, especially in the summer, and may be open on Monday. 1 January, 25 March, Good Friday, Easter Sunday, and Christmas Day are public holidays.

DIRECTIONS

Except where sites are relatively easy to find, we have given quite detailed directions. Nevertheless, a good map of Greece is essential. We particularly like the recently published 1 : 250,000 *Road Editions*, which cover mainland Greece in five sheets. The maps are widely available in Greece and from specialist shops in the UK.

xiv **How to use this Guide**

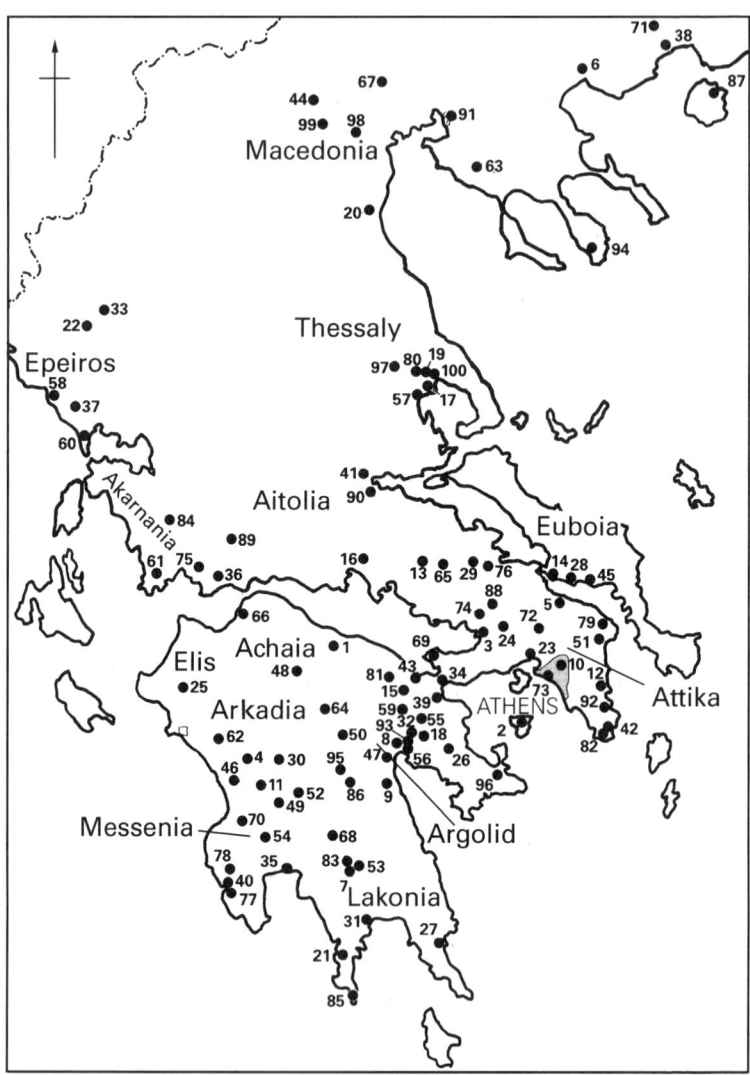

▲ Fig. 1. Map of Greece showing regions and locations of sites

1	Aigeira	51	Marathon
2	Aigina	52	Megalopolis
3	Aigosthena	53	Menelaion
4	Alipheira	54	Messene
5	Amphiareion	55	Mycenae
6	Amphipolis	56	Nafplion
7	Amyklai and Vapheio	57	Nea Anchialos
8	Argos	58	Nekyomanteion
9	Astros	59	Nemea
10	Athens	60	Nikopolis
11	Bassai	61	Oiniadai
12	Brauron	62	Olympia
13	Chaironeia	63	Olynthos
14	Chalkis	64	Orchomenos (Arkadia)
15	Corinth	65	Orchomenos (Boiotia)
16	Delphi	66	Patras
17	Demetrias	67	Pella
18	Dendra and Midea	68	Pellana
19	Dimini	69	Perachora
20	Dion	70	Peristeria
21	Diros	71	Philippi
22	Dodona	72	Phyle
23	Eleusis	73	Piraeus
24	Eleutherai	74	Plataia
25	Elis	75	Pleuron
26	Epidauros	76	Ptoion
27	Epidauros Limera	77	Pylos
28	Eretria	78	Pylos Palace
29	Gla	79	Rhamnous
30	Gortys	80	Sesklo
31	Gytheion	81	Sikyon
32	Heraion	82	Sounion
33	Ioannina	83	Sparta
34	Isthmia	84	Stratos
35	Kalamata	85	Tainaron
36	Kalydon	86	Tegea
37	Kassope	87	Thasos
38	Kavala	88	Thebes
39	Kenchreai	89	Thermon
40	Koryphasion	90	Thermopylai
41	Lamia	91	Thessaloniki
42	Laurion	92	Thorikos
43	Lechaion	93	Tiryns
44	Lefkadia	94	Torone
45	Lefkandi	95	Tripolis
46	Lepreon	96	Troizen
47	Lerna	97	Velestino
48	Lousoi	98	Vergina
49	Lykosoura	99	Veroia
50	Mantineia	100	Volos

For †Elizabeth and Hector Catling

Introduction

Environment and Ecology

The Greek landscape is dramatic, dominated by mountains and the sea. It is reckoned that only 20% of the country is flat and the mainland alone has over 4000 km. of coastline, more than Italy or Spain—mere statistics, but for the inhabitants of Greece vital statistics because the landscape has had a profound effect on their lives. In this section we will see how Greece was formed and how the Greeks have shaped and been shaped by their environment.

Geology

Geologically Greece is a young country. Most of the oldest rocks are in the north-east, in Macedonia and Thrace, and in southern Attika and the Cyclades. These rocks have been folded and altered by metamorphism into hard gneisses, schists, and, most importantly, marbles. In western and southern Greece the rocks are younger, mainly sandstones, marls and limestone, which is such a prominent feature of the landscape. These rocks were folded in a great arc around the older block of harder rocks at the time the Alps were formed. Subsequently the older and younger rocks were lifted by tectonic movements but the stresses and strains of this process caused faults and fractures. Because, in geological terms, much of this tectonic activity is recent, the jagged edges of the scarps have not been smoothed by erosion and so mountains, such as the Taygetos range which towers over Sparta, often rise abruptly from the plains.

Greece lies at the junction of two major tectonic plates, the Eurasian and the African. Because the African plate is being subducted under the Eurasian, this is a destructive plate margin marked by a volcanic island arc which runs from the peninsula of Methana in the Argolid, through Melos and Thera to the island of Nisyros in the eastern Aegean. Around 1600 BC Thera erupted spectacularly, an event which had serious environmental consequences and may well have weakened Minoan Crete. A more serious consequence of the geological instability of Greece has been the devastation caused by frequent earthquakes. Poseidon, the 'earth-shaker', was a god who quite justifiably inspired terror.

Volcanic eruptions and earthquakes can suddenly transform the landscape, but erosion, if more subtle, is no less potent. Water dissolves limestone and eventually produces the deep gorges, precipitous slopes, and gloomy caves typical of *karst* scenery. Alluvial deposition has

▲ Fig. 2. The Lakonia plain with Taygetos mountain range behind

completely altered the coastline in places. The Aliakmon and Axios rivers have filled in much of the gulf west of THESSALONIKI and 300 Spartans would no longer find it so easy to hold the pass at THERMOPYLAI. Elsewhere, because the sea-level has risen considerably since the last Ice Age, the coastline has receded and ancient harbours, such as KENCHREAI in the Corinthia, have been drowned. We should certainly not think of the landscape of Greece as static. When we look around us, we will not necessarily see what the ancient Greeks saw.

Communications

The mountainous terrain has a major impact on communications. The Pindos range runs like a spine down northern and central Greece, and the Peloponnese is also bisected by mountains. The passes which cross these mountains would often have been blocked by snow in winter and were difficult even in summer—the highest point on the Katara Pass between Thessaly and Epeiros is at 1707 m. Not that mountains need be a deterrent, as the Spartans demonstrated in the C8 BC when they conquered Messenia which is separated from Lakonia by the Taygetos range. Nevertheless, it is clear that the topography of Greece impeded political unification and fostered local independence and cultural diversity.

Few regions were entirely self-sufficient, however, and the sea offered additional resources which were soon exploited. As early as the 10th millennium BC, the inhabitants of the Franchthi Cave in the Argolid acquired obsidian, which they used for their chipped stone tools, from the island of Melos. The sea broadened horizons and ensured that the Greeks did not remain isolated from one another. Ultimately their ships reached the central and eastern Mediterranean and established the overseas contacts which would prove so fruitful. Yet the sea was not easily mastered. The numerous islands in the Aegean aided navigation and provided convenient landfalls but whipped up contrary winds and localized currents.

Resources

Journeys by sea could be hazardous. Nevertheless, the Greeks were dependent on maritime trade, especially for metals. The Mycenaean palaces required supplies of copper and tin for the production of bronze. Although some of the copper came from the mines in southern Attika, much was imported from Cyprus as there is no tin in the Aegean. Greece does have iron ore deposits but Italy became one of the main sources of iron once Greek settlers had arrived in the C8 BC. ATHENS benefited from the silver mines at LAURION and built the fleet which defeated the Persians in the battle of Salamis when a particularly rich vein was struck early in the C5 BC. Gold was mined in Macedonia and on Siphnos.

The other major mineral resource which Greece possesses is stone and in particular marble. Much of the marble used for sculpture came from Paros and Naxos in the Cyclades but the Athenians had their own quarries on Mt Pentelikon. There were also more exotic types of stone, such as Lakonian *lapis Lacedaemonius* (see THERMOPYLAI) and cipollino marble from Karystos, which the Romans prized.

Although it was undoubtedly useful that so much stone was available for construction, most Greeks would have settled for less bare rock and more agricultural land. Thessaly was certainly fertile and also Boiotia, even if Lake Kopais had not yet been drained (see ORCHOMENOS/GLA). But the Argive plain, cradle of the Mycenaean civilization, is at most 20 km. in length and the SPARTA plain is much the same size. No wonder the Spartans coveted fertile Messenia. The coastal plain of Elis has rich alluvial soils but north western Greece offers less scope for arable agriculture and was noted more for 'flocks of sheep and shambling cattle'.

Water is also scarce. The fame of Greek rivers can seem overstated at the height of the summer when they almost run dry, though their wide beds indicate the strength of the winter torrents. Rivers provide most water for northern and central Greece, in particular the Nestos in Thrace, the Strymon, Axios, and Aliakmon in Macedonia, the Peneios and the Spercheios in Thessaly, and the Acheloos in Aitolia, which was once navigable as far as STRATOS, 35 km. upstream. In the Peloponnese, only the Eurotas and the Alpheios could be described as major rivers.

Introduction

Climate

There is not much water in the rivers because most of Greece has a Mediterranean climate, warm wet winters and hot dry summers. The contrast between the seasons is summarized by Hesiod (*Works and Days* 543–58 and 582–92):

And when the chilly time approaches, stitch the hides of newborn kids with sinews from an ox into a cape to keep the rain off your back. A fitted cap of felt upon your head keeps your ears dry; when Boreas attacks the dawn is cold. From starry heaven at dawn a fruitful mist is spread upon the earth upon the lucky fields. The mist is drawn from ever-flowing rivers; stormy winds force it high above the earth; sometimes it falls as rain at evening, other times it turns to wind when Thracian Boreas stirs up the thick-massed clouds. Finish your work; get home ahead of him, so you will not be swallowed up in that black cloud from heaven and come home dripping with your clothing soaked. Be on your guard: this is the hardest month, stormy, hard on the stock and hard on men.

But when the thistle blooms and on the tree the loud cicada sits and pours his song shrill and continuous, beneath his wings, exhausting summertime has come. The goats are very fat, and wine is very good. Women are full of lust, but men are weak, their heads and limbs drained dry by Sirius, their skin parched from the heat. At this time, I love a shady rock, and Bibline wine, a cake of cheese, and goat's milk, and some meat of heifers pastured in the woods, uncalved, or first-born kids.

(translation Wender)

Hesiod lived in Boiotia which enjoys a true Mediterranean climate, though evidently he did not. He would have been mystified by the assertion that 'for those of normal constitution it is a tonic that tautens the sinews of body and mind'. Most of the rain falls in November, December, and January, almost none in June, July, and August. This is the climate of central Greece and the Peloponnese but there is more rain in the west than the east. Attika is particularly dry with less than 400 mm. of rain each year on average. Northern Greece has a modified Mediterranean climate in that the summer drought is not quite so severe. Nevertheless, it can be extremely hot in summer and cold in winter. Had Hesiod come from Larisa in Thessaly, his complaints would have been justified since temperatures of 44 °and -13 °centigrade have been recorded. Of course altitude is also a factor and in the mountains of northern Greece the climate is classified as continental, since it often rains in summer and there is snow in winter.

It is assumed that the climate was no different in the past, so the resources of our ancient Greek farmer consist of a field full of rocks and less water than he would like for his crops. Nature has another trick up her sleeve, because he cannot predict how much rain there will be and whether it will fall at the right time. The amount of rain can vary quite considerably, as Aristotle points out (*Meteorologica* 2.4):

> Sometimes drought or rain is widespread and covers a large area of country, sometimes it is only local. For often in the country at large the seasonal rainfall is normal or even above the normal, while in some districts there is drought. At other times, on the other hand, the rainfall in the country at large is meagre, or there is even a tendency to drought, while in a single district the rainfall is abundant in quantity.

Traditional Agriculture

In the days before state intervention and EC subsidies, how did farmers reduce risks and avoid starvation? Traditionally diversification has been seen as one solution. Farmers grew a range of crops and aimed at self-sufficiency. Because the next harvest might be disastrous, families would ideally have enough grain for two years and a supply of oil that would last four years, since the olive fruits biennially. If there was still a surplus, this could be traded but cash crops did not take priority. We also find that farmers did not cultivate a single block of land but had a number of plots which were often quite a distance apart. This is certainly inconvenient but scattered plots of land can minimize the risk of crop failure and may offer scope for diversification if they occupy different ecological niches.

The Countryside in Antiquity

The first farmers arrived in Greece in the Neolithic period (7000–3000 BC). Naturally they occupied the best agricultural land, which is why we find such a concentration of Neolithic sites in Thessaly. Over time the number of sites increased and also their size—this is especially true of SESKLO. More land was needed and improved techniques so that poorer soils could be successfully utilized. A simple type of plough was introduced; olives and vines were cultivated, as well as cereals and pulses, providing those essential ingredients of the Mediterranean diet, oil and wine; sheep and goats were raised as much for their milk and wool as their meat. In the Early Helladic period (3000–2000 BC), settlers spread across southern Greece and in due course created the economic conditions which the Mycenaean palaces exploited so effectively (1500–1200 BC). Then there is a decline in the level of activity in the countryside until the Classical period (480–323 BC) when rural sites proliferate.

These rural sites are also a feature of the Greek landscape in the Hellenistic and Roman periods (323 BC–AD 500). It is thought that they must have been farmsteads but we cannot tell whether they were occupied throughout the year or on a seasonal basis. Some may just have been storehouses but clearly more resources were being invested in the countryside.

Barley is not as nutritious as wheat but needs less water and was the staple cereal grown by most ancient Greek farmers. The Spartans dined on barley bread and barley stew in their communal messes. The fields were ploughed and cereals sown in the autumn, just before the winter rains. The harvest was in May or June. Once the cereals had dried out, they were threshed and winnowed. Most Greek cities had to import some of their grain. This was particularly true of Athens which relied on grain brought from the Black Sea.

We hear less about pulses—peas, beans, and lentils—but as a source of protein their role in the diet will have been important. Ancient agronomists realized that soil nutrients could be restored if cereals and pulses were alternated. There was also a system of bare fallow. Fields were left uncultivated but ploughed several times so that weeds could be kept down. On the golden shield which he made for Achilles, Hephaistos depicted (*Iliad* 18.541–9):

a large field of soft, rich fallow, which was being ploughed for the third time. A number of ploughmen were driving their teams across it to and fro. When they reached the ridge at the end of the field and had to wheel, a man would come up and hand them a cup of mellow wine. Then they turned back down the furrows and toiled along through the deep fallow soil to reach the other end. The field, though it was made of gold, grew black behind them, as a field does when it is being ploughed. The artist had achieved a miracle.

Olives, vines, and figs were usually cultivated on slopes, since they did not require as much soil as cereals. Theophrastus explains why (*De Causis Plantarum* 2.4.2–3):

Use your rich soils for grains and thin soils for trees. Grains and all other annuals take the nutriment from the surface soil, which therefore ought not to be thin or of a quality to be quickly exhausted, as happens in a shallow layer of earth. But trees, equipped with long and strong roots, draw their nourishment from the depths. In rich soils, trees run to wood and foliage, but yield little or no fruit. Hence a thin soil is superior from both standpoints; it produces a balanced foliage and fruitage.

(after Semple)

Olive trees mature slowly, though Hesiod exaggerates when he claims that a man who had planted an olive grove would not live to eat its fruit. Once productive, they did not make excessive demands on the farmer. The trees would be pruned in the winter and then tended occasionally. The olives were picked between November and January. The fruit was either pickled or crushed and pressed. Much of the oil was of course consumed but we must not forget that the Greeks also cleaned themselves and lit their lamps with oil.

Vines were much more labour intensive. The stocks were pruned in January or February and then the soil was constantly turned over, since this increases the amount of moisture which reaches the roots. The grapes were picked and pressed in September or October. Greece produced some fine wines. When Odysseus called on the Cyclops, a mistake since the giant thought that his companions had been brought along as snacks, he took 'a goatskin of dark and mellow wine' from Thrace which had to be diluted with twenty parts of water. The wines of THASOS, which were marketed so successfully in the Classical period, may have enjoyed a similar reputation.

Sheep and goats were grazed on arable land and consequently provided manure in return for their fodder. There was also plenty of rough pasture on the hills which could be used for larger flocks. The type of transhumance practised more recently by the Vlachs and Sarakatsani in northern Greece would not have been feasible, though some shepherds may have travelled quite a distance. Horses and cattle needed lusher pastures. Thrace, Thessaly, and Boiotia produced fine horses and the cattle bred in Epeiros were magnificent beasts.

The Impact of Agriculture on the Landscape

Agricultural terraces constitute one of the most visible and certainly laborious adaptations of the Greek landscape. It would appear that most of the terraces were built in the C19 or early C20 AD but they were not designed for tractors and so the less accessible have been abandoned. Unless the terrace wall collapses, the soil is not washed away and vegetation soon grows back. However, a more recent trend has seen bulldozers carve up hillsides and trigger erosion because the terraces have no protection from the elements. It is assumed that terraces were a feature of the ancient Greek landscape; yet they are seldom mentioned in our written sources and remain archaeologically elusive.

In the past Greece certainly had more woods but these disappeared as land was cleared for cultivation and trees were felled for timber. In this respect the landscape was different, if not quite as different as some have supposed. The character of the vegetation is determined by a number of factors. In central and southern Greece the climate favours drought-resistant species, whereas in the north there can be frost. The height above sea-level is also important. Trees on the lower slopes of the hills will usually be Aleppo pines, stone pines, or evergreen oaks. Higher up there are deciduous oaks, chestnuts, even beech trees, and at around 900 m. the firs and black pines of the coniferous belt. Few trees thrive above 1800 m.

Much of Greece is covered by *maquis* which can be impenetrable and thoroughly hostile. Typical *maquis* species include the prickly-oak, arbutus, laurel, broom, and myrtle. Where the *maquis* thins out, we find

▲ Fig. 3. Terraces on the Methana peninsula

phrygana, aromatic bushes such as cistus, origano, sage, and thyme. Shepherds graze sheep and goats on the *maquis* and *phrygana,* which does stunt the growth of some species. Goats in particular have been regarded as extremely destructive, though their reputation as the scourge of the Greek countryside is not entirely justified. In the summer the scrub-covered hillsides can look rather monotonous but you will see the most spectacular display of wild flowers if you visit Greece in the spring.

Historical Overview

The Palaeolithic, Neolithic, and Bronze Ages (350,000–1050 BC): From the First Settlers to the Age of the Heroes

The first humans arrived in Greece in the Lower Palaeolithic period. A skull from the Petralona Cave in Macedonia may be 350,000 years old and sites in Epeiros date from 200,000 BP (see IOANNINA). The Middle Palaeolithic (100,000–35,000 BP) settlers were Neanderthals who hunted deer and ibex in the mountains of northern Greece. Anatomically modern humans do not appear until the Upper Palaeolithic period (35,000–10,000 BP) when continental Europe was in the grip of the last Ice Age. As the ice sheets retreated, the climate became warmer and wetter, the sea-level rose and the landscape of Greece changed dramatically. Around 7000 BC the first farmers arrived, almost certainly from Turkey, and founded sites such as SESKLO in Thessaly. The crops and livestock which they introduced could support a much larger population than the hunter-gatherer lifestyle of their Palaeolithic predecessors and the number of sites increased rapidly over the course of the Neolithic period (7000–3000 BC). As communities grew in size, their internal organization developed in complexity. This is reflected in the architecture of Sesklo and DIMINI. There was also more contact between settlements.

In southern Greece there were fewer Neolithic sites. The Alepotrypa cave at DIROS in Lakonia is one of these. It was not until the end of the period that settlers spread across the Peloponnese. The rugged terrain, poor soils, and dry conditions presented a challenge which prompted a number of innovations. Hitherto most tools had been made of stone but in the Early Helladic period (3000–2000 BC), copper and then bronze became more common. Greece has sources of copper but not tin, the other constituent of bronze, which must have been acquired from overseas. The House of Tiles at LERNA in the Argolid and the White House at KOLONNA on AIGINA exemplify the sophisticated architecture of the Early Helladic period. Yet it is on Crete that the first palaces were built around 1900 BC, while Middle Helladic (2000–1600 BC) Greece seems remarkably impoverished by comparison. There is no obvious explanation for this decline which may have been caused by a combination of factors.

It was not until the end of the Middle Helladic period that the situation improved quite suddenly. In the shaft graves at MYCENAE some of the dead were literally covered in gold. Only rulers could have afforded such an ostentatious display of wealth, yet this was not simply conspicuous consumption. Those in power at Mycenae may not have felt entirely secure and needed to assert their authority. The same lavish treatment of the dead can be seen elsewhere in the Peloponnese at the start of the Late Helladic/Mycenaean period (1600–1050 BC), for example in the tholos tombs at VAPHEIO, PYLOS, and PERISTERIA. Except for the mansion at the MENELAION, the domestic architecture is much less impressive, although it is not out of the question that there were already palaces at Mycenae, Pylos, and TIRYNS. In the C16 and C15 BC Greece apparently consisted of a number of minor kingdoms whose rulers were fond of weapons and warfare. It is likely that they acquired some of their wealth through violence, although trade seems a better explanation for the close ties which developed with Crete. Nevertheless, the Mycenaeans may have been responsible for the destruction of the Minoan palaces in the C15 and certainly took control of Knossos subsequently.

The decline of the Minoan civilization benefited the Mycenaeans. In the C14 and C13 BC they settled on the islands and became much more involved in trade. Mycenaean pottery has been found on hundreds of sites in the eastern Mediterranean, in Italy and as far west as Spain. Diplomatic correspondence between Hittite and Mycenaean rulers is preserved in the archives of the Hittite capital at Boğazköy in central Turkey.

Although some magnificent tombs date from this period, such as the

Treasury of Atreus at Mycenae and the Treasury of Minyas at ORCHOMENOS, the construction of fortifications and palaces was evidently the main priority. Huge circuits were built at Mycenae, Tiryns, MIDEA, ATHENS, and GLA. Such an enormous investment of resources would make no sense if there were no threat but the fortifications were doubtless intended to impress as well as protect. Palaces have been excavated at Mycenae, Tiryns, Pylos, and THEBES. They were royal residences and also administrative centres. Clay tablets written in the Linear B script record the taxes which were paid to the palace in the form of agricultural produce. This was then used to support a labour force which manufactured bronzes, textiles, perfumes, and other luxuries. It is clear that the king of Pylos ruled the whole of Messenia but there were two palaces in the Argolid at Mycenae and Tiryns. In Boiotia Thebes and Orchomenos may have been rivals. It seems that Greece was still politically divided.

At the end of the C13 BC most of the major Mycenaean sites were destroyed and some, such as Pylos, were not reoccupied. A Dorian invasion from the north has been proposed. Alternatively the culprits may have been the mysterious Sea Peoples who attacked Egypt at this time. Yet there is no evidence that Greece had been invaded and it is thought that earthquakes caused some of the destructions. This catastrophe did have serious consequences, however. The political and economic system which the palaces had maintained was undermined and collapsed. There was depopulation and deprivation as Greece became more and more isolated. The Bronze Age had ended.

The Geometric and Archaic Periods (c. 1050–480 BC): The Emergence of the Greek City

From the style of pottery in general use over much of southern Greece, 'Geometric' is often used nowadays to designate the period c.1050–700 BC. Once an archaeological dark age, its early phases have been brightened by finds at LEFKANDI on Euboia (C11–C9 BC), revealing an early Iron-Age community with plentiful eastern contacts, able to build a precocious forerunner of Greek temple design. The C8 BC was a watershed, to which later Greek tradition assigned the first celebration of games at OLYMPIA (776 BC) and the first Greek settlements in Italy and the west. The earliest and greatest poetry in Greek literature, the epics of Homer, probably belong to this time, which saw the invention of the Greek alphabet, adapted from Semitic sources. Related to these developments was the emergence in central and southern Greece of the city-state (*polis*), typically a small, in origin agricultural, community occupying a given territory, with a central place or 'city', enjoying political independence and a strong separate identity. Many seem to have begun as a coalescence of separate villages, as at CORINTH and Athens.

Archaeologically perhaps the clearest sign of this momentous transformation is the appearance (C8 BC) of communal places of worship (see *The Gods and their Sanctuaries*), followed by temple-building, as at the ARGIVE HERAION or ERETRIA.

Temples, and the cult-statues inside them, were ideas probably borrowed by Greeks from the Near East, like the alphabet. This early Greek debt to the east emerges clearly too in the arts of the C7 BC, when Greek craftsmen adopted eastern techniques and styles, including (probably from Egypt) stone architecture and monumental marble sculpture. Here the significance of trade as a conduit for new ideas cannot be overemphasized. By 600 BC the Greeks were building specialized merchantmen and had founded trading stations in Egypt and Etruscan Italy. The stone haulway (DIOLKOS) across the Isthmus, built *c*.600 BC, reflects the strategic position of Corinth in this east–west trade.

The diolkos was probably the work of Periander, one of the usurpers called 'tyrants' who set up effective monarchies in many cities during the C7–C6 BC. Archaic tyrants had a later reputation for sponsoring civic building (see *Waterworks*), and some were credited with impressive gifts to the inter-state or panhellenic sanctuaries at Olympia and DELPHI, home of the most important Greek oracle. These sanctuaries were the glories of the Archaic age, their remains perhaps the most eloquent witness nowadays to the increasing wealth and artistry of the Greeks at this time.

Lavish dedications at panhellenic sanctuaries were a peaceful outlet for the inter-city rivalries of the Archaic Greek states. But these gifts were often funded by booty from the inter-city warfare increasingly endemic to Greek politics (see *Warfare and Defence*). By the later C6 BC superior force had allowed SPARTA to emerge as the leading power in the Peloponnese. Less embroiled in external ventures, Athens was distracted for much of the C6 BC by internal conflicts, prompting constitutional reforms (508/7 BC) which put her on the road to direct democracy.

People's power was the antithesis of the absolute monarchy practised by the ancient Persian kings, whose empire based on Iran had incorporated the Greek cities of western Turkey ('Ionia' in Greek parlance) from 546 BC. In 490 BC the Athenians beat off an attempted Persian landing at MARATHON. Nine years later, the Great King, Xerxes in person, led a full-scale Persian invasion of Greece. The Greek cities under Spartan leadership formed an alliance, and in two decisive battles, at Salamis (480 BC) and PLATAIA (479 BC), brought about a complete Persian withdrawal. This astonishing outcome, in which Athens played a key part, ushered in ancient Greece's golden age.

The Classical Period (479–338 BC): Imperial Cities

Victory over the Persians made a huge impression on the Greeks, fundamentally reshaping their views of themselves, and of 'barbarians', for centuries to come. A rash of monuments glorifying their success followed, such as the bronze tripod-monument at Delphi.

In 478 BC Athens took the first step towards creating something like an Athenian empire by assuming leadership of the Greek alliance, which now took the armed struggle against anti-Persian objectives as far as Egypt and Cyprus. Success depended on the allied fleet of triremes, war-galleys manned by Athenian rowers and based at PIRAEUS, where their shipsheds are still visible. After the original war-aims had receded by c.450 BC, Athens used force to maintain the membership and continued to collect allied tribute. Under the radical democracy promoted by the politician Perikles (died 429 BC), the Athenians funded (in part from the tribute, stored in Athens since 454 BC) an ambitious building programme, its centrepiece the Parthenon (447–432 BC). Athens now flourished as an innovative centre of Greek culture (see *Contests*), its prosperity reflected in public works not just in Athens (see *The Agora*) but also in the outlying villages or demes, such as RHAMNOUS and SOUNION.

Athenian power fuelled the suspicions of Sparta and her allies, prompting the great Peloponnesian War (431–404 BC), which ended in a decisive Spartan victory. Sparta now in turn became a (short-lived) imperial power, but her aggressive methods were unpopular, and in time provoked Thebes, which inflicted a shattering defeat on the Spartan army at Leuktra (371 BC). With Theban support, Peloponnesian geopolitics were now reversed with the liberation of the Spartan slave population (helots) in Messenia, reorganized into a heavily defended new city of MESSENE, and the creation of an anti-Spartan league of Arkadian cities, its capital at MEGALOPOLIS, another new city.

Meanwhile Macedonia, for southern Greeks a hitherto marginal area of dubious Greekness, was being transformed into a major military power under a dynamic hereditary king, Philip II (reigned from 359 BC). His gradual encroachments southwards provoked the polemic of ancient Greece's greatest orator, the Athenian politician Demosthenes, and, in 338 BC, a major battle with the allied Greeks led by Athens and Thebes at CHAIRONEIA. Philip's victory turned southern Greece into a Macedonian fiefdom, a state of affairs somewhat veiled by his creation of a unitary organization of Greek states based at Corinth. This league had just elected Philip commander of a planned invasion of the Persian empire when he was stabbed to death in the theatre at VERGINA, ancient Aigai (336 BC), leaving the overthrow of Persia to his son and successor, Alexander the Great. Philip's likely tomb at Vergina hints at the growing wealth and sophistication of the Macedonian elite at this time, as do the remains of the royal capital at PELLA, where grand palatial architecture now reappears in Greece for the first time since the Mycenaeans.

The Hellenistic Period (336–146 BC): Kings and Leagues

Alexander the Great (reigned 338–323 BC) spent most of his later years overseas in a staggering career of conquest which saw Macedonian arms triumph as far east as the Punjab. After his premature death at Babylon, his marshals (the so-called Successors) fell to fighting over these conquests, which in time were split into three major kingdoms ruled by Macedonian dynasties based respectively on Egypt (the Ptolemies), the Fertile Crescent (the Seleukids), and Macedon itself (Cassander and others; from 276 BC the Antigonids). Latecomers were the Attalids of Pergamon in western Turkey, who carved out a kingdom from Seleukid territory during the C3 BC. In Greece itself Alexander the Great's kinsman, King Pyrrhos (319–272 BC), built up a powerful state in his native Epeiros, its religious centre at DODONA.

Politically Alexander's conquests had shifted the Greek centre of gravity eastwards for a century. But a list of Delphic maxims inscribed *c*.300 BC in the remote Greek colony of Ai Khanoum (in modern Afghanistan) symbolizes the cultural orientation of the new 'Hellenistic' world towards the Aegean (see *Travellers and Tourists*). The Greco-Macedonian dynasties in Egypt and Asia used lavish gifts to the old Greek centres to win Greek support; in particular Athens, in the C2 BC a major cultural centre again, was a beneficiary of royal patronage.

In the eastern Balkans, the Antigonid kings of Macedon remained the dominant power, their navy allowing them to play an Aegean role in the C3 BC. In their own backyard, they maintained their influence through puppet regimes and control of the 'fetters of Greece'—fortified strongholds and naval stations at DEMETRIAS, CHALKIS, and Corinth. Against the superior resources of the kings, the individual Greek city counted for little: Athens, e.g., was ruled by a Macedonian nominee, Demetrios of Phaleron (317–307 BC), and in 222 BC Antigonos III was instrumental in putting down Sparta's attempted revival under Kleomenes III.

Partly in response, Greece saw the further development of military federations of cities and peoples. In Epeiros the dynasty of Pyrrhos was overthrown *c*.232 BC in favour of an Epeirote league with federal citizenship. In the C3 BC the Aitolian and the Achaian leagues, both based on backwoods tribal states of the Classical period, unexpectedly emerged as major (and inimical) mainland powers. Aitolian self-enrichment, by fair means or foul, turned THERMON, their central place, into a showcase. The Achaians, meanwhile, under the distinguished leadership of Aratos (died 213 BC) and Philopoimen (died 182 BC), in fits and starts absorbed the whole Peloponnese, including even a reluctant Sparta (195 BC). After an alliance with Rome, the league's heyday fell *c*.180–160 BC.

From the late C2 BC an expanding Rome found itself drawn into imperialistic ventures in Greece. Antagonized by Philip V of Macedon's alliance with Carthage, their bitter enemy, the Romans invaded the Balkans (200 BC), defeating Philip (197 BC) and confining him to Macedonia proper. The Aitolians, at first Rome's allies against Philip, fell out with the victor, prompting their defeat too (189 BC); the league survived, shorn of power. Suspicious of King Perseus, Philip's son and successor, Rome provoked him into a war, which he decisively lost (168 BC). Rome now suppressed Macedon's monarchy. Epeirote support for Perseus triggered Roman retribution: 150,000 Epeirote captives were deported and Epeiros never recovered. Mounting anti-Roman feeling among the Achaians, in spite of their alliance, provoked the return of the legions in 146 BC: in a short war Rome ruthlessly crushed the league, destroying Corinth. Greek independence was finished.

In the Hellenistic age more Balkan Greeks than ever lived in cities. This trend was most marked in the traditionally tribal regions of Aitolia, Epeiros, and Akarnania, as seen at the city-sites of KASSOPE, STRATOS, and PLEURON. Even on the Aegean side, new cities were still bring founded, such as Demetrias, as well as defunct ones restored, notably Thebes. Continuing urban directions already signalled in the C4 BC, a grid plan was now the mark of a modern city. So was a more developed architecture for civic amenities, as with the public buildings of Messene (see also *Warfare and Defence*).

The Late Roman Republic and the Pax Romana (146 BC–AD 267): Captive Greece

The Romans first imposed direct rule on the Balkans in 146 BC, when a revolt prompted them to turn Macedonia into a province. In the same year, having defeated the Achaian League, they put the cowed cities of Greece proper under the supervision of Macedonia's Roman governors. This arrangement continued even after parts of Greece ill-fatedly sided with Rome's enemy, King Mithradates VI of Pontos (88–86 BC). Following a generation of Roman civil wars, culminating with the battle of Actium (see NIKOPOLIS), Augustus, the first Roman emperor, created (27 BC) a separate province of Achaia, embracing the Peloponnese, central Greece, and the offshore islands. By the time of Hadrian (died AD 138), Greece west of the River Acheloos had been hived off into a separate province of Epeiros, its capital the Augustan city-foundation of Nikopolis, and Thessaly was attached to Macedonia.

The most visible traces today of these administrative dispositions are the Roman speaker's platform (*rostra*) at Corinth, and the palatial residence at OLYMPIA, both used by the Roman proconsuls of Achaia. Under the pax Romana the Roman emperor himself was a remote figure who rarely visited Greece in person. Provincial cities invoked his unseen presence by worshipping him with temples, statues, priests, and festivals. Sometimes old shrines were converted to this new use (as at Olympia).

Other cities built anew (Athens and Corinth). Roman ruler cult endured in Greece well into the C4 AD.

Roman rule opened Greece up to western, Italian, influences. Early on, *c.*130 BC, Rome engineered the via Egnatia, its rutted flagstones still walkable at PHILIPPI. This strategic highway linked the Adriatic and Macedonia, and brought Roman officials, soldiers, and businessmen into the Balkans. Caesar (died 44 BC) and Augustus (died AD 14) gave their veterans, along with poor urban Romans, Greek land to settle, notably at Patrai (PATRAS), Corinth, and Philippi. These Roman colonies formed showplaces of the Roman way of life; Latin inscriptions still dot their ruins.

From the C1 AD the provincial Greeks took to certain western customs: gladiatorial and wild-beast shows (see *Contests*) made converts even of the Athenians; and public baths of Roman type became a normal part of Greece's larger towns, along with ornate fountain houses (see *Waterworks*). New architecture acquired a more Roman appearance: mortared rubble (a Balkan version of Roman cement), brickwork, and the use of multi-coloured marbles, are common indicators of Roman-period work on Greek sites. But Greece still faced east as well, and the colonnaded streets which appear in Athens and Corinth in the C1 AD betray a Syrian influence.

Under Roman rule the Greek city became the basic unit of local administration. The Romans, like the Ottomans, preferred a hands-off approach to provincial governance, leaving local affairs in the hands of Greek big-wigs (the Romans called them the *primi*, 'first men'). Gifts of, or repairs to, public buildings were a favourite status-statement of these 'first men' (and sometimes women, like Epigone of MANTINEIA). Among them Herodes Atticus (pp. 117–118), an Athenian magnate of the mid-C2 AD, stands out for the scale of his works. His buildings can still be visited at Corinth, Olympia, and Athens.

In the C1–C2 AD Roman Macedonia developed into a tranquil, albeit prosperous, backwater (see DION). Further south, a much-admired Classical heritage transformed old Greece into a museum province (see *Ancient Travellers and Tourists*), and targeted it for dramatic interventions by two Roman emperors. Nero's addiction to the Greek stage brought him to Greece (AD 66–68) to compete (and predictably win) in the province's famous old festivals (see Olympia). He even 'liberated' Greece (his inscribed speech to this effect, in Greek, is displayed in Thebes museum), although after civil disturbances the proconsuls were soon back.

Hadrian, nicknamed 'Greekling' (*Graeculus*), made a more lasting impact. So enamoured of Greece that as emperor (AD 117–138) he paid it three extended visits, Hadrian poured money into the region, mainly in the form of buildings. His special favourite was Athens, which he also made the seat of a kind of ceremonial Greek senate called the

Panhellenion, its councillors recruited from all over the Aegean Greek world.

Outside observers, especially Romans, saw the 'captive' Greece of their own day as decadent, morally and economically. Some regions of Roman Greece were indeed in economic decline, their cities half-deserted, their shrines roofless. But the Greek city was an old and resilient institution; others now flourished, especially if an administrative or touristic centre, or on a major route. The grandiose architecture typical of cities in other provinces, however, did not find special favour in Greece, except where Roman influence was particularly strong, as at Nikopolis, Athens, and the colonies.

The military setbacks afflicting the empire during the C3 generated a new mood of insecurity in Greece, expressed in the gradual drying up of the flow of inscriptions on stone from the 240s on. But the Balkans were not directly affected until the mid-C3 AD, when the Goths, a Germanic people, launched successive assaults. In AD 268–270, the Herulian Goths overran Thessaly and southern Greece, attacking urban centres and sacking Athens. Although peace returned to Greece for most of the C4 AD, the old pax Romana was dead.

Greece in Late Antiquity (AD 270–675): The Age of Constantinople

The Gothic raids, by threatening Rome's lower Danube frontier, revived the strategic importance of Macedonia, Thessalonike (THESSALONIKI) in particular, where the emperor Galerius (AD 305–311) established his capital. Constantine I's foundation of Constantinople (AD 324) reflects this same eastwards shift in Roman military thinking. The clearest legacy today of Greece's new insecurity is the ubiquitous defensive wall, which reappears from the mid-C3 AD on. Where they enclose urban centres, these late circuits are often much smaller than their classical predecessors (for example Athens and Sparta), limiting their protection to the administrative core. Hard to date, some belong to the C3 AD (see Dion); others seem belated responses to the incursions of the Gothic leader Alaric in AD 396 (see Sparta); yet others belong to the reign of Justinian (AD 527–565), who worked hard to strengthen Balkan defences (see ISTHMIA). Generally, Roman governors and generals now took a prominent hand in public building, as imperial supervision of Greece's cities tightened from the C3 AD. By the C5 this supervision was exercised from Constantinople, seat of the eastern emperor following the division of imperial resources in AD 395.

Walls apart, the chief urban novelty of the C4–C7 AD is the construction of churches and related buildings, a development reflecting profound social and cultural changes in Greece. Christianity had been rooted in the Balkans since the mission of the apostle Paul, who founded Christian groups at Philippi and Corinth. The official promotion of

Christianity by the Roman state from Constantine I onwards, however, brought the faith out into the open. The earliest attested churches in Greece (from c. AD 340), as well as some of the most lavish, appear in central Greece and Macedonia. In southern Greece, the old gods continued to receive influential support from elite pagans, including sometimes the Roman governor. Famous sanctuaries, such as ELEUSIS or the Athenian Akropolis, flourished until Theodosius I banned public and private sacrifice in AD 391. Bucking the trend, Athens, a pagan bastion, maintained public ceremonies for Athena into the C5 AD, and kept some cult-statues on show into the 480s. Generally, in the C5–C7 AD churches appear all over the southern Balkans, not just in urban centres, but even in once-famous sanctuaries (Olympia and EPIDAUROS). All this implies the gradual emergence of active bishops and laity in southern Greece by 400 at the latest.

Christianity, continued insecurity, and actual attack all contributed to a gradual transformation of the urban fabric in late-antique Greece. In the C4–C5 AD major centres like Athens, Corinth, and Sparta still sought to keep up appearances, repairing public buildings and even acquiring new ones. Well paved streets and bath-houses, as well as grandiose churches, typify the urban habitat at NEA ANCHIALOS in Thessaly (C4–C6 AD). But Christian indifference to the old forms of civic life is symbolized at Philippi, where c. AD 550 a huge church was built over the earlier food-market, palaistra, and public latrines.

Changes in Greek towns in this period were matched in the countryside, where archaeological surveys are revealing a hitherto unsuspected density of occupation and activity during the C4–C7 AD. All over the Balkans, the real break with the past only came with the destructive incursions of the Slavs and Avars from the mid-C6 onwards. This discontinuity can be measured by the fact that only a tiny handful of the hundreds of early-Christian churches in the southern Balkans escaped ruin at this time. From AMPHIPOLIS a telling, and typical, sign of urban decay is the appearance of squatters in one of the basilicas. Finds of Slav pottery at ARGOS and elsewhere confirm that some Slav agriculturalists settled in the regions that they overran. In the upheavals, old centres were abandoned, part of the existing population fled, and Constantinople for a time lost control of most of Greece.

Warfare and Defence

Warfare is a recurrent theme in Greek literature and art. This emphasis on military prowess reflects the heroic ideal sanctified by Homer in the *Iliad*. Fortunately most Greeks were not as bloodthirsty as Achilles but political instability provided plenty of scope for conflicts until the Romans finally took control. Security was evidently a major concern and this is why you face a climb when you visit most of the sites. Bear in mind that it was even more inconvenient for the people who lived there. Fortifications were constructed at enormous expense because of the threat of attack. Warfare certainly had a major impact on Greek society.

In the Middle Neolithic period a wall was built around the akropolis at SESKLO. It is not clear whether this was defensive and doubts have also been expressed about the fortifications at Late Neolithic DIMINI. In time, as more sites were occupied, there must have been pressure on resources and this will have caused tension. The use of copper and then bronze led to the production of more sophisticated weapons which soon became status symbols. Some Early Helladic settlements, such as LERNA and KOLONNA on AIGINA, were fortified and the end of this period is marked by destructions.

The warrior ethos takes on a quite different dimension in the shaft graves at MYCENAE. Men were celebrated for their military exploits, real or supposed, in death. An arsenal of swords, daggers, knives, and spears was buried in the graves—the Mycenaeans clearly did not believe that they would rest in peace. Some of the swords and daggers were elaborately decorated and warfare is a favourite theme in the art of this period. Wounds on a number of the skeletons reveal the painful consequences of this violent lifestyle.

At first most Mycenaean settlements were not fortified but could have been defended if necessary. Even in the case of a site such as TIRYNS, which is on a low hill, the steep slopes would have impeded attackers. It was the palaces which were responsible for the development of defences in the C14 and C13 BC. We now know that PYLOS and THEBES as well as Mycenae and Tiryns were fortified. Mycenaean rulers must have felt threatened – but by whom? At Mycenae and Tiryns the fortifications did not protect the whole of the settlement and it could be argued that they separated those in power from their subjects. They were evidently intended to impress, since the weapons which were available at this time would not have necessitated the construction of such massive walls. Most of these citadels were on limestone outcrops and consequently had no water supply. It was only at the end of the C13 that this deficiency was remedied. These were troubled times for the Mycenaeans and there may have been a serious cause for concern. Despite these precautions, the palaces were in ruins by the C12.

Warfare in the *Iliad* is a curious affair. Heroes tour the battlefield and seek out opponents of appropriately high status. After an exchange of insults they fight a duel, oblivious of the turmoil around them. Sometimes the loser beats a hasty retreat but often dies in graphic detail. Did Homer have a specific period in mind? Since the heroes use bronze weapons, this could be a description of Mycenaean warfare, but it is likely that battles were still fought as a series of skirmishes in the C8.

Hoplites, heavily armed infantrymen, formed the core of Greek armies. They wore bronze helmets, often of the Corinthian type which covered the whole of the head, cuirasses, and greaves. Large circular shields provided further protection. Swords and spears were the main offensive weapons (there is a fine display of arms and armour in the museum at OLYMPIA). Citizens who could not afford this equipment, which must have been prohibitively expensive, fought as skirmishers. Hoplites were not particularly mobile and so a close order formation was adopted known as the phalanx. The fact that each of the hoplites shielded his neighbour ensured that the ranks kept close together. Those who turned and ran would have been extremely vulnerable. Most Greek cities did not make use of cavalry except for the Thessalians who could train on open plains.

These were the troops who proved more than a match for the Persians when they invaded Greece. However, the Greeks realized that they could not protect their cities and the construction of fortifications became a priority once the Persians had been defeated. Because they were afraid that the Spartans would intervene, the Athenians built their walls quickly from whatever they could find. A section of the fortifications can be seen in the Kerameikos. PIRAEUS was also fortified and connected to Athens by walls. The city could therefore be supplied by sea in the event of a blockade. This system proved extremely effective in the Peloponnesian War and frustrated the Spartans when they invaded Attika. Other circuits which were built in the C5 include THASOS, CORINTH, and ERETRIA.

In the C4 BC the Athenians constructed a series of fortresses on their northern border at RHAMNOUS, PHYLE, and ELEUTHERAI, while ELEUSIS guarded the approach from the west. These fortresses had towers spaced at regular intervals so that the defenders would be protected when they fired on attackers. Catapults, which operated on the torsion principle, were in use and could shoot arrows and stone projectiles. As they became more powerful, towers were built higher—the contrast between Eleutherai and AIGOSTHENA is instructive. Construction techniques also improved (see **box** on masonry styles). There is a particularly fine C4 city circuit at MESSENE which was founded in 369 BC. The broken terrain is cleverly exploited. MANTINEIA was also fortified at this time but here and at PLATAIA mudbrick was used above a stone base.

If the Macedonians could not win over a city by diplomacy, they would launch a direct assault rather than set up a blockade. Siege towers and rams had shifted the balance in favour of the attackers once again. After their defeat at the battle of CHAIRONEIA in 338 BC the Athenians hastily constructed an outer wall and a deep ditch. Late in the C4 the Spartans fortified their city for the first time. Inaccessible sites, such as ALIPHEIRA, KASSOPE, LEPREON, and PLEURON, could be defended more easily, which was just as well since warfare was a constant threat in the Hellenistic period. NIKOPOLIS, founded about 30 BC, was fortified by Augustus but the pax Romana brought security. It was only when the

> ### Masonry styles
>
> *Rubble:* the blocks of stone may be roughly finished but are not shaped or laid in courses. A masonry style which is found in most periods. *Cyclopean:* so called because the Cyclopes, a race of one-eyed giants, reputedly built the walls of Mycenae and Tiryns. Consists of large blocks, which are not shaped, with rocks and stones inserted between them. *Polygonal:* the blocks are jointed and carefully fitted together but are not laid in courses. The style appears in the C6 and was still in use in the Hellenistic period. *Trapezoidal:* the sides of the blocks are cut at an angle and they are laid in horizontal courses. A style which is common in the C5 and C4. *Ashlar:* rectangular blocks laid in horizontal courses, *isodomic* if the courses are of equal height and *pseudo-isodomic* if they alternate in height. Used in fortifications from the C5. The surface of the blocks may be *hammer-dressed, chiselled,* or *smoothed.* The late Roman defences of Greece were built of rubble and mortar. Care was taken with the faces of the wall, typically by the artful use of spolia or reused material, such as column drums, architrave blocks, and statue bases.

barbarian attacks started in the C3 that defences were restored, although often on a much reduced scale, enclosing only the nucleus of the settlement, as at Athens, Sparta, and AMPHIPOLIS. Sanctuaries, such as OLYMPIA and EPIDAUROS, also felt the need for fortifications at this time.

Residential Space

The introduction of agriculture at the start of the Neolithic period resulted in the construction of permanent settlements. For Palaeolithic hunter-gatherers mobility was essential, since their food did not remain stationary. Neolithic farmers could not leave their crops and consequently led more sedentary lives. This gave them the incentive to build houses which would withstand the winter rains and provide some home comforts. Predictably, they soon fulfilled more than just these basic needs.

The Middle Neolithic (5800–5300 BC) houses at SESKLO were solidly built. Stone was used for the lower courses and mudbrick for the superstructure. It seems likely that the roofs were thatched. Doors and window frames must have been made of wood. Apart from the fact that tiles eventually replaced thatch, this is how most Greek houses were constructed. Mudbrick does not sound particularly durable but can be protected by layers of plaster and is excellent as insulation. Most of the houses at Sesklo were of the megaron type—a shallow porch fronts two or more rooms set one behind the other. In the Late Neolithic period (4800–4500 BC) a large megaron dominated the summit of the akropolis at Sesklo and also DIMINI. Walls isolate the houses at Dimini and food was cooked indoors, whereas previously it had been prepared in the open spaces between the houses and must have been widely shared. The development of a more hierarchical and acquisitive society is implicit in the layout of these Late Neolithic settlements.

Domestic architecture becomes even more complex and sophisticated in the Early Helladic period. The House of Tiles at LERNA and the White House at KOLONNA on AIGINA are both corridor houses. Corridors divide and flank the main rooms on the ground floor. The first-floor rooms may have been surrounded by a veranda. Circulation around these houses was carefully controlled by doors and staircases. It is evident that they served a multiplicity of functions—residential, administrative, possibly even religious in the case of the House of Tiles. In some respects they anticipate the palaces of the Mycenaean period, although there is no direct connection.

Middle Helladic architecture is much less impressive. The megaron is once again the typical house type and the difference in standards can clearly be seen at Lerna. The quality of domestic architecture does not markedly improve at the start of the Mycenaean period, despite or possibly because of the construction of splendid tombs. If there were palaces at MYCENAE, TIRYNS, or PYLOS, they have not left much trace.

In the C15 BC a mansion was built at the MENELAION in Lakonia which had a central megaron unit, separated from rooms on either side by corridors. This basic plan was then expanded in the C13 palaces. Clearly these were positioned so that they would be conspicuous. The palace at Mycenae was supported on massive terraces which provided a superb view of the Argive plain. The ruler could see and be seen by his subjects. The configuration of the site determined the plan of each of the palaces, yet they do share similarities. This is particularly true of the throne room complexes at Mycenae, Tiryns, and Pylos where form and function were most closely interconnected. The circular hearth in the throne room was not simply a source of heat but must have had a ceremonial role which no doubt reflected or symbolized the duties of the ruler. Power quite literally centred on the palace. The scribes who ran the administration at Pylos had their offices by the main entrance and could check on every visitor. There were craftsmen based in the palaces and storerooms for oil and wine, much of which must have been consumed at state banquets. It is no wonder that the destruction of the palaces precipitated the collapse of the Mycenaean civilization.

After 1200 BC opulent palaces disappeared from Greece until the C4 BC. With the emergence of city-states, monumental architecture was reserved for sanctuaries and civic amenities. Residential housing was by contrast simple, which partly explains why the remains before the late C5 BC are generally scrappy. This modesty reflected social values as much as economics. The attitudes we know most about are, as usual, those of Classical ATHENS. Here houses were meant to be simple, since the male householder was expected to busy himself outside on civic business. Meanwhile his wife should stay indoors and manage the household. Within the house the total seclusion of women was an ideal, to protect them from threats to their sexual purity, and ancient writers refer to separate 'men's' and 'women's areas'.

Excavation shows that Classical houses were made of plastered mud-brick or rubble, with floors mainly of beaten earth. Nor were they spacious. Even on cities which had been laid out on a grid plan, such as OLYNTHOS or KASSOPE, the houses were built as blocks of back-to-back terraces, not on separate plots. Yet privacy was a major concern. Most houses conformed to essentially the same layout, not facing the street, but looking inwards for privacy, with a single entrance giving onto a central courtyard from which rooms opened off. Most rooms were probably multi-functional, and food could be cooked and heat delivered on portable hearths and braziers. A fixed bathroom is a feature of some houses at Olynthos, as is a workshop equipped with an olive press. This is a reminder that most male householders were farmers who walked to their fields from the city and stored and even processed the harvest in their houses.

The one room which had a specific purpose was the room 'of the men', the *androne*s. It was here that men from outside the family were entertained. The householder and his guests reclined on couches around the sides of the room and ate off tables set beside them. Where mosaics appear, they are usually confined to this room. It has been suggested that normally the rest of the house, comprising the family area, was what constituted the 'women's area'.

The Athenian politician Demosthenes claimed that C5 BC statesmen lived quite simply, whereas his contemporaries in C4 BC Athens demanded more luxurious houses (*Aristokrates* 207). Greater ostentation was a trend in this period, to judge from the C4 houses at ERETRIA, not to mention the palatial 'House of Dionysos' at PELLA, presumably a courtier's mansion. These houses are larger, with sumptuous fittings. They also have double courtyards, anticipating the Greek house-type described by the Roman architect Vitruvius (late C1 BC), in which the domestic rooms or *gynaikonitis* ('women's area') were ranged round one colonnade, and the public rooms or *andronitis* ('men's area') round another. Behind this change lay the increasing prominence in Greek city-politics of rich notables, who used their houses to display their wealth and status and, probably, do political business.

Roman rule (from 146 BC) promoted existing inequalities in Greek society. More people lived in sub-standard hovels which leave little archaeological trace. The houses of the richest Greeks now acquired greater political importance, since their guests included important Roman visitors. Heated baths, sculpture, marble veneer, and figured mosaics became normal for rich Greeks. By the C2 AD the Roman fashion for luxurious country retreats had reached Greece, and palatial villa-complexes belonging to the Athenian Herodes Atticus have been found at modern LOUKOU and at MARATHON. In late antiquity, the continuing taste for private opulence is shown by the sixteen-room 'Omega House' (C4 AD) near the agora in Athens, its creature comforts including a small swimming pool.

The rise of the Macedonian monarchy in the C4 BC reintroduced palaces to Greece as centres of power and luxury. Palaces are known in Macedonia from c.400 BC. They include the best preserved of all Greek palaces, at VERGINA, as well as the gigantic but ruinous palace in Pella. Like their Mycenaean predecessors, these palaces shared a desire to impress onlookers. As well as being large, they are all sited in commanding positions, and Vergina and Pella have imposing facades with colonnades and monumental entrances. The interiors were organized around one or more colonnaded courts, a feature taken from Greek houses. Although room-functions are usually hard to pinpoint, at Vergina the layout was dominated by dining rooms, in line with the prominence of banqueting and drinking parties in the life of the Macedonian court. In a development anticipating Roman palaces, Vergina formed a larger complex, including a theatre. Gardens, libraries, a throne room, archives, and private suites can also be predicted for these Macedonian palaces.

In Roman times the royal palaces were superseded as centres of power by accommodation for Roman emperors and officials. An imperial residence may be preserved at OLYMPIA, where the Leonidaion was rebuilt as a lavish mansion in the C2 AD, probably for Hadrian. At THESSALONIKI parts of the sprawling palace-quarter built by Galerius have been found, including a mausoleum, circus, and triumphal arch. An official residence has been recognized in the grandest secular building of late antiquity in Greece, the so-called Palace of the Giants, a massive and luxurious villa-complex built over the agora at Athens soon after AD 400.

Waterworks

Overcoming the disadvantages of the mainly arid climate to ensure sufficient water was one of ancient Greece's most remarkable achievements, and visitors to sites like PLEURON or PERACHORA, with their massive cisterns, cannot fail to be impressed by the scale of investment in the water supply. Many ancient communities were sited to exploit natural springs (CORINTH is a good example), although others, such as ATHENS, were notorious for their poor water supply. Where springs were lacking, the winter rains had to be collected in cisterns or drawn up from wells. From the C6 BC on, water-proof cement is the tell-tale sign of hydraulic works on Greek sites.

Among the earliest waterworks known in Greece are the impressive Mycenaean cisterns at ATHENS, MYCENAE, and TIRYNS. In historic times, cities needed water for houses and for a range of public amenities, including fountains, baths, and latrines. Water was also needed by industry, as at LAURION. Wells and cisterns for rainwater (collected from the pitched roof) are found in some house courtyards, as at OLYNTHOS. But residents in many cities depended on fetching water from public fountain houses.

These first developed in the C7–C6 BC and were among the more popular public works of Archaic tyrants. Public fountains were social places, as at Peirene in Corinth, not least because the chore was done by females. They were usually roofed, with a colonnaded entrance masking a draw-basin fed by bronze water spouts, as at LYKOSOURA. Fountains either tapped a source on the spot, as with the Kastalian spring at DELPHI or Upper Peirene on ACROCORINTH, or were the terminal of an engineered supply. A sub-surface aqueduct is known from Athens as early as the C6 BC, using terracotta pipes.

Although bathrooms are found in some Classical houses, as at Olynthos, the public baths common from the C4 BC presumably answered a widespread need. Wash-basins supplied with running cold water were provided for athletes in gymnasia, as at Delphi, which also featured a circular pool. The best idea of Hellenistic baths can be had at GORTYS, where they were heated. The link with Asklepios is not fortuitous, as Greeks had considered bathing therapeutic at least from the time of the doctor Hippokrates (C5 BC).

Under Roman rule Greece's cities shared in the impressive waterworks typifying urban life in the Roman empire. Greeks took to public baths of Roman type, the ancestor of the modern 'Turkish' baths, which favoured communal bathing over individual tubs and exposed the body to a successive range of temperatures. In Greece the best example of the developed type is from ARGOS, where marble-clad plunge pools and sweat rooms heated by underfloor hypocausts are grouped together into a lofty complex, one of the highest buildings to survive from ancient Greece.

Roman bath-facilities guzzled water, and mainly for this reason major Greek cities now acquired raised aqueducts tapping more remote supplies, as at NIKOPOLIS. Costly projects, they are specifically linked to the emperor Hadrian at Athens and Corinth. The elaborate fountain house (often called a nymphaion), lined with coloured marbles and statues, is also a feature of the period. A lavish example is the nymphaion of Herodes Atticus at Olympia c. AD 150. The Roman-style good life demanded landscaped water-gardens, as in the rebuilt Leonidaion, also at Olympia (C2 AD). More prosaically, it fostered better sanitation. Fine examples of communal male-only lavatories (called *Vespasianae* from the Roman emperor who first taxed them) can be seen near the commercial markets of Roman Athens and PHILIPPI, 68 and 42 seaters respectively.

The Agora and Gymnasium

The agora was the civic centre of a Greek city, a focus for administrative, legislative, judicial, commercial, social, and religious activities. Magistrates were based in the agora and it was here that the city council met. There were lawcourts, markets, shops, and shrines. Statues commemorated prominent citizens and benefactors. Inscriptions recorded laws, treaties, and decrees (see **box**).

In most Greek cities the agora was an open square. Although used primarily for civic and secular purposes, this was also a sacred precinct and so the perimeter was marked by stones inscribed: ΗΟΡΟΣ ΕΙΜΙ ΤΕΣ ΑΓΟΡΑΣ—I am the boundary of the agora. Stoas (see **box**) often lined the sides of the square. This type of agora can be seen at ATHENS, KASSOPE, MEGALOPOLIS, PELLA, SIKYON, and THASOS. In his description of ELIS, Pausanias (6.24) notes that the agora 'was constructed in the older manner with separate stoas and lanes between them'. By the Hellenistic period, most agoras were more carefully planned.

The architectural layout of an agora depended on a number of factors, not least the political system in the city concerned. This was the heart of democratic Athens, whereas at Pella, the Macedonian capital, decisions were taken in the palace which quite literally looked down on the agora.

The prytaneion contained the sacred hearth which symbolized the communal life of the city. Officials dined here and entertained visitors. At Kassope the prytaneion occupied one side of the agora. The council, or boule, typically consisted of appointed representatives, former magistrates or elders. The boule in C5 Athens had 500 members. They met in a purpose-built bouleuterion which was rather like a roofed theatre. There was also a bouleuterion in the agora at Sikyon. For the ekklesia, the assembly of adult male citizens, more space was required. Theatres were certainly used for this purpose. The Athenians held their assemblies on the Pnyx, the hill west of the Akropolis. The Thersilion at Megalopolis was built for the Arkadian federal assembly which numbered 10,000.

The Greeks evidently believed that justice should not only be done but should be seen to be done. Trials took place in the agora, often in front of several hundred jurors. Pausanias (1.28) lists a number of lawcourts in Athens. The most famous of these, the Heliaia, may have occupied the square structure on the south side of the agora. Courts also sat in the Painted Stoa and the Royal Stoa on occasion.

The agora was also a commercial centre. Aristotle did not approve of this (*Politics* 7.11). He recommended that there should be 'an agora of the kind customary in Thessaly which they call a free agora, that is one which has to be kept clear of merchandise and which no artisan or farmer or any other such person may enter unless summoned by the

Inscriptions: What do they say?

The Greeks set up inscriptions all over their cities, particularly in the agora, in sanctuaries and cemeteries. The most common kind of inscription you see is the epitaph on a tombstone. There are thousands of these to be found stacked in museum courtyards all over Greece. Later ones may end ΧΑΙΡΕ(ΤΕ)—'goodbye'. Another common category is the dedication to a deity, sometimes using the word ΑΝΕΘΗΚΕ or ΑΝΕΘΗΚΑΝ—'s/he (or they) dedicated' so-and-so. State dedications may start with the donor's name, such as Η (or Α) ΠΟΛΙΣ—'the City', or Η ΔΗΜΟΣ or Α ΔΑΜΟΣ—'the People'. The deity's name normally appears as well, such as ΔΙΟΝΥΣΙΩΙ—'for *Dionysos*'. Dedications of sculpture may record the artist's 'signature' with the word ΕΠΟΙΗΣΕ or ΕΠΟΕΣΕ—'so-and-so made (me)'.

Greek cities rewarded patriots, benefactors and foreign rulers with a portrait-statue set up on a base. Often you can still see marks for attaching the feet of the statue. ΕΥΕΡΓΕΤΗΝ—'benefactor', is a common word in this type of text. Sometimes you find ΣΩΤΗΡΑ—'saviour'. Many that you see on site were set up for Roman emperors. Their titles usually included the words ΑΥΤΟΚΡΑΤΟΡΑ ΚΑΙΣΑΡΑ ΣΕΒΑΣΤΟΝ—'Imperator Caesar Augustus'. Often honoured too, their empresses are called ΣΕΒΑΣΤΗΝ—'Augusta'.

Cities also committed to public view on stone or bronze a host of official documents and records. Often they are inscribed in line after line of small, close, letters on an upright stone slab or stele. This type of document sometimes begins ΑΓΑΘΗΙ ΤΥΧΗΙ—'in Fortune's name'. You can often tell accounts because they use distinctive numerals (see the EPIGRAPHIC MUSEUM in Athens). Decrees may have the word ΕΙΠΕ(Ν) near the start—'so-and-so spoke' to the motion. Further down they may have ΕΔΟΞΕ(Ν)—'it was resolved' by, for example, the ΒΟΥΛΗ—'council'.

Last but not least, the form of letters in Greek inscriptions can give you an idea of their date. As with handwriting today, letters had a different 'look' in different periods. With the Greek letter Ο, the larger it is, the later the date. If it is full-sized, you are looking at a Roman inscription. If you find an Σ, Greek 'S', the earlier the text, the more widely the horizontal bars are splayed. They do not become horizontal much before c.150 BC (see the Archaeological Museum in PIRAEUS).

magistrates. The agora for merchandise must be different from the free agora and in another place'. Herodotus (1.153) quotes this comment by Cyrus, the Persian ruler: 'I have never yet been afraid of men who have a special place in the centre of their city, where they swear this and that and cheat each other' and adds that 'the Persians never buy in an agora, indeed they do not have an agora in the whole country'. The rooms in

Stoas

Because of their versatility, stoas (colonnades) were used for a range of different purposes, particularly in the Classical and Hellenistic periods. Cool and airy in the heat of the summer, they also provided shelter from sudden storms. This would certainly have been one of their main attractions in sanctuaries and may explain why the first stoas were built. In the sanctuary of Apollo at THERMON, where the Aitolians met for a festival and fair each year, there were three enormous stoas. Delphi and Olympia had tracks covered by stoas, known as xystoi, so that athletes could train in bad weather. Dedications were displayed in stoas, such as the cables from the Persian bridge across the Hellespont in the Stoa of the Athenians at Delphi. Painted panels in the Painted Stoa in Athens celebrated military victories and statues of Persians supported the roof of the Persian Stoa in Sparta.

The rooms in some stoas—the South Stoa in Athens and the stoa at BRAURON—have off-centre doors so that dining couches could be fitted in. There were restaurants in the South Stoa at Corinth. Officials had their offices in stoas—the archon basileus in the Royal Stoa at Athens and the Hellanodikai at Elis—and they were also used as lawcourts. Tradesmen rented shops and storerooms. One of the stoas at Corinth may have been a fish-market. Stoas were also a place where people met and talked, most famously the philosopher Zeno who based himself in the Painted Stoa and whose followers became known as Stoics.

A number of different types of stoa can be identified. The simplest have just one row of columns—the Stoa of the Athenians at Delphi, the Echo Stoa at Olympia and the stoas in the agora on Thasos. In most stoas there was a second row of columns—the North and South Stoas in the ARGIVE HERAION, the stoas at KALYDON, AMPHIAREION, and Thermon. The West Stoa at Elis and the enormous Stoa of Philip at MEGALOPOLIS have three aisles. The exterior columns were usually Doric and the inner columns Ionic, since these took up less space. The late C5 Stoa of Zeus in Athens was one of the first to have projecting wings, an arrangement which can also be seen in the council-house at MANTINEIA and the Stoa of Philip. Several stoas have a row of rooms behind the portico—the reconstructed Stoa of Attalos at Athens, the South Stoa at Corinth, and the stoas at Brauron and SIKYON. Two-storey stoas include the Stoa of Attalos and the Stoa of Eumenes, also in Athens.

the Stoa of Attalos on the east side of the agora in Athens were used as shops. No doubt stalls were set up in the square as well. Craftsmen based in and around the agora included metalworkers, potters, coroplasts, sculptors, and cobblers. Officials known as agoranomoi ensured that traders did not cheat their customers. Weights and measures were regularly checked.

Aristotle would presumably have been more impressed by the

temples at Athens, Corinth, Megalopolis, Pella, and Thasos. The deities who had sanctuaries in the agora at Athens included Aphrodite, Ares, Apollo, Athena, Demeter, Hephaistos, and Zeus. The drama and musical competitions, held in honour of Dionysos, originally took place in the orchestra in the centre of the agora. Temporary wooden stands were constructed for the audience and it was only after these collapsed that plays were regularly performed in the Theatre of Dionysos. At Corinth there were chariot races in the agora. Under the pax Romana the agoras of famous cities such as Athens, SPARTA, and ARGOS became museums of local history and art and centres for the performance of traditional rites. In the C2 AD part of the agora at Sparta was known as the Choros, because boys danced there naked at the Gymnopaidia, a festival of Apollo. The Roman equivalent of the agora was the forum, of which there are good examples at Corinth and PHILIPPI, both Roman colonies.

It seems quite likely that athletes originally practised in the agora but the gymnasium soon became the place where Greek males exercised their bodies and also their minds. In the C4 philosophical schools were founded in the gymnasia in Athens. By the C3 BC a system of training for the city's youth (ephebes), based on the gymnasium, became universal. At first the facilities had been quite simple. Typically the gymnasium was sited in an open space, shaded by trees, on the outskirts of the urban centre. A supply of water would have been essential and there was often a shrine of Herakles or Hermes close by. But educational developments prompted the appearance of more formal facilities. From the late C4 on gymnasia often incorporated a range of structures, including baths, covered and open running tracks, and a peristyle court (palaistra) surrounded by rooms where the members could change, bathe, oil themselves, store equipment and attend lectures. Examples of this type of gymnasium can be seen at DELPHI, OLYMPIA, AMPHIPOLIS and SIKYON. At MESSENE the gymnasium incorporated a stadium as well.

Gods and their Sanctuaries
Prehistoric Greek Religion

Because of the lack of texts, the religious beliefs of the prehistoric period remain obscure, although archaeology does provide some evidence for the types of cult activity which took place. Even this is fairly speculative, however, and there is some truth in the observation that archaeologists tend to classify any object which has no obvious practical purpose as ritual. At those times when traces of cult activity have proved elusive it could be argued that religion was of no importance. This would almost certainly be a mistake because these early communities were completely at the mercy of their environment and surely regarded the climate and other natural phenomena as divinely ordained. Propitiatory rituals would therefore have been essential and those who could intercede with the supernatural powers must have been held in great respect. Communal cult activity does not necessarily have an impact archaeologically. This depends more on the level of investment which in turn reflects the social and political role of religion.

Female figurines, so characteristic of the Neolithic period, have been interpreted as symbols of a mother goddess, responsible for the fertility of her devotees, their crops, and animals. Although it is questionable whether there was just one deity, females certainly dominate. The role of religion in the Early and Middle Helladic periods is uncertain but at least the Mycenaeans have left us some clues. Gold rings in the shaft graves at MYCENAE and other early Mycenaean tombs depict scenes of cult activity. Ecstatic dancers shake the branches of trees, deities descend from the heavens and receive homage from worshippers. Similar scenes appear on gold rings and sealstones from Crete and it has been claimed that the Mycenaeans adopted Minoan religious beliefs and practices as well as other aspects of their culture. Alternatively it is possible that the Mycenaeans prized these rings because they were precious and had no interest in their symbolism.

The few Mycenaean shrines which have been excavated differ from those on Crete in a number of respects. The cult centre at Mycenae, just south of Grave Circle A, consists of a complex of rooms, none of which is particularly large. Not many people could have participated in or observed the rituals. Installations in the shrines include hearths, altars, and platforms on which terracotta figurines were displayed. Some of these can be seen in the museum in NAFPLION. Mainly female and quite grotesque, they could represent deities, priestesses, or worshippers. They would have been a fearsome spectacle in the dim light of the shrine. Female figurines were placed on a bench in the shrine at TIRYNS which was in the lower citadel.

It is significant that the shrines at Mycenae and Tiryns were not in the palace. Secular and religious authority may have been kept separate, although the circular hearths in the main room of the palace, the megaron, were surely the focus for ceremonies over which the ruler presided. A Linear B tablet from PYLOS (Tn 316) records some of the dedications which the palace had made:

(In the month of) Porowitos:
Pylos. A sacral ceremony was performed at Pakijana. Gifts were brought, po-re-na were purified. To the Lady: one gold cup and one woman. To Manasa: one gold bowl and one woman. To Posidaia: one gold bowl and one woman. To Triseros: one gold cup. To Dospotas: one gold cup.
Pylos. A sacral ceremony was performed at the shrine of Poseidon. The town was purified. Gifts were brought, po-re-na were purified: one gold cup and two women . . .

Pylos. A sacral ceremony was performed at the shrine of Pe-re-82 and at the shrine of Iphemedeia and at the shrine of Diwia. Gifts were brought, po-re-na were purified. To Pe-re-82: one gold cup and one woman. To Iphemedeia: one gold bowl. To Diwia: one gold bowl and one woman. To Hermes Areias: one gold bowl and one man.

Pylos. A sacral ceremony was performed at the shrine of Zeus. Gifts were brought, po-re-na were purified. To Zeus: one gold bowl and one man. To Hera: one gold bowl and one woman. To Dirimios the son of Zeus: one gold bowl...

(after Hooker)

There has been some speculation about the fate of the men and the women. It is possible that they were sacrificed or they may have been dedicated to the service of the deity concerned. Some familiar names appear on this tablet—Poseidon, Hermes, Zeus, and Hera—but also unknown gods and goddesses of whom the Lady, Potnia, was the most important. Although Mycenaean religious beliefs and cult practices were quite different from those of Classical Greece, clearly there was some continuity.

Greek Sanctuaries of Historic Times

A high proportion of sites in Greece, including some of the most spectacular like DELPHI and the Akropolis at ATHENS, take the form of ruined sanctuaries. The main reason why there are so many now is because there were so many then: at SPARTA alone, for instance, a visitor in the mid-C2 AD counted 64 sanctuaries. Shrines were everywhere because the gods were everywhere, their passage leaving tell-tale signs which their holy places often commemorated, as with the marks left by Poseidon's trident in the Erechtheion at Athens. The chief gods, known to all Greeks, were the twelve Olympians, envisaged as a fractious extended family living on Mt Olympos (Macedonia) under the loose authority of Zeus (see **box**). But there were obscure local gods too, such as Aphaia, worshipped only on AIGINA, not to mention a host of supernatural beings, the so-called heroes and heroines, such as Iphigeneia at BRAURON.

To an extent which is perhaps hard for us to credit in the C21, in ancient Greece worship of these gods was the cement which bound together human groups small and large, from the family to the state. Greek religion was mainly a public religion, something which you joined in doing with others. Above all, every city was a religious community of men and women who shared the worship of the same gods, and from childhood took part in the same festivals year after year. Citizens worshipped their 'ancestral gods' in sanctuaries both within and without the walls, as prescribed by a crowded calendar of festivals which allotted prominence in the rituals not only to men, but also to their wives and

The Olympian gods and goddesses

Zeus—lord of the heavens, the supreme power on Olympos, guardian of the law and of social order. A mature, bearded male, who sometimes holds a sceptre or thunderbolt.

Poseidon—god of the sea and the forces of nature, the 'earth-shaker'. Also depicted as a mature, bearded male, his attribute is the trident.

Hades—god of the underworld and of death, like his two brothers he is a mature, bearded male.

Apollo—god of music, prophecy, and the arts, but also sickness and medicine. A youthful figure, often shown with a bow or lyre.

Hermes—the messenger god who guided the souls of the dead to the underworld, he was also the protector of the house and the agora. Sometimes bearded, sometimes youthful, he wears winged sandals and carries a herald's staff.

Dionysos—the god of wine and intoxication. At first he is bearded and wreathed in ivy, but later he becomes a youthful, rather effeminate figure. He is often accompanied by satyrs and maenads.

Hephaistos—the god of craftsmen, a lame smith who carries tongs.

Ares—the god of war, he is seldom portrayed.

Herakles—a hero who was immortalized after his death. Wears the lion skin, which he removed from the victim of his first labour, and carries a club.

Hera—the wife and sister of Zeus, goddess of fertility and the sanctity of marriage. A matronly figure.

Athena—goddess of wisdom, patron of crafts, and a fearless warrior. She is usually helmeted and carries a spear and shield.

Artemis—the virgin huntress and goddess of childbirth. Like her twin brother Apollo, she often holds a bow.

Aphrodite—goddess of love and desire. At first scantily dressed, she later loses her clothes completely.

Demeter—goddess of crops and of female fertility, her daughter **Persephone** was the goddess of the underworld.

Hestia—the goddess of the hearth, she is usually enveloped in a cloak.

daughters. This communal character of Greek religion endured until the banning of open paganism in AD 391.

The countryside and cities of ancient Greece were dotted with shrines of all shapes and sizes. Small shrines, comprising an altar and not much else, can be seen in the agora at Athens. Larger sanctuaries were always in the public domain, belonging to cities or to leagues, as at THERMON, religious centre of the Aitolians. City-state shrines were controlled by the citizens through their assembly, council, and magistrates.

Priestesses and priests sometimes inherited their posts. Otherwise the city appointed them as it did its generals, usually for a set term; like the generals they were amateurs, with no special qualifications or training. Priestly personnel were often honoured with portrait-statues at the end of their service, which sometimes survive, as in the Asklepieion at MESSENE.

Excavation reveals sanctuaries as they had developed over many centuries. The combination of usually rudimentary planning at best, and a bewildering accumulation of monuments, can make the remains seem confusing. In essentials, however, most sanctuaries were shaped by the same core of ritual requirements. To prevent pollution, the sacred precinct was set apart from the profane world by boundary stones (EPIDAUROS) or a wall (Delphi), with stoops of holy water here and there where worshippers purified themselves by washing (one of these is on display in the museum at ISTHMIA). The most important kind of rite was the sacrifice of one or more farm-animals. Sacrifice required the only indispensable structure in most sanctuaries, an altar, usually of stone, incorporating a grate on which a fire was lit to burn off the fatty parts of the carcass to please the gods. In an irony not lost on the Greeks themselves, however, the edible flesh was consumed by the worshippers. This was usually done on the spot, and explains the sets of dining rooms in sanctuaries, as at Brauron or PERACHORA. Even on the stately Akropolis, we should imagine the sight and sound of livestock awaiting dispatch, not to mention the aromas of cooking, and the noises of banqueters. Unsurprisingly, incense-burning to mask smells was normal practice in sanctuaries.

Because open-air sacrifice was Greek religion's nearest thing to a standard religious service, worshippers had no need to congregate in an enclosed building like a church or mosque. The roofed shrines in sanctuaries housed, not people, but an image of the deity. Multiple shrines were a feature of major sanctuaries shared by several deities, such as OLYMPIA. The best-known form of shrine today, the stone temple enclosed by a colonnade, was costly and relatively rare; cheaper structures, like the small, one-room shrine at DODONA, were always more common. Divine effigies offered an obvious focus for the prayers of the faithful, especially on days of festival, when temple-doors were opened and the god 'watched' the sacrifice outside. Usually it is only their bases which survive, rarely the images which they supported, as at LYKOSOURA. Dimly lit, and often larger than life-size and glinting with precious metals, these sacred statues were designed and displayed to inspire maximum awe in onlookers.

Temples were the most elaborate in a near-endless spectrum of different kinds of gift offered by individuals and states to their gods. The underlying principal was reciprocity: one good turn, it was hoped, would deserve another. Much of the clutter on sanctuary-sites consists of stone settings once supporting offerings of sculpture or other objects, particularly thick on the ground around the temple or along the sacred way. Piety was fanned by a more worldly desire to outdo rivals. In interstate sanctuaries in the C6–C5 BC, states vied with each other in building elaborate 'treasuries', as at Delphi, Olympia, and NEMEA. Warfare between Greek states was a major dynamo of sanctuary-development. Booty, including the sale of prisoners, paid for new dedications, even whole temples. The winning side commemorated victories with gifts of captured arms, such as those hung on the outside of the Parthenon at Athens, or by commissioning artworks, like the personified Victory from Olympia, now in the museum there. These offerings were often 'votive', fulfilling vows. Individuals did the same, the vow made at a time of stress, such as the prospect of a sea-voyage, then as now dreaded by many Greeks (see ALIKI). Stoas or colonnades were commonly used to shelter and display offerings, as at Brauron.

A minority of sanctuaries had buildings reflecting special requirements. In mystery-cults where worshippers underwent initiation into secret knowledge, often at night, a roofed structure to hold a congregation might be deemed necessary, as at ELEUSIS, or else a stepped area where initiates sat and watched a sacred performance, as at Lykosoura. Oracles, where the divinity responded with a prophecy when questioned, did not require special architecture (see Delphi and Dodona), although the death oracle or NEKYOMANTEION in Epeiros featured an underground chamber, perhaps symbolizing the entrance to the underworld. Healing sanctuaries were also a type of oracle, since patients commonly received dreams in which the god prescribed a cure, as at Epidauros and the AMPHIAREION, both equipped with colonnades for ritual sleeping.

Every sanctuary had the equivalent of one or more 'open days' every one, two, or four years, when the community turned out in force for the god's festival. Typically the occasion involved a procession of worshippers and sacrificial beasts, which might follow a sacred way where the destination was a rural sanctuary. As well as a jolly get-together over sacrificial food and drink for men and women of all age-groups, many festivals featured entertainment in the form of *Competitions*. The large crowds on these occasions help to explain the concern of even minor sanctuaries to secure an adequate water supply (see *Waterworks*), as at Perachora.

This concern also reflects the importance of sanctuaries as inviolable places sheltering asylum-seekers, people who sought the protection of the gods in times of war, or to avoid capture or arrest. A good example is the heavily fortified sanctuary at Thermon, a well-attested place of refuge for the Aitolians and their property.

Apart from the incessant accumulation of offerings and the addition of modern amenities (notably heated baths in the Roman period, as at Olympia), the appearance of sanctuaries did not change greatly over time. The new sanctuaries of the Hellenistic and Roman periods were more regularly planned, as with the Asklepieion at Messene or the sanctuary of Isis at DION, but contained essentially the same features. Isis, in origin an Egyptian goddess, was one of a number of 'new' cults which gained in popularity after the eastern conquests of Alexander the Great (died 323 BC). The worship of living kings as gods, hinted at in Greece proper with the building of the Philippeion at Olympia (338 BC), was more common in the Hellenistic east. Ruler-cult only became standard in Greece under the Roman emperors (from 30 BC), although the architecture of imperial shrines was relatively restrained. Older religious buildings might be adapted to emperor-worship, as at Olympia or in the agora of Athens. But the custom-built shrine, as found on the Akropolis and in the forum of colonial CORINTH, is, on present evidence, rare.

From the C4 churches began to be built in the southern Balkans to meet the needs of Christian congregations for meeting halls in which to celebrate the liturgy. In Greece, the standard type was the basilica. Adapted from a secular structure common all over the Roman world (as in the forum at Corinth), it normally comprised an east-facing nave flanked by colonnaded aisles, with a projecting apse and a gallery, and sometimes a colonnaded forecourt (atrium) to the west. These early churches relied for impact on a richly decorated interior, using mass-produced components such as columns and capitals, often supplied by the quarry on the north Aegean island of Prokonnesos. Some, especially those which were the seat of a bishop, formed part of larger complexes, including a baptistery, a bishop's residence, bath-building, and storerooms, as can be seen at PHILIPPI and NEA ANCHIALOS.

Competitions

For Greeks from Homer onwards, displays of human excellence, measured by success in a competition, were a way of worshipping the gods. Strange though it may seem to us, the famous games of the ancient Greeks, along with countless more local contests, were all religious festivals, celebrated in or near sanctuaries and punctuated by sacrifices and prayer. Because they were hallowed by religious tradition, these games (the Greeks called them *agones*) achieved extraordinary longevity—the four-yearly contests at OLYMPIA, reputedly founded in 776 BC, were still celebrated in the AD 390s.

The games developed in a bewildering variety of fields—we hear of contests in male beauty, painting, and speechifying. But the most popular activities were athletics, along with equestrian events (a sport of the rich), music, and poetry. Boxing, wrestling, running, the javelin, and chariot-racing were all as old as Homer and formed the core of later athletic meets, which were generally contested naked. Athletes of the Archaic and Classical age were often aristocrats. Musical events featured choruses and soloists, both singers and instrumentalists. Professional reciters competed in declaiming the poets from memory, especially Homer. Boys, youths, and adult men competed in separate events, and athletic contests for women are also known. From the C6 BC four games—those at the sanctuaries of Olympia, DELPHI, ISTHMIA, and NEMEA—were recognized as preeminent, and timed so as to form a circuit; after them in repute came the Panathenaia games at ATHENS (founded 566 BC) and games for Hera at ARGOS.

Champions, above all Olympic victors, were celebrities, fêted by their home-cities and the subject of admiring poems, paintings, and statues. Competition at top events was extremely tough, with none of the modern notions of fair play; from the C4 BC we hear of the ritual cursing of sporting rivals. It is true that the prizes in the top games were symbolic wreaths of leaves. But winners in lesser games won valuables—at the Panathenaia in the C4 BC up to 4000 litres of Athenian olive-oil contained in so-called Panathenaic amphoras (see ERETRIA museum)—a substantial reward. In minor local games, cash prizes became the norm.

Western drama first developed in Athens at contests honouring Dionysos, god of impersonation and wine. In the C5 BC Athenian playwrights and their producers, who paid for the cast and the theatrical paraphernalia, competed for best comedy and best tragedy twice a year at the two major festivals of Dionysos. Nearly all the ancient Greek drama which survives was written for Athenian festivals; such is the enduring appeal of the comedies of Aristophanes and the tragedies of Aeschylus (died 456/5 BC), Sophocles (died 406 BC), and Euripides (died after 408 BC), that they continue to be performed today. The victorious producer (*choregos*), by definition an Athenian of means, was allowed to put up a commemorative monument displaying his prize, a bronze tripod. The so-called Street of the Tripods, running round the eastern side of the Akropolis, came to be lined with these 'choregic' memorials. One survives, the C4 BC Monument of Lysikrates. Elsewhere, they can be seen at the AMPHIAREION.

Sanctuaries developed a range of structures linked to contests. For athletics, the stadium was developed early, a running track *c.*200 m long, framed by seating areas, a bank of earth on one side or both, as at Olympia, and from the C4 BC stone seating, as at EPIDAUROS and DODONA. Equestrian events took place in hippodromes, although none of these survives.

Athenian drama at first was performed in the agora, using a dancing place (orchestra) for a chorus, and wooden grandstands. In the early C5 BC the venue was switched to a theatral area in the sanctuary of Dionysos on the south side of the Akropolis. The first phases of this theatre, coinciding with the golden age of Athenian drama, were simple—spectators sat on the natural hillside, and actors changed costume in a tent ('skene', whence scenery). From the C4 BC on, the demand for Athenian-style drama led to a proliferation of theatres in Greece. At the same time, actors increasingly took precedence over the chorus, which was dropped altogether in the so-called New Comedy of the Athenian playwright Menander (born in 342 BC). Surviving theatres in stone, mainly dating from the C4 BC or later, reflect this development. Typically they feature the skene, now a low building in stone, fronted by a colonnade (proskenion), the roof of which (by the early C3 BC) served as a raised stage for actors, as at the Amphiareion. Expensive to build, stone theatres became, and perhaps always were, multi-purpose. In particular, they were regularly used for citizen-assemblies. The odeion, a smaller version of the theatre which could be roofed, was used for musical competitions, and also (in Roman times) for the show-speeches of professional orators. The surviving examples are mainly of Roman date, as at Athens, Epidauros, and NIKOPOLIS.

Traditional Greek games flourished under the Roman empire—the stadia at Delphi and Athens, for instance, in their present form date from the C2 AD. Contestants were now mainly professionals; two fine examples of monuments documenting the careers of such men can be seen in the Isthmia museum. It is clear that the gladiatorial combats and beast-fights of the Roman west now made inroads into Greek life as well, usually as part of local celebrations of the cult of the emperors. The purpose-built amphitheatre, a western import, appears only in Greece's Roman colonies, as at PATRAS. Normally these Roman spectacles were held in stadia, as at Athens, or in existing theatres adapted for the purpose by the conversion of the orchestra into an arena, as at DODONA.

The Greek Way of Death

Like an oak or a poplar or a tall pine felled in the hills by men with whetted axes to make timbers for a ship, Sarpedon came to earth. Groaning and clutching at the dust his blood had stained, the captain of the Lycians lay stretched in front of his chariot and horses.

(*Iliad* 16.482–6)

Life may not have been nasty and brutish but it was often short. In Classical Greece most children died before they were 10. The average age at death for adult males was 44 and just 36 for females. War, pestilence, and famine ensured that Charon, the infernal ferryman who rowed souls across the River Styx, was never short of customers. When death is so common, it can elicit a set of responses which may seem excessive but have a cathartic effect. Many societies believe in a period of transition between life and death, a liminal phase. The soul must first make a journey before it joins the ancestors. Ceremonies ensure that this journey is completed successfully. Of course we do not know whether the soul benefits from this attention but the bereaved can come to terms with their loss gradually and readjust.

Funerals have often been used as an opportunity for lavish expenditure. Plato (*Hippias Major* 291 DE) stated that 'it is best to be rich, healthy, honoured by the Greeks, to reach old age and, after you have buried your parents well, to be laid out well by your children and buried magnificently'. This would enhance your social status and also the position of your family, an important consideration if the transfer of property or power was at stake. Those who were responsible for the organization of the funeral had their own priorities.

Prothesis

When someone died, their eyes and mouth were closed. A coin was often placed between their teeth to pay Charon. The corpse was washed by the women of the household, preferably in sea-water, and then laid out on a bier dressed in a robe or wrapped in a white shroud. Those who died before they had married were sometimes buried in their wedding outfits. The prothesis was held on the day after death at the home of the dead person. It is a favourite theme on Geometric pottery. Mourners stand or sit around the bier, their hands raised to their heads. This same gesture can be seen on the terracotta coffins from the Mycenaean cemetery at Tanagra (on display in the museum in THEBES). The women tear their hair and scratch their faces, consumed by grief. The mourners also chanted dirges in honour of the dead at the prothesis. Some of these dirges were improvised, others may have been more formal laments, led by professional mourners.

Ekphora

The funeral ceremony usually took place on the third day and involved a procession to the cemetery, the ekphora. Some cemeteries, such as the Kerameikos in ATHENS, lay just beyond the city boundary, whereas Mycenaean tombs can be quite a distance from the settlement. The corpse was carried by pall-bearers or pulled on a cart. Hired musicians accompanied the procession which stopped at each street corner and attracted as much attention as possible. Solon, the Athenian legislator, disapproved of this practice and insisted that the ekphora should take place before sunrise. Plutarch (*Solon* 21) tells us that:

he also passed a law which specified how women should appear in public, as well as their conduct at funerals and festivals, and put an end to wild and disorderly behaviour. When women went out of doors they were not allowed to wear more than three garments, or to carry more than an obol's worth of food and drink, or a basket more than eighteen inches high, or to travel at night except in a waggon with a lamp in front of it. Besides this he abolished the practice of lacerating the flesh at funerals, of reciting set dirges, and of lamenting any person at the funeral ceremonies of another. People were also forbidden to sacrifice an ox at the graveside, or to bury their dead with more than three changes of clothing, or to visit the tombs of those who were not members of their family, except at the time of burial. Most of these practices are forbidden by our laws in CHAIRONEIA which also provide that offenders shall be punished by the board of censors for women for weak and unmanly behaviour, and for carrying their mourning to extravagant lengths.

This type of legislation is quite common and reflects that fact that funerals were an occasion when families could seek attention and consequently spent more than was thought appropriate, hence the restrictions.

The Rite

Inhumation was the standard practice in the prehistoric period. The Mycenaeans sometimes provided wooden or terracotta coffins for their loved ones but usually the corpse was laid directly on the floor of the tomb, either stretched out or on one side with the knees drawn up. Later inhumations were not significantly different, except for the introduction of stone sarcophagi. Roman imperial sarcophagi can be extremely impressive, as in the case of the examples outside the museums at ELEUSIS and THESSALONIKI.

The number of cremations suddenly increases in the C11 BC, particularly in Attika and Euboia. There is no obvious explanation for this and the Athenians subsequently switched between cremation and inhumation. The choice may have depended on local custom, family tradition, or simply personal preference. At first the body was cremated on a pyre and then the calcined bones were placed in an urn, usually an amphora or a metal cauldron, and buried in a pit. The pyres used for some of the later cremations in Athens were actually in the grave which was provided with ventilation channels.

Children were seldom cremated and their treatment differs in other respects. Sometimes a separate section of the cemetery was set aside for them but often they were buried in the settlement. Possibly it was felt that they should not be removed from their parents even in death. Because of the high mortality rate, parents faced the prospect that some of their children would almost certainly die. It has been claimed that they must therefore have limited the extent of their emotional involvement but they would nevertheless have experienced a profound sense of loss.

War dead were another special category. At MARATHON tumuli mark the graves of the Athenians and Plataians who died in 490 BC. There was also a separate tomb for each of the contingents which fought at PLATAIA in 480 BC. Herodotus (9.85) notes that 'some of the funeral mounds which are to be seen at Plataia were erected merely for show: they are empty and were put up to impress posterity by states who were ashamed that they had taken no part in the battle'. An annual festival was held in honour of the heroes of Plataia. Under the stone lion at CHAIRONEIA there were 254 bodies laid out in rows, Thebans who died at the battle in 338 BC. The Athenians usually buried their war dead in Athens in communal tombs which lined the road between the Kerameikos and the Academy. Thucydides (2.34–46) records the speech which Perikles delivered at the funeral ceremony in 431 BC.

From the C4 BC on it became increasingly common for the deceased to be remembered in heroic guise, especially where they belonged to the elite. Hellenistic cities conferred 'heroic honours' on their most distinguished dead, including the right of burial in a heroon inside the city. There are examples at KASSOPE, KALYDON, and MESSENE. Private mourners also turned loved ones into heroes, and Polydeukion, a much-mourned foster-son of Herodes Atticus (see p. 115) is thus depicted in a relief (mid-C2 AD) now in the museum at BRAURON.

The Tomb

Most graves were simple pits cut in the earth or rock and covered by stone slabs. In the case of cist graves, slabs form the sides as well as the roof (reconstructions of both of these grave types can be seen in the museum in VOLOS). Sometimes the body was encased in roof tiles. Children in particular were often buried in jars or pithoi. In some cemeteries graves were grouped together, presumably in family plots. Middle Helladic tumuli (see DENDRA, Marathon, and VOIDOKOILIA) follow the same principle, in that the earth mound typically enclosed a number of pit, cist, or pithos graves.

The Mycenaeans clearly believed that families should be reunited in death, because most of their tombs were collective. In the shaft graves at MYCENAE there were relatively few inhumations but some tholos tombs and chamber tombs remained in use for centuries. Shaft graves do not differ significantly from pit and cist graves, except that the roof is lower down. Chamber tombs consist of a narrow passage, known as the dromos. The entrance of the tomb, the stomion, was blocked by stones. Through the stomion is the rock-cut chamber. The tombs at PELLANA have enormous circular chambers. There are also impressive chamber tombs at Dendra and Thebes. Nevertheless, they do not match the finest of the tholos tombs (see Dendra, DIMINI, Mycenae, ORCHOMENOS, PERISTERIA, PYLOS, and VAPHEIO) for sheer ostentation. Tholos tombs have the same basic plan as chamber tombs but the chamber is vaulted in stone.

Archaic and Classical graves seem rather modest by comparison. It is not until the C4 that the penchant for the grandiose revives, seen in Athens with the remarkable tomb of Nikeratos of Istria, now in the museum at PIRAEUS. Led by their kings, the Macedonians also buried in style, developing a new type of 'Macedonian' tomb (see p. 438), of which the finest examples are at VERGINA and LEFKADIA. From the C2 BC elite-families in the Greek cities took to erecting mausolea, as at Messene. But the monument of Philopappus in Athens, a tomb for deposed royalty, at present looks exceptional in its lavishness.

The Offerings

Most Greek museums contain cases full of grave offerings and we can see that this aspect of the funeral ceremony must have been considered especially important. The stupendous array of objects from the shaft graves at Mycenae (on display in the National Archaeological Museum in Athens) or from the cemetery at Sindos (in the museum in Thessaloniki) demonstrate how much wealth could be taken out of circulation for the benefit of the dead. There is no simple correlation between the character of the offerings and the status of the deceased but some attribute or achievement is often emphasized—a soldier buried in his armour, an athlete with his strigil and oil flask. Personal items also include jewellery, mirrors, and toys, a poignant reminder that so many children had their lives cut short. Other offerings were provided for the afterlife. It was evidently believed that they would be needed, even if they were never used. Cups and jugs, presumably full of wine or water, ensured that the dead could slake their thirst. Food was also supplied but some animals were clearly sacrificial victims. In one of the pits in the C10 'heroon' at LEFKANDI there were four horses. The other pit contained the cremated remains of a man and the skeleton of a woman, doubtless his wife or consort, who may have killed herself. Perfumed oil was one of the most common gifts. It was poured on the body, masked putrefaction, and symbolized purity. Oil lamps banished the darkness and terracotta figurines were a source of solace and protection.

Grave Markers

Plain or sculptured stone slabs, stelai, were set up over a number of the shaft graves at Mycenae. Since there were hundreds of tombs in some Mycenaean cemeteries, grave markers must have been quite common at this time but few can be identified. Possibly they were made of wood and have disintegrated. The location of tholos tombs would not have been in doubt because they were covered by earth mounds. This practice is echoed in the *Iliad* and the *Odyssey*. Heroes expect that their graves will be marked by a conspicuous mound. As Achilles remarks to Agamemnon posthumously (*Odyssey* 2.30–33): 'How I wish you could have met your fate and died at Troy in the full enjoyment of your royal status. For then the whole nation would have built you a mound and you would have left a great name for your son to inherit.' Circular mounds were also a feature of the Kerameikos and other Athenian cemeteries in the Archaic period.

Stone stelai, often tall and rather narrow, reappear in the C7 BC. Sometimes there is a profile figure carved on the front of the stele—an athlete or a soldier, not exactly a portrait but a reminder of what the person concerned had once been. A sphinx, the guardian of the dead, was placed on top of some stelai. The Athenians also used male and female statues, kouroi and korai, as grave markers. This practice was apparently prohibited in the late C6. Cicero (*De Legibus* 2.26.64) records that: 'on account of the size of the tombs in the Kerameikos, it was decreed that no one should make a tomb which required the work of more than ten men in three days, that no tomb should be decorated with plaster or have 'herms' [presumably statues] on it'. In the Classical period stelai in Athens take a different form, shorter and wider. As there was room for more figures, we often see family groups. Stelai and marble lekythoi line the facades of peribolos tombs in the Kerameikos. Grave stelai from Boiotia, on display in the museum in Thebes, have incised decoration and there is a fine series of painted stelai from Demetrias in the museum in VOLOS.

The Greeks were fond of epitaphs. Stelai usually tell us the name of the dead person and also their father. Sometimes the grave marker appeals to us. The inscription on the base of a kouros from the cemetery at Anavysos in Attika reads: 'Stand and mourn at the marker of dead Kroisos, whom one day wild Ares slew as he fought in the front rank.' A kore, also in the National Archaeological Museum, is identified as: 'The marker of Phrasikleia. I shall ever be called maiden, a title which the gods allotted me instead of marriage. Aristion of Paros made me.' Even more poignant is the inscription on the C5 stele of Ampharete in the Kerameikos: 'I hold here this dead child of my daughter. When in life we both beheld the rays of the sun, I held her thus on my lap and now, both dead, I hold her still.'

Other Ceremonies

After the funeral the relatives returned home and shared a banquet, the *perideipnon*. Further ceremonies were performed at the tomb on the third, ninth, and thirtieth days after death. The period of mourning was then at an end but the family would gather at the tomb every year for commemorative rites. The visit to the tomb is a favourite subject on Athenian white-ground lekythoi. Ribbons were tied around the grave stele and gifts of food and drink left. It seems that the Mycenaeans eventually reopened the tomb and performed a second funeral ceremony. There is a remarkable contrast between the care which they took when someone was buried and the lack of respect which they displayed subsequently. They may have believed that the spirit remained in the tomb for a time and therefore had to be appeased but eventually completed its journey, at which point the physical remains, in the form of the skeleton, need not be feared.

We do not know where the Mycenaeans thought that spirits went but by the time of Homer and Hesiod their destination was 'the misty house of cold Hades', a 'mirthless place' which was also dark and windy, not a particularly attractive prospect.

Ancient Travellers and Tourists

The modern traveller who seeks out traces of the past on a visit to Greece follows in the footsteps of the ancients themselves. The earliest surviving guide-book to Greece, by Pausanias, was written in the mid-C2 AD. Long before that, the existence in Greece of something like tourism is shown by a vivid description of Athens, dating from the C3 BC (Herakleides (?) 1.4–2.20):

> Most houses are mean, a few only are serviceable. At first sight visitors would doubt that this was the renowned city of the Athenians, but they would not take long to believe it. For the most beautiful things in the world are there: a remarkable theatre, large and wonderful. And a magnificent shrine of Athena, conspicuous and worth seeing, the so-called Parthenon, sited above the theatre; it makes a big impression on sightseers. The temple of Olympian Zeus, only half-built, even so is impressive for its layout, and, if finished, would have been outstanding... They have festivals of all kinds, and temptations and stimulation of the mind from many different philosophers; there are many ways of amusing oneself, and non-stop spectacles. The products of the land are all invaluable and excellent to taste, though on the scarce side. But the presence of foreigners, which all of them are used to and which suits their temperaments, makes them forget their hunger by turning their thoughts to agreeable things.
>
> (after Pfister)

Many of these visitors would have been overseas Greeks from the Hellenistic diaspora. From the C2 BC cultural tourism of this kind was taken up by the Roman elite, who travelled in style, as with the C1 AD nobleman whose butler (*sumptuarius*) inconveniently died while they were in Athens. The sightseeing itinerary of the Roman general Lucius Aemilius Paulus in 167 BC is described by the Roman historian Livy. His stops included DELPHI ('the famous oracle'); CHALKIS (to see the Euripos and its bridge); the AMPHIAREION, with its 'old temple made charming by springs and streams around it'; Athens, 'with many things to see', among them the Akropolis, the harbours, and shipyards, monuments to great generals and statues of gods and men; CORINTH, especially ACROCORINTH and the Isthmus; SIKYON and ARGOS, both 'famous cities'; EPIDAUROS, 'noted for the famous temple of Asklepios'; SPARTA, 'notable not for the splendour of its public works but for its upbringing and institutions'; and OLYMPIA, where Paulus 'saw many sights which he considered worth seeing', above all the cult-statue, which was 'as if Zeus himself was present'.

This surprisingly modern itinerary—not so different from one of the three-day coach tours—mainly involved sightseeing at cities and sanctuaries already old in the time of Paulus. This bias was in keeping with the preference among Roman admirers of Greek culture for Classical (C5–C4 BC) over contemporary Greece. This meant that Roman tourists side-lined the bits of Greece considered uncultured in Classical times, notably Macedonia, Aitolia, or north-west Greece.

Pausanias (died c. AD 180), a Greek from western Turkey, toured the Roman province of Achaia c. AD 140, then returned home to write up what he had seen, probably with overseas Greeks like himself in mind. He caught the old cities and sanctuaries of Greece in their final flowering under the pax Romana, and painstakingly documents their 'heritage'. He was not particularly interested in the present, but shared the Roman enthusiasm for the Greek past, right back to the age of the heroes, as with his eye-witness account—the earliest known—of the Bronze Age ruins of MYCENAE, in his time already 1500 years old (2.16.4–5):

There are parts of the circuit-wall remaining, including the gate with lions standing on it . . . In the ruins of Mycenae is a spring named Perseia, and the underground chambers of Atreus and his sons, where they kept the treasure-houses of their riches. There is the tomb of Atreus and of those who returned home from Troy.

Pausanias meant his guide to be a practical help, as is shown by his directions to the reader when describing the agora at Athens: monuments are 'next' or 'near' to, 'further up' from or 'above', each other—indications which can be frustratingly vague for modern archaeologists who excavate with Pausanias in hand, but probably adequate when the monuments still stood, and when the visitor could also call on a local guide, as Pausanias repeatedly did. He is modern in other ways too: his grouping of sights into regions anticipates the practice of modern guides (like this one), as does his helpful habit of digressing to fill in the background. But in other ways he was thumpingly not one of us, as he shows when he reaches ELEUSIS. Archaeologists would dearly love to have his description of this celebrated sanctuary, but Pausanias, a religious man and an Eleusinian initiate, tells his readers that 'the dream forbids me to write what lies inside the sanctuary wall, and what the uninitiated are not allowed to see they obviously ought not to know about'. The ancients would have understood this fear of committing sacrilege.

On the other hand, Pausanias describes many places which even in his day could be said to be 'of specialist interest only'—as when he visited a tiny, one-horse, place in Lakonia, to tell us that 'there is nothing at Zarax, except for a shrine of Apollo'. Zarax is not included in this Guide.

Roman tourists in particular had tabloid tastes. Licinius Mucianus, a Roman senator (C1 AD), marvelled at a transvestite who lived in ARGOS. A Roman governor was shown a pickled sea-monster or Triton displayed at Tanagra in Boiotia. Having scoffed, he was promptly shipwrecked nearby, much to local satisfaction.

Athens, Attika, and the Saronic

Attika

Thucydides (1.2) comments that 'because of the poverty of the soil ... Attika has always been inhabited by the same race of people'. Invaders presumably took one look and went elsewhere. The agricultural resources of Attika are certainly limited. It is reckoned that only around 25% of the land is cultivable, rainfall is low—less than 400 mm. per annum—and the rivers run dry in summer. No wonder the authorities were so concerned about the grain supply. But there were compensations. The mountains, Pentelikon and Hymettos in particular, produced high quality marble. Silver and copper could be mined in the LAURION hills. Attika also has a number of excellent harbours and was well placed for overseas trade.

Close ties with the Cyclades can already be seen in the Early Helladic period at MARATHON. The ore deposits around Laurion had been discovered and were being processed at THORIKOS. ATHENS seems less prominent at this time but does develop into a major centre in the Mycenaean period. There may have been a palace on the Akropolis which was impressively fortified in the C13 BC. Athens overshadows the other Mycenaean sites, which include ELEUSIS, Marathon, and Thorikos, and may have unified Attika.

In historic times Attika formed the rural territory of Athens, and down to 431 BC it was where most Athenians lived. Its political unification, attributed by the Athenians to Theseus, was probably completed c.600 BC, after a gradual resettlement in the dark ages, a process archaeologically visible by the C8 on numerous sites of future 'demes'. These were the rural districts, mostly based on older villages, such as Thorikos, into which Attika was reorganized politically by the politician Kleisthenes (508/7). In the C5–C4 demes were thriving local communities, some resembling Athens in miniature, with their own temples, theatres, and fortifications, as well as private houses and cemeteries, as at RHAMNOUS. Attika also contained important state sanctuaries at Eleusis and BRAURON. From the C3 Attika was unevenly affected by depopulation, and deme life declined in vitality. Large estates based on villas, such as at Marathon, were a feature of imperial times. In late antiquity there is evidence for renewed activity, in the silver mines at Laurion, and at border-forts like PHYLE.

Athens (Figs. 4–19)

The Athenian state of historic times emerged in the dark ages, which saw the repopulation and political unification of Attika under a central authority based on Athens. Archaic Athens was an aristocratic society, as its funerary monuments bear out, although reforms by the politician Solon (590s BC) eased the lot of Athenian peasant-farmers. From c.546–527 the Athenian aristocrat Peisistratos ruled as a tyrant, followed by his son Hippias (to 510); both were substantial builders and patrons of religious cults. In 508 the politician Kleisthenes founded the Athenian democracy. After the Persian wars (490–479 BC) Athens entered the peak of her prosperity under Perikles, before defeat by SPARTA in 404 BC (p. 12). In the early C4 the city staged a partial recovery as an Aegean power, a status lost for good after its defeat at CHAIRONEIA (338). Under the leadership of the politician Lykourgos there followed a new programme of public works (330s and 320s). In 322 Athens lost the Lamian War, and fought with other Greeks against the Macedonian ruler Antipater, who destroyed the Athenian fleet. For over a century Athens was little more than a Macedonian satellite. In 229 the city regained its autonomy, going on to acquire powerful new friends in Rome and the kings of Pergamon (Asia Minor). In the C2 Athens blossomed as a cultural centre; there was much new building, some of it sponsored by Hellenistic kings. This flowering ended when the city sided with king Mithradates VI of Pontos against Rome and was sacked by the Roman general Sulla (86). From now on Athens was more or less incorporated into the Roman empire, although Roman admiration for Classical Greece allowed the city to retain certain privileges and, from the 50s BC, prompted leading Romans to finance public works. Hadrian made Athens the capital of the Panhellenion, an assembly representing Greek cities from all over the Aegean founded in AD 131/2, and began an ambitious programme of public works, continued by the Athenian magnate Herodes Atticus (pp. 117–118) in the following reign. In the 250s AD the city's fortifications were repaired and extended, but failed to keep out the Heruli, Gothic raiders who caused extensive damage (AD 267). Athens was slow to recover, but its famous pagan cults still flourished in the C4, as did its schools of philosophy and rhetoric. Having survived a siege by the Gothic Alaric (396), the city enjoyed an architectural revival in the C5. Extensive damage by the Slavs in the 580s brought an end to normal civic life.

Akropolis (Figs. 4–7)

The entrance is at the west end of the site.

Special Features

The site which symbolizes the Classical Greek civilization.

History

The Akropolis was first occupied in the Neolithic period, but few traces of the prehistoric settlement have survived. In the C13 BC it was fortified and there may have been a Mycenaean palace on the summit. In historic times the Akropolis never entirely lost its role as a fortress, but by *c.*750 BC it had become a sacred precinct for Athena, patron-goddess of the Athenians. Amid all its increasingly fine monuments, it was always a sanctuary: in 485/4 BC, as an inscription shows, people had to be stopped from cleaning the intestines of sacrificed animals beside the sacred precincts. The Archaic monuments were all but obliterated by the Persian destruction (480 BC) and by extensive remodelling in the later C5. Nevertheless, it is known that there was at least one major temple by *c.*560 BC, and a second, the Old Temple of Athena, was added by 500. A wealth of votive sculpture survives from *c.*570 on, some of it stimulated by the four-yearly festival of the Great Panathenaia, first celebrated in 566/5 BC, and incorporating a procession up to Athena's altar, its centrepiece a ship on wheels, the 'sail' a newly woven robe for the goddess. The Athenian victory at MARATHON is seen as prompting the start of work on a grand new gateway, predecessor of the Propylaia, and the so-called Older Parthenon, both damaged when the Persians burnt the Akropolis (480). Under the leadership of Perikles the Athenian democracy launched a massive new building programme, funded from the tribute paid by the Athenian allies. The Parthenon (447–432) and Propylaia (436–432) were its chief glories. Athena's precinct now became tied in with Athenian imperialism. Somewhere here were huge marble blocks (see EPIGRAPHIC MUSEUM) recording the payments of her Greek allies, who also had to send a 'cow and a full suit of armour' to the Great Panathenaia. In spite of the Peloponnesian War, Athens went on to build the temple of Athena Nike and the Erechtheion, thereby completing the most ambitious renovation of a civic sanctuary ever seen in ancient Greece. It is likely that the Parthenon was always intended to commemorate Athenian victories over the Persians. From the C4 onwards, Athenians and other Greeks came to understand the whole of the Akropolis in this way, and both Alexander the Great (334 BC) and Attalos I or II of Pergamon (early C2 BC) made dedications here to mark their victories over 'barbarians'. In 295 the Athenian tyrant Lachares stripped the gold off the colossal gold and ivory statue of Athena Parthenos to pay his men. The deterence of a weakened Athens to the Hellenistic kings is marked by the massive base for Eumenes II overlooking the Panathenaic Way, her subjection to Rome by the temple of Roma and Augustus, the only major new structure on the Akropolis since the C5. This temple's architectural homage to the nearby Erechtheion reflects a new mood of nostalgia for the great monuments of the Classical Akropolis, said to by Plutarch to retain 'a certain bloom of newness in each building and an appearance of being untouched by the wear of time' (*Perikles* 13). The Panathenaia, its prizes upgraded by Hadrian, enjoyed a long Indian summer in the C2 – early C3. The Herulian attack on Athens (267) prompted the construction of the so-called Beulé Gate in front of the Propylaia. Its single door was ill-suited to the stately movement of Athena's procession, although this continued to take place into the early C5 (see **box**). A disastrous fire, best attributed to the Heruli, destroyed the cult statue, cella, and roof of the Parthenon. The temple was patched up, but by 485 a replacement statue had been destroyed by Christian Athenians. Conversion to a church of the Virgin Mary is dated to the late C6.

Description

You enter the Akropolis through the **Beulé Gate** [1], named from the French archaeologist who discovered it in 1852, built into a Turkish bastion, since demolished. It consists of a marble wall, central door, and two flanking towers, making artful use of earlier blocks, including (inner face, over the door) the inscribed entablature of an ostentatious temple-like monument set up by the *choregos* Nikias to celebrate victories in 320/19 BC.

Just below the north wing of the Propylaia stands a massive tapering **pedestal** [2] of Hymettos marble, nearly 9 m. high, inscribed in honour of Marcus Agrippa, an Athenian benefactor (27–12 BC). The inscription overcuts an earlier one, the shape of the base is Pergamene, and the plinth has cuttings for a chariot and four horses. All this suggests that the base originally commemorated the equestrian victory of Eumenes II, possibly at the Panathenaia of 178 BC, and was reinscribed—a notorious Athenian habit.

The Panathenaic Way terminated at the **Propylaia** [3], the formal entrance of the sanctuary. It was started in 437 BC, once the Parthenon had been dedicated, and was still under construction in 432 BC. The architect, Mnesikles, may have modelled the central hall on the earlier propylon which the Persians had destroyed but he altered the orientation so that it would have the same east-west alignment as the Parthenon. The hall has a portico of six Doric columns at either end. The ramp which runs down the centre is flanked by slender Ionic columns, a combination of the architectural orders which is also seen in the Parthenon. These columns supported coffered marble panels which Pausanias (1.22.4) describes as 'incomparable for the size and beauty of the stone'. The actual entrance consists of five doorways which were closed by

Athens, Attika, and the Saronic 49

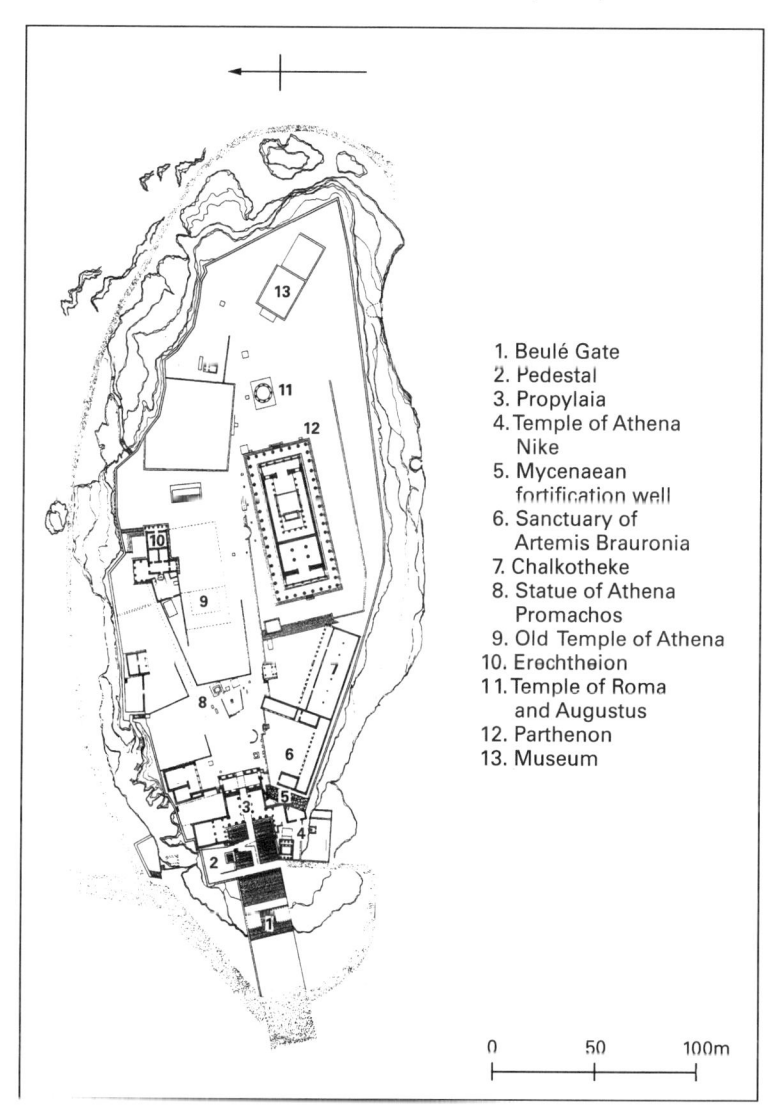

1. Beulé Gate
2. Pedestal
3. Propylaia
4. Temple of Athena Nike
5. Mycenaean fortification well
6. Sanctuary of Artemis Brauronia
7. Chalkotheke
8. Statue of Athena Promachos
9. Old Temple of Athena
10. Erechtheion
11. Temple of Roma and Augustus
12. Parthenon
13. Museum

▲ Fig. 4. Plan of the Akropolis

wooden doors. The top step of dark Eleusinian limestone contrasted with the white Pentelic marble. On the north side of the hall there is a room which has an off-centre door, so that the maximum number of couches could be fitted in for the officials who feasted here. Pausanias calls this room a picture gallery and lists the paintings which he could still identify. At least two were by Polygnotos, one of the most famous early C5 BC artists, so this really must have been a collection of old masters. We would expect a comparable room on the south side of the hall but in fact there is just a portico of three columns in front of a blank wall. Turn right once you have entered the sanctuary and you can see that the Propylaia was never finished, because the bosses have not been chiselled off the blocks. Indeed it would appear that Mnesikles had also planned two additional halls, although these were never built. The outbreak of the Peloponnesian War in 431 BC may have meant that there were no more funds available. Even incomplete the Propylaia rivalled the Parthenon for sheer magnificence in the opinion of some ancient commentators.

The best view of the **Temple of Athena Nike** [4] is from just south of the Propylaia. The temple was built on the bastion which had protected the main entrance of the Mycenaean citadel. The statue of Athena Nike was dedicated in 425/4 BC and it seems likely that construction of the temple started soon after 430. The architect may have been Kallikrates, who is named in an inscription, unless he was responsible for the shrine which the temple replaced. The use of the Ionic order creates a more delicate effect, especially set beside the severely Doric Propylaia. The plan of the temple is simple. Four columns form the porch. There is a short square cella and behind this four more columns. A sculptured frieze ran around the temple. An assembly of the gods is shown on the east side, followed by a series of battles in which the Athenians triumph over mythical and historical foes. There were battles in the pediments as well—the gods and the giants and the Greeks and the Amazons. The Mycenaean bastion was faced in limestone and crowned by a parapet of marble slabs on which Nikai sacrifice cattle in honour of Athena. A stretch of the **Mycenaean fortification wall** [5], built of Cyclopean masonry, is visible by the Propylaia.

Two more structures on this side of the Akropolis merit a mention, although they have been almost completely destroyed. The **Sanctuary of Artemis Brauronia** [6] may have been founded by the Peisistratid tyrants. It was an urban satellite of the sanctuary at BRAURON and no doubt attracted the same sort of dedications from women. These would have been displayed in the stoa on the north side of the sanctuary. Pausanias (1.23) mentions a statue of Artemis by Praxiteles and a colossal Trojan Horse. Between the sanctuary and the forecourt of the Parthenon was the **Chalkotheke** [7] in which weapons and armour were stored.

As Pausanias made his way around the Akropolis, he noted dozens of statues and we have to imagine a series of terraces on which dedications and official decrees would have competed for our attention. The **statue of Athena Promachos** [8], directly in front of the Propylaia, was certainly the most spectacular. It was made of bronze, stood approximately 9 m. high and apparently took Pheidias nine years to complete. Pausanias (1.28.2) claims that 'the spear-tip and helmet-crest of the Athena are visible as you come in by sea from SOUNION', although not any more because the statue was taken off to Constantinople.

▲ Fig. 5. The Temple of Athena Nike

The foundations between the Parthenon and the Erechtheion were laid for the **Old Temple of Athena** [9], the only C6 structure which can still be seen on the Akropolis. There is some uncertainty about the date of this temple. One theory is that it was built in 529–520 BC and would therefore be a Peisistratid dedication. Alternatively it may have been started after democracy was restored in 508 BC. The temple contained the venerable olive-wood statue of Athena Polias. There is no detailed description of the statue but it was certainly ancient and no doubt quite simple. We do know that it was dressed in a new peplos every four years and had gold jewellery. The plan of the temple is complex and there were clearly two cellas. It seems likely that the statue of Athena stood in the east cella and that the three rooms in the west cella served other deities. Athena also featured prominently in the battle between the gods and the giants on one of the pediments. The temple was destroyed by the Persians in 480 BC, although the opisthodomos may have been repaired and used as a treasury until the C4.

The **Erechtheion** [10] replaced the Old Temple of Athena but was not constructed on the same site. One consequence is that the view of the Parthenon from the Propylaia is not interrupted and there may also have been a religious motive, as it was evidently intended that the Erechtheion should take in a number of the cults located on the north side of the Akropolis. This was the temple of Athena Polias, identified in inscriptions as 'the temple on the Akropolis in which [there is] the ancient statue'. It was known as the Erechtheion because the hero Erechtheus, the foster-child of Athena, was worshipped here in conjunction with Poseidon. There were altars of Hephaistos and the hero Boutes as well. Pausanias (1.26–7) also mentions a well of sea-water, a golden lamp which only needed to be filled once a year and a bronze palm tree which drew away the smoke from the lamp.

The architect, possibly Mnesikles, did not have an easy task. He had to design a temple which served a rather disparate collection of cults on a site which sloped quite steeply from east-west and south-north. He opted for an asymmetrical structure which has a central hall flanked by porches. The temple is Ionic, constructed of Pentelic marble except for the dark Eleusinian limestone used for the frieze. Figures of white marble were attached to this—you can see the dowel holes—but the subject of the frieze is uncertain, despite the existence of an inscription which records the payments made to the sculptors. The temple may have been started in 421 BC and it was completed by 406/5. Some repairs were undertaken in the C4 and a fire *c.*27 BC necessitated a major renovation. The Erechtheion became a church in the C7 and was occupied by the harem of the Turkish commandant in the C15. Because of these alterations, it is not clear how the interior was originally laid out but the newly restored exterior is extremely impressive.

The main feature of the south side is the Caryatid porch which is

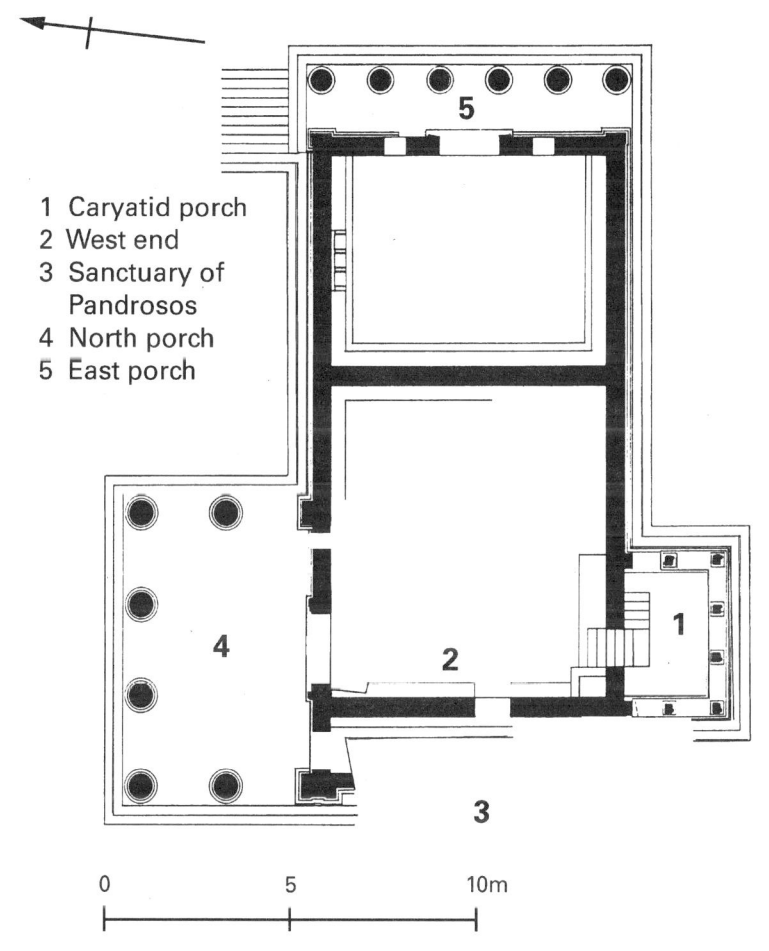

1 Caryatid porch
2 West end
3 Sanctuary of Pandrosos
4 North porch
5 East porch

▲ Fig. 6. Plan of the Erechtheion

connected to the west cella by a stairway. Female statues, commonly called Caryatids after Karyai in Lakonia, had been used as columns in the Archaic period, certainly at DELPHI and possibly on the Akropolis. In this case they may have represented the Arrhephoroi who wove the new peplos for the statue of Athena. The Caryatids also provided a visual counterpoint for the priestesses on the east frieze of the Parthenon. The west end of the temple can be reached by a flight of steps. It was rebuilt in the C1 BC and consists of a high basement which supports four engaged columns separated by windows. The famous olive tree of Athena, which the goddess produced when she and Poseidon competed for the control of Attika, has a C20 successor. This is in the sanctuary of Pandrosos, the enclosure west of the temple. The north porch of the

Erechtheion is superb. The tall columns have intricately carved bases and capitals, and the door-frame is also richly decorated. A gap was left in the floor where a thunderbolt supposedly struck the rock. The east porch now has six columns again, for the first time since the visit of Lord Elgin. A panel describes the most recent restoration. From the platform east of the temple you can see the inner face of the circuit wall, built of column drums and blocks from the Older Parthenon and further on there are two Doric column capitals from the Old Temple of Athena.

Just east of the Parthenon are blocks from the **Temple of Roma and Augustus** [11] (its ancient name is unknown). This was a circular Ionic colonnade, probably with a conical marble roof. The inscription on its architrave says that the Athenian People dedicated it 'to the goddess Roma and Augustus Caesar'. It may have marked the emperor's visit to Athens in 19 BC. Images of Roma and Augustus would have stood inside, with an altar nearby. The shrine is usually thought to have stood on the square foundation on the same spot, although another theory places it in front of the east facade of the Erechtheion, the Ionic order of which it closely copies, as you can see from the necks of the columns and the capitals.

Parthenon, or 'House of the Maid', originally described the rear chamber of the **Parthenon** [12], only giving its name to the whole temple from the C4. The temple you see today is at least the second on a deep masonry platform first built for the unfinished 'Older Parthenon'. It mainly served as a treasure-house, sheltering a cornucopia of silver and gold offerings, not to mention the gold and ivory colossus of Athena by Pheidias, which Perikles was prepared to strip in an emergency.

Currently the temple is the object of major conservation works begun in 1975, one aim being the replacement of original sculpture, in danger from atmospheric pollution, with concrete casts, as you can see with the metopes on the west and east front. Much of the sculpture, as well as architectural blocks, had already been removed by the 7th Lord Elgin (1801–5), and is now in the British Museum. When Elgin arrived, the temple was already a ruin, having been blown up by the Venetians (1687) while serving as a Turkish ammunition depot. Until then, apart from relatively minor interventions during its service as mosque (from 1460) and earlier a church (late C6–1456), its structure had survived largely unscathed from the time of the repairs following the fire of AD 267. These left the outer colonnade unroofed, with the colonnade of the cella recreated using parts of a dismantled Hellenistic stoa from the lower city. You can see a partial reassembly of this feature in the roped-off area south of the Parthenon. Some experts claim, but have yet to prove, that the ochre patina visible on parts of the building is the discoloured remnant of an original coating applied to protect the freshly cut marble.

The plan of the Parthenon is unique but was based on that of the Older Parthenon. This would certainly have reduced the cost. An

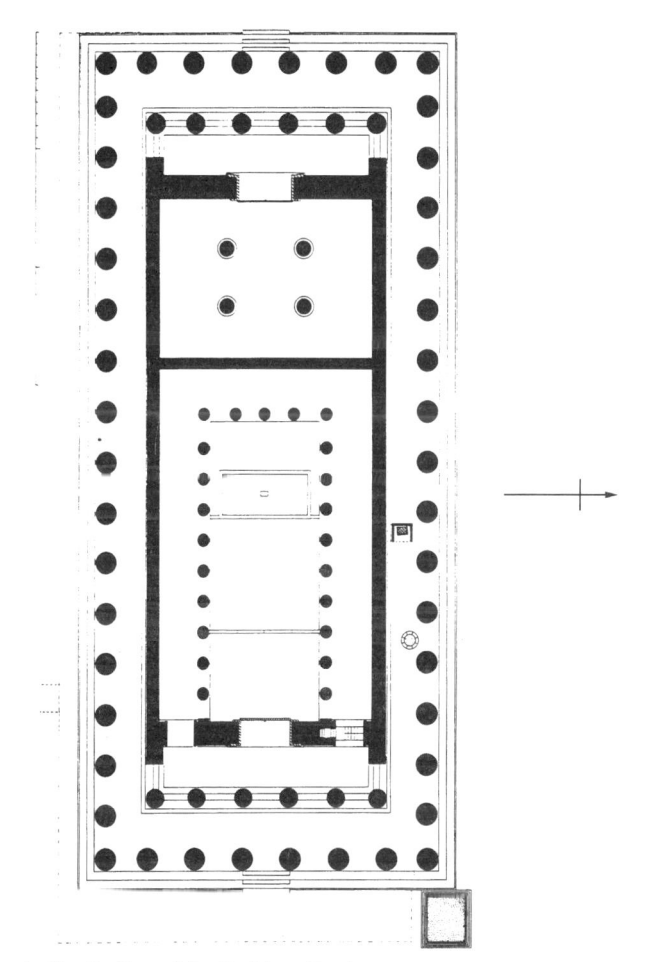

▲ Fig. 7. Plan of the Periklean Parthenon

enormous limestone platform had been constructed for the earlier temple which only needed to be extended by a few metres. Many of the marble column drums were reused. Nevertheless, it is clear that the Parthenon must have been conceived as a reincarnation of the temple which the Persians had destroyed and thus a celebration of the victory at Marathon, as well as the wealth and power of Periklean Athens. One of the main differences between the two temples is that the Parthenon has eight rather then six columns at each end. This increased the width of the cella and consequently made more space for the colossal cult statue. Pheidias, the sculptor of the statue, is described by Plutarch (*Perikles* 13) as the 'director and supervisor of the whole enterprise' and he may have been responsible for this adjustment. A canonical Doric temple has thirteen side columns but the Parthenon required seventeen because there were two cellas, each entered through a portico of six columns. The cult statue of Athena Parthenos stood in the east cella, framed on three sides by a colonnade which was replaced after the fire of AD 267. The west cella was the Parthenon proper. We know from inscriptions that treasures were stored here. The columns in this room were evidently Ionic.

The height of the exterior columns is 10.43 m., almost exactly the same as those of the temple of Zeus at OLYMPIA, which is surely no coincidence. On the east architrave you can see a row of dowel-holes and the weathering marks for fourteen circular shields, probably some of the captured arms offered to Athena by Alexander the Great after his first victory over a Persian army (Granikos, 334 BC). Between them you can also see the holes for the attachment of 345 letters (gilded bronze, each $c.$10 cm. high) of a Greek inscription set up by Athens in honour of Nero (AD 61/2), probably to mark imperial campaigns against Parthia (the new Persia).

Every one of the metopes was sculptured: the battle of the gods and the giants at the east end, the Trojan War on the north side, Greeks and Amazons at the west end, Lapiths and Centaurs on the south side. Athena was the focus of both pediments: her birth at the east and the contest with Poseidon at the west. The famous frieze ran around the outside of the cella, just below the ceiling. Even when freshly painted it would have been difficult to see. It is not mentioned by Pausanias, although he does not describe the metopes either. The best view may have been from the terrace below the temple. The visitor could follow the procession, almost as a participant. Nevertheless, the frieze was undoubtedly an extravagance and this is equally true of the statue of Athena Parthenos, almost 10 m. high, the wooden core covered in ivory and gold. Thucydides (2.13) tells us that the gold weighed 40 talents, over 1000 kg., and could be removed if there was a financial crisis.

The optical refinements were another expensive option. Look down the top step of the platform and you will find that it is curved. The columns tilt and have a convex profile. The corner columns are wider than the rest. The architrave and the frieze slant in. Vitruvius, who had read a manual on the construction of the Parthenon by Iktinos, says that this was done to correct the optical illusion whereby a perfectly level platform would look concave and a vertical column would appear to lean out. Yet some of the refinements could not have been visible and there are also subtle irregularities, for example in the distance between the columns, which may have been intended to create a more dynamic effect.

In the deep pits on the south side of the Parthenon, a section of the massive foundation wall of the Older Parthenon has been left exposed. There are fire damaged column capitals from this temple further on.

The **Akropolis Museum** [13] is well labelled in Greek and English. In **rooms I-III** there is early C6 architectural sculpture. The two pediments in which lions attack bulls come from the Hekatompedon, the likely predecessor of the Older Parthenon. Like the gorgoneion, this type of animal combat was an apotropaic device, intended to avert evil. In the corner of one of these pediments Herakles wrestles a sea-monster, possibly Triton or Nereus. In the opposite corner there is a curious creature which has three heads, three bodies, and a snaky tail, vividly painted blue, green, and red. He is known as Bluebeard but his identity remains a mystery. An early C5 inscription mentions that there were a number of oikemata, houses or chambers, which the treasurers of Athena had to open each month. The implication is that these oikemata were treasuries, possibly set up by aristocratic Athenian families rather than by other cities, since the Akropolis was not a panhellenic sanctuary like Delphi or Olympia. The oikemata must be the source of some of the other pediments on display. Herakles battles the Hydra in one and arrives on Olympos in another.

There is an impressive array of Archaic statues in **room IV**. Many were buried after the Persian sack and still have traces of paint. Korai were a favourite dedication in this period, maidens for a maiden goddess. Some may have represented Athena herself but most held out offerings and were evidently votaries. The dress style is quite understated at first but becomes more complex and flamboyant, no doubt in order to attract attention. Some of the korai were perched on columns so that they would stand out. The men who made these dedications, aristocrats and artisans, were determined that their piety should be noticed. At the far end of the room there is a rather battered Athena, possibly the statue by Endoios which Pausanias (1.26.5) saw and one of the few survivors of the Persian attack. **Room V** is dominated by sculpture from the west pediment of the Old Temple of Athena and in particular the goddess, an animated kore, who slays an awkwardly twisted giant. Sculpture from the temple of Athena Nike has recently been put on display in the alcove.

Room VI covers the transition from the Archaic to the Classical style. Note the more relaxed pose of the Kritian Boy and the introspective expression of the Blond Boy. Athena now wears a simple peplos. Figures from the west pediment of the Parthenon can be seen in **room VII** and sections of the frieze in **room VIII**. It is assumed that the frieze represents the Panathenaic procession, possibly at the first mythical festival. Or the occasion could be the Panathenaia of 490 BC, before the battle of Marathon, in which case these are the Athenians who will die. Or is this a generic Panathenaic procession? Because some key elements have been omitted, it is not out of the question that we have a fusion of the many festivals which the Athenians celebrated. There is a full complement of Olympian deities on the east frieze, not just Athena.

> ### The Panathenaic procession
>
> The Athenian orator Himerios who lived under Julian (AD 361–363) gives a flowery description of the Panathenaic procession as still celebrated in his day:
> 'The ship begins by putting to sea out of the gates as if from some calm harbour. (The trireme), being moved from there as if against a sea without waves, is pulled through the middle of the thoroughfare, which comes straight and level from the upper parts (of the city) and separates the stoas arrayed on either side of it, where the Athenians and other folk conduct business. Priests and priestesses, all of them Eupatrids, crowned with garlands, some of gold, others of flowers, are the complement of the ship. The ship, stately and high in the air, is led in circles as if with sea waves lying beneath, and the priests and priestesses, equipped with many wooden poles athwart, lead the ship without hindrance to the hill of Pallas (the Akropolis).'
>
> (*Oration for Basileios*, after Trombley)

Hills West of the Akropolis (Areiopagos, Pnyx, and Muses) (Fig. 8)

Special Features

The Pnyx was the engine-room of the C5 BC Athenian democracy, the Hill of the Muses has an extraordinary funerary monument, and all three hills provide splendid views of Athens.

Description

The **Areiopagos** ('Hill of Ares') is the treacherously smooth limestone hill, with no significant remains, just north-west of the entrance to the Akropolis. It gave its name to the oldest council of ancient Athens, addressed by the Christian apostle Paul. In the C1 BC the Roman architect Vitruvius (2.1.5) mentions here 'an ancient type of building, to this day covered in mud', possibly by then shown as the original home of the council. In historic times this seems to have met just below the summit to the north, on the site of the ruined church of St Dionysios the Areiopagite.

To reach the **Pnyx**, cross Dionysiou Areopagitou and follow the signs to the church of Ayios Demetrios Loubardiaris. Just beyond the church there is a paved road to the right which skirts the fenced site. Access is through the third gate along.

The Pnyx was the place where the all-male assembly of Athenian citizens (*ekklesia*) regularly met in the C5 and (to a lesser extent) the C4 BC. After *c*.450 BC all major decisions of the Athenian state were taken by

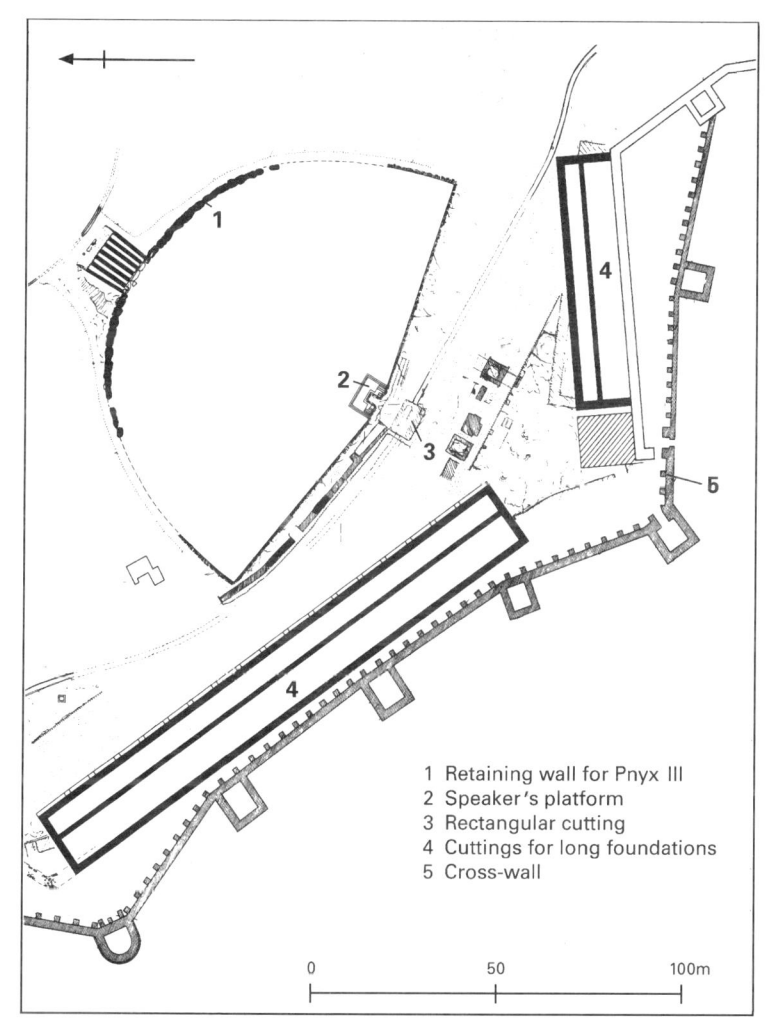

▲ Fig. 8. Plan of the Pnyx

1 Retaining wall for Pnyx III
2 Speaker's platform
3 Rectangular cutting
4 Cuttings for long foundations
5 Cross-wall

the assembly, and all citizens over twenty were entitled to speak and to vote (a show of hands). A quorum of 6000 was required, and pay (C4 BC) stimulated attendance-rates. Set speeches were made by political leaders, for whom mastery of public speaking was vital. In the 330s the assembly met forty times annually. Like all Greeks, Athenians sat during assembly-meetings, on either the ground or some kind of seat. Cushions are attested.

The present monument (Pnyx III) has recently been dated by pottery to the 330s BC. Never completed, it comprises an enormous semi-circular **wall** (visible) [**1**], retaining the earth filling for an auditorium now thought to be level with the new rock-cut speaker's **platform** (*bema*) [**2**], flanked by two rock-scarps created by the quarrying operations. Pnyx II was a smaller version of the same, and you can see a section of its stepped retaining wall and foundations of an access stairway. Plutarch (*Themistokles* 19) claims that this phase was the work of the Thirty Tyrants (404/3 BC), who 'turned the speaker's platform, which was constructed so as to look at the sea, so that it looked toward the countryside, believing that maritime empire was the origin of democracy, but that farmers bore oligarchy more easily'. This new arrangement reversed that of the primitive Pnyx I (dated *c.* 500 or 460 BC). A section of the foundations for its retaining wall is visible. Current estimates of Pnyx I's maximum seating capacity range from 6000 to 10,400.

By 88 BC at the latest, the assembly had given up the Pnyx for the theatre. Around AD 100, an open-air shrine to Zeus the Highest (*Hypsistos*) had been founded east of the *bema*. In the east scarp you can see a group of small niches for offerings, and one large one for a cult-statue. Inscribed votive plaques found here have relief images of body-parts (toes, breasts, eyes), indicating a healing cult, probably for fairly humble Athenians, to judge from their names.

On the terrace immediately above the *bema* is a large **rectangular cutting** [**3**], probably the original setting for the 'Altar of Zeus Agoraios' (C4 BC) in the Agora (the dimensions match closely). Behind you can also see cuttings for two **long foundations** [**4**], which go with Pnyx III. They were either for stoas which were never completed or (on a controversial theory) for earth spectator-embankments overlooking a racecourse. Behind these runs a section of the **cross-wall** (*diateichisma*) [**5**], an inner wall with towers linking the Hill of the Nymphs (north-west of the Pnyx, site of a modern observatory) to the Hill of the Muses. The visible stretch is dated by pottery to the C2.

To reach the **Hill of the Muses**, return past the church of Ayios Demetrios and follow one of the paths on the right up to the summit of the hill. Awaiting you is the impressive mausoleum of a Roman grandee dismissively described by Pausanias as 'some Syrian'. His full name, Gaius Julius Antiochus Philopappus, can be made out in the Latin inscription on the left pilaster of the facade, which details his Roman career as 'Consul, Arval Brother, adlected among the senators of praetorian rank by Emperor Caesar Nerva Trajan Optimus Augustus Germanicus Dacicus'. This Philopappus was grandson of the last ruler of Kommagene, a small Roman client-kingdom in south-east Turkey, and had settled in Athens, where he was a prominent citizen and benefactor. He is shown in the central niche, the Greek inscription below giving him the courtesy-title 'King', and is flanked by his father, another 'King Antiochos' (see LYKOSOURA), and (right, now missing, but known from early drawings) the Macedonian king Seleukos I (died 281 BC), his ancestor. The relief shows Philopappus in a chariot in the procession at Rome marking his inauguration as a consul (AD 109). The interior, housing his sarcophagus, is destroyed.

South Slope of the Akropolis (Fig. 9)
The entrance is at the eastern end of Dionysiou Areopagitou.

Special Features

The Theatre of Dionysos encapsulates the history of the ancient Greek theatre from the days of the great Athenian dramatists until the end of antiquity.

Description

'The most ancient sanctuary of Dionysos is by the theatre. There are two temples and two statues of Dionysos, the god of ELEUTHERAI and the one Alkamenes made out of ivory and gold' (Pausanias 1.20.2). The first **temple** [1] which you pass is C4 and contained the gold and ivory cult statue by Alkamenes who was a pupil of Pheidias. Behind this and less well preserved is a C6 **temple** [2] built for the ancient wooden statue of Dionysos which was brought from Eleutherai. A C4 **stoa** [3] closed off the north side of the sanctuary.

The **Theatre of Dionysos** [4] has a complicated history which may never be fully understood. It seems likely that there was a theatre on the south slope of the Akropolis by the late C6 and some of the most famous tragedies and comedies were first performed here in the C5. This theatre must have been quite basic. The audience sat on the hillside which was presumably levelled off. The action took place in the orchestra at the foot of the slope. It is not certain that this was circular—the theatre at THORIKOS has a rectangular orchestra. In the late C4 the theatre was rebuilt in stone as one of the projects initiated by the orator Lykourgos. He also commissioned the statues of Aeschylus, Sophocles, and Euripides which Pausanias saw. The auditorium had 64 rows of limestone seats divided into thirteen blocks. Another fourteen rows were subsequently added at the top and the theatre would then have had a capacity of around 17,000. The marble thrones in the front row were reserved for officials. In the centre is the seat ΙΕΡΕΩΣ ΔΙΟΝΥΣΟΥ ΕΛΕΥΘΕΡΕΩΣ—of the priest of Dionysos Eleutherios. The parapet of marble slabs was probably put up in the C1 AD when the theatre was used for gladiatorial contests. Dio Chrysostom (31.121) complains *c.* AD 100 that: 'the Athenians watch this fine spectacle in their theatre under the walls of the Akropolis, in the place where they bring Dionysos into the orchestra and stand him up, so that often a fighter is slaughtered among the seats in which the Hierophant and other priests

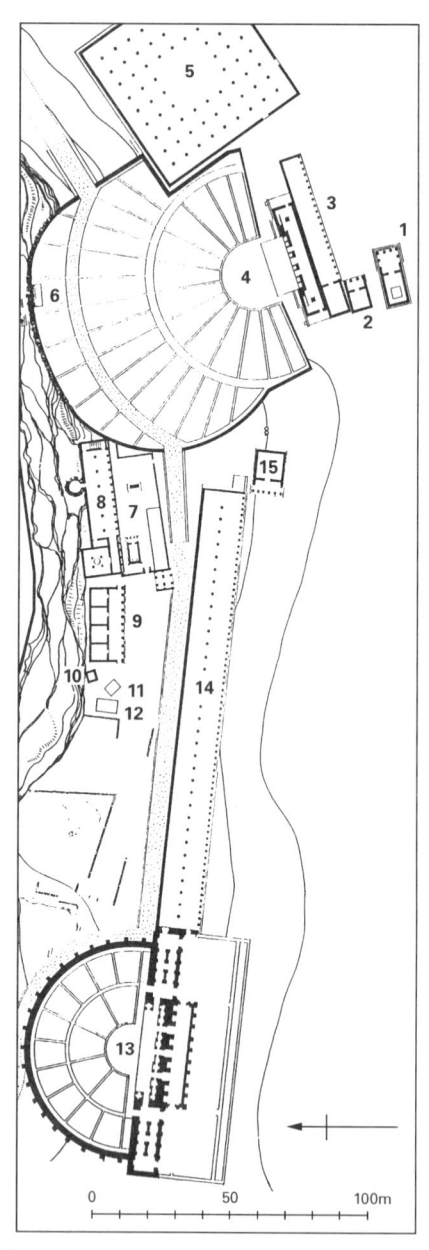

▲ Fig. 9. Plan of the south slope of the Akropolis. Key: 1 C4 temple 2 C6 temple 3 C4 stoa 4 Theatre of Dionysos 5 Odeion of Perikles 6 Choregic monuments (columns) 7 Temple and altar of Asklepios 8 Stoa 9 Ionic stoa 10 C6 Spring chamber 11–12 Temples of Themis and Isis 13 Odeion of Herodes Atticus 14 Stoa of Eumenes 15 Choregic monument of Nikias (base)

▲ Fig. 10. The throne of the priest of Dionysos in the theatre of Dionysos

must sit'. The theatre had other, more respectable, functions. It seems that the assembly often met here. Citizens who had performed some conspicuous service were honoured and the orphaned children of Athenians who had died in battle paraded at the Dionysia festival. The stage went through a series of transformations. At first it simply consisted of a stone facade. In the Hellenistic period a columned proskenion and paraskenia were placed in front of this. It was renovated in the C1 AD and given a sculptured frieze a century or so later. In the C4 AD this was incorporated in the *bema* of Phaidros which served as a platform for speakers in the assembly.

'Near the theatre and the sanctuary is a structure they say was built in imitation of the tent of Xerxes' (Pausanias 1.20.3). The **Odeion of Perikles** [5], just east of the theatre, was used for concerts and musical contests. It has almost completely disappeared but was evidently rectangular and had a wooden roof supported on nine rows of columns.

The two **columns** [6] above the theatre were once crowned by tripods and must have been choregic monuments set up to commemorate a victory at one of the festivals. The cave below the columns had an impressive marble facade and is identified by an inscription as the choregic monument of Thrasyllos and his son Thrasykles who both won victories.

From the path at the top of the auditorium you can look down on the **Asklepieion** which is currently a stone depot. Asklepios was a late arrival in Athens. His cult was introduced in 420/419 BC by Telemachos who may have come from EPIDAUROS and apparently founded the sanctuary at his own expense. Athens had recently been devastated by the great plague and it is not difficult to understand the appeal of a god who healed the sick. The **temple and altar of Asklepios** [7] were built in the C4 and also the two-storey **stoa** [8] on the north side of the court which must have been the abaton where patients slept and awaited a divinely inspired cure for their illness. It was here that Pausanias admired a Sauromatian breast-plate made out of hooves. An early Christian basilica was constructed in the court in the C5–C6 AD.

West of the sanctuary there is an Ionic **stoa** [9]. The rooms have off-centre doors and were evidently used for ritual feasts. The late C6 **spring chamber** [10], west of the stoa, was sacred to Pan and the Nymphs. Note the fine polygonal masonry which lines the sides of the drawbasin. **Temples of Themis and Isis** [11–12] stood on the platforms in front of the spring chamber and underline the importance of this terrace as a focus for cult activity and not only in the Classical period, since the temple of Isis is Hadrianic and the whole of the Asklepieion complex was renovated in the C4 AD. Pausanias also records sanctuaries of Aphrodite Pandemos, Ge Kourotrophos, and Green Demeter—clearly an eco-goddess.

At the west end of the terrace you can see the restored **Odeion of Herodes Atticus** [13]. This has a separate entrance on Dionysiou Areopagitou but access is often restricted. Pausanias (7.20.3) tells us that Herodes built the odeion in memory of his wife Regilla who died in AD 160–161. It has an immense facade, 28 m. high, which was once veneered in marble. Statues filled the niches behind the stage. Marble was also used for the floor of the orchestra and the rows of seats which could hold around 5000 spectators. Philostratus (*Lives of the Sophists* 551) tells us that Herodes 'made the roof of cedar wood, which is considered expensive even for statues'.

The enormous **Stoa of Eumenes** [14] on the lower terrace must have been one of the most costly and conspicuous benefactions which a grateful Athens received from the Hellenistic rulers of Pergamon, in this case Eumenes II (197–159 BC). Unfortunately the stoa was destroyed in the C3 AD. What remains is the series of buttresses, connected by semicircular arches, which supported the terrace behind. It was evidently a two-storey structure and may have been designed by the same architect as the Stoa of Attalos in the Agora which is identical in some respects—note in particular the Pergamene capitals. At the east end of the stoa is the base of one of the grandest **choregic monuments** [15], built by Nikias in 320/319 BC in the form of a Doric temple. In the C3 AD it was dismantled and used to construct the Beulé Gate on the Akropolis.

When you leave the site, turn left and then left again down Vironos for the **Monument of Lysikrates**, the best preserved of the choregic monuments on the Street of the Tripods. *Choregoi* were rich Athenians who covered the costs of one of the choruses which competed at drama and music festivals. The prize in some of these competitions was a bronze tripod which the victorious choregos could put on display. The Monument of Lysikrates was built in 335/334 BC and consists of a high limestone podium, crowned by a base which supports six columns of white Pentelic marble set between panels of blue Hymettian marble. This is one of the earliest structures on which we see Corinthian columns used externally. Above the architrave there is a sculptured frieze which depicts Dionysos and the pirates. The flamboyant acanthus finial on the roof was once topped by the bronze tripod which Lysikrates had won.

Agora (Fig. 11)

The main entrance is on Adrianou, but the site can also be entered from the south via a path which runs down from the Akropolis.

Special Features

This is the best preserved agora in Greece, and provides a palimpsest of the urban history of Athens.

History

The Agora was the civic heart of Athens at least until the C1 AD. A large open space, flanked by a haphazard accretion of public buildings, it acquired a bewildering mix of functions—centre of government and justice, a political assembly-place, a sacred precinct, a market, and the city's social hub. Its vibrancy was enhanced by the Street of the Panathenaia (an ancient name), a main road into Athens and sometime processional way running right across it. The vicinity was already settled in Neolithic times, and there was an extensive Mycenaean cemetery here. In the Geometric period the area continued in use for burials, but now was also inhabited, to judge from domestic well-shafts. The area began to be set aside *c.*600 BC for the communal use of the Athenians, and the first public buildings (east side) date from the early C6 BC. Perhaps before, and certainly after, the Persian occupation (480 BC) the Athenians of the C5 BC started to build here in a monumental style—chiefly multi-purpose stoas of increasing grandeur set around the periphery, and also a fine temple (the Hephaisteion). By contrast the specifically 'political' structures, like the council-house and lawcourts, remained unimpressive architecturally throughout the C5. The Agora also started to fill up with public statues and paintings, of gods, heroes, patriots, and from *c.*300 BC at the latest, Macedonian rulers. After the building boom of the C5, the Agora in essentials remained unchanged until the C2, when it was transformed by foreign investment from Hellenistic kings keen to proclaim their Greek cultural credentials. The chief novelties were two huge stoas at right angles along the south and east sides, going some way to regularize the Agora's appearance. Under Roman influence, the Agora took on the character more of a museum and high-brow cultural centre, with Romans replacing Macedonian royalty as donors. Marcus Agrippa under Augustus, who funded a concert-hall and (probably) the temple of Ares, is a prominent example. For reasons of tourism and sentiment, Roman Athens maintained some of the Agora's ancient political routines, as in the Tholos. The Heruli damaged the area (AD 267), although some buildings survived. A new post-Herulian city-wall incorporated ruined buildings along the east side of the old Agora. After Alaric (396) inflicted further damage, the area saw a revival with construction of the so-called Palace of the Giants, abandoned after the violent arrival of the Slavs (582/3).

Description

The Agora is a large and confusing site. Since its final form as a civic centre was essentially as described by Pausanias, it makes sense to see the site as far as possible through his eyes.

Before you enter the site, note the excavations on the north side of Adrianou. Amid the tangle of walls you can make out the marble remains of an **altar of Aphrodite** ([1]—*c.*500 BC), and the west end of the **Painted Stoa** or *Stoa Poikile* ([2]—*c.* 475–450 BC). This was one of the most famous buildings in the Agora, chiefly for its C5 BC paintings hung on the interior walls, including the battle of Marathon. If you now cross the road, you can look down on the remains of the **Royal Stoa** or *Stoa Basileios* ([3]—*c.*500 BC), between the street and the railway line. Pausanias began his account of the Agora with this historic monument, still used in his day as the office of the 'king' archon, a senior Athenian magistrate. You can see, in situ just outside the porch, the huge rectangular 'stone' where local officials swore to uphold the laws of Athens.

Once inside the site the description follows the route of Pausanias with some alterations for practical purposes. After seeing the Royal Stoa, Pausanias described the remaining buildings on the west side beginning with the adjacent **Stoa of Zeus of Freedom** or *Eleutherios* [4] of *c.*430–420 BC, in origin a sacred building fronted by an altar and statue, in

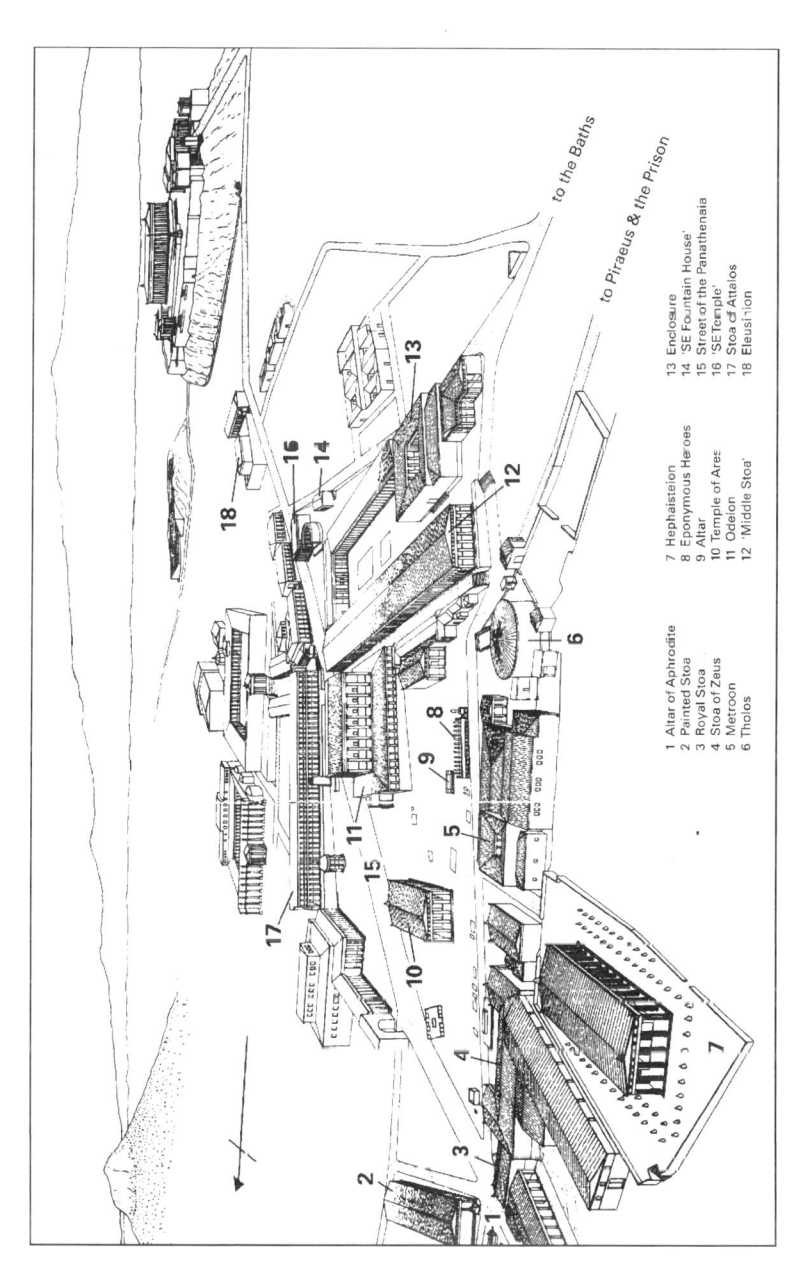

▲ Fig. 11. Reconstruction of the Agora in AD 150

1 Altar of Aphrodite
2 Painted Stoa
3 Royal Stoa
4 Stoa of Zeus
5 Metroon
6 Tholos
7 Hephaisteion
8 Eponymous Heroes
9 Altar
10 Temple of Ares
11 Odeion
12 'Middle Stoa'
13 Enclosure
14 'SE Fountain House'
15 Street of the Panathenaia
16 'SE Temple'
17 Stoa of Attalos
18 Eleusinion

his day a museum of C4 BC paintings on civic themes. You can see behind the building a two-room annexe, the one to the south with remains of a statue base. This discreet addition (early C1 AD) housed a cult of the Roman imperial family.

In front of the Metroon is a headless **statue of Hadrian**, originally set up before the Stoa of Zeus. It is striking for the scene on the cuirass of Athena supported by the she-wolf suckling Romulus and Remus—an allegory for Hadrian's vision of the Athenian cultural heritage nourished by Roman rule.

Pausanias next describes the **Metroon** [5] or shrine of Meter, Mother of the Gods (C2 BC), its front porch supported on foundations of coarse reddish stone. This was the record office of Athens where, in Pausanias' day, historic documents like the affidavit against Socrates could be inspected, perhaps while you sat on the partly preserved marble bench in a rear room. Beneath the porch, you can see much earlier walls (C6 BC), belonging to the oldest public buildings in the Agora.

Next comes the circular **Tholos** [6], built *c.*470–460 BC to provide meals for the fifty members of the Athenian council on round-the-clock duty at any one time. The marble floor belongs to a refit in Pausanias' time, when civic dinners were still cooked in the kitchen-annexe to the north-east.

From here we suggest a diversion to the **Hephaisteion** [7], ignored by Pausanias at this point. The steps up from the Tholos also provide a good vantage point over the Agora, with an information panel and reconstruction. The marble Doric temple (*c.*449–415 BC), the best-preserved in Greece, sits on the ancient Hill of the Agora (Kolonos Agoraios) and was designed to be viewed from below. Hephaistos, god of metalworking, shared it with Athena, goddess of crafts. Civic investment in these patrons of artisans seems to reflect the inclusive spirit of ancient Athenian democracy. The metopes, concentrated on the east end, show the Labours of Herakles and Theseus. Two visible friezes, one round the interior porch, the other at the rear, depict mythical battle-scenes. Excavation provided rare evidence for plants (C3 BC?) in formal rows of flower plots around the temple, now recreated. This was still a working temple in Pausanias' day, and owes its superb state of preservation to its conversion into a church, when the door was cut into the rear chamber.

A second detour from the Tholos takes you to the so-called prison and Classical houses. Follow the line of the 'Great Drain' southwards almost to the boundary of the site, into an area giving a feel for the mean houses and narrow streets for which ancient Athens was notorious. A large pile of marble marks the courtyard of the **prison** (*c.*450 BC), identified as such by its size and unusual plan and by finds of small clay bottles claimed as holders of poisonous hemlock, used in Athenian executions. From here you can visit two neighbouring **houses** (C and D,

▲ Fig. 12. Statue of the Emperor Hadrian in the Agora

rare Athenian examples of the C5 BC), impressive for being so unimpressive.

From the Tholos, Pausanias retraced his steps to describe monuments to his east, starting with the base (C4 BC) for the bronze statues of the **Eponymous Heroes** [8] after whom the citizen-tribes were named. Originally ten, by the time of Pausanias they had grown to twelve in honour of foreign benefactors. You can see where the base was extended south for a statue of Hadrian, eponym of the last new tribe, Hadrianis.

To the south, and worth noting while here, is the **Great Drain**, with its polygonal masonry (early C5 BC). and a **boundary stone** (*c.*500 BC) still in situ, inscribed 'I am the boundary of the Agora'. Entry to the Agora was a privilege, and citizens in bad standing, for example deserters, were excluded down to the C4 BC at least. In Pausanias' time the stone had long been covered up.

Opposite the Metroon Pausanias oddly omitted a fine marble **altar** ([9]—C4 BC) standing here in his day. Ancient guide-letters show that it was dismantled and moved to its present site (in the C2–C1 BC), perhaps from the Pnyx, where a cutting of just the right size exists. It may have belonged to Zeus 'of the Agora' (*Agoraios*).

We follow Pausanias down to the **Temple of Ares** [10], now a large, gravel-covered foundation. On some of the blocks from the superstructure, still on site, you can see finely-carved masons' marks of Roman date (C1 BC–C1 AD), but the superstructure is mid-C5 BC. Here too a structure, this time a whole temple, was reassembled in the Agora from an unknown site. The work was probably funded by Agrippa in homage to the Roman Ares, the war-god Mars, who was especially dear to Augustus.

From here Pausanias headed south for the **Odeion** [11], also called the Agrippeion, presumably after its Roman donor. In Pausanias' day this theatre was a venue for Greek 'show-orators' or sophists, celebrity-speakers who won fame for their rhetorical pyrotechnics. Shortly after his visit, the original theatre, of which you can still see the coloured marble floor of the orchestra, was rebuilt and it was now that the north colonnade of colossal marble Tritons and Giants (copied from the Parthenon) was added. In their present position they belong to the facade of the so-called **Palace of the Giants** (Fig. 13), a huge complex of *c.*410 overlying the Odeion (destroyed by the Heruli) and extending much further to the south. Probably not a gymnasium (as labelled), but a palatial residence of the late-antique type, it conceivably belonged to the Athenian Eudocia, empress of Theodosios II.

Wandering through, past a Corinthian capital from the first odeion, you reach the **Middle Stoa** [12], which the palace overlay. Pausanias also passed through this enormous Doric building (147 by 17.5 m.), but ignored it, probably because it was too recent (*c.*180 BC). On the south it

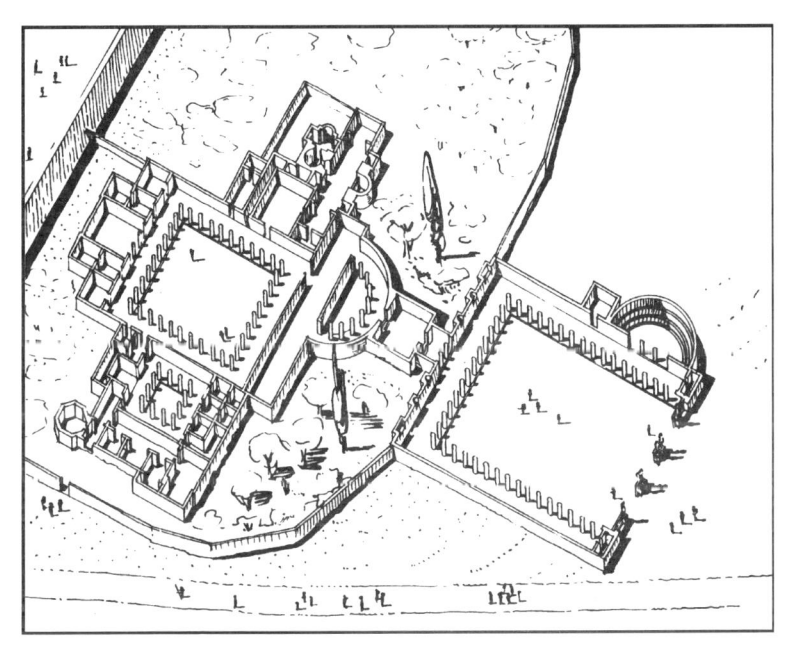

▲ Fig. 13. Reconstruction of the Palace of the Giants in the Agora

came to form part of a larger (administrative) complex, the **South Square** (*c.*150 BC), as did a much older (C6) and near-square walled **enclosure** [**13**], perhaps for the open-air meetings of a lawcourt, possibly the Heliaia.

After the Odeion, Pausanias pops up again at what he calls (probably in error) the Nine Spouts, now known as the **South-East Fountain House** [**14**], its scrappy remains (labelled) just south of the church of St George. He mentions it because it was extremely old, a survival from the Archaic Agora (*c.*550–525 BC). To its west you can see the mudbrick walls and off-centre doors of **South Stoa I** (*c.*430–420 BC), its rooms used for serving meals, perhaps to market officials.

Pausanias now took the **Street of the Panathenaia** [**15**] south-east out of the fenced area. The stone paving you see was laid either in his lifetime or not long before. He ignored the **South-East Temple** [**16**], its foundations just east of the church, built around the time of Augustus, the facade reusing Ionic columns brought in from the temple of Athena at SOUNION.

He also ignored the vast **Stoa of Attalos** [**17**], flanking the east side of the Agora, like the Middle Stoa unremarkable in his eyes either historically or architecturally. This two-storey colonnade, deliberately set down at right angles to its giant neighbour, was a gift of Attalos II, king of Pergamon (*c.*150 BC). It seems to have served as a high-class shopping mall. Rebuilt by the American School of Classical Studies, it now houses the museum.

The **museum** has excellent labels in English. Notable items include the ivory Mycenaean pyxis (Case 5); the Early Geometric warrior-burial (Case 9); the Middle Geometric female burial, including a model granary (Case 17); finds from the 'prison' (Case 20); inscriptions (Case 25), including the rules from the 'Library of Pantainos' (p. 74); and ostraka with names of famous historical figures (Case 38). In the C5 BC ostracism (from *ostrakon*, a potsherd) was a way of banishing a citizen by an assembly in the Agora of the citizens, who voted by writing on a potsherd the name of the citizen each wished to have banished.

Before following Pausanias out of the site to the Eleusinion, you pass just south of the stoa a fine stretch of the **Post-Herulian Wall**, visibly built from the debris of destroyed public buildings. Immediately east of the Street of the Panathenaia, overlooking the Agora, is the partly excavated **Eleusinion** [18], or sanctuary of Demeter and Kore, where the sacred objects were brought from the mother-sanctuary at ELEUSIS and then returned in procession during the mysteries. You can see (unlabelled) the foundations of the temple of Triptolemos (*c.*500 BC). On the opposite side of the street is a fenced and inaccessible area containing the so-called **Omega House**, a luxurious courtyard villa occupied from the C4–C6 AD, with a marble-paved apsidal pool which you can make out from the fence.

▼ Fig. 14. Reconstruction of the Omega House in the Agora

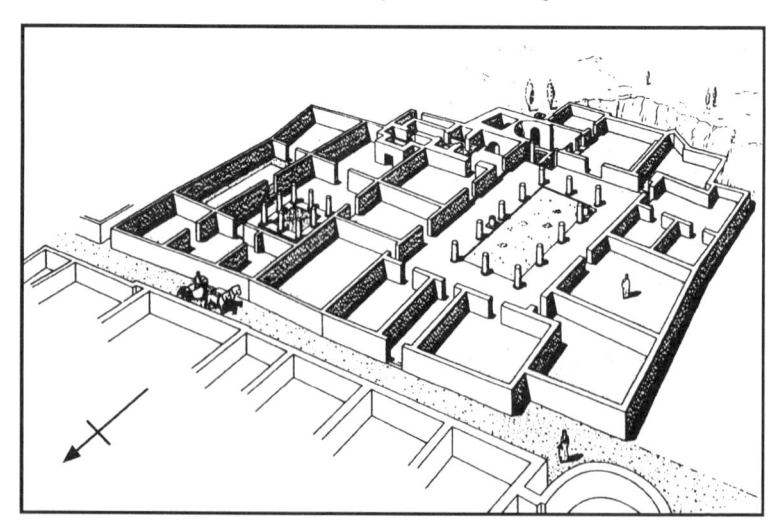

Athens, Attika, and the Saronic   73

Roman Agora and Library of Hadrian (Fig. 15)   ★

Special Features

These are impressive monuments which demonstrate Roman esteem for Athens, and provide an opportunity to stroll through Plaka, the old town of Athens.

Description

To reach the so-called **Library of Hadrian** [1] from the south entrance of the Agora, turn right down Adrianou until you reach the modern entrance on Odos Areos. The site is fenced and not accessible. From here you have a good view of the west facade (Pentelic marble, with columns of Karystos marble, or *cipollino*, from southern Euboia); the ancient gateway; and, in the distance, the niches of the **library** [2] proper lining the inner side of the east wall. However, the best view of the interior is from Aiolou, at the east end of the library, where you can look down into the colonnade, the east range of rooms and the later structures in the court.

   This huge complex was once the most luxurious public building in Athens. Pausanias (1.18.9) describes it as 'a hundred columns of Phrygian marble. The walls too are built of the same material as the colonnades. And there are rooms there decorated with a gilded ceiling, alabaster, and also with statues and paintings. Books are kept there.' The

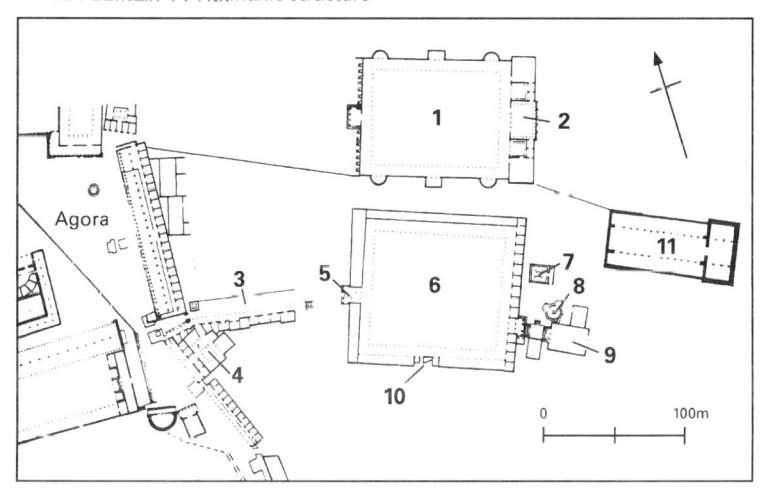

▼ Fig. 15. Plan of the Roman Agora and Library of Hadrian. Key: 1 Library of Hadrian 2 Library proper 3 Broad Street 4 Library of Pantainos 5 Gateway 6 Roman Agora 7 Latrines 8 Tower of the Winds 9 Public building 10 Fountain 11 Hadrianic structure

library proper was the central room behind the east colonnade, the rows of niches originally holding wooden cases with shelves for the books. The room at the north end has a raked floor and is best understood, like its south counterpart, as a lecture-room. The open court originally had an ornamental pool and (probably) a garden, and you can still see the holes for attaching the veneer of coloured marbles to the interior walls. The complex served as a cultural centre, its fortress-like walls creating an oasis of scholarly calm in the city-centre. The building was damaged in the Herulian raid (AD 267), and on three sides (not the south) it was then built into the post-Herulian city-wall. What dazzled Pausanias, the 100 costly columns of purple and white (*pavonazzetto*) marble from Dokimion (north-west Turkey), had been taken off for re-erection elsewhere by the early C5 AD, when the colonnades were crudely rebuilt as part of a general renovation. The unusual building with four apses in the centre of the court was a church, perhaps the earliest in Athens, built *c*.425–450.

If you continue up Odos Areos from the west entrance you will see the north edge of the *Plateia* or **Broad Street** [3] as an inscription calls it, a marble-paved and colonnaded way of *c*. AD 100 linking the Agora and the Roman Agora. What you see now is a rebuilding (C5 AD). At the east end of the excavations you can make out the remains (at an angle to the street) of the rectangular colonnade of the **Library of Pantainos** [4], a privately-funded public library (also *c*.100), its inscribed rules now in the Agora museum.

A massive Doric **gateway** [5] marks the west entrance to the [6] **Roman Agora** (ancient name unknown) and underlines its ancient link with the old Agora to the east. An inscription on the gateway's entablature (*IG* 2^2.3175, from 11–9 BC) says that the gate (and probably the whole complex) was dedicated to 'Athena the Originator' (of Athens) and funded from 'the gifts given by Gaius Julius Caesar the god and Emperor Caesar Augustus, son of a god'.

The entrance to the Roman Agora is near the north-east corner. On your right as you enter the site is a fine 68-seater public **latrine** ([7]—C1 AD), originally roofed except for a central opening for ventilation, with a system of running water to flush away the sewage. Its presence here confirms that this market-quarter was a much frequented part of the later city, as does the well-preserved **Tower of the Winds** [8], a modern name for the House of the Kyrrhestian, as the Athenians called it, after its designer Andronikos of Kyrrhos, a famous Macedonian astronomer. Called a clock (*horologion*) by ancient authors, this elegant marble octagon was also a weather-station, with a water-driven clock inside (currently inaccessible), sun-dials on each face, and on top a weather-vane in the form of a bronze Triton or sea-monster, which held its rod above the prevailing wind, as represented in the reliefs giving the building its name. It used to be dated to the C1 BC, but the tendency nowadays is to

▲ Fig. 16. The Tower of the Winds in the Roman Agora

place it *c.*150–125 BC, long before the Roman Agora was built, but when the neighbourhood already functioned as a market.

Just to the south of the tower is the arched facade of an unidentified **public building** ([9]—C1 AD), dedicated to Athena and the deified Roman emperors, who are mentioned in the inscribed entablature-block still in place. This structure is sometimes misleadingly called the Agoranomion or office of the market-supervisor.

You enter the Roman Agora by its east gateway. In plan it is a large open square, presumably once full of temporary stalls, with marble paving added in the C2 AD. It was flanked by Ionic colonnades screening shops (east side) or large market halls (north side), and there was a public **fountain** [10] on the south side. You can see a long inscription cut on the north face of a door jamb in the west gateway in which the emperor Hadrian intervened to regulate the Athenian trade in olive-oil—part of the ancient business carried out in this now rather soulless place. The top line reads ΚΕ ΝΟ ΘΕ ΑΔΡΙΑΝΟΥ: 'chief points from the law-giving of Hadrian'.

Just to the east of the Roman Agora there was another massive **Hadrianic structure** [11], its identification uncertain. Traces of this can be seen in a vacant plot (no. 78) on the north side of Adrianou, just east of the Hotel Adrian. The outer faces of the blocks have the artfully rough finish typical of Hadrianic masonry in Athens.

Odos Venizelou, just to the east, takes you to the **church of Theotokos Gorgoeipikoos and Ayios Eleftherios**, also known as the Little Metropolis, and now dwarfed by the cathedral of Athens next to it. The fabric of this early C13 church consists almost entirely of reused masonry, sculpture, and inscriptions from Classical Athens. A Doric frieze above the side door comes from the (Hadrianic?) gate to the City Eleusinion and depicts poppies and myrtle-bundles (left) and a *plemochoe*, a top-shaped vessel peculiar to Eleusinian ritual. Above the main entrance are two lengths of sculptured frieze side by side. From an unknown structure, probably of the C2–C1 BC, they show the Attic months personified as youths or men, along with signs of the zodiac and emblems of religious festivals. The month Hekatombaion and the Great Panathenaia held in that month appear in the middle of the left-hand block respectively (left) as a youth flanked by a crab and (right) Procession personified, with the Christian cross not quite obliterating the wheels of the car supporting the Panathenaic ship.

Olympieion (Fig. 17)

Special Features

The Olympieion is the largest temple in mainland Greece, and lies in an ancient quarter of the city renovated by Hadrian.

Description

The **Arch of Hadrian** [1] on Amalias spanned a venerable thoroughfare linking the Street of the Tripods and the south-east sector of the city, the line of which is followed by Odos Lysikratous. It carries two inscriptions, one (facing west) reading 'this is Athens, the ancient city of Theseus', the other (facing east) 'this is the city of Hadrian and not of Theseus' (*IG* 2^2.5185). The 'city of Theseus' was the old city to the west. By 'Hadrian's city' may have been meant the even older quarter to the south-east, pre-dating the time of Theseus (Thucydides 2.15), and 'refounded' thanks to Hadrian's public works in the area. The axis of the passage through the arch is exactly aligned with the middle of the lowest step on the east front of the Olympieion, to which the arch was evidently a kind of architectural preface.

The modern entrance to the Olympieion is on Leoforos Olgas. In front of the Hadrianic gateway to the precinct is a section of the Themistokleian **city-wall** [2] and one of its gates, identified as the so-called Cavalry (Hippades) Gate. The column-drums here, reused in the fortifications, came from the unfinished Peisistratid Olympieion. West of the wall, and dating from Hadrianic times, is the best-preserved example to be seen in Athens of Roman public **baths** [3], richly decorated with multi-coloured marble and mosaic pavements, with a small fountain at the east end.

The cult of Olympian Zeus at the **Olympieion** [4] was ancient. A small Doric temple with a colonnade, dated *c.*590–560 BC, stood on foundations found beneath the present temple. The family of the tyrant Peisistratos began work (*c.*520 BC) on a gigantic temple over twice the size of its predecessor. It had a double colonnade in the Doric order, and was inspired by the huge Ionic temples of this type at Ephesos and

▼ Fig. 17. Plan of the Olympieion and the Panathenaic Stadium. Key: 1 Arch of Hadrian 2 City-wall 3 Baths 4 Olympieion 5 Temple of Apollo Delphinios 6 Temple of Kronos and Rhea 7 Wall of Valerian 8 Panathenaic stadium 9 Lysikrates monument 10 Theatre of Dionysos

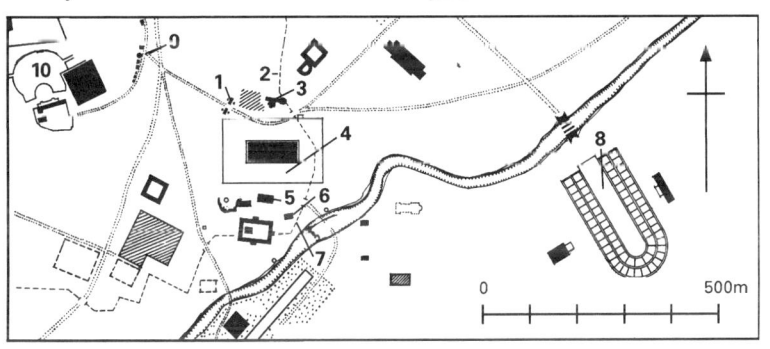

Samos. The temple was abandoned with the fall of the tyranny, although in the C3 BC, only 'half-finished', it was still thought a sight worth seeing. The Seleukid king Antiochos IV Epiphanes (175–164 BC), now known to have spent several years of his youth in Athens, undertook a completely new temple on the same platform, using a Roman architect, Decimus Cossutius. The new temple followed its predecessor's plan, but used the Corinthian order and Pentelic marble instead of poros stone. This temple, although unfinished when the king died, became one of the most admired in the Greek world. All the surviving columns but one date from this phase, which left the temple well-advanced, with work at least started on the double colonnade of the cella, since this must be where the more portable columns shipped to Rome by Sulla (84 BC) came from. Further work was carried out under Augustus by a consortium of client-kings, and the easternmost column of the three on the south-west flank is thought to be from this phase. Hadrian took the credit for completing the temple, and attended its dedication ceremony in the winter of AD 131. But a recent study has shown that the imperial additions were mainly the precinct, its surrounding wall (originally much higher, so that you could not see out or in), and the gateway, along with a colossal gold-and-ivory statue of the god (kept in the rear chamber). The cella was an open court, in accordance with the plan of Cossutius, to judge from Vitruvius (3.2.8). The real deity was Hadrian, who called himself 'Olympian' and who, unlike Zeus, had his own altar here. The precinct, moreover, was 'full' (Pausanias) of statues of him, set up for the most part by cities from all over the Roman east. You can still see two of the bases in the north-east corner (not in situ), one the gift of the small city of Koropissos (southern Turkey).

Excavations south of the Olympieion are now fenced and inaccessible, and best viewed from the platform. The large foundations are those of a colonnaded Doric temple of *c*.450 BC, identified as that of **Apollo Delphinios** [5]. The smaller ones to the south-east belong to a Roman podium-temple of *c*. AD 150, probably of **Kronos and Rhea** [6]. Just to the east you can see the line of the **fortification wall** [7], dated under Valerian (AD 253–60) and here following the old city-wall. To build it both temples seem to have been dismantled.

Continue east along Olgas to reach the **Panathenaic stadium** [8], which has unrestricted access. What you see is a modern restoration (1896) of the ancient stadium on the site. This was a controversial gift of Herodes Atticus which he paid for, Philostratus says, by withholding his father's cash-legacy to the Athenians, who apparently 'hated' him in consequence. Built in time for the Great Panathenaia of 143, it is usually thought to have replaced a simpler stadium (late C4 BC) located on the same site. Of Pentelic and Hymettian marble, it had a huge seating capacity of 50,000, as large as the Colosseum. Fragments of the original structure include the westernmost of the two herms at the far end of the stadium and some blocks of the parapet. This feature, along with the continuous podium behind it, apparently once supporting a fence or nets, shows that from the outset the stadium was used for wild-beast shows as well as traditional athletics. When Herodes died, the Athenians gave him a public burial here. The find of a small altar dedicated 'to He[rodes] the Marathonian hero' on the east hillside above the stadium (no access) suggests that his tomb lay in this vicinity.

Kerameikos (Fig. 18)

The entrance is on Ermou, just before the junction with Peiraios, a short distance from the Thisio metro station.

Special Features

The most important and informative Greek city cemetery.

History

The Kerameikos was named after the potters who had workshops in this part of the city and contained the state cemetery, the Demosion Sema, where the Athenians buried their war dead, military heroes, statesmen, philosophers, and even painters. This stretched from the Dipylon Gate to the Academy, a distance of approximately 1.5 km. The Agora was also in the Kerameikos. Pausanias in fact identifies the Agora as the Kerameikos, although this is rather an eccentric view.

The urban and suburban character of the Kerameikos is perfectly exemplified by the sector which has been excavated. This is bisected by the Eridanos stream which first became the focal point of a cemetery in the C11. The Submycenaean graves were simple pits in which the dead were buried in an extended position. In the Protogeometric period (*c.*1050–900 BC) most of the graves were on the south bank of the Eridanos and cremation was the preferred rite. Thereafter the Athenians switched between cremation and inhumation, possibly in response to social pressures or just from choice. Geometric (*c.*900–700 BC) graves can be quite rich and it is evident that funerals were an occasion when differences in wealth and status would be made apparent. Some of the graves were marked by massive kraters or amphorae which depict the dead person laid out on a bier and surrounded by mourners. The Archaic period (*c.*700–480 BC) saw a reduction in the number and quality of the offerings but there is much more of an emphasis on the external appearance of graves. Some were covered by enormous circular tumuli and crowned by statues or sculptured stelai. This lavish expenditure on funerals was eventually curbed by sumptuary laws.

Most of the statues and stelai were retrieved from the fortification wall which the Athenians hastily built in 478 BC. As Thucydides comments (1.93): 'one can see that it was done in a hurry. The foundations are made of different sorts of stone, sometimes not shaped so as to fit, but laid down just as each was brought at the time. There are stelai taken from tombs and sculpture mixed in.' After the Athenians were defeated by the Spartans in 404 BC the fortifications were pulled down but they were rebuilt early in the C4. Tombs soon lined the roads which ran from the Dipylon Gate and the Sacred Gate. Some take the form of a rectangular enclosure which contained a number of graves, usually members of the same family who were commemorated by stelai or marble lekythoi. The cycle of increased ostentation followed by enforced austerity was repeated at the end of the C4 when Demetrios of Phaleron prohibited expensive funerary monuments. In the Hellenistic period graves were marked by kioniskoi, small columns which simply recorded the name of the deceased, their father and deme. In 86 BC the Romans captured Athens and left a trail of destruction which Plutarch (*Sulla* 14.4) describes in graphic detail: 'the blood that was shed in the Agora covered the whole of the Kerameikos inside the Dipylon Gate. Indeed many say that it flowed through the gate and flooded the suburb'. Potters subsequently set up workshops around the Sacred Gate. The cemetery remained in use until it was eventually buried under a layer of silt.

Description

The **Oberländer Museum** is well labelled in English, German, and Greek. In **room 1** there is the late C5 stele of Ampharete, who holds her dead grandchild (p. 41), and the relief which commemorates the death of the cavalryman Dexileos at Corinth in 394 BC. The room on the left contains Archaic grave stelai. The dead person is sometimes represented as a soldier, although the nudity is of course an artistic convention, sometimes as an athlete. On a relief at the far end of the room there is a boxer with a broken nose and cauliflower ear. The stele was crowned by a palmette or a sphinx, the sinister guardian of the dead. In **rooms 2–4** you can see how grave offerings varied over time. Room 2, opposite the entrance, covers the Submycenaean, Protogeometric, Geometric, and early Archaic periods. Pottery is the common denominator in these graves. In time more metalwork appears—bronze and iron weapons which include a 'killed' sword—and some jewellery. The stylistic development of Athenian pottery continues in **rooms 3 and 4**. There is Archaic and Classical black-figure and red-figure. White-ground lekythoi were a favourite gift and often depict mourners at the tomb. Pottery also fulfilled a political role in C5 Athens when an ostracism was held (see Agora museum). The names of the candidates were inscribed on sherds or ostraka—over 7000 have been found in the bed of the Eridanos. There were inexpensive unguentaria in most of the Hellenistic graves which were replaced by blown glass vessels in the Roman period. On one of the reliefs outside

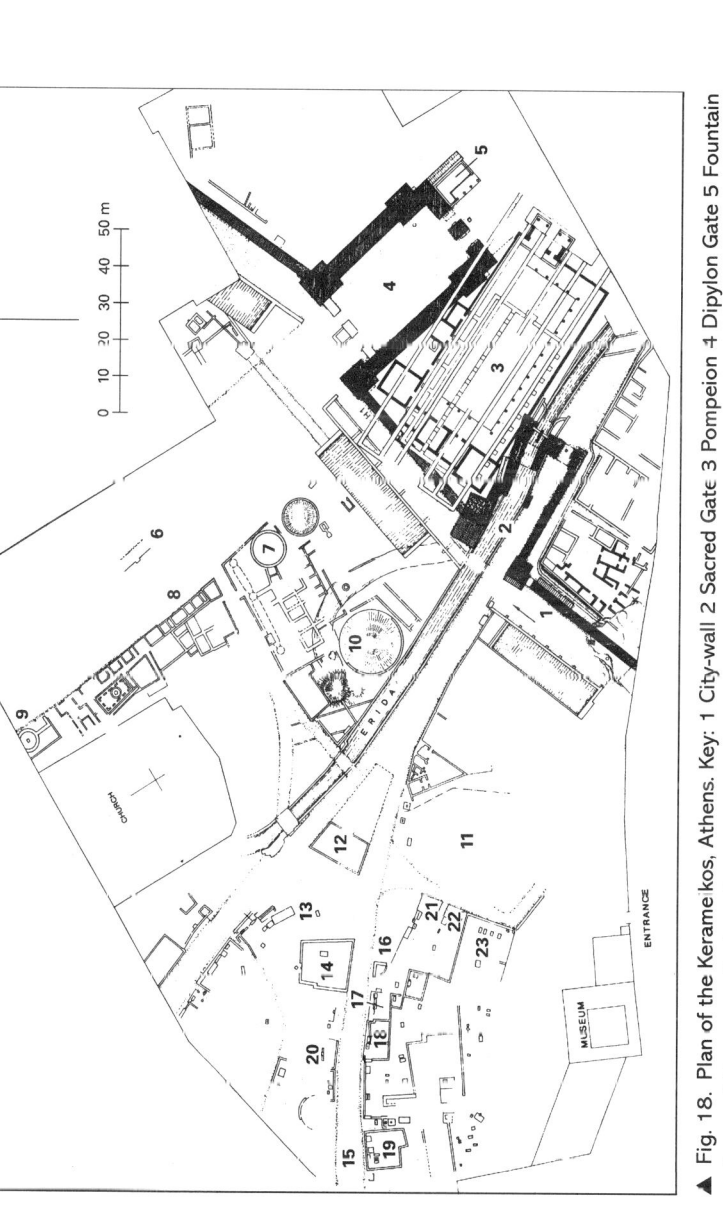

Fig. 18. Plan of the Kerameikos, Athens. Key: 1 City-wall 2 Sacred Gate 3 Pompeion 4 Dipylon Gate 5 Fountain house 6 Dromos 7 Baths 8 Tomb of the Lakedaimonians 9 C4 tomb 0-11 Tumuli 12 Sanctuary of the Tritopatres 13 C6 tumulus 14 Enclosure 15 Street of the Tombs 16 Grave precinct 17 Peribolos tomb 18 Marble bull 19 Grave precinct 20 Stele of Hegeso 21-3 Grave precincts

the museum two couples sit behind a table and contemplate their funeral meal while Charon waits below them in his boat.

The best preserved section of the **city-wall** [1] is south of the Sacred Gate. It is obvious from the different masonry styles that the wall had a chequered history. Three main phases can be identified—early C5, early C4, and late C4. There is also evidence of C3 AD repairs. The wall consisted of a stone base which supported a mudbrick superstructure. The base was raised each time the wall was rebuilt, hence the hybrid character of the masonry. As siege engines became more powerful and sophisticated, the need arose for a second line of defence and so an outer wall, the proteichisma, was constructed and in front of this a moat. The **Sacred Gate** [2] guarded the road to Eleusis, the Sacred Way. The Eridanos was also channelled through this gate which is of the courtyard type. Attackers would be penned in the court in front of the gate, at the mercy of the defenders on the ramparts. The gate formed part of the Themistokleian fortifications but underwent a number of modifications. The **Pompeion** [3] was built in the C4 in the space between the Sacred Gate and the Dipylon Gate. It consisted of a peristyle court, entered from a propylon at the east end. The rooms on the north and west sides of the court were provided with couches. The Panathenaic procession set out from the Pompeion and privileged citizens feasted on the meat from the sacrificial victims here. It was destroyed by Sulla in the C1 BC and lay in ruins until the C2 when a basilica was constructed. This only lasted until the arrival of the Herulians in the C3 and was replaced by two stoas in the C4. As the name implies, the **Dipylon** [4] was a double gate. Originally it had a stone base and a mudbrick superstructure but was rebuilt in conglomerate and limestone in the late C4. A second pair of gates was added between the outer towers in the Hellenistic period. Thirsty travellers would certainly have appreciated the **fountain house** [5].

The Kerameikos seems such a tranquil place now but this was not the case in antiquity. The Dipylon was the main gate of the city and people will naturally have gathered here. Some came for a particular reason because, as several scholiasts drily note, the Kerameikos was 'where the prostitutes stood'. The excavators have identified one of the houses by the Sacred Gate as a brothel and the cemetery must also have been used by prostitutes and their clients. This is quite a thought as you stroll down the **Dromos** [6], the road which runs north-west from the Dipylon. The funeral ceremony for the war dead was held here and there were torch races on the Dromos. You pass a round **bath** [7] where travellers could freshen up and then the **Tomb of the Lakedaimonians** [8], Spartan officers who were killed in 403 BC. Note the boundary stones marked ΟΡΟΣ ΚΕΡΑΜΕΙΚΟΥ. Where the Dromos disappears under Odos Peiraios there is an extremely impressive late C5 or early C4 **tomb** [9] in which another of the Spartan casualties, the Olympian victor Lakrates, may have been buried.

▲ Fig. 19. Boundary stone by the Tomb of the Lakedaimonians in the Kerameikos

One of the **tumuli** [10] between the Dromos and the Sacred Way, is linked with an Athenian clan, the Kerykes. The enormous **tumulus** [11] on the other side of the Sacred Way was built over the grave of a man who evidently came from Ionia. Envoys from Corcyra and Selymbria were buried at the foot of this tumulus, opposite the **Sanctuary of the Tritopatres** [12], ancestral spirits who were worshipped for their procreative powers. The boundary stones on the north-east and south-east corners of the sanctuary state that entry is forbidden. Behind the Tritopatreion there is a C6 **tumulus** [13] and just west of this a mudbrick **enclosure** [14] of the late C5 which may be the grave precinct of the Alkmaionids, one of the most powerful Athenian families. The **Street of the Tombs** [15] was laid out in the C4 and you can see how the cemetery would have looked at this time. Many of the monuments were destroyed in 338 BC, when the Athenians hastily reinforced the city-walls, but were later restored. The **grave precinct** [16] of Lysanias of Thorikos, one of the most prominent, is crowned by the memorial for his son Dexileos who would have been buried with his comrades in the Demosion Sema. Next there is a typical **peribolos tomb** [17]. The white plaster on the facade covered up the poor quality masonry which was used when the tomb was restored. The stelai commemorate Agathon and Sosikrates, two brothers from Herakleia on the Black Sea, and Agathon's wife Korallion. The marble **bull** [18] towers over the grave of Dionysios from the deme of Kollytos who had served as treasurer in the sanctuary of Hera on Samos. He died unmarried but his mother and sisters ensured that his tomb would be conspicuous and that his name would therefore live on. The **grave precinct** [19] of Lysimachides has one of the best preserved facades and must have been set up after 338 BC but before Demetrios of Phaleron introduced sumptuary laws in 317–307 BC. On the north side of the street is a cast of the fine late C5 **stele of Hegeso** [20]— the original is in the National Archaeological Museum. The path up to the museum passes the **grave precincts** of the poet Makareos [21], of Demetria and Pamphile who were sisters [22], and of Philoxenos who came from MESSENE [23]. This was not an exclusively Athenian cemetery but had quite a cosmopolitan character. Note the forest of kioniskoi just below the museum, a case of 'sic transit gloria profundi' after the splendid excesses of the C4.

National Museum (Fig. 20)
The main entrance is on Patission.

Special Features

The spectacular finds from the shaft graves at MYCENAE, masterpieces of Greek sculpture, an exemplary display of sculpture from Roman Greece, and a comprehensive collection of Greek ceramics.

Athens, Attika, and the Saronic 85

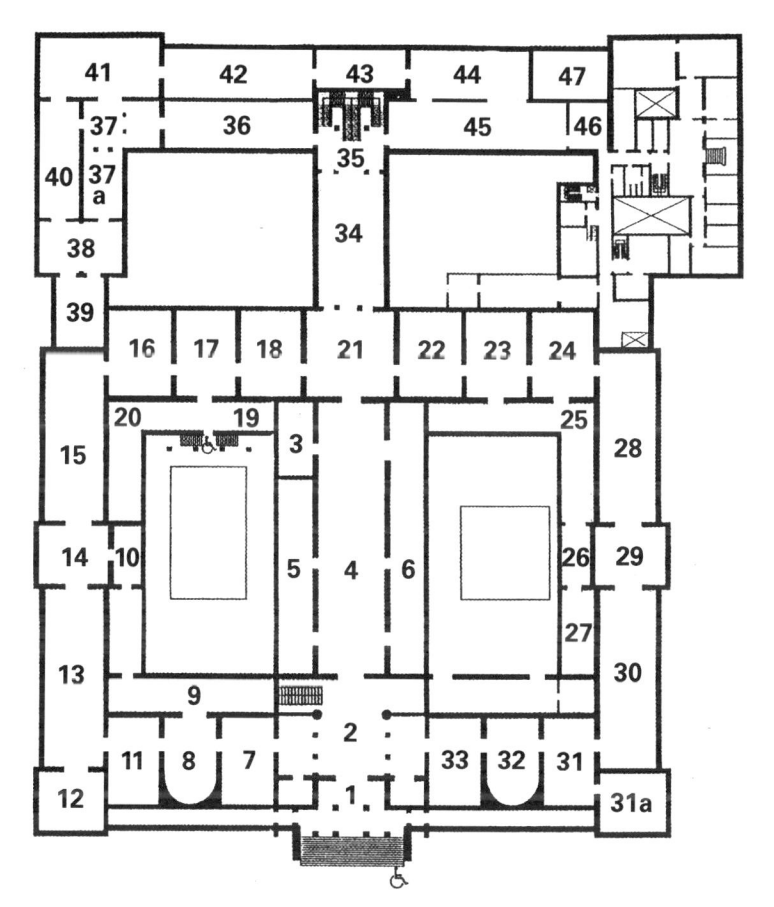

▲ Fig. 20. Plan of the National Archaeological Museum

Description
Prehistoric Collection: Rooms 3–6

These rooms have recently been reorganized and have excellent display boards in English and Greek. **Room 5**, on the left, covers the Neolithic, Early, and Middle Helladic periods. Note in particular the vividly painted Neolithic pottery from SESKLO and DIMINI in Thessaly—also finds from Troy which were presented by Sophie Schliemann.

The Mycenaean collection in **room 4** is stupendous. The six shaft graves in Grave Circle A at MYCENAE naturally come first. Many of the burials were marked by stone stelai on which battle and hunt scenes demonstrate the Mycenaean predilection for blood sports. The dead were buried in shrouds covered in gold rosettes. They wore jewellery and some of the men had gold masks placed over their faces. Weapons emphasize their military prowess. Do not miss the inlaid daggers which have figures of gold and silver set into an oxidized silver plate on either side of the blade. Details are picked out in niello, a blue-black paste. Like so many of the objects from the shaft graves, these daggers represent a hybrid artistic style which combines the refined skills of Minoan craftsmen and the flamboyant tastes of the Mycenaean aristocrats who commissioned them. The gold cups also epitomize this love of ostentation. Grave Circle B is not as rich but note the bowl carved from a block of rock crystal. In the centre of the room there is a display of gold rings and sealstones. The Warrior Vase comes from one of the houses on the citadel at Mycenae. The gesture of the woman who bids the soldiers farewell implies that they may not survive their encounter with the ruffians on the back. The Linear B tablets were not intended as permanent records but you can see that they have been burned and consequently preserved. The lively boar hunt fresco is from the palace at TIRYNS. Gold cups and inlaid daggers were also buried in the tholos tombs at PYLOS, DENDRA, and VAPHEIO. Columns from the Treasury of Atreus at Mycenae frame the door at the far end of the room.

There are finds from sites in the Cyclades on display in **room 6**. The marble figurines and vases from Early Cycladic (3000–2000 BC) graves stand out. The purity of the marble makes the figurines particularly attractive but they were once painted and would have looked quite different. As is so often true of Greek sculpture, first impressions can be deceptive.

Sculpture Collection: Rooms 7–35

The Late Geometric amphora in **room 7** was a grave marker in the Kerameikos cemetery and underlines the fact that the Greeks did not make use of stone for sculpture in the C8. Mourners file past the dead woman who has been laid out on a couch and covered by a checked shroud, which is cut away so that she is visible. Marble eventually provided a more durable medium for funerary monuments and also for votives, such as the statue of Artemis from Delos which Nikandre dedicated in the mid-C7. The triangular face, framed by braids of hair, is characteristic of the Daedalic style, which was inspired by imported terracottas of the Near Eastern goddess Astarte. The nudity of the ivory statuettes in this room is also typically Near Eastern but not the slim proportions. By the early C6 Egyptian influence can be seen in the sheer size and the system of proportions used for the colossal kouros from SOUNION in **room 8**. The kouros pose is also derived from Egypt, although in the case of male statues nudity is a Greek convention. Most of the Attic kouroi were grave markers. The fine, if disembodied, Dipylon Head is one of the earliest. In due course the treatment of the anatomy becomes more realistic and you can follow this development in rooms **9–13**.

Note in particular the kouros from Melos (**room 9**), the Volomandra kouros (**room 10**), the statue of Aristodikos and the Anavysos kouros (**room 13**). That naturalism was the conscious aim of the sculptors seems unlikely since the rigid posture of the kouroi is clearly not taken from life. Also in **room 9** there is one of the most graceful korai, the 'marker of Phrasikleia' (see p. 41). Because many of these Archaic statues only stood in the open for a relatively short period of time, they still have traces of paint preserved. The splendid grave stele of Aristion in **room 11** was painted blue and red. There is sculpture from the temple of Aphaia on AIGINA in **room 12** and a remarkable kouros base at the far end of **room 13** which shows us how aristocratic Athenian youths passed their time.

The contrast between the Archaic and Classical styles is quite stark. Look at the relief from Sounion in **room 14** which depicts a victorious athlete. He has a more introspective expression than the kouroi and the sculptor has attempted a three-quarter view of the torso. As you enter **room 15** there is a votive relief from ELEUSIS on the left. Triptolemos is in the centre, flanked by Demeter and Persephone. The superb bronze statue of Poseidon was recovered from the sea off cape Artemision minus his trident. Once Greek sculptors could cast life-size bronze statues, which were made in several pieces and then soldered together, they could attempt much more ambitious poses. The mass of a marble statue had to be carefully balanced, whereas bronze is a much more flexible medium. Unfortunately it is also a more valuable commodity and most bronze statues have been melted down and the metal recycled. Particularly in the Roman period, Classical masterpieces were copied in marble but the effect is not the same. Compare the Poseidon and the Omphalos Apollo which is a copy of an early C5 statue.

Much of the sculpture in **rooms 16–28** is funerary. A law may have been passed in Athens at the end of the C6 which limited expenditure on funerals but sculptured grave stelai appear once more in the late C5. The scenes on these stelai can be quite complex and often enigmatic. In **room 16**, on a stele from Salamis or Aigina, a youth has rescued a bird from a predatory cat. Below the cat is a boy, possibly a slave who grieves for his master. The funerary lekythos of Myrrhine is more explicit. She is led away by Hermes while her family bid farewell. **Room 17** has sculpture from the late C5 temple of Hera in the ARGIVE HERAION. Roman copies of Classical statues can be seen in **rooms 19–20**, in particular the Varvakeion Athena which is a one-twelfth scale version of the Athena Parthenos by Pheidias. It does not quite recapture the majesty of the original. On the late C5 stele of Hegeso in **room 18** the dead woman selects a necklace from a box of jewellery which a slave girl has brought. It is a mundane scene and yet poignant because it can never happen again. The bronze horse and jockey in **room 21** were found in the sea off cape Artemision. The scruffy but determined boy is typically

Hellenistic. Also in this room is a copy of the Diadoumenos by the famous C5 sculptor Polykleitos. The pedimental sculpture from the temple of Asklepios at EPIDAUROS is in **room 22**. The east pediment depicts the capture of Troy and the west pediment the battle of the Greeks and Amazons. Grave monuments increase in size in the C4. The relief is often set in a separate frame which enshrines the figures. A handshake is a common motif, an adieu which holds out the prospect of a reunion in the future. The Ilissos stele in **room 23** is one of the finest. The dead youth leans against his tombstone, mourned by his aged father, but the boy at his feet is fast asleep. **Rooms 25–27** contain Athenian decree reliefs and also votive reliefs, many of which were dedicated to Asklepios. The grave stele of Aristonautes in **room 28** is one of the latest. They were subsequently banned by Demetrios of Phaleron (317–307 BC). The Marathon Boy is reminiscent of statues by the C4 sculptor Praxiteles. Like the Antikythera youth and so many other bronzes, he was lost at sea and therefore survived. Also in this room there is the bronze head of a boxer from OLYMPIA and a marble head from TEGEA which may be the goddess Hygieia.

The Hellenistic sculpture in **room 29** includes a C3 statue of Themis from RHAMNOUS and some of the colossal heads which Damophon carved in the C3 for the sanctuary of Despoina at LYKOSOURA. There is a powerfully modelled statue of Poseidon from Melos in **room 30**, the head of the Zeus by Eukleides which Pausanias saw at AIGEIRA, and a playful but quite possibly painful encounter between Pan and Aphrodite. The recently opened display of Roman sculpture in **rooms 31–33** is excellent. The emphasis is on imperial portraiture. The Julio-Claudians and the Flavians occupy **room 31**. An equestrian statue of Augustus is particularly impressive. The rows of heads in the side room commemorate the Athenians who served as kosmetai of the Diogeneion gymnasium. **Room 32** has portraits of Hadrian and Antinoos (see p. 314), a fine bust of Herodes Atticus and of his favourite Polydeukion (see p. 115). **Room 33** covers the Severan dynasty, the Tetrarchs and Constantine. Note the bronze statue from SPARTA of a Roman empress, possibly Julia Mamaea who was murdered in AD 235. The statue was removed from its pedestal, flattened and then buried.

Bronze and Egyptian Collections: Rooms 36–37 and 40–41

Most of the bronzes in **room 36** come from the sanctuary of Zeus at DODONA. There is also a dedication which the Athenians made after a sea victory and attachments from a triumphal chariot found at Nikomedia in Bithynia, possibly in the palace of Diocletian. In **room 37** you can see how a bronze statuette was cast. The Egyptian collection, recently installed in **rooms 40–41**, is well presented and labelled. Greeks from Egypt have donated many of the items. In **room 40** there is a statue from the sanctuary of the Egyptian gods at MARATHON.

Thera Exhibition and Pottery Collection: Rooms 48–56 (First Floor)

An exhibition of finds from Akrotiri on Thera has been put on display in **room 48**. The site was overwhelmed by a volcanic eruption in the late C17 BC and is often described as a prehistoric Pompeii because the houses and their contents have been so well preserved by the ash. Much of the pottery is Cycladic but Minoan influence can also be detected. Evidently there were close ties between Thera and Crete at this time. The finds in the first section of the room also include bronze and stone vessels and a remarkable bed which materialized when voids in the ash were filled with plaster. Most of the frescoes from Minoan Crete and Mycenaean Greece consist of scraps which defy restoration. At Akrotiri there were entire frescoes still in situ. They were painted in a style which is clearly Minoan but have a quite distinctive character. Two boys box, a fisherman carries home his catch, swallows flit through a volcanic landscape. The most complex scene is of a flotilla of ships, apparently decked out for a festival.

The history of Greek pottery is set out in **rooms 49–56**. The dominant role of Athens is evident from the start of the Protogeometric period (**room 49**). At first the decoration is quite simple and restrained. Glossy black paint covers more and more of the body. In the Geometric period (**rooms 49–50**) bands of abstract motifs steadily encroach and create a much richer effect. Figures make an appearance in the C8. A common scene, no doubt because most of the pottery comes from graves, is the prothesis. Men and women, rendered as silhouettes, mourn the dead or drive past in chariots, the mode of transport favoured by heroes. The painters now have certain idiosyncrasies and can be differentiated. The pioneer of this figure style is known as the Dipylon Master. In the C7 Near Eastern motifs were introduced and Orientalizing pottery styles developed (**rooms 50–51**). CORINTH specialized in the production of exquisitely painted perfume flasks which were widely exported. The Athenians favoured more ambitious but often rather crude compositions on their Protoattic amphorae. Late in the C7 they adopted the black-figure technique from Corinth. The figures, painted in silhouette, have details incised so that the clay shows through. In time this style became more refined and Athens took control of the market for decorated pottery. As well as early examples of Athenian black-figure pottery, **room 52** has a terracotta model of the temple of Hera in the Argive Heraion, finds from the sanctuary of Hera at PERACHORA and Artemis Orthia at SPARTA, terracotta metopes from the temple of Apollo at THERMON, and wooden panels from Pitsa, west of SIKYON. The black-figure in **room 53** includes pieces by some of the best painters—Lydos, the Amasis Painter and Exekias who was responsible for the terracotta plaques. The red-figure technique was invented c.530 BC and is the reverse of black-figure. The decoration is reserved in the colour of the clay and the background is blacked out. Details are painted rather than incised and this allows for much more subtle effects. In the late Archaic period both techniques were used but black-figure died out in the C5 except for the Panathenaic amphorae which were given as prizes at the games. You can follow the development of red-figure in **rooms 54–56**. Much of the pottery made in Athens was exported to Italy. There was less demand for white-ground lekythoi which were one of the most common grave gifts in the late C5. The visit to the tomb is a favourite theme. The figures, painted in outline on the white background, have details added in a range of colours.

Epigraphic Museum
The entrance is at Tositsa 1, the street on the south side of the National Museum.

Special Features

This houses the most important collection of Greek inscriptions in the world. Inside you get a good impression of a working environment—a library of stones.

Description

The earliest stones are in **room 11**, and some of the most historic from all periods in **room 9** (closed for repairs in 1999). Most of the important stones are labelled in English and a knowledge of ancient Greek is not essential. The labels give an idea of the great range of purposes for which the ancient Athenians and other Greeks committed documents to stone. Particularly striking is the preponderance of official records, especially decrees, accounts of officials, and lists of war dead. Much of this reflects the accountability and openness of the Athenian democracy. Many are carved on stone slabs (stelai), originally slotted into bases for display in public areas.

One set of inscriptions here that you should not miss are the so-called **tribute lists** (**room 1**). The tallest (over 3.5 m. at least) is also the earliest (from 454/3 BC). Once displayed on the Akropolis, these huge blocks from the hey-day of the C5 BC Athenian empire listed the tenth part set aside for Athena from the annual payments to Athens by her allies. You can see how individual contributors were grouped regionally under headings like hΕΛΛΕΣΠΟΝΤΙΟΣ ('Hellespont', modern Dardanelles) and ΘΡΑΙΚΕΣ ('Thrace'). The amounts are rendered by a system comprising a numerical sign, I, which could be repeated (IIII = 4), along with the first letters of words for numbers, representing the number itself: so Π = 5, from *p(ente)*, 'five' ; Δ = 10, from *d(eka)* and so on. These lists are extremely important for reconstructing Athenian history of the period. Standing in front of them you start to grasp the enormous skill of the specialist scholars (epigraphers) who painstakingly reassembled these enormous jigsaws.

Numismatic Museum

The museum is at 10–12 Eleftheriou Venizelou. It was closed in September 1999 because of earthquake damage.

Description

The museum is housed in the superb Iliou Melathron ('Troy Mansion'), the Athenian residence of Heinrich Schliemann, excavator of MYCENAE, and worth visiting for its architecture and historical associations alone. The Greek national coin collection, displayed here since 1999, is exceptionally fine and accessibly laid out.

The display is on the ground floor. **Room 1** is devoted to Schliemann and the history of the house. **Room 2** focuses on the invention, evolution, and uses of currency down to the modern day, with a section on techniques and good examples of hoards. **Room 3** contains coins from Athens, Greek federal organizations, Macedon under Alexander the Great, and the Greek settlements in Asia Minor and Italy. **Room 4** is devoted to the varied imagery on ancient coinage, including portraits. **Room 6** contains mainly private collections and **room 7** focuses on the history of the museum. There are plans to open further rooms on the first floor to display Roman, medieval, and modern coins.

Piraeus (Fig. 21)

Special Features

The ancient Piraeus was once the greatest port in the eastern Mediterranean, and has an archaeological museum which you should not miss.

History

The development of Piraeus as the chief harbour of ATHENS was begun by the statesman Themistokles, who built the first walls in 493/2 BC. Its attractions were an easily fortified peninsula-site, proximity (*c.*7 km.) to Athens, and three natural harbours (Kantharos, the largest; Zea, modern Pasalimani; and Mounychia, modern Mikrolimani). The home of the Athenian war-fleet, Piraeus was also, for a while (C5–C4 BC), the biggest commercial entrepôt in Greece; as such, it was a cosmopolitan place, with an estimated 5000–6000 foreign residents at its peak. By far the biggest of the dependent settlements (demes) of Athens, it had a population reputed to be 'more democratic' than Athens itself. Unlike Athens it was a planned city. Few traces of this plan survive, although recent rescue excavations point to a grid of wide (8 m.) and narrow (5 m.) streets. In the mid-C5 BC the statesman Perikles linked Athens and Piraeus with the Long Walls, allowing Athenian access to the sea even in war-time. After Alexander, Piraeus was occupied on and off by a

Mikrolimani (Mounychia)

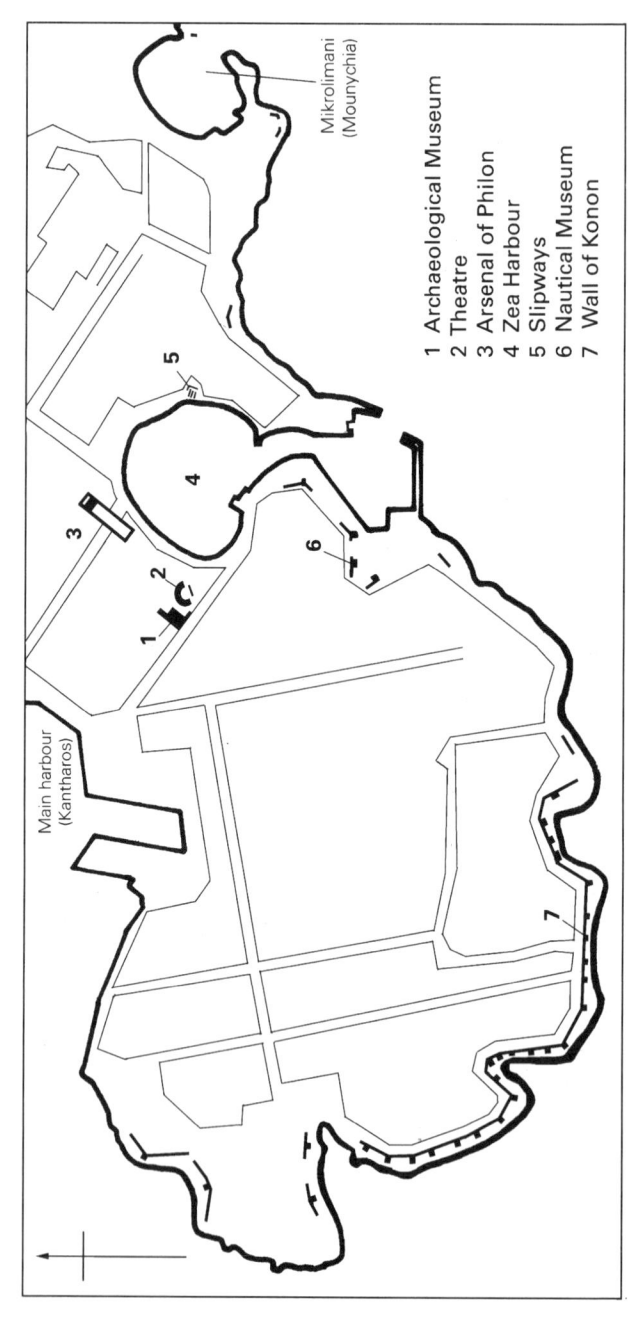

1 Archaeological Museum
2 Theatre
3 Arsenal of Philon
4 Zea Harbour
5 Slipways
6 Nautical Museum
7 Wall of Konon

Main harbour (Kantharos)

▲ Fig. 21. Plan of Piraeus

Macedonian garrison and lost its commercial dominance to Rhodes and Alexandria. In 86 BC the Roman general Sulla destroyed the docks and public buildings during his war against Mithradates. Piraeus now became a byword for Greece's decline. By the late C1 BC the settlement had shrunk to the area immediately around the harbours. Little of the ancient city is now preserved.

Description

The **Archaeological Museum** [1] is on Charilaou Trikoupi, just off Zea harbour, and is well signed. This museum contains exceptional finds, not only from Piraeus but also from other sites in Attika, the Saronic area, and the island of Kythera. The labels, in English and Greek, are exemplary.

Displayed in the entrance hall is a **boundary-stone** inscribed 'boundary of the agora', dated *c.*450 BC partly from the letter-forms. At the end of both lines you can see the early form of the Greek letter *sigma* (S), with three bars instead of four (Σ). The boundary-stone belongs to a group of fourteen, reflecting the original town-plan of Hippodamos of Miletos (early C5 BC), the most famous Greek town-planner, after whom this agora was called 'Hippodamian'. The site has yet to be located.

Room 1 (first floor) has finds illustrating the religious cults of Attika and the commercial and naval life of Piraeus. Of particular note are the finds from a Minoan peak sanctuary on Kythera, the only one outside Crete; pottery from the sanctuary of Artemis Mounychia (now under the yacht club in Mikrolimani), including ritual vessels, the so-called *krateriskoi*, decorated with scenes of running girls, similar to finds from BRAURON; a bronze ram from a trireme, perhaps C4 BC; and a market inscription (C1 BC) shedding light on the gastronomic preferences of the Athenians, with maximum prices set for pigs' trotters, belly of pork, goats' udders, and beef lungs.

Room 2 has a well chosen and displayed range of pottery and small finds from Mycenaean to Hellenistic times, above all the remarkable finds from the tomb of a musician-composer at Daphni, including a type of harp (*trigonon*), the tortoise-shell soundbox of a lyre, and a flute, along with wax tablets with faintly preserved lettering, taken to show that the deceased wrote his own songs.

Rooms 2–3 contain the museum's star attractions, a group of bronzes and two marble herms found by chance (1959) in mysterious circumstances (see **box**). The Apollo is the oldest known full-length bronze statue from Greece, usually dated *c.*520 BC on stylistic grounds. It once held a bow and shallow bowl, and may have been a cult-statue from a shrine. The Athena once held a spear and shield, drapery and proportions would fit a C4-BC date, although it could be a late Hellenistic copy of an earlier work. The large Artemis is usually dated to the C4 BC, as is the small Artemis.

Room 4 recreates a Greek sanctuary, mainly based on finds from a sanctuary of the goddess Kybele in modern Moschato. **Room 5** (in 1999 closed by an earthquake) contains funerary monuments.

Rooms 6–7 (ground floor) have more funerary monuments (c.350–317 BC, the acme of Athenian funerary art). Two are noteworthy for their size: the colossal lion (room 7), from Moschato, and, dominating room 6, the uniquely lavish monument (c.350 BC) of a foreign resident, Nikeratos, and his son Polyxenos. The epitaph calls him Istrianos, 'citizen of Istria', a Greek colony on the Romanian coast (modern Constanza); he owed his wealth, no doubt, to the lucrative Black-Sea trade. The tomb was found at modern Kallithea inside the Long Walls, and presumably once lined the ancient Athens road. The stepped base with its frieze of Greeks fighting Amazons (traces of ancient paintwork) recalls, and perhaps was influenced by, the famous Mausoleum of Halikarnassos (modern Bodrum). The stele of Panchares (room 6), son of Leochares, has a relief scene in which a heavily armoured Greek foot-soldier (Panchares) defends a fallen comrade against a spear-wielding cavalryman, identified as Macedonian from his 'Alexander' -like hairstyle; if so, the battle may be CHAIRONEIA (338 BC).

Rooms 8–9 are devoted to Hellenistic and Roman sculpture. The most remarkable finds (room 9) are a group of 'mass-produced' reliefs in Pentelic marble (C2 AD), made by local workshops for export to Italy and other Roman destinations, to adorn the walls of public buildings and wealthy homes. Found by chance during dredging of the main harbour of Piraeus, they seem to have been cargo on an ancient vessel which foundered just after departure. A total of 88 pieces (including fragments) are known. The style ('neo-attic') copies or adapts Archaic and Classical works for a Roman clientele, as with the panels 'quoting' the battle of Greeks and Amazons on the shield of Pheidias' statue of Athena in the Parthenon. The mirror composition of the two Archaizing plaques with Herakles and Apollo disputing the Delphic tripod shows their decorative purpose (probably to flank a door).

In the grounds of the museum (inaccessible but visible) is a **theatre** [2], dated c.150 BC from inscriptions on the stage-building. Its preserved foundations include a proskenion with projecting wings. Remains of an older theatre have been excavated on Mounychia hill, probably dating back to the C5 BC, and now built over.

Nearby, at 170 Ipsilandou, preserved beneath an office-block, you can see from the street a small section of the foundations of the so-called **Arsenal of Philon** [3], one of the most admired buildings in Piraeus until its destruction by Sulla in 86 BC, and named after its architect, who wrote a book about it. A naval warehouse (*skeuotheke*) for storing the rigging, sails, and rope of triremes wintering in the nearby shipsheds of Zea, it was commissioned in 347/6 BC. Its renown in part derived from its size, with a length of 400 Attic feet (c.118–23 m.), as stated in a remarkable 97-line inscription setting out the specifications for contractors. The section here, found in 1988, preserves the arrangements for the double-doors at the north entrance of the building, described as follows:

> leaving two doorways at each end of the warehouse, 9 feet wide; and to build a partition wall between the doorways at each end, 2 feet wide and 10 feet deep towards the inside, and make a return in the wall against which each door opens, as far as the first columns.
>
> (*IG* 2².1668, lines 22–6)

In antiquity the harbour of **Zea** [**4**] was the main base for the Athenian fleet, lined with over 196 shipsheds according to inscriptions (C4 BC). Nowadays the nearest you can get to viewing their remains is the basement of 1 Serangiou, where narrow grilles give a dimly lit view from the street of the inner end of three **slipways** ([**5**]—C4 BC), originally separated by colonnades supporting a shared roof.

There is a reconstruction of shipsheds in the **Nautical Museum** [**6**] which is in the bay south of Zea, and has other exhibits illustrating Athenian naval history. A stretch of the **wall of Themistokles** can be seen here, built of unbaked brick supported by a masonry socle. It was begun in 493/92 BC, and enclosed the whole of the Piraeus peninsula. It was demolished by the Spartans in 404 BC.

If you follow the road around the Akte peninsula, you will see, edging the shore, well-preserved stretches of ashlar masonry belonging to its successor, also at least partly of baked brick. This so-called **wall of Konon** [**7**] is named from the Athenian general who rebuilt and enlarged the fortifications of Piraeus after 394 BC with money from the Persian king. Inscriptions show that the walls were kept in good repair down to *c.*229 BC at least.

The Piraeus bronzes

The bronzes were found by workmen digging a ditch for a sewer a block behind the waterfront of the main harbour, in what was probably an ancient warehouse, later burnt down around them. They were in storage at the time of the fire, which was probably the work of Roman troops in 86 BC. Their origin is a mystery. Damage to the left foot of the Athena points to hurried removal from a base. Since there is one statue of Apollo and two of his sister Artemis, the statues perhaps were among the 'sacred things' sent to Athens for safekeeping in 88 BC from Delos, following an attack by Mithradates of Pontos on the sanctuary of Delian Apollo.

Sounion (Figs. 22–25) ★

The site is just off the road which runs down the west coast of Attika.

Special Features

A fine Classical temple in a spectacular location.

History

Pausanias starts his description of Greece at Sounion and soon makes his first mistake when he says (1.1.1): 'on the point of the cape is a temple of Athena'. In due course we will see why he misidentified the temple of Poseidon but it does underline the fact that this once prestigious sanctuary had become redundant by the C2 AD. The 'sacred cape of Sounion' is first mentioned in the *Odyssey* (3.278) as the place where Phrontis died at the helm of Menelaos' ship and was buried. Homer does not tell us why the cape was sacred but it was an obvious location for a sanctuary of Poseidon. This was the last landfall before sailors faced the Aegean and they will no doubt have offered up prayers to the god of the sea for their safe return or thanks when a voyage had been completed successfully. There is evidence of cult activity in the C7 and early in the C6 a number of marble kouroi were set up in the sanctuary. One of these, a colossus 3.05 m. high, is on display in the National Archaeological Museum. Soon after 500 BC a temple was under construction for Poseidon. This was more or less the same size as the later temple and had the same basic plan. Given that there was so much animosity between ATHENS and AIGINA at this time and that the temple of Aphaia had recently been completed, it seems quite likely that the project was financed by the state rather than the deme of Sounion. In 480 BC the Persians sacked the sanctuary and destroyed the temple. After the battle of Salamis the Greeks dedicated a captured Phoenician warship as retribution for this sacrilegious act. It was not until the middle of the C5 that the temple of Poseidon was replaced and a temple was also built in the sanctuary of Athena Sounias. In the winter of 413/412 BC the Athenians fortified Sounion to protect the sea-route around the cape and consequently their corn supply. The Macedonians extended the fortifications and constructed shipsheds in the C3. Thereafter Sounion declined in importance. The temple of Athena was partially dismantled and reassembled in the Athenian agora in the C1 AD. This was presumably why Pausanias made his mistake which was not rectified until the late C19. By then the temple of Poseidon had become famous as one of the most romantic ruins in Greece, painted by Turner and celebrated by Byron (*Don Juan* canto III, stanza L16):

Place me on Sunium's marbled steep,
Where nothing save the waves and I,

May hear our mutual murmurs sweep;
There swan-like, let me sing and die.

Description

The path takes you through the fortifications on the east side of the site and you then enter the **Sanctuary of Poseidon**. The impressive Doric **propylon** [1] was built at around the same time as the Classical temple. By the propylon is a **room** [2] with an off-centre entrance which could accommodate eleven couches and was presumably used for ritual meals.

▼ Fig. 22. Plan of the Sanctuary of Poseidon at Sounion. Key: 1 Propylon 2 Room 3 Stoa 4 Stoa 5 Temple of Poseidon 6 Streets 7 Bastion 8 Shipsheds

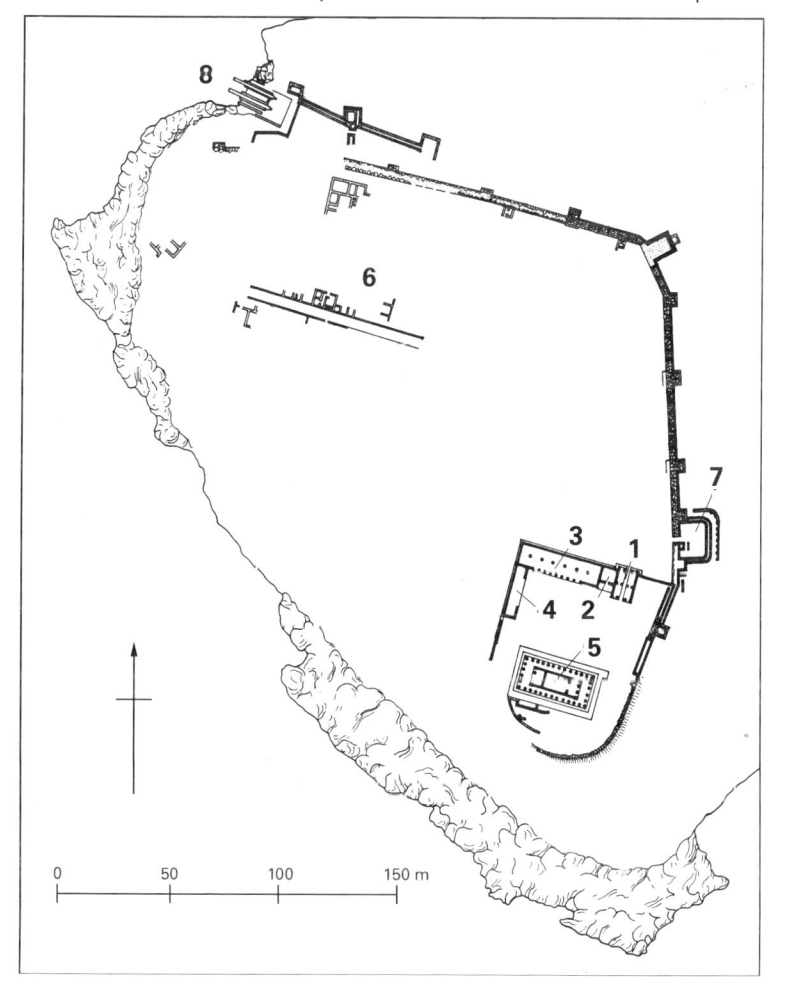

▲ Fig. 23. Isometric reconstruction of the Temple of Poseidon at Sounion (after W. H. Plommer, *Annual of the British School at Athens* 45 (1950) pl. 8)

West of this there is a Doric **stoa** [3] which adjoins a second, much simpler **stoa** [4]. A date *c.*444 BC has been proposed for the **Temple of Poseidon** [5]. It was constructed of local Agrileza marble which is quite coarse and soft but attractively veined. The peristyle consisted of six by thirteen slender Doric columns which only have sixteen rather than the conventional twenty flutes. One theory is that this would have made the columns seem correctly proportioned and not foreshortened when viewed from the sea. A rather recherché but nevertheless significant point is that the columns of the porch were aligned with the third column of the peristyle. This is also a feature of the temples of Ares and

Athens, Attika, and the Saronic 99

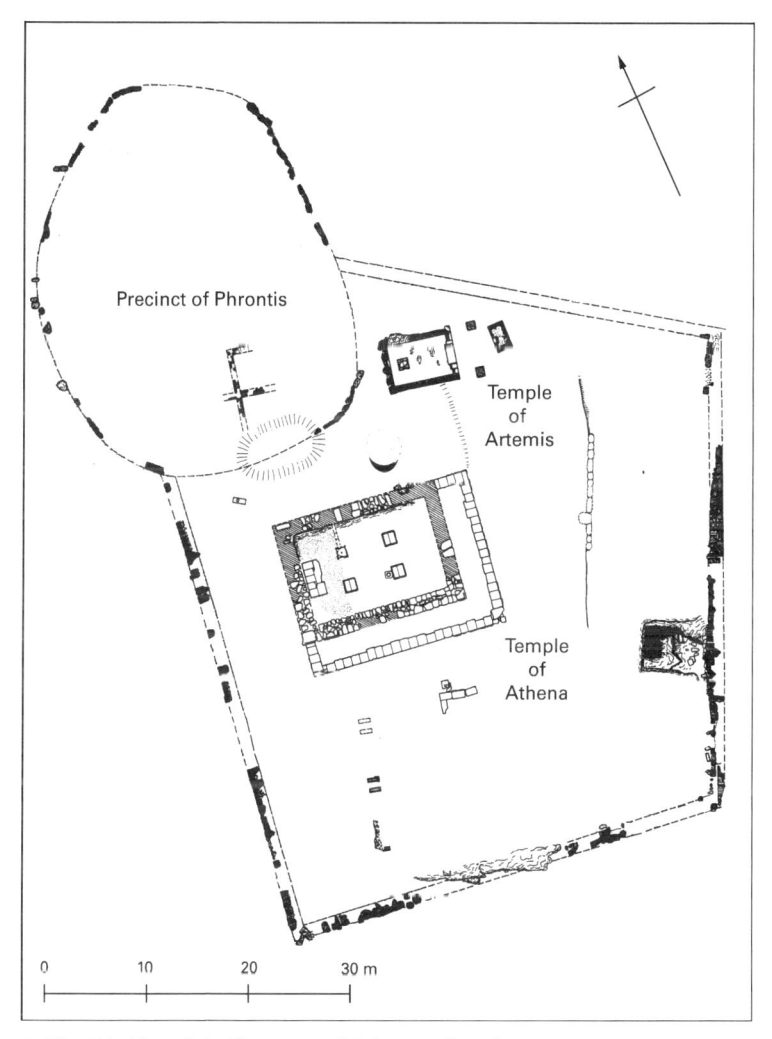

▲ Fig. 24. Plan of the Sanctuary of Athena at Sounion

Hephaistos in the Athenian agora and Nemesis at RHAMNOUS which may well have been designed by the same anonymous architect. A continuous frieze ran above the columns in front of the porch and depicted the battle of the Gods and the Giants, the Lapiths and Centaurs, and the exploits of Theseus. There is no ancient description of the cult-statue of Poseidon which must once have stood in the cella.

From the sanctuary you can see one of the **streets** [**6**] of the town which was laid out on a grid plan. This was not in fact the centre of the deme of Sounion. An inscription mentions an agora in the Agrileza valley, although the situation is complicated because there was also an

▲ Fig. 25. The Temple of Apollo at Sounion

agora at Pasa Limani, 5 km. up the coast from Sounion. As you leave the sanctuary, you pass an impressive **bastion** [**7**] constructed of marble blocks. This was added in the C3 when the Macedonians took control of the fortress. From this bastion the line of the C5 fortifications can be followed north and then west.

A short distance down from the tourist pavilion there is a sign for the temple of Athena which is on the low hill east of the road. The foundations of the temple can clearly be seen in the centre of the sanctuary but much of the superstructure was removed in the C1 AD and used in the construction of the South-East Temple in the agora at Athens. One of the Ionic column capitals is on display in the Stoa of Attalos. The temple was built around the middle of the C5 and is unusual in that there were columns on the east and south sides but not the west or north. The roof of the cella was supported by four columns and the base of the cult-statue is still preserved. The other temple in the sanctuary, possibly of Artemis, has a fine statue base of Eleusinian limestone in the cella. The oval enclosure may have been the precinct of the hero Phrontis, the helmsman who died off Sounion.

If you wish to look at the shipsheds and/or have a swim, follow the track on the opposite side of the road from the sanctuary of Athena which skirts the fence and runs down to the sea. There is a path along the shore to the bay in which the **shipsheds** [**8**] were constructed, presumably in the C3. The two slipways meet the sea at quite a steep angle and may not have been intended for triremes. The ships were winched out of the water and would have been protected by a roof.

Thorikos (Figs. 26–27)

Take the turn signed Thorikos Ancient Theatre just north of modern Lavrion on the Athens road. The site is unfenced.

Special Features

Thorikos was an important industrial centre, provides our best impression of the architectural features of an Attic deme town, and has a unique series of Mycenaean tombs.

History

The prominent conical hill of Velatouri, the akropolis of ancient Thorikos, dominates the harbours of Frankolimani and Portomandri on either side of the Ayios Nikolaos promontory and hence the sea route down the east coast of Attika. In addition there were ore deposits on Velatouri and we now know that these were already being exploited in the Early Helladic period, the third millennium BC. The technique of lead isotope analysis has shown that LAURION was the source of much of the copper in circulation in the Aegean in the second millennium and Thorikos clearly benefited from the trade in metals. By the end of the Middle Helladic period the settlement had spread across the southern and eastern slopes of Velatouri and some impressive early Mycenaean tombs were constructed. It seems quite likely that Thorikos was an independent political centre at this time but may have been overshadowed by ATHENS subsequently. Most of the evidence for the Early Iron Age comes from a cemetery of Protogeometric and Geometric graves on the west slope of Velatouri. The town subsequently became the centre of one of the Attic coastal demes and even had a theatre, but Thorikos is seldom mentioned by ancient writers. The promontory of Ayios Nikolaos was fortified *c.*412 BC to protect the sea route and the Laurion silver mines after the Spartans had taken over Dekeleia as a base for their operations in Attika. Industrial activity intensified in the C4— ore washeries and workshops were constructed in the town—and then just as rapidly declined. This was disastrous for Thorikos which is pithily described as 'once a city, now just a name' by Pomponius Mela (*De Chorographia* 2.3.46) in the C1 AD and is completely overlooked by Pausanias.

Description

The **theatre** [1] at Thorikos is one of the earliest in Greece. It seems that the orchestra was first laid out in the late C6 BC. In the middle of the C5 the orchestra was extended and 21 rows of stone seats were fitted in the cavea which is not circular but elliptical. A temple of Dionysos occupied

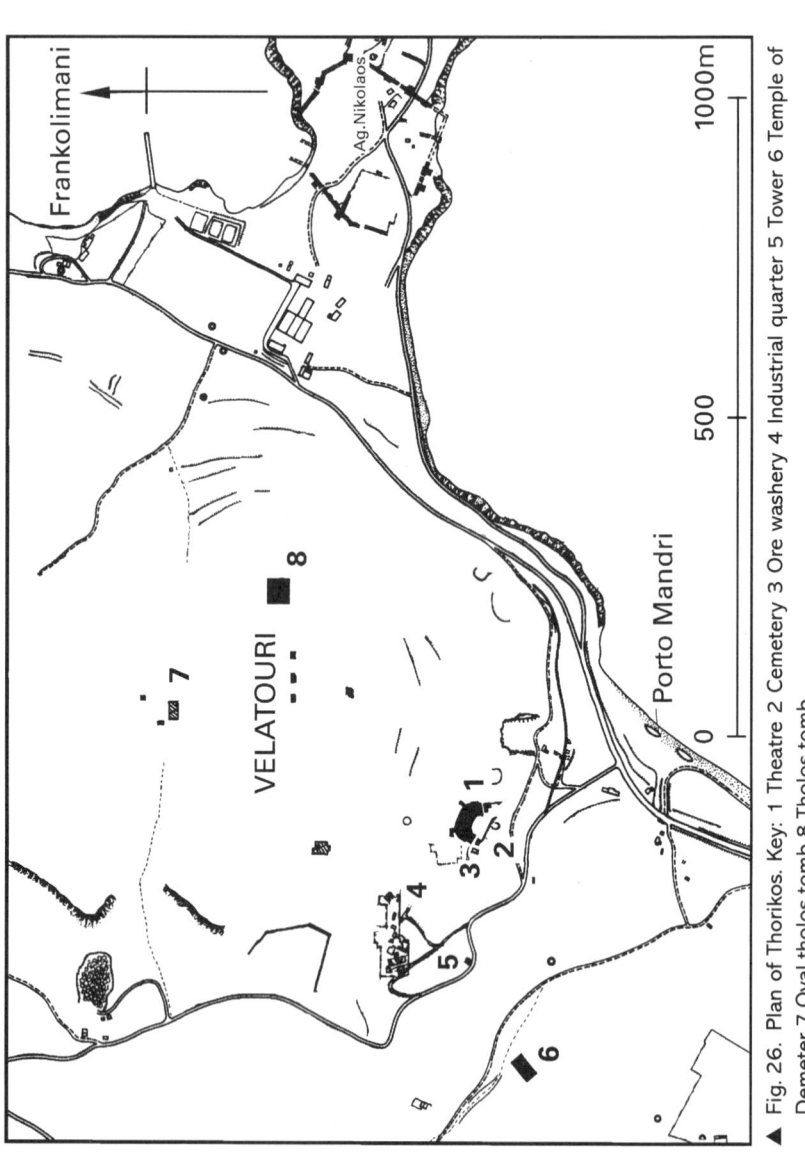

Fig. 26. Plan of Thorikos. Key: 1 Theatre 2 Cemetery 3 Ore washery 4 Industrial quarter 5 Tower 6 Temple of Demeter 7 Oval tholos tomb 8 Tholos tomb

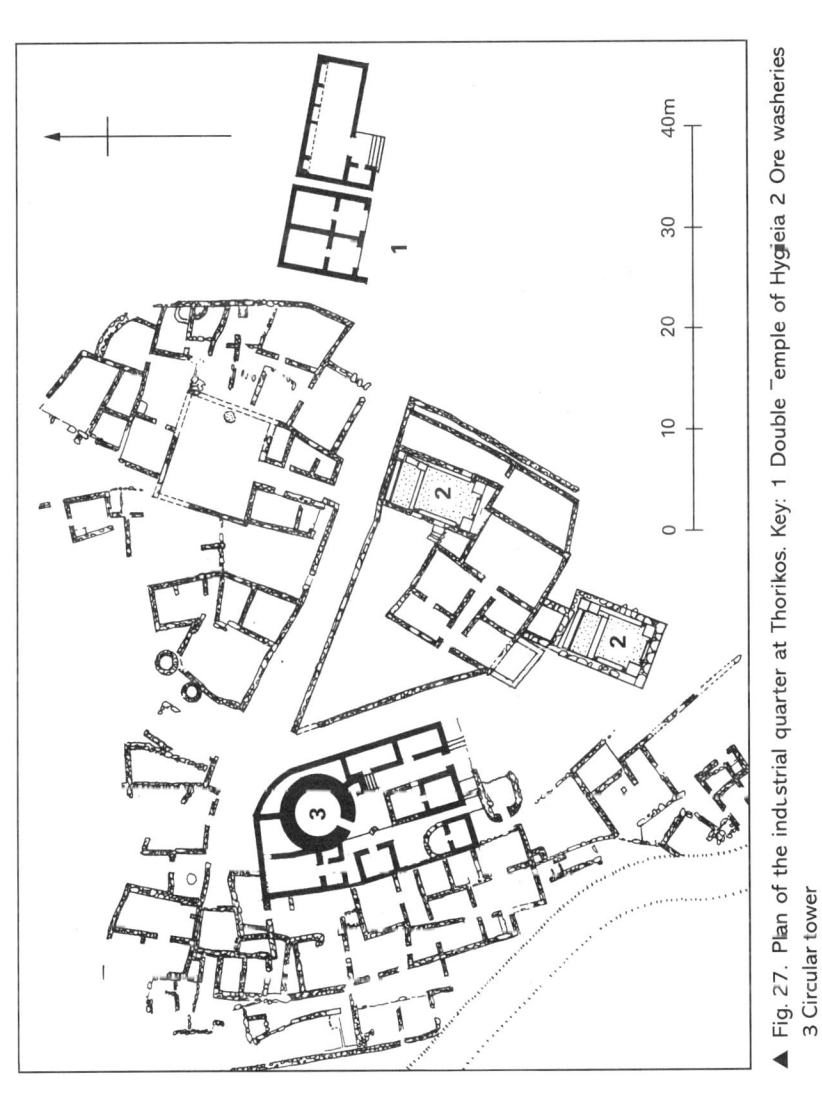

▲ Fig. 27. Plan of the industrial quarter at Thorikos. Key: 1 Double Temple of Hygieia 2 Ore washeries 3 Circular tower

the rectangular platform in the western parodos. The altar is on the opposite side of the orchestra in front of the first row of seats. The massive isodomic wall at the back of the theatre was added in the C4 and supported a further twelve rows of benches which could be reached by two ramps. There would then have been room for around 6000 spectators. A **cemetery** [2] has been excavated just in front of the theatre. This was in use in the Archaic-Classical periods and the graves had evidently been grouped around a funerary monument. West of the theatre there is a restored **ore washery** [3] (see p. 105) and beyond this a **mine gallery** which is kept locked. Nevertheless, you can appreciate the awful conditions which the miners faced as they hacked through the rock. Continue west and you will find yourself in one of the industrial quarters of the **town** [4]. A narrow street runs past a double temple of Hygieia [**27.1**] which is flanked by a stoa and then through blocks of houses. These were built in the C6–C5 and then adapted or replaced in the C4. Note the ore washeries [**27.2**] and also the circular tower [**27.3**] in one of the houses. Security must have been a particular concern at Thorikos because of the threat posed by the slaves who worked in the mines. Below the houses there is a **tower** [5] and on from this a C5 **temple of Demeter** [6].

To see the **Mycenaean tombs** [7–8], climb around the east slope of Velatouri until you reach the saddle between the two peaks. A Middle Helladic tumulus, some 25 m. in diameter, has been excavated in the saddle. This was superseded by the tomb on the hillside [7], a unique oval tholos which was built in the early Mycenaean period, presumably for the ruler of Thorikos. Now make for the bend in the dirt track which runs up the east side of Velatouri. Here there is a more conventional Mycenaean tholos [8]. Note the wall which cuts across the dromos and retains the mound over the tomb and also the pits cut in the floor of the chamber.

Laurion (Figs. 28–29) ★

Take the road for Ayios Konstantinos on the outskirts of modern Lavrion. Just before the village, there is a turn on the left signed Χάος—Αγία Τριάδα. If you approach the turn from Ayios Konstantinos, it is signed Ancient Mine Workshop. After 3.3 km. you reach the church and picnic spot of Ayia Triada where there is a second sign. A 25-minute walk down the rough dirt track will bring you to the site of Agrileza.

Special Features

A pleasant walk in quiet countryside through a remarkable industrial landscape.

The operation of the mines

Because of erosion, ore deposits will have been exposed and, initially at least, could be extracted by open-cast mining. When a vein of ore ran below the surface, the miners tunnelled through the rock. However, the 'third contact' lay at a much deeper level and was reached by vertical shafts, some of which descended 100 m. or more. Once the vein had been located, galleries were opened up. These were never more than 1 m. high and so the miners had to lie on their backs or sides. The tools which they used were simple—hammers, chisels, picks, and shovels. For light they relied on torches or lamps which must have made the atmosphere in the cramped galleries even more intolerable. Shafts were often sunk in pairs so that one could provide ventilation but some miners suffocated.

When the ore had been lifted to the surface, it was processed in a workshop a short distance from the mine. First it was crushed and ground in a mill. Then the ore was washed in order to separate out the lead. The ore washeries are one of the most distinctive features of Laurion and clearly represented a considerable investment on the part of their owners. They usually consisted of a rectangular stand tank from which water could be released at high pressure through funnel-shaped holes into wooden troughs. These contained the crushed ore which was stirred so that the heaviest particles of lead sank and remained in the trough. The dross was swept into a channel and ran around the plastered platform on which the concentrated ore was dried. Sedimentation basins ensured that the lighter particles were also precipitated and that the water could eventually be recycled. Massive circular cisterns were constructed in order to collect rainwater and can be seen in the vicinity of most of the workshops.

The furnaces in which the ore was smelted have proved more elusive. They may have been sited away from the mines and workshops because they gave off noxious fumes, although the health and safety of the work force does not appear to have been a major concern. A source of fuel was possibly more important, since Laurion was soon deforested. Two furnace complexes have been excavated on the coast and one at Megala Pefka. Layers of charcoal and ore were loaded into the bottle-shaped furnace which was then fired. Bellows raised the temperature until the metal melted and ran out into tap holes. When the metal had solidified it was reheated in a cupellation furnace so that the lead oxidized and could be skimmed off or removed with iron rods which had been dipped in water. Once refined, the silver was ready for use.

History

In antiquity Laurion was the toponym used for the south-eastern tip of Attika, a rugged and waterless district which would have been of no consequence but for the fact that there were metalliferous ore deposits.

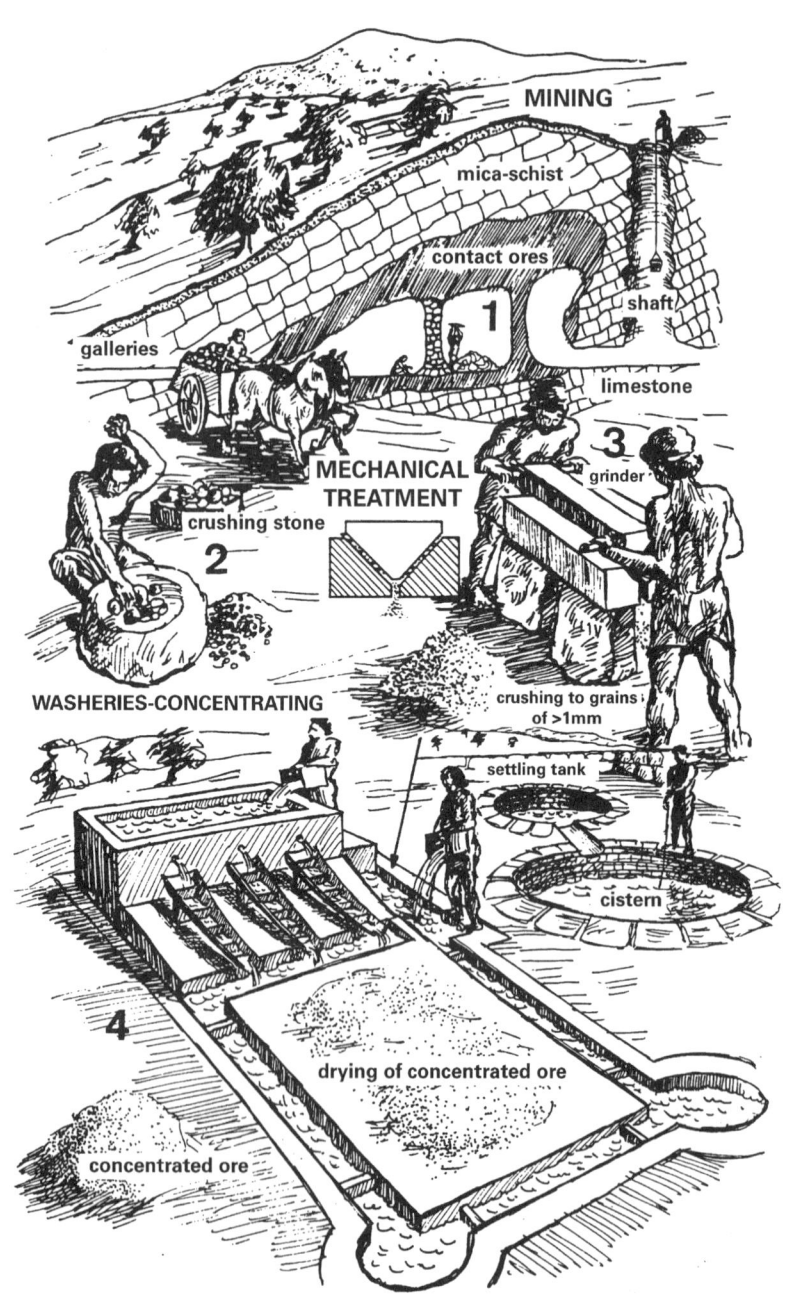

▲ Fig. 28. Processing and smelting ore at Laurion (after H. Mussche, *Thorikos: A Guide to the Excavations* (Brussels 1974) 60–1, fig. 81)

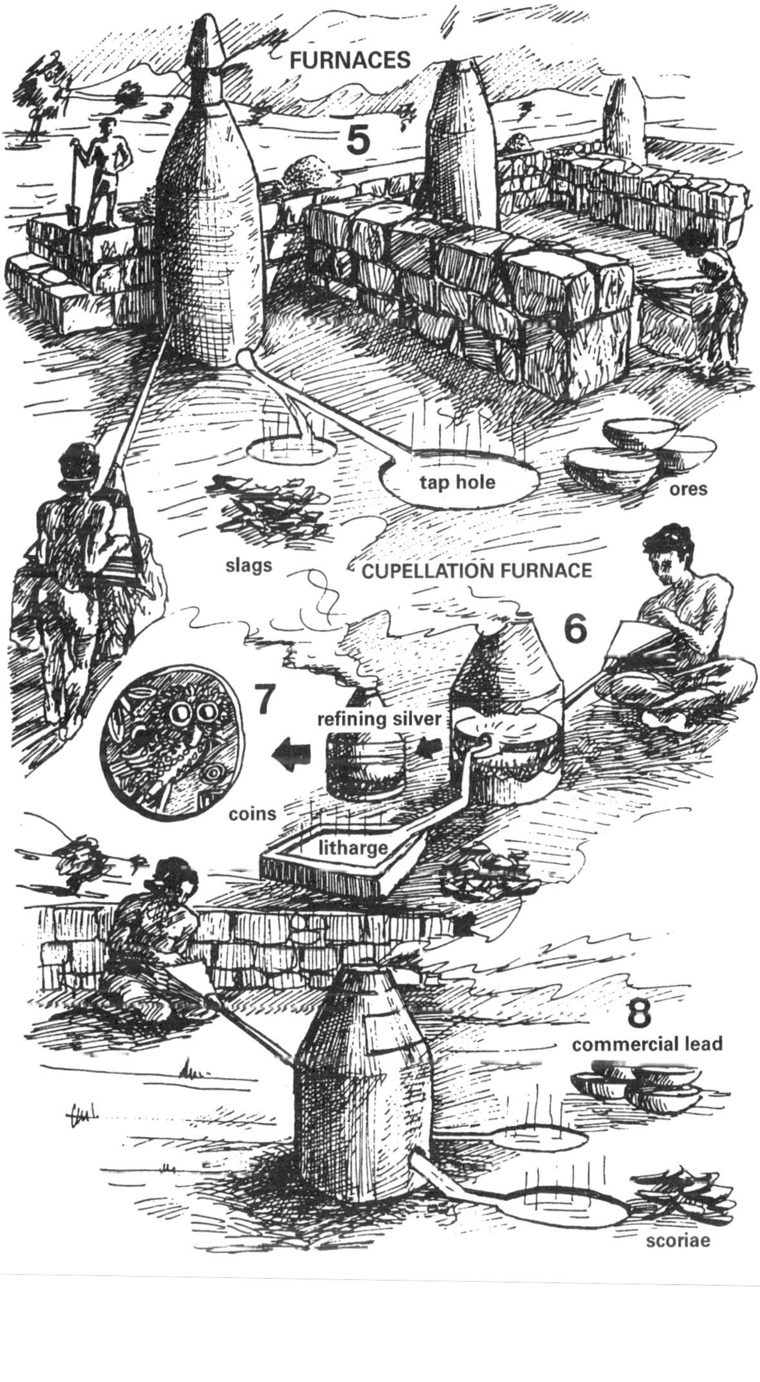
FURNACES
5
tap hole
ores
slags
CUPELLATION FURNACE
6
7
refining silver
coins
litharge
8
commercial lead
scoriae

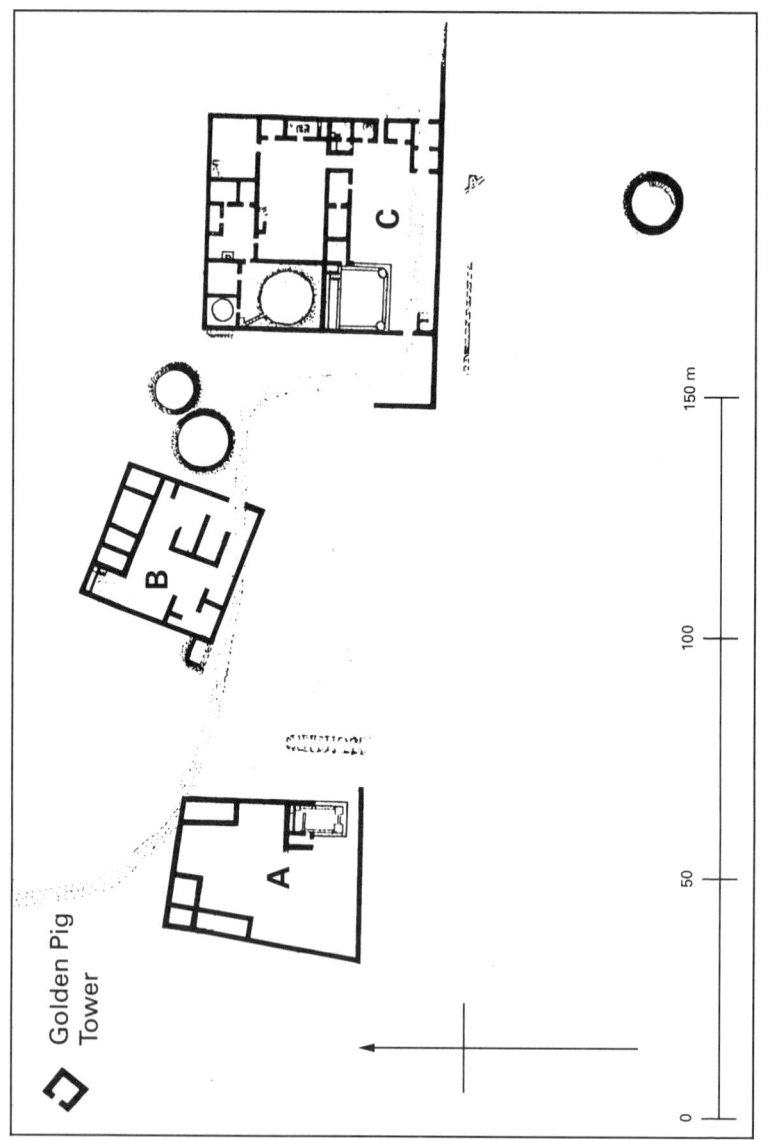

▲ Fig. 29. Plan of the workshop complexes at Agrileza

Geologically Laurion consists of superimposed beds of limestone and schist which have been folded and eroded. At the junction or contact zone between the beds, veins of lead, zinc, and iron ore were deposited by hydrothermal action. The lead ore is argentiferous galena from which silver could be extracted by cupellation.

Ores were being mined and processed at THORIKOS in the prehistoric period but elsewhere there is not much evidence of activity until the C6. It was then that ATHENS first issued the famous silver coins known as owls which had the head of Athena on the obverse and an owl plus the name of the city in the form AΘE on the reverse. Early in the C5 the revenue from the mines increased dramatically when the 'third contact', a deeper but richer ore deposit, was discovered. Herodotus (7.144) tells us that Themistokles persuaded the Athenians to use this windfall to build a fleet of triremes and thereby made the city a naval power. It was not only the state which prospered. The Athenian general Neikias had 1000 slaves for hire in the mines at an obol per man per day. Many of these slaves fled when the Spartans occupied Dekeleia in 413 BC and the industry collapsed. The next boom period was in the second half of the C4. Inscriptions set up in the agora at Athens by officials known as *poletai* recorded the leases which individuals had taken out. The state apparently controlled the mines but they were operated by private contractors, some of whom made enormous profits. It was claimed that Epikrates of Pallene and his associates received 300 talents in three years from one concession (Hypereides 4(3).35). In the C3–C2 there was a decline in the level of activity which was exacerbated by a slave revolt. By the C2 AD Laurion was the place 'where the Athenians once had silver mines' (Pausanias 1.1.1), although there are signs of renewed activity in late antiquity.

Description

As you walk down the track you first pass the detritus of modern industrial operations. From the C19 until quite recently manganese and zinc were mined and lead was resmelted from ancient spoil heaps. You then come across traces of earlier activity, in particular a large circular cistern, plaster-lined and with access steps near the fenced area. Where the track divides into three, after approximately 1 km., continue straight on down the middle fork until you reach the **Agrileza workshop complex** which has been partially fenced.

Workshop **C** is late C4 BC. The washery, one of the largest in Laurion, is of the conventional type. Note the three column bases which supported a roof over the stand tank and the washing floor. This would have kept the sun off the workers and also reduced evaporation—water was a precious commodity. East of the washery is a court with rooms on three sides. These had lower courses of stone and a mudbrick superstructure. Ore may have been stored in the plaster-lined room by the washery. There were also workrooms and a possible bathroom. A ramp leads up to a second court. One of the rooms on the east side of this has four stone orthostats embedded in the concrete floor, presumably for a work surface, and a bloomery hearth. Water for the washery came from a circular cistern, 11.20 m. in diameter, which could be entered by a flight of steps and cleaned out periodically. The smaller cistern may have supplied drinking water.

Across the track from Workshop **C** there is another circular cistern. The Agrileza complex also includes two more workshops, **A** and **B**, which have recently been excavated. Just beyond Workshop **A** is the **Golden Pig Tower**, ruggedly built in trapezoidal masonry. Traces of an enclosure can be seen west of the tower which may well have been a farmhouse. Although this is not prime agricultural land, the miners created a demand for food but evidently there was also a need for security.

When you reach the point where the track divides into three, you may wish to follow the path on the left which drops down to skirt the fence around the excavations at Soureza where there is another workshop complex of cisterns and washeries.

Brauron (Figs. 30–32)

The sanctuary is south of Loutsa and is signed Temple of Artemis Vrauronia. The museum is c.1 km. beyond the site.

Special Features

Brauron, which still retains its rural setting, is a well-preserved sanctuary offering a unique insight into the role of religion in ancient Athenian women's lives, with many of the finds on display in the nearby museum.

History

The sanctuary lies in a fertile plain beside a small bay, c.38 km. from ATHENS. The marshy, rural setting suits a cult of Artemis, a goddess of the wild and the wet. She was also concerned here with fertility and the life-cycle of Athenian women, whose social marginality was reflected in the location on Attika's eastern edge. In the C5 BC Artemis shared the site with a heroine also linked to childbirth, Agamemnon's daughter Iphigeneia. She was said by the Athenians to have escaped sacrifice by her father and become priestess of Artemis here, where she was buried. Cult-activity took root just north of a low hill, the site of a prehistoric settlement, with the earliest votive finds from the C8 BC. During the C6 BC Brauron came under the control of Athens, and a subsidiary shrine was established on the Akropolis. The state celebrated a major four-yearly festival here, the women's Brauronia, starting with a procession from Athens. Although a temple already existed in the C7–C6 BC, most of the known buildings date from the C5–C4 BC, when the sanctuary flourished. The preserved offerings from the site are typically to do with female beautification and textile production, such as mirrors and loom weights. Inscribed inventories confirm that the dedicators were chiefly female, and reveal that women's work in the form of clothes was also a popular offering. Cult-activity is particularly linked with a ritual, the *arkteia*, or 'being a bear'. A representative sample of Athenian girls selected on a tribal basis served Artemis as 'bears'—interpreted today as a rite of passage preparing them for physical puberty and marriage (see **box**). The sanctuary still functioned in Hellenistic times, when an unpublished inscription (C3 BC) mentions repairs needed to a list of buildings, among them a gymnasium, palaistra, and stables, yet to be found. The work was probably occasioned by flooding of the river north of the site, which eventually buried the site under mud. North of the sanctuary is a large basilican church (C6 AD).

Description

When you enter the site, the path leads you towards the stoa, partially reconstructed. Note on your left a heavily-rutted **bridge** [1], taking the processional route from Athens over a stream (C5 BC).

The site is dominated by the huge Doric **stoa** ([2]—*c*.420 BC) in the form of a Greek letter *pi*, creating an open court in its centre. Its limited use of marble shows a desire for economy, and it was never finished. Behind the north colonnade is a corridor with a carefully arranged line of stelai and bases for offerings, one with a well-preserved inscription recording the name of a female donor, Mnesistrate (ΜΝΗΣΙΣΤΡΑΤΗ). Behind the north and west colonnades is a series of eleven **dining rooms** [3], nine of them equipped with couches. You can see the holes where the wooden couch-legs were fixed with lead, as well as the base-blocks for some of the marble-topped tables placed before the couches. They may be the 'rooms' (*oikoi*) of the inscription mentioned earlier. It remains to be established if the users of this *c*.100-couch 'restaurant' were women or men. At the rear is an open-air corridor overlooked by a long **colonnade** [4] featuring a row of stone slots. One theory is that these held wooden panels on which textile offerings were displayed.

On a platform retained by a stepped **terrace** [5], perhaps once used for viewing, are the foundations of a **temple** ([6]—*c*.500 BC), presumably the 'old temple' of inscribed inventories, where valuable offerings were on display. It replaced an early Archaic predecessor. Doric, with no external colonnade, it had a porch giving access to a main chamber,

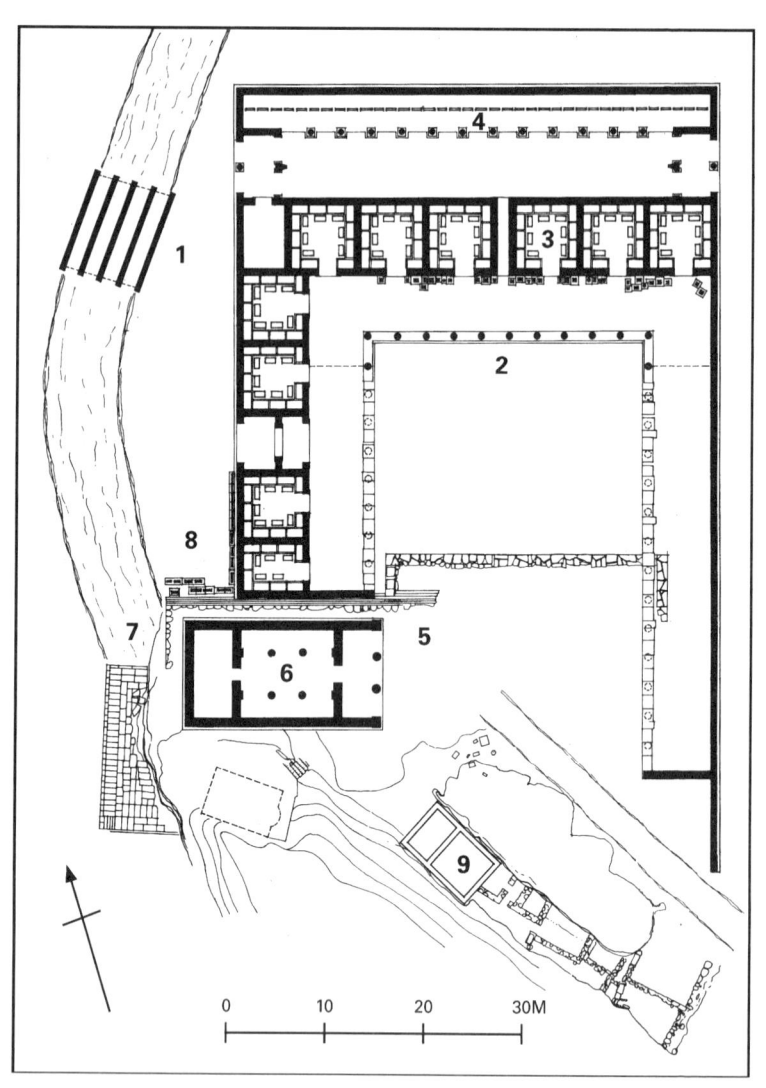

▲ Fig. 30. Plan of the sanctuary of Artemis at Brauron. Key: 1 Bridge 2 C5 stoa 3 Dining rooms 4 Colonnade 5 Terrace 6 Temple 7 Spring 8 Stone slots 9 Hero-shrine of Iphigeneia

beyond which was an inner room. Fragments of the temple's once-imposing entablature are still on site, including a worn triglyph block of massive size.

From the platform you can look down on a **spring** [7] forming a pool, a place of particular sanctity, into which offerings were thrown. Thousands of objects of the C8–early C5 BC were found here. Even in midsummer the small stream issuing from this pool gives Brauron a marshy aspect, especially fitting for Artemis. In front of the terrace you can also see stone **slots** [**8**], originally for displaying inscribed inventories.

South of the temple is a cleft in the rock, perhaps a collapsed cave, the crude walls to the rear having the look of the site's earliest architecture. At the mouth are remains of a small temple-like structure, perhaps a **hero-shrine of Iphigeneia** [**9**], since the Greeks saw caves as entrances to the underworld. It may have been the Parthenon or 'House of the Maid' of the inventories, a repository of valuable offerings.

The vestibule of the **museum**, with labels in Greek and English, has models of the sanctuary and stoa (here identified as quarters for the 'bears'), as well as an inscribed inventory from the site. **Room 1** has offerings from the sanctuary of a mainly female character, including fragments of *krateriskoi* (see **box**), mirrors, jewellery, and trinket boxes (*pyxides*), pottery inscribed with dedications to Artemis, and fragments of *epinetra*, or pottery knee-covers used by women combing wool; there are also two cases with Geometric and C7-BC sherds from the sanctuary. **Room 2** has marble statuettes of girls and boys dedicated in the stoa (the ritual context is unclear), and reliefs showing family-pilgrimages processing towards Artemis. **Room 3** includes a relief of a seated woman spinning, terracotta plaques of Artemis, and a relief (C2 AD) of a reclining Polydeukion (see **box**). **Rooms 4** and **5** contain material, mostly pottery, from cemeteries at modern Merenda (east Attika, ancient Myrrhinous) and Anavysos (south-west Attika, ancient Anaphlystos)

▼ Fig. 31. The stoa at Brauron

▲ Fig. 32. Inscription of Mnesistrate, Brauron

Krateriskoi

The central case against the far wall of room 1 (top two shelves) contains a special class of pottery from the sanctuary, so-called *krateriskoi*, shaped like a chalice with double handles. The figurative decoration, often fairly basic, shows young girls dancing, racing, or processing near the altar of Artemis, usually paired with a palm-tree (the goddess was born under one on Delos). Girls are shown both naked and dressed, and often hold a wreath. One fragment shows a tilted *krateriskos* beside an altar, as if its contents had been ritually poured onto the ground. These images seem to depict the rites of the bear-girls, including athletics, which explains the presence of training facilities.

respectively—important evidence for the growth of Attika's rural population in the C8 BC, perhaps by recolonization from Athens. There are also finds from the Mycenaean chamber-tomb cemetery at Perati.

Marathon (Fig. 33)

Beyond Nea Makri there is a turn on the left for Marathonas Museum and then two more signs for the Archaeological Museum which is 2.5 km. from the junction.

Special Features

Marathon, where the Athenians defeated the Persians in 490 BC, is one of

> ### Polydeukion
>
> Polydeukion was a kinsman and favourite foster-son of Herodes Atticus (pp. 117–118) who died prematurely. The emotional and learned Herodes mourned him extravagantly as a Homeric-style hero, founding private funerary games in his memory and depicting him in sculpture set up on his properties in Attika, including this relief. The dead youth is shown here in the traditional pose of an aristocratic hero, reclining with a drinking cup as if at a banquet. When the Roman governors of Greece berated Herodes for such self-indulgence, he boldly retorted, 'What's it to you if I play with my marbles?' (Philostratus, *Lives of the Sophists* 559).

the more evocative Greek battlefields, and the museum should not be missed.

History

The plain of Marathon is prime agricultural land which has been cultivated since the Neolithic period when the settlement at Nea Makri and the Cave of Pan were first occupied. It is possible that settlers from the Cyclades were buried in the Early Helladic cemetery at Tsepi, although the Cycladic style pottery and figurines could simply reflect close cultural contacts rather than colonization. Middle-Late Helladic tumuli and a fine tholos tomb in which two horses had been sacrificed underline the importance of Marathon in the prehistoric period.

In 546 BC Peisistratos landed at Marathon and made himself tyrant of ATHENS. This may be why his exiled son Hippias advised the Persians that they should disembark here in 490 BC. The Persian king Darius I wished to punish the cities who had assisted the Ionian Greeks when they revolted. No doubt his ultimate aim was the conquest of Greece. The Persians attacked Euboia, sacked ERETRIA and then set sail for Marathon. When the Athenians heard that the Persians had landed, they sent their army, supported by a contingent from PLATAIA, to prevent an advance on the city. For several days the two armies kept their distance until Miltiades persuaded the Athenians that they should attack. Because they were heavily outnumbered, the Athenians weakened the centre of their line so that they would not be outflanked by the Persians. Then they set off at a run. Herodotus (6.112–13) tells us that:

The Persians, seeing the attack develop at the double, prepared to meet it confidently enough, for it seemed to them suicidal madness for the Athenians to risk an assault with so small a force—at the double, too, and with no support from either cavalry or archers. Well, that was what they imagined. Nevertheless, the Athenians came on, closed with the enemy all along the line, and fought in a way

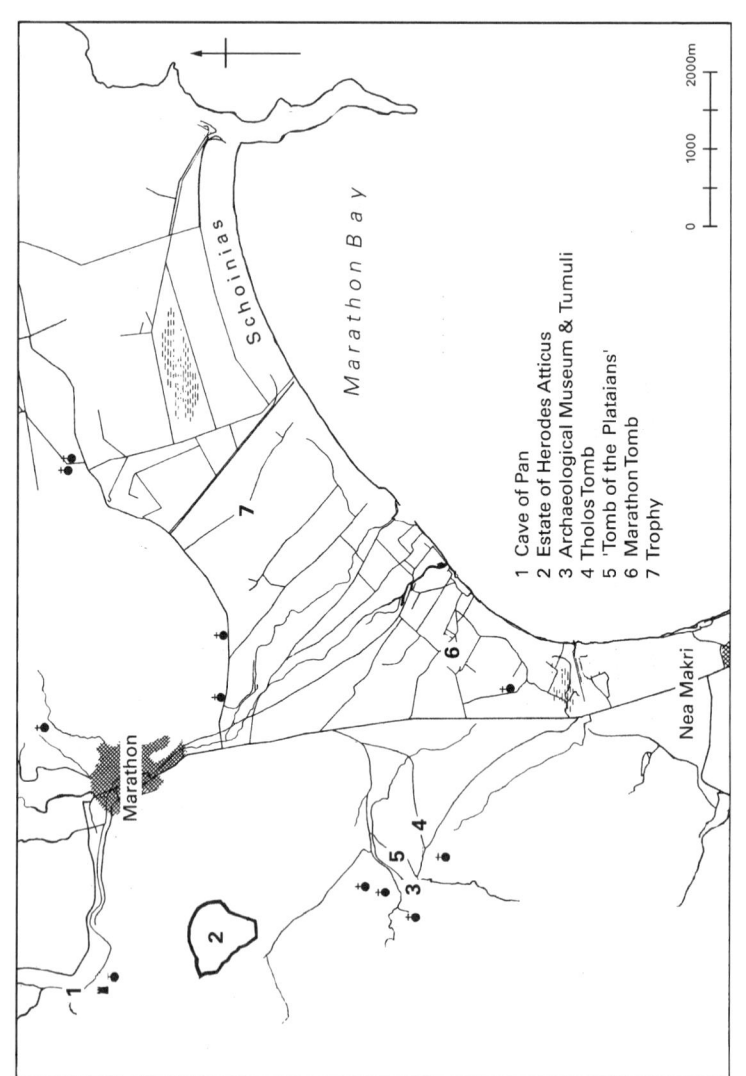

1 Cave of Pan
2 Estate of Herodes Atticus
3 Archaeological Museum & Tumuli
4 Tholos Tomb
5 'Tomb of the Plataians'
6 Marathon Tomb
7 Trophy

Fig. 33. Plan of the area around Marathon

not to be forgotten. They were the first Greeks, so far as I know, to charge at a run, and the first who dared to look without flinching at Persian dress and the men who wore it. For until that day came, no Greek could hear even the word Persian without terror. The struggle at Marathon was long drawn out. In the centre, held by the Persians themselves and the Sakai, the advantage was with the foreigners, who were so successful as to break the Greek line and pursue the fugitives inland from the sea. But the Athenians on one wing and the Plataians on the other were both victorious. Having got the upper hand, they left the defeated Persians to make their escape and then, drawing the two wings together into a single unit, they turned their attention to the Persians who had broken through in the centre. Here again they were triumphant, chasing the routed enemy, and cutting them down as they ran right to the edge of the sea.

Herodotus claims that 6400 Persians were killed and just 192 Athenians. Although the Scythians had already demonstrated that the Persians were not invincible, the impact of the Athenian victory at Marathon was profound and gave the Greeks a psychological advantage when Xerxes invaded ten years later.

So much for the battle, what about the race? An Athenian herald named Pheidippides apparently ran from Athens to SPARTA to ask for assistance and then back again, a distance of approximately 500 km. Fortunately for fun runners the race does not commemorate this feat but the Athenian soldier who ran from Marathon to Athens in full armour, announced the victory, then collapsed and died.

Aside from the events of 490 BC, the only other historical point of interest is that Herodes Atticus was born at Marathon and had an estate here [2].

Description

Finds from a number of sites around Marathon have been put on display in the **Archaeological Museum** [3]. In **room 1** there is Neolithic and Early Helladic pottery from the Cave of Pan. **Room 2** contains pottery, figurines, jewellery, and obsidian from the Early Helladic graves at Tsepi. Note the 'frying pans', a type of vessel which is also common in Cycladic cemeteries at this time. There is an enormous flint blade from the settlement at Nea Makri. The Middle Helladic and Mycenaean pottery comes from the tumuli by the museum. Graves were also the source of the Geometric and Archaic pottery. In **room 3** there are Ionic column drums and a capital from the trophy which the Athenians set up after the victory in 490 BC. The pottery in the two cases is from the tumuli in which the Athenian and Plataian dead may have been buried. **Room 4** has Classical grave stelae and two marble amphorae on which the family of Theogenes is commemorated.

Room 5 and the courtyard focus on Herodes Atticus, the provincial Greek potentate of the C2 AD who dominated Athens for much of his life. His family came from the deme of Marathon, where he was the biggest landowner and liked to reside. You can see (courtyard) the keystone from the arched gateway to an estate of his c.2.5 km. north-west of the museum. Inscribed 'Gate of eternal harmony. This is the property of Regilla which you are entering', it proclaims the concord of his marriage to Regilla, a Roman patrician from Italy, whose death (AD 151) the emotional Herodes mourned extravagantly. The lintel (courtyard) and two Egyptianizing statues (room 5) come from a Roman sanctuary of Isis c.4 km. south-east of the museum (modern Brexiza), probably also belonging to Herodes. In imitation of Hadrian's Egyptian-style portraits of his beloved Antinoos, these may portray Polydeukion, one of Herodes' two much-loved foster-sons who died young (see BRAURON). The other, Memnon, an African black, was portrayed in the now-headless herm (courtyard), still inscribed with his nickname ΤΟΠΑΔΕΙΝ, 'Little Topaz'. It also has a curse to protect it from vandalism by Herodes' many Athenian enemies, who eventually brought him to trial (174) before the emperor Marcus Aurelius in Sirmium. In room 5 is the inscribed poem recording the hypocritically rapturous welcome which all Athens gave the acquitted Herodes, still high in the emperor's favour: 'Blessed were you, O Marathon, just now, and an object of care to men more than before, as you looked down on the glorious descendant of Alkaios [Herodes], who returned from the Sarmatian nomads at the outermost edge of the world, whither he had followed the far-travelled emperor of the Ausonians [Marcus Aurelius]' (*IG* 2².3606, after Oliver).

To the right of the museum there is a row of **tumuli**. Two have been protected by a concrete shelter and can be glimpsed through the windows even if this is closed. The tumuli consisted of a circular mound of earth bordered by stones. The graves were inserted in the mound. Although the earliest of the tumuli is Middle Helladic, they were still in use in the Mycenaean period. It is remarkable that this tradition should have been maintained for at least five centuries. The **Mycenaean tholos tomb** [4] is a further 600 m. beyond the museum. There is a shelter covered by an asbestos roof on the right of the road but it is unlikely that this will be open.

To the left of the museum there is a dirt track which climbs to a vantage point from which you can see the battlefield. The Athenians camped by the sanctuary of Herakles, which was almost certainly at the southern end of the plain. The Persians had landed on the beach at Schoinias and the battle must have been fought to the north of the Soros where the **trophy** [7] was later set up in commemoration of the victory.

As you return from the museum, you pass a **tumulus** [5] on the left of the road after approximately 300 m. This contained the remains of eleven males and the associated pottery indicates that they had been buried early in the C5. It is possible that these were the Plataians who died at Marathon but this is not certain.

Also on the left of the road, approximately 2 km. from the museum, is the **Early Helladic cemetery** at Tsepi which is covered by a concrete shelter. This may well be closed but the graves can be seen through the windows. They were built of stone and covered by massive slabs.

Join the main road and head for Nea Makri. After 2 km. take the left turn for the **Marathon Tomb** [**6**] which is 800 m. from the junction. Also known as the Soros, this enormous tumulus is 9 m. high and 50 m. in diameter. It was here that the cremated remains of the 192 Athenians who died in the battle were buried. The Athenians usually held the funerals of their war dead in the Kerameikos cemetery but Thucydides (2.34) notes that the heroes of Marathon were treated differently because of their exceptional valour.

Rhamnous (Figs. 34–36)

The site can be reached from the plain of Marathon via Kato Souli and is well signed.

Special Features

The site is set in unspoilt countryside and is worth a visit for the temples of Nemesis and Themis, although the fortress is currently inaccessible.

History

Rhamnous was the most remote of the demes of ATHENS, on the northeast coast of Attika overlooking Euboia, providing an anchorage for ancient shipping on an otherwise inhospitable coastline. It was the centre for a local population of 'Rhamnousians', self-governing under their chief officer or demarch. Some of them lived around the sanctuary of Themis and Nemesis, others down by the sea, reached by an ancient route descending from the sanctuary, lined with their tombs (C4 BC). Deme-cult for the two goddesses can be traced back to the C6. The sanctuary was rich enough to act as a local bank by *c.* 440, as shown from inscribed accounts, although the new (and relatively costly) temple of Nemesis may have been part-funded by the Athenian state, which had a strategic interest in Rhamnous as a base for surveillance of shipping. The Athenian garrison, first attested in 342/1, was probably much older, as the earliest fortification of the coastal akropolis, where it resided, is dated to the C5 BC. From 336/5 Rhamnous was patrolled by Athenian ephebes, young men aged eighteen or over, as part of their military service. After Alexander the garrison played a part in Athenian struggles against Macedon and Aegean pirates. In 262–229 BC the fortress was occupied by Macedonian troops, and the demesmen now included worship of Macedon's king (Antigonos II) in the festival of Nemesis. Severe damage to her temple, apparently deliberate, has been attributed to raids by Philip V of Macedon (200 BC). In AD 45/6, as an inscription on the east architrave shows, Athens rededicated the temple to Livia, the deified wife of Augustus, and it is probably to this time that ancient repairs to the building should be dated.

Description

You approach the sanctuary along a path lined with C4 BC **tombs**, the first circular, the rest of the enclosure (*peribolos*) type. This was the ancient route from Marathon.

The **Sanctuary of Nemesis** (see **box**) comprises two temples built on a terrace partly supported (north and east) by a fine **retaining wall [1]** of isodomic masonry. The **smaller temple [2]**, with polygonal masonry and, unusually, a plain wall with a door instead of columns at the front, is dated to the early C5 BC. Two inscribed thrones (C4 BC) once flanking the door to the inner chamber show that both Themis and Nemesis were honoured here. Inside the chamber was found an inscribed base for a well-preserved marble statue of Themis over 2 m. high (*c*.300 BC), a dedication by the demesman Megakles, 'signed' by the Rhamnousian

▼ Fig. 34. Plan of the Sanctuary of Nemesis at Rhamnous. Key: 1 Retaining wall 2 Smaller temple 3 Larger temple 4 Altar

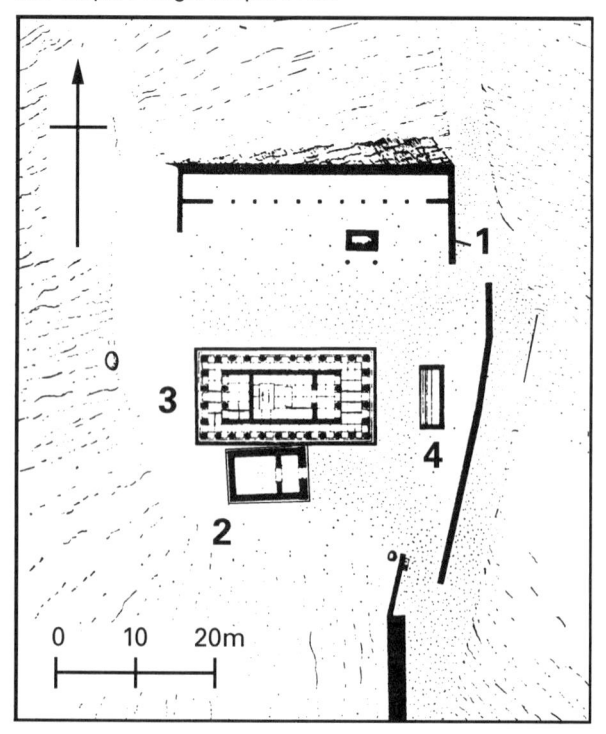

▲ Fig. 35. Reconstruction of the cult-statue of Nemesis at Rhamnous (after Keliakis in N. D. Papachatzis, *Pausaniou Ellados Periegesis, I: Attika*, 1974)

sculptor Chairestratos, and now in the National Archaeological Museum.

The **larger temple** [3], or 'Nemesion' as an inscription (C3 BC) describes it, was conceived, at least in later times, as a memorial to the victory at MARATHON. It is built strikingly close to its neighbour (less than 8 cm. away at one point), perhaps to reuse the foundations of a predecessor. Foundations of its **altar** [4] lie to the east. The Doric architecture suggests a start-date in the 420s BC, during a lull in the Peloponnesian War. Tell-tale signs of an unfinished project are the column-shafts (not completely fluted), and the pavement (never smoothed). On one (debated) view, the roughly stippled bands on the risers of the steps were deliberately left for aesthetic effect. The lower step is in a grey, the rest of the temple in a white, marble (both local). The change of colour may have been meant to grade the optical transition from the soil colours of the ground to the white marble.

Two blocks from the pavement in the interior chamber (cella) have channels cut into them, perhaps for an offering table. An inscription (C3 BC) shows that painted portraits ('icons') of Athenian officers were displayed here. The main attraction was a colossal marble **cult-statue** by Agorakritos of Paros. Pausanias says that it showed Nemesis standing, holding an apple-branch and a ritual bowl (*phiale*), her crown decorated with a stag and victory-figures, supported on a base, decorated with reliefs. The statue and its base were deliberately broken up in late antiquity, presumably by Christians. Many fragments of both have been collected from the site since 1812/13.

A nearby **shed** (inaccessible) houses the reassembled entablature of the temple of Nemesis, a partial reconstruction of the cult-statue and its base by Greek archaeologists, and sculptured tombstones from the funerary enclosures.

The chief features of the (currently closed) **fortress**, reached by the continuation of the 'street of tombs', are its fortifications (C5–C3 BC) and a small theatre (*c.*350 BC), used for dramatic performances and meetings of the demesmen.

▼ Fig. 36. The Temple of Nemesis at Rhamnous

> ### Themis and Nemesis
>
> Themis and Nemesis were both abstract concepts and also concrete goddesses, the former meaning 'justice' or 'order', the latter 'retribution' or 'righteous anger' at an injustice. Rhamnous had the best-known cult of Nemesis. A later tradition about her cult-statue, whether true or not, shows how the Greeks conceived her avenging power:
>
> ... the most implacable of the gods towards arrogant men. It seems that the anger of this goddess fell upon the barbarians who landed at Marathon. For they were so sure that nothing could stop them from capturing Athens that they brought a block of Parian stone for fashioning into a trophy to their deeds. Pheidias worked this block into a statue of Nemesis.
>
> Pausanias here (1.3.2–3) is wrong about Pheidias, and may have been misinformed by the local guide. The sculptor was in fact his less famous pupil, Agorakritos.

Amphiareion (Fig. 37) ★

Leave the National Road at the Markopoulo junction and after c.7 km. turn right at the sign for the Archaeological Site. The site is a further 3 km., the entrance being c.200 m. after a final sign.

Special Features

The site is attractively located in a wooded glen and is of considerable historical and archaeological interest as an ancient healing centre.

History

Amphiaraos was a heroic warrior-prophet from ARGOS, who in one myth vanished into a cleft in the earth through the machinations of Zeus. By the C6 BC he had re-emerged in Greece as a famous source of oracles. Supposedly he was first worshipped as an Olympian god at the Amphiareion, his chief sanctuary from the late C5 BC on, with cult firmly attested by 414, but perhaps much older. The site is a cleft-like ravine on the border between Boiotia and Attika in the territory of the Oropians, constantly disputed between ATHENS and the Boiotians, so that one or other controlled the sanctuary for long stretches during the C5–C2 BC, and again in imperial times. The shrine's popularity was helped by its ease of access, by sea or overland from Athens—a day's journey 'for a traveller without luggage' (Herakleides (?) 1.6). Athenian patronage was probably crucial in establishing its credentials for faith-healing (attested by 414), for promoting festivals and games (known from c.400, with five-yearly 'Amphiareia' from 329 BC), and for building works. The hero-god's healing and oracular powers were interlinked, as shown by the ritual: 'Those who come to inquire of Amphiaraos are wont to purify themselves first of all. Purification consists in sacrificing to the god [...] After these preliminaries they sacrifice a ram, and spreading the skin under them go to sleep, awaiting a revelation in a dream' (Pausanias 1.34.3.). As at EPIDAUROS, during ritual sleep (incubation) on the sacrificial fleece, the god either cured you miraculously or suggested how your disease could be treated. In the C4 BC the proverbially greedy Oropians charged nine obols to consult the god—over double a sailor's daily pay. You could also take the waters here, famously refreshing; there were also therapeutic baths. The sanctuary was supervised by a priest, an important personage, his duties known from an inscription (see **box**). It enjoyed a first flowering in the C4 BC, when major buildings (temple, stoa) were put up, and a second in the C2–C1 BC, when it was a 'must-see' for Roman visitors to Greece. In the Roman phase of Athenian control it seems to have declined in panhellenic importance, although the renovation of buildings is well attested, and inscriptions take the cult into the C3 AD at least.

Description

The sanctuary, originally defined by inscribed boundary-stones, is laid out on two sides of a ravine, with the precinct proper on the north-east side, and on the south-west the ancillary area.

As you enter the site from the west, once on level ground the Doric **Temple of Amphiaraos** ([1]—C4 BC) is immediately on your right, its external colonnade limited to the facade. The porch gave access to a single chamber, flanked by two Ionic colonnades fitted with screens, the base for the marble cult-statue visible in the central aisle. Other features are known from a C3 BC inscription: offerings of precious metals displayed on 'the table of Amphiaraos' and on the walls, and a 'strong-room' (*thesauros*), possibly the small chamber to the rear which was added later.

To the east is the **altar** [2], nearly 9 m. long in its final form and divided into five sections for Amphiaraos and a long list of other gods and heroes (Pausanias 1.34.2). The three steps to the west are the remains of '**the theatre by the altar**' [3], known from an inscription of the late C4 BC, when it was dismantled, having previously served spectators standing to view events in the open space later filled with statue-bases. The first two of these (extreme south-west) were erected over the foundations of a **small temple** [4], with remains of a **stoa** [5] behind, its back wall retaining the terrace, perhaps the 'dormitory' known from an inscription (see **box**).

South-east of the altar, and Roman in its present form, is the sanctuary **spring** [6], where Amphiaraos had allegedly reappeared as a god, and where cured pilgrims were encouraged 'to drop silver and gold

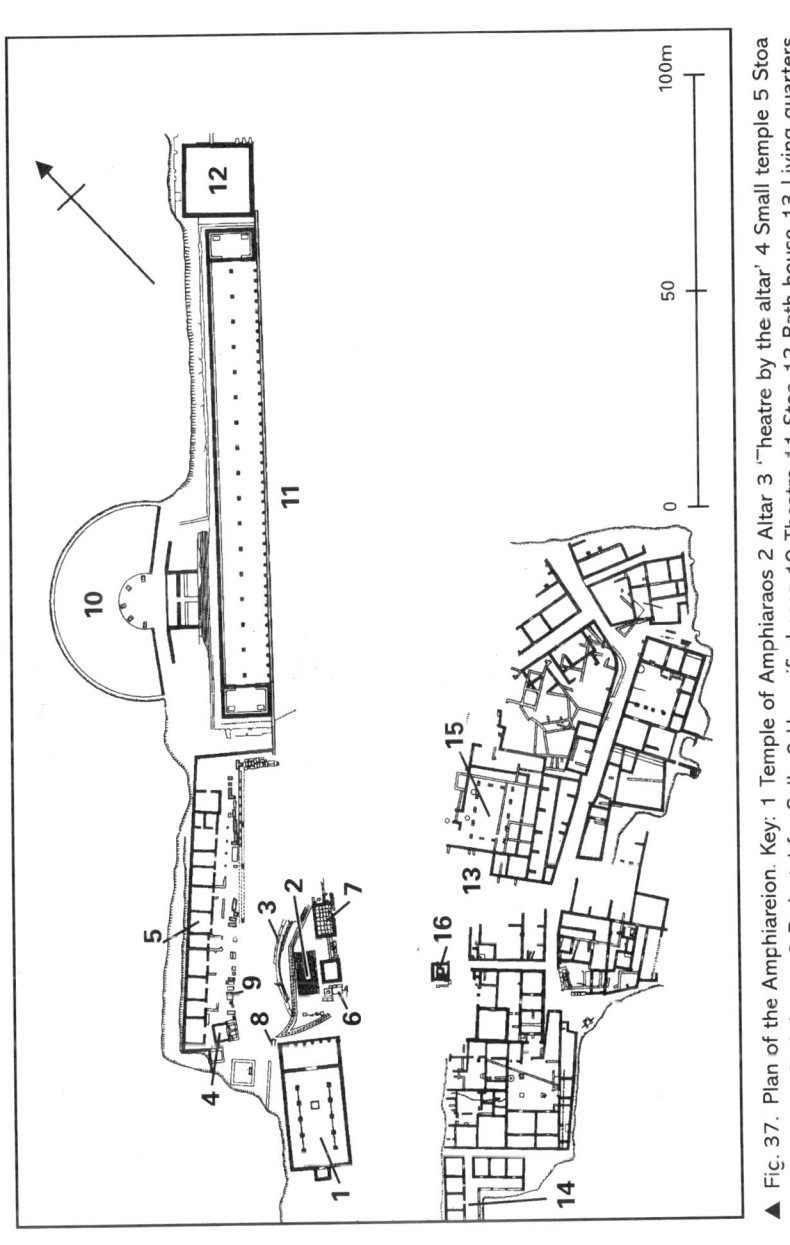

▲ Fig. 37. Plan of the Amphiareion. Key: 1 Temple of Amphiaraos 2 Altar 3 'Theatre by the altar' 4 Small temple 5 Stoa 6 Spring 7 Bath-house 8 Pedestal for Sulla 9 Honorific bases 10 Theatre 11 Stoa 12 Bath-house 13 Living quarters 14 'Guesthouse' 15 'Market' 16 Water clock

coins' (Pausanias 1.34.3). The adjacent **bath-house** ([**7**]—C4 BC), with traces of basins, water-channel, and floor-grooves to prevent slipping, seems to be the 'men's baths' placed in this vicinity by an inscription.

Flanking the temple entrance (west side) is the inscribed **pedestal** [**8**] for a statue honouring the Roman dictator Sulla (see **box**). It occupies the place of honour in a great series of **honorific bases** [**9**], the remainder lined up opposite the altar. They illustrate the calibre of external patron which the sanctuary managed (or sought) to attract in the C3–C1 BC. For instance, the 6th, 7th, 16th, 20th, and 21st along from the temple honour respectively Hadeia, a daughter-in-law of king Lysimachos, Agrippa, the henchman of Augustus, Brutus, Caesar's assassin, King Ptolemy IV and his sister-queen, Arsinoe, and Appius Claudius Pulcher, the Roman consul of 54 BC.

Sulla

Sulla's benefactions to the Amphiareion lay behind the extraordinary events described in a Greek inscription (68 lines) found in the sanctuary. It details the outcome (73 BC) of a journey to Rome by the then priest to head off an attempt by Roman tax-collectors (*publicani*) to make the sanctuary pay tax, even though Sulla had declared it exempt some years previously. The tax-men had argued that this exemption applied only to sanctuaries of gods, whereas Amphiaraos was just a hero. They lost, thanks probably to prior services to Rome by the priest, a 'friend for all time of the Roman people' (*IG* 7.413).

All the bases for Romans are reused, with earlier inscriptions for the original (and long dead) honorands either erased or blatantly left there. Greek cities like Oropos which engaged in this penny-pinching practice attracted public criticism, as with the Rhodians, berated by Dio of Prusa, a Greek intellectual (*c.* AD 100): 'What occurs is quite absurd. For your chief magistrate merely points his finger at the first of the statues already set up. Then, after the previous inscription has been removed and another name engraved, the business of honouring is finished' (*Oration* 31.10, trans. Cohoon).

The **theatre** [**10**], built with donations from wealthy sanctuary personnel, was partly re-erected in 1960–62. The 'stage-building' was the gift of a priest *c.*200 BC, according to the inscription on its facade. A second inscription, on the projecting proskenion, gives its donor (C2 BC) as an ex-president of the games, who also paid for the *pinakes*, the wooden panels with painted scenery which were slotted between the columns. Another priest, Nikon, paid for the five marble thrones for VIP spectators *c.*80 BC.

Inscribed lists of victors (C2–C1 BC) in the five-yearly games record the entertainments offered in the theatre. As well as the traditional events for solo musicians, poets, and playwrights, there were innovations reflecting the latest cultural fashions, such as contests for solo actors performing extracts from the classics, and one for professional speakers ('sophists'). The itinerant performers came from as far afield as Naples and the Greek cities of Asia Minor.

In front of the theatre is a Doric **stoa** [11], its extraordinary size (nearly 109 m. long) reflecting the number of pilgrims at the time it was built (*c.*350 BC on architectural grounds). An inscription naming the (unknown) donor originally ran above the columns of the facade. The screened off rooms at either end of the stoa (for incubants?) were later additions, as was the continuous stone bench. Contests in the stadium, known from inscriptions and thought to have occupied the space between the stoa and the ravine, would have been watched from here. The tile and mortar in the rubble walls indicate a major repair well into imperial times, to achieve which most of the building must first have been dismantled.

At the east end is a second **bath-house** [12], in origin C4 BC, and perhaps the 'women's baths' of an inscription, marginally sited and well away from those of the men. It was completely rebuilt in imperial times as a suite of heated baths.

In the courtyard of the **museum** (closed) are reassembled sections of the temple pediment (traces of its painted-plaster decoration) and the Doric frieze of the stoa, and three bases from **choregic monuments** supporting the prize-tripods of victorious producers of drama (*choregoi*) at the Amphiareia.

This is the best place to cross the ravine (in ancient times bridged) into the remains of the **living quarters** [13] of the sanctuary. These are well worth seeing, as they give you a definite feel of streets and buildings, among them a '**guesthouse**' [14] and '**market**' [15]. The most notable single feature, near the ravine and opposite the altar, is the sanctuary's **water clock** [16]. The water escaped from its central chamber through a bronze aperture (visible), lowering a float linked to some kind of time-gauge.

Rules for the sanctuary

Extracts from an inscribed 'sacred law' (early C4 BC) laying down rules for the sanctuary:

'Gods! The priest of Amphiaraos shall attend the shrine from the end of winter until the time of final ploughing, not being absent more than three days at a time, and shall remain in the shrine no less than ten days each month.

'Whoever intends to seek remedy from the god shall pay a fee of no less than nine obols of legal currency and drop it into the offertory box in the presence of the temple attendant.

> 'Whoever is in need of the god shall incubate . . . complying with the rules. The name of the incubant, as soon as he pays the money, is to be recorded by the temple attendant—both of (the incubant) himself and of his city—and shall be displayed written up in the dormitory register, so that anyone who wishes may inspect it. In the dormitory men and women shall recline in separate places, the men to the east of the altar and the women to the west'.
>
> (*SEG* 31 [1981] 416, lines 44–50, trans. Petropoulou)

Phyle (Figs. 38–39) ★

Go through the village of Phyle and after 2.5 km. take the left fork, which has a small sign for the αρχαιο φρουριο Φυλης (7.5 km.)—do not turn right for the Monastery of Kliston. You will eventually see the fortress on a hill on your left. At 9.6 km. turn left onto a dirt track which runs to the foot of the fortress.

Special Features

The impressive C4 border fortress at Phyle makes a pleasant excursion out of Athens and there are excellent tavernas in the village.

History

We first hear of Phyle in 404 BC. In *Hellenika* 2.4, Xenophon describes the events after ATHENS had been defeated by SPARTA and was under the control of the Thirty Tyrants. One of their opponents, Thrasyboulos, had fled from the city but

> presently he set out from Thebes with about seventy of his companions and seized Phyle. The Thirty marched out from the city against him with the three thousand and the cavalry in fine weather. When they reached Phyle, some of the young men attacked at once. However, they accomplished nothing and suffered a number of casualties before they retreated. The Thirty wanted to set up a blockade, so as to cut off access to supplies and force a surrender, but a heavy snow storm started in the night and continued on the next day. Consequently they returned to the city in the snow and many of their camp followers were killed by the men from Phyle.

As the fortress was not built until the C4 BC, it is not clear where Thrasyboulos and his companions were positioned but they had presumably occupied the hill which is protected by steep slopes on three sides. Phyle was a strategically important site, because it lay on the most direct, if not the easiest, route between Athens and THEBES. It was an obvious location for one of the Athenian border forts. A date in the early C4 has been proposed for the construction of the fortress which was garrisoned by ephebes who spent one year of their military service on frontier duty. The fortress was still in use in the C3.

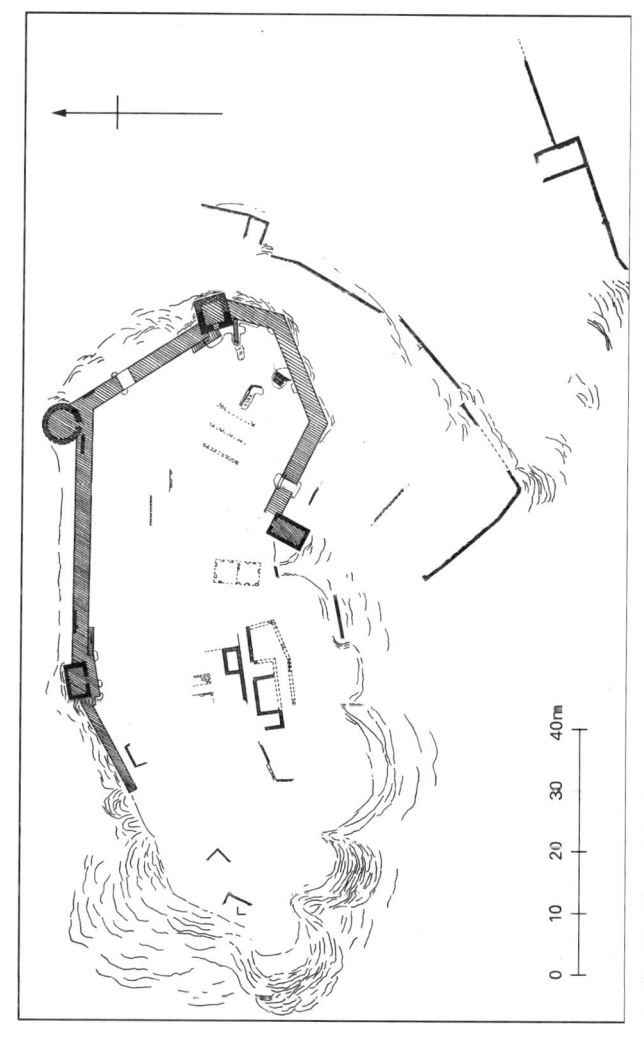

Fig. 38. Plan of the fortress at Phyle

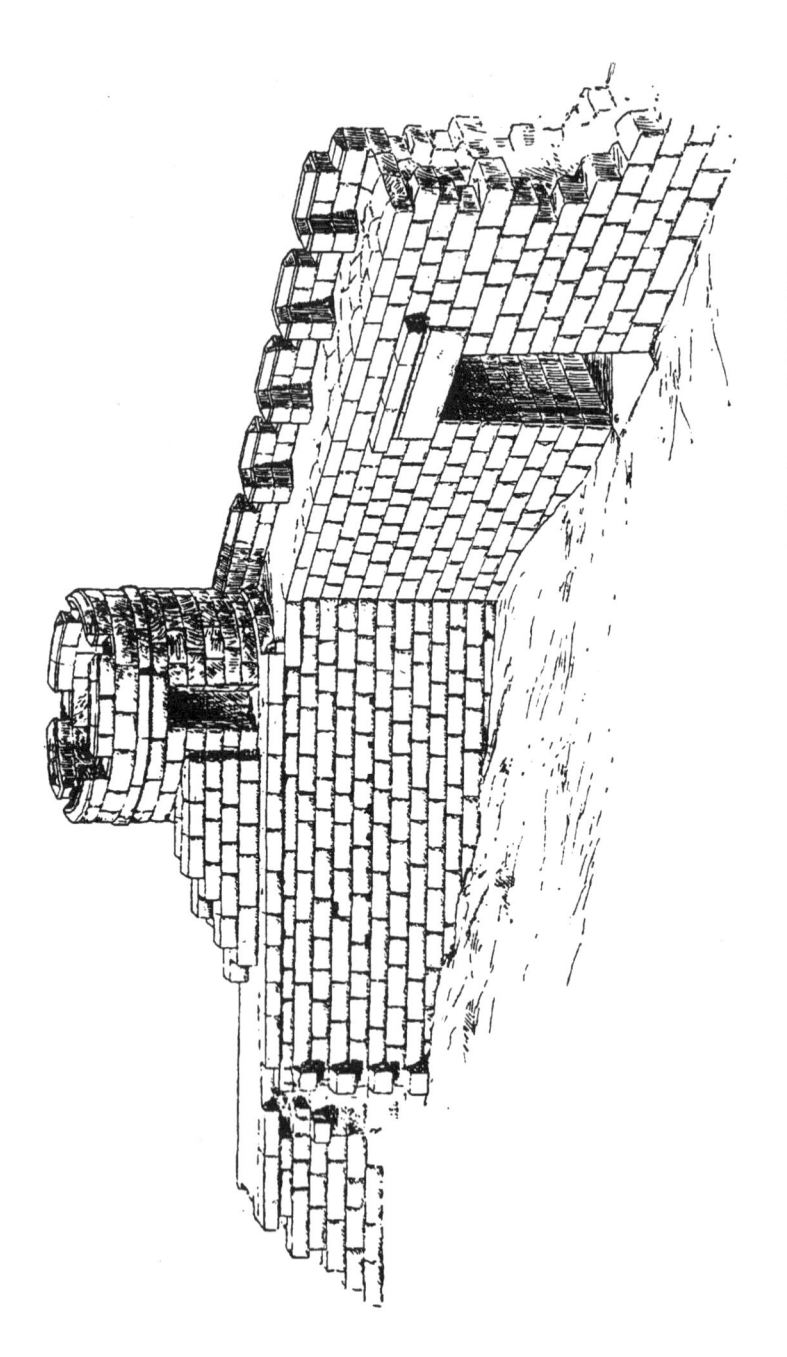

▲ Fig. 39. Reconstruction of the round tower at Phyle (after W. Wrede, *Athenische Mitteilungen* 49 (1924) 207, fig. 11)

Description

The eastern end of the hill was fortified in ashlar masonry but it was evidently felt that there was no need for a complete circuit since an attack from the west would have been suicidal. The main gate is flanked by towers, one of which is circular. It is curious that the Greeks did not make more use of circular towers which provide a better field of fire. As the plan of the fortress demonstrates, ashlar walls were built in straight lines if possible and no doubt this is why square or rectangular towers were preferred. Those defenders stationed on the walls were protected by a crenellated parapet. There is a second gate on the south side of the fortress and traces of the barracks in which the ephebes ate and slept. They had a fine view of the city of Athens which may have been some consolation for those who did not enjoy life on the frontier.

Eleutherai (Figs. 10 11)

The site is on the old Athens–Thebes road. From the restaurant in Kaza (Κάζα), follow the track signed Ancient Fortress of Eleutherae, which takes approximately ten minutes on foot.

Special Features

An impressive C4 fortress which dominates the Kaza pass between Attika and Boiotia.

History

The fortress is known as Gyphtokastro, the gipsy castle, and it seems likely that this is the site of ancient Eleutherai which was on the border between Attika and Boiotia. Pausanias (1.38) comments that 'the city built just above the plain towards Kithairon is clearly Eleutherai', a description which fits Gyphtokastro. There is less support for the theory that the site is ancient Panakton.

Eleutherai was originally Boiotian but switched sides and joined ATHENS in the C6 BC. Pausanias claims that this move was prompted by a 'desire for Athenian citizenship and hatred of THEBES'. In the sanctuary of Dionysos below the Akropolis in Athens there was a wooden statue of the god which came from Eleutherai, possibly as a result of this alliance. The fortress was built in the C4—the type of masonry and the architecture of the towers indicate a date around 370–360 BC. Eleutherai guarded one of the roads between Athens and Thebes. Either the fort is Theban work, as recently suggested, or it formed part of a system of border forts set up by the Athenians so that raids on their territory could at least be impeded if not prevented. On this view the enemy could attempt to capture the fortress, not a particularly attractive proposition since there were powerful catapults installed in the towers, or force the

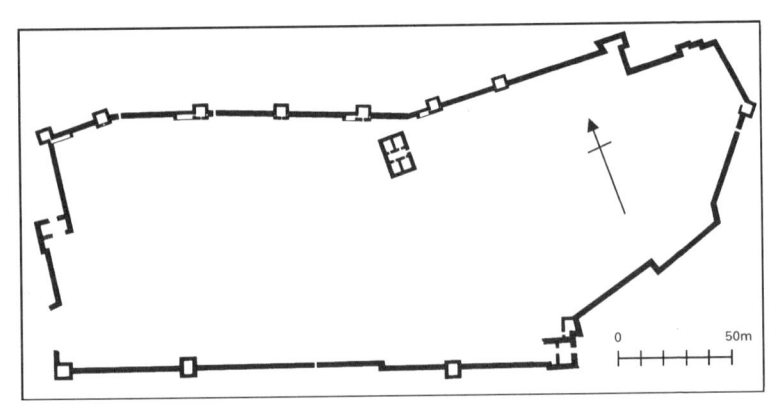

▲ Fig. 40. Plan of the fortress at Eleutherai

▲ Fig. 41. The fortification walls at Eleutherai

pass and have their lines of communication cut. Later in the C4 the fortifications were repaired and strengthened, possibly because of the threat posed by Philip of Macedon. When Pausanias saw Eleutherai the fortress and the settlement were in ruins.

Description

The fortress is an irregular rectangle, 300 m. east-west and 125 m. north-south. There were gates at each end of the circuit and four posterns. The walls have an inner and outer face, constructed of trapezoidal and ashlar blocks of limestone, and a rubble core. A parapet protected the defenders. The towers on the north side of the fortress were three storeys high. Archers fired through the slits at second-floor level. The windows on the top floor were for catapults. The garrison must have slept or dined in the rectangular structure. They needed some shelter from the elements. When it snows, an icy wind whips off Kithairon. Do not visit Eleutherai in a blizzard—we have and it was a serious mistake.

Aigosthena (Figs. 42–43) ★

Take the Αιγόσθενα turn on the old road between Athens and Thebes, then follow signs for Porto Germeno. Aigosthena is 19 km. from the turn. There is a sign for the Archaeological Site on the road by the beach.

Special Features

A site for connoisseurs of Greek military architecture which also has a fine beach.

History

Aigosthena is at the eastern end of the Corinthian Gulf on the slopes of Mt Kithairon. The settlement, which certainly existed by the C8 BC, was in the territory of Megara and, although rather remote, controlled the direct route between Boiotia and the Peloponnese. Xenophon (*Hellenika* 5.4.18 and 6.4.26) records that the Spartans passed through Aigosthena in 378 BC and after their defeat at the battle of Leuktra in 371 BC. It was a difficult road and on the first occasion a tremendous wind blew up while the Spartans were still on the mountain. Pack animals were swept down the slope and the soldiers could not keep hold of their shields which fell into the sea. Aigosthena is seldom mentioned otherwise and consequently it is not clear when or why the fortifications were built. Dates in the early C4, the late C4, and the early C3 have been proposed on the basis of their architectural style. Since the Megarians would presumably have required some assistance, one theory is that the Athenians were involved because they needed a naval base on the Corinthian Gulf. This would indicate a date around 340 BC. Alternatively the Macedonian king Demetrios I may have fortified Aigosthena later in the century when he campaigned against his fellow-king Cassander. The city joined the Achaian Confederacy in 243/2 BC and then came under Boiotian control. Pausanias (1.44) simply notes a sanctuary of Melampous, an obscure and not particularly helpful deity who 'gives no oracles even through dreams'. A statue base describes Hadrian as the founder of the city and it is conceivable that the indefatigable emperor even visited Aigosthena. There is an impressive early Christian basilica.

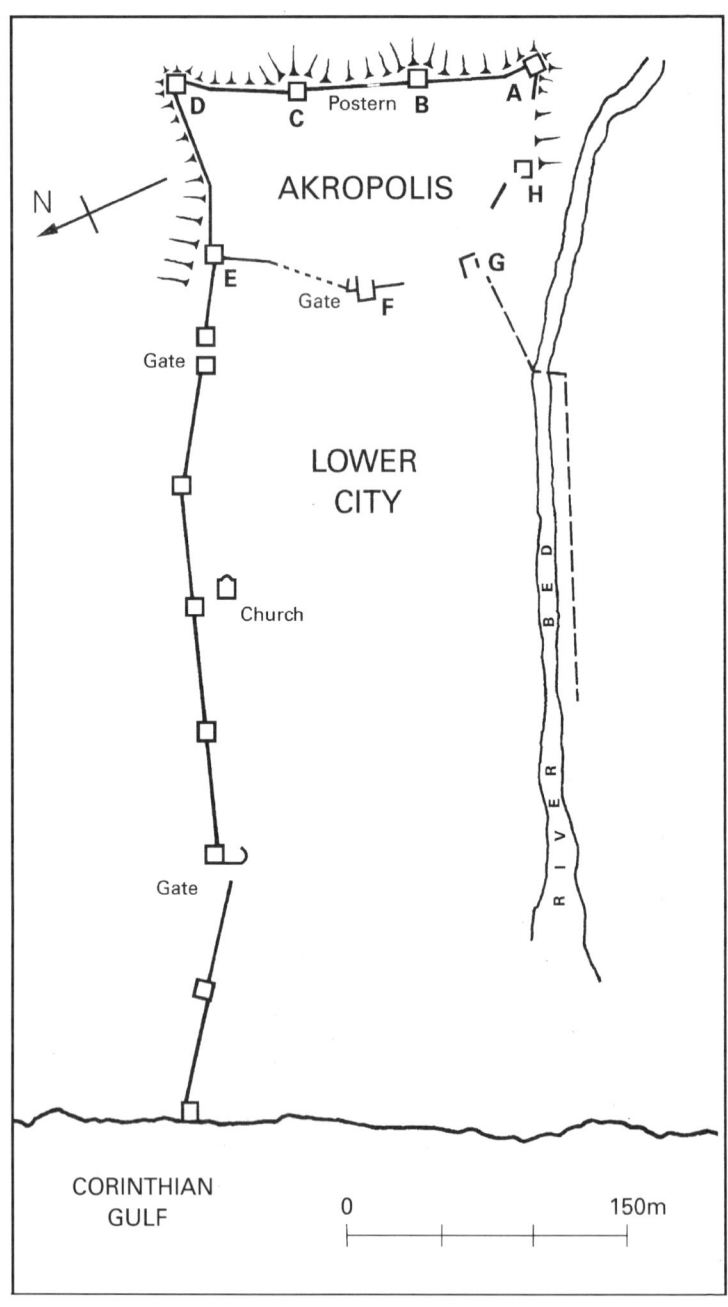

▲ Fig. 42. Plan of the fortress at Aigosthena

Description

We suggest that you make your way up to the akropolis first and then follow the line of the fortifications back down to the beach for a swim.

The best-preserved section of the fortifications is on the east side of the akropolis, although an earthquake in 1981 caused considerable damage. Tower A, at the south-east corner of the circuit, had remained more or less intact until then but now looks decidedly precarious. Built of limestone and conglomerate, it was 9 m. square and 18 m. high. There were windows on the top floor, evidently for catapults which fired bolts or stone projectiles. Archers were stationed on the next two floors and the tower has a solid base. Developments in siege warfare in the C4 resulted in the construction of much more massive fortifications. The contrast between Aigosthena and ELEUTHERAI is instructive in this respect. Ashlar masonry was used for the towers, trapezoidal and polygonal blocks for the curtain walls. The defenders would have made sorties from the postern gate between towers B and C. The main gate was evidently by tower F, between the akropolis and the lower city which was also fortified. Few traces of the wall on the south side of the city can be seen but the north wall is still in situ. It runs down to the sea, a distance of approximately 450 m., and is protected by a line of eight towers. There were at least two gates. The church of the Theotokos is on the site of a three-aisled early Christian basilica. A square baptistery opens off the south aisle. Spolia built into the church include a statue

▼ Fig. 43. The fortification walls at Aigosthena

base set up by Η ΠΟΛΙΣ ΑΙΓΟΣΘΕΝΕΙΤΩΝ which shows that Aigosthena was still a 'city' (polis) in the C4 AD.

Eleusis (Figs. 44–46)

The site is in the centre of modern Elefsina, just off the old Athens–Corinth road. The akropolis is crowned by a clock-tower.

Special Features

Eleusis was the centre of the most successful religious cult in the Greek world, which for a time rivalled Christianity. The architecture of the site, although complex, is still impressive.

History

Eleusis was the best-known centre of the cult of Demeter, goddess of corn, who found a welcome here in her torch-lit search for her daughter Kore (or Persephone), abducted by Hades, god of the underworld. In return Demeter taught the Eleusinians her secret mysteries. After Kore's return, she made the earth fertile again, and told Triptolemos, an Eleusinian hero, to teach agriculture to the rest of humankind. The historic mysteries probably originated in farming concerns, but owed their enormous later appeal to a ritual 'which inspires in those who partake of it sweeter hopes regarding both the end of life and all eternity' (Isokrates, *Panegyrikos* 28, *c.*380 BC), perhaps by placing human transience within nature's eternal cycle of regeneration. The mysteries took place every August, beginning with a great procession along the sacred way from ATHENS. Although initiates were sworn to secrecy, we know that they watched a ritual pageant of Demeter's search for Kore, and that the nocturnal climax in the hall of initiation was marked by 'a great light', and the displaying of 'sacred objects' by the hierophant or chief priest.

Although Eleusis was a Mycenaean settlement, cult at the later sanctuary for the moment extends no further back than *c.*750 BC. Incorporation of the village of Eleusis into the Athenian state (by 600) prompted new works in the precinct, in particular a hall of initiation ('of Solon'), rebuilt on a larger scale, perhaps under the Peisistratid tyrants. Imperial Athens vigorously promoted the cult (C5 BC), rebuilding the hall (burnt by the Persians in 480 BC) with a doubled capacity; by now the mysteries were open to all Greeks. From the C1 BC on the cult attracted the patronage of the Romans. Hadrian, himself an initiate, as was his favourite, Antinoos, began a major programme of building works, and made Eleusis a concern of the Panhellenion, his new organization of Aegean Greeks. The 'common precinct of the world', as Aristides, a contemporary orator described it, was badly burnt in an attack (AD 170) by the Costoboci, a Sarmatian people. It recovered, with more building, including repairs, by Marcus Aurelius (an initiate in 176), and in the early

Athens, Attika, and the Saronic 137

C3 AD the mysteries were described as 'the most populous' of all Greek festivals. They were still celebrated not long before 392, when Nestorios, the last legitimate hierophant, was holding office. Like all his predecessors, he was a 'descendant of Eumolpos', the mythical first hierophant. Alaric's Goths pillaged the precinct (396); by c.500 a church had been built just outside the forecourt.

▼ Fig. 44. Plan of Eleusis. Key: 1 Forecourt 2 Fountain house 3 Roman arches 4 Temple of Artemis 5 Altar 6 Kallichoron 7 Peisistratid fortification wall 8 'Pits' 9 C5 BC fortification wall 10 Greater Propylaia 11 Lesser Propylaia 12 Mirthless rock 13 Stepped area 14 Telesterion 15 So-called anaktoron 16 Roman temple 17 Museum 18 South gate 19 Sacred house 20 Late C4 BC fortification wall 21 Cisterns

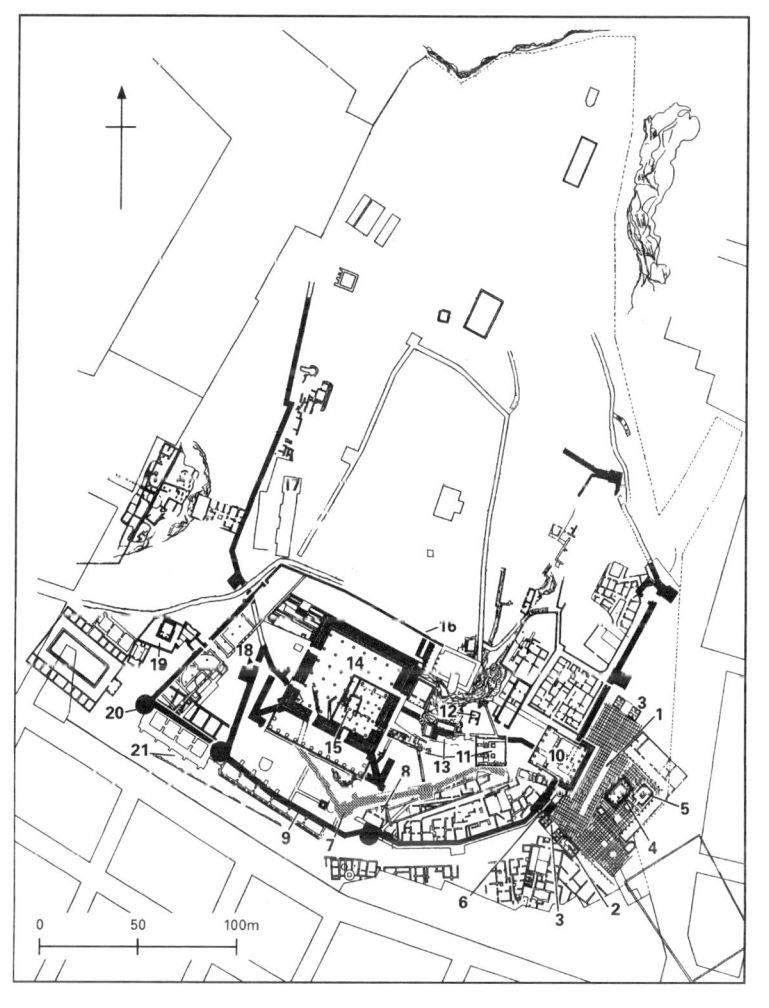

Description

What the visitor sees is the sanctuary in the final stages of its long development in the C2–C3 AD. You enter by an imposing **forecourt** [1] paved with Pentelic marble, flanked by stoas to the north-east and north-west, with a large **fountain house** ([2]—east side). All this is Roman-imperial, probably part of a single (Hadrianic) plan. Of the same period (east side) are the partly-reassembled remains of a **Roman arch** [3] in Pentelic marble, spanning the road from the harbour, with a matching arch (poorly preserved) opposite, both identical to Hadrian's arch in Athens. The building inscription reads ΤΟΙΝ ΘΕΟΙΝ ΚΑΙ ΤΩ ΑΥΤΟΚΡΑΤΟΡΙ ΟΙ ΠΑΝΕΛΛΗΝΕΣ: 'The Panhellenes (offered this) to the two Goddesses and the Emperor'. The unnamed emperor is nowadays taken to be Hadrian, founder of the Panhellenion.

In the centre of the court is the podium (rubble set in concrete) of a **Temple of Artemis** [4], Roman-style with a Doric colonnade across the front only. Mentioned by Pausanias, it was probably begun by Hadrian, although the cult was ancient, to judge from the curving Geometric wall underneath.

To the north-west is an unusual **altar** [5] of Roman brick build, again superseding older structures beneath it. Set into the ground rather than raised above it, it looks like a rectangular well, with a projecting shelf half-way down, probably for a grill or grate. Called an *eschara* or sacrificial hearth, this type of altar is linked with underworld deities and is mentioned in inscriptions as a feature of Eleusinian sacrifices.

Just east of the main gate is one of the sacred landmarks of Eleusis, the well called **Kallichoron** [6], said by Pausanias to be where 'the women of Eleusis danced and sang for the goddess' (1.38.6), consoling her after Kore's abduction. In the C5 BC initiates offered ritual dances by torchlight here 'for the golden-crowned Kore and her august mother' (Euripides, *Ion* 1085–86). Roman buildings respected the well, dated by its polygonal masonry to the C6 BC.

Before entering the sanctuary you will see a wooden staircase on your left permitting a visit to the **Peisistratid fortification wall** [7] of the sanctuary, replacing and extending a Geometric circuit (*c.*750 BC) with a much stronger wall of unbaked brick on a polygonal stone socle. A range of other masonry styles is also visible, including the pseudo-isodomic repairs under Kimon (479–461 BC) to a Persian breach in the Peisistratid wall. The two lines of conspicuous piers supported the roof of an underground building identified with the **'pits'** or *siroi* [8] for storing the gifts of grain for the goddesses demanded by Athens from her allies in (perhaps) the 420s BC (*IG* 1³.78). The **wall** [9] enclosing these piers to the north belongs to the extension of the circuit under Perikles.

The so-called **Greater Propylaia** [10], the monumental north gate

▲ Fig. 45. Kallichoron well at Eleusis

▲ Fig. 46. Shield-bust of a Roman emperor, Eleusis

to the precinct, faithfully replicates the central part of the Propylaia on the Akropolis. This homage to Classical Athens was probably begun by Hadrian. On grounds of hairstyle, the badly preserved figure of a cuirassed emperor on the pediment is thought to be Marcus

Aurelius, who evidently completed and/or repaired his predecessor's project.

Once inside, a paved way leads you up to the so-called **Lesser Propylaia** [11], an earlier version of the north gate, its patrician donor, Roman consul in 54 BC, known from the Latin inscription on the architrave: 'Appius Claudius Pulcher, son of Appius, promised the propylon for Ceres and Proserpina as consul, and began (the work) as imperator. Pulcher Claudius and Rex Marcius completed (it) in accordance with his will.' This Pulcher, perhaps an initiate, died in 52 BC, and his heirs inherited the project. The block is decorated with symbols of the cult: sacred chests, wheat-sheaves, and poppy flowers. The grooves were for the double-leaved door, flanked on the inside by a pair of colossal caryatids (in the museum).

In antiquity the cave above the gate was seen as a gateway to Hades. Bounded by a precinct wall, with foundations of a small shrine just outside the mouth, the whole area used to be claimed as a shrine to Pluto. More recently it has been identified as the **Mirthless Rock** or *Agelastos Petra* [12], another sacred landmark, where Demeter sat and grieved for her daughter. Inside the cave, a natural outcrop may have been shown as the goddess's actual seat.

Passing, on the right, a **stepped area** [13] for standing spectators, thought to be Roman, you reach the heart of the sanctuary, the vast hypostyle **Telesterion** [14] or hall of initiation. This was the most sought-after setting for honorific statues, known from their inscribed bases dotting the site, mainly set up for Athenian priests and other Hellenistic and Roman worthies. As seen now, the hall is a drastic Roman rebuilding, and also slight enlargement, of a venerable structure built by a team of C5-BC architects, including Iktinos. Probably realized by Marcus Aurelius *c.* AD 170–175, this final version was roughly square (*c.*56 by 54.5 m.), the roof supported by 42 columns, with grandstands for thousands of initiates around all four sides, cut from the bedrock on the north-west. In front ran a huge colonnade in the Doric order (the column drums in situ are Roman), the so-called 'prostoon of Philon', its architect, originally built in the C4 BC, and already anticipated in the C5 BC, when its massive foundations were constructed.

Inside, near the centre, are the remains of an enigmatic rectangular structure, the so-called **anaktoron** [15], completely rebuilt in the Roman renovations. It is usually seen as a 'holy of holies', but an alternative suggestion is a stage-like platform for the 'visions' (*phasmata*) of the reunited goddesses, perhaps illuminated effigies. A jumble of earlier remains is visible beneath the Roman floor-level: polygonal and poros walls assigned to (respectively) the 'Solonian' and 'Peisistratid' halls; also Geometric and Mycenaean walls.

To the east of the hall the later floor of the court has been lifted to expose the fortifications at this point: a circular corner-tower in the

C5 BC circuit, and the join with the south extension added in the late C4 BC.

On top of the akropolis by the small chapel of the Panayitsa are remains of a **temple** ([16]—C2 AD), Roman in plan with a frontal colonnade only, reached from the hall by monumental rock-cut steps and a terrace.

Steps lead north-west from the hall to the **museum** [17], labelled in English. The fine sarcophagus of Pentelic marble outside (early C3 AD; without the original lid), showing the myth of Meleager, was made in Athens, which exported sarcophagi all over the Roman empire. Room 1 has a copy of a red-figure Athenian votive tablet (*c*.370 BC, original in the National Archaeological Museum) showing (right) the seated goddesses (Demeter, below, on her rock), and dancing initiates carrying wands, torches, and libation-vessels, led by the god Iakchos. The large burial-amphora (C7 BC, an important example of the Protoattic style), has early scenes of the blinding of Polyphemos and Perseus decapitating Medusa. Rooms 2–3 have sculpture from the site. Room 4 has models of the sanctuary and a statue of the deified Antinos (see p. 314) represented as Asklepios. Room 5 has a 'caryatid' from the Lesser Propylaia. She has a ritual chest (*kiste*), of the kind used for the 'sacred objects' (*hiera*) carried by priestesses in the procession from Athens which is decorated with an image of a *plemochoe* (see p. 76). Room 6 has examples of the clay *kernos*, a distinctive Eleusinian vessel used in the ritual 'carrying the *kernos*', and described by Athenaeus (C3 AD, citing an earlier authority) as 'holding within it a large number of small cups cemented together. "In these", Polemo says, "are white poppy-heads, grains of wheat and barley, peas, vetches, okra-seeds and lentils" ' (*Deipnosophists* 476–8, ed. Loeb).

From the museum we suggest that you leave the precinct by the **south gate** [18], part of the fortified extension of the sanctuary in the late C4 BC. An architrave inscribed in big letters ΕΛΕΥΣΙΝΙΩΝ ΑΓΩΝΩΝ, 'games of the Eleusinian festival', belongs to an unidentified building in the vicinity (C2 AD?), where, as the inscription suggests, management of the contests was now based.

Just outside the gate you can see the '**sacred house**' ([19]—a modern designation), important evidence for the early sanctity of the site. Built *c*.750 BC, its rooms were full of vessels (C7 BC) containing ashes from offerings, perhaps from a hero-cult for the previous occupants.

The path round the outside of the sanctuary allows you to view the late C4 BC **fortification wall** [20] and circular corner-tower, with decorative pecked masonry in the lower courses. Next come massive brick-built **cisterns** [21], fed by a vanished aqueduct, all probably Hadrianic. The circuit-wall from here to the Great Propylaia shows evidence of Roman repairs, usually dated to the reign of Valerian (AD 253–259).

Aigina (Figs. 47–50) ★

Kolonna: The site closes off the northern end of the harbour and is crowned by a solitary column. As you leave the quay, there is a sign for the Archaeological Museum. After approximately 300 m. there are further signs for the Archaeological Site and the Archaeological Museum.
Aphaia: The sanctuary is 12 km. from Aigina town on the Ayia Marina road.

Special Features

An attractive island which is easily accessible from Athens and has two major sites. The history of Aigina is encapsulated by the Kolonna site which includes the recently reopened Archaeological Museum. At Aphaia there is one of the best-preserved temples in Greece and a museum which has a unique display of painted architecture.

History

The location of Aigina in the centre of the Saronic Gulf created opportunities, but also problems, and proved a potent factor in the history of the island. It was not until late in the Neolithic period, the fourth millennium BC, that the Kolonna site was first occupied. Pausanias (2.29.2) comments that 'Aigina is the most unapproachable island in Greece' because it is surrounded by rocks and this may have deterred settlers. However, most Aegean islands were only colonized at this time. Limited agricultural resources and low rainfall were much more of a hazard. By the middle of the third millennium, Kolonna was a substantial settlement. The remains of a corridor house have been excavated just south of the temple of Apollo. Known as the Weisses Haus, because the walls were plastered and painted white, it is like the House of Tiles at LERNA and may have been built for the ruler of Kolonna. Despite the fact that the settlement was fortified late in the third millennium, there is evidence of a major destruction horizon. Nevertheless the fortifications were reconstructed and over the course of the Middle Helladic period became more and more impressive. That the prosperity of Kolonna was based on trade seems certain. Pottery was imported from Greece, Crete, and the Cyclades but just as much was exported. The boats painted on barrel jars (on display in the museum) emphasize the maritime dimension of the local economy. The fact that some of the sailors have spears hints at less savoury activities such as piracy. One warrior, a man whose status or achievements must have been quite exceptional, was buried in front of the main gate in a built grave which also contained a gold diadem, a sword, a spear, and a boar's tusk helmet. The treatment of the dead in the shaft graves at MYCENAE is of course similar but in this, as in other respects, Aigina anticipates and may well have influenced developments on the mainland. Unfortunately we know less

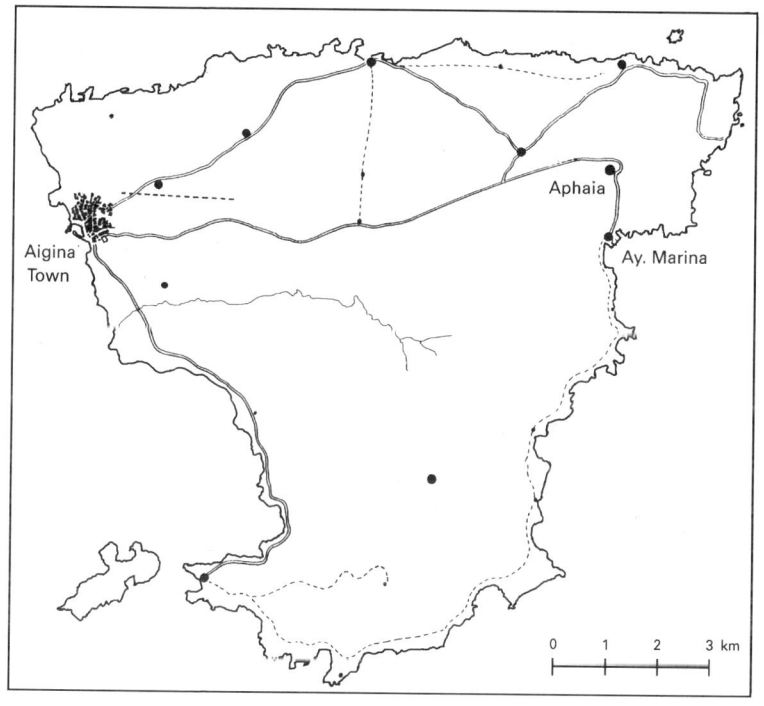

▲ Fig. 47. The island of Aigina showing location of Kolonna and Aphaia

about the Mycenaean period, although cult activity at Aphaia is attested.

The Aiginetans of historic times, Dorian Greeks, enjoyed their heyday in the C7–early C5 BC as a naval power with extensive commercial interests. Aiginetans took part in the foundation of the Greek emporium of Naukratis on the Nile delta c.630 BC, and Herodotus says that a certain Sostratos of Aigina was the richest of all Archaic Greek traders. The wealth of Archaic Aigina stimulated the arts, and her sculptors in bronze were much in demand on the mainland. In the C6 BC Aigina and Athens became deadly rivals, although in 480 Aiginetan and Athenian ships combined to defeat the Persians at Salamis. Aigina's independence ended in 458/7, when the Athenians forced the 'eyesore of the Piraeus', as Themistokles called the island, into their empire. In 431 BC an Athenian colony was installed and the Aiginetans exiled. Hellenistic Aigina was a plaything of the great powers, and at one point was even sold (209 BC) for 30 talents. By the mid-C1 BC the island, like Piraeus, was a byword for Greece's decline, although in the early Christian era there was some recovery.

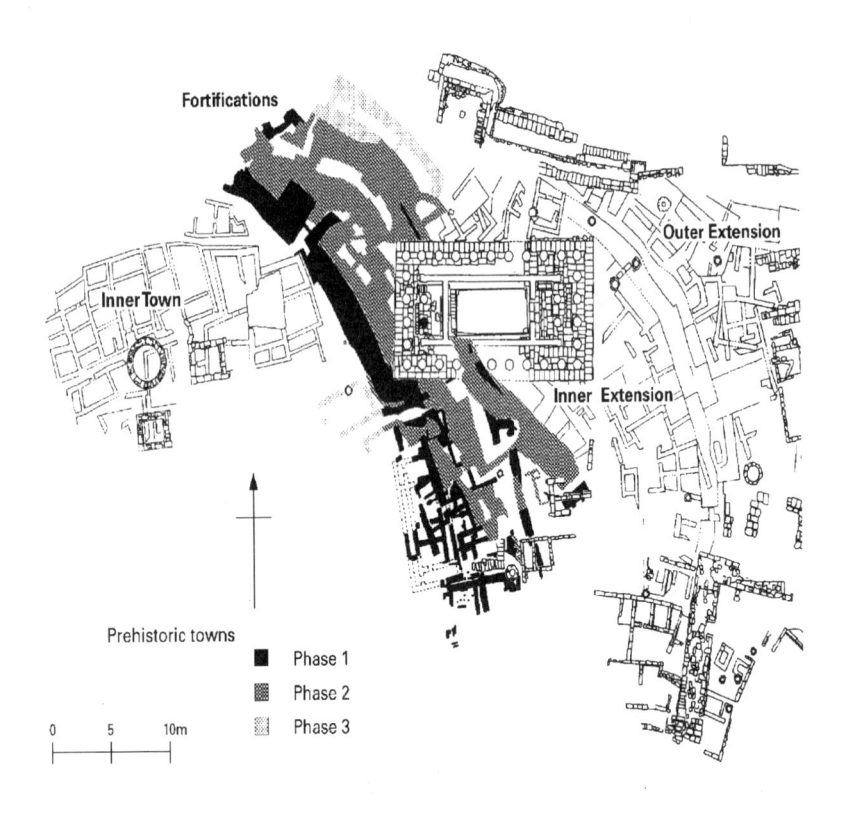

▲ Fig. 48. Plan of Kolonna site on Aigina

Description
Kolonna

In the vestibule of the **museum** there is an Early Helladic kiln and a model of the Weisses Haus. It is not certain that there was a veranda around the first-floor rooms but this would have provided a pleasant blend of light and shade. Most of the grave reliefs in the courtyard came from the cemeteries on the island of Rheneia and formed part of the collection of the first National Museum. Across the courtyard there are three rooms. The first of these, on the left, contains prehistoric finds from Kolonna. There is Final Neolithic, Early Helladic, and Middle Helladic pottery—note the ships on the matt-painted barrel jar—excellent Mycenaean pottery and terracotta figurines. In the main room there is a case of imported Athenian pottery—Protogeometric-Geometric, Protoattic, and early black-figure—and another case which contains Corinthian imports and a stone mould for an aryballos. Archaic sculpture from the temple of Apollo includes a Herakles from one of the

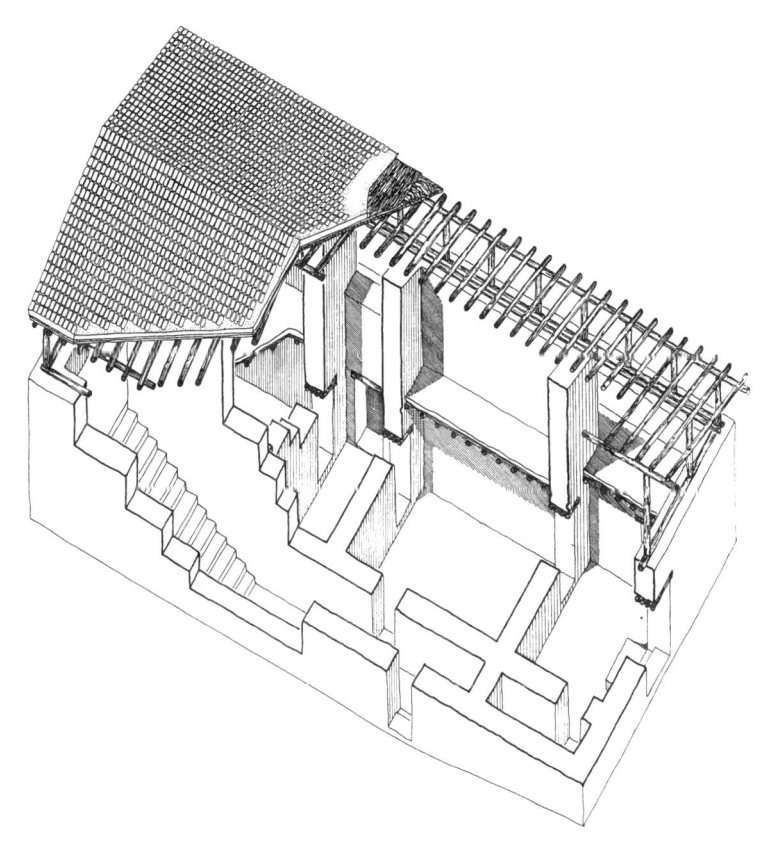

▲ Fig. 49. Reconstruction of the Weisses Haus at Kolonna on Aigina (after H. Walter and F. Felten, *Alt-Aigina III.1: die vorgeschichtliche Stadt* (Mainz 1981) 19, fig. 14)

pediments. A C6 inscription records construction activity at Aphaia (see p. 146) and there is a fine Early Classical sphinx. The room on the right contains Classical sculpture, in particular two cases of disiecta membra from the Aphaia pediments, a nice C5 grave relief and a Hellenistic Cybele.

As you enter the site, you first pass the **Harbour Wall** which was built in the C3 AD and runs around the eastern end of the promontory. No doubt it was the threat of attack by the Herulian Goths which prompted the construction of the fortifications. You then climb up to the platform of the **Temple of Apollo**. There is a fine view of the town and the port which occupies the ancient commercial harbour. The military harbour was in the bay south of Kolonna. The first temple of Apollo was built c.600 BC and replaced in 575–550 BC by the second temple, which was apparently destroyed by fire. The third temple, dated c.510 BC, had a peristyle of Doric columns and the conventional porch, cella, and opisthodomos. It is one of the monolithic limestone columns in the opisthodomos which has survived and provided the name of the site (from the Italian *colonna*). The **altar** can be seen east of the temple and south of this the scanty remains of a **temple**, possibly of Artemis. A section of the **temenos wall** which enclosed the sanctuary is preserved just north of the temple.

You will not easily make sense of the **prehistoric settlement** which has ten architectural phases. The sequence of fortifications which protected the promontory in phases V-IX can best be understood if you look south from the temple platform. In each successive phase the line of the fortifications was moved further east and this has created an architectural time line. Cross the temple platform for a view of the face of the later **Middle Helladic wall** which is over 6 m. wide in places. The **warrior grave**, cut into earlier houses, is approximately 25 m. from the south-east corner of the temple.

Aphaia

We strongly recommend that you time your visit to include the site museum which is opened at set times in the morning.

Mycenaean pottery, terracottas, and seals suggest that there was an open-air cult on this prominent hill-top site in the Late Helladic period. The deity of the historical sanctuary was first identified by a fine Archaic inscription (*c*.550 BC) found in 1901, and now in the Aigina museum: 'When Theoitas was priest, for Aphaia the temple (*oikos*) was made, and the altar and the ivory were added, and the [throne] was finished off' (Guarducci, *Epigraphica* 46 (1984) 9ff.).

The name of Aphaia, a little-known goddess, probably derives from *phainein*, 'to appear'. Writers of Roman date identified her with the Cretan goddess Britomartis, a virgin huntress pursued by Minos who took refuge on Aigina. Although late, this myth fits nicely with the prehistoric island's Minoan connections (see Kolonna). The small finds suggest Aphaia's importance for women as a 'child-nurturer', and include bronze rings for offerings of hair, perhaps from initiation-rites. Her cult here goes back to Geometric times. Archaeological continuity from the Mycenaean sanctuary has yet to be demonstrated.

Aphaia's shrine received monumental treatment in the C6 BC, when an earlier building was replaced with a small, brightly painted, Doric temple, without a colonnade. Work began *c*.570 BC, and the Theoitas inscription describes the finishing touches, perhaps including ivory additions to the cult-statue. Not long after the temple burnt down, while the paintwork was still fresh, and the blocks were used in the fill of the terrace supporting its much larger successor, the temple you see now.

Along with this new temple, overlying its predecessor, the sanctuary was enlarged and reorganized, with a new gateway. The programme may have begun *c.*510 BC, although pottery in the terrace-fill suggests operations continuing into the period *c.*490–480 BC. Parts of four sets of pedimental groups have been found, two of them (the later ones) now displayed in the Munich Glyptothek. It seems that the first pair were taken down, put on show in the precinct, and replaced (at different times *c.* 500 to 490 or even 480 BC on stylistic grounds) with a new subject, the Greek sack of Troy (at both ends), which stressed the glorious deeds of the sons of Aiakos, Aiginetan heroes. Modern explanations for this costly operation see the new sculptures referring to Aigina's defeat of Athens (possibly *c.*495 BC) or even her contribution to the Persian defeat at Salamis (480 BC). An inventory of the temple's fittings inscribed in Athenian Greek shows that the Athenian colonists kept up the cult (*IG* 4.39), which only went into final decline in the C1 BC. The temple's metope slabs are missing and may have been looted in Roman times.

There are a number of helpful display boards scattered around the site with information in Greek, German, and English, and reconstructions of what the temple would have looked like.

As you ascend to the temple, the modern path runs to the left of the main **gateway** (propylon) through which the sanctuary proper was entered. The ashlar **precinct wall** (peribolos) stretches west of the gateway, under the modern terrace wall, and can be traced right round the temple.

To the east of the gateway is a **bath-building**, comprising two rooms, one equipped with three flat baths (protected by a modern roof). It dates from the C3 BC. South and east of the baths is a **complex of rooms**,

▲ Fig. 50. The Temple of Aphaia on Aigina

seemingly the *amphipoleion* or 'house of the attendants' of the inscribed inventory (*IG* 4.39). This lists eating and drinking equipment stored here, showing that some rooms were used for feasting.

North of this complex, which partly overlies older ancillary structures, is the **altar**. To the north, overlying an earlier **altar**, are foundations of a **base**, perhaps for a display of discarded pedimental sculpture. Just northwest of this is a **base** for a column supporting a votive sphinx (6C BC).

The **temple**, approached by a **ramp** leading to the altar, is now roped off and cannot be entered, but it is possible to see all of the main details. The material is limestone, originally stuccoed and painted cream, with details picked out in red, black, and dark blue. Metal grilles, their slots still visible, originally closed off the porch and the columns of the rear chamber. The double colonnade of the main room (cella) is well preserved, and you can see the U-shaped cuttings in some blocks for lifting them into position. As an after-thought a doorway (visible) was made linking the cella to the opisthodomos, perhaps to allow access to the cult-statue during the lengthy job of replacing the east pediment.

A section of the **earlier precinct wall** is visible in a triangular cutting on the temple's north side. The crude **circular wall** projecting beneath the west end belongs to the temple's construction-phase, and was buried once the temple was finished.

The **museum** has excellent information panels in English covering the sanctuary's history. The ground floor is devoted to the later sanctuary, and includes a model, as well as reconstructions of parts of the pedimental groups, showing the marked contrast in sculptural styles between the west (more Archaic) and the east (more Classical) ends. The basement is given over to the C6 BC temple, with a model, and reconstructions of the facade, a column (note the early, cushion-like, form of the Doric capital) and part of the porch. Tests show that the pigments for the paintwork include chalk, red ochre, malachite (green), and Egyptian blue (see **box**). The capital of the sphinx column is here; also a replica of the Theoitas inscription.

Paint

The Greeks routinely painted their buildings and sculpture, giving them a brightly coloured appearance at odds with today's romantically weathered buildings and denuded marble statues in museums. The white marbles of Paros and Mt Pentelikon near Athens were prized partly because they took paint so well. The Aigina pediments now in Munich were brightly painted, with artists incising and then colouring in the patterning on garments. In the C5–C4 BC it was normal for a sculptor and painter to work as a team. Although sculptors in the C5 BC came to rely more on form and moulding in carving costume, pale washes were probably still used for flesh colours and dark paint for picking out folds in drapery.

Corinth and Environs

CORINTH is an excellent example of the way in which nature blessed and cursed Greek cities. The akropolis of ACROCORINTH dominates the Isthmus and consequently the land corridor between central Greece and the Peloponnese. Moreover, Corinth had ports on either side of the Isthmus, at KENCHREAI and LECHAION, and could therefore control sea traffic as well, particularly after the construction of the DIOLKOS. However, the coastal plain, although famously fertile, is not particularly extensive. This lack of land was often a source of tension. Earthquakes have also been a common occurrence because the Corinthian Gulf is essentially a rift valley or *graben*, bounded by fault lines. This tectonic instability explains why Kenchreai is now underwater, whereas the harbour at Lechaion has silted up.

There is a cluster of prehistoric sites around the Isthmus but none of these is an obvious administrative centre and MYCENAE may well have controlled the Corinthia in the Late Helladic period. Of course it is possible that there was a major prehistoric settlement on the site of ancient Corinth which has been destroyed. In historic times the Corinthia was coterminous with the boundaries of Corinth, the ancient city commanding the Isthmus crossings from a site made near-impregnable by the natural fortress of Acrocorinth. The ports of Lechaion and Kenchreai, and the haulage or diolkos, illustrate Corinthian exploitation of this strategic position. PERACHORA and ISTHMIA offer contrasting types of Corinthian sanctuary, the one local and small-scale, the other a panhellenic player. Corinth's third natural asset was the 'land of most noble fruitfulness' as Livy described the fertile coastal strip, which it shared with a neighbouring city to the west, SIKYON.

Corinth (Figs. 51–53)

The site is in the village of Ancient Corinth, approximately 5 km. south of New Corinth.

Special Features

The site is of exceptional historical interest, and there is a fine museum.

History

Corinth, the natural centre of the Corinthia, is sited on the terraces immediately below ACROCORINTH, and was famously well-watered. Continuous settlement here goes back to the C10 BC. In the C8 BC the

Corinth and Environs

Corinthians profited from their geographical position to take a leading part in Greek trade and colonization in the west. The city was less inhospitable than most to craftsmen, and Corinth's bronzes were much admired by the ancients, as its Archaic painted pottery is today. In the C7–early C6 the city was ruled by the tyrants Kypselos and Periander. Classical Corinth was usually an ally of Sparta. The city at this time had a vast system of mudbrick fortification-walls embracing the city and LECHAION and running up to Acrocorinth. From 338 to 243 BC the city was held by the Macedonians. Its manual workers helped to incite the Achaian League, of which Corinth was a member, to an ill-judged war against Rome (146 BC): the consul Mummius pillaged and burnt the city, and massacred or enslaved the inhabitants. Caesar refounded Corinth as a Roman colony (44 BC) peopled mainly with ex-slaves from Rome; Italian businessmen also flocked here. Roman planners laid the new city out on a grid and divided up the territory into farming plots. From 27 BC Corinth was the seat of the provincial administration of Achaia. It was a centre of the imperial cult, and grew steadily in commercial importance, especially in the reign of Claudius, under whom Paul founded a Christian community here. By the mid-C2 the colony could be described as the 'capital of Achaia'. Its Latin, Italian culture, strong at first, had become a typical Greek and Roman mix by the early C2 AD, when Greek became the dominant tongue. In the C2 AD many public buildings were rebuilt and, with the help of Herodes Atticus (pp. 117–118), Corinth became a marble-clad showplace. The city suffered from severe earthquakes in AD 77, 375, and 521. It was taken by Alaric (396), and new walls were built in the early C5, enclosing about one-third of the area defended by the Classical wall. The city remained the seat of the governor, surviving into the C7. Conditions here in the C8 await clarification.

Description

We suggest that you begin your visit at the museum, at the furthermost site entrance, opposite the car park.

The **museum** is well-labelled in English. The room on the right is devoted to Greek material, including: a limestone sphinx at the back of the room (C6 BC) and cases of Corinthian pottery and terracottas from Neolithic to Hellenistic times. On the left of the entrance-hall is a gallery with Roman and medieval finds. Items include Augustus and other imperial statues from the Julian Basilica; wall-paintings (c. AD 100) from a house by the theatre; colossal figures from the Captives Facade (c. AD 160–170); and two marble statues of officials (C5–C6 AD), one holding the handkerchief (*mappa*) rolled into a ball which he dropped to mark the start of public shows. Among finds in the cloister is the tombstone (c. AD 100) of Gaius Valerius Valens, a Roman legionary seconded to the governor's staff in Corinth for office duties (he is shown holding a writing-case); the relief friezes from the Hadrianic stage-building of the theatre; and a Christian inscription (*IG* 4.204) from the trans-Isthmian wall beseeching the 'Light of light, true God of true God' to 'guard the emperor Justinian and his faithful servant Victorinus, along with those who dwell in Greece according to God'. In the courtyard are honorific statues (C1–C3 AD), their missing portrait-heads inserted separately, and inscriptions of Roman date, including the base for Regilla found at Peirene.

Just south of the museum, before you enter the site, is the massive podium of **temple E** [**1**], one of the grandest temples in the colony, dedicated either to Octavia, the sister of Augustus, or to Jupiter Capitolinus. It was lavishly rebuilt in the Corinthian order after the earthquake of 77 AD by a family of donors, including children (*liberi*), recorded in the Latin inscription on display (its letters once of bronze).

Inside the site we suggest that you go first to the low hill on which stands the **Temple of Apollo** [**2**], built *c*.550 BC on the site of a predecessor (*c*.670–650 BC) which had the earliest known tiled roof. The C6 temple had a peristyle of six by fifteen poros limestone columns. Note the traces of stucco still preserved on some of the columns and the wide capitals which are typical of this period. The arrangement of the interior is uncertain because the Roman colonists collapsed the two rooms inside into one and removed the interior columns which were re-erected as a colonnade in the south-west forum.

From here you have a panorama over the marble-paved **forum** [**3**], which is unusually large. It was divided into upper and lower areas by the Central Shops. You can see the Lechaion road, the colony's principal north–south axis (*cardo maximus*), entering it at the north-east. In Greek times the area was dominated by shrines, a race-course, victor-monuments, and the South Stoa. The agora seems to have been elsewhere, to the north or north-east of the Temple of Apollo.

Immediately below to the north, you can see the excavated third of the **North Market** ([**4**] early C1 AD?), a colonnaded court housing forty units, perhaps commercial offices.

Along the north side of the forum run the **North-West Shops** ([**5**] early C2 AD), fronted by a colonnade; the vault of the central shop is still preserved. This structure masks the **North-West Stoa** [**6**], a long two-storey colonnade of Augustan date.

The west side of the forum is lined by the **West Shops** [**7**], and in front of them is a row of small podium-temples, their dates and identifications not always settled. Of note is the square podium once supporting the **Babbius monument** ([**8**] early C1 AD), a circular Corinthian colonnade, roofed but open, originally for a statue. By the side is an ornate block from the facade recording in Latin the rich donor, Babbius Philinus, who was probably an ex-slave, as his father is unnamed. Just south

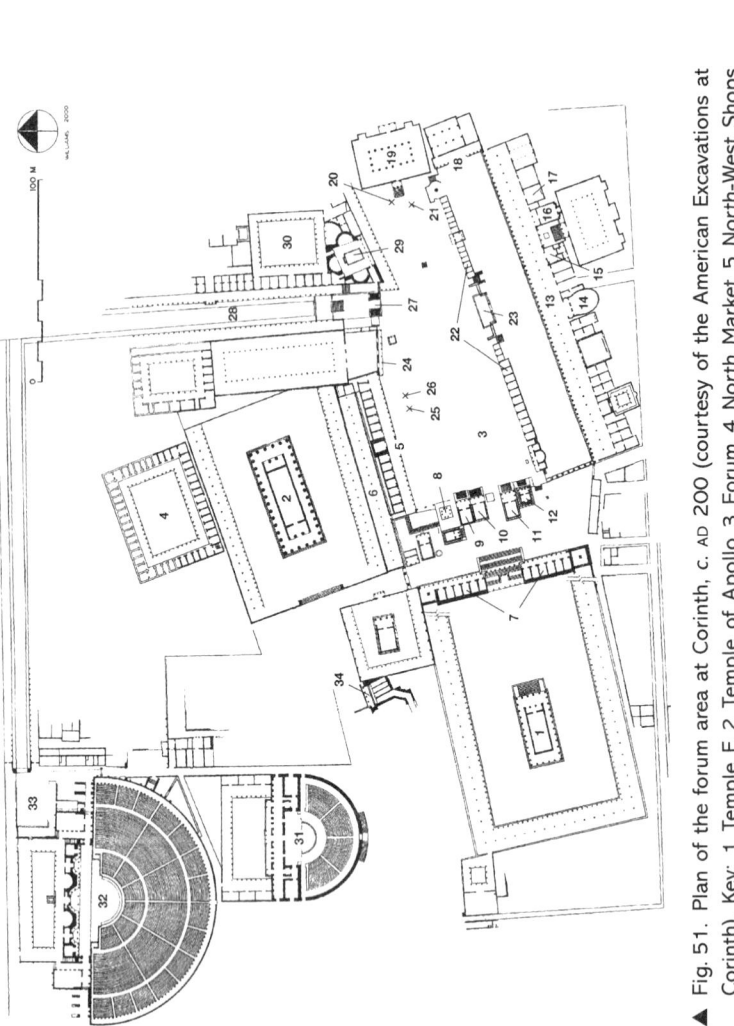

Fig. 51. Plan of the forum area at Corinth, c. AD 200 (courtesy of the American Excavations at Corinth). Key: 1 Temple E 2 Temple of Apollo 3 Forum 4 North Market 5 North-West Shops 6 North-East Stoa 7 West Shops 8 Babbius monument 9 Temple J 10 Temple H 11 Temple G 12 Temple F 13 South Stoa 14 Council house 15 Fountain house 16 Rectangular hall 17 ?Isthmian office 18 South-East Building 19 Julian basilica 20 Starting platforms 21 Terrace 22 Central shops 23 Rostra 24 Captives façade 25 Terrace wall 26 Sacred spring 27 Gateway 28 Lechaion

are **temples J [9]** and **H [10]**, set side by side and both Corinthian. They were dedicated respectively by and to the emperor Commodus (AD 180–192), as shown by Latin inscriptions still on site from their facades (in both the name of Commodus was later erased). The donor of temple H was the estate of Cornelia Baebia, a rich Corinthian woman. In the south-west corner is **temple G [11]**, dedicated to the oracular Apollo of Claros in western Asia Minor, which the colony consulted. **Temple F [12]** alongside was dedicated to Venus, progenitor of the imperial house (early C1 AD).

The south side of the forum is bounded by the huge two-storey **South Stoa [13]**, a late C4 BC structure. Originally a row of 33 double-roomed shops opened off from the double colonnade, many of them used as restaurants to judge from the finds. The colonists repaired the stoa, and in the course of time converted many of the old ground-floor units for administrative use. Of note are the massive elliptical walls of a **council-house** ([14] C1 AD) for the colonial councillors (*decuriones*), against which was a continuous bench, of which only one fragment is preserved; a **fountain house [15]**, lavishly coated in marble veneer (C1 AD); a **rectangular hall [16]**, the door flanked by statue-bases, one of them inscribed for Gaius Cerealis, provincial procurator under Hadrian. The procurator was a powerful man, the emperor's chief personal agent in the province; this looks like his office. The next unit east ([17] roofed) perhaps was used by officials of the Isthmian games, as the fine floor mosaic (AD 50–100) depicts a victorious athlete standing beside a seated figure of Good Fortune.

The south-east end of the upper forum is closed by the **South-East Building** ([18] AD 25–50), a civic office fronted by the portico mentioned in a Latin inscription from the facade, still on site. Just to its south is the much larger **Iulian basilica** ([19] Augustan?), a columnar hall with a basement (*cryptoporticus*), the hall decorated inside with marble veneer and the statues of Augustus and other imperial figures now in the museum. Its purpose may have been commercial.

In front of the basilica the Roman paving has been taken up to reveal two **starting platforms [20]** for race courses; the earlier (C5 BC) is now reburied. Its Hellenistic successor has seventeen pairs of toe grooves, laid out in a straight line on a more east–west orientation. A low curved wall just south retains a **terrace [21]**, perhaps used as a combat ring.

Separating the two levels of the forum are the **Central Shops [22]**, a series of well-fitted rooms (AD 25–50), perhaps used by the bankers for which the colony was well-known. Their focus was a high speaker's platform or **rostra [23]**. An inscription (late C2 AD) shows that a letter to the Corinthians from the Roman governor was 'read from the rostra', which must have been where he made official appearances. A C10 church on top suggests that medieval Christians identified the spot, perhaps rightly, with the platform (*bema* in Biblical Greek) of the proconsul Junius Gallio (*c.* AD 52), who refused to hear the case of the Corinthian Jews against the Christian Paul (*Acts* 18.12–16).

Opposite the rostra and bounding the forum west of the Lechaion road are architectural fragments and foundations of the richly sculptured **Captives Facade** [24], a portico closing the space between the North-West Shops and the Lechaion Road, and so called from its upper storey, comprising a line of piers to which were attached colossal figures of eastern barbarians, two of them now in the museum. It probably dates *c.* AD 160–170 and commemorated the victory of the emperor Lucius Verus over the Parthians. Many architectural elements (but not the barbarians) are Augustan and were taken from some earlier monument.

Next to the facade are three stretches of a **terrace wall** [25] decorated with a Doric frieze of triglyphs and metopes, buried in Roman times. Cuttings and bases show that the wall once supported victory-tripods and statues. Here a dark limestone **base** for a life-size bronze figure preserves the 'signature' of a famous C4 BC sculptor: ΛΥΣΙΠΠΟΣ ΕΠ[ΟΗΣΕ], 'Lysippos made (it)'.

A flight of steps in an opening in the wall leads down to the C5 BC **Sacred Spring** ([26] closed by a grate). A low tunnel, entered by a door formed by a metope, links the terrace wall to a nearby **shrine** to the north, buried under the North-West Shops, and (on one theory) was used to conceal a priest who delivered oracles from under the floor of the shrine. In Greek times the whole area was sacred, as shown by an inscription in place (cement replica of an original in the museum) which reads 'Inviolable. Let no one go down. Fine eight (obols)' (C5 BC).

Pausanias records, as he left the forum by the Lechaion road, a **gateway** [27] decorated with two gilded chariot groups driven by Helios and Phaithon. The foundations of this triple-bayed arch survive, originally perhaps Augustan, but rebuilt *c.* AD117, and decorated with historical reliefs, of which many fragments have been found. Below, reached by monumental steps, is the impressive **Lechaion road** [28], a paved and colonnaded street with sidewalks, the earliest of its kind in Roman Greece (later C1 AD).

Immediately on your right is the **Fountain of Peirene** [29], one of the best-known landmarks of the ancient city, its water 'sweet to drink' (Pausanias 2.3.3). In Roman times the locals believed that it was fed by its namesake fountain on Acrocorinth. In fact, it was supplied like the 'sacred spring' to the west by surface water filtering through Corinth's higher terraces until trapped underground by a layer of clay. The fountain was a social centre, and the young women who came to draw water no doubt were part of its charm; the playwright Euripides (C5 BC) has old men playing drafts here (*Medea* lines 68–9). As you see it now, the square fountain court is essentially Roman. The screen of poros stone with its six arched openings was added under Augustus, the sunken

▲ Fig. 52. Ship relief at Corinth

draw-basin, supplied through nozzles from reservoirs under the paving, in the C1 AD. You descended the steps in the north wall into the lower area to gather the water. In its present form the square court, with semi-domed apses for lounging and talking set into its massive high walls, dates to a rebuilding in the later C2 AD, as does its rich marble veneer. The white marble cladding admired by Pausanias may belong to an earlier phase (early C2 AD); it was paid for, as a Latin inscription shows, by the family of Antonius Sospes, a rich Corinthian orator and friend of Plutarch (see CHAIRONEIA). A base found here (now in the museum) for a statue of Regilla, 'image of modesty', has given rise to the erroneous view that her husband Herodes paid for work at Peirene. Greek arrangements survive in the four reservoirs behind the arched facade: the three draw-basins facing them, over the front wall of which water was drawn in the C6–C5 BC; the six later chambers in front; and the screen of Ionic columns (C2 BC).

Immediately north is a complex (late C1 AD) described by Pausanias as an **enclosure** [30] (*peribolos*), adorned with a statue of Apollo and a painting of Odysseus slaying Penelope's suitors. It had Ionic colonnades round the sides and an apse for relaxing. A block with a relief of a ship on one face, and inscribed on the other, comes from a Latin inscription on the colonnade recording its donors. The complex replaced an Augustan market (*macellum*) for fish, to judge from Latin inscriptions found nearby. Its circular central structure, visible below the floor, may have been used for preparing the fish.

Fig. 53. The Lechaion Road at Corinth

If you turn left on leaving the site and walk up the village road you reach (right) the **odeion** ([**31**] fenced but accessible). This roofed theatre is listed among the gifts of Herodes Atticus (Philostratus, *Lives of the Sophists* 551). Excavation has shown that in fact he reconstructed a building of the late C1 AD, his chief contribution being to pay for marble veneers, and an open court to the north linking the odeion to the theatre. Herodes' work was consumed by fire (early C3 AD). The odeion was then rebuilt as an arena, mainly by removing the stage and adding the clearly visible wall, *c*.2 m. high, in front of the lowest row of seats.

The north-facing **theatre** ([**32**] inaccessible), making use of a natural slope in the terraced terrain, dates to the C4 BC, and was rebuilt by the colonists (early C1 AD?) for drama. Under Hadrian a lavish, marble, stage-building was constructed, each of its three stories decorated with relief friezes, their remains displayed in the museum courtyard. In the early C3 AD the theatre was converted into an arena for wild-beast shows by removing the first ten rows of seats and quarrying the rock in front back to a natural scarp (visible). The arena wall so formed had murals (now totally lost) with scenes of a beast-hunt (*venatio*), including a contestant pole-vaulting over a leopard, and another performing a handspring to avoid a lion. Later in the C3 the arena in turn was converted into a water-basin for aquatic shows.

East of the stage-building you can see a square open **court** [**33**]. A Latin inscription (C1 AD) on a paving-slab records that the pavement was paid for by a market-official (aedile) called Erastus, often identified as the Christian of the same name known to Paul (*Romans* 16.23), his office rendered in New Testament Greek as 'steward (*oikonomos*) of the city'.

In front of the museum, and visible from the car park, you can see the **Fountain of Glauke** ([**34**] C6 BC, rehabilitated by the colonists). This large cube of rock was cut into what originally was a natural ridge, the rest of which was quarried away in antiquity. Inside are four reservoirs, fronted by draw-basins approached by steps. Pausanias was told (2.3.6) that Glauke, a Corinthian princess, flung herself into the water here after being poisoned by the witch Medea, whose children the Corinthians then stoned to death in revenge.

Acrocorinth (Fig. 54) ★

Take the road which runs past the museum and turn left at the sign. From the car park (café) at Acrocorinth it is quite a steep climb to reach the summit (575 m. above sea-level).

Special Features

On a clear day Acrocorinth commands outstanding views. A springhouse is the chief ancient attraction.

Description

The **fortifications**, as preserved, are mainly medieval, with some Ottoman Turkish additions. For the most part these walls were built directly on the base of the ancient circuit (*c.*3 km). This was in ruins by the late C1 BC, Roman legionaries having dismantled all but the lowest courses (146 BC) in most places. One exception is the large ancient **tower** [1] to the right of the second medieval gateway, preserving its original front to a height of over 11 m., with fine vertical drafting of the corner stones. It flanked a lost ancient gate, sited like its successors on the west side, the only relatively gentle approach. No earlier than the C4 BC, the tower may well be evidence for improvements to the circuit in 335–243 BC, when a Macedonian garrison occupied Acrocorinth, one of the 'fetters of Greece'. Even so, in 243 BC the Achaian commander Aratos with 400 men mounted a successful surprise attack at night, using ladders to scale the wall where it was accessible only with difficulty and therefore relatively low (a point on the north side probably).

The **summit** is marked by a trigonometrical point. Some displaced ancient blocks are visible, thought to belong to the 'small **Temple of Aphrodite**' (C5 BC) [2], seen here by Strabo (8.6.21), who sketched its racy past before the Roman sack:

The sanctuary of Aphrodite was so wealthy that it possessed as temple-slaves more than a thousand prostitutes who were dedicated to the goddess both by

▼ Fig. 54. Plan of Acrocorinth

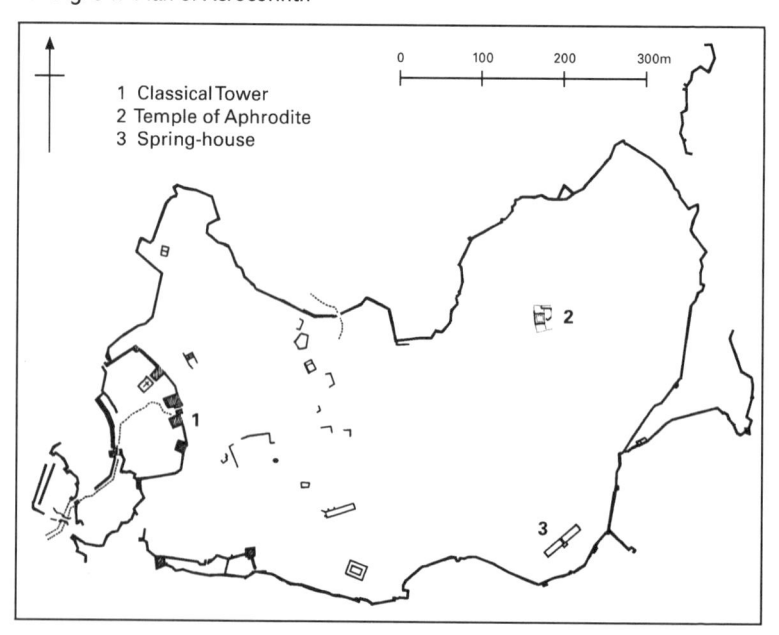

1 Classical Tower
2 Temple of Aphrodite
3 Spring-house

men and by women. And so, by reason of them, the city was thronged and enriched; for the sailors spent their money easily, and on that account the proverb says: 'Not for every man is the voyage to Corinth'.

The underground **spring-house of Peirene** [3], now protected by a modern concrete roof, is accessible with care. Strabo noted that (in his day) it was 'always full of clear and drinkable water'. Steps (the lower ones ancient) lead down to an ancient screen (C4 BC, now partly submerged) and on into an inner chamber. The barrel-vaulted ceiling is C3 BC. The winged horse Pegasos was said to have been caught here by Bellerophon while drinking. That the place had a sacred character is suggested by ancient graffiti, on the walls and screen, in which the writer 'remembers' a loved one. In an example on the left wall (C2 AD), inscribed by marble-workers or MAPMAPIOI, 'Euporos remembered his son and brother, Apellas (remembered) Nepsis, and Philonas (remembered) Dionysios' (*Corinth* 3.1.51, no. 1).

Isthmia (Figs. 55–57)

From the Isthmus take the road for Epidavros and turn right at the sign for the Archaeological Museum in Isthmia. The site is actually in the village of Kyra Vrysi.

Special Features

Although poorly preserved, the site of this panhellenic sanctuary is still interesting, and the museum is well worth seeing.

History

The site owed its panhellenic character to its location on the most direct land route from the Peloponnese to central Greece and Attika, as well as from Corinth to the Saronic gulf. There was a Mycenaean settlement here, and the earliest evidence for cult dates from the C11 BC. The first temple and altar were built in the early C7. The Corinthians refounded the local games as a biennial, panhellenic festival *c*.582 BC; the prize was a wreath of celery, and the programme included chariot, horse, and musical contests. In 196 BC the Roman general Flamininus used the games to announce the freedom of Greece. In 146 BC the games were transferred to Sikyon and the sanctuary abandoned. It was rehabilitated by the Roman colonists, who founded (mid-C1 AD) a cult of Palaimon, an Isthmian boy-hero who drowned and was brought ashore by a dolphin; identified with the Roman Portunus, he now became the object of nocturnal mysteries. The games only returned under Nero, who performed here himself, and (AD 66) imitated Flamininus by declaring the province free to the assembled Greeks (see THEBES museum). The main

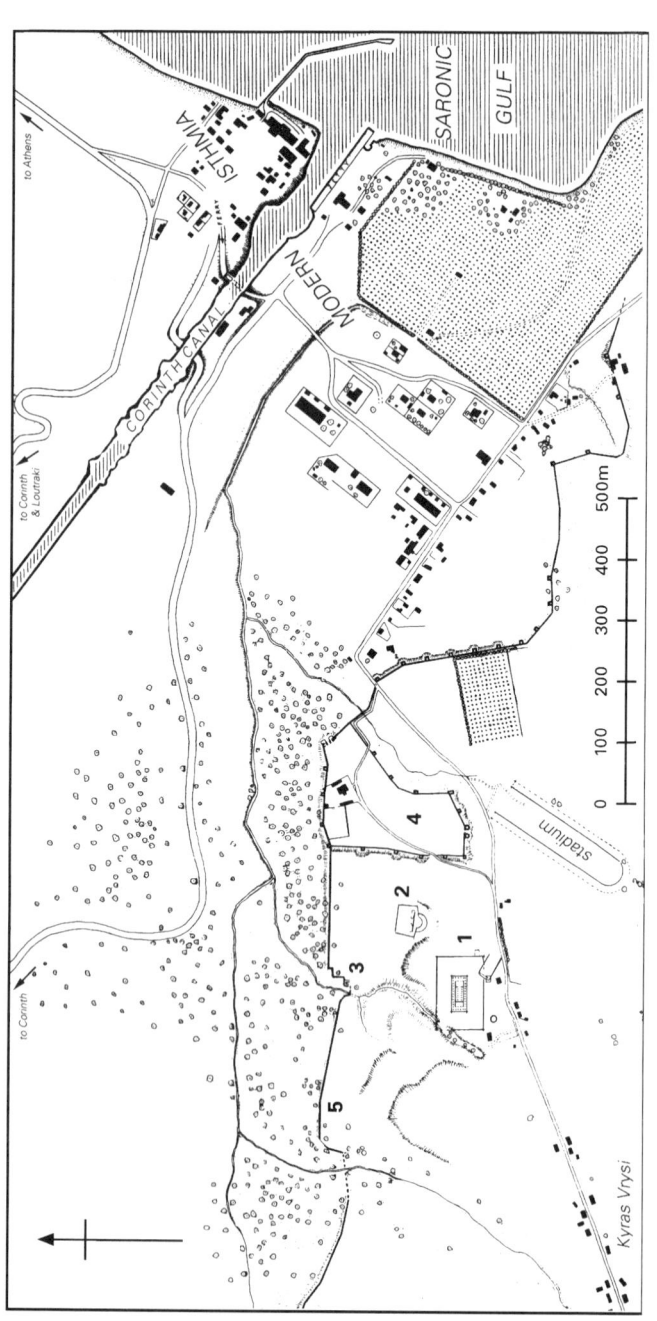

▲ Fig. 55. Plan of Isthmia. Key: 1 Sanctuary (site plan, Fig. 56) 2 Theatre 3 Baths 4 Fortress 5 Trans-Isthmian wall

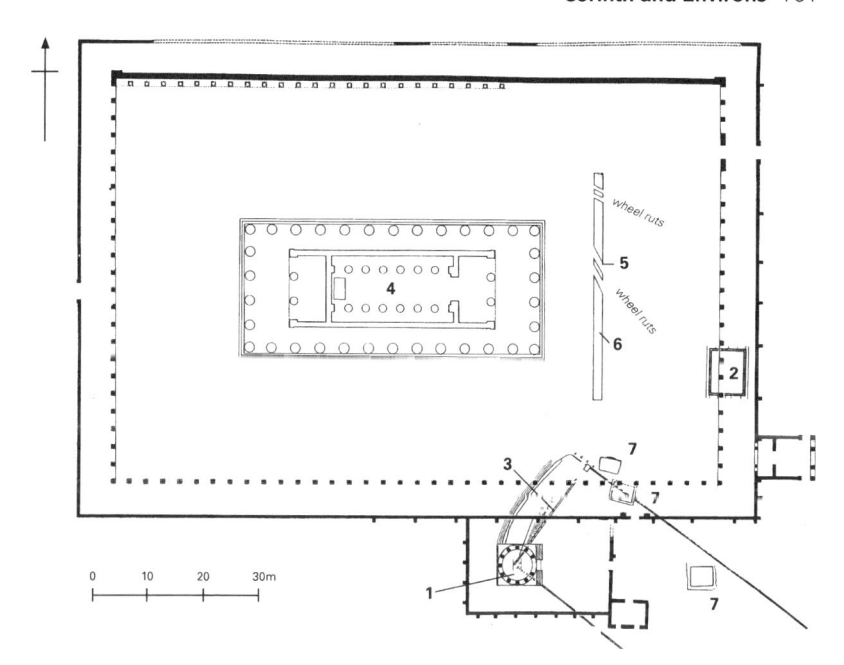

▲ Fig. 56. Plan of the Sanctuary of Poseidon at Isthmia. Key: 1 Palaimonion 2 Foundations 3 Starting gate 4 Temple of Poseidon 5 Wheel-ruts 6 Altar 7 Palaimonion pits

refurbishment of the sanctuary took place c. AD 100. A shrine of Palaimon was built under Hadrian, when it first appears on local coins. After the mid-century the temple was enclosed by colonnades and the Palaimonion resited. A major building programme instituted by the colonial priest Publius Licinius Priscus Juventianus may also belong to the later C2. The sanctuary continued to function into the late C3 AD at least, and perhaps into the C4. Its abandoned buildings were used as a quarry for the trans-Isthmian wall and fortress to the north and north-east of the site, both built c. AD 410–420 as a defence against barbarian incursions.

Description

After you enter, you see on the right the square podium for the resited **Palaimonion** ([**56.1**] after 150 AD), earlier placed on **foundations** [**56.2**] to the south-east of the temple of Poseidon. As shown on coins, this was a circular colonnade with a conical roof housing a tree and a statue of Palaimon on the dolphin. Below was a crypt: 'here, they say, Palaimon is hidden' (Pausanias 2.2.1). In fact, it covered a disused water-channel once used to maintain the stadium, and in Roman times reinterpreted as the hero's tomb. A succession of nearby **pits** [**56.7**]

▲ Fig. 57. Reconstruction of the Palaimonion at Isthmia

('A-C'), full of animal bones and lamps, were used for the nocturnal sacrifices.

Nearby is the Classical **starting gate** [**56.3**] for the stadium. From the starter's pit a series of grooves fan out in a stone sill. They once held string controlled by the starter and linked to a line of horizontal bars hinged on vertical posts. When the starter dropped the (sixteen) bars, the race began.

To the north are the foundations of the 'not very large' (Pausanias) Doric **Temple of Poseidon** [**56.4**], built *c.*465 BC, rebuilt after a fire in 390 BC, and patched up in Roman times. Inside Pausanias saw a colossal gold and ivory group given by Herodes Atticus. It depicted Poseidon and Amphitrite in a chariot drawn by four horses and escorted by sea-monsters (Tritons), and replaced colossal marble figures of the same two deities, of which fragments survive. You can see the **wheel-ruts** [**56.5**] of the late-Hellenistic road running over the foundations of the **altar** [**56.6**] after the abandonment of the sanctuary in 146 BC.

80 m. north-east of the temple is the poorly preserved **theatre** (*c.*400 BC) [**55.2**]. It was refurbished three times, and the white marble cladding

admired by Pausanias was only added in the later C2 AD. An inscription found nearby (*BÉ* 1954, no. 111) tells of an innovative performer here (C2 AD), the musician Themison, 'who set to music, to perform himself, the verses of Euripides, Sophocles and Timotheus'.

To the west you can see the Roman **baths** (C2 AD) [**55.3**], built over a swimming pool of the Greek period. The central hall has a fine mosaic depicting Nereids, Tritons, and other sea creatures.

The **museum** is so clearly and thoroughly labelled that we do not offer a detailed description. Highlights include the glass panels from KENCHREAI and the fragments of painted plaster murals from the early Archaic temple of Poseidon. In the vestibule are two fine monuments from the Greek games, both commemorating champions. One, for an athlete, has eight victors' wreaths, each carefully differentiated. The other (C1–C2 AD) portrays a professional flute-player from Corinth, with nineteen wreaths for his victories in musical games. What the four, small, round objects in his right hand are is a mystery.

Kenchreai (Fig. 58)

The site is in the village of Kehries, 5.3 km. from the museum at Isthmia. There is no sign but it is obvious from the road. The site is not fenced.

Special Features

With its Roman harbour-works now mostly submerged, Kenchreai dramatically demonstrates the changes to Greece's coastline since antiquity.

History

Kenchreai, the further of Corinth's two ports, gave the Greek and Roman city access to the eastern Mediterranean. It was from here *c.* AD 50 that the Christian Paul took ship to Syria. In the C2 AD the port was a bustling place, 'busy with a multitude of people' (Apuleius, *Metamorphoses* 10.35). The tomb here of a colonial worthy hints at its economic importance for the Corinthian elite. For Pausanias (2.2.3) its attractions were 'a shrine of Aphrodite with a stone statue, and beyond it, on the mole that extends into the sea, a bronze figure of Poseidon, and at the other end of the harbour [. . .] the sanctuaries of Asklepios and Isis'. The port facilities were remodelled for the Roman colony (C1 AD), and pottery finds suggest that they remained in use into the middle ages.

Description

The clearest feature is the **south pier** [**1**] on the right side of the bay, perhaps based on a natural promontory. It has a (now submerged) ancient mole joined to it, once a breakwater. On the pier identified

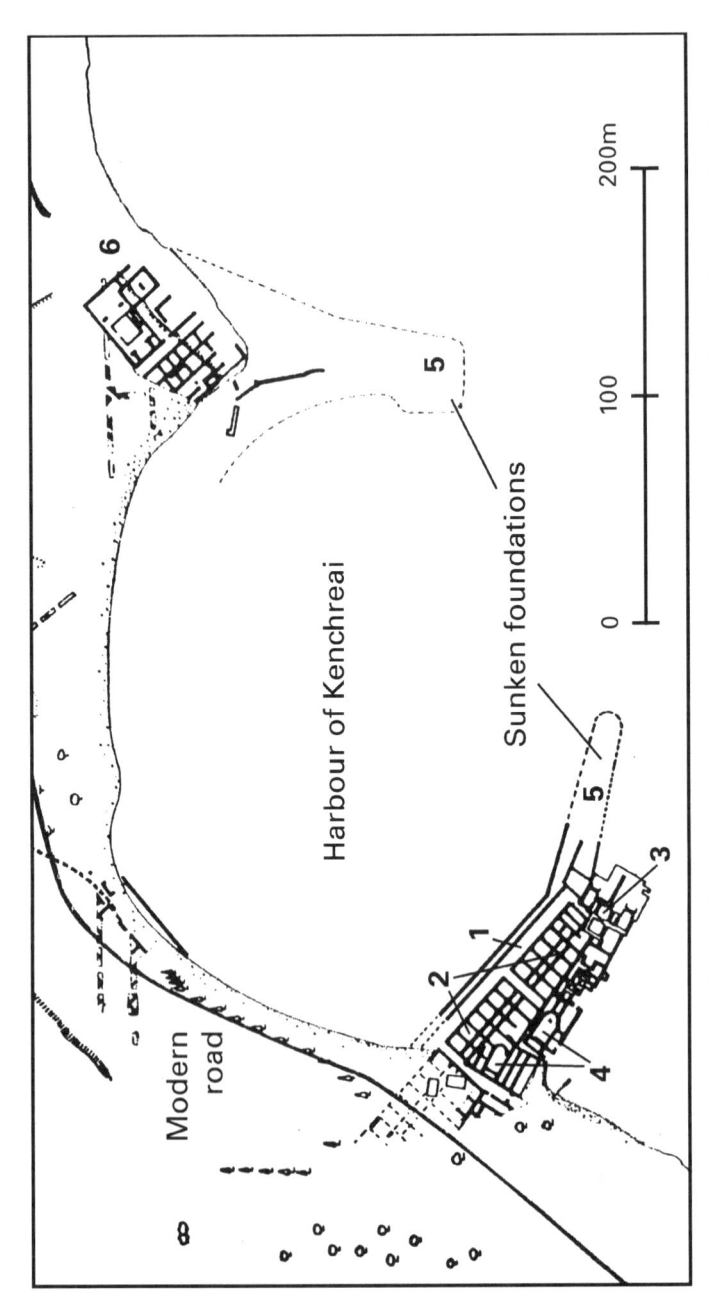

▲ Fig. 58. Plan of Kenchreai. Key: 1 South pier 2 Warehouses 3 Fish-tanks 4 Sanctuary of Isis 5 Submerged moles 6 Brick-built complex

structures include **warehouses** ([**2**]—early C1 AD) and (further out) basins identified as commercial **fish-tanks** [**3**] for the storage of live catch (late C1 AD). An apsidal area (*c.* AD 100), mostly underwater, and on dry land a conspicuous apsed hall (late C1 AD), both formed part of the **Sanctuary of Isis** [**4**]. In the former were found remains of fifty ancient wooden crates containing the superb coloured-glass panels now in ISTHMIA museum. They had arrived by sea and been stored here, probably to decorate the sanctuary, when an earthquake (AD 375) irreparably damaged them, and they were abandoned. In the C5 the sanctuary was converted into a church.

At the left end of the bay is the **north mole** [**5**], the one mentioned by Pausanias, now completely submerged, and marked by the massive walls of a **tower** (C6 AD or later), probably a lighthouse or look-out. Nearby is an elaborate **brick-built complex** ([**6**]—*c.* AD 100 with later alterations). In an isolated position behind, on a ridge jutting into the sea, are limestone foundations of a monumental **tomb** (C1 AD), originally clad in white marble with elaborate mouldings and inscribed with a Latin epitaph, which may preserve part of the occupant's name, *Reg[ulus]*, a colonial notable.

Lechaion (Fig. 59)

Leave New Corinth by the old Patras road. 1 km. beyond the town limit you will see prominent dune-like hills by the sea on your right. Immediately before the first, turn right onto a dirt track which will take you to the harbour site.

Special Features

Lechaion was one of the largest engineered harbours in the ancient world. The site offers excellent views of the Corinthia.

History

Lechaion was the harbour linking Corinth with the west, including Italy. As such, it must have already been in use by the C8 BC. It was the home of the Corinthian fleet (C5 BC), linked to Corinth by a highway and a pair of 'long walls' (by 394 BC), and had shipsheds. Later it was a Macedonian naval base. With the foundation of the Roman colony its importance revived, marked by the lavish architecture of the road linking Lechaion with the forum. Improvements to the harbour were still being made *c.* AD 355, when an inscription found here names the Roman governor as 'benefactor and founder of the harbour'. Lechaion was a settlement in its own right, with sanctuaries of Aphrodite and Poseidon. Of modest size under Augustus (Strabo 8.6.22), it was much larger in late antiquity, to judge from the basilican church here (*c.* AD 450), the biggest in Greece. The site has never been excavated. Pottery on the surface is mainly C1–C3 AD, and much of the harbour may be the work of the Roman colonists. A Corinthian coin of AD 177–192 showing a sailing vessel passing a tall lighthouse may depict Lechaion.

Description

A good vantage point can be had from the top of the easternmost **dune** [**1**], crowned by a trigonometrical point. This dune is one of three artificial mounds created in antiquity from dredging activity. From here you can see the silted-up **harbour mouth** [**2**], and the stonework of the narrow channel giving access to the two **inner basins** [**3**], edged by stone quays, and also linked by a channel. The larger basin, which is dried up in summer, has an artificial **island** [**4**] in the middle (C2–C3 AD), perhaps a base for a sculptural monument. All this was the inner harbour, possibly created from a natural lagoon. There was also a corresponding outer harbour, formed by a pair of engineered **basins** [**5**] opening directly to the sea and flanked by **moles** [**6**], of which traces remain. These gave some protection from the prevailing north-west wind while ships manoeuvred themselves into the sheltered inner waters. Further west by the shore you can make out the **basilica** (fenced with no access).

Diolkos (Fig. 60)

Leave New Corinth by the old Athens road, passing the railway station on your left. Turn left at the fork, signed Poseidonia/Loutraki, cross the railway and drive c.2 km. as far as the sign Ancient Diolkos on your right, just before the canal bridge.

▼ Fig. 59. Plan of Lechaion. Key: 1 East dune 2 Harbour mouth 3 Inner basins 4 Island 5 Outer basins 6 Moles

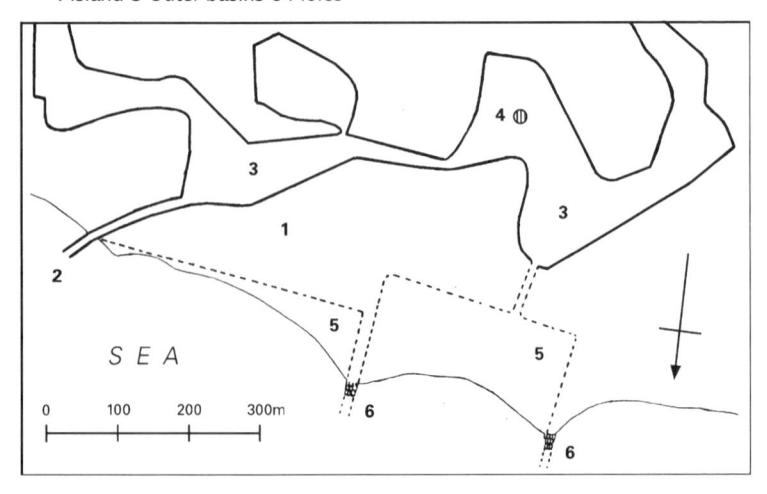

Special Features

A remarkable demonstration of Archaic engineering makes this site worth visiting, as well as its proximity to the modern Isthmus canal.

History

In antiquity the Isthmus had something of the strategic importance of the Panama isthmus today. The ambitious project of piercing it by a canal was attributed to a succession of autocrats from Periander (see CORINTH) to Herodes Atticus. Only Nero's attempt, abandoned after his death (AD 68), has left visible traces. In addition, there are ample remains of a 'haulway' or *diolkos* (*c*.600–550 BC?). This took the form of a stone 'railway' 6–7 km. long for the movement of heavy loads overland from one gulf to the other, on which ran wheeled carts, pulled probably by oxen (muscle) and men (guidance). The texts only mention its use for warships (C5 BC to C9 AD), although the chief aim was probably commercial, whether the movement of indivisible cargo (such as stone) or whole merchantmen. At least in the later C5 BC it was much in use to judge from the Athenian playwright Aristophanes, who employs its frequent movements 'up and down' as a comic metaphor for sexual intercourse (*Thesmophoriazusae* lines 647–48).

Description

The best-preserved stretch is to the west of the road, and it is worth walking as far as the pilot station to view it. The preserved paving rises out of the water by an ancient quay and climbs gently east, as if vessels were manoeuvred onto a wheeled cradle while still in the water and then hauled off. The channels for the cartwheels are still visible in the stretch nearest the road. You can also see transverse grooves which are the marks made by the cables.

Perachora (Figs. 61–62) ★

Take the main road to Loutraki and continue through the town to modern Perachora where you follow the signs for Lake Vouliagmeni/Λ. Βουλιαγμενη (9 km.). Carry on

▼ Fig. 60. Plan of the Corinth canal and the Diolkos

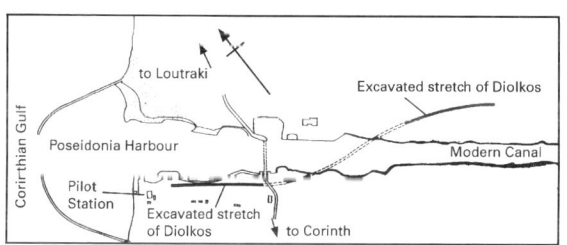

past the lake until you see the lighthouse ahead of you. From the car park, a sign (ΑΡΧΑΙΟΛΟΓΙΚΟΣ ΧΩΡΟΣ ΗΡΑΙΟΥ) directs you to the site.

Special Features

This is a gem of a site: archaeologically important, scenically situated, and provided with a delightful beach.

History

The site lies on a promontory opposite Corinth known in ancient times as Peraion. Here an isolated Heraion or rural sanctuary of Hera Akraia ('of the headland') developed in Geometric times to serve the scattered inhabitants of the area north of the Isthmus. They used it as an asylum in times of danger, as shown by an episode in 391–390 BC, when the whole local population, 'men, women, the slaves and the free, along with most of their flocks' took refuge here from a Spartan army (Xenophon, *Hellenika* 4.5). The shrine was absorbed into Corinthian territory by *c.*750 BC, Corinth asserting her ownership by investment in the first temple. The sanctuary flourished in the C7–C6 BC, and inscriptions on the pottery suggest that most visitors at this time were Corinthians. There is good evidence for eating and drinking here, most of it probably done at an annual festival, when pilgrims would have camped out on the upper terraces. Hera may have had a nurturing aspect, to judge from the numerous finds of clay cakes. According to Strabo in the late C1 BC, an oracle existed here 'in ancient times', although unconfirmed by other evidence. In the late C4 BC there were new building works, possibly reflecting benefaction by the Macedonian king Demetrios I when he held Corinth. The sanctuary seems to have declined in Hellenistic times, and signs of violent destruction have been linked to the Roman sack of Corinth (146 BC), which probably marked the end of the cult. In the C2 AD a small farming community set up house among the ruins.

Description

We suggest that you start at the bottom by the little harbour and work your way up. This area was the focus of the cult. The earliest building here was a small **apsidal temple** ([1]—*c.*750 BC), its stone footings still visible. The crude superstructure was mudbrick, with a thatched roof, and its appearance is reflected in a votive clay model from the site (on display in the National Archaeological Museum in ATHENS). To its west you can see the foundations of a much larger **temple** ([2]—*c.*525 BC), a long, narrow building (over 9 m. by perhaps 31 m.) with a Doric facade but no outer colonnade. This was probably the third temple down here, although the second has left no traces. The **altar** [3] in front, originally as wide again to the south, was faced with triglyph- and metope-panels,

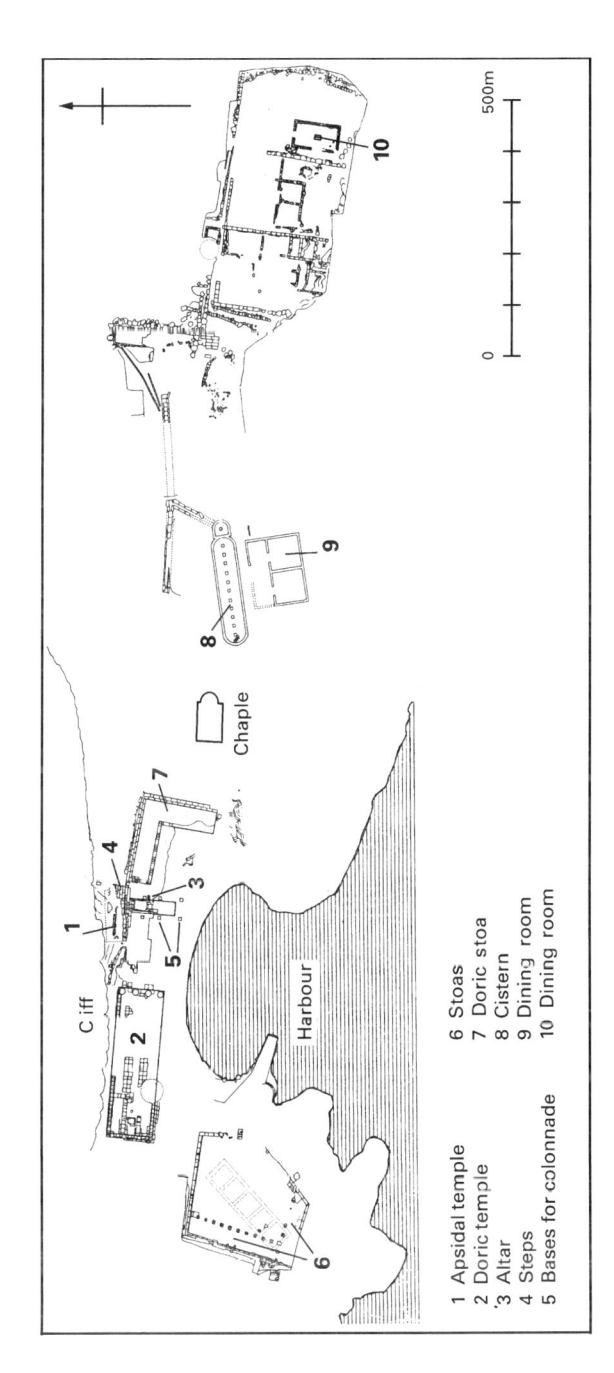

▲ Fig. 61. Plan of Perachora

1 Apsidal temple
2 Doric temple
3 Altar
4 Steps
5 Bases for colonnade
6 Stoas
7 Doric stoa
8 Cistern
9 Dining room
10 Dining room

an altar-type peculiar to the north-east Peloponnese and perhaps invented by Corinthian architects. The **steps** [4] to the north were probably for spectators watching the ritual. You can see **bases** [5] for an unusual Ionic colonnade added round the altar in the C4 BC, possibly once supporting a canopy. In the small courtyard west of the harbour are traces of two simple **stoas** [6] with continuous benches inside. To the east of the altar are remains of a more impressive Doric **stoa** ([7]—late C4 BC), L-shaped with two stories and unusually high barriers between the upper columns, perhaps to screen a secret ritual.

A path now leads up past the modern chapel of Ayios Ioannis to an impressive double-apsidal **cistern** ([8]—c.525 BC), the inside lined with waterproof plaster. Access was by means of an ingeniously cantilevered stone staircase, and a row of internal piers once supported a flat, wooden roof. The water supply, which was filtered through a settling tank, came from a drain channelling surface rainwater from the terraces above. To the south, and built at the same time, is a pair of eleven-seater **dining**

▼ Fig. 62. The cistern at Perachora

rooms [**9**] sharing an anteroom. The stone couches would originally have been softened by mattresses; slots for the legs of wooden tables can be made out in the pebble plaster floor. The rooms were used for sacrificial feasts, perhaps by privileged worshippers such as city magistrates.

The path continues up to the easternmost terrace and an Archaic **dining room** ([**10**]—C7 BC). All that remains of this rectangular structure are the stone footings, once supporting mudbrick walls and a tiled roof. The identification is based mainly on the discovery inside of a central hearth, full of ash when found, and enclosed by kerbstones (since removed). One of these had an inscription (C7 BC) beginning 'I am a drachma, O white armed Hera', where 'drachma' has its earliest sense of a set of six iron spits: the dedicator had made a gift of utensils for cooking the sacrificial meat.

When you leave the site, a few hundred metres back from the car park, a small circular sign on the left (**ΑΡΧΑΙΑ ΚΡΗΝΗ**) leads you to a **fountain house** (late C4 BC) in the upper plain (not on the plan). Originally this had a facade of Ionic columns protecting three drawbasins. These in turn were supplied by three storage-chambers running 26–29 m. underground to the east. At its extremity the central one was linked to an open-air shaft, probably for a wooden wheel raising water for animals.

Sikyon (Fig. 63)

Take the turn by the main church in the centre of Kiato, which is on the old Corinth–Patras road, and head for Vasiliko, also known as Sikiona. Once in Vasiliko, which is approximately 5 km. from Kiato, follow the signs for the Archaeological Museum. This is just over 1 km. from the centre of the village.

Special Features

Sikyon was a wealthy and at times politically powerful city, renowned as a major artistic centre. The archaeological site is not particularly spectacular but the location is congenial.

History

Like a number of other Archaic Greek cities, Sikyon was ruled by tyrants, the Orthagorid dynasty which remained in power for approximately a century, *c.*650–550 BC. Aristotle (*Politics* 1315B) comments that the Orthagorids: 'treated their subjects with moderation and generally obeyed the laws, Kleisthenes in particular was worthy of respect because of his warlike character, and through their attention to detail they were popular leaders'. The tyrants promoted themselves as patrons of the arts. Sculptors and poets settled at Sikyon and Kleisthenes was responsible for the construction of a tholos and monopteros at DELPHI.

When the tyranny ended Sikyon became a Spartan ally until the

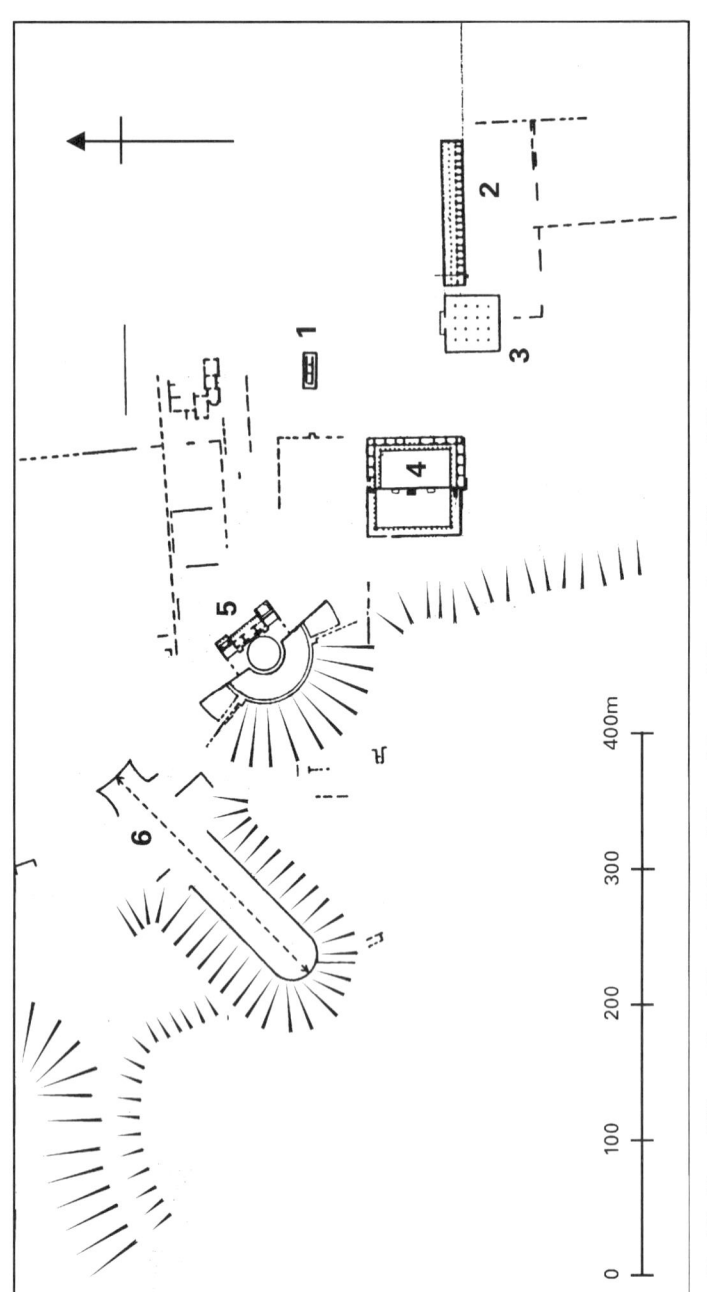

▲ Fig. 63. Plan of Sikyon. Key: 1 Temple 2 Stoa 3 Council-house 4 Gymnasium 5 Theatre 6 Stadium

Thebans and then the Macedonians took control of the city in the C4 BC. There was a Sikyonian school of painters at this time, which included Pausias, and the sculptor Lysippos was also from Sikyon. In 303 BC Demetrios I captured and subsequently moved the city to a more secure site inland. Sikyon joined the Achaian League in the C3 and enjoyed some success under the leadership of Aratos but Roman rule ultimately proved more beneficial for CORINTH. An earthquake in the C2 AD 'left the city nearly deserted' (Pausanias 2.7).

Description

The site of Archaic and Classical Sikyon has not been identified, although it was certainly in the plain. The new city was founded by Demetrios on the plateau which stretches west of Vasiliko, between the Asopos and Helisson rivers. This may have previously been the akropolis and is protected on three sides by steep slopes. Some traces of fortifications have been noted but it is not clear whether the whole of the site was enclosed. The city was evidently laid out on a grid plan.

The **museum**, in a restored Roman bath, is currently closed for repairs. The site entrance is opposite, on the north side of the **agora**. You pass the foundations of an Archaic **temple** [1] which was restored in the Hellenistic period. This may be the temple of Artemis Limnaia. The Hellenistic **stoa** [2], on the south side of the agora, is rather overgrown but evidently had a double row of columns, behind which there were twenty rooms, presumably shops. West of the stoa is the **council-house** [3] which was built in the C3 BC in the form of a hypostyle hall. The roof was supported on sixteen Ionic columns and the seats for the members of the council were on earth embankments. The council-house subsequently became a Roman bath. The **gymnasium** [4] occupies two terraces below the Hellenistic akropolis. It is also C3 and may have been the Gymnasium of Kleinias, the father of Aratos. On the lower terrace there is an open court, lined on three sides by Ionic porticoes with rooms behind. Fountains flank the steps which connect the two terraces. The court on the upper terrace had Doric porticoes but no rooms. Above the gymnasium there is a sanctuary of the Nymphs.

Up the road from the museum is the **theatre** [5], one of the largest in Greece. The cavea once had 60 rows of seats, most of which were cut from the rock. The upper rows of seats could be reached from the vaulted tunnels on either side of the cavea. It seems that the theatre had a raised stage when it was built early in the C3 BC. This was modified in the Roman period. The Achaian League met at Sikyon, apparently in the theatre, and this would explain the statue of Aratos which Pausanias saw, since he was elected general (*strategos*) of the League seventeen times. The **stadium** [6] is just beyond the theatre but has not been excavated. There is no trace of the temples on the **akropolis** which Pausanias mentions.

Argolid

Much of the Argolid is mountainous and barren. However, the alluvial plain which opens off the Gulf of Argos is extensive and the soil is fertile if thirsty. Now it is covered by citrus groves but once raised horses. Sediment deposited by the River Inachos has pushed the shoreline back and TIRYNS, formerly a harbour town, is several kilometres from the sea. The plain is hemmed in by mountains and consequently rather cut off but does command one of the main routes into Arkadia and Lakonia.

LERNA and Tiryns were already local administrative centres in the Early Helladic period and ARGOS is an important Middle Helladic site. Nevertheless, the wealth buried in the shaft graves at MYCENAE is still unexpected and in some respects inexplicable. The rise of Mycenae almost certainly presupposes control of the Argive plain, yet there were other prosperous and presumably powerful settlements at this time. The situation does not become any clearer in the C14 BC when palaces were constructed at Mycenae, Tiryns, and possibly MIDEA. Even Homer could not make his mind up; Agamemnon is described as the lord of the Argolid but he and Diomedes, the ruler of Tiryns, share the plain in *Iliad* 2.559–80.

The destruction of the Mycenaean palaces and the collapse of the political system marks a contraction of settled life in the Argolid. From *c.*900 BC the Geometric community at Argos rose to prominence on the Argive plain, which it contested with neighbouring Mycenae and Tiryns, eventually destroying both (*c.*470). Argive power, reflected in early embellishments to the ARGIVE HERAION, peaked in the C7 BC, retreating before the rise of SPARTA. Off the plain NEMEA to the north-west emerged as a panhellenic sanctuary at this time. In the hill country of the eastern Argolid the inland shrine of Asklepios at EPIDAUROS saw the same development, but later (C4), and lasting far longer. The Epidaurians lived in one of the small cities on the Argolid's eastern shore, like TROIZEN to the south. The history of both was influenced by Saronic contacts, also felt at LOUKOU in Argive territory, site of a palatial villa (mid-C2 AD) belonging to the Athenian Herodes Atticus (pp. 117–118). In Roman times Argos with its nearby harbour remained the region's chief centre, Epidauros its major sanctuary.

Nemea (Figs. 64–65)

There is a sign for Ancient Nemea on the road between Nafplion and Corinth. You turn into the site, which is well signed, just before you enter the village of Archaia Nemea.

Argolid 175

Special Features

Nemea was one of the four panhellenic sanctuaries. Architecturally the site is of considerable interest and there is a fine museum.

History

In the first of his twelve labours Herakles fought and killed the Nemean lion. In one version of the legend he subsequently founded games in honour of Zeus. Alternatively, it was said that they were instituted by Adrastos of Argos in memory of the infant prince Opheltes who was bitten by a snake and died at Nemea.

On the Tsoungiza hill, above Archaia Nemea, a prehistoric settlement has recently been excavated but there is not much evidence of cult activity in the sanctuary until the C6 when the first panhellenic festival was held, possibly in 573 BC. The sanctuary was then under the control of the city of Kleonai, which is just east of Nemea. A temple and altar were constructed early in the C6 and also a heroon, presumably for Opheltes. The first of the panhellenic festivals was established at OLYMPIA in 776 BC. DELPHI followed in 582 BC, then ISTHMIA in 582/80 BC and finally Nemea. In the C5 the Argives took control of the sanctuary and removed the festival from Nemea. It returned around 330 BC, almost certainly under the auspices of Philip II of Macedon, and a phase of renewed architectural activity followed. The temple and stadium were rebuilt and the hostel and bath added.

Whereas the festivals at Olympia and Delphi were quadrennial, Isthmia and Nemea held games every two years. There were no musical contests at Nemea, only athletic and equestrian events. The athletes competed over various distances in the stadium, boxed, wrestled, or fought in the pankration, a particularly brutal sport. The horse and chariot races took place in the hippodrome which has not been discovered. Victors received a wreath of wild celery. In the Hellenistic period the festival led a rather peripatetic existence but was permanently based in Argos by 100 BC, and was still celebrated there in the C3 AD. When Pausanias visited Nemea in the C2 AD, he noted that the roof of the temple had collapsed and that there was not a statue left (2.15.2). In the C5–C6 AD an early Christian community settled in the sanctuary and built the basilica.

Description

The displays in the **museum** cover the archaeology of the site in depth. Views of Nemea by early travellers can be seen in the foyer. The cases in the main room focus on the interpretation of the finds—the different types of dedications, coins and pottery, athletic equipment, evidence for industrial activity, how wells encapsulate the history of the site. There is a model of the sanctuary and a reconstruction of the roof of the C6 BC temple of Zeus. This room also contains finds from the prehistoric settlement at Tsoungiza and other sites around Nemea. Columns, capitals, and architectural elements from the C4 temple of Zeus and one of the oikoi have been put on display in the courtyard.

The path which runs from the museum to the temple of Zeus first passes through a row of C4 **houses** which may have been used by priests or officials. North of the houses and also built in the late C4 is the **xenon**—a hostel, possibly for the athletes who competed in the games. There is evidence that food was prepared and eaten in the rooms on the southern side of the complex. The athletes would presumably have slept in the rooms behind. Much of the xenon is obscured by the **basilica** which was constructed in the C5–C6 AD by the early Christian community. The temple of Zeus provided a convenient source of cut stone blocks for the basilica which has a central nave and side aisles entered through a narthex. A baptistery was added on the north side in the C6. On the 'nearer my God to thee' principle, some members of the community were buried by their church—one of these graves can still be seen.

West of the xenon and protected by a roof is the C4 **bath**. No doubt

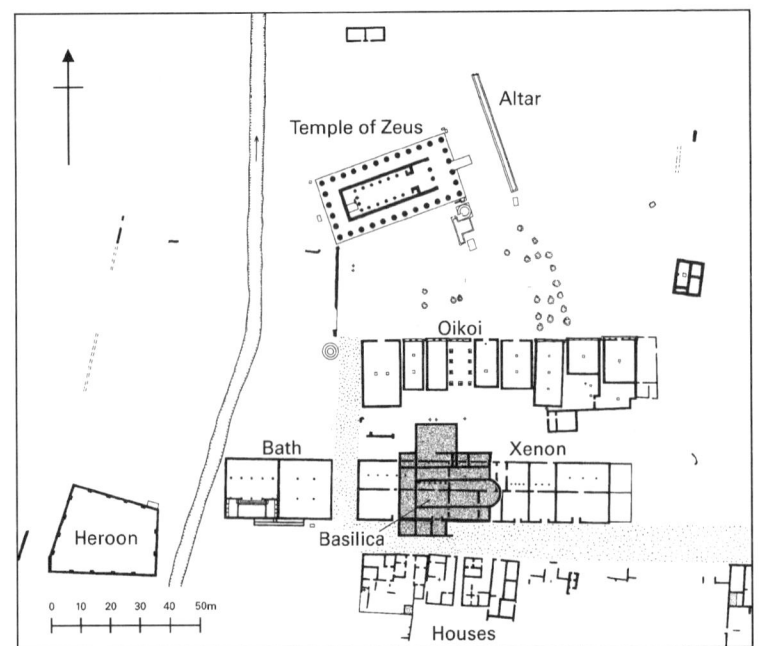

▼ Fig. 64. Plan of Nemea

this was used by the athletes but need not have been exclusively for their benefit. The west half of the complex contains the main facilities: a rectangular plunge bath entered by a flight of steps and two side rooms, in each of which there is a row of four stone basins. Water came from a spring east of the sanctuary and fed a reservoir on the south side of the bath. Waste water was channelled into the Nemea River.

Across the river from the bath is the **heroon**, almost certainly of Opheltes, which was in use by the early C6 BC. The perimeter wall was rebuilt in the Archaic period and then again in the late C4 or early C3. Essentially the heroon consisted of an open enclosure surrounded by a stone fence. There were a number of altars and presumably the grave of Opheltes.

North of the xenon is a row of nine **oikoi**. Given their position and that fact that Nemea was a panhellenic sanctuary, it is assumed that these oikoi were treasuries, although they do not have the same plan as the treasuries at Delphi and Olympia. Since the structure behind the easternmost oikoi was evidently a dining room, they may also have served as club-houses or leschai. The oikoi were built in the early C5 but had been either destroyed or remodelled by the C4 when two became a sculptor's workshop.

The first **Temple of Zeus** was built in the early C6 BC and destroyed by fire in the C5. It was replaced c.330 BC by a rather austere Doric temple, constructed of limestone from the quarry at Klenies on the Corinth–Tripolis road, which epitomizes the architectural developments of the late Classical and early Hellenistic periods. The temple had a peristyle of 6 by 12 Doric columns, rather than the more conventional 6 by 13. The columns are extremely slender compared with those of C5 temples. There was no sculpture in the pediments or metopes. The columns which ran around three sides of the cella were Corinthian below and Ionic above. This use of the three orders recalls other temples in the Peloponnese, such as Apollo at BASSAI and more particularly Athena at TEGEA which is similar in other respects. At the rear of the cella, originally separated by a bronze grille, is a crypt entered by a flight of steps. This was evidently an adyton, the purpose of which is unclear. It may have been an oracular pit, although there is no mention of an oracle at Nemea. East of the temple is an altar, built in the C6 and extended in the C4 so that it was 41 m. in length. Cypress trees were planted between the temple and the oikoi.

For the **stadium**, turn left when you leave the main site and then take the first left turn. There is a sign for the Ancient Stadium which is approximately 400 m. from the museum. You pass through a peristyle court, where the athletes must have waited and prepared for their events, and enter a vaulted tunnel which leads into the stadium. Graffiti (see p. 428) incised on the walls of the tunnel extolled the beauty of particular individuals: ΕΠΙΚΡΑΤΗΣ ΚΑΛΟΣ—Epikrates is beautiful. The

▲ Fig. 65. The Temple of Zeus at Nemea

stadium was constructed in the C4 and could accommodate 40,000 spectators. There were no seats but a stand was provided for the judges. The start line is preserved at the southern end of the track and there was evidently a wooden mechanism which prevented false starts. The length of the track will have been 600 feet, approximately 178 m.

Mycenae (Figs. 66–70)
Take the turn for Mikines on the Argos–Corinth road. The archaeological site is 2 km. beyond the village. We suggest that you visit the citadel first and then the Treasury of Atreus.

Special Features

The site of a civilization.

History

Although Mycenae controls the routes which run north from the Argive plain, the site is rather secluded and was relatively insignificant until the C17 BC, late in the Middle Helladic period. Then the grave circles were constructed. The size of the graves and the quality of the offerings imply that the first rulers of Mycenae were buried in Grave Circle B. They must have felt that this ostentatious display of wealth would enhance their status. The level of conspicuous consumption is even more impressive in Grave Circle A which replaced Circle B. The six shaft graves contained the stupendous and exotic array of items—weapons, jewellery, gold and silver vessels—in the National Archaeological Museum in ATHENS. It was once assumed that a foreign dynasty had settled at Mycenae but in most respects the treatment of the dead continues Middle Helladic traditions, although on a much more lavish scale. If, as seems likely, the rulers of Mycenae were Greek, how did they acquire their riches? Life in Middle Helladic Greece was fairly grim and there is no evidence of an affluent elite then. Given their fondness for warfare, it is possible that the Mycenaeans had looted Cycladic towns or Cretan palaces. They may even have served as mercenaries in Egypt. Yet it is curious that there is a gradual increase in their wealth, not the sudden prosperity which would have resulted from a successful raid. Trade could well have been a more lucrative and less risky source of revenue. There were certainly close links between Greece and Crete at this time.

In the C16 BC aristocrats at Mycenae discovered a new and even more flamboyant type of tomb. No fewer than nine tholos tombs were constructed over the course of the next three centuries. Unfortunately they have been robbed but there can be no doubt that the dead were buried in style. The construction of a shaft grave would have taken approximately 100 man days. For the Treasury of Atreus, the finest of the tholos tombs, the estimate is 20,000 man days. The Treasury of Atreus was built in the C14 and is clearly a tomb fit for a king. It seems likely that the three tholoi by the citadel were also royal tombs but this is not necessarily true of those some distance away.

It was not until the C14 and C13 BC that the mighty fortifications were built. Significantly, they only protect the citadel, not the whole of the settlement. Obviously they were defensive, although it is clear from their sheer size that they were designed to impress as well. The ruler also gets a decent palace at last. This was not simply a royal residence but will have been the administrative centre of the kingdom. How extensive was this kingdom? Mycenae must surely have controlled the whole of the Argolid, yet there was a palace at TIRYNS and possibly at MIDEA. While it is not out of the question that these sites were bitter rivals, constant warfare would have been ruinous. We should at least think in terms of an alliance dominated by Mycenae. That there was a Mycenaean empire ruled by Mycenae seems less likely. Because of the rugged topography, Greece is not a country which can easily be subjugated and the Linear B documents from the palace at PYLOS do not even hint at the existence of some higher authority.

A fire destroyed the houses south of Grave Circle B in the middle of the C13 BC. It is not clear whether Mycenae had been attacked but the fortifications were subsequently strengthened. Then at the end of the C13 the citadel was devastated. The cause of this destruction may have been an earthquake rather than an enemy assault. Nevertheless, the consequences were catastrophic and Mycenae never recovered. Although the site was still occupied, the great days were over. Mycenae was not forgotten, however. As the 'well-built' city of Agamemnon, 'rich in gold', it was made even more famous by Homer. He drew on an oral tradition which preserved quite detailed information about the past. Nevertheless, it must be remembered that the *Iliad* and the *Odyssey* were composed as epic stories not historical texts. To use *Macbeth* as a source for Scottish history would rather miss the point of the play and the same is true of the Homeric poems. Fact and fiction are brilliantly yet inextricably blended.

By the C6 BC ARGOS had become the dominant city in the Argolid, although Mycenae may have retained some degree of independence. The Argives remained neutral when the Persians invaded Greece in 480 BC but the Mycenaeans fought at the battles of THERMOPYLAI and PLATAIA. Pausanias (2.16) claims that the Argives were so jealous that they destroyed Mycenae *c.*468 BC and left the city 'utterly ruined and desolate'. It was not until the C3 that Mycenae was resettled as a dependency of Argos. The fortifications were repaired, a temple of Athena or Hera was built on the summit of the citadel and a theatre. This period of reoccupation was relatively brief, however, and Mycenae was finally abandoned in the C2.

Pausanias visited the site in the C2 AD and other travellers followed in his footsteps from the late C18 onwards. They included Lord Elgin who removed some of the carved decoration from the facade of the Treasury of Atreus. This is now on display in the British Museum. In 1876, fresh from his triumphs at Troy, Schliemann began the first systematic excavations at Mycenae. Because Pausanias mentioned that Agamemnon and his followers were buried inside the citadel, he opened a trench by the Lion Gate, found Grave Circle A and rediscovered a civilization. Schliemann had enhanced his own reputation and immortalized Mycenae.

Description

The citadel occupies a limestone outcrop which is protected by ravines and can only be approached from the west. There is no evidence that it was fortified before the C14 BC, although a mudbrick or timber palisade cannot be ruled out. At first the line of the **fortifications** followed the edge of the limestone. The walls were constructed in the Cyclopean technique, so called because Pausanias was told that they had been built by giants, the Cyclopes. Large blocks of limestone, unworked or roughly dressed, form the inner and outer face around a fill of earth and rubble. In the C13 the fortifications were extended, the Lion Gate was built and also the postern gate on the north side of the citadel. Ashlar masonry was used for the walls in front of the Lion Gate. This consists of rectangular blocks of conglomerate laid in regular courses

Fig 66. Plan of the citadel, Mycenae. Key: 1 Lion Gate 2 Grave Circle A 3 Cult centre 4 Palace 5 Palace entrance 6 Court 7 Megaron 8 House of Columns 9 Cistern 10 Postern gate

and looks most impressive. You can also see stretches of polygonal masonry which date from the Hellenistic period when the fortifications were repaired.

The ramp which leads up to the **Lion Gate** [**66.1**] is quite steep. Attackers would have found themselves hemmed in by the bastion on the right side of the ramp and under fire from the defenders stationed on top of the walls which must originally have been at least 10 m. high. Four massive blocks of conglomerate frame the Lion Gate. Above the lintel is a triangular space, blocked by a limestone slab on which two lions or lionesses are carved. A different type of stone was used for their heads which have disappeared. Between the lions there is a column, which may represent the palace, and they rest their forepaws on two altars. Did the lions symbolize the political and religious authority of the ruler? The pivot holes indicate that there were double wooden doors, held in place by a bar. Holes were cut in the lintels for the handles of the doors, so that they would lie flush.

Just beyond the gate is **Grave Circle A** [**66.2**]. This lay outside the citadel until the C13, when the fortifications were extended, and it was then that the parapet of limestone slabs replaced the original enclosure wall. Since the grave circle had last been used three centuries or so before it was carefully restored, the dead were evidently held in great respect. Presumably the later rulers of Mycenae saw themselves as their descendants. The six graves consist of a rectangular shaft which was cut through the earth and rock. Ledges at the lower end of the shaft supported a roof of stone slabs. Nineteen individuals—men, women, and children—were buried in the circle. They had been laid out on the floor of the grave, surrounded by their spectacular offerings. The roof was then set in place and the shaft filled with earth. Stone stelai marked the position of the grave. On either side of the grave circle are the basements of C13 and C12 houses—the Granary, the Ramp House, and the House of the Warrior Vase. Further south, covered by a roof, is the **cult centre** [**66.3**]. This is not accessible at present but consists of a number of shrines. There is a fresco from one of these shrines on display in the museum in NAFPLION and also some bizarre terracotta figurines.

The **palace** [**66.4**] is on the summit of the citadel and would certainly have been conspicuous. The ruler had a fine view of his or her domain. Unfortunately, much of the palace has been destroyed, although not the main suite of rooms. From the entrance on the west side [**66.5**] a corridor runs south and then east to a paved court [**66.6**]. The staircase south of the court may have been the official entrance. The **megaron** [**66.7**] consists of a porch which had two wooden columns, a vestibule, and the throne room. This was dominated by a circular hearth surrounded by four columns. There were battle scenes painted on the walls and gypsum slabs on the floor. The effect must have been quite splendid. The rooms north of the megaron were covered by an

Argolid 183

▲ Fig. 67. The Lion Gate at Mycenae

Archaic/Hellenistic temple. On a lower terrace at the east end of the citadel is the **House of Columns** [**66.8**]. It is now recognized that this formed part of the palace. The adjacent rooms were occupied by craftsmen.

The north-east extension was built at the end of the C13 and protected a secret **cistern** [**66.9**]. This ensured that there would be a supply of water, even if the citadel was under siege. The cistern is not always open and you will need a torch. A flight of steps runs under the fortification wall, turns west, then east and finally reaches the plaster-lined draw-basin which was fed by a system of terracotta pipes. From the north-east extension a path leads west, past a row of storerooms, to the **postern gate** [**66.10**] which was built to protect the water supply and also provided an escape route.

When you have left the citadel, turn off the path for **Grave Circle B** [**69.15**]. There is not much left of the wall which enclosed the circle. The fourteen shaft graves were not as large as those in Circle A and there were also a number of pit graves. Although Circle B is the earlier of the two circles, their period of use does overlap. It is therefore unlikely that Circle A represents a separate dynasty. Yet the later treatment of the circles is quite different. Circle A was carefully restored in the C13 but at

▲ Fig. 68. Interior of the Treasury of Atreus at Mycenae (after E. Dodwell, *Views and Descriptions of Cyclopian Remains in Greece and Italy* (1934) pl. 10)

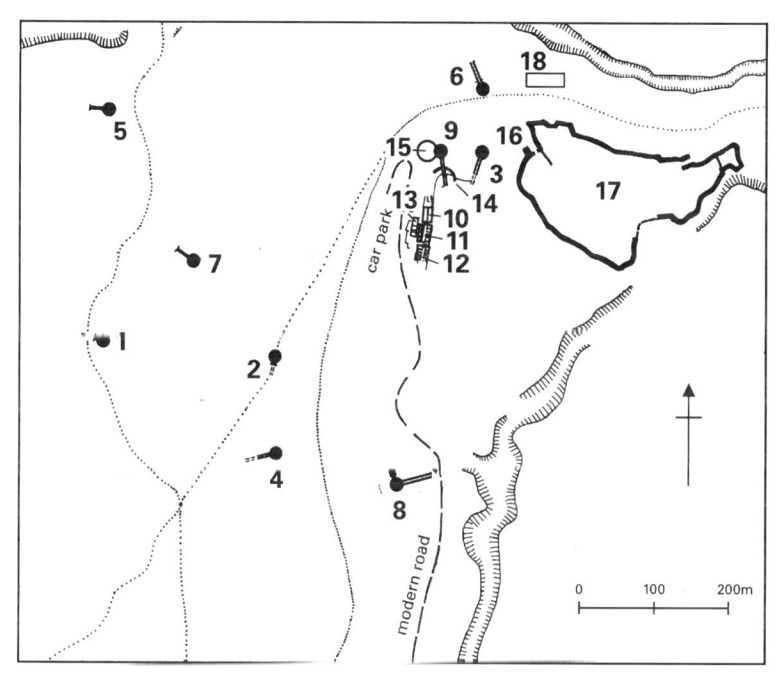

▲ Fig. 69. Plan of Mycenae. Key: 1 Cyclopean tomb 2 Epano Phournos tomb 3 Tomb of Aegisthus 4 Panagia tomb 5 Kato Phournos tomb 6 Lion tomb 7 Tomb of the Genii 8 Treasury of Atreus 9 Tomb of Clytemnestra 10 House of the Shields 11 House of the Oil Merchant 12 House of Sphinxes 13 West House 14 Theatre 15 Grave Circle B 16 Lion Gate 17 Citadel 18 Museum

much the same time Circle B was almost obliterated by the **Tomb of Clytemnestra [69.9]**, the last of the nine tholos tombs constructed at Mycenae. Ashlar masonry lines the sides of the dromos. The facade was once decorated and you can still see the bases of the columns. The corbel vault of the chamber collapsed in the C19 and has been restored. There is a row of stone seats from the Hellenistic **theatre [69.14]** above the dromos. The **Tomb of Aegisthus [69.3]**, one of the earliest tholos tombs, is currently being consolidated. Four **houses [69.10–13]** have been excavated south of Grave Circle B—the West House, the House of Shields, the House of the Oil Merchant, and the House of Sphinxes. Jars full of olive-oil were stored in the houses and luxury items of ivory, faience, and stone. Linear B tablets suggest that the palace was involved in this enterprise.

Just beyond the site entrance there is a path on the right. This passes another tholos tomb, the **Lion tomb [69.6]**, and leads to the **museum [66.18]** which will soon be open.

The **Treasury of Atreus [69.8]** is a short distance down the road to

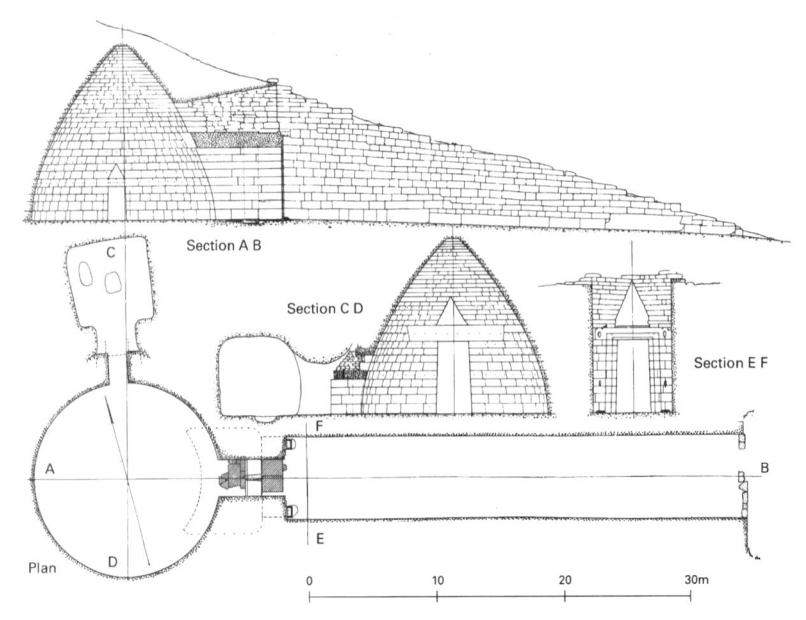

▲ Fig. 70. Plan and elevation of the Treasury of Atreus at Mycenae (after A. J. B. Wace, *Annual of the British School at Athens* 25 (1921–23) pl. 56)

Mikines. When Pausanias visited Mycenae (2.16), he was shown 'the subterranean chambers of Atreus and his sons, where they kept the treasure-houses of their wealth'. Presumably these were the tholos tombs, although we cannot be sure. It seems quite likely that most had already been robbed. If the contents of the tombs were as impressive as their architecture, it is no wonder that they were described as treasure-houses.

The dromos is 36 m. in length and is lined with ashlar masonry. Note the wall which closes off the end. The Mycenaeans filled in the dromos once the funeral had taken place and the Treasury of Atreus was evidently no exception, despite the fact that it had a decorated facade. Half-columns of green marble flanked the door. The triangular space above the lintel was filled by a slab of red marble on which there were rows of spirals, again framed by half-columns. The entrance of the tomb was sealed by a double wooden door. It should be pointed out that the lintel block above your head weighs approximately 120 tons and yet it has been carefully cut so that the inner side follows the curvature of the vault. The effort and skill required to quarry, transport, lift, and finish this one block almost defy belief. The vaulted chamber, over 14 m. in diameter and 13 m. high, has never collapsed. Bronze nails indicate that there was once applied decoration, possibly rosettes. The Treasury of Atreus is unusual in that it has a side chamber where the ruler who commissioned this extraordinary tomb was doubtless buried.

Argos (Figs. 71–75)
The remains of ancient Argos are historically important, and the museum has some well-known finds. The Larisa offers incomparable views.

History

Argos occupied a central place in Greek legend, mainly because Homer calls Agamemnon's kingdom 'Argos' and his host against Troy 'Argives'. As a result Strabo (late C1 BC) classed Argos with SPARTA as the most 'renowned' cities in the Peloponnese. Historically Argos was a good deal less significant than all this suggests. Prehistoric activity is well attested, but Dorian Argos of historic times originates with a settlement at the foot of the Larisa, by far the higher of two hills which dominate the site, the other being the rounded Aspis ('Shield'). A vigorous Geometric culture followed. In the early C7 BC Argos produced a powerful tyrant, Pheidon. By the C6 Sparta had won the leadership of the Peloponnese, and Argos was reduced to a regional power, by *c.*475–450 controlling the whole Argive plain. In this same period Argos became a democracy, a change stimulating public works in the agora and elsewhere. The city was allied with Philip II of Macedon, who claimed an Argive ancestry, and later was a member of the Achaian League. Included in the province of Achaia, Argos traded on the prestige of its legends to win Roman favour, especially from Hadrian, who funded a 30-km. long aqueduct. At the same time a patriotic local elite paid for celebrations of the Nemean and Heraian games and new public works. From the C4 AD on the old civic buildings and spaces fell into increasing disrepair, although rich private houses are attested into the C5. Alaric sacked the city (396 AD), hastening the ruin of its pagan shrines. Christian churches are known from the later C5. The incursions of Avars and Slavs left their mark at Argos, where so-called Slav pottery has been found. From the C7–C9 the history of settlement is obscure.

Description

We suggest that you start your visit with the **Archaeological Museum** in the centre of town near the main square, on Odos Vasilisis Olgas. The ground-floor gallery has Early and Middle Helladic, Mycenaean and Geometric pottery and bronze and iron objects from tombs. The display illustrates the development of the Geometric pottery style in some detail. A fragment of an Argive mixing bowl (C7 BC) shows the blinding of the giant Polyphemos by Odysseus and his companions, one of the earliest identifiable scenes of myth in Greek art. There is also a bronze

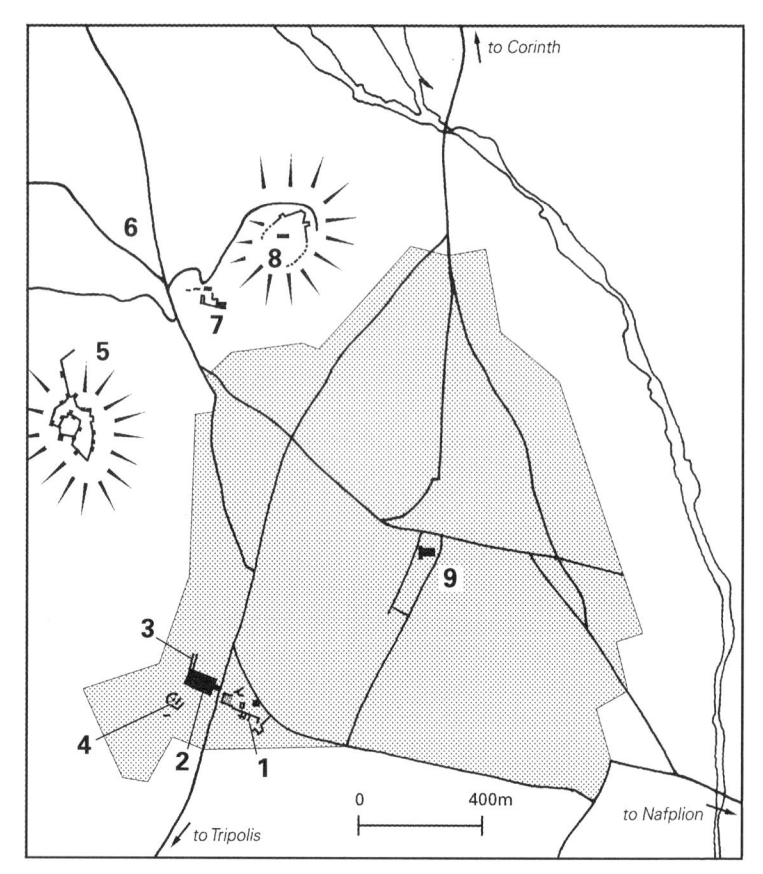

▲ Fig. 71. Plan of Argos. Key: 1 Agora 2 Roman baths 3 Theatre 4 Odeion 5 Larisa (citadel) 6 Deiras 7 Sanctuary of Apollo and Athena 8 Aspis

helmet and cuirass (C8 BC), the only complete Geometric armour found in Greece, along with the bronze fire-dogs and a set of iron roasting spits (see PERACHORA), all from the same tomb. Upstairs Roman sculpture is displayed, mostly from the theatre baths, and including a headless version of the Herakles attributed to the famous sculptor Lysippos (C4 BC). In the basement there is prehistoric pottery, clay seal impressions, and a ceremonial hearth from LERNA. In the garden are important mosaics: the seasons, from C5 AD baths 4 km. south of Argos, and months, hunting scenes and Dionysos from a C5 AD house north of the agora.

For the agora and the theatre, take the Tripolis road. On the right of the road, left of the path, are the remains of Roman **baths**, the most imposing of their kind in Greece. The dominating feature is a brick-faced hall with a vaulted apse, its north wall preserved to its full height. Beneath the floor is a burial-crypt in which three sarcophagi were found.

▲ Fig. 72. West apse of the Roman baths at Argos

190 Argolid

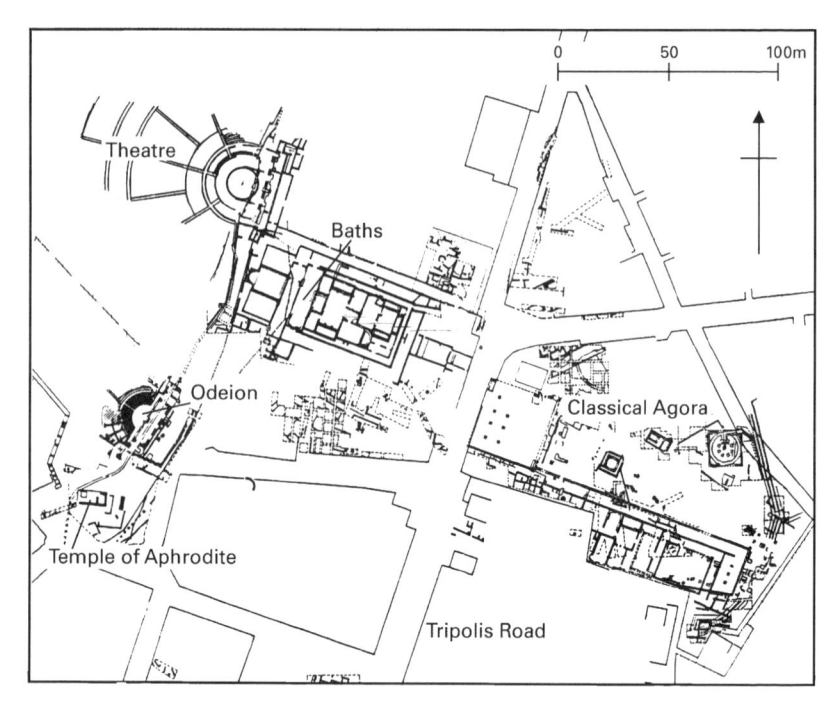

▲ Fig. 73. Plan of the ancient civic centre at Argos

This hall, once adjoining a vast colonnaded court (beneath the later baths), belongs to the original complex (late C1 AD), provisionally identified as a sanctuary for the worship of Asklepios, Serapis, and the Roman emperors. In the C2 AD a roofed bath-complex was installed in the courtyard. The large central hall, a *frigidarium* or cold room, contained three pools screened by columns of veiny green marble from Karystos, where bathers sat and had cold water poured over them after visiting the hot baths. These were the three rooms with hollow floors supported by well-preserved pillars of tiles for a heating system (hypocaust), each equipped with one or more hot-water pools.

Overlooking the baths is the **theatre**, the seating mainly rock-cut in the natural slope of the Larisa, with an estimated seating capacity of 20,000. Dating from *c.*300–275 BC, its construction reflects the transfer to Argos of the games from NEMEA and the ARGIVE HERAION. On the south retaining wall is a rock-cut relief showing the Heavenly Twins (Dioskouroi) Kastor and Polydeukes. Of the Greek stage-building, little survives apart from foundations and an underground passage. It was largely destroyed by its Roman successor, a broad stage backed by a two-storey facade, in marble-veneered brickwork of which there are conspicuous remains. According to an inscription this was a gift from Hadrian following a fire. The theatre was also used for wild-beast and gladiator shows, as shown by the holes in the foot-rests of the first row of seats for a temporary system of posts and nets. In the C4 AD the orchestra was converted into a pool for aquatic shows, and six blocks of the basin-wall are still visible.

A path to the left of the theatre runs past the **aqueduct** supplying water for these shows, and leads on to the **odeion**, or roofed concert-hall of the early C2 AD, with alterations later in the century. In the orchestra, and no longer visible, a poorly preserved mosaic depicts a table for prizes at the Nemean and Heraian games. The odeion overlies a series of slightly concave rock-cut steps belonging to a **theatre** of c.450 BC, seating 2300–2500 people and thought to be used for meetings of the Argive assembly (Haliaia) and perhaps music and drama. Beyond the odeion you can see the foundations of a small Doric **Temple of Aphrodite** (c.450 BC).

The **agora** is on the left of the road and was fairly overgrown in 1998. Although not easy to follow, the site is of considerable interest. The area was liable to flooding by a torrent until drained c.500 BC, permitting its development as a public space. The agora was never regularly planned. It had a strongly religious character, and its festive facilities included a

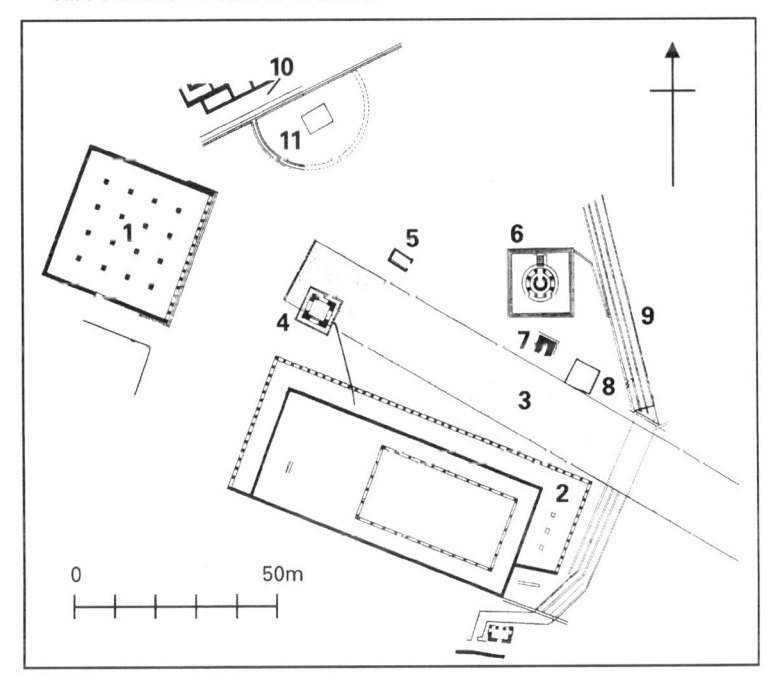

▼ Fig. 74. Plan of the agora at Argos c. AD 200. Key: 1 Colonnaded hall 2 Palaistra 3 Racetrack 4 Fountain 5 Temple 6 Nymphaion 7 Tomb 8 Marble base 9 Drains 10 Stoa 11 Orchestra

race-course and a dance-floor. At first renewed under Roman rule (C1 AD), this traditional function was compromised by later building works (late C2–C3), which emphasized instead the role of the agora as a market.

On the west edge of the fenced site, by the road, are the foundations of the earliest building found in the agora. This was a **colonnaded hall** ([1]—*c*.460 BC), entered from the east through a Doric facade, its roof supported by sixteen Ionic columns inside. Originally it was probably a council-chamber. It survived into the C4 AD. East of the hall you can see the colonnade of a long stoa. Originally this began *c*.25 m. east of the hall, forming the north side of a long, rectangular building flanked by Doric stoas on three sides (*c*.450–425 BC), identified as a **palaistra** [2]. This function was retained after a complete reconstruction (early C1 AD), but lost *c*. AD 200, when public baths were installed here. Now or later the north stoa was extended up to the colonnaded hall, with some of the new rooms behind perhaps serving as shops.

The north stoa looked over a **racetrack** ([3]—C1 AD), some of its starting-blocks still visible to the east of the hypostyle hall. This probably replaced a much earlier (C4 BC) track, likewise orientated north-west to south-east. Nearby, partly built over the track, which it must have put out of action, is a square, brick-faced **fountain** ([4]—late C2 AD), originally veneered in marble and topped by a small four-arched feature set over a water-jet. An inscription records its donors as a rich Argive family of Tiberii Julii. Just north-east are the foundations of a small **temple** ([5]–C3 AD) on the site of an older monument, its blocks reused in the large base for the cult statue.

To the east are the prominent remains of a circular **nymphaion** [6] on a square platform, succeeding an earlier building on the same site. The white-marble, colonnaded rotunda was built over a crypt, entered by a spiral staircase which you can still see, and supplied with water. An inscribed block from the rotunda-frieze refers to these hydraulic works: '[the water from] the springs and the nymphaion with the reservoirs'. The function of the building is uncertain, although the similarity to the Palaimonion at ISTHMIA makes a religious use likely, and suggestions include a shrine of the local nymph Amymone or the heroon of the mythical Argive king Danaos. It was converted *c*. AD 200 into a normal fountain and the crypt closed.

Nearby to the south is the square foundation of a monumental **tomb** [7]. Ten gold leaves were recovered from the skeleton found in the grave ditch. Burial on the agora was an exceptional privilege in this period, reserved for civic benefactors. The deceased perhaps was the rich Argive who funded the nymphaion. His tomb may be linked to a **marble base** [8] nearby to the south-east, the lost superstructure perhaps a memorial. Along the east side of the site are the three parallel **drains** [9] which prevented the agora from flooding by canalizing the Kephisos torrent

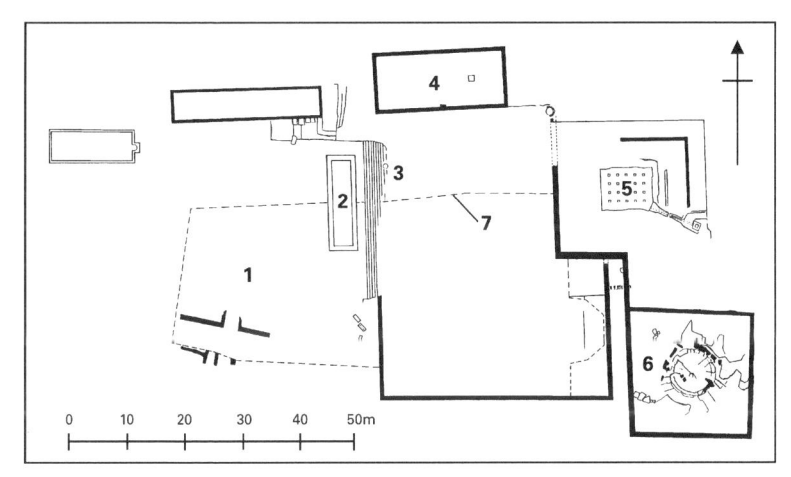

▲ Fig. 75. Plan of the Sanctuary of Apollo and Athena at Argos. Key: 1 Court 2 Altar 3 Steps 4 Rectangular building 5 Courtyard building 6 Rotunda 7 Dotted outline of Christian basilica

(C4 BC replacing an Archaic channel). They were covered originally with limestone slabs, replaced by brick vaults in the C5 AD. In the north-west corner of the site, near the entrance, are remains of a **stoa** [**10**], abutted by a semi-circular, stepped **orchestra** ([**11**]—C4 BC), probably for use by religious choirs. *c.* AD 200 it was converted into a pool.

To reach the **Aspis** (the modern hill of Prophitis Ilias), follow the old Mantineia road running between the Aspis and Larisa and take the turn signed ΛΟΦΟΣ ΑΣΠΙΔΟΣ. Half-way up on the south-west side, just right of the road which runs round the summit, is the **Sanctuary of Apollo and Athena** (Fig. 75), an important Argive cult-centre. Pausanias saw here a temple of Apollo with a bronze statue of the god, who was called Deiradiotes from Deiras, the ravine between the Larisa and the Aspis; also a shrine of Athena, nicknamed Oxyderkes, 'far-seeing'. There was an oracle, its mouthpiece in his day a prophetess banned from sexual intercourse and possessed by the god once a month at night, after tasting the blood of a sacrificed lamb (2.24.1–2). An earlier inscription (*c.*340 BC) mentions a consulting room (*manteion*) and a replica of the omphalos, the ovoid stone marking the centre of the earth at DELPHI. The actual remains are chiefly rock-cuttings, and the temple has completely disappeared. Approaching from the west you find yourself in a large **court** [**1**] with rock-cut foundations for an **altar** [**2**] and, beyond, a flight of rock-cut **steps** [**3**] leading to a second terrace, with remains of a **rectangular building** ([**4**]—C5 BC?). The highest terrace has a **courtyard building** [**5**] possibly used for dining, with a pillared cistern visible below the floor (C3 BC?). On a slightly lower level to the south-east are the remains of a colonnaded **rotunda** [**6**], perhaps the shrine of Athena.

Especially on the middle terrace there are clear traces of the early C6 AD basilican **church** [**7**] built on the site. Some sections of polygonal **fortification wall** are visible on the summit of the Aspis.

From the Deiras ravine a road heads west for the summit of the **Larisa**. The chief reward of the ascent is a superb view of the Argolid. The imposing medieval fortress incorporates stretches of Archaic and Hellenistic fortifications.

Argive Heraion (Figs. 76–77) ★

Go to the village of Honikas, also known as Neo Iraio, which can be reached from Mycenae, Argos, or Agia Triada. In the village there is a sign for the Ancient Ireo.

Special Features

The Heraion was the main sanctuary of ARGOS and is one of the best-preserved and most scenic classical sites in the Argolid.

History

Herodotus (1.31) tells the story of

two young men of Argos, Kleobis and Biton. The Argives were celebrating the festival of Hera, and it was most important that the mother of the two young men should drive to the temple in her ox-cart. But it so happened that the oxen were late in coming back from the fields. Her two sons therefore, as there was no time to lose, harnessed themselves to the cart and dragged it along, with their mother inside, for a distance of nearly six miles, until they reached the temple. After this exploit, which was witnessed by the assembled crowd, they had a most enviable death. Men kept crowding round them and congratulating them on their strength, and women kept telling the mother how lucky she was to have such sons, when in sheer pleasure at this public recognition of her sons' act, she prayed the goddess Hera, before whose shrine she stood, to grant Cleobis and Biton, who had brought her such honour, the greatest blessing that can fall to mortal man. After her prayer came the ceremonies of sacrifice and feasting, and the two lads, when all was over, fell asleep in the temple—and that was the end of them for they never woke again.

This may not have been quite what their mother had in mind but Herodotus does not record her reaction. Why had the Argives built their main sanctuary such an inconvenient distance from the city? The superb view from the upper terrace offers us a clue. Argive political power depended on control of the plain and the prominent position of the Heraion would have been a conspicuous symbol of their authority. The choice of this site for a sanctuary may also have been prompted by traces of a settlement and tombs which date from the 'heroic age'. On the summit of the hill are the vestigial remains of prehistoric houses and a Mycenaean cemetery has been excavated west of the Heraion.

The massive wall which supports the upper terrace of the sanctuary resembles the Cyclopean fortifications of MYCENAE and TIRYNS and was once considered Mycenaean but should be C8 or C7 BC. Nevertheless, this is still an early date for such a major stone structure and implies that there must have been a temple on the terrace. A terracotta model from the Heraion in the National Archaeological Museum in ATHENS suggests that the earliest temple was built of mudbrick and had a thatched roof. In the mid-C7 this was replaced by the Old Temple of Hera which burned down in 423 BC. Chryseis, the priestess of Hera, apparently fell asleep and did not notice that a lamp had set old wreaths and garlands on fire. The roof timbers were soon ablaze and the temple destroyed. The New Temple of Hera was built $c.420$–410 BC, although it may have been planned earlier. Most of the other structures in the sanctuary also date from the Archaic and Classical periods.

Description

The **Old Temple of Hera** [1] occupied the upper terrace but has almost completely disappeared except for a stretch of the platform which once supported the peristyle columns. This was one of the earliest colonnaded temples in Greece and underlines the prominent role of cities such as Argos and CORINTH in the development of Greek architecture. Because the walls of the cella were of mudbrick, the plan of the temple is uncertain.

The middle terrace is dominated by the remains of the **New Temple of Hera** [2]) which was built by the architect Eupolemos. Local limestone was used for the steps and platform, poros for the superstructure and imported marble for the tiles and sculpture. Pausanias tells us that the birth of Zeus and the battle of the gods and giants were depicted in the pediment and metopes at the east end of the temple, while the capture of Troy and scenes from the Trojan war appeared at the west end. Some of the sculpture can be seen in the National Archaeological Museum. The peristyle of the temple consisted of twelve by six Doric columns. The plan of the interior is less clear and the C19 excavators have not left much of the platform intact. Nevertheless, it would seem that there was a porch, cella, and opisthodomos. In the cella stood the gold and ivory cult-statue of Hera by Polykleitos. Since he was one of the finest C5 BC sculptors, the statue must have been magnificent and it is praised by ancient writers, but inevitably we can only imagine what it must have looked like. Pausanias provides a brief description and also lists some of the offerings which he saw in the temple. They included a golden peacock which was dedicated by Hadrian and a purple cloak from Nero.

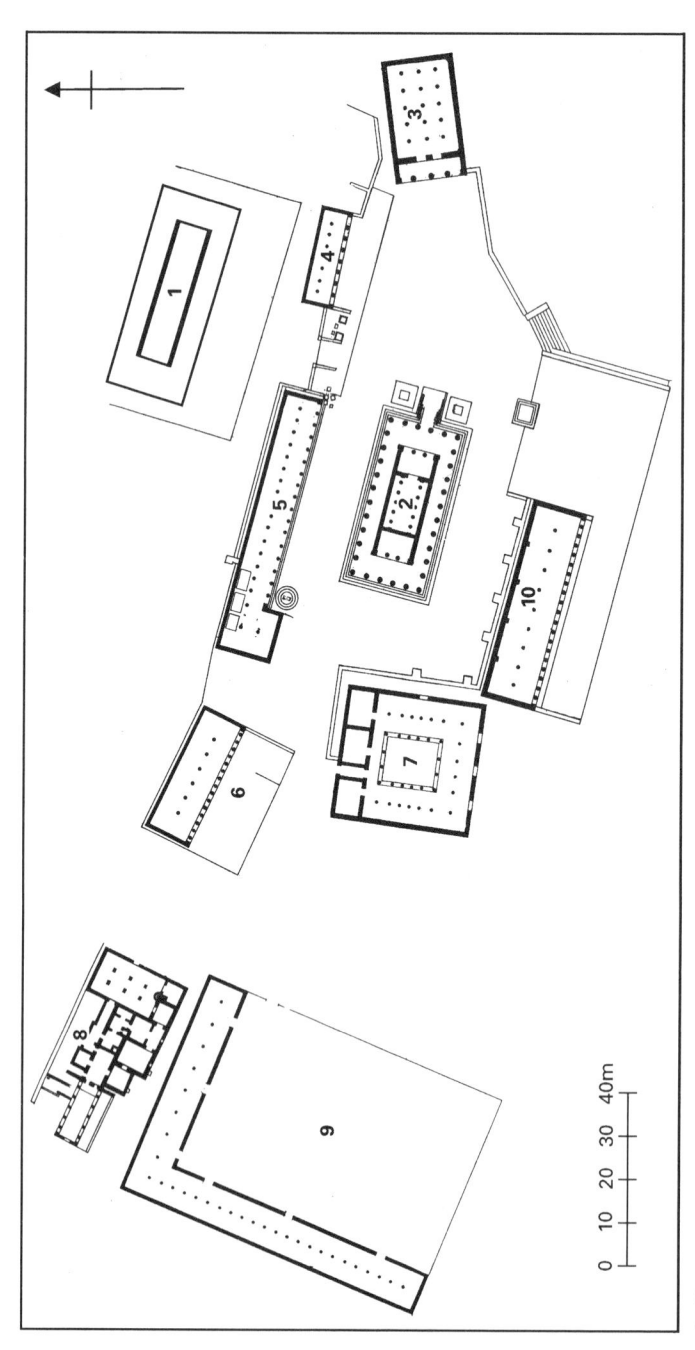

Fig. 76. Plan of the Argive Heraion. Key: 1 Old temple 2 New temple 3 East building 4 North-east stoa 5 North stoa 6 North-west building 7 West building 8 Bath-house 9 Palaistra 10 South stoa

▲ Fig. 77. The New Temple of Hera at the Argive Heraion

Most of the other structures on the middle terrace were built in the C7 or C6 BC. The **east building** [3] is divided internally by three rows of columns. Statues and stelai once stood on the bases in front of the **north-east** [4] and **north stoas** [5]. There is a cement-lined cistern at one end of the north stoa. Just beyond this is the **north-west building** [6]. The **west building** [7] is at a lower level and has stone couches on which privileged Argives dined in style. More couches may have been set up in the peristyle court. Further west and rather overgrown there is a Roman **bath-house** [8] and a **palaistra** [9].

Below the New Temple is the **south stoa** [10] which dates from the C5 BC. This occupied one end of a flight of steps which ran the length of the middle terrace. The height of these steps is such that this must in fact have been a stepped terrace wall which would nevertheless have provided a splendid vantage point for worshippers who watched the sacred processions as they crossed the plain from Argos in the footsteps of Kleobis and Biton.

Nafplion ★

Special Features

Nafplion, the first capital of modern Greece, is an extremely attractive town, has a fine archaeological museum, and makes an excellent base for the Argolid.

History

In view of the number of chamber tombs which have been excavated on the slopes of the Palamidi, it would seem that Nafplion, ancient Nauplia, was a major Mycenaean settlement. In the C7 BC the Argives, determined that their domination of the Argolid should not be threatened, took control of the city and the inhabitants fled. Its Kale, the citadel which dominates the old town, was fortified in the C3 BC but Pausanias found Nafplion deserted. Captured from the Venetians by the Turks in 1540, it was recovered by the Venetians in 1686. They built the fortress on the Palamidi, seized by the Turks in 1715. Between 1828 and 1834 the Greek government was based in Nafplion.

Description

The **Archaeological Museum** occupies the Venetian arsenal in the central square, Plateia Syntagmatos. The prehistoric collection is particularly impressive, although it should be noted that some of the most spectacular finds from sites in the Argolid are in the National Archaeological Museum in ATHENS.

In the vestibule there is a display of Palaeolithic and Neolithic stone tools and two stone 'menhirs' from the Mycenaean cemetery at DENDRA.

The room on the first floor contains Early Helladic pottery from Asine, Berbati, and TIRYNS, Middle Helladic pottery from Asine, Berbati, and MYCENAE, and Late Helladic pottery from Dendra, Mycenae, and Nafplion. In the tholos tomb at Kazarma there were the remains of a calf, which had presumably been sacrificed, bronzes, and jewellery. The suit of bronze armour from one of the chamber tombs at Dendra is particularly impressive and not as cumbersome as it appears. The helmet is plated with boars' tusks and recalls *Iliad* 10.260–5:

Meriones gave Odysseus a bow, a quiver and a sword, and set a leather helmet on his head. Inside it there was a strong lining of interwoven straps, under which a felt cap had been sewn in. The outer rim was cunningly adorned on either side by a row of white and flashing boars' tusks.

The warrior also wore bronze greaves.

Finds from Mycenae include two of the stelai from Grave Circle B, one of which was recut so that it could be used as the base of a stele, bronze weapons and tools, jewellery, pottery, stone vases, fresco fragments, and Linear B tablets. Note the faience plaque which bears the cartouche of the pharaoh Amenhotep III and may indicate that Egyptian officials had visited Mycenae. There is Late Helladic pottery and jewellery from Asine, Berbati, MIDEA, and Tiryns. It is not clear whether the terracotta figurines from the cult centre at Mycenae and the shrine at Tiryns represent goddesses, priestesses, or worshippers. Similarly the woman in the fresco has been interpreted as a goddess but wears a sealstone around her wrist which may signify that she is a priestess.

On the upper floor there is a Submycenaean helmet from Tiryns; Protogeometric and Geometric pottery from Mycenae, Tiryns and Asine; Geometric figurines, weapons, pins and jewellery; Archaic figurines and masks from Tiryns; Corinthian, Boiotian and Athenian pottery; Hellenistic pottery, lamps, figurines and a bathtub.

For an excursion from Nafplion we recommend **Asine**, not least because it is situated between two excellent beaches. From the village of Asini, on the Nafplion–Tolo road, follow signs for Ancient Asini. The site is not fenced.

Excavations have revealed an extensive prehistoric settlement but Asine was apparently subjugated by the Argives in the C8 BC. The peninsula was fortified in the Hellenistic period and there is a particularly fine tower on the east side of the akropolis.

Tiryns (Figs. 78–79)

Tiryns is 4 km. from Nafplion on the Argos road.

Special Features

Pausanias (9.36) states that 'the walls of Tiryns are no less marvellous' than the Egyptian pyramids. He might have added that the site can easily be reached from Nafplion.

History

Tiryns was already a major settlement in the Early Helladic period. There is evidence of impressive structures on the upper citadel in the late Middle Helladic and Early Mycenaean periods. Fresco fragments suggest a 'maison de chef' if not a palace. In the early C14 BC the upper citadel was fortified. Pausanias (2.25) believed that the fortifications were built by giants, the 'Cyclopes with natural rocks so huge that a pair of mules would not begin to shift the smallest', hence the term Cyclopean. A similar date has also been proposed for the first palace and it may well be that the construction of the fortifications represented a display of power by the ruler rather than simply a need for protection. MYCENAE was fortified soon after Tiryns and this raises the question of the relationship between the two sites. Were they enemies or allies, independent or interdependent? No doubt the situation fluctuated over time but there was surely some connection, whether political or economic. Tiryns may have been the main port for Mycenae, since the coastline was then much closer, approximately 1 km. from the citadel.

In the early C13 the fortifications were extended. The entrance was made more secure and the lower citadel fortified in mudbrick. An earthquake then necessitated a major reconstruction in the later C13. Galleries were added at the southern end of the citadel, the west bastion was built and the mudbrick fortifications replaced by stone. The palace was also completely rebuilt. Another earthquake devastated the site at the end of the C13. It would seem that the palace was left in ruins but the citadel was still occupied and the lower town apparently covered 25 hectares in the C12. The armour and weapons buried in a Submycenaean grave—on display in the museum in NAFPLION—imply that Tiryns was still an important site in the C11 but the city was eventually destroyed by ARGOS c.470 BC.

Description

The citadel occupies a low hill which only rises 18 m. above the plain. In this respect it would not have been as formidable a prospect for attackers as Mycenae or MIDEA. The fortifications, built entirely in the Cyclopean technique, encircle the whole of the hill, a circuit of 725 m. Their average thickness is 7.50 m. and the maximum preserved height is also 7.50 m. but must once have been at least 10 m. The fortifications can best be seen from the road.

The site entrance is on the east side of the citadel. It should be noted that access is restricted because there is a risk that some sections of the fortifications might collapse.

A steep **ramp** [1] leads to the **main entrance** [2] but because this is not in use at present you first enter the **lower citadel** [3]. Turn left and you will pass the main entrance which evidently could not be closed. This does seem curious but you soon reach a **gate** [4]. The stone used for this is conglomerate which may have been brought from Mycenae. Moreover, the gate has almost the same dimensions as the Lion Gate. Note the pivot holes for the double doors in the threshold and the cylindrical bolt hole in one of the jambs. Then there is a narrow corridor and a second **gate** [5]. Attackers could have been trapped in this confined space and picked off by the defenders. It is a sophisticated system which must have impressed and also disorientated visitors. From the court beyond the second gate you can see the **gallery** [6] on the southeast side of the citadel. Six rooms open off a corbel-vaulted corridor. It is assumed that supplies were stored in these rooms, presumably in case the citadel was besieged. You now pass through an impressive **propylon** [7]. There were wooden columns on the stone bases on either side of the door. The rooms at the southern end of the citadel, which include a second **gallery** [8], can be entered from the **forecourt** [9], although not at present.

The **propylon** [10] at the north end of the forecourt takes you into the core of the palace, the plan of which recalls Mycenae and PYLOS. The **court** [11] had columns on three sides which would have supported

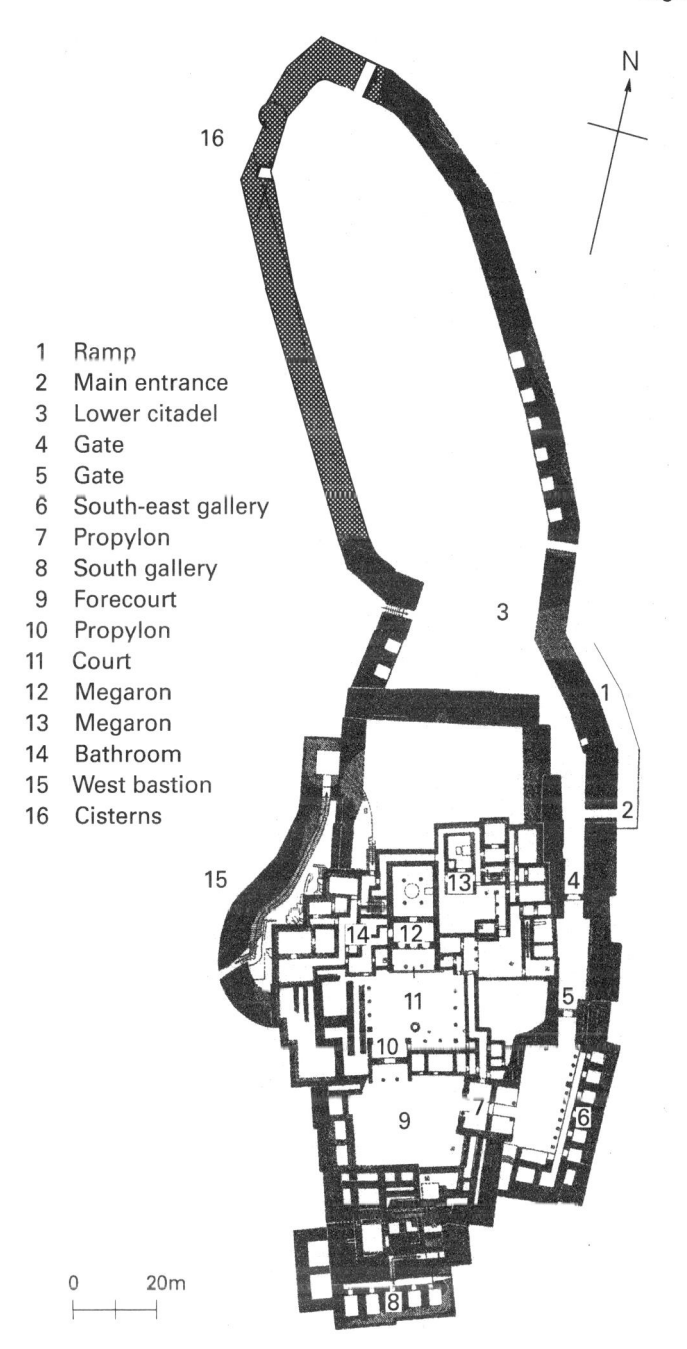

1 Ramp
2 Main entrance
3 Lower citadel
4 Gate
5 Gate
6 South-east gallery
7 Propylon
8 South gallery
9 Forecourt
10 Propylon
11 Court
12 Megaron
13 Megaron
14 Bathroom
15 West bastion
16 Cisterns

▲ Fig. 78. Plan of the citadel at Tiryns

balconies at first floor level. The circular structure on the axis of the megaron may have been an altar and it is certainly likely that ceremonies, whether religious or secular, were held in the court. You enter the **megaron** [**12**] through a porch—note the stone bases of the two massive wooden columns. There were three doors between the porch and the vestibule, which also served the rooms on the west side of the palace. Finally you reach the throne room, dominated by an enormous circular hearth flanked by four columns. It is assumed that there was a throne on the right side of the room, opposite the hearth. You may be puzzled by the wall which runs the length of the throne room. This is clearly later in date and it is possible that repairs were undertaken in the C12, although this structure has also been interpreted as a Geometric temple. East of the throne room there is a second **megaron** [**13**]. The earlier phases of the palace have been investigated in the deep trench in the court.

The rooms west of the throne room include a **bathroom** [**14**]. The floor consists of a single block of limestone, tilted so that water drains away. Panels, possibly of wood, were fixed in the shallow holes around the edge of the block. The **west bastion** [**15**] is not accessible but protects a flight of 65 steps down to a postern gate. It is not clear why the bastion was built, although it seems that there were springs on this side of the citadel.

From the throne room you can see the lower citadel. Recent excavations have revealed a complex sequence of architectural phases. The finds from a C12 shrine include some of the terracotta figurines in the museum in Nafplion. Two **passages** [**16**] run under the fortifications on the west side of the lower citadel to underground cisterns which would have provided a secure supply of water in the event of a siege.

There was a substantial settlement around the citadel which is now covered by citrus groves. Two tholos tombs and a cemetery of chamber tombs have been excavated on the slopes of Profitis Ilias, east of Tiryns.

Dendra and Midea   (Fig. 80)

Take the turn for Agia Triada, just north of Tiryns on the Argos–Nafplion road. From the village follow the numerous signs for the Archaeological Site of Dendron/ Dendra. The site is 3 km. from Agia Triada and access is unrestricted. Then follow signs for the Mycenaean Citadel of Midea which is 4 km. from Dendra. Access is again unrestricted at present.

Special Features

Midea is one of the largest Mycenaean citadels. A tholos tomb and a number of fine chamber tombs have been excavated in the Mycenaean cemetery at Dendra.

▲ Fig. 79. The west bastion of the citadel at Tiryns

Description

Three Middle Helladic tumuli have recently been excavated at Dendra. Since there were horses buried in two of the tumuli, it would appear that they were reserved for individuals of high status. The prestige of the cemetery is further underlined by the size of the tholos tomb and chamber tombs. Consequently it is assumed that Dendra served Midea, despite the distance between the two sites.

The tumuli are at the far end of the cemetery but have been protected by corrugated sheets and cannot easily be seen. Most of the chamber tombs have deep entrances which create a rather claustrophobic effect, no doubt intentionally. The chambers were more carefully cut than is the case in most Mycenaean cemeteries. There were some spectacular grave offerings in these tombs, in particular the suit of armour which is on display in the museum in NAFPLION. The vault of the tholos tomb has collapsed but the excavators found a number of intact pits in the floor of the chamber. A man and a woman, the 'king' and the 'queen', were buried in one of the pits with an impressive array of offerings which included bronze swords and daggers, gold and silver cups, sealstones, jewellery, and an ostrich egg rhyton.

Midea was clearly a major Mycenaean centre but must have been dominated by MYCENAE and TIRYNS. Although the citadel was fortified in the C13 BC, there is no evidence of a palace. Nevertheless, Midea did have an administrative role, since inscriptions written in Linear B have

▼ Fig. 80. Plan of the citadel at Midea

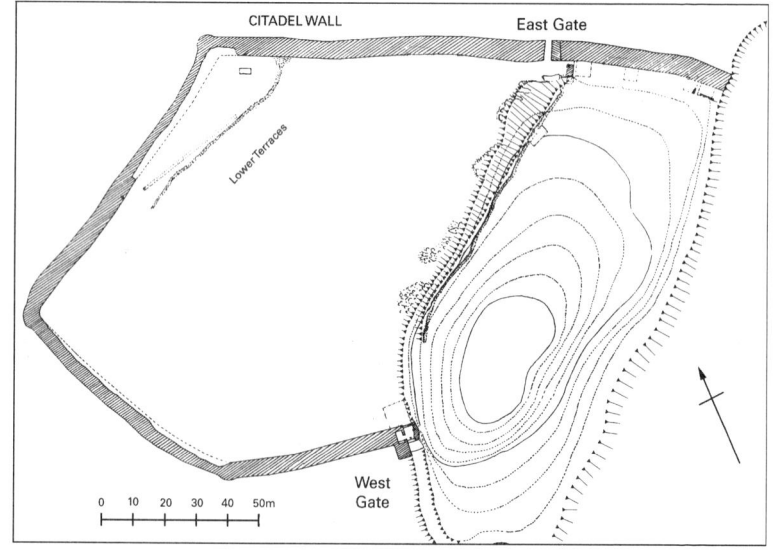

recently been found. The site was destroyed, possibly by an earthquake, at the end of the C13.

The best-preserved stretch of the Cyclopean fortifications is on the north-east side of the citadel and can be seen from the road. In places the height of the wall is still over 7 m. A path leads from the road to the excavations on the lower terraces. It is not easy to distinguish the architectural phases in this trench but the most substantial structure is a C13 megaron. Follow the path up the slope and you will reach the west gate which was protected by a tower. The view across the Argive plain is spectacular. Storerooms and workshops have been excavated just north of the gate. There is also a complex of rooms by the east gate, on the other side of the citadel.

Epidauros (Figs. 81–83)
Drive through Ligourio and then follow the signs for Ancient Theatre Epidavros.

Special Features

This site is of outstanding interest for the history of Greek architecture, medicine and religion. As well as the famous theatre, its sheer size is one of its most impressive features.

History

The sanctuary here lies in an isolated valley belonging to ancient Epidauros, a small city *c*.7 km. away on the Saronic coast, famed for its vineyards. In Geometric times Apollo took over a prehistoric site on Mt Kynortion, above the later Asklepieion, assimilating a local hero, Maleatas. Apollo's son, the healing god Asklepios, still only a hero in Homer, had arrived by *c*.500–475 BC, the date of the earliest inscribed offering from the site (*IG* 4^2.136), and of the first mention of his Epidaurian festival. His cult was imported, perhaps from Messenia or Thessaly, although by *c*.280 BC Epidauros claimed to be his birthplace. Its panhellenic reputation was fostered by the plague at ATHENS, prompting the establishment of the Epidaurian cult there (420). In 370 the Epidaurians launched a lavish programme of building which transformed the sanctuary. The money was partly raised locally, partly from pilgrims. Inscribed accounts of this work survive, with fascinating details about the craftsmen and the materials they used. Insight into the temple medicine of this period comes from slabs inscribed with records of faith healing: the sick undertook ritual sleep in the sanctuary, during which the god appeared to them in dreams and effected miraculous cures. The Epidaurian cult was exported to Rome in 293 BC, although this did not prevent Sulla from looting the sanctuary *c*.86 BC. Under the pax Romana it enjoyed a new prosperity, with major works in both sanctuaries, many

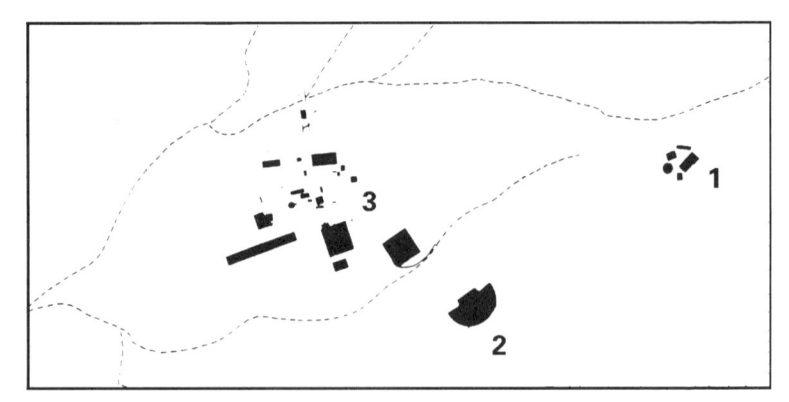

▲ Fig. 81. Plan of the site at Epidauros. Key: 1 Sanctuary of Apollo Maleatas 2 Theatre 3 Main sanctuary

funded by Antoninus, a magnate from western Asia Minor (mid-C2 AD). A defensive wall around the heart of the sanctuary is thought to reflect the troubles of the mid-C3. In the early C4 inscriptions emphasize the character of the cult as a mystery. Its latest-known priest and 'hierophant', one Mnaseas, held office in AD 355. A basilican church close to the ancient entrance is generally dated to the late C4, making it one of the earliest churches known in Greece. The thorough destruction of most of the pagan buildings may reflect Christian dismantlement.

Description

The **theatre** is one of the best preserved in Greece, and struck Pausanias as 'most especially worth seeing' for its 'symmetry and beauty' (2.27.5). Its construction is dealt with in inscribed accounts dated c.330–320 BC— too late for the famous sculptor Polykleitos to have designed it, as Pausanias wrongly believed. The 55 rows of seats, taking 13,000–14,000 spectators, rest on a natural slope, except at the north-west end where they are held up by artificial fill. The ancient stage, by contrast, is poorly preserved, and its remains are often covered by arrangements for modern performances. The surviving foundations are for a building with a narrow stage flanked by ramps. The orchestra is a stone circle enclosing a floor of beaten earth, with an off-centre slab of uncertain purpose. The theatre was used for musical and dramatic contests during festival-time.

The **museum** is mainly of interest for its architectural reconstructions, along with quite good plans and elevations. Left of the entrance are two Corinthian columns from inside the Tholos. **Room 1** includes the inscriptions recording cures and the building accounts, as well as surgical equipment showing that conventional medicine was also practised here. **Room 2** has casts of the pedimental groups from the temple of Asklepios, the originals displayed in the National Archaeological

Museum in ATHENS, and the reconstructed entablature of the ancient gateway (propylaia). **Room 3** has reconstructions of the temple of Asklepios and parts of the Tholos (here called the Thymele), although not the entablature, currently being restored and out of view.

After you enter the main site, the first building you see (early C3 BC) is remarkable for its size (*c*.76 m. square). It is identified as a **hostel** from its internal arrangement of four courtyards, each surrounded by eighteen rooms, and perhaps had an upper storey. The stone footings once supported walls of unbaked mudbrick. Nothing is known about who used this complex, although its proximity to the heart of the sanctuary suggests that it housed high-status visitors, such as festival-ambassadors.

From here on consult the separate plan of the main sanctuary (Fig. 82). Passing a small courtyard building identified as a **bath** ([1]—early C3 BC) by the presence of a water-channel and finds of water-basins, you reach a second courtyard building only slightly smaller than the hostel, probably a **banqueting hall** [2] and not, as first thought, a gymnasium. It was entered by a once-imposing Doric gateway, currently being restored, to which a ramp leads up from the north. As first built (*c*.300 BC?), the courtyard was a colonnaded square surrounded by rooms of varying size, some with off-centre doorways to accommodate dining couches round the walls, others with traces of couch-fittings. The meals eaten here presumably were part of *thusia*, the ritual consumption of animals after their sacrifice on the altars to the north. In the C2 AD a small, quite well-preserved **theatre** [3] was installed in the courtyard, built of rubble and brick. Its function is unclear.

You see next (to the north-east) a large, near-square **building** [4] of mortared Roman construction, its central hall featuring stone benches and a base for a cult-statue. The mysteries of Asklepios implied by C4 AD inscriptions perhaps were celebrated here.

A detour to the west at this point brings you to the **stadium** ([5]—late C4 BC), with stone seating (rare in Greece at this date) making use of natural slopes topped up with fill. A vaulted tunnel (C3 BC or earlier) links the race-track with a **palaistra** [6] to the north. The water supplied by the channel and basins round the edge of the track was intended for use by athletes. Women's races were held here by *c*. AD 45, when Dionysia of Tralles won the sprint at the festival of Asklepios.

Returning to the central area you reach the core of the sanctuary, enclosed (later C3 AD?) by a defensive **wall** [7], incorporating sections of Classical buildings and column-drums. Just north-west of the courtyard building are the foundations of a small **Temple of Artemis** ([8]—*c*.330 BC), the Doric facade linked by a ramp to the altar. Just north is so-called **Building E** ([9]—450–400 BC), a large courtyard structure, the north and east wings faced by screen-walls. This may be the first shrine of Asklepios, with the earliest facilities for ritual sleep. It faces the square foundations of the **altar of Apollo** [10].

208 **Argolid**

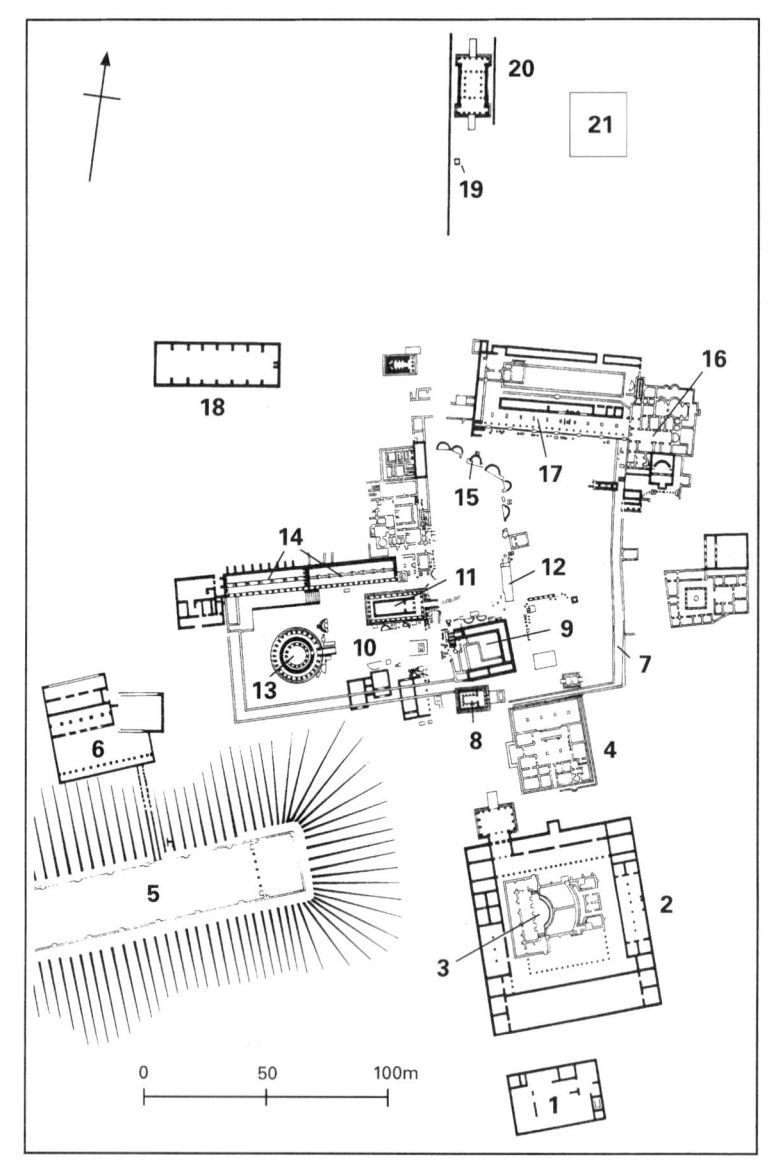

▲ Fig. 82. Plan of the sanctuary of Asklepios at Epidauros. Key: 1 Bath 2 Banqueting hall 3 Theatre 4 Building for mysteries? 5 Stadium 6 Palaistra 7 Defensive wall 8 Temple of Artemis 9 Building E 10 Altar of Apollo 11 Temple of Asklepios 12 Altar of Asklepios 13 Tholos 14 Abaton 15 Apsidal seats 16 Roman baths 17 Doric stoa 18 Cistern 19 Well 20 Gateway 21 Basilica

North of this are the foundations of the Doric, colonnaded **Temple of Asklepios** ([11]—*c*.375–370 BC), approached from the east by a ramp. Its build shows a certain thrift, with clay roof-tiles, and marble reserved chiefly for the pedimental sculpture. Pausanias describes the cult-statue as seated, in gold and ivory, the work of a Parian sculptor, Thrasymedes. Striking here is the clutter of bases for votive offerings jostling for space and attention around the god's temple, especially by the ramp. To the east are the foundations of the long **altar of Asklepios** [12].

South-east of the temple are the circular foundations of the **Tholos** ([13]—*c*.360–330 BC), a colonnaded rotunda which Pausanias thought 'well worth seeing' (2.27.3), while misattributing its design to (once more) the sculptor Polykleitos. Its former luxuriousness shows that it rivalled the temple of Asklepios in religious importance. The building is currently being restored. Approached by a ramp, it had an outer Doric colonnade supporting elaborate coffering. Beyond was a circular walled chamber floored in black and white marble, intricately patterned, and supporting an inner ring of Corinthian columns. In the middle of this floor was a hole giving access (by wooden steps) to a crypt comprising six concentric rings, pierced by doors to form a maze. These enigmatic and much-debated arrangements recall the Nymphaion at ARGOS and the Palaimonion at ISTHMIA, likewise rotundas with ritual crypts, both for hero-worship. Probably the rites here focused on Asklepios, not as a god, but in his primal character as an earth-bound hero.

North of the Tholos are the foundations of the **abaton** [14], literally '(place) not to be stepped on', an Ionic stoa facing south which was reserved for ritual sleeping, the rite at the heart of faith-healing here. It is currently roped off and being restored. Two large slabs inscribed with records of miraculous cures (*c*.350–300 BC) were found here in 1881 and are now in the museum (see **box**). They were seen by Pausanias, who says that 'of old there were more of them, in my time six were left' (2.27.3). The original abaton (C4 BC) was doubled in size to the west in Hellenistic or Roman times, the drop in the ground requiring a basement for the extension.

Heading north with the abaton on your left, you pass by a curving row of **apsidal seats** or exedrai [15], still in place, for the use of pilgrims, some once topped by honorific statues (C1 BC–C1 AD). On your right you reach substantial **Roman baths** ([16]—C2 AD), now being restored. The main hall terminated in a cold-water pool, and the heated rooms were to the north. These baths had a therapeutic function, as shown by the god's prescriptions for a rich invalid from south-west Asia Minor (*c*. AD 160), which include 'bathing without help' and 'walking around barefoot in the baths before plunging into the hot water' (*IG* 4².126).

Abutting this complex is a south-facing **Doric stoa** ([17]—early C3 BC?) fronted by a drainage channel, and proposed as the 'Stoa of Kotys'

Two miraculous cures

Two inscribed cures found in the abaton:
Ambrosia from Athens, blind in one eye. She arrived as a suppliant to the god. As she walked about in the sanctuary she laughed at some of the cures as incredible and impossible, that the lame and the blind should be healed by only seeing a dream. In her sleep she had a vision. It seemed to her that the god stood by her and said that he would cure her, but that in payment he would ask her to dedicate in the sanctuary a silver pig as a memorial to her ignorance. After saying this, he cut the diseased eyeball and poured in some drug. When day came she walked out healthy.

Hermodikos of Lampsakos [in western Asia Minor] was paralysed in body. The god healed this man when he slept and ordered him on coming out to bring to the sanctuary as large a stone as possible. He brought the stone which now lies before the abaton.

(*IG* 4^2.121, lines 33–41 and 107–10, after E. and L. Edelstein)

repaired by 'the Roman senator Antoninus' of Pausanias (2.27.6), in fact a rich Asia-Minor Greek, Sextus Julius Maior Antoninus Pythodorus from Nysa. The senator acted out of family piety, since he was distantly related to Kotys of Thrace, a philhellene king living under Augustus, who perhaps had paid for earlier repairs.

If you take the path north out of the central area, there is a Hellenistic **cistern** [18] away to your left (overgrown) and, further on, a fine masonry-lined **well** ([19]—C6 or early C5 BC), before you reach the grand **gateway** [20]. This was a roofed lobby fronted by Ionic colonnades and approached by ramps (early C3 BC), and was the main approach from the coast. The boundaries of the sacred precinct were otherwise marked by stones, inside which certain human functions proscribed as polluting were banned, including childbirth and dying—for all that this was, in effect, a vast sanatorium. The basilican **church** [21] to the east is likely to be overgrown.

To reach the **Sanctuary of Apollo Maleatas** on Mt Kynortion (fenced—check accessibility at the main site), go to the Xenia Hotel and Restaurant, which is signed from the car-park, and take the dirt track which runs from the back of the hotel. Continue for 1.3 km. and you will see the sanctuary on your left.

There was a Middle Helladic settlement on the site and an open-air altar was set up in the Mycenaean period, on which fires were lit and animals sacrificed. Cult activity resumed in Geometric times, although the surviving structures mainly belong to the C4 BC or to a wholesale rebuilding in the C2 AD by the senator from Nysa. As Pausanias says, 'everything about the sanctuary of Maleatas, including the cistern in

Argolid 211

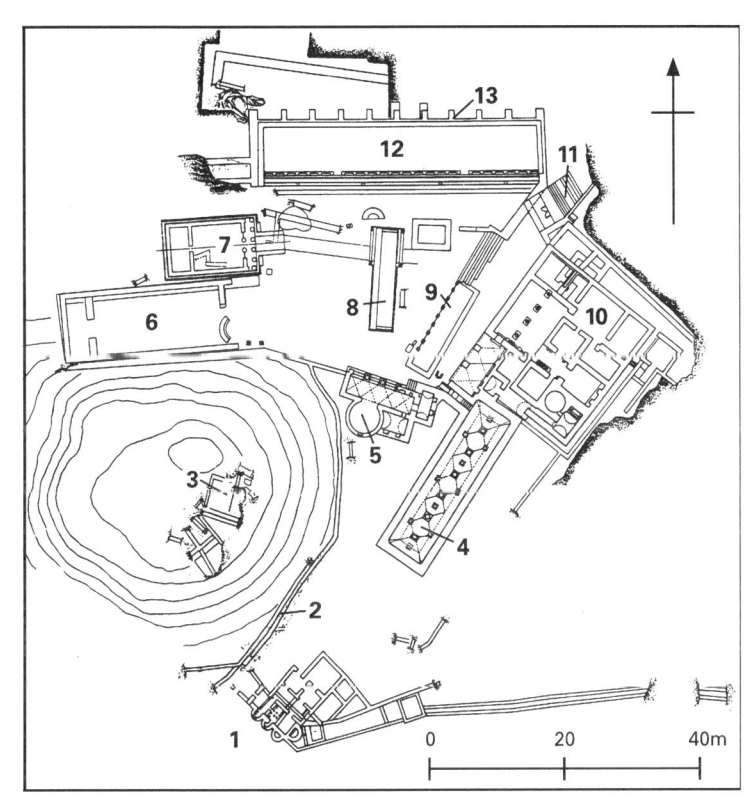

▲ Fig. 83. Plan of the Sanctuary of Apollo Maleatas at Epidauros. Key: 1 Roman baths 2 Retaining wall 3 Prehistoric settlement 4 Cistern 5 Fountain 6 Open-air building 7 Temple of Apollo 8 Altar 9 Shrine of the Muses 10 Skana 11 Gateway 12 Stoa 13 Retaining wall

which the holy water is collected, is also a gift of Antoninus to the Epidaurians' (2.27.7). Pottery takes the sanctuary's life into the C4.

As you enter you pass a complex of **Roman baths** [1] on your right. On your left are remains of a Roman **retaining wall** [2] to prevent falls of earth from the hill above. On top of this hill are remains of the **prehistoric settlement** [3]. Continuing, you pass (right) the impressive underground **cistern** [4] of Antoninus, with a modern roof, and (left) a Roman **fountain** [5]. Arriving in the central area, on your far left is an enigmatic **open-air building** [6], temple-like in plan (C1 BC?), overlying a Mycenaean terrace. Immediately to its north are the remains (roofed) of the small, Doric **Temple of Apollo** [7], non-colonnaded (C4 BC) and, in front of it, under scaffolding and being restored, its long **altar** [8], originally with piers supporting some kind of canopy over the north end. Just to the east is a line of re-erected piers marking the facade of a

shrine of the Muses [9], identified by an inscription. Behind this is a large complex of rooms (mid-C2 AD), its tiles stamped '(of) Antoninus'. This is identified as the **skana** [10] of four Roman inscriptions, or 'living quarters' for sanctuary staff, and included a bath-suite (south-east corner). In AD 183 it served the priest of Apollo, the 'fire-bearer' (his son), two women attendants, and two temple guards. The restored steps of a Roman **gateway** [11] separate it from the slight remains of a **stoa** ([12]—late C4 BC), supported by an impressive, buttressed **retaining wall** [13], the *analamma* of inscriptions (*c*.330 BC), which has to be viewed from the next level down.

Troizen (Fig. 84)

Take the turn for Trizina on the Methana–Galatas road. Once in the village, follow signs for the Antiquities (sic). The site is 1.6 km. from Trizina and is not fenced.

Special Features

Troizen, where the hero Theseus spent his childhood, is an attractive site in the countryside.

History

Troizen is more famous as the scene of mythical triumphs and disasters than historical incidents. It was here that Theseus was born and his son Hippolytos died. The latter, a chaste youth, was pursued by his stepmother Phaidra. He spurned her advances but was nevertheless accused of rape. Cursed by his father, he fled and was killed when a sea monster attacked his chariot.

Troizen was an independent city-state in the Archaic period and provided a safe haven for Athenian women and children when the Persians invaded Attika in 480 BC:

As soon as the decree was passed, most of the Athenians sent their wives and children to Troizen, where the citizens vied with one another to make them welcome. They even voted to maintain the refugees at public expense. They gave each family two obols a day, allowed the children to pick the fruit wherever they pleased as soon as it was ripe, and went so far as to pay schoolmasters to teach them.

(Plutarch, *Themistokles* 10.3)

There were statues of the Athenian refugees in a stoa in the agora. The Greek fleet which defeated the Persians at Salamis included five triremes from Troizen and the city contributed a contingent of 1000 hoplites at the battle of PLATAIA in 479 BC. The alliance between ATHENS and Troizen, forged in the age of heroes, did not survive the polarization of Greece in the C5. Athens sought control of the harbours around the Saronic Gulf but Troizen became a staunch member of the Peloponnesian League which was led by SPARTA. In the early C4 the city was still

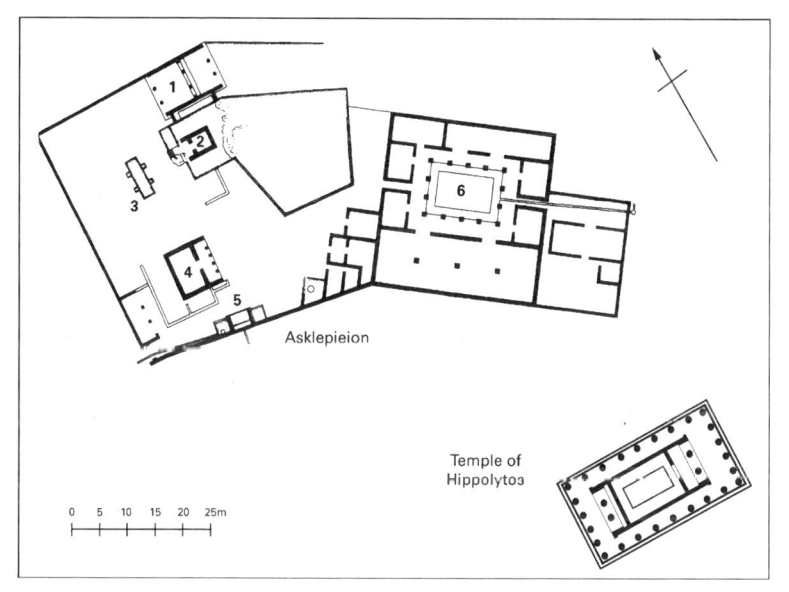

▲ Fig. 84. Plan of the Asklepieion and the Temple of Hippolytos at Troizen. Key: 1 Propylon 2 Temple? 3 Altar 4 Temple of Asklepios? 5 Fountain house 6 Abaton?

a Spartan ally. A rapprochement with Athens followed and eventually Macedonian rule. Despite these vicissitudes several major construction projects were undertaken in the late C4 and early C3. In the Hellenistic period Troizen joined the Achaian League. The emperor Hadrian paid a visit in the C2 AD and was followed by Pausanias (2.31–2) who lists eleven temples, one of which became the early Christian church of Palaia Episkopi.

Description

The architectural complex which you see first has been identified, plausibly if not incontrovertibly, as an **Asklepieion**. The sanctuary was entered through a **propylon** [1] which must once have been quite impressive. In the enclosure south of the propylon there is evidence of cult activity as early as the C8. The **structure** [2] at the west end of the enclosure was presumably a temple, since it faces an **altar** [3], but may be the house of Hippolytos which Pausanias mentions. The **temple** [4] south of the altar was built in the late C4 or early C3, possibly for Asklepios. It had a porch and cella. The **fountain house** [5] on the south side of the sanctuary was fed from a source of mineral water which relieved bowel and stomach problems. No doubt this was one of the attractions of the Asklepieion but there were evidently unwelcome side effects, since Pliny (*Naturalis Historia* 31.11) claims: 'it is the fault of the waters of Troizen that everyone there suffers from diseases of the feet'. The **complex** [6] at the east end of the sanctuary also dates from the late C4 or early C3. In the centre there is a peristyle court and south of this a room which has six square hearths and stone supports for wooden couches and tables. There were evidently more couches in the rooms east and west of the court. If the sanctuary is an Asklepieion, this should be the *abaton* or *koimeterion* in which patients slept and dreamed of a cure for their illness. Alternatively or additionally the rooms may have been used when sacrificial meals were served, since a system of drains ensured that they could be sluiced out and kept clean.

Hippolytos was worshipped as a hero at Troizen. Pausanias (2.32) saw his temple and cult-statue. He tells us that there was 'a tradition of annual sacrifices ... and every virgin girl cuts off a lock of hair for him before her marriage and dedicates it in his shrine'. It is believed that the cult of Hippolytos centred on the C4 **temple** south of the Asklepieion. The temple had a colonnade of 11 by 6 columns and consisted of a porch, cella, and opisthodomos. Some of the columns were reused in the early Christian church of **Palaia Episkopi** which is also on the site of a temple. This could well be the shrine of Aphrodite Kataskopia which overlooked the stadium of Hippolytos. 'Whenever Hippolytos exercised, Phaidra would watch him from here and lust for him. The myrtle still grows here with perforated leaves. When Phaidra was in despair of a way to ease her love, she wantonly ruined the leaves' (Pausanias 2.32). The **stadium** presumably occupied the rather narrow terrace north of the church.

When you return from the site, turn right at the sign for the Devil's Bridge. You pass the barrel-vaulted ΙΕΡΟ ΜΟΥΣΩΝ—the shrine of the Muses but actually a Roman bath, and then a fine Hellenistic **tower** which was restored in the Frankish period. The tower is on the line of a cross wall which separated the akropolis from the lower city.

Lerna (Fig. 85)

The site is just off the Argos–Tripolis road, at the southern end of the village of Myloi.

Special Features

Lerna, where Herakles slew the Hydra, is one of the most important and informative prehistoric sites in Greece, particularly for the Early Helladic period.

History

Lerna was first occupied in the Early and Middle Neolithic periods (6500–5300 BC). Since the site controls a strip of fertile arable land, has a source of fresh water and is on the coast, it must have seemed perfect. Nevertheless, despite these irresistible attractions, there was then a break in settlement and the site was not reoccupied until the Early Helladic period. Lerna evidently prospered, since the inhabitants felt the need and had the resources to build massive stone and mudbrick fortifications. In a dominant position on the summit of the mound the House of the Tiles was constructed, presumably for the ruler, although this is not certain. In one of the rooms there were dozens of impressed clay seals (on display in the museum in ARGOS) which had come from jars, wooden chests, and wicker baskets. A simple system of taxation must have been in operation and, in this respect at least, the House of the Tiles anticipates Minoan and Mycenaean palaces. Lerna was then destroyed by fire and the character of the settlement becomes quite different. Caskey, the American excavator of the site, wondered whether southern Greece had been invaded. This is now thought less likely but Lerna never seems as advanced again. In the Middle Helladic period several hundred of the inhabitants were buried in the settlement. Study of their skeletons has revealed that the men were 1.60–1.70 m. tall (5′ 3″–5′ 7″) and the women 1.48–1.56 m. (4′ 10″–5′ 1″). There was high infant mortality and those who survived childhood had short lives. Most of the women died between 25 and 40, the men between 30 and 45. They suffered from malnutrition, arthritis, malaria, and had poor teeth—not much of an advertisement for the Middle Helladic lifestyle. On the site where the House of the Tiles had once stood, two shaft graves were constructed early in the Mycenaean period and it may well be that an awareness of the past prompted this choice of location.

Description

Just beyond the entrance of the site there is a deep trench in which one of the **Neolithic houses** [1] can be seen. The fact that this is at a much lower level illustrates how the site increased in height over time, as the stone and mudbrick houses were demolished and rebuilt. The best preserved section of the **Early Helladic fortifications** [2] is on the southern side of the mound. Stone was used for the lower courses of the wall and mudbrick for the superstructure. Between the inner and outer face of the wall there is a series of rooms divided by mudbrick partitions which have been protected by tiles. Supplies were presumably stored in these rooms. A tower was built at the point where the wall turns north-east. This was originally horseshoe-shaped but was later replaced by the solid tower.

Before you enter the concrete shelter which covers the House of the Tiles, note the **Middle Helladic cist grave** [8], covered by a massive stone slab. The **House of the Tiles** [3] is a corridor house, in that it consists of two main rooms separated and flanked by corridors. Houses

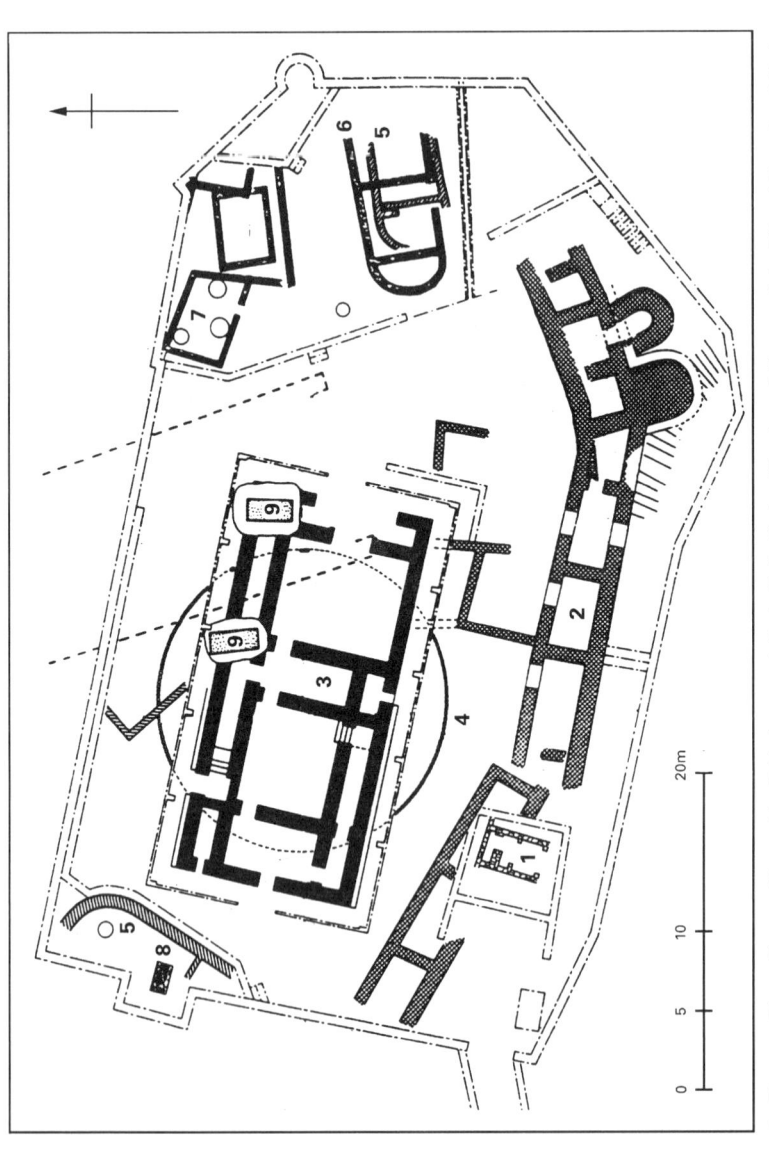

▲ Fig. 85. Plan of Lerna. Key: 1 Neolithic houses 2 Early Helladic fortifications 3 House of the Tiles 4 Tumulus 5 Early Helladic house 6 Middle Helladic house 7 Storeroom 8 Middle Helladic cist grave

of this type have been identified at a number of other Early Helladic sites, in particular at KOLONNA on AIGINA. Staircases indicate that there were two storeys and it is thought that a veranda may have run around the rooms on the first floor. The walls were of mudbrick, protected by a layer of lime plaster. In places the final coat of plaster had not been applied and it is possible that the house was incomplete or being renovated when it was destroyed. A thick layer of yellow clay had been spread on the floors. Some of the terracotta tiles from the roof have been used to fill gaps in the walls. The plan of the house is quite complex and it seems clear that it was designed to serve a range of functions. The later treatment of the House of the Tiles was most curious. After it had been destroyed, a circular tumulus was built over the ruins. The stone border of this **tumulus** [4] can be seen on the south side of the shelter. Evidently the site of the house was considered sacred but we do not know why.

Middle Helladic architecture is not as impressive. The typical house of this period is apsidal, built of mudbrick on a stone socle. At the eastern end of the site one of these **Middle Helladic houses** [6] is superimposed on an **Early Helladic** predecessor [5]. An adjacent **storeroom** [7] contains several large pithoi.

Astros and Loukou

Special Features

Loukou is the site of the most spectacular Roman villa so far found in Greece, although as yet inaccessible. Some of the finds are on display in the museums at Astros and TRIPOLIS, as well as the National Archaeological Museum in ATHENS.

History

In antiquity the fertile plain of modern Astros overlooking the Gulf of Argos was a distinct sub-region known as Kynouria, its coastal strip as Thyreatis. The region was disputed border-country, taken by SPARTA from ARGOS c.545 BC, but in Roman imperial times once more Argive. In the C2 AD the chief settlement was a village, Eva (modern Hellenikon, south-west of Astros). The major archaeological site is at modern Loukou: an exceptionally rich Roman villa. Inscriptions and sculpture show that this was the property of the Athenian magnate Herodes Atticus (pp. 117–118). To judge from the funerary inscription (C2 AD?) of one Gellius Carpus, an Athenian 'steward of the Thyreatic land' (*SEG* 13.1956.261), the villa was associated with a large estate on the plain. How Herodes came by this property is unknown, although his family had close ties with Sparta and CORINTH, Argive neighbours. The villa site has been known since 1806, and its sculpture is in museums in western Europe as well as Greece. There are currently Greek excavations, with sensational new finds of sculpture in 1995–6, including fragmentary versions of well-known groups like the Flaying of Marsyas.

Description

The **Archaeological Museum** in Astros is by the school. It is signed, although rather erratically. There are labels in English and Greek.

The room on the left has sculpture from the villa at Loukou, including two extremely fine grave reliefs, and an Egyptianizing head in Pentelic marble, perhaps Polydeukion (see p. 115). The next room has more sculpture from the villa, including a C4 BC Athenian relief of a banqueting hero, perhaps an antique dedicated by Herodes in the sanctuary of Polemokrates, son of Asklepios, which Pausanias saw at Eva. In the next room there are grave offerings—pottery, lamps, glass, and iron weapons—from the Classical and Hellenistic cemetery at Hellenikon. The room on the right has sculpture and architectural fragments, mainly from the villa, including portraits of Lucius Aelius Caesar, the adopted son of Hadrian who died before the emperor, and Commodus, perhaps originally helmeted. Monolithic granite columns in the courtyard come from the nymphaion area of the villa.

Continuing on the Tripoli road for 4 km., you reach the **monastery of Loukou** ('Luke'), where sculpture and architectural fragments of Roman date can be seen in the courtyard and the fabric of the church. On the way up to it you pass an aqueduct, its brickwork foundations confirming a Roman date, which probably supplied the fountain-house (nymphaion) of the villa.

A short distance further on the main road brings you to the **villa** (to your right and signed). Although excavations are still in progress and the site is not yet accessible, the sheer size and magnificence of the villa, set in delightful countryside, can be appreciated.

Elements of the villa so far reported include a colonnaded hall, a large courtyard, a luxurious nymphaion, a bath-complex, a dining hall and, probably, an 'Egyptian' shrine. The decor included granite columns (above), Amazon caryatids, figured mosaic floors including the myth of Achilles and Penthesileia, the labours of Herakles, and Dido and Aeneas. There was a profusion of free-standing sculpture, the subject-matter apparently influenced by Hadrian's villa at Tivoli, which Herodes must have seen.

Lakonia

Lakonia is bordered by mountains, hence the Homeric epithet 'hollow Lakedaimon'. Parnon cuts off the east coast and Taygetos provides an even more dramatic barrier between Lakonia and Messenia. The precipitous slopes of Taygetos reflect the fact that a major faultline runs along the base of the range. The consequence is geological instability and frequent earthquakes which form a leitmotif in Spartan history. Plutarch (*Kimon* 16) records that in 464 BC, 'the country suffered the most terrible earthquake in its history. The earth opened in many places, several of the peaks of Taygetos were torn away and the whole city of Sparta was destroyed, with the exception of five houses'.

Because of the mountains, land which can be intensively cultivated is restricted. The SPARTA plain is certainly fertile and the Eurotas is one of the few perennial rivers in the Peloponnese. When Telemachos visits Menelaos in the *Odyssey* (4.602–4) he admires the 'wide plain, where clover grows in plenty and galingale is found, with wheat and rye and broad-eared white barley'. But much of the Helos plain in southern Lakonia is recent alluvium, the Mani peninsula is extremely barren and the Malea peninsula is also quite rugged. No wonder the Spartans coveted Messenia. Lakonia did have mineral resources: deposits of iron ore around Neapolis, the *lapis Lacedaemonius* quarries at Krokeai and the *antico rosso* quarries at Kyprianon. Yet harbours were few and, except for GYTHEION, relatively inaccessible from Sparta. Inevitably there were times when the city became isolated and this must have fostered a sense of independence.

Evidence for the Neolithic period comes from the Alepotrypa cave at DIROS in the Mani but there has been more interest in the later prehistory of Lakonia, not least because Sparta is the home of Menelaos, brother of Agamemnon, husband of Helen, and one of the most powerful Greek chiefs in the Homeric epics. This has reinforced the belief that there must be a Mycenaean palace in Lakonia. Since Sparta may not have been settled until the C10 BC, attention has focused on the MENELAION, PELLANA, and VAPHEIO. In the early Mycenaean period these sites benefited from the economic opportunities created when the Minoans colonized Kastri on Kythera. The Cretan connection is particularly apparent in the spectacular offerings from the Vapheio tholos tomb, and the mansions at the Menelaion anticipate later Mycenaean palaces, such as PYLOS. But the major administrative centre which we would expect in the C14–C13 remains elusive. Although there is evidence of continuity at AMYKLAI, few other sites were still occupied in the C12.

Amyklai apart, Geometric Lakonia saw serious depopulation, simplifying Sparta's project of conquest which was complete by *c.*700 BC. The

Lakonians, Doric speakers like their masters, now became 'dwellers around' (*perioikoi*), locally self-governing but otherwise subjects. Gytheion, the most important of these communities, was Sparta's port and naval base. Their history now merges with that of Sparta until 195 BC, when Rome liberated the Lakonian cities. Either now or in 146 BC they were federated into a 'League of the Lakedaimonians' which formally excluded Sparta, although the old hegemon reasserted control in the later C1 BC, until a second and final divorce under Augustus, who founded the 'League of the Free Lakonians'. Originally made up of 24 cities, its membership was reduced to eighteen in the time of Pausanias (3.21.7). In the imperial era the Free Lakonian towns like EPIDAUROS LIMERA, TAINARON, and Gytheion, enjoyed a modest prosperity as ports.

Sparta (Figs. 86–87)

Special Features

Although traces of ancient Sparta's greatness are hard to find, the natural setting is stunning, and the museum has interesting finds from nearby sites as well as Sparta itself.

History

The site of Sparta with its low akropolis may have been settled by the C10 BC. The Spartans, newcomers who spoke Doric Greek, expanded south by conquest, taking AMYKLAI by *c.*750 BC and then the rest of the Spartan plain, reducing the subject population to helots or state serfs, and going on to make all Lakonia a Spartan dependency. From the C6 into the C4 the Spartans, at the head of a Peloponnese-based military alliance, were the most formidable land power in Greece. With their victory in the Peloponnesian War (404 BC) they even became heirs for a brief time to the Aegean empire of ATHENS. To the Athenians it seemed extraordinary that such a great city 'is not brought together in a single town and is not adorned with magnificent temples and public edifices, but composed of villages after the old fashion of Greece' (Thucydides 1.10.2). This contrast is borne out by the modesty of the sanctuary of Artemis Orthia. The finds here shed light on the harsh public education of the young which contributed to the city's success in war. Attributed to the law-giver Lykourgos, this martial way of life had gradually displaced the more cultured milieu of Archaic times, reflected in the C6 BC refinements of Amyklai. Defeat by THEBES at Leuktra (371 BC) reduced Sparta to a middling Greek power. Internal problems triggered attempts at reform (C3 BC), continued under Nabis (207–192 BC), Sparta's last king. Most surviving remains date no earlier than the C1 BC, when Sparta was a favoured 'free' city under Roman rule. Sparta now was little different from other prosperous provincial cities of comparable size, except that Roman admiration for the Sparta of old prompted a reinvention of the 'Lykourgan customs', an archaizing veneer of public rituals which the Spartans kept up from the later C2 BC at least to the early C4 AD. The city seems to have escaped an attack by the Herulian Goths (268) relatively unscathed. It was attacked again by Alaric (396), prompting a new inner-city wall. The city had a bishop by 457, and a major church on the akropolis by the 600s.

Description

The **Archaeological Museum** is in the centre of the modern town. In the porch, as you go in, is a large inscribed block from a statue-base (AD 202–204), with examples of Roman 'damnation of memory' (*damnatio memoriae*), the official erasure of the titles of a disgraced person, here enacted against the wife and father-in-law of the emperor Caracalla. In the hall (on the walls) are stone stelai for dedications of sickles from the sanctuary of Artemis Orthia (**box**). **Room 1** has mosaics from luxurious buildings in Roman Sparta, home to a thriving local school in this art (C3–C4 AD). **Room 2** includes marble architectural elements from the 'Throne of Apollo' at Amyklai; reliefs of the heroized dead, their worship particularly popular in Lakonia, and including one (no. 1005, late C6 BC) inscribed with the name of the Spartan statesman Chilon, whose hero-shrine was seen by Pausanias (3.16.4); and reliefs of the demigod twins Kastor and Polydeukes (the Dioskouroi), also Spartan favourites, no. 575 showing the swan's egg from which Helen their sister was born (see MENELAION), as well as lidded amphorae, perhaps prizes in games. **Room 3** has Sparta's most famous statue, of an armoured Spartan warrior (*c.*490 BC); also the Damonon inscription (*c.*450–425 BC), a record of horse-races in Lakonian festivals won by teams from a rich Spartan's own stables. **Room 4** (left of entrance) includes finds from various Spartan sanctuaries, including remarkable votive masks (C6 BC) from the shrine of Artemis Orthia, probably clay replicas of ones worn by

Spartan initiations

The iron sickles (one is still preserved) were prizes awarded to Spartan youths victorious in contests held in honour of Artemis Orthia. Most were won for songs and dances to do with hunting, the domain of Artemis. The oldest (with sockets for five sickles) dates from the C4 BC, although the majority are no earlier than the C1 BC. In origin the contests were initiation rites for the rising generation of Spartan warriors. In Roman times they were put on more as 'heritage' performances for rich tourists from all over the empire.

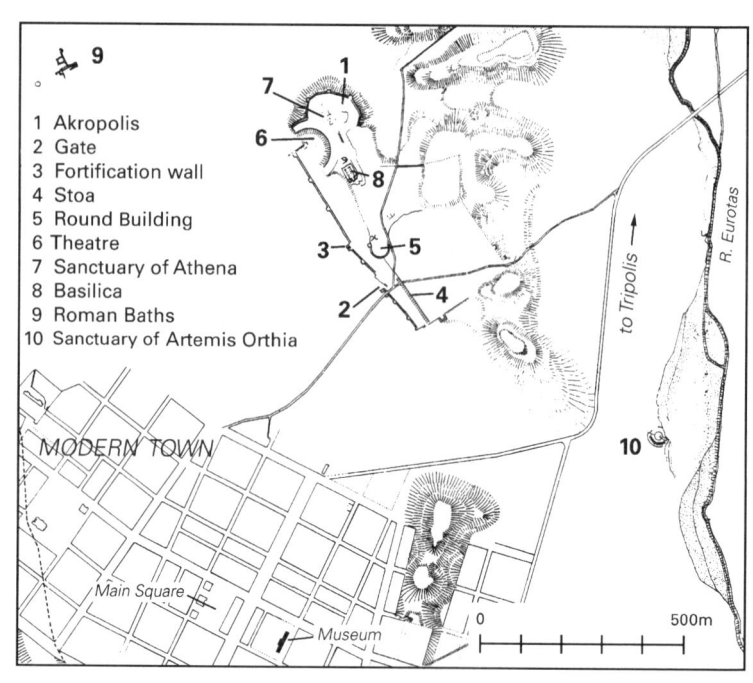

▲ Fig. 86. Plan of Sparta

Spartan youths in initiation practices. **Room 5** features a model of a Roman galley from Cape Malea, **room 6** (by the stairs) prehistoric finds from the Alepotrypa cave at DIROS in the Mani. **Room 7** has material from Mycenaean cemeteries in Lakonia.

The **akropolis** [1] and remains in the vicinity, the heart of the ancient city, lie north of the modern town amid olive groves and can be reached by following the main street up to the modern statue of Leonidas, then taking the track to the left of the sports ground. The surviving ruins mostly date from Roman imperial times.

Follow the track up until you reach a **gate** [2] in the late-Roman **fortification wall** [3]. The builders reused many pieces of older classical architecture in the lower courses as a device against battering rams. The wall encloses the whole Spartan akropolis, and is now thought to date from soon after 396, with later repairs.

From here on your right are the remains (fenced and inaccessible) of a huge brick-faced **stoa** ([4]—C2 AD). Its barrel-vaulted compartments, perhaps used as shops, were originally faced with coloured marble, with a public fountain in the middle. The colonnade in front of this once-impressive structure has long since gone. Pausanias wrote (3.11.3) that 'the most striking monument in the agora is called the Persian Stoa, built from the spoils of the Persian wars. It was altered in the course of time until it reached the size and decorative splendour you now see.' Could this be it, after its final reconstruction?

To the west c.60 m. is the so-called **Round Building** [5], a prominent mound retained by a circular wall of pre-Roman date. It was remodelled in Roman times when it supported an open circular colonnade with statues inside.

To reach the **theatre** [6] c.300 m. to the west from here, follow the track below the Round Building. Built into the south slope of the akropolis, with a fine facing of local marble admired by Pausanias, it dates to c.20 BC, although the Spartans repeatedly upgraded its stage. In 1997 British archaeologists found clinching evidence for an old theory that the first stage was on wheels and could be moved out of sight into a scenery store (*skanotheke*) of stone and brick in front of the west retaining wall, where an excavation trench preserves sections of two of the three rows of grooved blocks for the wheels. The idea for this moving stage (presumably wooden) looks Roman. In AD 78 a fixed stage of Roman type was built, with a Corinthian facade. To this belongs an inscribed block (*IG* 5.1.691) now near the south gate to the site. The letters ΟΥΕΣΠΑΣ, from the Greek for 'Vespasian', identify the Roman emperor who funded the work. The Spartans used the theatre for normal theatrical events, for ball contests between teams of young Spartans, and probably also for political meetings. On the east retaining wall there are 37 or so commemorative inscriptions of c. AD 80–180. They record either names of annual boards of local politicians, or their individual careers, as with the Hadrianic Eudokimos (lowest inscribed course, about half way along), who boasts that 'in none of my three missions to buy grain for the city did I have to throw overboard any of my cargo', in order to save ships in a storm.

Above the theatre are scrappy foundations of the C6 BC **Sanctuary of Athena Chalkioikos** ([7]—Athena of the Bronze House), named for the lost cladding of bronze reliefs on the temple, and (to the east) an impressive three-apsed **basilica** ([8]—C5–7 AD).

For the mustard-keen, some 600 m. north-west of the theatre are overgrown remains of **Roman baths** [9], perhaps once part of the Gymnasium of Eurykles, a Spartan senator of the early C2 AD (Pausanias 3.14.6).

The **Sanctuary of Artemis Orthia** [10] is north-east of the town-centre, on the right bank of the Eurotas. Take the road on the left (signed) at the junction where the main road from Tripolis turns right into the modern town. A short distance along this road, take the dirt track which branches off to the right. The site, 200 m. further down, is fenced but accessible. You can make out the foundations of a small, non-colonnaded, Doric temple (C2 BC, the third on the site), a low altar (Roman) over a C6 BC predecessor, and a massive substructure of rubble masonry. This once supported a near-amphitheatre (late C3 AD), with

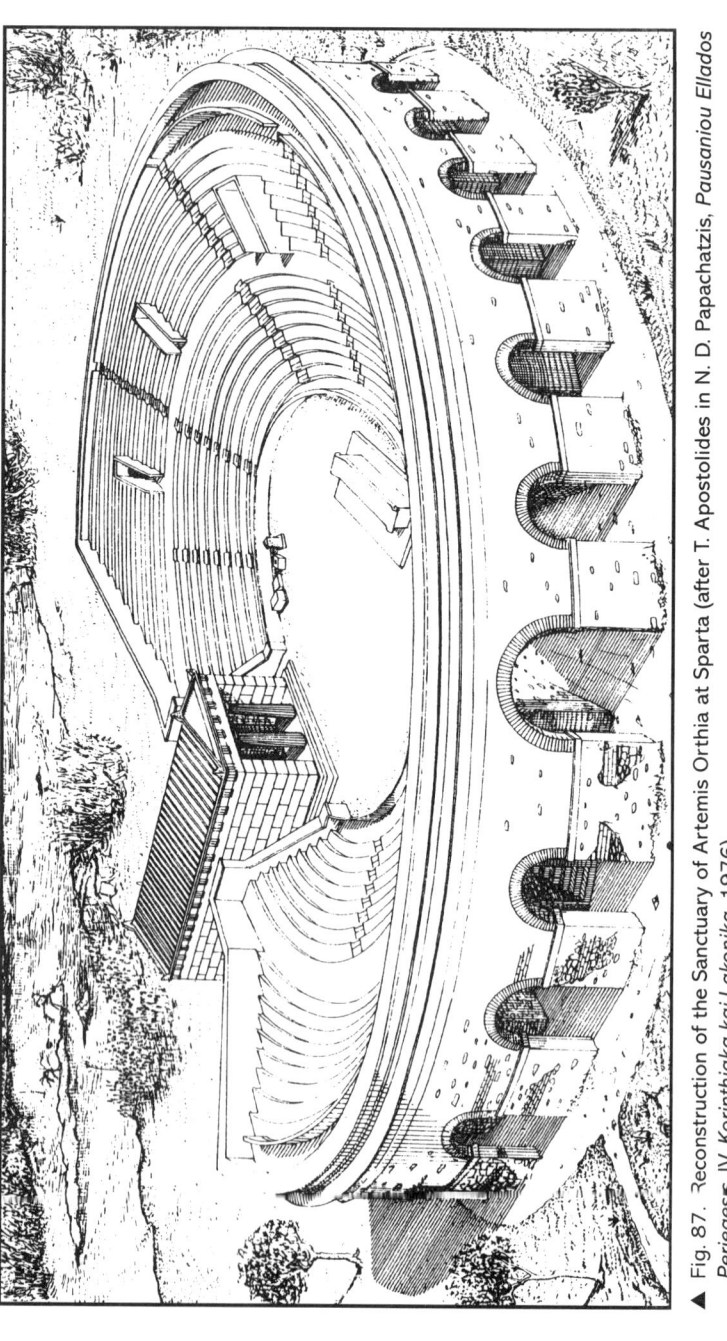

▲ Fig. 87. Reconstruction of the Sanctuary of Artemis Orthia at Sparta (after T. Apostolides in N. D. Papachatzis, *Pausaniou Ellados Periegeses*, IV, *Korinthiaka kai Lakonika*, 1976)

the facade of the temple instead of a stage-building. It was built for the audience at the goddess's annual contests, held in the 'arena' so formed (see **box**). The chief draw was 'The Whips', in which relays of Spartan youths 'with hands held up' endeavoured to stay silent while being flogged over the altar, hard enough for their blood to flow—a later reinvention of a C4 BC ritual played around the altar. Not far from the site entrance is a well-preserved statue base (early C3 AD) praising a local official for his 'championing of the customs of Lykourgos', which these gruesome contests claimed to represent.

Menelaion (Figs. 88–90)

Leave Sparta on the Tripolis road. After the bridge over the Eurotas, take the first turn on the right which is signed Geraki/Chrysapha. Continue straight along this road for 3 km. until you see a sign for the Menelaion Archaeological Site. A track, surfaced in concrete, leads to the church of Zoodochos Piqi where you should park. The track continues beyond the church and climbs quite steeply at first. A walk of 10–15 minutes will bring you to the Menelaion ridge which is marked by a sign.

Special Features

The Menelaion is the site of one of the best-preserved early Mycenaean architectural complexes and the hero shrine of Menelaos and Helen. There is a fine view of the Eurotas valley and the Taygetos mountains.

History

A number of ancient writers mention the shrine of Menelaos and Helen. Herodotus records that (6.61):

When Ariston was king of Sparta, although he married twice, he had no children. Unwilling to admit that this might be his own fault, he married a third time—and in the following circumstances: he had a friend, a Spartan citizen, with whom he was particularly intimate, and this friend's wife was much the most beautiful woman in Sparta. Oddly enough, she had been as a child extremely plain, and owed the transformation to her nurse, who, seeing that she was not much to look at, and well aware, moreover, that her parents, who were people of substance, were distressed at having such an ugly baby, conceived the idea of carrying her every day to the shrine of Helen at Therapne, above the temple of Apollo. She would then take the baby in, lay it down in front of Helen's statue, and pray the goddess to take away its ugliness. One day as the nurse left the shrine, a woman appeared and asked what it was that she had in her arms. The nurse replied that it was a baby. The woman asked to see it, but the nurse refused, for the child's parents had forbidden her to show it to anybody. The woman, however, persisted, and at last the nurse, seeing how extremely anxious she was to have a look at the baby, showed it to her. Thereupon the stranger stroked the baby's head and declared that it would grow up to be the most beautiful woman in Sparta. From that very day there was a change in its appearance. The child grew up, and, as soon as she was old enough, was married to Agetos, the son of Alkides—Ariston's friend.

The conspicuous monument on the Menelaion ridge, high above the River Eurotas, was tentatively identified as the site of Therapne in the C19. Schliemann came in search of the palace of Menelaos but was unsuccessful for once and it was not until 1909 that the existence of a major Mycenaean settlement was revealed by the British School at Athens. Excavation of the site resumed in 1973.

The Menelaion was first occupied in the Middle Helladic period and the settlement eventually stretched for over a kilometre along the ridge. In the C15 BC a mansion was constructed, presumably for the ruler. Architecturally it anticipates the plan of later Mycenaean palaces, in particular PYLOS, and may have served as an administrative centre. The Menelaion was clearly one of the principal early Mycenaean sites in Lakonia. The mansion was rebuilt early in the C14 but only remained in use for a short time. There is no trace of a palace and consequently we still do not know whether the Menelaion was Mycenaean SPARTA, although this does seem quite likely. In the late C13 the mansion was repaired and reoccupied. It was then destroyed by fire and for several centuries the site was neglected.

The first dedications were made in the late C8 BC, almost certainly in honour of Menelaos and Helen, although their names do not appear in inscriptions until the Archaic period. It is surely no coincidence that the Spartans should have chosen this site for the shrine. The Homeric epics had inspired an interest in the past but these hero-cults had a contemporary relevance. Although their claim on Menelaos might have been rather tenuous, the Spartans saw themselves as his heirs, the rightful rulers of Lakonia. At first there may simply have been an altar but in the late C7 or early C6 a shrine was built of poros limestone. The conglomerate platform was added in the C5 and no doubt commemorated the victory over the Persians. There is a steady decline in the number of votives in the Classical period and Hellenistic Spartans were even less interested, although a cult for Helen persisted on the plain below into Roman times.

Description

The early Mycenaean mansions were constructed on a natural terrace at the eastern end of the site. Mansion 1 consisted of three units separated by corridors, an arrangement which is replicated in the Palace of Nestor at Pylos two centuries later. Moreover, the central unit of Mansion 1 has exactly the same plan—porch, vestibule, and inner room—as the throne room at Pylos. It is likely that there were similar early Mycenaean

Lakonia 227

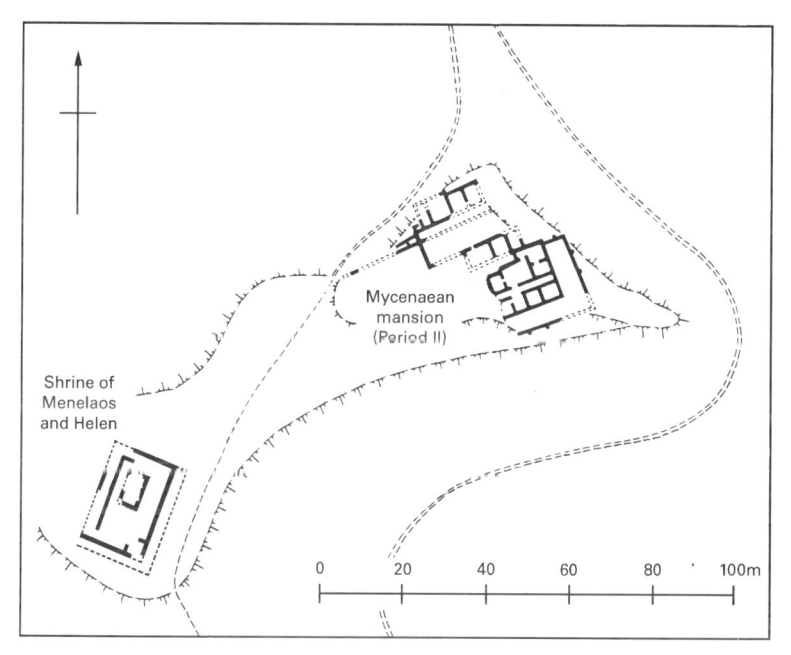

▲ Fig. 88. Plan of the Menelaion

▼ Fig. 89. The shrine of Menelaos and Helen at the Menelaion

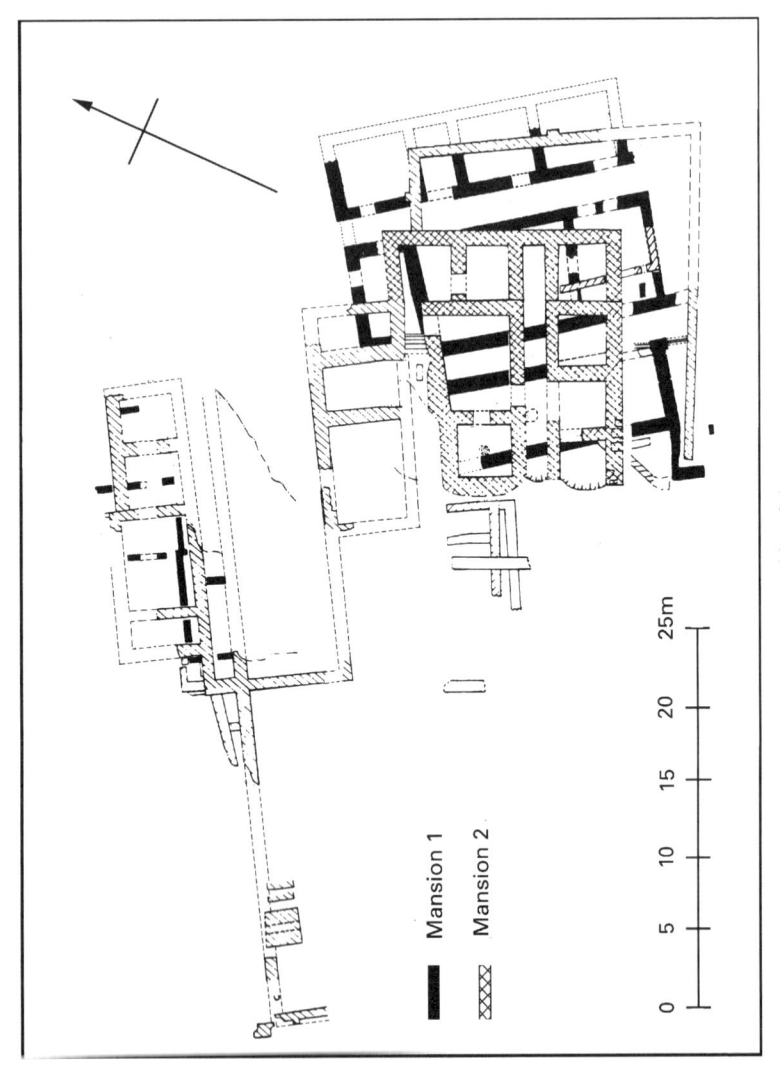

▲ Fig. 90. Plan of the Mycenaean mansions at the Menelaion

architectural complexes at MYCENAE, Pylos and TIRYNS which were levelled when the palaces were built in the C14 BC.

The mansion evidently became unsafe, possibly because of an earthquake, and was rebuilt further from the edge of the terrace. Mansion 2 faces west rather than south but has the same basic plan, despite the fact that it is on two levels. Bear in mind that Mansion 1 is underneath Mansion 2 and the tangle of walls should make sense. Some modifications were made when the mansion was reoccupied in the late C13.

The shrine of Menelaos and Helen consists of a rectangular platform built of blocks of conglomerate, which must once have been at least 5 m. high. There is a ramp on the west side of the platform, thoughtfully provided for the sacrificial victims which might have balked at steps. The structure on top of the platform is not well preserved. There may have been an altar and/or a shrine for the statues of Menelaos and Helen.

Pellana

Leave Sparta by the Tripolis road and take the left turn for Kastori/Georgitsi just before the bridge over the Eurotas. Continue along this road for 20 km. and then turn right at the sign for Πελλανα/Κονιδιτσα. After 4 km. you enter the village of Pellana. Bear left at the sign for the Archaeological Territory and then straight on at the sign for the Graves of Mikines which are 750 m. from the centre of the village.

Special Features

A pleasant excursion into the foothills of Taygetos which follows the line of the ancient road between SPARTA and MEGALOPOLIS. Pellana is the site of some of the most impressive Mycenaean chamber tombs.

History

The akropolis of Palaiokastro was occupied from the Early Helladic period but it is the Mycenaean chamber tomb cemetery which has prompted speculation about the role of Pellana as a political centre. Although the tombs have been plundered, their sheer size implies wealth and status. It has been argued that Pellana, rather than the MENELAION or VAPHEIO, must have been Homeric Sparta but the site seems rather remote. The akropolis was fortified in the C4 or C3 BC when Sparta was under threat. Pausanias mentions a barricade and also (3.21): 'the sanctuary of Asklepios and the spring called Pellanis. They say that a young girl fell into this spring and disappeared, and her scarf came up in another spring called Lankia.'

Description

Five chamber tombs have been excavated in the cemetery. A narrow passage leads to the entrance of the tomb which was carefully blocked by stones at the end of each funeral. The circular chambers were clearly inspired by tholos tombs. The shape of the chamber is identical but the method of construction is different, since tholos tombs were stone-built rather than rock-cut. One of the tombs is enormous, over 10 m. in diameter. The vault has collapsed and the tomb is now protected, rather appropriately, by a bronze roof. Note the deep pits in the other tombs. These were used as ossuaries when there was no more room in the chamber. Pottery from the tombs is on display in the museum in Sparta.

As you re-enter the village, the akropolis of Pellana, Palaiokastro, is on your left. Recent excavations have revealed circular Early Helladic structures, a paved Mycenaean road, Classical-Hellenistic houses, and a Byzantine cistern.

Amyklai and Vapheio

For Amyklai, leave Sparta on the Gytheion road. Just after you enter the village of Amikles there is a turn on the left for the Temple of Apollo Amyklaios. Further signs direct you to the sanctuary.

Just beyond Amikles there is a sign for the Ancient Place Vafeio. Turn right in the village of Vapheio and 2.4 km. from the main road you will reach a sign for the Vaulted Tomb of Vafio. There is a stone-paved path which leads to the tomb.

Special Features

Neither of these sites has particularly impressive architectural remains but they can easily be reached and are attractively located amongst citrus and olive groves.

Description

Amyklai

The hilltop view still evokes the fertility of ancient Amyklai, which had 'the finest trees, and the most fruitful crops, in Lakonia' (Polybius 5.19.2). The double-sanctuary of Apollo and Hyakinthos here was one of SPARTA's most famous shrines throughout antiquity. In myth Hyakinthos was accidentally killed by Apollo, his lover. He may have been a local hero worshipped by the Amyklaians, with Apollo installed by Spartan conquerors c.750 BC. The Spartans held a major annual festival here, the Hyakınthıa, when they mourned the dead hero, boys sang hymns and girls raced chariots, 'and the city is emptied to see the spectacle' (Athenaeus 4.139–40).

The chapel of Ayia Kyriaki is on the site of the **Throne of Apollo** (C6 BC), an innovative structure commissioned from an east Greek architect, Bathykles of Magnesia, comprising columns, caryatids, and mythical reliefs which framed the god's open-air statue (C7 BC?). This was an eye-catching 15 m. high bronze pillar with helmeted face, feet and hands, standing on a hollow base, supposedly where Hyakinthos was buried. Downslope from the church, to the south, an original retaining wall is still in place, running round the east end of the church and standing to a height of four courses in places.

To the north-west of the church is a conspicuous base showing that the cult was flourishing in the early C3 AD. The inscription praises an aristocratic Spartan grandmother, Pompeia Polla, for her 'modesty and reverence' while performing ceremonial tasks during the Hyakinthian games here.

Vapheio

The Mycenaean tholos tomb at Vapheio was excavated in 1888 by Christos Tsountas, one of the pioneers of Aegean archaeology. The vault of the tomb had collapsed and the chamber had been looted. However, the robbers had not noticed that there was a grave cut in the floor. The cover slabs were removed and revealed a fabulous array of items but no skeleton—this had evidently disintegrated. Since the offerings included a bronze sword, nine knives and daggers, two spears, and two axes, it is assumed that a man was buried in the grave. Where his hands would have been there were two gold cups, the famous Vapheio cups on display in the National Archaeological Museum in ATHENS. Sealstones, some of the finest from Mycenaean Greece, lay by his wrists and may have been worn as bracelets. Some of these sealstones were certainly imported from Crete, others may been commissioned by this wealthy individual who died in the C15. He came from the settlement at Palaiopyrgi, the prominent flat-topped hill south-east of the tomb, which he must once have ruled.

The tomb is surrounded by a fence and is not accessible at present because the walls have been shored up. The size of the tomb is impressive and you can see how the chamber was constructed. There is not much visible on the hill of Palaiopyrgi.

Epidauros Limera (Fig. 91) ★

4.5 km. north of Monemvasia there is a sign for Epidauros Limera Archaeological Site. After 1.3 km. turn right for Επίδαυρος Λιμηράς. The site is a further c.2 km. and is marked by a sign.

Special Features

The site has fine fortifications, an excellent beach (Pausanias admired its multi-coloured pebbles) and can easily be combined with a visit to the Byzantine town of Monemvasia.

Lakonia

History

There was a Mycenaean settlement on the akropolis and chamber tombs have been excavated nearby. The small classical city was allegedly a colony of its famous namesake in the Argolid, and its epithet already baffled the ancients. Occupying an akropolis overlooking the sea, it was a gateway to the interior of Lakonia like its Byzantine successor to the south, Monemvasia, and its harbour offered a way-station for ships coasting the Peloponnese. Freed from Spartan domination in 195 BC, the Epidaurians joined the Lakedaimonian, and then the Free Lakonian, League. Pausanias came here by sea, and noted as many as four sanctuaries 'worth seeing' (3.23.10), implying a certain prosperity in imperial times.

Description

The principal feature is the Classical fortifications. The best-preserved section, enclosing the slopes on the east side of the akropolis, can be seen from the road. An extension inland (after 350 BC), now badly preserved, took in the flat land behind the akropolis, and encloses ruins of ancient buildings, some with traces of wall-plaster (C2 BC).

▼ Fig. 91. Plan of Epidauros Limera

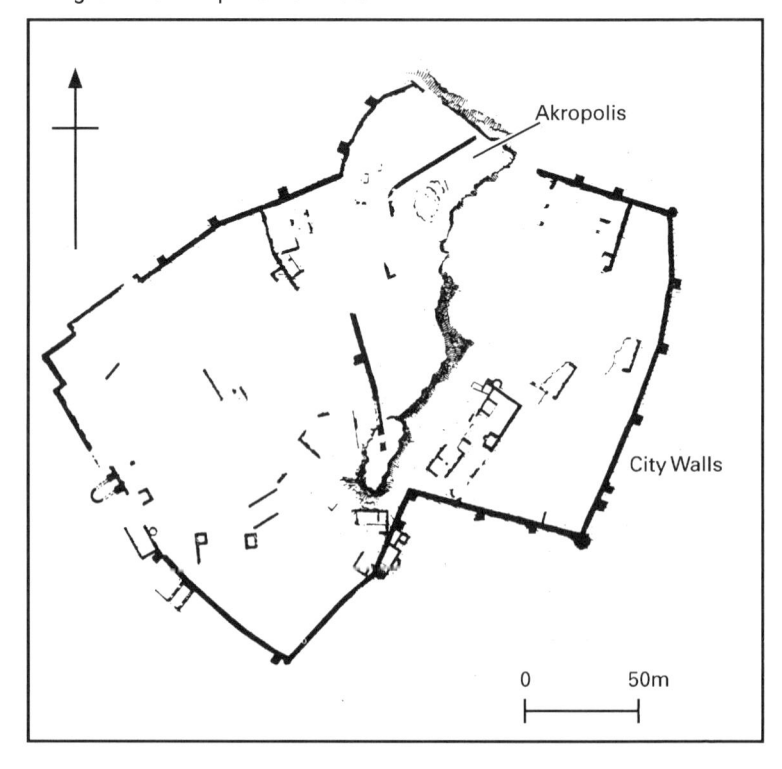

Gytheion

Special Features

Except for the theatre, there is not much to see in Gytheion, but it is an attractive seaside town and a good base from which to explore southern Lakonia. There is a superb beach at Mavrovouni, 5 km. to the south.

History

Gytheion, the chief port of Lakonia, was also the main harbour of SPARTA, even after the city's liberation by the Roman general Flamininus, whose memory its citizens still venerated in AD 15. The two cities were linked by a highway, sturdy enough in imperial times for the transport of heavy goods. There was an engineered harbour, formed by a jetty linking the islet of Krana to the mainland, protecting ships from the south wind. Roman businessmen were attracted here, and a famous inscription from Gytheion (71 BC) shows a pair of bankers, the brothers Cloatii, lending money at 48% interest per year so that the city could pay taxes to Roman officials who were cosily housed in the brothers' mansion. From Augustus on Gytheion was the capital of the Free Lakonian League. The Roman city was important enough to merit an aqueduct.

Description

Soon after you enter the town, before you reach the harbour, there is a left turn signed **Ancient Theatre**, which is c.400 m. straight down this road, by an army camp. Perhaps late Hellenistic, it seems to be mentioned in the inscription for the Cloatii (above) who were given the right to front-row seats at festivals. Some thrones are preserved. Another inscription from Gytheion, of c. AD 15, shows the theatre in action during a festival for the Roman emperor. Before the assembled townsfolk, incense was burnt in front of images of Augustus, Livia, and Tiberius on a table in the orchestra. There were also shows, for which local officials had to supply 'the platform for the chorus and four doors for stage performances'.

Diros ★

Take the road south from Areopolis and after 8 km. turn right at Pirgos Dirou for the Diros Caves.

Special Features

The Vlichada cave, which you tour by boat, has spectacular stalagmites and is one of the major tourist attractions in the Mani. The adjacent Alepotrypa cave was occupied in the Neolithic period.

Description

The Alepotrypa cave is not open at present but there is a display of finds in the **Archaeological Museum** and panels in Greek and English which outline the history of the site. The cave was occupied from *c.*5300 BC, in the Late Neolithic period. It was not the agricultural land around the cave which attracted the first settlers. Like so much of the Mani, Diros is dry and rugged and must have been a poor prospect for Neolithic farmers. However, the deep bay would have made this an obvious port of call for sailors and fishermen, since the southern coast of the Peloponnese can be extremely treacherous. No doubt they sheltered in the cave, where they discovered that there was a fresh water lake, and eventually a group of families made this their base. The presence of fish bones and sea shells confirms that the sea was a source of food and there is evidence of trade activity as well. Obsidian, the volcanic glass used for chipped stone tools, marble, copper, and silver were imported. The animal bones from the cave indicate that the settlers kept cattle, sheep, and goats, while deer and boar were hunted.

The cave is 280 m. in length and consists of a series of chambers. Families occupied niches in the sides of these chambers but apparently stored and cooked their food communally. The cave was a home for these people in death as well as in life. Adults were buried in pits and then in due course their skulls were placed in ossuaries. Some of the children had been cremated. Study of the skeletons suggests that conditions may not have been ideal. Anaemia, arthritis and malaria were common and the average life expectancy for adults was only 35 years. Occupation of the cave ended dramatically *c.*3200 BC, in the Final Neolithic period. It seems that an earthquake blocked the entrance of the cave. Those who were not killed instantly died of starvation and in time a layer of calcium carbonate formed over their bones. The final display case in the museum conveys a sense of how awful this disaster must have been.

Tainaron (Fig. 92) ★

Just beyond Vathia, at the southern end of the Mani peninsula, there is a blue sign for Ταίναρο. *Approximately 3.2 km. from this sign take the right fork down towards the sea—follow the sign for the* ΨΑΡΟΤΑΒΕΡΝΑ. *After 0.6 km. bear left at the junction for* Πάλυρος *and then after a further 1.0 km. turn right onto a dirt road at the sign for the Sanctuary and Death Oracle of Poseidon Tainarios. A short distance down this dirt road take the left fork for* Ταίναρο. *The site is 2.4 km. down the dirt road on a headland which is marked by the ruined church of Ayioi Asomatoi.*

Special Features

Archaeologically this is not a particularly important site, but you have to travel the length of the Mani and pass through a number of traditional villages set in splendidly austere countryside. It does feel like a journey to the ends of the earth.

History

Cape Tainaron, modern Cape Matapan, is the south tip of the Mani peninsula. It forms a promontory some 5 km. long, its isthmus flanked by two bays, of which modern Porto Kayio ('Quail Harbour') to the east is the likely site of Psamathous, the chief ancient port here. Tainaron proper is a small bay *c*.1.6 km. short of the point to its east, and is also known as Porto Asomato from its chief feature, a chapel of the Ayios Asomatos. In antiquity the region belonged to Lakonia, and until 195 BC was dependent on SPARTA. Depopulated today, it was far busier in antiquity, as a staging point for coast-hugging ships, and (late C4 BC) as a market for mercenaries, with up to 10,000 men camped probably at Porto Kayio. In Roman times, its quarries of 'Tainarian' marble were popular, both red (*rosso antico*) from a site north of the peninsula and black, from quarries north-west of the chapel.

The sanctuary of Poseidon here is attested from the C5 BC. Sparta allowed it to function as an asylum for refugee helots or state serfs, although they were dragged out on one occasion and killed (Thucydides 1.128.1). It must have been frequented by passing ships, and in Hellenistic times was wealthy enough to attract pirates. It had a

▼ Fig. 92. Plan of Tainaron

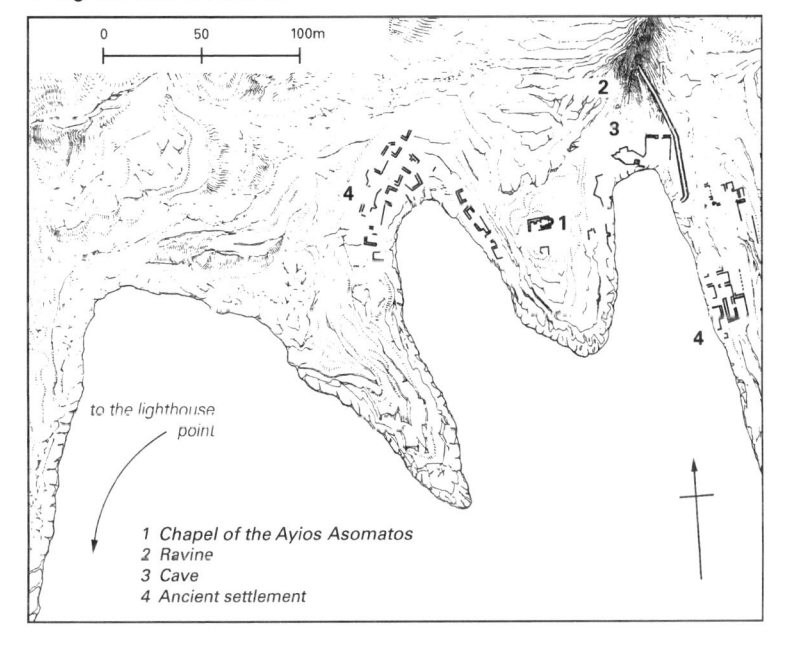

1 Chapel of the Ayios Asomatos
2 Ravine
3 Cave
4 Ancient settlement

long-standing reputation as an entrance to Hades, based on the existence of a cave, although this claim was scorned by Pausanias. The ancient evidence for the oracle of the dead which some scholars place here is poor. The sanctuary was used by the Lakedaimonian League for the display of inscribed decrees, and still existed in the C2 AD. By the late C1 BC the settlement had relocated to 'New City', officially also called Tainaron, a roomier site to the north at modern Kiparissos (on the west coast, 2 km. south of Yerolimena).

Description

Ancient blocks reused in the **chapel** [1], especially the north side, come from a rectagular (?) Hellenistic structure on the same site. Could this have been the oracle? In the bay 60 m. to the east of the church is a small shallow **ravine** [2] and a **natural cave** [3] with blocks in front, part of a rectangular ancient foundation, partly buried in the shingle. This seems the most likely candidate for the 'shrine like a cave with a statue of Poseidon in front of it' seen by Pausanias (3.25.4). There are ample traces of the ancient **settlement** [4] both further east and around the bay to the west of the church (rock-cut platforms, perhaps for the huts of asylum-seekers, and also cisterns). Further west, the bay beyond this has a rather fine **mosaic** with a spiral motif in the central emblema.

Messenia

Euripides described Messenia as a land 'with fine fruit, watered by innumerable streams, with excellent pasture for cattle and sheep, not too stormy in the blasts of winter, nor made too hot by the chariot of the sun ... more fertile than words can express' (quoted by Strabo in *Geography* 8.5.6). The flood plain of the River Pamisos, which stretches north from KALAMATA, was known in antiquity as Makaria—blessed. The west of the province, a plateau dissected by rivers, is also intensively cultivated. Although much of the coast is rather exposed, Messenia does have a number of fine harbours, in particular Navarino, Koroni, and Methoni (ancient Methone).

In the early Mycenaean period Messenia enjoyed a degree of prosperity rivalled only by sites in the Argolid. It was the dead who were the principal beneficiaries of this wealth. The elite were buried in tholos tombs with gold cups, intricate jewellery, and inlaid daggers. It seems unlikely that Messenia was politically unified at this time and we can tentatively identify a number of independent centres which include Nichoria, PERISTERIA, and PYLOS. The source of their wealth is more of a mystery but trade may have been a contributory factor. By the C13 BC Pylos had become the capital of Messenia. This is clear from the Linear B tablets which were found in the Palace of Nestor. There were two provinces, subdivided into districts, each under the jurisdiction of a governor. The head of state was a king who presided over an economic system which seems remarkably sophisticated. The tablets were preserved by accident, baked in the fire which destroyed the palace at the end of the C13. Pylos never recovered from this disaster which had serious repercussions for most of the Mycenaean sites in Messenia.

The inhabitants of historic Messenia, like those of Lakonia, were speakers of Dorian Greek. The region went into arrested development after conquest *c.*700 BC by the Spartans. The surviving Messenians either fled into exile or became agricultural serfs, compelled, 'like donkeys worn out with huge burdens', as the poet Tyrtaios grimly put it (fragment 6 West) to give half the harvest to their Spartan masters. Despite revolts, the Spartans remained in control until the liberation of Messenia with the help of the Theban leader Epaminondas in 369 BC. The coastal communities emerging as autonomous cities at this time included Methone on the west peninsula. The history of the region now merges with that of MESSENE, the new city founded in 369, and a central place for Messenia as a whole.

Kalamata

The recently reopened **Archaeological Museum** is in the centre of Kalamata on Odos Benaki, a short distance from the church of Ayioi Apostoloi. There are information boards in English and Greek. Most of the items on display in the four rooms are Roman and come from Koroni (ancient Korone), which is 40 km. from Kalamata on the west side of the Messenian Gulf. There is sculpture, inscriptions, and a fine mosaic of Dionysos. Note in particular the *sekomas*, standard measures made of stone. In the garden there is a huge Geometric burial pithos from Nichoria.

Pylos (Fig. 93)

Special Features

Pylos is an attractive town and makes an excellent base.

History

The precise location of Pylos was the cause of some confusion in antiquity. Strabo (8.3.7) quotes this verse: 'there is a Pylos in front of Pylos and indeed there is still another Pylos'. We now know that Mycenaean Pylos was at Epano Englianos, the site of the Palace of Nestor which is *pu-ro* or Pylos in the Linear B tablets. Classical Pylos was on the Koryphasion promontory, at the north end of Navarino Bay. Modern Pylos only developed as a port in the C16 when the Turks built the Neokastro fortress.

Navarino Bay is one of the finest natural harbours in Greece and has been the scene of two epic military encounters. The first of these was in 425 BC when an Athenian force occupied Pylos and eventually captured 292 Spartans who had been blockaded on the island of Sphakteria. This episode is discussed in detail by Thucydides (4.2–41) who comments that 'it caused much more surprise among the Greeks than anything else that happened in the war—the general impression had been that the Spartans would never surrender their arms'.

In 1827 a British, French, and Russian fleet, which had been instructed to end the conflict between the Greeks and the Turks through peaceful interference, entered the bay and sank most of the Turko-Egyptian fleet commanded by Ibrahim Pasha. This 'untoward event', as it was described in the King's Speech of 1828, ensured that an independent Greek state would be established. Some of the Turkish wrecks can still be seen off Sphakteria.

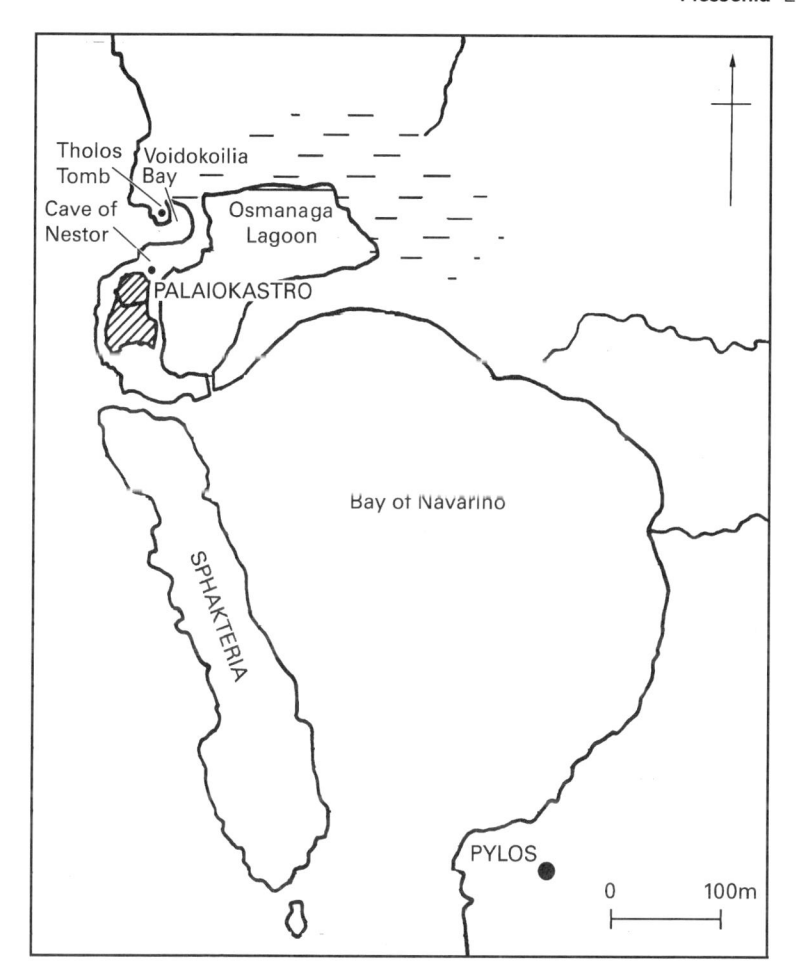

▲ Fig. 93. Plan of the area around Pylos

Description

There is a sign in the square for the **Archaeological Museum** which is on Odos Philellinon (but has recently closed for renovation). The first room has a display of stone tools from various sites in Messenia and Mycenaean pottery, bronzes, jewellery, and sealstones from the tholos tombs at Koukounara, Tourliditsa, Vlachopoulo, VOIDOKOILIA, and the tumulus at Kissos. Note in particular the boars' tusk helmet from Koukounara and the terracotta bathtub from Paleochoria. In the second room there is Hellenistic pottery from the cemetery at Divari, two bizarre Late Roman bronze statues, possibly the Dioskouroi, also fine Hellenistic glass bowls, pottery, lamps, jewellery, iron knives, and strigils from the tumulus at Tsopani-Rachi.

Neokastro, the Turko-Venetian fortress which overlooks the town, is occupied by the Ephorate of Underwater Antiquities and will become a Centre for Underwater Archaeological Research. It has recently been landscaped but when Leake visited Pylos in 1805 there were 'about 300 Turkish families in the fortress, most of them in a wretched state of poverty' (*Travels in the Morea* 1.400). The restored Maison Mansion houses the collection of René Puaux, mainly prints of the Greek War of Independence. In the hexagonal keep, which was formerly a prison, there is information (in Greek) about harbour and wreck sites investigated by the ephorate and also a display of amphorae. The view from the ramparts is superb.

Methoni is 11 km. from Pylos and can be recommended as an excursion. Although few traces of the ancient city remain, the Venetians made Modon—as Methoni was then known—one of their main bases in the Aegean and built the massive fortress which protects the promontory. There is also a sandy beach.

Koryphasion and Voidokoilia ★

Take the Pyrgos road and turn left at the sign for Voidokoilia, 7 km. from Pylos. From the turn it is 4 km. to a path signed Voidokoilia/Nestoros Cave which runs along the western shore of the Osmanaga Lagoon. It will take approximately 15 minutes to reach Voidokoilia. Alternatively continue along the road to Pyrgos and take the turn for Romanos, 11 km. from Pylos. Follow the signs for Voidokoilia/Navarino which is just over 3 km. from the turn.

Special Features

There is a wonderful beach at Voidokoilia—partners should enjoy this site.

Description

On the headland at the northern end of the bay is a Mycenaean **tholos tomb**. It is one of the earliest of these tombs and had been built in a Middle Helladic tumulus which consisted of a stone platform covered by an earth mound. Clearly there was a tradition that the elite buried their dead in this prominent location. Furthermore, a direct link can be made between tumuli and tholos tombs because of their juxtaposition at Voidokoilia. It is therefore likely that the Mycenaeans created the tholos tomb as a more impressive version of the tumulus and Messenia certainly took the lead in this development. As there is evidence of Classical and Hellenistic cult activity, the tomb may be the site of the hero shrine of Thrasymedes which is mentioned by Pausanias (4.36).

The **Cave of Nestor**, on the north slope of the ridge occupied by the castle, can be seen from the bay. Pausanias tells us that this is where

Nestor and his father Neleus herded their cattle. The cave, which is impressive but not spectacular, was occupied in the Neolithic period and there is also Mycenaean pottery.

The **castle** can be reached from the cave by a steep path which is quite a scramble at first. It was on the Koryphasion promontory that the Athenians established their base in 425 BC (see PYLOS). The summit was later fortified and there is Classical masonry incorporated in the walls of the castle. Slavs and Avars settled here in the C6 AD, hence Navarino. The castle was built by the Franks in the C13 and became known as Palaiokastro—the old castle—when it was superseded by Neokastro—the new castle at Pylos—in the C16. The interior is rather overgrown but there is a fine view.

Pylos Palace and Chora Museum (Fig. 94)   ★

The Palace of Nestor is at Epano Englianos, 17 km. from Pylos, on the Pyrgos road.

Special Features

Pylos is the best-preserved and most comprehensible Mycenaean palace. In Chora museum there is an extensive display of finds from the site.

History

In the *Iliad*, the squadron led by Nestor, 'king of sandy Pylos', is exceeded in size only by that of Agamemnon. But whereas the location of MYCENAE was never in question, there were three cities in the western Peloponnese named Pylos, each of which claimed that Nestor was their ancestral ruler. Although Pylos in Messenia seemed the most likely candidate, even Schliemann could not find a Mycenaean palace. It was Blegen who saw the potential of the site at Epano Englianos and by lunch on the first day of his excavations he had discovered substantial walls, fresco fragments, and Linear B tablets. Unfortunately this was in 1939 and he could not continue until 1952. Excavation of the palace was completed in 1966 and there has recently been a survey of the site.

Pylos was evidently a prosperous community in the early Mycenaean period, since three tholos tombs were constructed and have produced some impressive grave offerings, despite the fact that they had been disturbed. It is not clear whether there was a palace at this time, although the akropolis was evidently fortified. Early Mycenaean Messenia may have consisted of a number of independent principalities but by the C13 BC Pylos was the capital of a unified state. This has been deduced from the Linear B tablets preserved in the palace archive, which also tell us that this site is Pylos, even if they do not mention Nestor. It would appear that a palace had been built for the ruler of Pylos by the C14 and this was completely reconstructed in the C13. The settlement stretched for approximately 1 km. and may have been fortified. Pylos does not have the massive Cyclopean defences of MYCENAE or TIRYNS but a geophysical survey on the western side of the ridge has detected a wall at least 60 m. in length. On the coast south-west of Epano Englianos, between Romanos and Tragana, an artificial harbour was constructed. At the end of the C13 the palace was destroyed by fire. We do not know the cause of this catastrophe but Pylos never recovered.

Description

The akropolis has quite steep sides which would have inhibited an attack. Nevertheless, it is curious that the early Mycenaean fortifications were apparently dismantled before the palace was built in the C13. It consists of four units: the Main Building, the South-western Building, the North-eastern Building, and the Wine Magazine. Only the Main Building is accessible at present. It was a two-storey structure, built of rubble and mudbrick. The Mycenaeans made use of a technique which had originally been developed by the Minoans, possibly because of the threat of earthquakes. This was a system of horizontal and vertical timbers which provided a framework for the walls and made them less rigid but also more combustible. You can see where these timbers were placed. Interior walls were plastered and painted in bright colours. The palace may look rather dull now but the main rooms were once decorated in an extremely exuberant style.

The **Main Building** was entered through a propylon [**1–2**]. The stucco collars protected the bases of the wooden columns. In the rooms on the left of the propylon [**7–8**] there were hundreds of Linear B tablets. These were evidently archive rooms, conveniently situated so that palace officials could check what came in and went out. In front of the megaron there is a court [**3**], as at Mycenae and Tiryns. Blegen thought that visitors might have waited in the room [**10**] on the left of the court which has a bench and two wine jars set in a stuccoed stand. They would certainly have enjoyed themselves because there were hundreds of cups stored in the next room [**9**]. Some of these have been left on the floor where they fell and shattered. A quite extraordinary amount of pottery was kept in the rooms on the western side of the Main Building. Over 6000 vessels were recovered from rooms **18–22**, mainly plain cups and kylikes. Consumption of wine—as a social activity, on state occasions or at religious festivals—was clearly encouraged by the palace and no doubt enhanced the reputation of the ruler.

The megaron consists of a porch [**4**], which had two wooden columns and a stand by the door, possibly for a sentry. There is a vestibule [**5**] which could also be entered directly from corridors **13** and **35**. The throne room [**6**] is dominated by an enormous circular hearth, 4 m. in diameter. This must have been symbolic and not simply a source of heat.

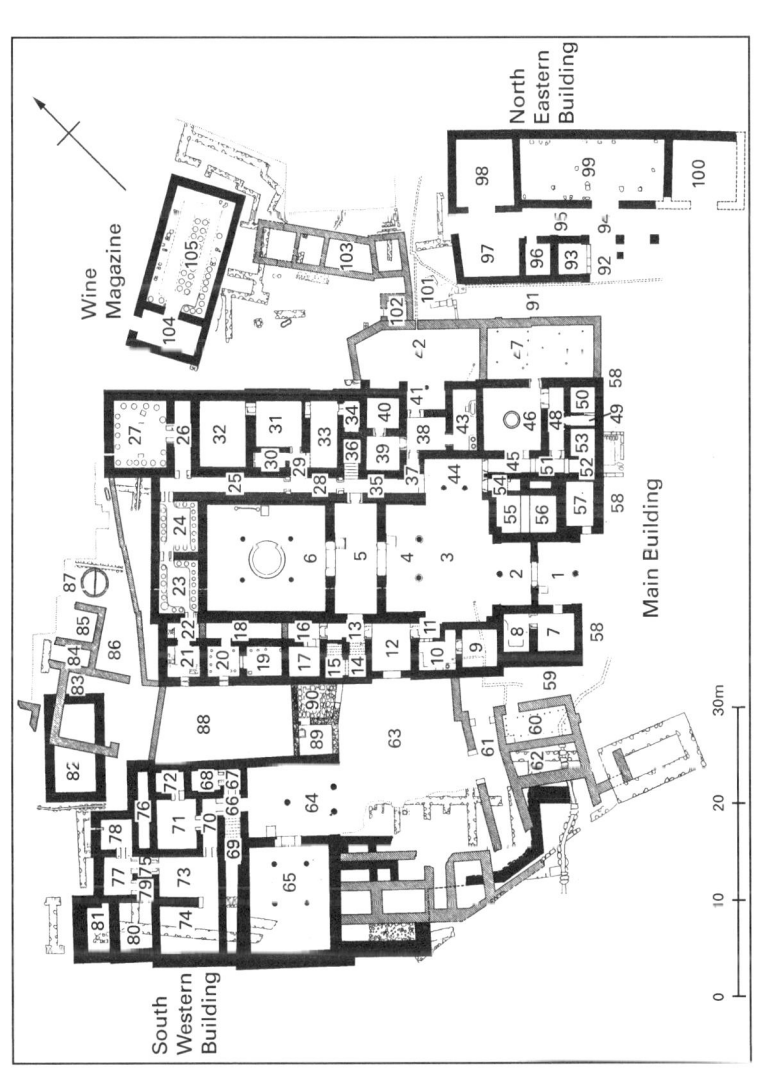

▲ Fig. 94 Plan of the Palace of Nestor at Pylos

Four wooden columns supported a balcony at first-floor level. There was no throne in place but it is assumed that this occupied the base on one side of the room. Two hollows in the floor connected by a shallow channel may have been used for libations. The whole room was sumptuously decorated.

Olive-oil was stored in the clay jars in rooms **23–24** and also in room **27**. Linear B tablets mention oil which is rose-scented and sage-scented, so it would seem that the palace was also a *parfumerie*. The function of the rooms which open off the corridor on the east side of the throne room is uncertain but note the staircase [**36**]; presumably there were domestic apartments on the first floor. Rooms **38–43** form an independent suite, possibly the private quarters of a member of the royal family, since there is a splendid terracotta bathtub in room **43**. The two jars set in a stand may have contained water which was presumably poured over the bather. The adjacent suite of rooms [**45–53**] includes the Queen's Hall [**46**]. The circular hearth in the centre of the room was plastered and painted and the walls were frescoed. There is a drain in the corner of room **53**, which may have been a toilet. It is possible that the palace guard occupied rooms **54–57** beside the main entrance.

The **South-western Building** is covered over at present. It may have been built before the Main Building and is similar in certain respects, in that there is a spacious hall [**64–65**] and rooms full of pottery [**67–68**]. Linear B tablets from the **North-eastern Building** mention repairs and this unit was evidently used by craftsmen who made chariots. It is also on the basis of Linear B inscriptions that rooms **104–105** can be identified as the **Wine Magazine**.

A path leads from the car park to the **tholos tomb**. The vault has been restored and would once have been covered by an earth mound. Although the tomb was robbed, there were some fine pieces of jewellery in the fill.

The **Archaeological Museum** in Chora is 4 km. from the Palace of Nestor. In **room I** there is a display of finds from the Mycenaean chamber tomb cemetery at Volimidia, just north of Chora. Evidence of later cult activity has been observed in several of the tombs. Quite a number of tholos tombs have been excavated in western Messenia. Note in particular the bronze vessels from Tragana, the swords and daggers from Routsi, one of the few tholos tombs which had not been plundered, and the gold cups and jewellery from PERISTERIA. Early Mycenaean Messenia was as wealthy as the Argolid and those in positions of power used funerals as an opportunity for conspicuous consumption. It is significant that expenditure on the dead was curbed once Pylos became the capital of Messenia.

Room II contains some of the pottery from the palace. The capacious goblets would have quenched the thirst of a hero and recall the gold cup which Nestor used at Troy (*Iliad* 11. 632–7): 'anyone else would have found it difficult to shift the cup from the table, but Nestor, old as he was, could lift it without trouble'. The frescoes, although blackened by the fire which destroyed the palace, still retain traces of their polychrome decoration and can be reconstructed, at least tentatively. There is a curious battle scene from room 64 in which warriors who wear helmets and greaves, presumably Mycenaeans, fight men clad in skins. Does this commemorate a foreign expedition? The fire also preserved the Linear B tablets which would otherwise have disintegrated. There are plaster copies of tablets on display. The offering table was in the throne room by the hearth and reinforces the impression that religious ceremonies were performed here.

There is more unpainted pottery from the palace in **room III**—votive kylikes, braziers, enormous pithoi—also the chimney pot which was found in the throne room. Grave goods from the tholos tomb at Vagenas, just south of the palace, include fine bronze weapons and vessels.

Peristeria (Fig. 95)

5 km. north of Kyparissia there is a turn for the Peristeria Archaeological Site. Go straight through the village of Peristeria. The site is 5 km. from the turn.

Special Features

Peristeria is not an especially spectacular site but it is relatively accessible and makes a pleasant diversion which takes you into the countryside.

History

Peristeria was one of the wealthiest Early Mycenaean sites in Messenia. Three tholos tombs were built on the akropolis in this period and one of these is extremely impressive. The tombs had been plundered but still contained some superb objects. It seems quite likely that Peristeria was the centre of an independent principality at this time but may have been annexed by PYLOS in the C14 or C13 BC and certainly became less important.

Description

On the right of the path which leads from the entrance, and rather overgrown at present, is the East House. This was built in the C16 BC, possibly for the ruler of Peristeria. It is remarkably unpretentious but this is true of much Early Mycenaean architecture. Resources were invested in the construction of tombs not palaces. Tomb 3 is the earliest of the three tholoi on the akropolis. There were three gold cups, a silver cup, and a gold diadem in a pit in the chamber. Tomb 2, built in the C15,

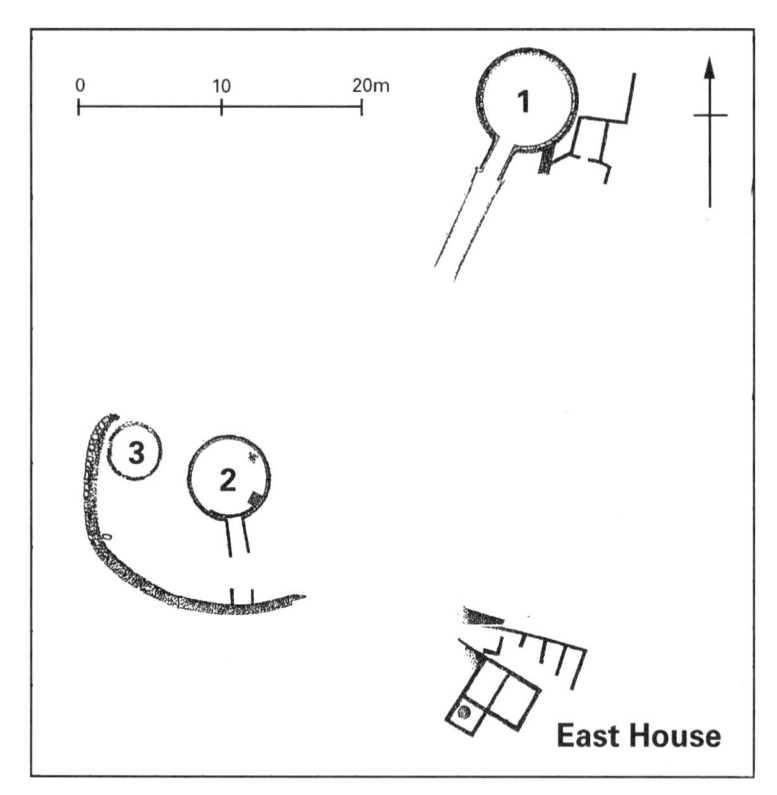

▲ Fig. 95. Plan of Peristeria

is over 10 m. in diameter. Gold jewellery had been deposited in the dromos. A wall runs around the western and southern sides of the tombs. It is thought that this may have separated the akropolis from the rest of the settlement but was not defensive. The vault of tomb 1 has been restored and would have been covered by an earth mound. The piece of glass on the facade protects two symbols, a double axe and a branch, which were incised on the stone blocks. Marks like these can be seen on Crete and may have been made by Minoan stone masons. The chamber is 12 m. in diameter and had evidently been a focus for cult activity in the Hellenistic period.

Messene (Figs. 96–99)

For the main part of the site, take the road signed Ithomi Archaeological Site on the edge of the village, just before the museum, if you have come from the direction of Kalamata. Note that the museum has recently reopened. You can park by the modern cemetery.

Special Features

Messene lies in an impressive natural setting below Mt Ithomi. Its fortifications are among the most admired in Greece, and it has one of the best preserved Hellenistic sanctuaries.

History

Messene, named after the legendary first queen of the region, was an artificial foundation (369 BC), its Messenian inhabitants drawn from liberated helots and returned exiles following the collapse of Spartan power in the region. Commanding the famously fertile Messenian plain, the site, on the west slope of Mt Ithomi, has revealed traces of earlier settlement (Geometric and Archaic). Its obvious defensive advantages were now reinforced by an impressive circuit of walls and towers, within which the new settlement was laid out on a grid. The work was supervised by the Theban general Epaminondas, later revered here as a founder. The city was conceived as an anti-Spartan bastion (see MEGALOPOLIS), and in the C3 it successfully maintained itself against the old enemy and Macedon, but later succumbed to forcible incorporation by the Achaian League (from 182 BC). Under Roman rule (from 146) Messene was a cultural backwater, but an important administrative and

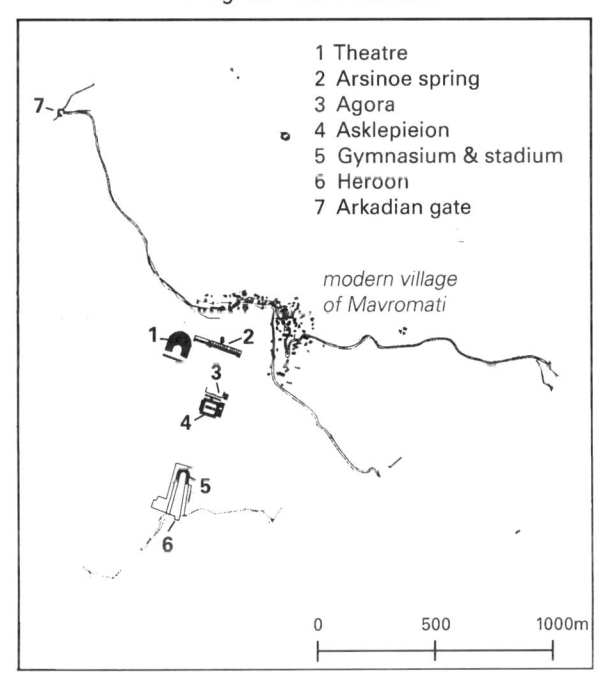

▼ Fig. 96. Plan of Messene

1 Theatre
2 Arsinoe spring
3 Agora
4 Asklepieion
5 Gymnasium & stadium
6 Heroon
7 Arkadian gate

economic centre, hosting a wealthy community of Roman businessmen and (probably) the assize-court of the governor, as well as producing (C2 AD) a family of Roman consuls. The Asklepieion remained in use until *c.* AD 400, and at least one basilican church is known.

Description

Just below the cemetery is the fortress-like **theatre** [1] mostly unexcavated, but note the pointed doorways in the west retaining wall. An inscription records an extraordinary meeting here (C1 BC), uncomfortable no doubt for some of those present, to listen to a statement of unpaid taxes owing to Rome.

Just to the east is a large **fountain house** ([2]—C3 BC with repairs in the C1 AD and *c.* AD 400), the Arsinoe spring of Pausanias (4.3.1), named after the daughter of a mythical Messenian king. It has an oblong rear cistern featuring a semi-circular base for bronze statuary, and two more cisterns to the front. To the east is the north-west corner of the **agora** [3] which is largely unexcavated.

Proceeding south you reach the 'four stoas of the **Asklepieion**' [4, site plan Fig. 97], as the Messenians called their religious show-place,

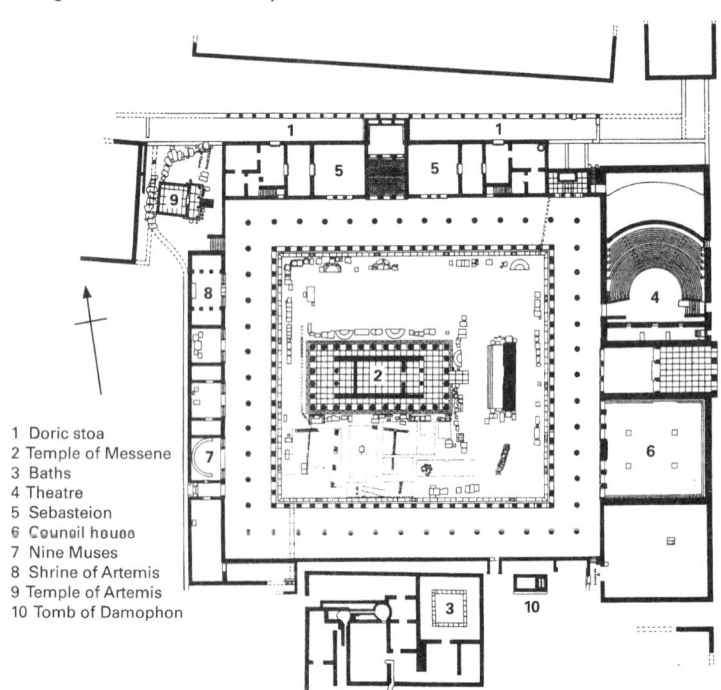

▼ Fig. 97. Plan of the Asklepieion at Messene

1 Doric stoa
2 Temple of Messene
3 Baths
4 Theatre
5 Sebasteion
6 Council house
7 Nine Muses
8 Shrine of Artemis
9 Temple of Artemis
10 Tomb of Damophon

▲ Fig. 98. The theatre in the Asklepieion at Messene

just south of the agora. Its north side facing the agora is fronted by a 90 m. long Doric **stoa** ([**97.1**]—late C3 AD), apparently unfinished. As Pausanias (4.31.10–11) shows, the Asklepieion honoured a host of deities:

The majority of the Messenian statues really worth seeing are in the sanctuary of Asklepios. For as well as images of the god and his sons, and ones of Apollo, the Muses and Herakles, there are also statues of the city of Thebes, Epaminondas the son of Kleommis, Fortune and Artemis Bearer of Light. The marble images are works of Damophon, and I know of no other Messenian sculptor worth noting. The iron image of Epaminondas is not his work, but another's. There is also a temple of Messene the daughter of Triopas, with a statue in gold and Parian marble. At the rear of the temple are paintings of the kings of Messene . . .

The centrepiece, a **temple** [**97.2**] (C3 BC) in the Doric order (six by twelve columns), with a massive altar axially aligned to its east, and a ramp added later, is built in the local stone. Its recipient, to judge from Pausanias, was probably Messene, the city's eponymous heroine, rather than Asklepios (as is often thought).

The surrounding complex of **four stoas**, with the buildings entered off them, is dated c.200 BC. Beneath the court an earlier shrine (C7–C6 BC) was discovered in 1993–4, the finds including clay and bronze miniatures of body parts, tending to confirm the tradition of Archaic cult for Asklepios in Messenia. A Hellenistic hypocaust identifies the first phase of the building immediately to the south as **baths** [**97.3**], also a feature of Asklepieia; likewise the small **theatre** [**97.4**] and stage, perhaps the *deikterion* or 'place for showing' (possibly a religious drama) of an Augustan inscription; the polychrome floor is Roman. The north wing with its inner rooms, at first perhaps serving Asklepios, became (under Augustus) a **Sebasteion** [**97.5**] or shrine for the worship of the Roman emperors. The spacious hall south of the theatre, with its continuous bench around three sides, was the **council-house** [**97.6**]) of the 76 'sacred elders of Oupesia' (an epithet of Artemis), the body of senior citizens who supervised the whole complex (not to be confused with the city-council, a much larger body which must have met elsewhere). On the west side a **room** [**97.7**] with a semi-circular base probably housed Damophon's group of the Nine Muses. More interesting is the cluttered little **shrine** [**97.8**] of Artemis (roofed), worshipped here as Upright (Orthia) and Bearer of Light. You can see the base for Damophon's colossal marble cult-statue, of which fragments are preserved, cuttings for the legs of the offering table in front, just to the right a collecting box, now missing its lid, and all around bases once supporting statues of the goddess's female attendants. The outside altar is flanked by a mysterious pillar, its function revealed by an inscription from the shrine (*SEG* 23 [1968] 220):

To you the Maiden, O Mistress Orthia, Damonikos and his partner Timarchis, daughter of a good father, dedicated (the statue of their daughter) Mego, who held your image in her hand, O Artemis, and stretched her torch before your altars ...

Mego's ritual task was to carry in and out of the shrine a portable, wooden image of the goddess, inserted into the top of the pillar for temporary display, and to light the sacrificial fire with her torch. For Messenian girls these nocturnal ceremonies may have had an initiatory character. The shrine superseded a small, earlier, ramped **Temple of Artemis** [**97.9**] just outside the north-west corner of the complex (*c*.300 BC).

Just outside the south wall of the south stoa is a rectangular **tomb** ([**97.10**]—early C2 BC) with two burials, which in this location should be a city-sponsored monument for a prominent citizen. He can probably be identified with the celebrated Messenian sculptor Damophon (see LYKOSOURA), since an inscription with decrees from seven cities in his honour was found here. Such public tribute to an artist was unusual in ancient Greece.

A short distance to the south-west you come to the imposing **stadium** [**96.5**], where the semi-circular end (*sphendone*) has been partly cleared. The boys' athletics marking the birthday of Tiberius presumably took place here among other events. The stadium was framed by three Doric stoas, now being restored, the middle one a double colonnade.

▲ Fig. 99. C4 tower at Messene

Beside their north-west junction are remains of a Doric propylon or gateway (c. C2 BC) giving access to the colonnades from the north, with four columns still in place. Inscriptions from the facade show that the whole complex was a gymnasium, probably the Old Gymnasium, with its Middle (= north) and Olympic (= west) Stoas, known from an Augustan inscription. The east stoa, like the gateway, was the gift of a citizen; generally, as inscriptions show, the gymnasium relied heavily on rich Messenians for its funding. Another inscription (C1 BC) lists names of ephebes, Messenian youths who trained here. In front of the east stoa is a stone war memorial, decorated with shields, suggesting the linkage between training and military service. At the south end of the stadium, resting on a massive podium which projects beyond the city-wall at this point, are remains of a building with a Doric facade identified as the **heroon** ([**96.6**]—C2–C1 BC) of a prominent Messenian family.

From here you can walk north-west along the line of the walls, or return to the main road to go past the museum to the '**Arkadian' gate** [**96.7**] for the ancient highway to Megalopolis, the most spectacular feature of the city-walls. Built entirely in stone, these form a vast circuit of c.9 km. running up the slopes of Mt Ithomi, and were surely meant to permit agricultural self-sufficiency during sieges. The towers were for catapults. The gate is an open circular court with two doorways, the one on the inner side in the form of a pair of two-leaved gates separated by a central post—the partly fallen monolith. One of the niches in the court held the statue of Hermes, god of travellers, seen by Pausanias (4.33.3), with an inscription recording its repair by Quintus Plotius Euphemio, who sounds like one of Messene's Roman businessmen.

Just outside are two mausolea side by side, part of an ancient extra-mural cemetery lining the road. One, fronted by a Doric stoa, has two chambers, each for a sarcophagus burial (C2 BC). The other produced fragments of an imported Athenian sarcophagus (C2–C3 AD).

Arkadia

Arkadia is in the centre of the Peloponnese, surrounded by mountains and cut off from the sea, except in the west where the territory of ancient PHIGALEIA included a stretch of the coast. There are plains in eastern Arkadia, dominated in antiquity by TEGEA, MANTINEIA, and ORCHOMENOS, but these are karstic basins, drained by sink-holes, which often flood. The problem in Arkadia is an excess, rather than a deficiency, of water. As the floods recede they do leave behind rich meadows. Western Arkadia is extremely rugged, although also well watered by tributaries of the Alpheios. The mountains were a source of timber, fir, and oak in particular. They also provided excellent pasture for sheep and goats. This was the home of the goat-god Pan and Arkadia became the idealized setting for the simple, pastoral lifestyle dreamed of by Roman poets.

There are no major prehistoric settlements. The historic Arkadians shared a collective identity, expressed in their distinctive Greek dialect, akin to Cypriot, and cult practices. They were organized into cities, chief among them Tegea and Mantineia, sharing the eastern Arkadian plain. Smaller cities in this mountainous terrain included Orchomenos and ALIPHEIRA, both perched on akropolis sites, and GORTYS, overlooking a dramatic gorge. Dominated by Spartan power from the C6 BC until its overthrow in 371, the Arkadians thereafter united under Theban guidance, with MEGALOPOLIS founded as the federal centre. In Hellenistic times most of Arkadia joined up with the Achaian League, peaceful conditions in the late C3 BC permitting embellishment of the sanctuary of LYKOSOURA, a member city. Under Roman rule, much of the area was depopulated, although Roman businessmen found opportunities here. Tegea survived as an important centre into the C5–C6 AD.

Tripolis

The **Archaeological Museum** is signed from the central square of Tripolis. It occupies an ochre-coloured, neo-classical mansion and is well-labelled in English and Greek.

Among the reliefs and inscriptions in the vestibule is a decree from Augustan MANTINEIA, here called 'Antigoncia', in praise of local benefactors, Euphrosynos and his wife, Epigone, who paid for extensive public works (*IG* 5.2.344). The first room on the left contains finds from the Mycenaean chamber tomb cemetery at Palaiokastro and the Neolithic settlement at Sakovouni. Further adjoining rooms display Geometric pottery from Mantineia, Archaic and Classical material from MEGALOPOLIS, and some sculpture. The room on the right of the vestibule has sculpture (Archaic to Roman), including two gravestones from the villa of Herodes at LOUKOU. A further room has small finds from Arkadian religious sites, including an akroterion from the temple of Poseidon at Mantineia. An adjoining room has bronzes from Megalopolis. The basement includes (vestibule) two akroteria from the temple of Despoina at LYKOSOURA and a sacred law from Mantineia inscribed on the flutes of a column (C6 or C5 BC). Adjoining rooms include more material from Palaiokastro, Mantineia, Megalopolis, and TEGEA, including sculpture and glass. There is also a display of finds from Loukou, including a portrait head of Polydeukion (see p. 115), antique sculpture displayed at the villa, and plans and photos of mosaics.

Tegea (Figs. 100–101)

We suggest that you visit the museum and the Temple of Athena first. Take the turn signed Anc. Tegea (2 km.), just south of Tripolis on the Sparta road. In the village of Alea, there are signs for the museum and the temple.

Special Features

Pausanias declared that the temple of Athena Alea 'surpassed the other temples in the Peloponnese in size and construction'. Although the temple is not well preserved, together with the theatre at Palaia Episkopi it does give some idea of the wealth and importance of ancient Tegea.

History

Mycenaean sherds and figurines from the sanctuary of Athena may indicate cult activity but it is not until the C9 BC that the number of dedications reaches a significant level. By the C8 the first temple had been constructed. This rather flimsy structure was extended and then in the late C7 replaced by a much more impressive temple. Tegea originally consisted of nine separate communities which merged and formed a polis. It is not entirely clear when this 'synoikism' (union) took place but the reconstruction of the temple may be connected. The main route between the Argolid and Lakonia passes through Tegea and it was inevitable that SPARTA would become a threat. Herodotus (1.66) tells us that the Spartans consulted the oracle at DELPHI about their proposed invasion of Arkadia and were informed:

I will give you Tegea to dance in with stamping feet

And her fair plain to measure out with the line.

The Lakedaimonians failed to perceive the ambiguity of this oracle and decided to leave the rest of Arkadia alone and march against Tegea. So confident were they of reducing the men of Tegea that they took chains with them. But they lost the battle and those who were taken prisoner were forced to wear on their own legs the chains they had brought and to 'measure out with the line' the plain of Tegea as labourers. In my own lifetime the fetters they were bound with were still preserved in the temple of Athena Alea.

Tegean resistance ended around 550 BC when the city joined the Peloponnesian League. At the battle of PLATAIA in 479 BC the contingent of 1500 hoplites from Tegea was stationed beside the Spartans, 'out of respect for their worth' (Herodotus 9.28). Tegea fought on the Spartan side in the Peloponnesian War and remained an ally until the battle of MANTINEIA in 362 BC. The bitter rivalry between Tegea and Mantineia was renewed at this battle after a brief period of reconciliation when they jointly founded the Arkadian League. Neither city can have benefited from these constant disputes which often arose because Mantineia had been flooded by water drained from the Tegea basin. A fire destroyed the Archaic temple of Athena in 395/4 BC and it was quite some time before the funds for a replacement were available. In 174 BC Antiochos IV paid for the reconstruction of the theatre and the emperor Hadrian was also a benefactor. From the detailed description provided by Pausanias (8.45–53), it would seem that Tegea was still an attractive city in the C2 AD but suffered when Alaric invaded the Peloponnese in AD 395. Even so, an enormous early Christian basilica was built at Palaia Episkopi in the C6.

Description

Most of the items on display in the **Archaeological Museum** come from Tegea. The room on the left has sculpture from the C4 BC temple of Athena—heads and torsoes from the pediments and akroteria. Pausanias mentions that the architect of the temple was Skopas of Paros, one of the most famous C4 sculptors. He was also responsible for the statues of Asklepios and Hygieia which stood on either side of Athena in the cella. His style is often described as expressive, a characteristic of the figures from the pediments which must have been made under his supervision. The sculpture focused on Tegea rather than Athena. Atalanta, a local heroine, was one of the main protagonists in the Kalydonian boar hunt, the myth depicted in the east pediment. The west pediment featured the fight between Achilles and Telephos who was born in Tegea. This celebration of the heroic past must have seemed particularly appropriate at a time when Tegea was once again independent. Note also the richly decorated marble blocks from the interior of the temple. There is more sculpture from Tegea in the room on the right. The room behind this contains prehistoric pottery from Asea, Geometric and Archaic bronzes, Classical pottery, and terracotta votives.

The **Sanctuary of Athena Alea** was on the southern outskirts of Tegea. From literary and inscriptional evidence it would seem that the deity worshipped in the sanctuary was initially Alea, whose votives indicate a concern for fertility. She may also have been seen as a protectress, a role often assumed by Athena who later appropriated the cult but retained Alea as her epithet. Recent excavations in the cella of the Classical temple have revealed traces of two earlier temples which were built in the C8 BC of wattle-and-daub around a framework of wooden posts. Pausanias describes their Archaic successor as 'a great and impressive' temple. It was much the same size as the Classical temple and had a colonnade of six by eighteen columns. The Archaic temple burned down early in the C4 and was not replaced until 345–335 BC. Skopas received the commission and it was his temple which Pausanias saw and so admired.

You enter the sanctuary from the east. The temple was shattered by an earthquake in the C6 AD but the plan and elevation can be restored. The peristyle consisted of six by fourteen Doric columns which were 19 m. high. The use of fourteen columns, rather than the conventional thirteen, was presumably dictated by the fact that there was a door approached by a ramp on the north side of the temple, as well as at the east end. Except for the sculptured pediments, the exterior of the temple must have been rather plain but the treatment of the interior was much more decorative. There was sculpture in the metopes above the columns of the porch and opisthodomos—the exploits of Telephos and other Tegean heroes. Engaged columns, Corinthian below and Ionic above, lined three sides of the cella. In his account of the dedications on display in the cella, Pausanias (8.46–7) complains that Augustus had removed the ancient statue of Athena Alea and the tusks of the Kalydonian boar after the battle of Actium. A replacement for the Athena had been acquired and on either side of this were the statues of Asklepios and Hygieia by Skopas. Pausanias also saw 'the hide of the Kalydonian boar, which time has withered and left without a single bristle, and the chains which the Lakonian prisoners wore while they cultivated the Tegean plain . . . a sacred couch of Athena and a painted picture of Auge', the mother of Telephos. Just north of the temple, accessible from the side door in the cella, was the fountain where Herakles raped Auge.

From the sanctuary follow the road signed ΠΑΛΑΙΑ ΕΠΙΣΚΟΠΗ for just over 1 km. until you see a church on your left. This is built on the ashlar wall which supported the cavea of the ancient **theatre**. Livy (41.20) tells us that the Seleukid king Antiochos IV Epiphanes was responsible for the 'magnificent theatre of marble at Tegea' which must have been started around 174 BC. Antiochos, noted for his generosity as a benefactor even if 'some said that he was unquestionably insane', evidently spared no expense, since the semi-circular cavea is over 80 m. in diameter. The enormous early Christian **basilica**, which has been uncovered just north-west of the church, is on the site of the **agora**. Pausanias states that this was the shape of a brick and lists the shrines and statues which he saw there.

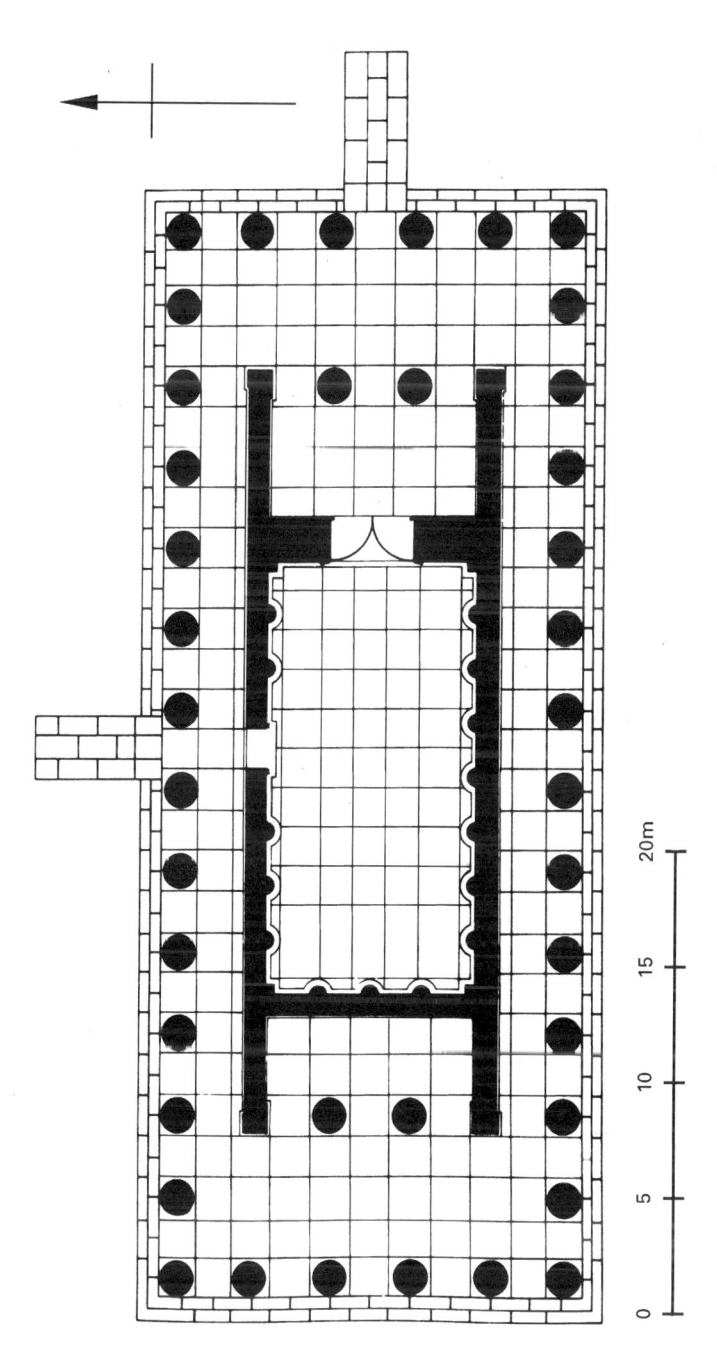

▲ Fig. 100. Plan of the Temple of Athena Alea at Tegea

▲ Fig. 101. Reconstruction of the interior of the Temple of Athena Alea at Tegea (after A. Stewart, *Greek Sculpture: An Exploration* (New Haven 1990) fig. 541)

Mantineia (Fig. 102)

Take the Patras/Pyrgos road north out of Tripolis. After 2 km. leave the main road where it bears left, at the sign for Ancient Mantineia which is straight ahead (do not turn right). The site (fenced but open) is opposite the extraordinary church of Ayia Photeini.

Special Features

The site is not especially impressive, but it is set in pleasant countryside and is historically interesting, as well as being easily accessible.

History

Mantineia was one of the two ancient cities (with TEGEA to the south) dominating the great plain of eastern Arkadia. An artificial foundation, it was created by the political and physical 'synoikism' (union) of five agricultural villages (C6 or early C5 BC). Location made its territory a strategic route for military traffic, and two major battles were fought here (371 and 362 BC). SPARTA sought to dominate Mantineia, and in 385 BC went so far as to dissolve the union, sending the Mantineians back to their ancestral villages. Following Sparta's defeat at Leuktra, the city was refounded on the same site (370 BC). In 223 BC the Macedonian king Antigonos III destroyed the city. Resettled by the Achaian League, Macedon's ally (221 BC), it was forced to take the name 'Antigoneia' (see TRIPOLIS). Repairs to public buildings were carried out under Augustus. The city reverted to its ancient name at the instigation of Hadrian, a visitor. He instituted a cult and festival here for Antinoos, his dead favourite (see p. 314), whose home-town in Asia Minor, Bithynion, claimed to be a Mantineian colony. The city continued to be inhabited into the C6–C7 AD.

Description

The ovoid wall-circuit of the refounded city encloses an area of 1.24 km^2. Within it the most prominent feature is the small **theatre** [1], of the C4 BC, supported on an artificial slope retained by a polygonal wall; the lowest rows of seats are preserved. Overlooking the **agora**, it presumably served for political assemblies as well as shows. Of the other scrappy structures visible, flanking the south side of the agora is a **stoa** [2] with two projecting wings (C4 BC), its walls originally of unbaked brick. A back-to-back, south-facing stoa was added in the C2 BC or later. A block found inside, inscribed 'of Zeus who gives good council', suggests that this was Mantineia's council-house. On the north side of the agora, starting from the theatre, are traces of the colonnade of another **stoa**. Next come semi-circular foundations (baked brick and rubble) of a vaulted feature identified as the inscriptionally attested **exedra** [3], 'on its own sufficient to adorn the whole city' (*IG* 5.2, lines 47–8), funded by a rich benefactress called Epigone (see Tripolis) under Augustus. In a further fenced enclosure to the east (not accessible) are remains of the east side of the agora.

If you continue along the road you pass through the **circuit-wall** [4], of which the trapezoidal masonry socle survives, although the mudbrick superstructure has vanished. Nearly 4 km. long, it once had 120 towers, of which 118 have been traced. Originally a small river, the Ophis, was diverted to fill an artificial moat encircling the wall.

A track following the line of the wall leads (right) to the hill of **Panayia Gourtsouli**, the ancient Ptolis, where Pausanias saw 'the ruins of ancient Mantineia' (8.12.7), meaning the pre-union settlement. From here there is an excellent panorama of the ecological niche of the ancient city, with its treeless plain liable to flooding and too high for the olive, but suited to cereals, and framed by scrub-covered hillsides providing grazing, as well as firewood and herbs.

260 **Arkadia**

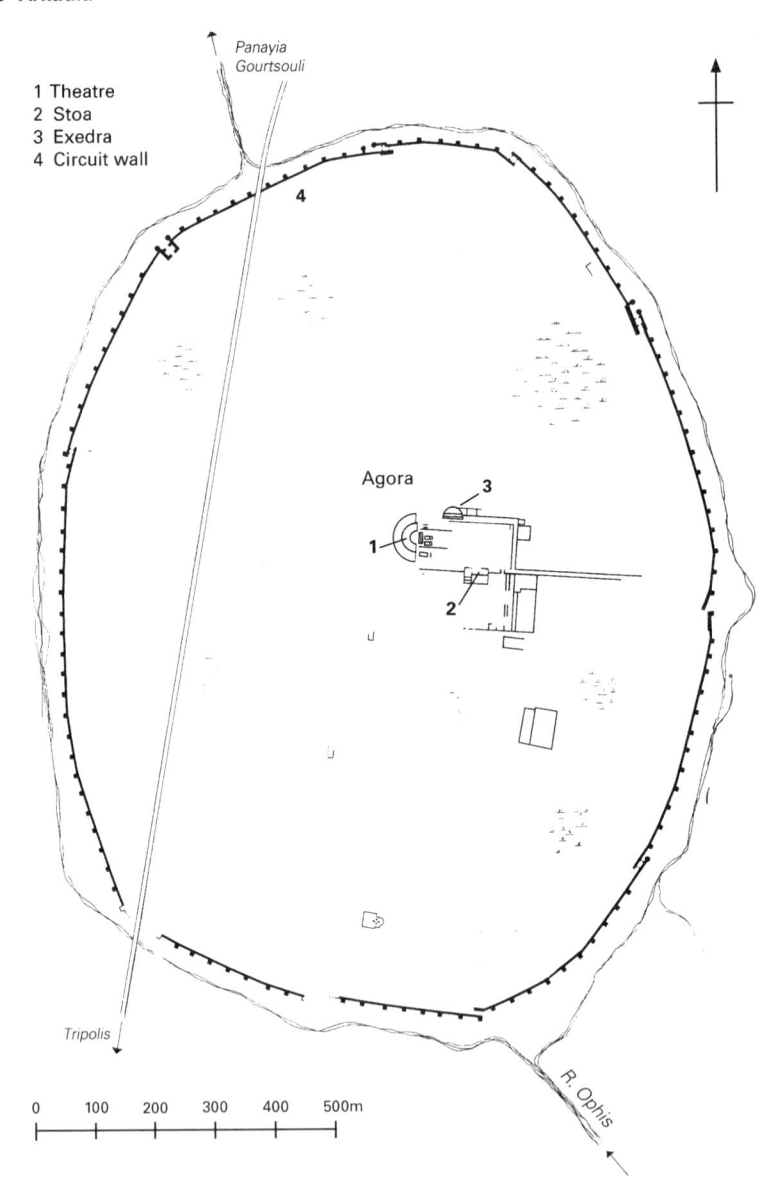

1 Theatre
2 Stoa
3 Exedra
4 Circuit wall

▲ **Fig. 102.** Plan of Mantineia

Orchomenos (Fig. 103) ★

From the square in Levidi take the road signed Ancient Orchomenos (said to be 5 km. but nearer 8). Turn left at a further sign for the site, pass through the village, and where the tarmac stops take the left-hand dirt track which ends (after c.1 km.) at an ancient tower.

Special Features

The mountain setting is scenic, and the site is quite easy to reach.

History

Orchomenos is a fortified akropolis site, strongly positioned on a conical hill dominating a basin prone to flooding and framed by mountains. Mentioned in Homer's *Iliad*, the city reputedly helped the Archaic Messenians in their struggle against SPARTA. In the C5 BC it was a Spartan ally and expanded its territory at the expense of near neighbours but in 370 BC surrendered to MEGALOPOLIS. The decree admitting Orchomenos to the Achaian League (*c*.230 BC) is preserved in the vestibule of the museum at TRIPOLIS. When Pausanias visited, the akropolis site was in ruins, and he comments that 'the present inhabited city is lower down than the circuit of the walls' (8.13.2). The city survived at least into the C3 AD.

Description

After the dirt track ends, a 3–4 minute walk along the path brings you to the **theatre** [**1**], which is fenced but accessible. Dating to the C4–C3 BC, it rests on a natural hillside, with ten rows of seating partly preserved. The marble seats in the front row were a gift, as is shown by the inscribed dedication to Dionysos, of a local citizen who had served as festival-president (agonothete). Two thrones are preserved in the orchestra, as well as a large circular altar of Concord (Homonoia), a deified abstraction popular in Hellenistic times when Greek cities were plagued by civil strife.

Above and to the south of the theatre you can climb up onto a plateau with the remains of the **agora**. On the north side it is flanked by the remains of a two-aisled **stoa** [**2**] *c*.70 m. long, combining an Ionic (inner) with a Doric (outer) colonnade (C4 BC) and on the east by another **stoa** [**3**], *c*.40 m. long (C5 BC). Inside were found twelve bronze tablets inscribed with civic decrees, showing the official character of this building, which may have been the council-house. Lower down to the south, on a platform retained by a wall, is the **Sanctuary of Artemis Mesopolitis**, 'she who resides in the middle of the city'. It consists of foundations of a medium-sized Doric **temple** [**4**] without an exterior colonnade (undated), and of an **altar** [**5**], perhaps C3 BC, set at an

Arkadia

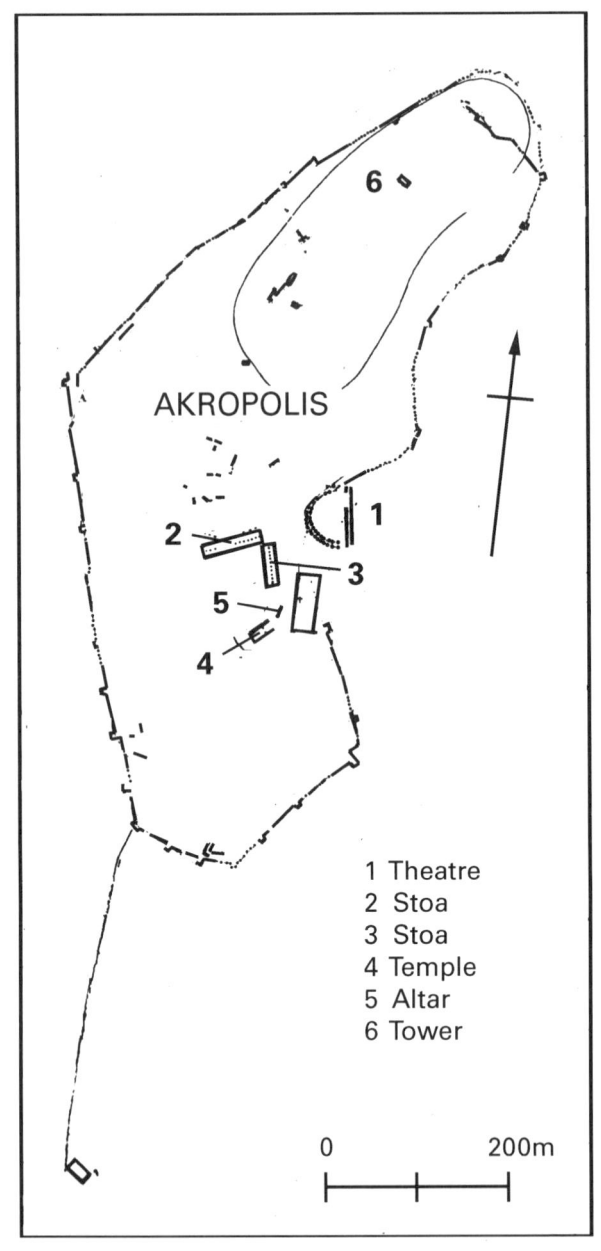

Fig. 103. Plan of Orchomenos

1 Theatre
2 Stoa
3 Stoa
4 Temple
5 Altar
6 Tower

obtuse angle to the east. The base for a statue of the Spartan king, Areus (died 265 BC) was found here. From the shrine a climb to the summit of the akropolis, crowned by a ruined Frankish **tower** [**6**], provides a panorama of Orchomenian territory.

Lousoi (Fig. 104) ★

Take the turn for Klitoria on the Tripolis–Patras road. From the square in Klitoria follow the road signed Cave of the Lakes 9 km. Continue beyond the cave and just before the village of Kato Lousoi take the left turn for Σιγούνι. There is a handpainted sign Πρός Νάο Αρτέμιδος. Approximately 4 km. along the Sigouni road turn left on a dirt track (further handpainted sign). After 2 km. you will reach the sanctuary of Artemis.

Special Features

The site is rather remote but in a scenic location and the sanctuary of Artemis is architecturally idiosyncratic. You also pass the Cave of the Lakes, a speleological marvel which we highly recommend.

History

'They say that Lousoi was once a city'—but when Pausanias toured Greece in the C2 AD 'there were not even any ruins left'. It was at Lousoi that the daughters of Proitos, who had been driven mad by the goddess Hera, were purified and cured. Their grateful father founded a sanctuary of Artemis Hemera which was certainly in existence by the C8 BC, since the dedications include fine Geometric bronzes. It is not clear whether there was also a settlement at this time. Several houses have recently been excavated on the site below the sanctuary but they date from the Hellenistic period. It is possible that the sanctuary served a number of communities and may have been patronized by shepherds in particular. Although Lousoi is rather remote, it does control one of the routes through the mountains and would have been a point of contact for the highlanders of northern Arkadia. By the end of the C7 BC a temple had been built for the goddess and the number of dedications increases. Games were held, the Hemerasia, which attracted competitors not only from the Peloponnese but even from cities in the east. The sanctuary flourished and in the early C3 the temple was rebuilt. Then in 240 BC disaster struck in the form of the Aitolians who had invaded the Peloponnese and captured the city of Kynaitha, just north of Lousoi. Polybius (4.18) tells us that they next

advanced towards Lousoi. When they arrived at the temple of Artemis, which lies between Kleitor and Kynaitha and is regarded as inviolable by the Greeks, they threatened to seize the animals of the goddess and other property around the temple. But the people of Lousoi sensibly gave the Aitolians some of the

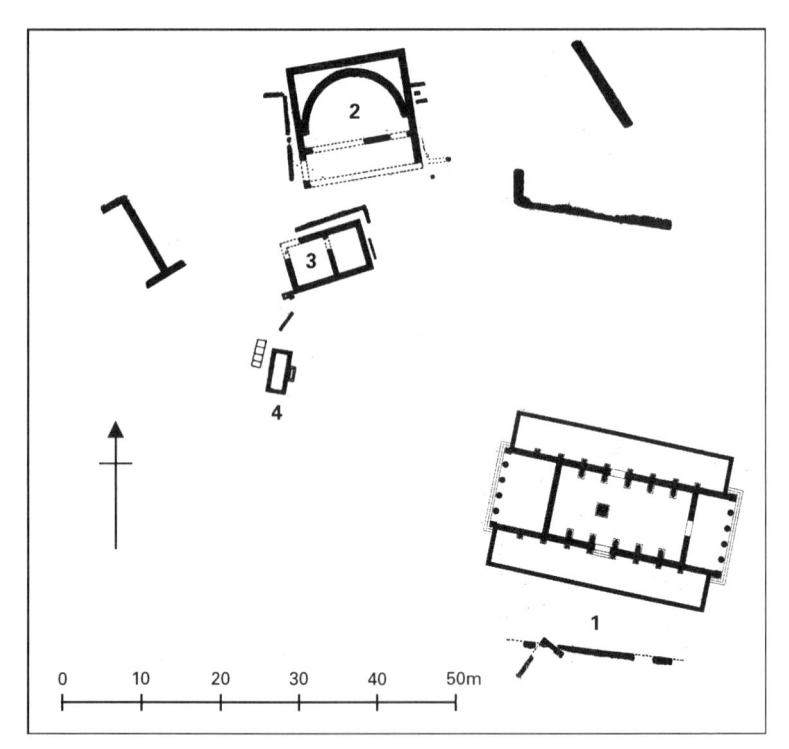

▲ Fig. 104. Plan of the Sanctuary of Artemis at Lousoi. Key: 1 Temple of Artemis 2 Council-house 3 Propylon 4 Fountain house

sacred furniture and so induced them to refrain from impiety and commit no outrage.

They left and attacked the city of Kleitor but were repelled, so they returned and 'drove off the sacred animals'. One theory is that there was a herd of deer in the sanctuary but it seems more likely that the people of Lousoi had sought asylum for themselves and their animals. The city later came under the control of Kleitor and this may explain the decline which Pausanias observed when he passed through Arkadia.

Description

Because there is no access at present, the **Temple of Artemis** [1] must be viewed from the fence. It was built in the early C3 BC and has an unconventional plan. There were evidently four Doric columns in the porch and opisthodomos. The cella had five semi-engaged columns on either side, backed by pilasters externally, and recalls the temple of Apollo at BASSAI. The sekos was apparently flanked by galleries which could only be entered from the cella. It is not clear how these galleries should be restored and their role in the cult is even more mysterious. The base of the statue of Artemis is preserved in the cella and it is assumed that this was transferred from the C7 temple.

On the terrace below the temple there is a structure which consists of a porch and a semi-circular auditorium. This was originally interpreted as a bouleuterion or **council-house** [**2**] but it could have been used in some ceremonial capacity. The council-house was built in the late C4 or early C3, almost certainly at the same time as the temple and also the **propylon** [**3**] through which processions would have passed. South of the propylon is a **fountain house** [**4**], presumably on the site of the spring which cured the daughters of Proitos. It was said that those who drank the water from this spring would be put off wine—an inscription warned thirsty shepherds of the consequences, should they succumb.

When you return down the dirt track you pass a fenced enclosure where a number of Hellenistic houses have been excavated. In the house on the upper terrace there is a peristyle court and a bathroom. One of the houses on the lower terrace has an andron (dining room) with room for eleven couches.

Megalopolis (Figs. 105–106)

From the centre of modern Megalopolis, take the Andritsaina road. After 1 km. turn left at the sign for the Ancient Theatre.

Special Features

The site has the remains of impressive public buildings, including the largest theatre in ancient Greece.

History

'Great City' (*Megalê Polis*) was an ambitious artificial foundation, probably of 370 BC. The largest Arkadian city, it was created as the capital of the Arkadian federal state which came into being following SPARTA's military collapse in 371 BC, and formed part of a ring of cities (see MESSENE) aimed at containing Spartan power. Occupying the centre and south of Arkadia, its vast territory incorporated perhaps as many as 40 previously independent communities, such as GORTYS. The city itself was laid out on level ground at the centre of a wide plain astride the River Helisson, a tributary of the Alpheios (see OLYMPIA), and was defended by a circuit wall *c.*9 km. long. Traditionally anti-Spartan and pro-Macedonian, the city joined the Achaian League in 235 BC, and was sacked by Kleomenes III of Sparta, the league's enemy, in 223 BC. Recovering, it went on to play a prominent part in federal affairs, producing the Achaian statesman and general Philopoimen, at whose death (182 BC), wrote Pausanias, 'Greece ceased to be the mother of the brave' (8.52.1). At his funeral here, his ashes were carried by Polybius, the

Arkadia

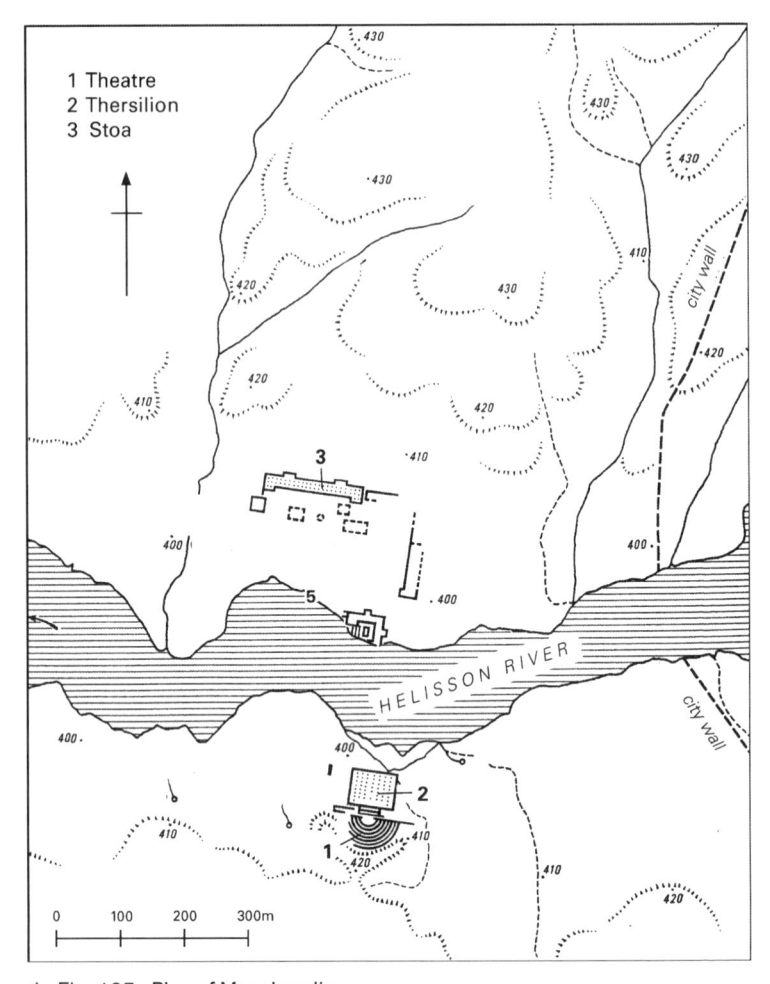

▲ Fig. 105. Plan of Megalopolis

future historian, also Megalopolitan. Under the Roman peace the city's political *raison d'être* ceased to exist, and Pausanias claimed that it 'now lies mostly in ruins, shorn of all its beauty and ancient prosperity' (8.33.1), although inscriptions reveal building-activity by Roman patrons, including the emperor Domitian (AD 94). It survived into the C7 AD as the seat of a bishopric.

Description

The site is closed at present, but both the theatre and the Thersilion can be seen from the fence. The **theatre** [1], dating from soon after 370 BC and claimed by Pausanias as the largest in Greece, was built into a natural hillside and had an estimated capacity of 17,000–21,000. The seats are inscribed with names of citizen-tribes, which seem each to have had their own section of the auditorium. Instead of facing a conventional stage-building, spectators looked onto the projecting Doric portico of the Thersilion. Roof-tiles stamped *skanatheka* show the existence of a shed where the west passageway (*parodos*) would normally be. This was for storing theatrical props, or even a wooden stage. These unique arrangements presumably reflect an original conception of theatre and Thersilion as a single unit for use by the political and military assemblies of the Arkadians. Later (possibly C2 BC) a fixed stone *proskenion* was built, replaced in imperial times by a Roman-style stage. The **Thersilion** [**2**], named after its donor, was the meeting place of the Arkadian primary assembly, the so-called Ten Thousand. It was a huge, rectangular hall, the roof held up by columns, their bases still visible. They are arranged in lines radiating from the centre, so as to maximize sight and sound of the speaker for an audience estimated at up to *c*.10,000 standing or *c*.6000 seated. The building was in ruins in the mid-C2 AD.

If you continue on the Andritsaina road for 500 m. from the turn to the theatre, just across the bridge over the river, you will see to the left of the road the foundations of the massive **Stoa Philippeios** [**3**], flanking the north side of the **agora** for a length of roughly 155 m., in keeping with the generally gargantuan pretensions of the new city. A winged stoa with three internal colonnades, the facade was Doric, with Ionic columns for the inside. The Megalopolitans named it in honour of Philip II

▼ Fig. 106. The theatre and Thersilion at Megalopolis

of Macedon, suggesting a date in the 340s BC. In the open ground of the agora in front, various bases for statues can be seen.

Lykosoura (Figs. 107–108)

Take the Kalamata road out of Megalopolis. After 13 km. turn right at the sign for Lykosyra. Just before the village of Choremi (Χορεμι) turn left at the T-junction signed ΑΡΧΑΙΑ ΛΥΚΟΣΟΥΡΑ. Beyond the village of Apiditsa and a further sign to Lykosoura, turn left where the road forks (signed). After c.2 km. take the gravel road which branches off to the left (signed but not clearly) and climbs up to the museum.

Special Features

This was one of the most important sanctuaries in the Peloponnese. It was famous for its colossal sculpture, some of it on display in the museum.

History

Lykosoura was a small Arkadian polis, said to be the oldest city on earth. Its main claim to fame was an extra-urban sanctuary of the two 'Great Goddesses' : the Mistress (Despoina), a venerable Arkadian deity, and Demeter, here playing a secondary role. Worshippers were initiated into nocturnal mysteries presided over by a hierophant as at ELEUSIS. Other elements were Arkadian, notably a savage sacrifice in which, as Pausanias recounts, 'they do not cut the throats of the victims as in other sacrifices, but each man lops off a limb of the victim, it matters not which' (8. 37.5). Not much is known about the sanctuary before 371 BC, when on the strength of its fame the Arkadians permitted Lykosoura to remain an independent enclave within the territory of the newly founded MEGALO-POLIS. The chronology has been clarified thanks to a new inscription suggesting that Damophon, the Messenian sculptor who made the cult-group, was active *c*.223–190 BC. It now looks as if the main development of the sanctuary belongs to the period of peace after 217 BC, during which the Peloponnesians restored traditional cults and festivals. The sanctuary rules were tightened up at the same time, to judge from an inscription (see **box**). Lykosoura later had trouble maintaining the cult, and an inscription claims that in the C1 AD the 'temple was about to collapse' when a rich Megalopolitan came to the rescue (*IG* 5.2.515). If it continued nonetheless to flourish into the C3, this was largely because the religious experience appealed to elite Greeks from elsewhere, including a strong contingent from Roman SPARTA.

Description

The main feature in the **museum** is the massive cult-group by Damophon (the heads are casts of the originals, now in the National Archaeological Museum in ATHENS). A reconstruction on paper is displayed. From left to right the original group comprised Artemis, Demeter,

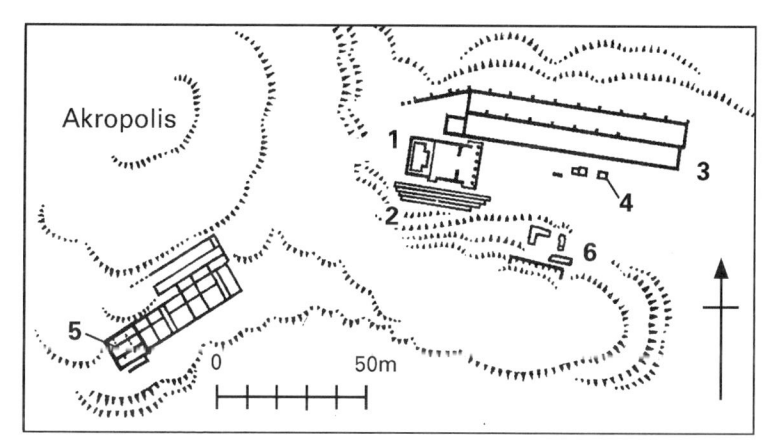

▲ Fig. 107. Plan of Lykosoura. Key: 1 Temple of Despoina 2 Steps 3 Stoa 4 Altars 5 Fountain house 6 Megaron

Despoina, and Anytos, a pre-Olympian god (Titan) who reared Despoina. Despoina's veil shows dancing animals in female clothing, perhaps referring to masked dances during the mysteries. The original height of the group on its base was *c.*5.60 m. To the right of the door is a marble lampstand, evoking the cult's nocturnal rites. Its dedicator, the Syrian 'King (Antiochos) Epiphanes Philopappus' (*IG* 5.2.524), was father of the more famous Philopappos buried at Athens (p. 60). Note the terracotta votives of water-carriers and figures with animals' heads, presumably masks, in the left-hand glass case.

The site is in two parts. Below the museum is the **Temple of Despoina** ([1]—late C3 BC), built of marble (columns), limestone, and brick (superstructure of the walls). A Doric facade and front porch lead into the main chamber, most of it taken up by the base for the cult-group. A curious feature is the side door in the south wall. This faces a series of ten **steps** [2] built against the natural slope. Perhaps they were for spectators, addressed by a priest from the door. To the east a poorly preserved **stoa** [3] overlooks foundations of three **altars** [4]. There are bases for honorific statues in the temple-porch.

Across the road from the museum are two ancillary structures. One is a well-preserved **fountain house** ([5]—possibly late C3 BC) with three chambers, fronted by a draw basin. The hydraulic cement, tiled floor, and spouts are all visible. Below this is a large stone-lined cistern with a brick floor and access-steps for servicing.

Just north-east of the temple on the slope (inaccessible) is a building which consists of an enclosure and a closed stoa, identified as the **Megaron** ([6]—late C3 BC?) or Hall where, says Pausanias, the mysteries were held. The animal-headed votives in the museum, some Archaic in date, were found here.

Fig. 108. The Temple of Despoina at Lykosoura

Sanctuary rules

These sanctuary-rules showing how the conduct of worshippers was hedged by rituals and taboos are contained in an inscription from Lykosoura dating to c.200 BC (*IG* 5.2.514):

'Concerning Despoina ... Let no one be allowed to pass into the sanctuary of Despoina who is carrying any gold objects not destined for dedication, or clothing that is purple, flowered or black, or sandals, or a ring. If any person does enter with any of the things which this stele forbids, let it be dedicated in the sanctuary. Nor is anyone to be allowed to enter with curled hair, or the head veiled. Nor is anyone allowed to bring in flowers, or a woman who is pregnant or breast-feeding to be initiated.... Those making sacrifice should use for sacrifice olive, myrtle, honeycomb, barleycorns clear of darnel, an image, white poppies, lamps, incense, myrrh, spices. Those sacrificing animals to Despoina white ...'

Bassai and Phigaleia (Figs. 109–111) ★

Bassai is 15 km. from Andritsaina and can also be reached from Lepreon.

Special Features

Pausanias (8.41) believed that the temple of Apollo Epikourios at Bassai was 'second only to the temple at TEGEA for its proportions and the beauty of its stone'. He does not point out that this is also a spectacularly wild site.

History

Cult-activity is attested at Bassai in the late C8 BC when the first dedications were made. C7 votives include miniature bronze helmets, cuirasses, greaves, and shields. Arkadian mercenaries (*epikouroi*) may have honoured Apollo as their protector (*epikourios*). Pausanias claims that Apollo was given the epithet *epikourios* because he prevented a plague but a military connection seems more likely.

The first temple was built *c.*625 BC, presumably by the city of Phigaleia which controlled the sanctuary. It is curious that the Phigaleians should have chosen such an isolated, if dramatic, site for one of their major sanctuaries. As shepherds and hunters they may well have felt that they should worship their gods in the countryside on which they were so dependent. Early in the C6 the temple was rebuilt and extended. There is evidence of a third temple which is dated *c.*500 BC. This was subsequently dismantled and the stone reused in the construction of the Classical temple. Pausanias states that the architect was Iktinos who had been responsible for the Parthenon. It is thought that the temple was built between 430–400 BC, no doubt in stages. For a city the size of Phigaleia this was an ambitious project which must have been financed on an *ad hoc* basis, when funds were available. There is a decline in the number of votives in the C4, particularly after MEGALOPOLIS became established as a religious, as well as political, centre for the Arkadians. A bronze statue of Apollo Epikourios was removed from Bassai and set up in the agora in Megalopolis. Nevertheless, the temple was still intact when Pausanias visited Arkadia in the C2 AD.

Description

The Classical temple is covered by a tent at present, while the structure is made more secure. Because it is in such an exposed location, the severe weather conditions have caused some damage. Moreover, this is a region which often experiences earthquakes. The builders were evidently aware of this and constructed a massive platform which cushions the temple from seismic shocks.

The temple faces north rather than east. Since the ridge runs north–south, this orientation had practical advantages and made the temple more conspicuous. However, it should be noted that the Archaic temple also faced north. This is true of a number of other temples in Arkadia, such as the temple of Athena at ALIPHEIRA. The local grey limestone was used, except for the interior metopes, the frieze, some of the column capitals, and the roof tiles which were of marble. The source of this marble was apparently TAINARON in Lakonia.

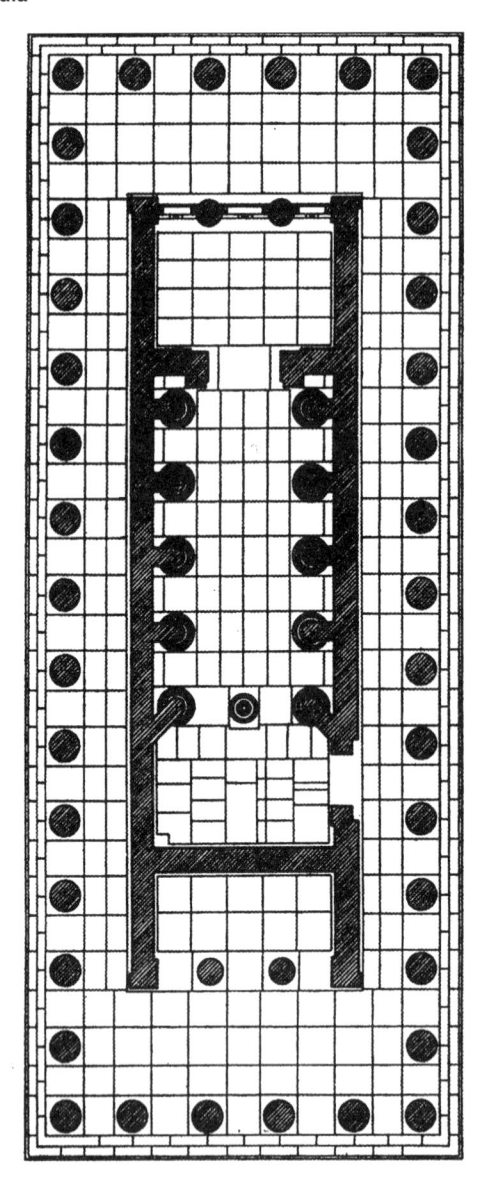

▲ Fig. 109. Plan of the Temple of Apollo at Bassai

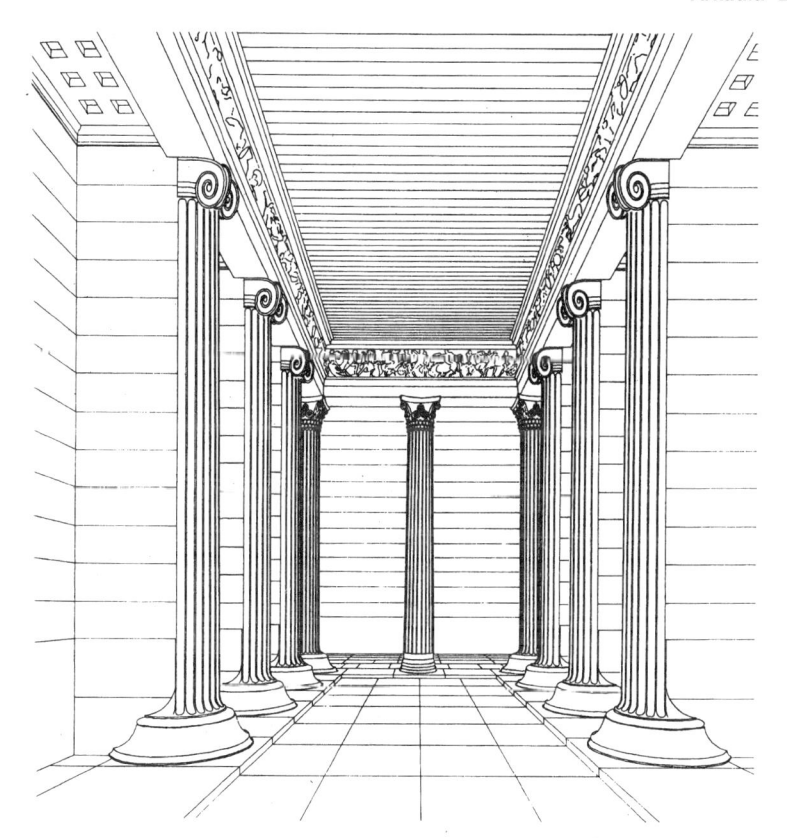

▲ Fig. 110. Reconstruction of the interior of the Temple of Apollo at Bassai (after A. Mallwitz, *Athenische Mitteilungen* 77 (1962) 167, fig. 2)

The peristyle consists of six by fifteen Doric columns and looks decidedly antiquated. There was no sculpture in the pediments or the exterior metopes, so the effect will have been rather severe. The reliefs in the metopes above the columns of the porch and opisthodomos have been badly broken. They may have depicted the return of Apollo from the Hyperboreans and the rape of the daughters of Leukippos by the Dioskouroi but this is not certain. The design of the cella was revolutionary. On either side there were semi-engaged Ionic columns and at the end of the cella the earliest known Corinthian column. In the reconstruction this is flanked by Corinthian columns but it seems more likely that these were Ionic. A frieze of Greeks and Amazons and of Lapiths and Centaurs ran around the interior of the cella. Excavated by the Society of Travellers in 1812, it is now in the British Museum. Beyond the cella is an adyton (holy of holies) which has a separate door. This faces east and so the adyton would have been lit when the sun rose.

The claim that Iktinos designed the temple has been disputed but does not seem out of the question. The interior is quite remarkable and the rather conservative exterior may have consciously echoed the third temple. Elements of the plan were certainly derived from the Archaic temple. This was built on the rocky knoll to the south and also had two interior rooms, a cella and an adyton which was entered through a side door.

If you wish to visit **Phigaleia**, continue on the road beyond Bassai to Perivolia and follow the road signed Phigaleia (3 km., partly tarmac). Turn right at the yellow sign for the Archaeological Site. After approximately 100 m., where the dirt road bears left, there is a narrow path on the right between ancient blocks and high hedges. In approximately 4 minutes you will reach an overgrown stretch of the Classical city-wall. Just beyond the path, on the left of the dirt road, you can see the remains of a stoa. Return to the fork and follow the yellow sign for the Ancient Fountain House, which is through the village and just beyond the cemetery. The fountain, shaded by a mighty plane tree, dates from the C4–C3 BC and is still in use. Pausanias (8.39–41) provides quite a detailed description of Phigaleia which, as he points out, 'is mostly precipitous'. In the agora he saw a statue of Arrachion who was an Olympic victor in the pankration, a particularly brutal event. Pausanias (8.40) tells us that

he won in the fifty-fourth games [in 564 BC] by the just decision of the umpires and by his own fortitude. He was fighting his last opponent for the wild olive when the opponent caught Arrachion and held him with a scissors grip and at the same time throttled him with his hands, so Arrachion broke one of this man's toes. Arrachion died by strangling, and at the same time the strangler gave in from the pain in his toe. The Eleians crowned the dead body with the wreath and proclaimed it as the winner.

Lepreon (Figs. 112–113) ★

Take the turn for Lepreon on the Kyparissia–Pyrgos road. In the village turn left at the sign for Taxiarches and also (yellow sign) Archaeological Site 1.7 km. A further yellow sign marks the entrance to the site (unfenced) on your right.

Special Features

The site is easily accessible and commands superb views.

History

Although small, Lepreon was the most important community in the region of Triphylia, south of ELIS. A contingent from here fought at PLATAIA (479 BC). Its citizens claimed to be Arkadians, but they were dependent on Elis for long periods. SPARTA liberated them *c.*400 BC, but

Arkadia 275

▲ Fig. 111. The Temple of Apollo at Bassai

they reverted to Eleian control 245–218 BC, and again in 146 BC. By the mid-C2 AD, when Pausanias paid his unrewarding visit, Lepreon was in decline.

Description

The site is a fortified akropolis forming part of a much larger city-circuit. Its dating is insecure. Features include square towers, gates, and a substantial cross-wall lined with what may be **barrack-buildings** [4]. Their construction has been linked with Philip V of Macedon, who garrisoned Lepreon in 219/218 BC. A more general resemblance to MESSENE has also been claimed, especially for the west part of the fortress.

You enter past a modern structure which incorporates part of the

▼ Fig. 112. Plan of Lepreon. Key: 1 Temple of Demeter 2 Altar 3 Gate 4 Cross-wall and barrack-buildings?

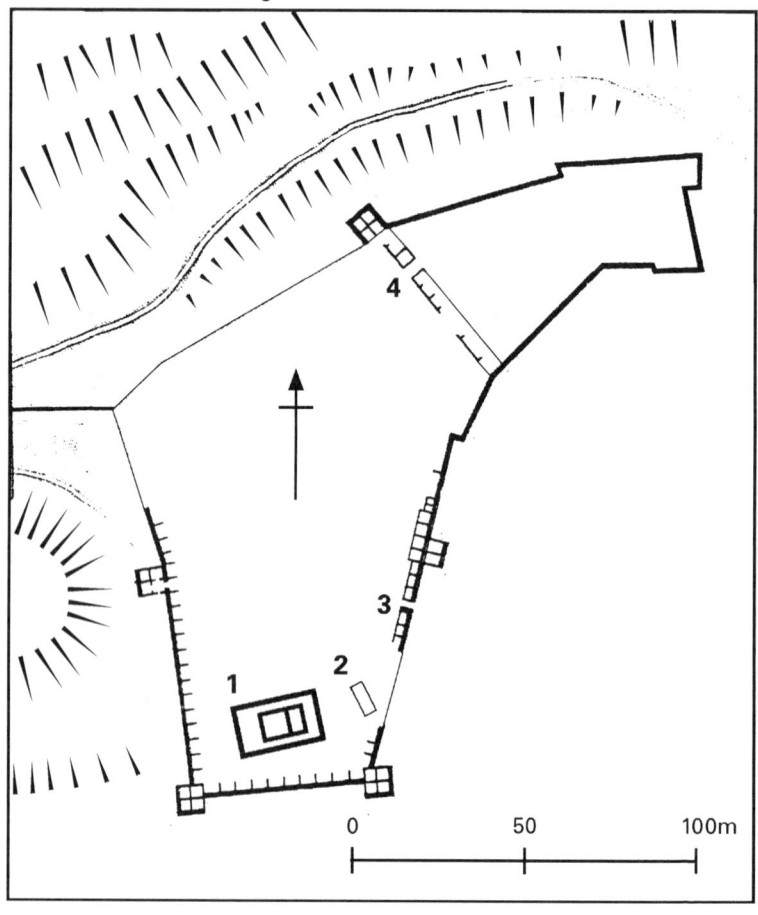

west wall. Continuing south-east you reach the main feature of the site, the foundations of a medium-sized Doric **Temple of Demeter** ([1] – C4 BC), conspicuously sited on a terrace with commanding views. There was an external colonnade of six by eleven columns. The material is coarse local limestone, originally plastered and painted. An **altar [2]** lies at an oblique angle to the east. The temple was noticed by Pausanias, who says that it was built of unbaked brick, by which he may mean the walls of the inner chamber. In his day the statue had gone (5.5.6). The temple is enclosed on two sides by the fortification walls. You can follow the line of these around the summit, passing a **gate** [3] in the east wall.

Alipheira (Figs. 114–115)

Take the turn marked Αρχαία Αλίφειρα/Alifira in the village of Amygdalies on the Andritsaina–Pyrgos road. When you reach modern Alifira, turn right at the sign for the ancient site. Just beyond the village, turn right again onto a dirt road signed Αρχαία Αλίφειρα 2 km. After a short distance there is a dirt track off to the left. From here the site is quite a steep 20 minute walk. Where the dirt track forks, turn left. Where it forks again, after about 10 minutes, follow on the right the first of a series of faded red arrows. A rather faint path leads up to the site.

Special Features

This is a site for lovers of impressive ruins set in remote countryside, a precipitous akropolis transformed into an urban centre by massive terrace walls.

▼ Fig. 113. The Temple of Demeter at Lepreon

History

There is evidence of cult-activity in the sanctuary of Athena in the Archaic period and this culminated in the construction of a temple for the goddess early in the C5 BC. Alipheira was one of the cities in the Arkadian League and Pausanias (8.26) claims that most of the inhabitants moved when MEGALOPOLIS was founded in 371 BC. Yet the temple of Asklepios dates from the late C4 and a number of fine tombs were built for prominent citizens in the C3. ELIS took control of the city in 244 BC and consequently it was attacked by Philip V of Macedon in 219 BC in the course of his campaign against the Aitolians and their Eleian allies. Polybius (4.78) tells us that Philip led the assault in person. The defenders capitulated and a Macedonian garrison was installed. This had evidently been removed by the C2 when Alipheira was once again free. Although of modest size, it was still officially a city in the C2 AD (Pausanias 8.28).

Description

The **Sanctuary of Asklepios** [1] is at the north end of the site on the first of a series of terraces. The temple, built in the late C4 BC, consists of a porch and cella. The base of the cult-statue is preserved in the cella. Pieces of ivory were found when the temple was excavated and it seems likely that they came from the statue to which an ivory head and hands were attached. There was originally a marble table in front of the statue, presumably for dedications. East of the temple is the base of the altar. A short distance above this is a peristyle court which was evidently surrounded by rooms. It is possible that this was a hospice for the sick who came in search of a cure, whether divinely inspired or medically supervised, for their illness.

The wall which supports the terrace above the Asklepieion is protected by a tower and must have been defensive. There is an even larger tower just east of this and the line of the **fortifications** [2] can be followed around the summit. The masonry style is irregular trapezoidal and a C4 BC date seems likely. At the highest point on the citadel there is a separately fortified **akropolis** [3]. Here the masonry is polygonal and could be C5 except for the tower at the west end of the akropolis which was evidently added later. When Philip attacked Alipheira, 'he led a picked force of men up the steep slope and reached the space in front of the akropolis unperceived'. It is possible that he had climbed up the west side of the citadel which was apparently left unfortified.

The signal was now given and the troops at once planted their ladders against the walls and began the assault of the city. The king was the first to enter and took the space in front of the akropolis, which he found unoccupied. When this

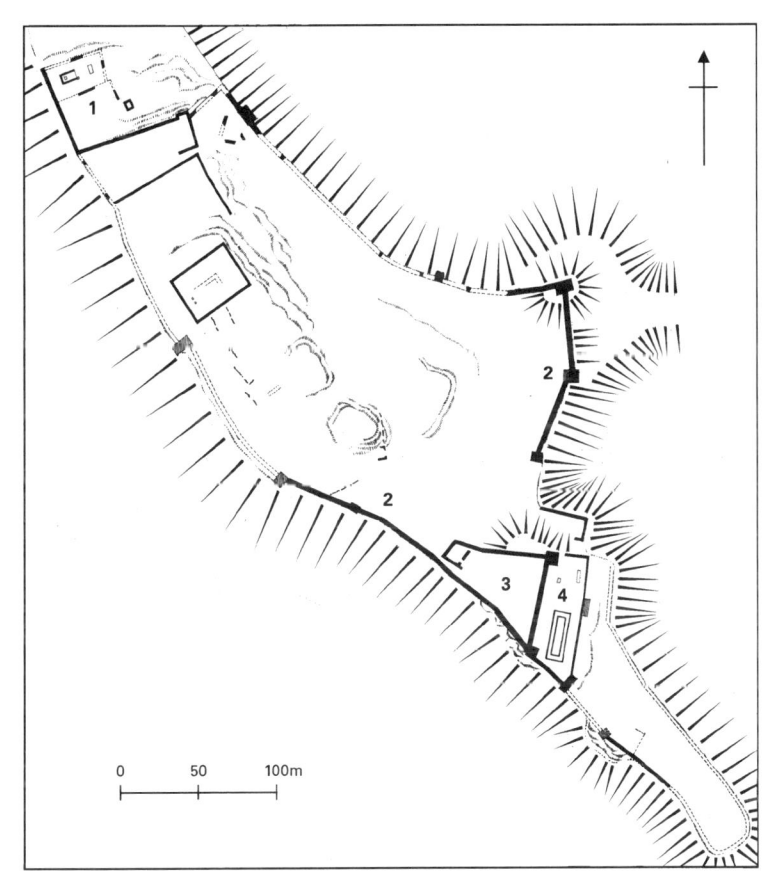

▲ Fig. 114. Plan of Alipheira. Key: 1 Sanctuary of Asklepios 2 Fortifications 3 Akropolis 4 Sanctuary of Athena

was in flames, the defenders on the walls, realizing what was likely to happen and afraid that they would find their last hope gone, left the walls and rushed to take refuge on the akropolis. The Macedonians at once captured the walls and the city. Afterwards the garrison of the akropolis sent commissioners to Philip and, as he promised to spare their lives, they surrendered it to him by treaty.

(Polybius 4.78)

On the terrace south of the akropolis is the **Sanctuary of Athena [4]**. The temple was built c.500–490 BC and is oriented north–south rather than east–west because of the configuration of the site. The peristyle consisted of six by fifteen Doric columns and there was no porch or opisthodomos. The cella may have retained the plan of an earlier temple. There were marble tiles on the roof. The altar is at the north end of the

▲ Fig. 115. The Temple of Athena at Alipheira

terrace and evidently faced east. Opposite is the square base of the colossal bronze statue of Athena by Hypatodoros of Thebes—'one of the most magnificent and artistic statues in existence' in the opinion of Polybius.

Gortys (Figs. 116–118) ★

From the central square at Karitaina, take the road for (11 km.) Atsicholos (Ατσίχολος). Just before the village there is a right turn onto a dirt road signed To Ancient Gortyna (3 km). At a second blue sign keep straight on until you descend into the gorge of the Lousios, passing a small Byzantine church on your left, and stoppng at the third blue sign. The main part of the site is in the field above.

Special Features

The drive takes you through the attractive medieval town of Karitaina to the dramatic gorge of the River Lousios (Gortynios) where the site is located. The Hellenistic baths are the chief attraction.

History

Gortys was a small and insignificant Arkadian polis included by Pausanias (8.27.3) in his 'list of the cities which the Arkadians in their zeal and out of the hatred they bore the Spartans were persuaded to abandon' in

Arkadia 281

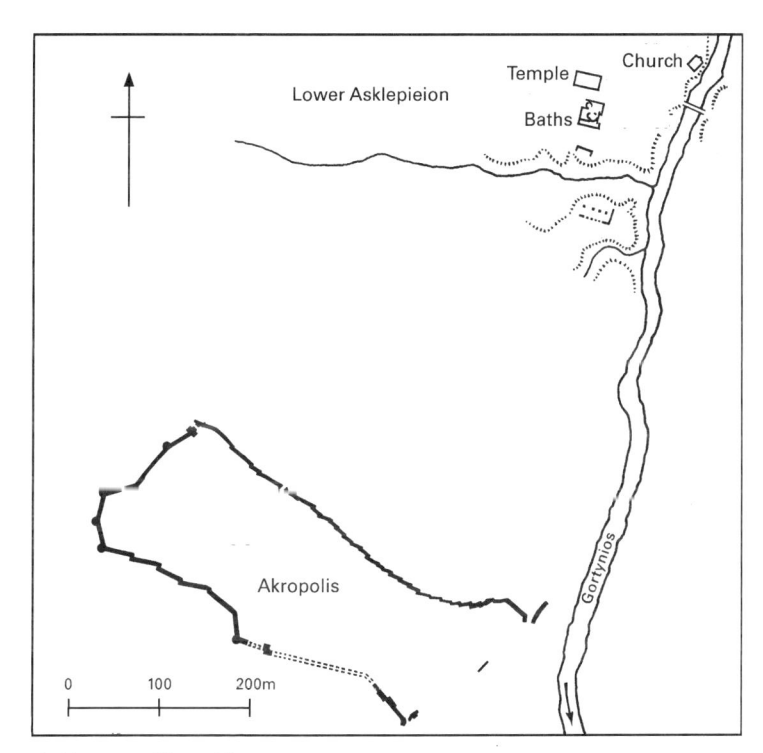

▲ Fig. 116. Plan of Gortys

order to found MEGALOPOLIS (371 BC). It survived as a dependent village. The refreshing waters of the Lousios, claimed by Pausanias to be colder than any other river, encouraged Gortys to develop as a spa based on a shrine of the health-god Asklepios. In the C4 BC this shrine was rich enough to hire Skopas, a top sculptor (see TEGEA), and famous enough to attract (or so it was later said) a dedication of arms by Alexander the Great (Pausanias 8.28.1). Another prominent figure, the Achaian leader Philopoimen of Megalopolis, dedicated a statue of his daughter here, as an unpublished inscription shows.

Description

The site comprises a fortified akropolis and Asklepieion to the south-west, and below, on a natural terrace overlooking the ravine, a second **Asklepieion**. Its best-preserved, and most interesting feature, is a **bath-complex** (C4 BC with Hellenistic alterations). As first built, this took the form of a rubble-walled rectangle divided up into rooms supplied with water by a conduit, and equipped (c.300 BC) with a pool for bathing by immersion. From c.250 BC to c. 100 BC, a series of alterations converted

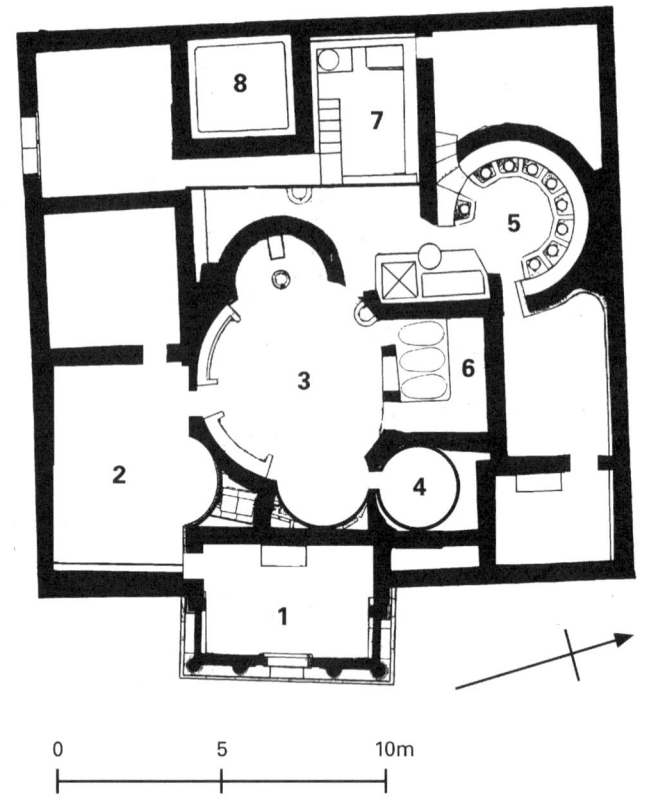

▲ Fig. 117. Plan of the baths at Gortys. Key: 1 Porch 2 Changing room 3 Central hall 4 Sweat-room 5 Rotunda 6 Immersion-baths 7 Furnace 8 Reservoir

this bath building into what has been seen as an Arkadian prototype for Roman baths. The building was now entered through an east-facing Ionic **porch** [**117.1**], giving access to a heated **changing room** [**117.2**]. From here you entered a large **central hall** [**117.3**], equipped with two fountains and a bench, and again heated. Off this room was a small circular **sweat-room** [**117.4**], with a very thin floor, also heated from below. To the north-west was a circular **rotunda** or tholos [**117.5**] with individual hip-baths round the wall, where hot water would be poured over the seated bather. In [**117.6**] there were three **immersion-baths**. The service area was on the south-west side, including the **furnace** [**117.7**] and **reservoir** [**118.8**]. The complex could deal with 20–30 bathers at a time. Its most original feature was the hypocaust-system, which circulated heated air from the furnace through brick channels below the floor. It appears here for the first time in Greece.

▲ Fig. 118. The baths at Gortys

Just to the north are the massive foundations for a colonnaded **temple** (c.370 BC), abandoned before the superstructure was begun, perhaps c.362 BC, when the Thebans were called in by the Arkadian League to suppress a revolt by Gortys.

Achaia and Elis

Achaia consists of a narrow coastal plain backed by the Panachaikon mountains. The alluvial soil of the plain is intensively cultivated and the mountains were a source of cedar, fir, and oak in the past. This region is particularly earthquake prone. In 373 BC severe shocks struck the city of Helike which was then overwhelmed by a tidal wave and submerged. Pausanias (7.24) reports that the ruins were still visible underwater. Elis has one of the most extensive and fertile plains in the Peloponnese, excellent pasture for cattle and horses. Flax was also cultivated and taken to PATRAS (ancient Patrai) to be turned into linen dresses.

In Elis prehistoric settlement is limited except around OLYMPIA which was evidently a site of some importance by the Early Helladic period and is surrounded by Mycenaean cemeteries. Worship of Zeus here is attested at least from the 900s BC. The evolution of the games transformed this regional shrine into a panhellenic one by the C6. Control of the Archaic games was contested, by the Pisatans and Eleians among local communities, who also included the men of LEPREON. In the 470s BC a new political centre for the region was founded at ELIS, on which Lepreon and other smaller neighbours were now dependent. The Eleians by now were the recognized hosts of the Olympian games, and Elis remained the region's political centre down into Roman imperial times. The whole area was well-known for its rural character, with a dense population scattered mainly in villages.

By the Mycenaean period Achaia was quite densely settled but most of our evidence comes from cemeteries and no site stands out as an obvious regional centre. There was apparently an influx of settlers in the C12 BC. On the basis of pottery found at AIGEIRA it has been claimed that they came from outside Greece, although this seems unlikely. The region was inhabited in Geometric times by the Achaian 'people' (*ethnos*), and produced an early (C8 BC) temple at Aigeira, one of the twelve cities forming the Achaian federation. First heard of in 453 BC, the league expanded into a major land power in the C3, before defeat and dissolution by Rome (146 BC). Achaia's chief port at Patrai, made a Roman colony by Augustus, thereafter dominated the region until the close of antiquity.

Olympia (Figs. 119–121)

Special Features

This is one of the most impressive classical sanctuary sites in Greece and there is an outstanding museum.

History

The site lies in a wooded, well-watered, valley at the confluence of the rivers Alpheios and Kladeos, overlooked by a low akropolis (the Hill of Kronos). Prehistoric settlement in the vicinity is well attested. Cult-activity from the C11 BC is shown by finds of votive offerings, including figurines of animals and chariots, suggesting the prominence of stock-breeding chieftains from the western Peloponnese among the early worshippers of Olympian Zeus. The Greek writer Strabo (C1 BC) claimed that Olympia owed its initial fame to its oracle, which specialized in military matters, and was interpreted by two long-lived lineages of local diviners, the Iamidai and the Klytiadai. Greek tradition dates to 776 BC the creation of a four-yearly festival here, featuring sporting competitions. It acquired a special renown, and by the C6 BC contestants came from all over the Greek world, including Sicily and southern Italy. In the course of the C6 BC the citizens of ELIS, some 40 km. away, came to manage both sanctuary and festival. In the C5 BC this lasted five days, and there were horse and chariot races as well as athletics for both boys and men. Winners, or 'Olympionikai' as they were known, won an olive-wreath, the right to display their image in the sanctuary, and great renown, enjoying distinctions in their home cities such as free dinners for life. Athletics made Olympia politically important: inter-state treaties were displayed here, and Greek states rivalled each other in building treasuries and monuments marking success in war. Philip II of Macedon was honoured at Olympia with the Philippeion (338 BC), a building which advertised his family's divine pretensions to the Greeks. Architectural embellishment had got under way c.650 BC; by Philip's day Olympia was an artistic showcase rivalled only by DELPHI. In Hellenistic times Olympia continued to expand its athletic facilities, but suffered in the early phase of Roman rule in Greece. Sulla looted it (86 BC). Imperial patronage prompted a revival, and the games and cult-statue by the sculptor Pheidias, now one of the Seven Wonders of the World, became potent emblems of Classical Greece for nostalgic contemporaries. Agrippa, the son-in-law of Augustus, repaired the temple, Tiberius won the chariot race (4 BC), and Nero, who competed as a musician in specially convened games (AD 67), was also a benefactor. In the C2 AD, with Olympia once again the premier athletic meet of the ancient world, a final expansion of amenities took place, including the installation of an up-to-date water-supply, paid for by the ubiquitous Herodes Atticus (pp. 117–118). The visit of Pausanias, whose admiring description takes up 41 chapters of his guide-book, took place c. AD 173. In the mid-C3 the barbarian threat prompted the construction of a defensive wall around the temple and bouleuterion, incorporating many demolished monuments. The temple was restored c.300 for a last time, and the games continued in an unbroken tradition until at least the late C4, as shown by a recently found inscription recording two Athenian brothers who were boy-victors in 381 and 385 respectively. In the early C5 the workshop of Pheidias was converted into a church for a community of local Christians, whose houses and workshops nestled in the former sanctuary. By the close of antiquity the classical monuments had succumbed to earthquakes and flooding, and Slavs had settled in the vicinity.

Description

The **museum** has helpful models of the sanctuary in the vestibule. **Gallery 1** contains prehistoric and Geometric material, including parts of bronze cauldrons and horse-models. **Gallery 2** has Orientalizing bronzes; a collection of C8 BC and Archaic dedications of arms and armour, reflecting the military character of the early cult; architectural terracottas from the Heraion; and a striking limestone female head (*c.*600 BC), often identified (erroneously) as part of a cult-statue, but perhaps from a sphinx. **Gallery 3** includes pottery dedications, the bronze head of a battering ram (C6 BC), and sculpture and architectural terracottas from the treasuries. **Gallery 4** has a votive helmet of Asiatic type captured in the Persian wars (490–479 BC) and inscribed 'the Athenians after taking (it) from the Medes (dedicated it) to Zeus' ; also a Corinthian helmet, baldly inscribed 'Miltiades dedicated (it) to Zeus', a gift from the future hero of Marathon; a half life-size group in terracotta shows Zeus purposefully abducting the beautiful Ganymede as his winesteward; clay moulds from the workshop of Pheidias for making the gold drapery of the statue of Zeus; and the Winged Victory (*c.*420 BC), originally displayed on a pillar *c.*10 m. high, and marking a victory by the Messenians and Naupaktians, Athenian allies, in the Peloponnesian War. **Gallery 5** has assorted sculpture. **Gallery 6** has a controversial masterpiece, a Hermes holding the infant Dionysos, found in the temple of Hera on the spot where Pausanias had seen it. Pausanias attributed it to Praxiteles, the famous C4 BC Athenian sculptor, but nowadays it is increasingly seen as a derivative work of the C2 BC, a date which would suit the post-Classical footwear. **Gallery 7** has seven of the eight imperial statues from the Metroon, the head of Titus (AD 79–81) fitted onto a reused statue of Nero; also statues from the nymphaion of Herodes, including a bull, Zeus's sacrificial victim, with the dedicatory inscription 'Regilla, priestess of Demeter, (dedicated) the water and the (objects) around the water to Zeus' (*IVO* no. 610).

The **Central Gallery** contains the architectural sculpture from the temple of Zeus, with good information-panels which give details of the myths. The arrangement of the pediments is new and (in 2000) as yet unpublished. The choice of subject-matter demonstrates how Elis sought to promote Olympia's larger importance The east pediment shows a local myth with a pan-Peloponnesian relevance, the preparations for the murderous chariot race between Pelops, who gave his name to the peninsula, and Oinomaos, king of Pisa. They flank the central Zeus respectively on his right and left; the woman on Pelops' right is normally identified as his bride-to-be, Hippodamia. The west pediment depicts the wedding-feast of the Thessalian prince Peirithoos, a grandson of Zeus, after some of his guests, the half-equine centaurs, have rioted from alcohol and are attacking the women. The central figure is Apollo, ancestor of the Iamids, with Peirithoos and Theseus, his Athenian friend, to left and right respectively. The metopes illustrate the Twelve Labours of Herakles, and were placed over the front and rear porches, six at either end. Herakles was a local hero, the mythical founder of the games, but also a universal figure, the greatest of Greek heroes and the ancestor of the Dorian Greeks, whose heartland was the Peloponnese.

A bridge takes the main road from the modern town across the **Kladeos** [1], in antiquity channelled away from the sanctuary by a wall at least 800 m. long and 3 m. high. There is a helpful information-panel just inside the entrance to the site with a reconstruction and a plan.

On your right you pass a collection of buildings forming the **gymnasium**, originally an open space for athletic training, but in time given an architectural form. First come the remains of a large irregular court originally framed by four Doric colonnades. The one nearest the path is a **xystos** [2], housing two parallel practice-tracks (C2 BC). Its counterpart on the west side, since washed away by the Kladeos, accommodated athletes. A monumental **gateway** [3] in the Corinthian order was added c.100–50 BC to this complex, which directly abuts (next on the right) the **palaistra** [4], of c.300–250 BC. This was a wide courtyard framed by Doric colonnades, in turn masking a series of rooms and halls, one identified as a dining room (south-west corner), the three on the north side as a library. The donor of this splendid facility may have been a Hellenistic king. To its south was a **heroon** ([5]—c. 450 BC), a feature of gymnasia, with a circular room, perhaps for sacred meals. A central altar was found here inscribed 'belonging to the Hero' (*IVO* no. 662), his identity unknown. To the south-west athletes were served by a sequence of **bath-buildings** ([6]—inaccessible), including the earliest (c.100 BC) Roman-style bath in Greece (see GORTYS).

Immediately east of the heroon are the remains, now difficult to understand, of two **courtyard houses** (c.450 BC) of uncertain function. The earlier [7], of c.450 BC, may have been an old palaistra, rather than (the usual identification) the *theokoleion* or 'house of the priests (*theokoloi*)' of Pausanias 5.15.4. In the C1 BC it was partly overlaid by a much larger **residential house** [8] to the east, possibly for sanctuary workers.

Just south is what Pausanias describes as the '**workshop of Pheidias**' [9], where 'Pheidias fashioned the image piece by piece' (5.15.1). It was the second highest building in Olympia, big enough for a statue over

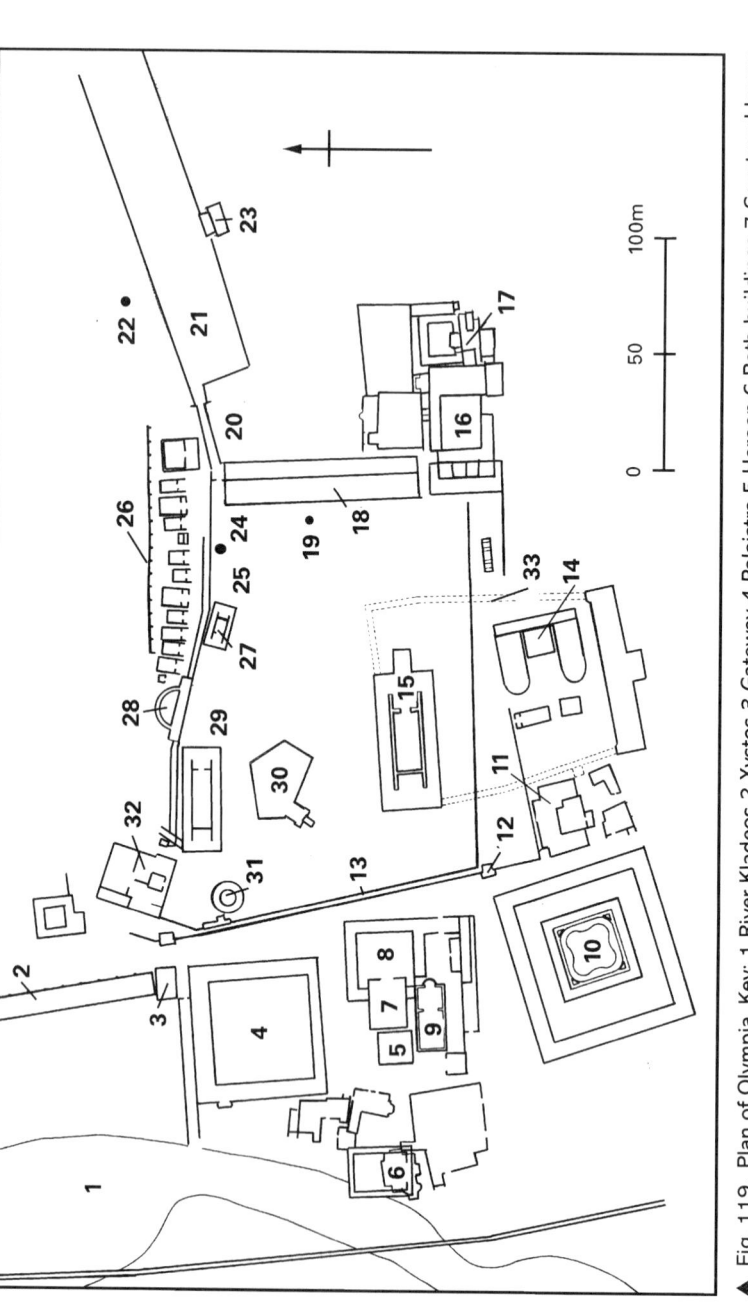

▲ Fig. 119. Plan of Olympia. Key: 1 River Kladeos 2 Xystos 3 Gateway 4 Palaistra 5 Heroon 6 Bath-buildings 7 Courtyard house 8 Residential house 9 'Workshop of Pheidias' 10 Leonidaion 11 Club-house 12 Processional entrance 13 Wall 14 Bouleuterion 15 Temple of Zeus 16 House of Nero 17 Roman baths 18 Doric colonnade 19 Honorific monument 20 Secret entrance 21 Stadium 22 Altar 23 Umpires' stand 24 Bases 25 Terrace 26 Treasuries 27 Metroon 28 Nymphaion 29 Temple of Hera 30 Precinct of Pelops 31 Philippeion 32 Prytaneion

12 m. tall, and its internal plan was temple-like, resembling the cella of the temple to which the image was transferred. In the C2 AD the workshop housed an altar of all the gods. In the C5 it was converted into a church, the old entrance being closed by an apse. The inside was now clad in marble, and the last two inscriptions from ancient Olympia record the two lectors from the local church, Kyriakos and Andreas, who saw to this work.

To the south is the **Leonidaion** (c.350 BC), at 6000 m.² the largest building in Olympia [**10**]. It was the gift of 'Leonides son of Leotes, the Naxian', as he records on an inscription in large letters once displayed on two sides of the building's architrave (*IVO* no. 651). Pausanias mistakenly calls him a local man. The building, surrounded by Ionic columns, with rooms ranged round a colonnaded court, served as a sumptuous guesthouse and banqueting area, perhaps mainly for aristocratic Greeks come to race their horses. In the mid-C2 AD it was used as a residence by the Roman governor, having been rebuilt after a severe fire. Its inner court was now converted into a cool water-garden, the centrepiece a circular island, in spirit recalling Tivoli, the great villa of Hadrian outside Rome.

Just east of the Leonidaion (inaccessible, but tidied up and visible) is a Roman building of brick construction recently identified as a **clubhouse** [**11**] for the Greek guild of athletes. It was probably begun through Nero's patronage, was in use by the later C1 AD, and was still functioning in the late C4. Its most prominent feature is a facade c. 10 m. high with three arched statue-niches. This overlooked a swimming pool and a court, all once veneered in coloured marble. Two large training rooms flanked the court.

Opposite the north-east corner of the Leonidaion are the remains of what Pausanias called the '**processional entrance**' [**12**] into the **Altis** or sacred grove (5.15.2), set into a poorly built precinct-wall of (probably) C2 AD date, originally high enough to prevent outsiders seeing in. This enlarged a space originally bounded by the roughly parallel wall to the east [**13**], dating from c.300 BC and in effect just a parapet. By the time of Pausanias the Altis bristled with centuries of accumulated dedications and statues of victors. Bases for many remain more or less in place.

Further down on the right are the remains of the **bouleuterion** [**14**], in Roman times the seat of the Olympic council, the Eleian body which administered the games and sanctuary, and the place where participants swore to observe the rules of the games. The odd plan, hard to make out on the ground, features two apsidal chambers built at different times, the older one (to the north) c. 550 BC, the other c. 500 BC. It has been suggested that the old-fashioned architecture may reflect a local vernacular tradition, the peculiar dualism the ancient rivalry between the Eleians and Pisatans, who lived in the district round Olympia. Later a large room (c. 370 BC) linked the two chambers, and the whole was fronted by an Ionic colonnade, also C4 BC. South of the complex is the large '**South Stoa**' (*c.*350 BC), a double colonnade with a projecting centre, perhaps a viewing stand for VIPs. It faced south, overlooking the processional route from Elis and the hippodrome.

To the north is [**15**] the **Temple of Zeus** (*c.*470 BC), even now the most imposing structure at Olympia. Temple and statue were a thank-offering, paid for by Elis with booty from a successful war against Pisa. And they put into the shade, as they surely were meant to, the more modest temple of Hera (below), funded by Scillus, another neighbour and rival. The temple was Doric, built mainly from the local shell-limestone, the coarse finish disguised by a plaster coating. A ramp gave access to the temple-platform. Within the colonnade of six by thirteen columns was a conventional tripartite chamber consisting of a front porch entered through bronze doors, a main room containing the statue, and a rear porch which could be used as a lecture-hall; the historian Herodotus read out his work here. Inside the main room towered the god, made of gold and ivory, seated on a richly adorned throne, in turn supported by a base with gold figures. A barrier limited access, but visitors could ascend to a first-floor viewing gallery. The sculptor was the Athenian Pheidias, and the dignity of his conception of Zeus was widely admired in ancient times, prompting one Greek poet to write: 'Either Zeus descended to you from heaven, or you, great artist, ascended and saw the god' (*Greek Anthology* 16.81). For the sculpture decorating the exterior of the temple, see above pp. 286–287. The temple was frequently repaired in antiquity. Probably it was already a roofless ruin by the

▼ Fig. 120. Column drums from the Temple of Zeus at Olympia

C6 AD, when an earthquake destroyed the colonnade. The statue had been removed to Constantinople by AD 395.

To the north-east of the temple, its rough site marked by a stone cairn, was the **altar of Zeus**, the true focus of his cult, and one of the wonders of Olympia. Made of sacrificial ashes mixed ritually with water from the Alpheios, by the C2 AD it rose *c.*7 m. high.

South-east of the temple is a roped-off area, the remains practically invisible through the undergrowth. They include the so-called **House of Nero** [16], a palatial residence for which earlier Greek buildings were demolished. In fact the imperial link is doubtful, as the known building-phases are later (C2–C3 AD). In the early C3 Olympia's largest **Roman baths** [17] were built just to the east.

Just north of the 'House of Nero', its plan no longer very clear, is all that remains of a once-imposing **Doric colonnade** [18], the 98-m. long **Stoa Poikile** (late C4 BC, with a major rebuilding, possibly under Augustus). Named like its Athens counterpart from paintings once (but by the C2 AD no longer) displayed there, it was also called the **Echo Stoa**, 'for the echo repeats a word seven times or even oftener' (Pausanias 5.21.7). The same architect is thought to have worked on the Philippeion (below), and the stoa may have been a Macedonian gift. It replaced an earlier earth grandstand, and likewise served as a tribune for spectators of ritual in the Altis (below).

In front are remains of the largest **honorific monument** [19] in the Altis: an oblong pedestal *c.*20 m. long which once supported a pair of marble Ionic columns, each *c.*9 m. high, in turn topped by statues, now lost. Two inscriptions show that they depicted the Egyptian rulers Ptolemy II (282–246 BC), a leading player in Peloponnesian power-politics, and his sister-wife, Arsinoe II.

Just north of the stoa is what Pausanias (6.20.5) calls the **secret entrance** [20], a vaulted tunnel (*c.*200 BC) leading to the stadium, for use by the umpires (*Hellanodikai*, usually ten) and the contestants only. It was entered by a gate set into an arch, re-erected in modern times.

The present **stadium** ([21]—C4 BC, with later alterations) is an enlarged version of a predecessor on roughly the same site. Throughout its history up to *c.*40,000 spectators sat directly on earth embankments, which were never upgraded with the stone seating increasingly common elsewhere from the C4 BC on. Another old-fashioned feature was the ritual exclusion of married women from the games. The one exception was the Eleian priestess of Demeter Chamyne. The stone **altar** [22] on which she sat (C2 AD) has been reassembled on the north embankment. On the south you can see the paved **umpires' stand** ([23]—C4 BC, with later enlargements), placed a surprising 60 m. short of the start/finish line, one of two at either end, with places for twenty runners. The course is 191.78 m. long. The unexcavated site of the **hippodrome** lies to the south.

Re-entering the Altis you pass (right) a row of **bases** [**24**] for bronze images of Zeus called Zanes. Pausanias says that they were funded from fines paid by athletes who broke the Olympic rules, mainly by offering bribes. He knew of a modest fourteen for the period from 388 BC to his own day.

The Zanes back onto a stepped **terrace** [**25**] at the foot of the Hill of Kronos, part of the 'theatre' attested in 364 BC. It was probably used chiefly for watching the procession and sacrifices occupying a whole day of the C5 BC festival. On the terrace is a row of eleven poorly-preserved **treasuries** [**26**]. These temple-like monuments were offerings by Greek cities, spanning the period *c.*560–450 BC. Eight were set up by overseas colonies, five of them in southern Italy or Sicily, one in north Africa. From left to right (after a small shrine just east of the nymphaion) the row starts with Sikyon (*c.*450 BC, some modern reconstruction), then Syracuse (early C5 BC), Epidamnos (*c.*525 BC), Byzantion, Sybaris (before 510 BC), ?Cyrene, ?Cyrene again, followed by an ?altar, and then Selinous, Metaponton, Megara (510 BC), and Gela (*c.*560 BC). In Pausanias' time they acted as display-units for miscellaneous antiquities, such as 'the sword of Pelops with a golden hilt' which he saw in the Sikyonian treasury (6.19.3).

Below the terrace are the substantial remains of a small Doric temple (*c.*400 BC), the **Metroon** [**27**] or shrine of the Mother, also known as Rhea, the mother of Zeus. Under Augustus there was a far-reaching renovation, and the Eleians rededicated the temple to the first Roman emperor, hailed in an inscription on the architrave as 'saviour of the Greeks and the whole inhabited world' (*SEG* 42 [1992] 390). The eight imperial statues once set up inside were discovered by the excavators and are on display in the museum, except for one now in Berlin.

West of the Metroon is a monstrous **nymphaion** [**28**] or fresh-water fountain of *c.* AD 153, the terminal for an aqueduct bringing water from a source to the east, all paid for by the Athenian magnate Herodes Atticus (pp. 117–118) in the name of Regilla, his wife. The water flowed into an upper basin, whence lion's-head spouts fed it into a rectangular basin below, flanked by circular pavilions (*monopteroi*). An apsidal rear-wall carrying two stories of niches for a total of 24 statues (see museum), depicting Herodes and his clan above and the imperial family below, towered over the installation, the whole clad with coloured marble. The amenity replaced the brackish wells for which Olympia was notorious. But it caused fierce debate in its day, with a Greek philosopher denouncing it as a threat to the traditional simplicity of the games, and Pausanias ignoring it entirely.

West of the nymphaion are the well-preserved remains of the Doric **Temple of Hera** ([**29**]—early C6 BC), who was honoured in the C2 AD with four-yearly games for women only. The temple, the earliest at Olympia, may originally have been dedicated to Zeus. The limestone

▲ Fig. 121. Reconstruction of the nymphaion of Herodes Atticus at Olympia (R. Bol, *Olympische Forschungen*, Bd XV, *Das Statuenprogram des Herodes-Atticus-Nymphäums*, 1984)

walls were finished in sun-dried brick, and the all-wood columns were gradually upgraded to stone, although one still survived in Pausanias' day. By then the temple was a crowded museum for a miscellany of valuable antiques, among them *c.*21 gold-and-ivory statues of early date and one of Olympia's marvels, a cedarwood chest (possibly early C6 BC) with intricate appliqué figures in gold, wood, and ivory.

Just south is the (inaccessible) **precinct of Pelops** ([30]—C10 BC with later alterations), an artificial mound built over prehistoric remains—Early Helladic houses and a tumulus—which was claimed as the hero's grave. Pelops was a hero in the folkloric mould of the stranger (from Asia in this case) who turns up and marries the king's daughter (here Hippodamia). In the time of Pausanias a black ram was sacrificed to him each year (5.13.2).

Nearby to the north-west is the **Philippeion** ([31]—after 338 BC), a circular and temple-like Ionic structure of stone and marble built to house a gold-and-ivory statue-group of Philip II of Macedon, his parents, his wife, and Alexander, their son. The material of the statues, the form of the building, and the location inside the Altis must have combined to present the Macedonian royals to Greek onlookers as superhuman—a distasteful notion to many in Greece.

Not far to the north are the indistinct remains of the **Prytaneion** [**32**], the *hôtel de ville* of the Eleians, which Pausanias says housed the city's sacred hearth and a dining room where the Eleians feasted the Olympic victors (5.15.7). Its date is uncertain, perhaps as late as the C1 AD. The original Prytaneion was in the south-east of the sanctuary, on the site of the 'House of Nero'.

Elis (Fig. 122)

The turn off the main road is signed 'Ancient Ilida'. In the village of Avgeio take the left-hand fork and continue for another 2 km. to the museum.

Special Features

A small museum, remnants of once substantial architecture, and rich farmland all around evoke one of the largest and most populous civic communities of the ancient Peloponnese.

History

The city-site in the plain of the river Peneios was already occupied by the C12 BC, but became a 'city' only *c.*471 BC, when it emerged as the political centre for the region. There were three fine gymnasia, used by athletes training for the games at OLYMPIA. The city was a Spartan, and later an Aitolian ally, before forced incorporation into the Achaian League (191 BC). Under the early emperors Elis was immune from Roman tribute, and new buildings, including baths, attest to its prosperity. The landowning elite now mixed families claiming descent from Eleian heroes with Italian incomers. The civic centre was badly damaged in the C3 AD, perhaps by barbarian raids, and in late antiquity a large cemetery grew up in the former agora and vicinity. In AD 450–500 a Christian basilica with fine mosaics was built on the south side of the old agora.

Description

In the main room of the **museum** there is a plan and a reconstruction of the site. On display are Early and Middle Helladic finds from the akropolis; Submycenaean pottery from tombs by the theatre; finds from the theatre which include Roman lamps depicting gladiators and a wild-beast show, as well as bronze 'tickets'; fragments of Archaic and Classical architectural terracottas; coins; black- and red-figure, Hellenistic and Roman pottery; and Hellenistic and Roman sculpture, including a fine male portrait (C2–C3 AD). The courtyard has two circular mosaics

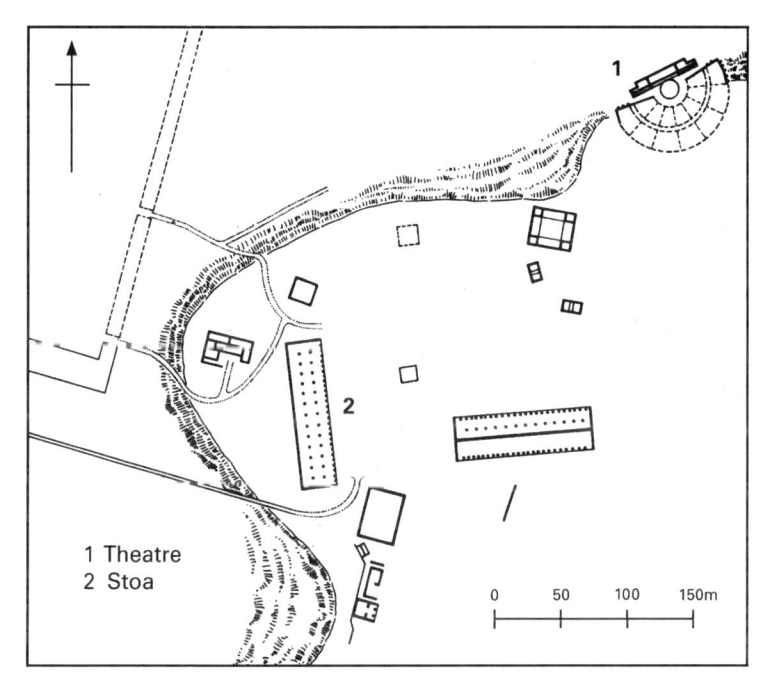

Fig. 122. Plan of Elis

(C3 AD) found in a large Roman building south-west of the agora, one depicting Apollo and the Twelve Muses, the other the Twelve Labours of Herakles.

The **theatre** [1], which is C4 BC, with later alterations, is by the museum, the audience looking out towards the river Peneios. Pausanias (6.26.1) calls the theatre 'ancient' : there were no stone seats, and the stone stage is one of the earliest in Greece. The building went out of use in late antiquity, when the area was used for burials.

About 200 m. south of the museum remains of a massive **stoa** [2] straddle the modern road. This is identified with the Doric stoa 'divided into three aisles by the columns', in which 'the Hellanodikai (the umpires at the Olympian festival) usually spend the day' (Pausanias 6.24.2). Facing east, this overlooked the agora, said by Pausanias to be 'old-fashioned', since its stoas were separated by streets, instead of forming a continuous enclosure as was normal in his day. The agora had a rustic feel, being called Hippodrome, because the Eleians used it to train their horses.

A further 200 m. back along the road there is a Roman complex on the right, reusing earlier material, and on the left, after the modern aqueduct, you can see a brick-built complex, also Roman.

Patras (Fig. 123)

Special features

Ancient Patrai, like its modern successor on the same site, was the chief city of the north-west Peloponnese. The substantial Roman odeion should be seen, and there is a small museum.

History

The Patras area was already settled and flourished in Mycenaean times. Founded by the Achaians on a spur of Mt Panachaikon, Greek Patrai was relatively insignificant until the C3 BC, when mounting contacts between Italy and Greece gave it a new importance as a port. Antony and Cleopatra stayed here before the battle of Actium (31 BC). Augustus founded (officially in 16/15 BC) a settlement of legionary veterans at Patrai, its official name now known from coins to be *Colonia Augusta Achaica Patrensis*. The new colony was endowed with a vast territory on both sides of the Corinthian gulf, and the emperor transferred the cult of Artemis Laphria from KALYDON to the akropolis here, where she was worshipped as Diana Laphria Augusta and served by priestesses of Italian descent. The city was one of the chief centres of Roman Greece, located on a Roman trunk road linking the west Peloponnese with Corinth. Especially from the Flavian period (C1 AD), excavations attest extensive building activity, including public baths, a bridge, an aqueduct, and luxurious private houses, as well as the odeion and amphitheatre. Tombstones attest a Christian presence from the C3–C4 on. The city survived, its population much reduced, into the middle ages.

Description

The only major structure from antiquity is the brick-faced **odeion** [1] next to Plateia 25 Martiou, its date uncertain, but earlier than the visit of Pausanias in the late C2 AD, who rated it with the odeion of Herodes Atticus in ATHENS, as the most impressive of all Greek odeia. It was rediscovered in 1889, and has been heavily restored since, including the new marble seating. How it was used is uncertain, although dramatic and musical contests are known for the Roman city (below). Pausanias sites it next to the agora.

Below the square, and best viewed from the pedestrian street (Ifestou) below, you can see part of the massive barrel-vaulted substructure of the **amphitheatre** [2], of *c.* AD 100–150, sited to take advantage of the natural slope of the akropolis, and possibly the 'theatre' seen by Pausanias. Only one other amphitheatre is known in Greece, at Corinth. Its chief use would have been for wild-beast shows and gladiatorial combats, the last well-attested in Roman Patrai.

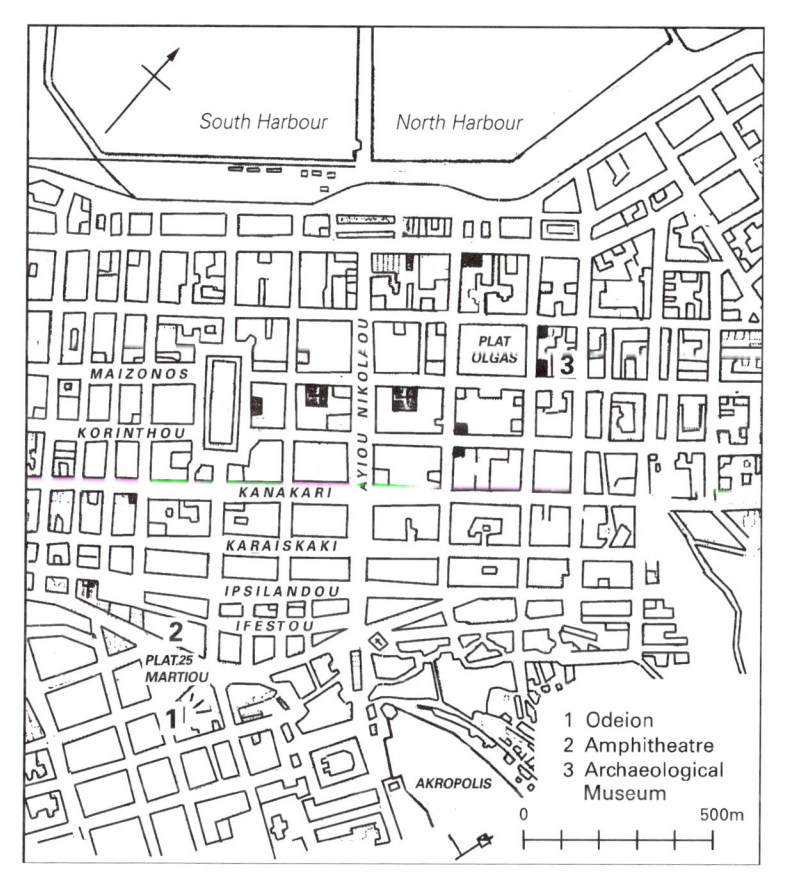

▲ Fig. 123. Plan of Patras

The **Archaeological Museum** [3] is on Odos Maizonos on the east side of Plateia Olgas. The room to the left has a large mosaic from a Roman house, with scenes of Greek athletic (below) and (above) dramatic and musical contests. Greek games remained part of the cultural scene in the Roman colony, as inscriptions also show. The same room also has sculpture from Classical to (mainly) Roman times. A gravestone depicts the deceased, a Roman soldier, in the pose of the Spear-Bearer, a famous statue by the sculptor Polykleitos (late C5 BC). In the room on the right there is Mycenaean pottery, jewellery, and bronzes from chamber tombs in Achaia—note in particular the swords and greaves in case 2—also pottery and weapons from Late Geometric graves. Some of the gold jewellery from the Classical-Hellenistic cemeteries in Patras is particularly impressive. Roman finds include glass and alabaster vessels, and an extraordinary disc with an ivory frame in which pieces of blue glass have been inset, possibly from the window of a C2 house in the city.

Aigeira (Fig. 124)

Take the turn for ΑΙΓΑΙ which is on the left as you leave Egira on the Old National Road in the direction of Corinth. There is also a battered sign ΠΡΟΣ ΑΡΧΑΙΟ ΘΕΑΤΡΟ ΑΙΓΕΙΡΑΣ. The road climbs steeply and after 5.2 km. there is another sign for the ΑΡΧΑΙΟ ΘΕΑΤΡΟ which is a short distance down a track.

Special Features

Aigeira has a fine Hellenistic theatre and the view across the Corinthian Gulf is superb.

History

Prehistoric settlement is attested on the akropolis, in particular C12 BC levels which date from the period when the Mycenaean palaces were destroyed. The appearance in these levels of a type of hand-made burnished pottery is of particular interest because it has been argued that this was introduced by invaders. It is certainly quite unlike Mycenaean pottery but could reflect a decline in the level of specialized production rather than the arrival of ceramically impoverished northerners. At this time Aigeira was apparently called Hyperesia but was renamed as a result of an incident in the C7 which Pausanias mentions in his description of the city (7.26).

A hostile army from SIKYON was about to invade. The people knew that they were no match for the Sikyonians so they collected all the nanny-goats in the countryside, herded them together, and tied torches on their horns, then late at night they set fire to the torches. The Sikyonians thought that help had come to Hyperesia and these were the fires of their allies, so they went home again, and the Hyperesians renamed their city after the nanny-goats (*aiges*).

After this bestial reincarnation we do not hear about Aigeira again until the Hellenistic period. The city evidently benefited from the revival of the Achaian League in 281/280 BC, since the theatre and the shrines were constructed in the C3. The Aitolians attacked Aigeira in 219 BC but were repulsed. Polybius (4.57) explains that 'a certain Aitolian deserter, who had spent some time at Aigeira, noticed that the guards of the Aigion gate were constantly drunk'. So a force of 1200 Aitolians crossed the gulf, killed the guards, and entered the city. However, 'they only stayed together for a short time in the vicinity of the agora and then their passion for plunder caused them to disperse'. The men of Aigeira regrouped on the akropolis and fought back. The Aitolians fled and most 'were either trampled to death or dashed to pieces when they attempted to escape down cliffs where there was no path'. The theatre and the shrines were remodelled in the C2 AD, around the time that Pausanias visited the city. He records a number of sanctuaries and certainly does not give the impression that Aigeira was in decline, although the theatre became a stone quarry later.

Description

The **theatre** was set back against the side of the hill so that the rows of seats below the diazoma could be cut from the conglomerate bedrock. The stone used for the upper rows of seats has been removed. A water channel separates the cavea from the semicircular orchestra. When the theatre was constructed in the C3, there was a rectangular skene flanked by paraskenia. The proskenion, in front of the skene, was supported on a row of Doric columns and formed a raised stage. In the C2 AD the Hellenistic skene was dismantled. A wall was built across the orchestra and considerably increased the size of the stage. The row of buttresses behind this wall supported a high scaenae frons which was no doubt richly decorated.

The two **shrines** (*naiskoi*) just north of the theatre have recently been covered by a roof. A colossal marble head from shrine D, now in the National Archaeological Museum in ATHENS, has been identified as the Zeus by Eukleides which Pausanias (7.26) saw. There were four Ionic columns in the porch. The pebble mosaic in the cella depicts an eagle, the symbol of Zeus, and a serpent. The statue would have stood in the niche at the back of the cella. In his list of sanctuaries at Aigeira,

▼ Fig. 124. Plan of Aigeira

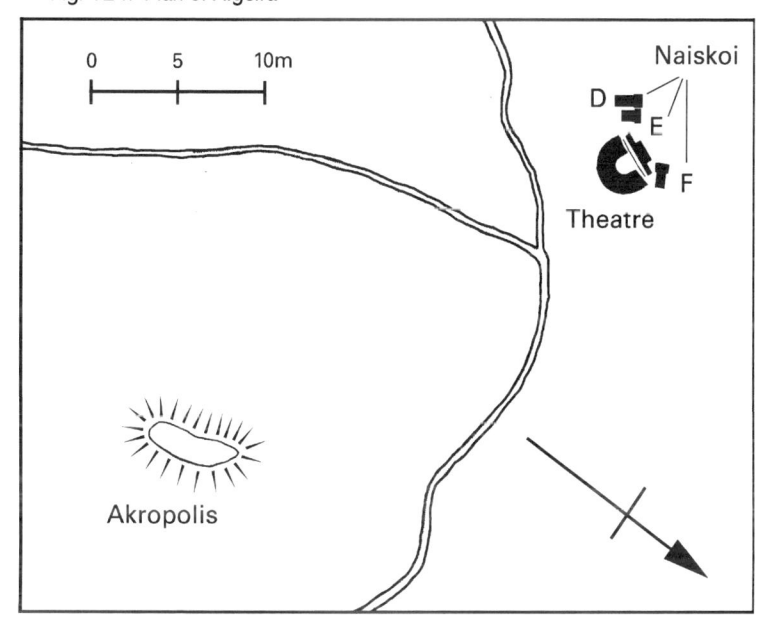

Pausanias juxtaposes Zeus and Artemis whose temple and statue were evidently quite new. Shrine E was restored in the C2 AD and may be the temple in question. If so, it also contained an ancient statue of Iphigeneia which had possibly come from the Archaic temple on the akropolis. Shrine E consists of a prostyle Ionic porch and cella. Likewise shrine F which has a mosaic in the cella but in this case composed of tesserae rather than pebbles. A C2 date for shrine F seems likely, whereas shrines D and E should be C3.

At the east end of the terrace in front of the theatre there is a classic box grid of square trenches separated by balks. Pieces of a colossal Hellenistic statue have been found which could be the Tyche mentioned by Pausanias. She held a cornucopia and had 'a winged Eros beside her, the implication being that human passion succeeds more by luck than by beauty'. The row of five stone basins would have been used by bathers and it seems likely that there was a **gymnasium** on the terrace in the Hellenistic period. This was superseded by pottery kilns in the C3 AD. The excavations at the northern end of the terrace have revealed two more Hellenistic structures, presumably temples since one matches shrine D and the other had a peristyle. They may have replaced a Classical temple. Traces of the agora have been found lower down the hill.

The view from the **akropolis** is particularly impressive. This was the site of the Mycenaean settlement and subsequently of a sanctuary. The tutelary deities may have been Artemis and Iphigeneia. A modest C8 BC shrine was succeeded in the C7 by a temple which remained in use until the Hellenistic period.

Central Greece and Euboia

This section covers sites in Boiotia and Phokis as well as Euboia. Except for the Kephisos river valley and the plain around Krisa, Phokis is mountainous and would have been rather insignificant but for the sanctuary at DELPHI. Boiotia has two fertile plains, separated by low hills and surrounded by mountains. The dominant city in the southern plain has always been THEBES. In antiquity the northern plain was often under the control of ORCHOMENOS and inevitably the cities were fierce rivals. They cultivated some of the best land in Greece which produced high quality wheat.

Euboia is the second largest island in the Aegean but was only separated from the mainland relatively recently and the narrowest point of the channel can be bridged. The island has a number of excellent harbours and also mineral resources—iron ore deposits around CHALKIS and cipollino marble in the south at Karystos.

Thebes was already a fortified settlement in the Early Helladic period and is the site of a Mycenaean palace. Orchomenos also has impressive Mycenaean architectural remains and may have directed a project to drain Lake Kopais. The reclaimed land was protected by the citadel at GLA. Manika on Euboia is a major Early Helladic site which had close links with the Cyclades. LEFKANDI was also occupied in this period and became extremely wealthy in the Early Iron Age when the Heroon was constructed.

In the C8 BC Euboians from Chalkis and ERETRIA had a prominent role in the trading and colonizing ventures which spread a Greek presence over much of the Mediterranean seaboard at this time. Delphi's guidance to would-be colonists helped to make its oracle the most important in Archaic Greece. Of lesser renown were the local oracles of Boiotia, of which the PTOION in particular flourished at this time. From the late C6 the numerous cities of Boiotia were organized into a federal state dominated by Thebes, its apogee in the mid-C4 under the Theban statesmen Epaminondas and Pelopidas, when Boiotian power was felt as far south as Messenia. Straddling the land-routes to north Greece, the region was a battlefield, as at PLATAIA and CHAIRONEIA. Macedonian rulers destroyed, and resurrected, cities in Boiotia, and Euboia was a Macedonian enclave for much of the C3 BC. Both regions supported Rome's opponents in the C2 and early C1 BC, suffering accordingly. In imperial times by and large they were depopulated backwaters, although Delphi's sanctuary still enjoyed a certain renown. Rustic life in Boiotia, where the chief cities were now Lebadeia (modern Livadia) and Thespiai, is admirably captured in the Latin novel *The Golden Ass* by Apuleius (mid-C2 AD). Archaeological survey has shown that from the

C4 on rural Boiotia saw a marked recovery, lasting until the Slav incursions.

Delphi (Figs. 125–131)

The site is on the road from Livadia to Itea, a short distance east of the modern town. We recommend that you see the sanctuary of Apollo first, then the sanctuary of Athena and finally the museum. But if you intend to head east after your visit, you should start in the museum.

Special Features

Delphi has the most spectacular location of any classical site in Greece, and is of incomparable historical and archaeological interest.

History

As he makes his way to Delphi, Pausanias (10.5) complains that the road 'is precipitous and difficult even for an active man'. This does seem a remote location for such a major sanctuary, yet it ensured that Delphi was in neutral territory, away from the political power brokers. Furthermore, the sanctuary is peripheral but not isolated. It could be reached by sea and was just off one of the main routes north. The Greeks believed that Delphi was the centre of the world and from their point of view this is quite understandable.

There was a Mycenaean settlement and a deposit of figurines in the sanctuary of Athena may indicate cult-activity. It seems that the site was then abandoned until the C10 BC. Votives first appear around 800 BC, mainly Argive and Corinthian, and the oracle (see **box**) was certainly in operation by the C8. It was consulted by states on fundamental policy issues, such as colonization, and became renowned as a source of informed and impartial advice. The sanctuary and the oracle remained under the jurisdiction of the local community until the early C6 when the Delphic Amphictyony took control, supposedly after the First Sacred War. The Amphictyony was a federation of twelve peoples from central Greece, Attika, Euboia, and the Peloponnese. The first Pythian Games were held in 591/0 or 586/5 BC. Delphi was now established as a panhellenic sanctuary and soon developed an international reputation. A number of Greek cities built treasuries in the C6 and foreign rulers also made dedications, especially Croesus of Lydia. Herodotus (1.50–51) describes some of the gifts which Croesus sent to Delphi. These included a gold lion on a base of gold ingots, a gold bowl which weighed a quarter of a ton, a silver bowl with a capacity of 5000 gallons, and a gold statue of the woman who baked his bread. When he then asked the oracle what would happen if he marched against Persia, he was reputedly told that he would destroy a great empire. Croesus therefore attacked Persia and was defeated—the empire he destroyed was his own.

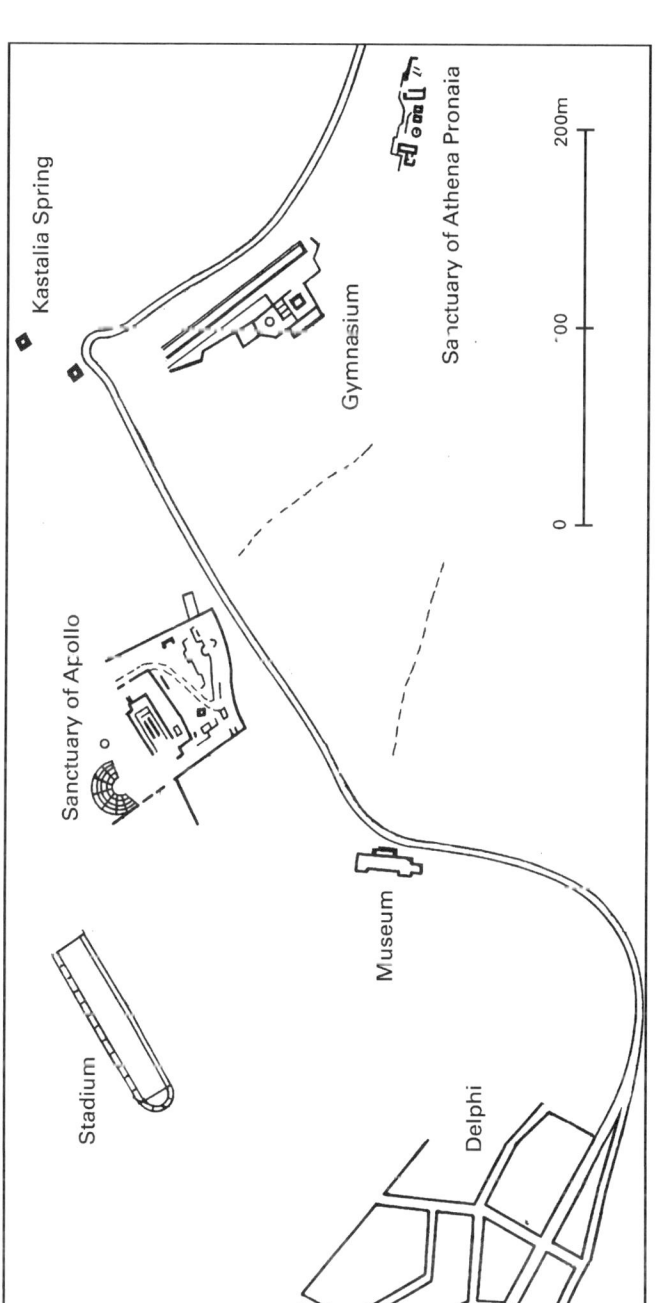

▲ Fig. 125. Plan of Delphi

In 548 BC the temple of Apollo burned down and was rebuilt with assistance from the Alkmaionids, an exiled Athenian family. Thereafter, whenever Spartans consulted the oracle they were informed that they must first free Athens from the Peisistratid tyrants. The impartiality of the oracle was further compromised when the Persians invaded Greece. The Argives were advised to remain neutral: 'guard the head well and the head will save the body' (Herodotus 7.148). The Athenian envoys were given an even more gloomy response: 'haste from the sanctuary and bow your hearts to grief'. Dissatisfied they tried again and the prophetess predicted that 'the wooden wall only shall not fail but help you and your children' (Herodotus 7.140–41). The Athenians decided that the wooden wall must be their fleet, so they abandoned Attika and prepared to meet the Persians at sea. After their victories at Salamis and PLATAIA, the Greeks set up a number of commemorative monuments at Delphi which had also been attacked by the Persians and apparently defended by Apollo himself.

There is less construction activity in the C5 BC but the early C4 saw several major developments, in particular the restoration of the temple which was destroyed by an earthquake in 373 BC. This took almost half a century and evidently proved difficult to fund. In 356 BC the Phokians seized the sanctuary and melted down gold and silver votives to pay their troops. Philip of Macedon was invited to intervene and the ultimate outcome was the battle of CHAIRONEIA in 338 BC which ensured Macedonian domination of much of Greece. The Aitolians took control of Delphi in the C3 and helped to thwart an attack by the Gauls in 279 BC. Hellenistic rulers, such as Attalos I of Pergamon, made dedications in order to enhance their prestige. The Romans succeeded the Aitolians and certainly left their mark. The sanctuary was plundered by Sulla in 86 BC and Nero removed 500 statues but Domitian repaired the temple and Hadrian was a major benefactor. Tourists, like Pausanias, were another source of income at this time and Delphi became a 'place of memory' for subject Greeks. The rise of Christianity was not a complete disaster and a fine basilica was constructed in the C5 AD.

Description

Sanctuary of Apollo

In front of the entrance there is a **Roman agora** [1] which contained shops and has niches for statues. Note the opus reticulatum brickwork. This would have been covered by marble veneer. The sanctuary is surrounded by an enclosure wall but does not have a propylon. The Sacred Way initially runs past a series of **Classical monuments** [2–7], stone bases now bereft of statues. The Corcyraeans dedicated a bronze bull after they had trapped an enormous shoal of tunny [2]. Most of the other monuments celebrated military victories and were placed so as to cause maximum aggravation. Directly opposite a Spartan dedication [**5**], commemorating the sea battle at Aigospotamoi in 405 BC, was a monument set up by the Arkadians [**3**] after they had defeated the Spartans in 369 BC. Delphi offered tremendous scope for the spirit of competition on which Greek cities thrived. They could publicize their achievements and at the same time humiliate their rivals. The two semicircular **exedrai** [**8–9**] were Argive dedications. Next on the left is the first of the **treasuries** [**11**]. This was built by the city of SIKYON in the late C6 but incorporates blocks from two earlier structures, one evidently a circular monopteros. From c.600–570 BC Sikyon had been ruled by the tyrant Kleisthenes who won the first chariot-race at the Pythian Games. He may well have put his chariot on display in one of these structures. They were no doubt dismantled by the Sikyonians when the tyranny fell.

Herodotus (3.57) mentions that the Siphnians had 'gold and silver mines so productive that a tenth part of their output was sufficient for a treasury at Delphi not inferior in value to the most splendid there'. The Ionic **treasury** [**12**] they commissioned c.525 BC was certainly ornate. It was constructed of marble, had Caryatid columns, a carved frieze and pedimental sculpture. The treasuries on this stretch of the Sacred Way would have presented quite a contrast, in that they reflected the architectural traditions of the city concerned—Doric in mainland Greece and the western colonies, Ionic in the Cyclades and the eastern Aegean. This juxtaposition of styles doubtless inspired experimentation. The fact that the Athenians used marble for their **treasury** [**24**] may be a case in point. Pausanias (10.11) says that it was built from the spoils of MARATHON, that is after 490 BC, although he may have been misled by the inscription on the base just south of the treasury and a date c.500 BC is not out of the question. It was reconstructed by the city of ATHENS in 1903–06 and you can see how well the marble accentuates the simple lines of Doric architecture. Like most of the treasuries it consists of a porch and a cella in which votives were kept. The metopes, replaced by casts, depict the exploits of Herakles and Theseus. Dozens of inscriptions were incised on the walls. Many record Athenian victories in the games.

Opposite the Athenian Treasury is the mid-C6 **Knidian Treasury** [**22**]. This was built of marble and had Caryatid columns. The Sacred Way now turns north-east and passes the rectangular **council-house** (bouleuterion) [**23**], where the Delphic council met, the rock of the **Sibyl** [**35**] and the base of the **Naxian Sphinx** [**36**] which stood on an Ionic column over 9 m. high. At this point the Sacred Way reaches the **Halos** [**34**], originally a circular area, where the festival of the Septerion was held every eight years. In one of the rituals an adolescent boy set fire to a wooden structure which represented the palace of Python, the serpent whom Apollo supposedly killed when he took over the sanctuary, hence the epithet Pythian. The hoard of gold, silver, and ivory votives in the museum was buried here. On one side of the Halos is the **Stoa of**

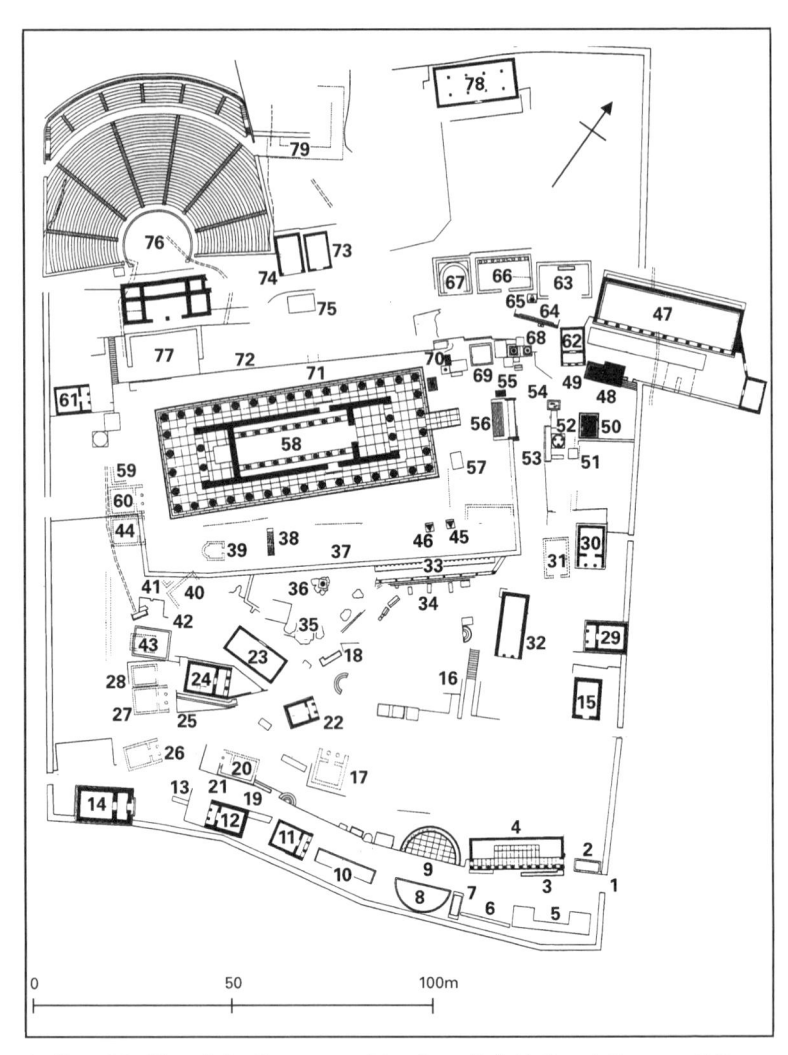

▲ Fig. 126. Plan of the Sanctuary of Apollo at Delphi. Key: 1 Entrance 2 Base of the bull of Corcyra 3 Bases of the Arkadians 4 Stoa 5 Monument of the Admirals 6 Site of Miltiades monument 7 Base of the horse of the Argives 8 Base of the Seven and Epigones 9 Monument of the kings of Argos 10 Base of the Tarentines 11 Treasury of the Sikyonians 12 Treasury of the Siphnians 13 Base of Liparaians 14 Treasury of the Thebans 15 Treasury 16 Staircase 17 Treasury 18 Base of the Boiotians 19 Base of the Aitolians 20–21 Treasury and terrace of the Megarians 22 Treasury of the Knidians 23 Council-house 24 Treasury of the Athenians 25 Base of Marathon 26 Treasury of 'The Boiotians' 27 Treasury 28 Treasury 29 Treasury of the Kyrenaians 30 Treasury 'of Brasidas and the Akanthians' 31 Treasury 32 Treasury of the Corinthians 33 Stoa of the Athenians 34 Halos 35 Rock of the Sibyl

▲ Fig. 127. Reconstruction of the Treasury of the Siphnians at Delphi (after G. Daux and E. Hansen, *Le Trésor de Siphnos* (Paris 1987) 225, fig. 133)

the Athenians [33]. It was constructed soon after the Persian Wars and had a portico of eight Ionic columns. The inscription on the top step reads:

ΑΘΕΝΑΙΟΙ ΑΝΕΘΕΣΑΝ ΤΕΝ ΣΤΟΑΝ ΚΑΙ ΤΑ hΟΠΛ[Α Κ]ΑΙ ΤΑΚΡΟΤΕΡΙΑ hΕΛΟΝΤΕΣ ΤΟΝ ΠΟΛΕ[ΜΙΟ]Ν—'the Athenians dedicated this stoa and the hopla and the prows they captured from the enemy'.

The hopla were evidently cables from the Persian pontoon bridge across the Hellespont. Behind the stoa is the remarkable **polygonal wall [37]**

Fig. 126. Plan of the Sanctuary of Apollo at Delphi. Key (con.): 36 Column and sphinx of the Naxians 37 Polygonal wall 38 Fountain 'of the Muses' 39 'Shrine of Ge', 40–41 *Oikoi* 42 Fountain of the Asklepieion 43 Treasury under the Asklepieion 44 Treasury 45 Approximate site of the pillar of Messene 46 Suggested site of the black limestone column 47 Stoa of Attalos 48 Pillar of Eumenes II 49 Pillar of Attalos I 50 Chariot of Helios 51 Tripod of Plataia 52 Krotonian base 53 Base of the Tarentines 54 Location of the Apollo of Salamis 55 Aitolian column of Eumenes II 56 Altar of Apollo 57 Column of Aemilius Paulus 58 Temple of Apollo 59 *Oikos* 60 Treasury 61 Treasury 62 Treasury 63 Precinct and unfinished base 64 Base of Corcyra 65 Base of acanthus column 66 Base of Daochos 67 Semicircular base 68 Tripods of Gelon and Hieron 69 Base of 'Apollo Sitalkas' 70 Pillar of Prusias 71 Niche used as a fountain 72 Ischegaon 73 Treasury of the theatre 74 Treasury of the theatre 75 *Oikos* 76 Theatre 77 Niche of Krateros 78 Lesche of the Knidians 79 Unidentified monument

▲ Fig. 128. The Athenian Treasury at Delphi

which supports the platform of the temple. The inscriptions on this wall, mainly Hellenistic and Roman, deal with the emancipation of slaves. After the scanty remains of the **Corinthian Treasury** [**32**], in which the gifts presented by Croesus were stored, and the **Treasury of Kyrene** [**29**] just beyond this, the Sacred Way turns north. The **Tripod of Plataia** (recently identified as **51** rather than **52**) was a joint dedication by the Greek cities which had repelled the Persian invasion. The gold tripod stood on a column in the form of three bronze snakes, their bodies intertwined. The Phokians melted down the tripod and the snakes were taken off to Constantinople by Constantine I, who also removed the **Chariot of Helios** [**50**] from the adjacent base. It now seems unlikely that the four horses in the Basilica of St Mark in Venice came from here.

There were a number of votives at the east end of the temple: the **pillar of Eumenes II** of Pergamon [**48**], the **pillar of Prusias II** of Bithynia [**70**], the base of the colossal **statue of Apollo Sitalkas** [**69**] and the **tripods** [**68**] dedicated by Gelon, the tyrant of Syracuse, and his brother Hiero. The Roman general Aemilius Paulus rather pointedly reused a Macedonian dedication for his **victory monument** [**57**] after he had defeated Perseus at Pydna in 168 BC. Chians built and then paid for the restoration of the **altar of Apollo** [**56**], a black limestone pedestal in pseudo-isodomic masonry with white marble on the top and the base.

The first three **temples** [**58**] were reputedly made of laurel, beeswax and feathers, and bronze. By the late C7 BC Apollo had a more substantial temple. This burned down in the C6 and was replaced by the Alkmaionid temple, which was reconstructed after an earthquake in the

▼ Fig. 129. The polygonal wall behind the Stoa of the Athenians at Delphi

C4 [**58**]. It is really quite modest. Rough blocks of conglomerate were used for the foundations, limestone for the platform, and poros from Corinth for the columns. The peristyle evidently consisted of six by fifteen columns but it is not clear how the interior was laid out because much of the temple has been demolished so that the metal clamps could be removed. The oracle (see **box**) was in an adyton, presumably at the back of the cella, but we cannot see how it would have operated. Pausanias (10.19) mentions the sculpture in the pediments and also shields, captured from the Persians and the Gauls, which were fixed on the metopes. In the rectangular **niche** [**77**] on the north side of the temple platform there was a bronze lion hunt by the sculptors Leochares and Lysippos which commemorated the occasion when the Macedonian general Krateros saved the life of Alexander.

A flight of steps leads up to the **theatre** [**76**], used for Delphian citizen-assemblies and music contests at the games. There were hymns in honour of Apollo and instrumental pieces played on the cithara and flute. The theatre was completed by Eumenes II of Pergamon in the

The oracle

The oracle originally operated on one day each year. This was subsequently extended to one day in each of the nine months when Apollo was in residence at Delphi. The enquirer first had to purify himself with holy water and pay a consultation fee. An animal was then sacrificed on the altar outside the temple. If this proved auspicious, the enquirer entered the temple and sacrificed on an inner altar. Finally his question was put to the Pythia in the adyton of the temple. The Pythia was a woman of over 50. Once appointed, she had to remain chaste. She bathed in the Kastalian Spring, burned laurel leaves and barley meal, and then sat on a tripod in the adyton. The notion that vapours emanated from a chasm and inspired her is almost certainly a later invention, although she may well have entered a self-induced trance. Her response to the enquirer was interpreted by the prophetai but could still be ambiguous, literally Delphic, as Croesus discovered. Most responses were more direct and recommended a particular course of action on policy issues and religious questions. This reliance on divination provided an acceptable solution to particularly difficult problems, especially in the Archaic period. The political role of the oracle diminished later on. Apollo could be blunt. The city of Aigion won a naval victory and asked whether any Greeks were better. The reply was as follows: 'The land of Pelasgic ARGOS is better, as are Thessalian horses, Spartan women and the men who drink the water of fair Arethusa. Better still are those who live between TIRYNS and Arkadia rich in flocks, the Argives with linen cuirasses, spurs to war. You Aigians are neither third nor fourth nor twelfth but uncounted and unreckoned.'

C2 BC. It has 35 rows of seats, separated by a diazoma, and could hold around 5000 spectators. The orchestra would originally have been circular but the stage was evidently extended forward in the Roman period. There is a spectacular view of the sanctuary from the cavea.

Directly east of the theatre the Knidians built a **lesche** or club-house [**78**] in the mid-C5. Pausanias (10.25–31) tells us that this is where the Delphians 'used to meet for old tales and serious conversation'—it sounds rather like a kafeneion—and then provides an invaluable description of two murals painted by Polygnotos. These have been lost and there is not much of the lesche left. Below this is the **monument** [**66**] dedicated by Daochos II of Thessaly in the C4 and the C2 **stoa** [**47**] built by Attalos I of Pergamon which was later bricked up and turned into a reservoir.

A steep path climbs from the theatre up to the well-preserved **stadium** where the athletic competitions took place. Originally they were held in the plain below Delphi and this continued to be the venue for the equestrian events. The stadium was moved in the C3 BC and given its present form in the C2 AD. The athletes entered through an arch. The start and finish lines are still in position, 600 Roman feet apart, with seventeen lanes marked out. There was room for approximately 6500 spectators on the stone seats. Officials sat in the tribune in the middle of the north side.

On the left of the road down to the sanctuary of Athena is the **Kastalian Spring**. The water, described by Pausanias (10.8) as delicious, was used in purification rituals. The rock-cut fountain is Hellenistic or Roman. At the back of the court there is a narrow reservoir and niches for votives above this.

Sanctuary of Athena Pronaia

The sanctuary of Athena is also known as Marmaria, the marbles. You first pass the **Sanctuary of the hero Phylakos** [**2–3**] who helped to fight off the Persians. Below this is the C6 **altar of Athena** [**4**]. There were also **altars of Hygieia and Eileithyia** [**5**], the goddess of childbirth, by the precinct wall. The poros **Temple of Athena** [**7**] was constructed in the late C6 and incorporates column capitals from a C7 predecessor. The walls between the columns were added after an earthquake, possibly in 480 BC. The boulder at the back of the temple arrived more recently in 1905. The first of the two **treasuries** [**8-9**] is Doric. The second was dedicated by the city of Massalia, modern Marseilles, in the late C6 and is Aeolic—the columns have palm capitals rather then Ionic volutes. Note the bead and reel at the base of the walls. The **Tholos** [**11**] is one of the most famous monuments at Delphi but we do not know why it was built, although the name of the architect, Theodoros, is recorded. It had a peristyle of twenty Doric columns. Three of these have been

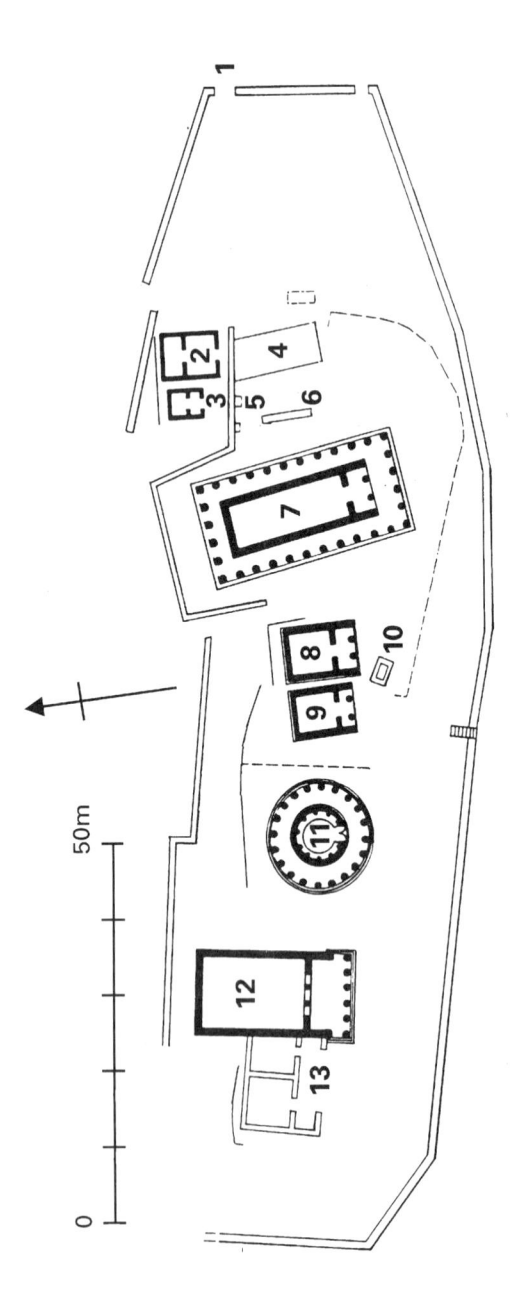

▲ Fig. 130. Plan of the Sanctuary of Athena Pronaia, Delphi. Key: 1 East gateway 2–3 Heroon of Phylakos 4 Main altar of Athena 5 Altars of Hygieia and Eileithyia 6 Archaic altar 7 Temple of Athena 8 Doric treasury 9 Massalian treasury 10 Base attributed to a Persian trophy 11 Tholos 12 Limestone temple 13 Rectangular building

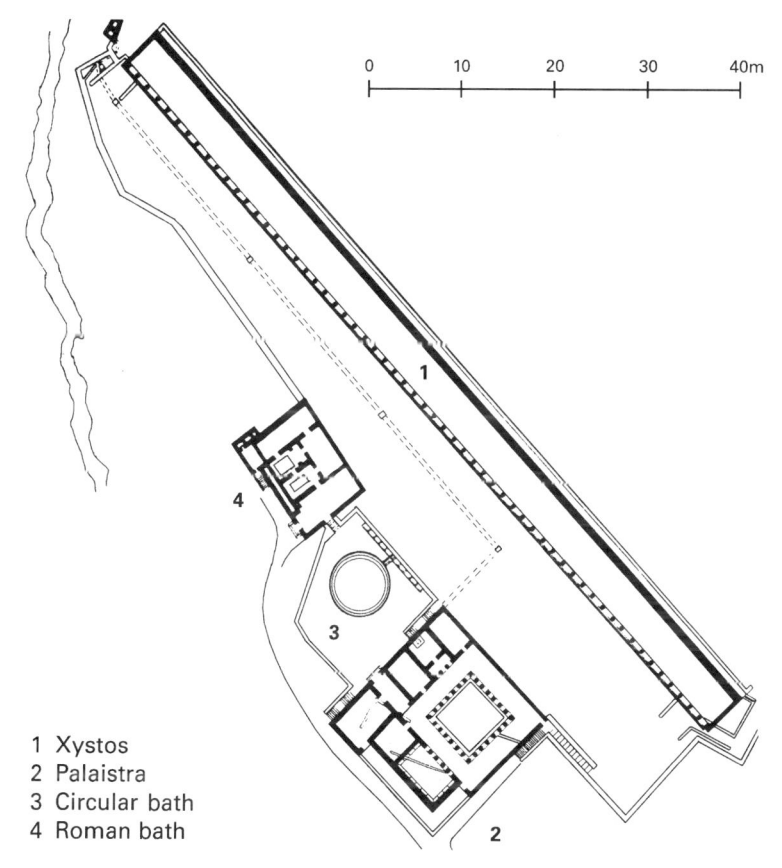

1 Xystos
2 Palaistra
3 Circular bath
4 Roman bath

▲ Fig. 131. Plan of the gymnasium at Delphi

restored and also a section of the frieze. The columns inside the cella were Corinthian and stood on a bench of blue marble. The Tholos and the adjacent limestone **temple** [12] were both constructed in the early C4 and one theory is that this was in expiation for a murderous feud. Alternatively the C6 temple of Athena may have been destroyed by the earthquake which struck Delphi in 373 BC and had to be replaced. The prostyle porch is unusual in a Doric temple.

The **gymnasium** (Fig. 131) is a short distance east of the sanctuary of Athena and can also be viewed from the road. On the upper terrace there were two tracks, one a **xystos** or covered track [1] so that athletes could train in bad weather. The **palaistra** [2] below has rooms on two sides of a peristyle court. The boxers and wrestlers practised here. After their exertions they could immerse themselves in the circular **bath** [3] (which must have come as quite a shock given the temperature of the water) or wash in the basins by the wall. The Romans sensibly built a **bath-complex** [4] so that they would have hot water.

Museum

As there was an extension under construction at the time of our most recent visit, it is likely that the displays have been altered and so they are not described room by room.

The museum has an exceptional collection of sculpture. There are early C6 BC metopes from the Sikyonian monopteros in which Kleisthenes may have displayed his chariot. The frieze from the Siphnian Treasury is especially impressive. In the battle scenes the relief is subtly varied and this successfully creates an illusion of depth. The compositions on the metopes from the Athenian Treasury are much simpler but just as effective and the crisply carved figures would have stood out well. The pedimental sculpture from the Archaic temple of Apollo is sadly fragmentary and difficult to interpret. Archaic statues include two early kouroi, conventionally identified as Kleobis and Biton, the Naxian Sphinx and the remarkable gold and ivory figures from the deposit of votives buried under the Halos. There is also a life-size silver bull.

The charioteer is one of the few Classical bronze statues to have survived. He was saved by a rockfall but lost his horses. Polyzalos, the tyrant of Gela, made this dedication after he won the chariot race in 478 or 474 BC. There is no hint of emotion in the face, no sense of anticipation or triumph. The C4 is represented by sculpture from the Tholos, the ornate Acanthus Column and statues from the Daochos monument. These were copied from bronze statues by Lysippos at Pharsalos in Thessaly. Agias, the great-grandfather of Daochos and a famous athlete, has a powerful physique. The finest of the Roman statues is a superb Antinoos (see **box**) and there is a headless herm of the historian Plutarch (see p. 320) who was a priest at Delphi for thirty years.

Antinoos

Antinoos was a strikingly handsome youth from the city of Bithynion in what is now north-west Turkey, chiefly famous for his death and its extraordinary aftermath. Hadrian's companion and probably boyfriend, he drowned mysteriously in the Nile in AD 130. Hadrian must have been distraught with grief to judge from his reaction, which was to found a city at the place where Antinoos had died, and to declare him officially a god, with MANTINEIA a centre of the new cult. He was the subject of many posthumous statues, which depict him as a muscular, brooding beauty. There are other examples at ELEUSIS and the National Archaeological Museum.

Thebes

The museum is by a C13 Frankish tower at the northern end of the town on Odos Pindarou and is well signed.

Special Features

It is not obvious that Thebes was once one of the great cities of Greece but the excellent museum does compensate for the lack of impressive remains.

History

If the Thebans had wanted a slogan, 'city of legend' would certainly have been appropriate. Kadmos the Phoenician supposedly founded the city and so the akropolis was known as the Kadmeion. Dionysos and Herakles were both born in Thebes. Oedipus became ruler after he had outwitted the sphinx, murdered his father Laios, and married his mother Jocasta. When he abdicated, his sons Eteokles and Polynikes quarrelled over the throne. Polynikes led the Seven against Thebes and the brothers killed one another. No wonder Aeschylus and Sophocles based tragedies on these stories.

Excavation of the ancient city has been opportunistic rather than systematic, as land is redeveloped or services installed. Consequently the jigsaw is far from complete and interpretation can be difficult, particularly in the case of the prehistoric levels which have often been disturbed. Nevertheless, it seems that the settlement already occupied much of the Kadmeion in the Early Helladic period and was fortified. Mycenaean Thebes was a palatial centre. This is evident from the discovery of hundreds of clay tablets inscribed in the Linear B script. Tablets have only been found on Mycenaean palace sites. Frescoes, ivories, and exotic cylinder seals indicate the level of refinement which we would expect. The architectural history of the palace is not entirely clear, however. The likely sequence of events is that the palace was built in the C14 BC, destroyed by fire in the early C13, rebuilt on a different alignment and then finally destroyed in the late C13. The palaces at MYCENAE, PYLOS, and TIRYNS have similar plans but we still do not know whether this is also true of Thebes. The settlement was extensive, 300,000 m.², and apparently fortified. Around the Kadmeion there were chamber tomb cemeteries. The rulers may have been buried in the impressive tombs on the Megalo Kastelli hill, some of which were frescoed. Thebes presumably controlled the whole of southern Boiotia at this time but ORCHOMENOS was also a major Mycenaean centre and it is likely that the two cities were already rivals.

In the C6 Thebes formed a federation of Boiotian cities which did not initially include Orchomenos. When the Persians invaded, the

Thebans went over to their side and fought against the Greeks at the battle of PLATAIA in 479 BC. ATHENS, an old adversary, attacked Boiotia in 457 BC. As a result the Thebans became staunch allies of SPARTA and remained so until the early C4. By then Thebes was firmly in control of the Boiotian Confederacy and made a bid for the hegemony of Greece under Epaminondas. He defeated the Spartans at the battle of Leuktra in 371 BC and freed Messenia but was killed at MANTINEIA in 362 BC. The Thebans opposed Philip II and led a revolt against the Macedonians in 335 BC. This was crushed by Alexander who destroyed Thebes. The city was refounded in 316 BC but suffered a further disaster in 86 BC. Because the Thebans had supported Mithradates, the Roman general Sulla confiscated half of their territory. When Pausanias (9.7.4) visited Boiotia in the C2 AD, 'the whole of the lower city was deserted, except for the sanctuaries. They live in the akropolis and call it Thebes instead of the Kadmeion'.

Description

The **Archaeological Museum** is well labelled and has excellent information panels. In the entrance hall there are grave stelai and inscriptions which include the proclamation by Nero that he had freed Greece. **Room A** contains C7 statues in the Daedalic style, a number of fine C6 kouroi from the sanctuary of Apollo at PTOION, and Classical grave stelai from Thespiai. The displays in **room B** cover a range of sites and periods. There is Early and Middle Helladic pottery from Eutresis, Lithares, and Thebes, Mycenaean pottery, bronzes and jewellery from Orchomenos, and horns of consecration from GLA. Finds from the Mycenaean palace at Thebes include a fresco which depicts a line of women, presumably a religious procession. The collection of Near Eastern cylinder seals is remarkable. The fact that most of the seals were made of lapis lazuli will certainly have been their main attraction. It is possible that they were destined for one of the workshops in the palace. Jewellery was produced and also furniture—note the legs of an ivory throne. The Linear B tablets emphasize the role of the palace as an administrative centre. A number of stirrup jars, used for the bulk transport of olive-oil, also have Linear B inscriptions. Analysis of the clay has revealed that the stirrup jars were imported from western Crete. There is Archaic pottery from the cemetery at Rhitsona and splendid figurines—do not miss the cheese grater. Most of the Classical and Hellenistic figurines come from the cemetery at Halai. Grotesque characters caper on the votive skyphoi from the sanctuary of the Kabeiroi, just west of Thebes. **Room C** contains Classical grave stelai and Roman sculpture from the sanctuary of Artemis at Aulis and from Thespiai. The technique used for the warriors on the black stone stelai is unusual in that the details were carefully incised and then painted. In **room D** there is a display of finds from the

Mycenaean chamber tomb cemetery at Tanagra. Although the Minoans often buried the dead in terracotta coffins it was not a common practice in Mycenaean cemeteries. The scenes depicted on the coffins from Tanagra may lack finesse but they offer us a rare glimpse of the funeral ceremony. Women have a prominent role. They stand in a line and tear their hair or scratch their faces. The expressions of grief seem stylized but were no doubt heartfelt, especially as some of the coffins were clearly made for children.

From the museum, stroll up Odos Pindarou and you will pass the site of the **Mycenaean palace**, which is obscured in places by later walls. If you have time, the C4 **Electra Gate** on Odos Amphionos is flanked by round towers. East of the Kadmeion is the Mycenaean chamber tomb cemetery on the **Megalo Kastelli** hill.

Plataia (Fig. 132)

From the modern village of Erythrai a road heads west signed Platea Archaeological Site (said to be 5 km. but only 4). The site itself is not signed but is difficult to miss, as the road passes through a breach in the ancient wall, just before reaching a roundabout outside the modern village of Plataies.

Special Features

The site, set in attractive countryside, gives you a good sense of a small Boiotian city. There is a fine panorama over the fertile plain of the River Asopos, including the general area of the famous battle to the east.

History

Plataia was a small city at the north foot of Mt Kithairon, west of the Gyphtokastro pass from Boiotia into Attika, and this geography helps to explain the close ties between ATHENS and the Plataians, who fought at MARATHON (490 BC) and could be called 'Athenians among Boiotians' (C3 BC). The city's most famous hour was the battle of 479 BC, when Plataians fought with the allied Greeks and Persia was decisively ejected from Greece. It was twice destroyed by its eastern neighbour THEBES and twice refounded, the second time by Philip II *c.*338 BC. In the early C3 BC the playwright Posidippos joked of Plataia that 'most of the time it is a desert, and only at the Freedom-festival (Eleutheria) does it become a city'. There was truth in this, in that the chief resource of the city, apart from a small but fertile territory, was the memory of the famous battle, kept alive locally by the four-yearly Freedom-festival, its high-point a race in armour between the battle-trophy and the altar of Zeus, and a cult of Greek Concord, added in the C3 BC. These ceremonies were administered by a 'League of the Greeks', including Athens and SPARTA. They attracted renewed outside interest under the pax Romana, and

318 Central Greece and Euboia

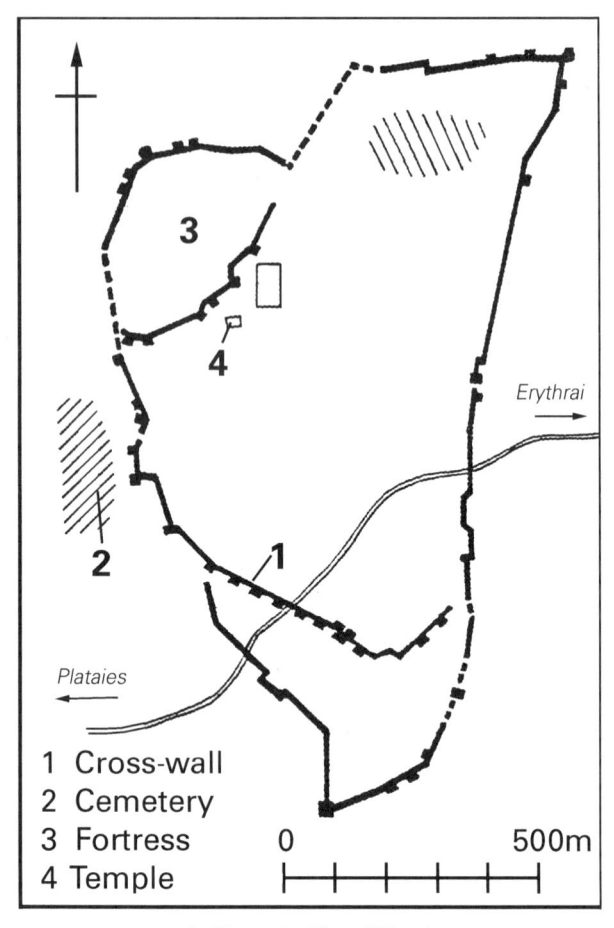

▲ Fig. 132. Plan of Plataia

Plutarch admiringly describes the annual rite here of washing the Greek war-graves, conducted by the city-officials. The city seems to have shared in the expansion of population in Boiotia from the C4 on, and its refortification by Justinian implies an administrative role of some importance in the mid-C6 AD.

Description

The most prominent feature of this plateau-site is the **city-wall**, rebuilt when Plataia was refounded by Philip. The towered **cross-wall** [1] on the west side of the site, breached by the modern road, belongs to this phase. Its ashlar masonry has a 'rusticated' finish, and originally supported a mudbrick superstructure. On the west of the site is an extra-mural **cemetery** [2], with carved stone sarcophagi still in place. The overgrown north sector of the site will reward only the specialist, although most evidence of ancient occupation was found here, including a late-antique (Justinianic?) **fortress** [3], and remains of a Doric **temple** [4], with a large public building nearby. The tombs, shrines, and altars commemorating the battle have never been firmly identified.

Chaironeia (Fig. 133)

The site is in the village of Khaironia, on the old road between Thebes and Lamia. There is a brown sign for the Archaeological Museum, but you can hardly miss the lion, right beside the road. The museum is currently closed for repairs.

Special Features

The site is mainly of historical interest, and also conveniently located by the road.

History

Chaironeia was a small Boiotian city commanding a fertile plain of strategic importance, carrying the main road between THERMOPYLAI and southern Greece. The city gave its name to two ancient battles fought outside its walls, one in 86 BC, when Sulla defeated Archelaos, general of Mithradates VI of Pontos, the other, more famous, in 338 BC, when Philip II of Macedon defeated the allied Greek army with the help of the future Alexander the Great, his son, who led the cavalry. Chaironeia's other claim to fame is as the birthplace and residence of Plutarch, the most widely read of the Greek writers under Roman rule whose work has survived (see **box**).

Description

The **Lion Monument** [1] is described by Pausanias (9.40.10): 'As you approach the city, you see a common grave (*polyandrion*) of the Thebans who were killed in the contest with Philip. It has no inscription, but is topped by a lion, probably referring to the spirit of the men.' It was rediscovered in 1818, and restored and reinstated on its plinth at the beginning of the C20. The monument is part of a rectangular enclosure, found to contain 254 skeletons stacked in layers, along with weapons. As Philip was unlikely to concede such a conspicuous memorial to a defeated THEBES, it probably dates after the refoundation of the city in 316 BC, when the Thebans may have been hard up, to judge from the rather second-rate artistry.

About 200 m. further on from the lion is a blue sign for the **ancient theatre** [2]. This is a short distance from the road at the north-east foot

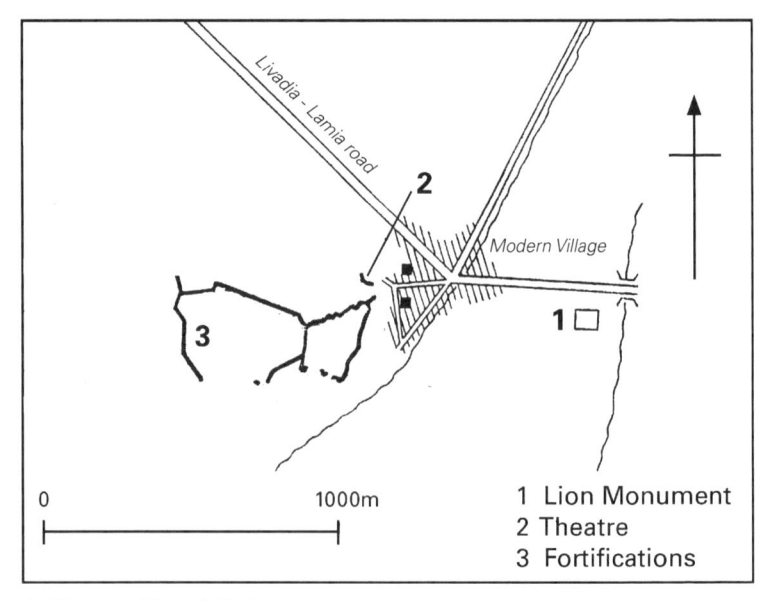

▲ Fig. 133. Plan of Chaironeia

of the akropolis, which has ancient **fortifications** [3], and is a good measure of Chaironeia's size and resources. The fourteen rows of seats, narrow and uncomfortable, are poorly cut into the rock, but give a fine view over the plain. There are no visible stage-buildings, although these once existed, since an inscription (C2–C1 BC) mentions the gift of a proskenion for the god Dionysos.

> ### Plutarch
>
> Plutarch (lived c. AD 42–120) was a philosopher and biographer. He wrote voluminously, and his most popular work, the *Parallel Lives*, pairs biographies of famous Greeks and Romans, including such classics as Alexander, Caesar, and Mark Antony. Plutarch was a local landowner, and, in spite of his growing reputation, loyal to Chaironeia, once writing: 'I live in a small city, and I prefer to stay there, lest it becomes even smaller' (*Life of Demosthenes* 2.2). His fellow-Chaironeians eventually honoured him with a herm-portrait at DELPHI, now (headless) in the museum there. He had a wide circle of friends among the notables of the province and even leading Romans, and they used to come and stay with him at Chaironeia, where learned conversation over leisured dinners was the order of the day. Plutarch also ran his own private academy in his house for sons of friends. His cultured life at Chaironeia belies Boiotia's ancient reputation for boorishness.

Orchomenos (Fig. 134)

Take the turn for Orchomenos on the old road between Thebes and Lamia. Continue through the village and you will come to a sign for the Archaeological Site, by the monastery of the Koimesis Skripou.

Special Features

Pausanias (9.34–36) claimed that Orchomenos was 'as famous and glorious as any city in Greece' and that the Treasury of Minyas was 'no less marvellous than the Egyptian pyramids'.

History

The wealth of Orchomenos was proverbial, at least amongst the Greeks at Troy. 'Not even the revenues of Orchomenos' would have placated the wrath of Achilles (*Iliad* 9.381). This reputation for affluence was linked with Minyas, a mythical ruler of the city. Pausanias observed that 'he was the first man to build a treasury'.

Although the early occupation levels have been disturbed, it is clear that Orchomenos was a major prehistoric site. There is a distinctive type of Middle Helladic pottery which is known as Minyan because it was first discovered at Orchomenos by Schliemann. The Treasury of Minyas, one of the finest Mycenaean tholos tombs, was constructed in the late C14 or early C13 BC. Only a powerful ruler could have afforded such a lavish tomb. It may be no coincidence that the Mycenaeans fortified GLA at around this time and apparently drained Lake Kopais. If Orchomenos led this project, as seems likely, THEBES would have faced serious competition for Boiotian supremacy.

Although the two cities remained rivals in the Classical period, Orchomenos joined the Boiotian Confederacy and consequently fought on the Persian side at the battle of PLATAIA in 479 BC. Orchomenos seceded from the confederacy in the C4 and was destroyed by Thebes in 364 and then again in 349. Philip II and Alexander rebuilt the city which flourished for a time but became relatively insignificant under Roman rule.

Description

We suggest that you visit the monastery first. The **church** was built in 874 in a style inspired by Bulgarian architecture. The ashlar blocks and column drums used in its construction were clearly recycled. Recent excavations by the south-west corner of the church have revealed the disturbed remains of a substantial Mycenaean structure. It is possible, although not certain, that this was the palace. The finds include pieces of fresco which depict a boar hunt—reminiscent of the fresco from TIRYNS on display in the National Archaeological Museum in ATHENS.

Opposite the church is the **theatre**, which can be seen from the road

▲ Fig. 134. Plan of Orchomenos

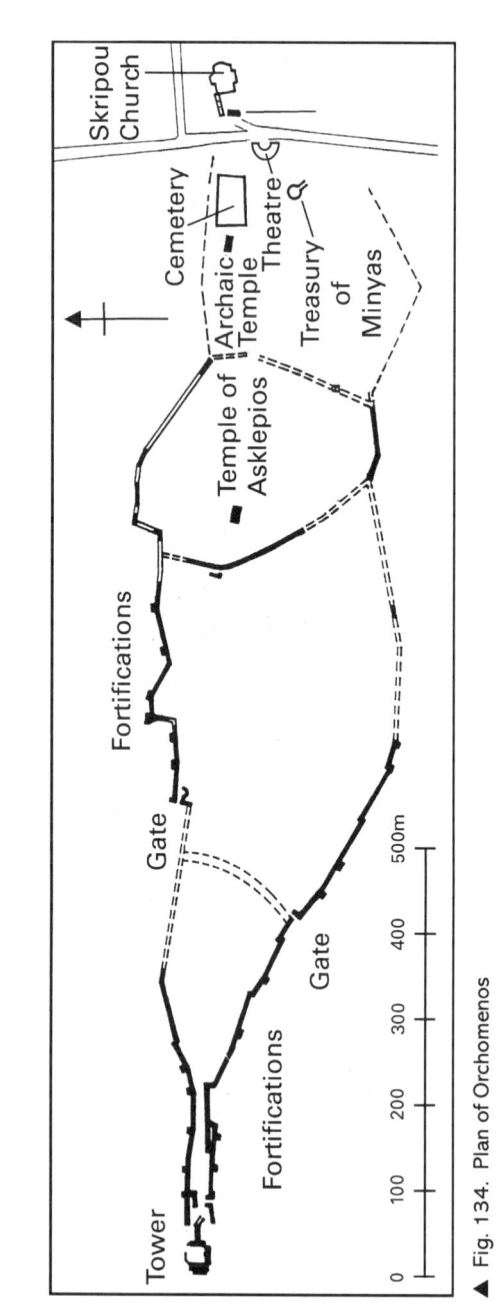

if access is restricted. It was built in the late C4 BC and has twelve rows of seats preserved. The orchestra is intact but the stage has been dismantled. Inscriptions mention musical contests in honour of Dionysos and the Graces, who were especially revered at Orchomenos.

The **Treasury of Minyas** is a short distance south-west of the theatre. The enthusiasm for tholos tombs which you see in the Argolid and Messenia was not shared by the Mycenaeans in Boiotia. It would seem that the rulers of Thebes were buried in chamber tombs. The fact that the Treasury of Minyas is not simply a tholos tomb but one of the most impressive must be an ostentatious assertion of independence. Pausanias (9.38) was certainly an admirer:

The Treasury of Minyas is one of the greatest wonders of Greece and of the world. It is built in stone, the shape is circular but the top does not stick up too sharply. They say the topmost stone is a keystone which keeps the entire structure in place.

Unfortunately someone must have tested this theory because the vault has collapsed. The dromos was originally around 30 m. in length. Limestone blocks were cut for the stomion, the entrance of the tomb which was evidently closed by a wooden door. Notice how the inner side of the lintel block follows the curve of the vault. The chamber is 14 m. in diameter and would have been approximately the same height. The statue base in the centre was added much later and used in Roman times for the imperial cult. The Treasury of Minyas resembles the Treasury of Atreus at MYCENAE in a number of respects, not least in that there is a side-chamber. Like the main chamber this had already been cleared when Schliemann excavated the tomb in 1880–86 but you can still marvel at the crisply carved rosettes and spirals on the panels which form the roof.

There is a road up to the citadel just beyond the theatre. This passes the modern cemetery and then, on the right, the remains of an **Archaic temple** constructed of massive blocks of stone. The road ends on a terrace, a short distance from the foundations of a **Hellenistic temple**, almost certainly of Asklepios. The summit of the akropolis is quite a steep climb up rough paths/goat tracks. The **fortifications** were built in the late C4 and protected the Hellenistic city. The **tower** right at the top, reached by a flight of rock-cut steps, is particularly well preserved. There is a fine view of the Kopais basin.

Gla (Figs. 135-136)

Take the Kastro exit on the Athens–Lamia road and follow signs for Larimna. After a short distance turn down the side road signed Archaeological Site of Gla. When you reach the site, keep straight on until you see the south gate on your left. The road makes a complete circuit of the citadel.

Special Features

Gla is one of the largest and most impressive of the Mycenaean citadels but why was this extraordinary site built? Go and join in the speculation.

History

There may have been a settlement at Gla in the Neolithic period but it was the Mycenaeans who developed the site. Around 1300 BC they fortified the whole of the limestone outcrop, a circuit of approximately 3000 m. The 900 m. of fortifications at MYCENAE seem modest by comparison. Two architectural complexes, the palace and the agora, were constructed but only occupy a fraction of the 230,000 m.^{2} available. Then in the late C13 the site was destroyed and abandoned.

In antiquity Gla was an island in Lake Kopais. This natural basin, formed by erosion and solution of the limestone, is drained by *katabothroi* or swallow-holes. Eventually the *katabothroi* were blocked by sediment, the basin flooded, and a lake was created. In the heat of the summer this dried up and became a marsh but the water level rose again in the winter. The lake was artificially drained in 1886 and 20,000 hectares of prime agricultural land became available for the cultivation of cotton and cereals. The emperor Hadrian funded dyke-building and Strabo (9.2.18) mentions an unsuccessful attempt at reclamation in the C4 BC. There is also evidence of an earlier system of dykes, constructed in the same distinctive technique as the fortifications around Gla. It would appear that Mycenaean engineers tamed Kopais, a remarkable achievement even if the level of the lake was lower in the prehistoric period. The farmers and their crops must have needed protection and so Gla was built. ORCHOMENOS would certainly have benefited and possibly initiated the project, although other communities may also have been involved.

Description

The **fortifications** at Gla were constructed in the Cyclopean technique—an inner and outer face of limestone blocks separated by a rubble core. The builders were fortunate because they could obtain stone which split into rectangular blocks. The indentations mark changes in the direction of the wall, which is 5–6 m. wide and follows the edge of the limestone outcrop. Given the length of the circuit, four gates were needed so that the citadel would be easily accessible in the event of an attack.

You reach the **south gate** [3] by a steep path rather than the paved ramp which the Mycenaeans used. The bastions on either side of the gate form a narrow court. An enemy force could be hemmed in and would then come under fire from defenders positioned on the bastions. The gate was evidently made of wood sheathed in bronze. Note the guard

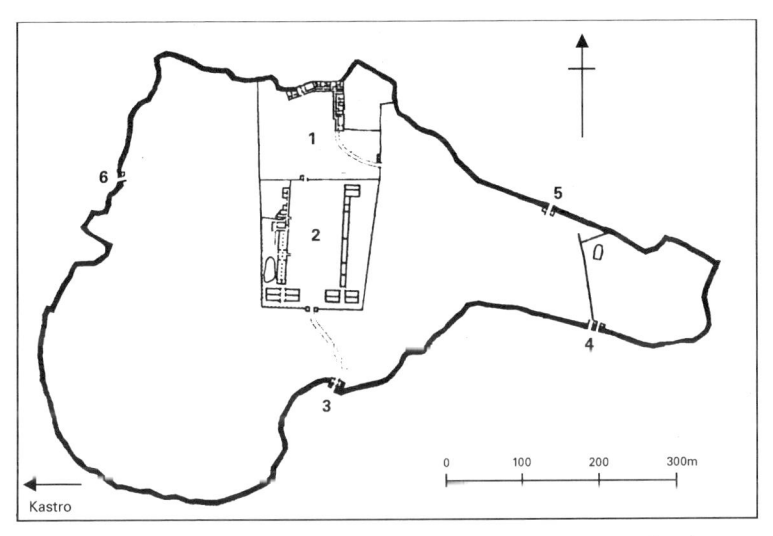

▲ Fig. 135. Plan of the citadel at Gla. Key: 1 Palace 2 Agora 3 South gate 4 South-east gate 5 North gate 6 West gate

rooms and also the ramp behind the east bastion. None of the other gates [4–6] is quite as impressive.

Now head for the highest point on the citadel and after approximately 100 m. you will be in the first of the two architectural complexes, although this may not be obvious if the site is overgrown. The so-called **agora** [2] is a rectangular enclosure, 160 by 170 m. The buildings on either side of the enclosure look rather like stoas. Stone was used for the lower courses of the walls and mudbrick for the superstructure. It was originally thought that this was a place of assembly, hence the agora. However, recent excavations in the rooms at the southern end of the enclosure have revealed masses of carbonized grain and it is clear that these were store rooms. The agora would have provided storage space for around 2000 tons of cereals.

A gate connects the agora and the enclosure which contains the **palace** [1]. This is quite unlike other Mycenaean palaces. It has a north and an east wing which meet at right angles. The two wings duplicate one another. Essentially they consist of a series of separate apartments connected by a system of corridors. There is a megaron unit at the end of each wing by the entrance. Some of the rooms were frescoed. Poros horns of consecration, on display in the museum in THEBES, hint at Minoan influence.

The use of the term palace is almost certainly inappropriate, since there is no evidence that Gla was a political centre. The palace has been more plausibly interpreted as the residence of two individuals of equal

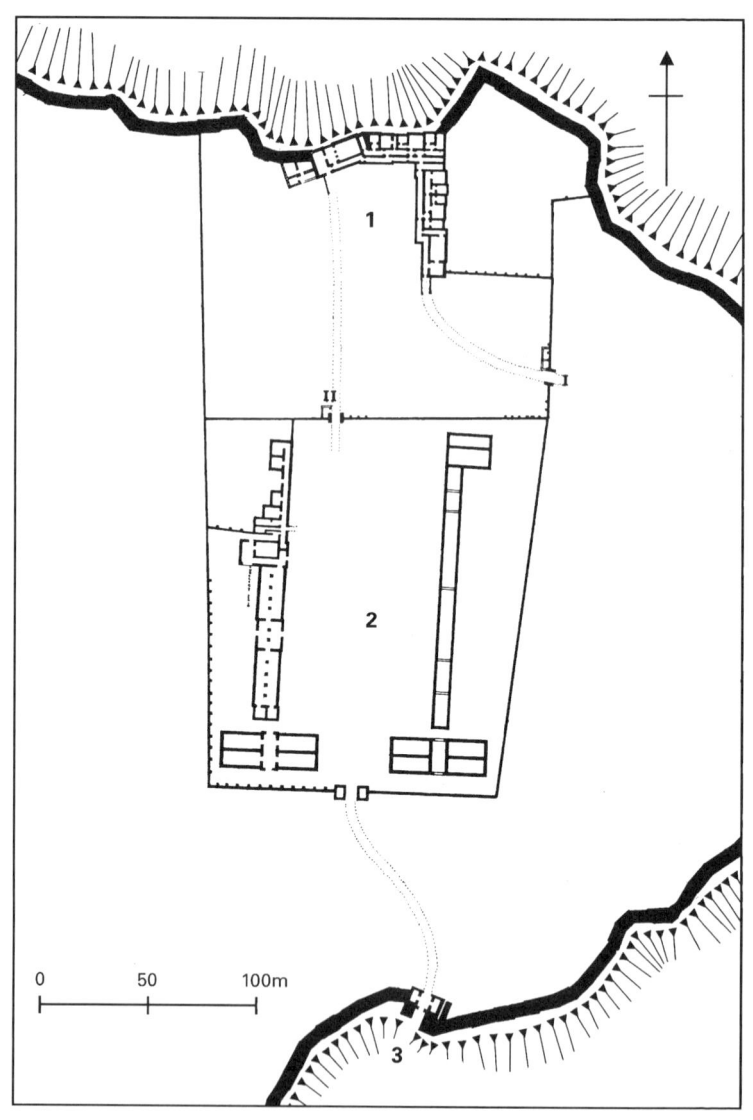

▲ Fig. 136. Plan of the palace and agora at Gla. Key: 1 Palace 2 Agora 3 South gate

status, possibly an officer who commanded the garrison and an official who was responsible for the dykes and storerooms.

Ptoion (Fig. 137) ★

Take the exit for Akrefnio on the Athens–Lamia road (this exit, still under construction, is not marked at present, but does exist). From the central square in Akrefnio, follow the signs for the Sanctuary of Apollo Ptoos and then take a side road, also signed. This soon becomes a dirt road. When you reach a junction, take the left fork for Ιερα Μονη Οσιας Πελαγιας (Holy Monastery of Agia Pelagia). At the next junction do not take the fork signed ΠΡΟΣ ΙΕΡΑ ΜΟΝΗ but keep right and you will soon pass another sign for the site, which is just above the road, shortly before the chapel of Ayia Paraskevi.

Special Features

This out-of-the-way site is rather overgrown and there is not much to see. But it is accessible and has a nice view, as well as getting you into the mountainous wilds of eastern Boiotia.

History

The worship of Apollo on Mt Ptoion was well established *c.*640 BC, but the earliest offerings go back to the C8 BC. The site may well mark the eastern frontier of the territory of nearby Akraiphia, and lay on an ancient route linking THEBES with north-east Boiotia. Apollo's epithet 'Ptoios' links him with a local hero of that name, worshipped in a nearby shrine to the west, and said by the poet Pindar (early C5 BC) to be the god's son. As at DELPHI, Apollo shared the sanctuary with Athena Pronoia, her cult known from inscriptions. The cult particularly flourished in the Archaic period, when *c.*100 statues of young males (kouroi) were dedicated here (see THEBES museum). Its clientele was regional rather than local, and included Hipparchos, son of the Athenian tyrant Peisistratos. The chief attraction was an oracle, its mouthpiece a prophet, whose inspired ravings in Boiotian dialect were mistaken for Karian, a language of south-west Asia Minor, during a famous consultation by the Persian general Mardonios in 480 BC (Herodotus 8.135). In 226–224 BC Akraiphia, which controlled the sanctuary, refounded the local games, the Ptoia. The programme was artistic (music, singing, poetry), although there were also team-races for cavalry. By the C1 AD an impoverished Akraiphia was dependent on local magnates to keep the games going, such as the Epaminondas who *c.* AD 37–42 lavishly revived them after a 30-year lapse. In Plutarch's time (*c.* AD 100) the oracle had fallen silent, and at the sanctuary 'for most of the day you will hardly see a single shepherd with his flocks' (*Decline of the Oracles* 8.414A), although the now-yearly games lingered on as late as the C3 AD.

Description

The sanctuary is laid out on three levels above the road. On the lowest level are substantial installations belonging to a **fountain** fed by spring water. From its first phase (*c.*500 BC) comes a fine, bronze, serpent's-head water-spout. The most impressive feature today, albeit rather overgrown, is a vast **cistern** ([1]—possibly C3 BC), with seven interconnected chambers. In front are remains of two Archaic **basins** [2] with polygonal masonry, cut through by a later **aqueduct**. A prominent base for a private dedication has a Latin inscription naming the donor as Curtius Certus, one of the local Roman businessmen.

On the large, sloping middle level, as well as other structures of unknown purpose, are two parallel, rectangular buildings, interpreted as **stoas** [3], the one to the south overlying what may be foundations of an Archaic **altar**, perhaps of Athena. The uppermost level is an artificial terrace, retained above and below by walls, for the **Classical temple** [4], of which some foundations for the colonnade and cella are preserved. Normally dated c.350–300 BC, it perhaps should be placed a century earlier, to match the date of a group of architectural terracottas from the

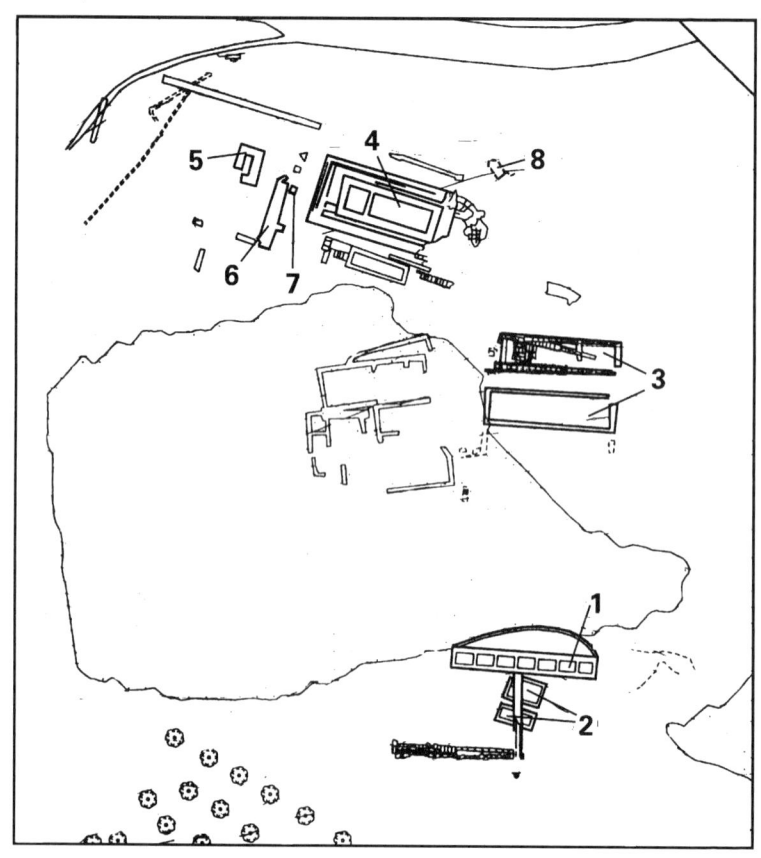

▼ Fig. 137. Plan of the Ptoion. Key: 1 Cisterns 2 Basins 3 Stoas 4 Classical temple 5 Altar 6 Foundation 7 Bases 8 Grotto

site. In front of the temple is a rectangular limestone foundation identified as an **altar** [**5**]. Between the two is a 12-m. long **foundation** [**6**], possibly once supporting the kouroi-dedications. Four **bases** [**7**] for bronze tripod-cauldrons are aligned on this foundation. Above the temple is a ancient man-made **grotto** [**8**], conceivably used in the oracular ritual. A theatre and dining rooms (*trikleina*), mentioned in an inscription of the C1 AD, have yet to be found.

Thermopylai

The site is on the national road halfway between Lamia and Kammena Vourla. It is marked by a conspicuous modern memorial (N side of the road).

Special Features

Although there is little to see, the site of the famous 'last stand' against the Persians by Spartans and Boiotians is evocative.

History

Thermopylai ('Hot Gates', so called from its hot sulphur springs which are still in use) was once a strategic pass carrying the chief ancient route linking north and south Greece. The lie of the land is now radically altered by alluvial deposits from the River Spercheios, pushing the sea back *c*.5 km. In ancient times the road ran between Mt Kallidromos and the sea along a thin strip of land, narrowest here at the 'Gates'. In 480 BC a force of 6000–7000 Greeks led by Leonidas, king of SPARTA, tried to defend the pass against the vastly larger host (100,000 men?) of the Persian king, Xerxes I. As the story goes, when his scouts reported seeing the Spartan troops at the pass 'exercising naked and combing their hair' (Herodotus 7.209), Xerxes laughed. But the restricted space and better weapons allowed the Greeks repeatedly to repel the Persian attacks, and the king was at a loss until a local Greek, later a refugee with a price on his head, offered to guide the enemy over a mountain path bringing them out in the Greek rear. A Persian force duly set off at night. At dawn, realizing what had happened, Leonidas dismissed the Greeks to fight another day, except for his 300 Spartans and the Boiotians who all fought to the death. At the end, pulling back to some high ground, they 'defended themselves with knives, if they still had them, and otherwise with their hands and teeth, while the Persians buried them in a hail of missiles' (Herodotus 7.225). The Greek dead were buried where they fell, and after the war three inscribed monuments were set up on the same spot. The Spartans were still celebrating the memory of Leonidas with an annual festival in the 200s AD, and the battle's importance for today's Greece is shown by the modern monument, augmented in 1997 with a memorial to the 700 dead from Boiotian Thespiai. The defile retained its strategic importance into the C6 AD, when the Emperor Justinian built new fortifications.

Description

There is a car park opposite the modern monument. From here you can climb up to the knoll where the last stand took place, identified by excavations which unearthed many C5 BC arrow-heads, as well as Hellenistic fortifications and Roman and Byzantine houses, suggesting the presence here of an ancient harbour. The modern memorial, decorated with green 'porphyry' (*lapis Lacedaemonius*) from quarries at Krokeai south of Sparta, reproduces the poignant epigram attributed in ancient times to the poet Simonides:

Stranger, tell the people of Lakedaimon (Sparta) that we who lie here obeyed their commands.

(Herodotus 7.228)

Chalkis

Special Features

Although few traces of the ancient city can be seen, Chalkis is worth a visit for the well arranged museum and for a rare tidal phenomenon which attracted tourists in antiquity.

History

Chalkis was already a settlement of some importance in the Mycenaean period. Control of the narrow Euripos channel and therefore of the sea route down the more sheltered western side of Euboia provided commercial opportunities which the city soon exploited. Chalkis and ERETRIA founded colonies in Italy and Sicily in the C8 BC. The two cities then fell out and fought a protracted war over the Lelantine plain, through which the Chalkis–Eretria road passes. The outcome of this war, in which the two sides apparently forswore the use of long-range weapons, is uncertain. Colonists from Chalkis settled in the northern Aegean in the C7 and the city was renowned as a trade centre and for the production of metalwork. It was inevitable that imperialist ATHENS should threaten the independence of Chalkis which became a tributary ally after an abortive revolt in 446 BC and remained so until 411. It was only then that the first bridge across the Euripos was built. Philip of Macedon realized that this made Chalkis one of the key points from which he could control Greece and in 338 BC imposed a garrison as one of his 'fetters'. The city nevertheless flourished in the C3 but fought for the Achaian Confederacy against Rome and was partially destroyed in 146 BC.

Description

We suggest that you enter the city by the old bridge, across the narrows. The Euripos was dreaded by ancient mariners because tidal rips form here. The current can change direction six times or more in 24 hours and sometimes flows at a speed of seven or eight knots. The first bridge across the channel was built in 410 BC after Chalkis had left the Athenian Confederacy. Because the Athenians were masters of the sea, it was vital that reinforcements could cross from Boiotia if the city was threatened. Originally there were two channels separated by an island, each of which was spanned by a wooden bridge. In 334 BC the bridge was rebuilt and it may have been then that the western channel was filled in. The present structure, which retracts so that ships can pass through, dates from 1962.

From the bridge there are signs to the **Archaeological Museum** which is on Odos El. Venizelou. **Room 1**, on the right of the entrance hall, covers the Palaeolithic-Geometric periods. The finds from the extensive Early Helladic settlement and cemetery at Manika, just north of Chalkis, are of particular interest. Some of the pottery, the marble figurines, and marble vases could well have been imported from the islands and it has been argued that the site was a Cycladic colony. However, it seems more likely that this cultural eclecticism simply reflects the extent to which the Euboians were already involved in trade. Also note the quality of the Mycenaean pottery and bronzes. In **room 2**, on the left, there is Archaic and Classical sculpture—kouroi, grave and votive reliefs. The cases contain Archaic, Classical, Hellenistic, and Roman pottery, figurines, jewellery, and coins. The Roman sculpture in **room 3** includes a statue of Antinoos (see p. 314) and a bust of Polydeukion, the favourite foster-son of Herodes Atticus, who died in AD 147/8 (see p. 115). There is more sculpture in the two porticoes which face the museum and also inscriptions. The four Doric column capitals in the courtyard, possibly from a C5 temple of Zeus, serve as a reminder that Chalkis was powerful and prosperous, even if this is not obvious from what is left of the ancient city.

Eretria (Fig. 138)

Special Features

There are exceptional finds from Eretria and Lefkandi on display in the museum. The many remains of the ancient city include the sumptuous House of the Mosaics.

History

Eretria was one of the two chief cities of Euboia down to the C1 BC. It was probably founded c.825 BC from LEFKANDI, on a strategic site with akropolis, harbour, access to fertile land, and control of Euboia's chief east–west land-route. Eretria's glory days fell in the C8–C6 BC, when Euboians were at the forefront of Greek overseas ventures. Close political ties with ATHENS began in the C6 BC. In retribution for aiding a revolt of Persia's Greek subjects (499), a Persian expedition captured the city (490), ending its early greatness by burning the sanctuaries and deporting the inhabitants. Eretria now entered the Athens-dominated ambit of the Delian League, revolting in 446, whereafter it was occupied by Athens until it revolted again in 411. From 338 until 198 the city was usually under Macedonian control, in the early C3 exercised through the philosopher-politician Menedemos, founder of an Eretrian 'school' of philosophy. In 189 BC the city was captured and sacked by Titus Flamininus, his plunder mainly artworks (Livy 32.16). For a while Eretria still ranked as Euboia's second city (Strabo 10.1.10, drawing on an earlier source), and luxurious new houses were built near the west gate. After the city sided with Mithradates against Rome (87 BC), it passed into Athenian hands once more, regaining autonomy in the late C1 BC. In imperial times there was modest prosperity, partly based on a purple-dye industry.

Description

We suggest that you start at the **museum**, which is well signed. This has excellent displays with informative labels in French and Greek. Highlights in **Room 1** are the finds from Lefkandi, including a vessel depicting a griffin (1200–1100 BC) and a model centaur (c.1000 BC); bronze burial cauldrons and other finds from the heroon by the west gate (case 10); and (case 12) the earliest finds from the sanctuary of Apollo Daphnephoros, including a bronze horse's blinker, Syrian work of the C9. **Room 2** displays fragments from the west pediment of the late C6 temple of Apollo, remarkable for depicting an Athenian myth, the abduction by Theseus of the Amazon Antiope in the presence of Athena. There are also (case 2) objects from the C4 houses of Eretria, (case 18) Panathenaic amphorae (see **box**), and (case 22) material from a 'Macedonian' tomb to the north of the walled city, used by three generations (of a pro-Macedonian local family?). In the courtyard is a Middle Helladic pottery kiln found near the agora. If you plan to visit the House of the Mosaics, you should collect the key from the museum.

On the other side of the main road is the fenced but accessible **area of Classical and Hellenistic houses** [1] with excellent information panels in English and Greek. This should be visited for its palatial houses and a well-preserved stretch of the fortifications. The large (1260 m.²), one-storey, House II (C4 BC) is a double courtyard design, with an impressive entrance leading into the public area, centred on a large colonnaded court, with a seven-couch dining room to the north, and a

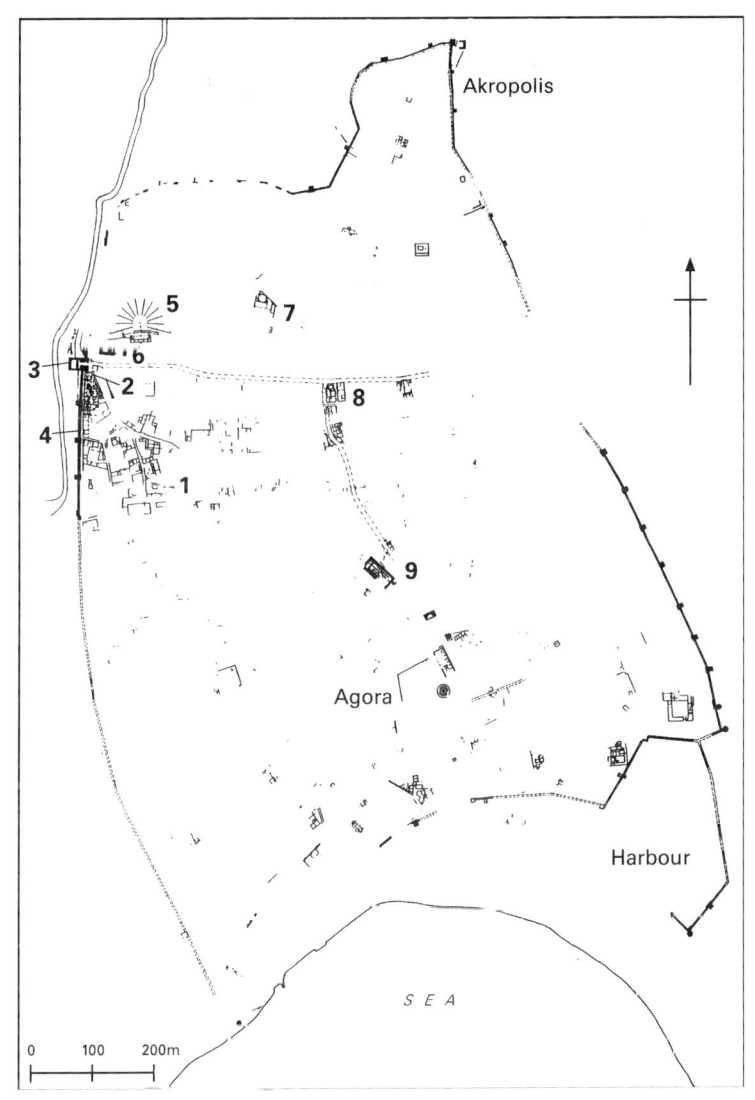

▲ Fig. 138. Plan of Eretria. Key: 1 Classical and Hellenistic houses 2 Heroon 3 West gate 4 Curtain wall 5 Theatre 6 Temple and altar of Dionysos 7 Gymnasium 8 House of the Mosaics 9 Sanctuary of Apollo Daphnephoros

domestic area to the west centred on a secondary court, and including a room ('kitchen') with a hearth.

To the north the wall-footings of an earlier courtyard house (House I) of c.400 BC, altered c.300 BC, and destroyed in 198 BC, were partly reused in a much larger complex of c.170, also one storey. This

> ### Panathenaic amphorae
>
> The so-called Panathenaic amphorae were prizes awarded to victors in the Panathenaia, the four-yearly games for Athena at Athens. The jars contained valuable olive-oil, and in the C4 BC at least 1400 were awarded at each gathering. The ones on display show the canonical black-figure decor: an armed Athena on one side, a contest on the other, and two inscriptions, one of them saying 'one of the prizes from Athens', the other giving a date by the Athenian archon. These come from a spectacular cache of nine, dated to 363/2 and 360/59 BC. They were found near the House of Mosaics, to which they perhaps belonged, since fragments of a further four from the same two years were found in the house itself, where they are thought to have been displayed in the colonnade of the west court. Perhaps an inhabitant of the House of the Mosaics, an athletic youth c.360, won them all in two consecutive victories at Athens.

comprised two houses, Ib (to the north, with a single courtyard) and Ia (with a double courtyard). Dwarfing its neighbour, Ia had a monumental entrance wide enough for carts, giving access (north) to a mix of public, domestic, and work rooms grouped round a colonnaded court, including a heated bathroom, and (south) to more rooms off a secondary court. Finds of an oil press, lead weights, wine amphorae, and storage jars suggest a house combining the agricultural workshops and residence of a large landowner. After alterations, the house fell into ruin in the C1 BC.

Below the house's most northerly rooms can be seen a triangular 'pavement' of large stones marking the site of an early Archaic **heroon** [2] built over an aristocratic family group of fifteen burials, both inhumations (children) and cremations (adults of both sexes, the men buried with swords and lances), dating c.720–680 BC. Ashes were wrapped in cloth and placed in bronze bowls, in one case (the preeminent burial, a male) in a bronze cauldron covered by a second. Burials ceased c.680, when the triangle was built, and a hero-cult instituted, as revealed by a nearby pit for the debris of sacrificial banquets. About 625–600 a rectangular building, perhaps a kind of club-house, was added, and the triangle itself enclosed by a curving boundary wall. The cult is thought to have centred on the dead warriors and the supernatural protection which they offered to the west-gate area. By the time the site was built over c.400, the heroon must have been long forgotten.

The **west gate** [3] is strategically sited at the point where the ancient highway from Chalkis crossed a winter torrent, originally by means of a ford. A gate already existed in late Archaic times, along with the first (wooden) bridge; there are traces of earlier defensive works. The surviving features are mainly those of a rebuild after the Persian wars to a new design, renovated at the end of the Athenian occupation (411 BC), in which the torrent-bed now acted in effect as a moat. A stone bridge (seven piers survive under the bastion), led the road through a bottleneck courtyard, flanked by a pair of bastion-like towers with mudbrick cores, to a two-leaved wooden door, its socket-settings still visible in the floor. Finally, at a date no earlier than *c.* 200 BC, and perhaps through the agency of Antiochos III, active in the area in 192/1, a massive protective bastion was built in front of the gate, with entrances on the north and south sides, and a vaulted channel below for the overflow from the stream, now diverted to the west. A well-preserved stretch of **curtain wall** [4], punctuated by three square towers, can be followed from the west gate to the museum. The polygonal socle dates from *c.* 400 and supported a mudbrick superstructure. The circuit as a whole encloses an area from the seashore to the summit of the akropolis to the north.

From the western quarter a gate leads to the **theatre** [5], fenced and currently inaccessible. The seating, with an original capacity of *c.*6300, rests (unusually for a Greek theatre) on a man-made hill, ensuring proximity with the nearby **temple and altar of Dionysos** [6] to the south-west, also C4 BC, but with an Archaic predecessor. The theatre's architecture evolved broadly in line with the theatre of Dionysos at ATHENS, with a first skene (stage-building) in stone dated to the late C5 BC, and a major rebuilding to the later C4. This included the stone seating, and moving the orchestra 8 m. north to allow enlargement of the skene, which now acquired a second storey fronted by an Ionic proskenion, with an underground passage linking the inside to the middle of the orchestra, probably for staging appearances from the Underworld. The skene was rebuilt and enlarged after 189 BC.

From the theatre a track runs north-east to the fenced but accessible **gymnasium** [7], dated to the late C4 BC, but renovated after 198 BC. Rooms were ranged round a colonnaded court, not fully excavated. The bathing amenities are interesting. A wash-room in the north-east corner was equipped with interconnecting basins fed by running water, three of them replaced after 198 with foot-baths. Also after 198, under Roman influence, a vaulted sweat bath was installed in an oval-shaped room to the north, the heat provided by a hearth on its tiled floor. In one of the rooms was found an intact 49-line inscription honouring an overseer of the gymnasium (gymnasiarch) called Elpinikos (late C2 BC), who paid an orator and an arms-trainer to 'devote themselves in the gymnasium to the boys, ephebes, and whomever else wanted to receive profit from such training' (*IG* 5. 2. 9, no. 234, now in the museum courtyard).

Below and *c.* 150 m. to the south-east (on Odos Ktesikleous) is the so-called **House of the Mosaics** [8], unique for Eretria in the quality of its mosaics, now protected by a tiled roof. The key can be obtained from the museum. This large house, the most luxurious yet found at Eretria, dates to *c.*370 BC and was destroyed by fire a century later. It was one-storeyed, with plastered mudbrick walls on stone footings and clay rooftiles. The plan is a double courtyard, the domestic rooms to the east ranged round an open court and divided from the public rooms to the west by a wall. The west rooms were grouped round a colonnaded court. To the north and west are three formal dining rooms, with couches for up to 21 guests. The eleven-couch room, partly overlaid by a later tomb (below), yielded fine clay ornaments once attached to the walls (museum, case 17). The mosaics in the seven-couch room include the mythical conflict between griffins and one-eyed women-warriors, the Arimaspians.

The **monumental tomb**, built over the ruined house, dates to *c.*120–70 BC, in the early phase of Roman rule. Massive blocks form a rectangular enclosure. Inside, the primary burial (to the north) was a male of *c.*20 years, later joined by a second sarcophagus-burial. The rare privilege of intra-mural burial here apparently marked the premature death of the son and heir of a leading local family, in an era when the rich dominated city politics.

The **Sanctuary of Apollo Daphnephoros** [9] is signed, fenced, and inaccessible (1999). Apollo was the patron deity of the Eretrians. His sanctuary was founded soon after the city itself, and the surrounding area was one of its original nuclei. Precociously early structures, and exotic offerings from the east (museum, case 12), class it among the most important sacred sites in Archaic Greece.

The massive foundations visible through the fence are those of the badly robbed Doric temple built *c.*530–520 BC (its east facade is nearest the street). The two colonnades of the cella were axially aligned with the short sides of the outer colonnade, a unique feature in Doric temples of the time, but found in the contemporary great Ionic temples. This Ionic influence, reflecting early Eretria's eastern contacts, went back to a predecessor (*c.*670–650), one of the major mainland temples of its time. Its foundations, which underlie the C6 BC temple, show a plan closely resembling the second temple of Hera on Samos, with a wooden colonnade (40.10 by 11.70 m.) enclosing a single elongated chamber. Underneath this in turn are the stone foundations of two apsidal structures, both dating to the C8 BC. The smaller, and earlier could be a votive replica of Apollo's legendary hut of laurel leaves at DELPHI or (a more recent theory) the residence of a priestly leader. The bigger and later (*c.*725 BC), a hundred Greek feet long (a hekatompedon), is the largest known building in C8 Greece, and the first temple on the site. Its foundations project to the north of the C6 BC temple. After the Persian destruction the sculpture from the west pediment of the C6 BC temple, showing Theseus abducting the Amazon Antiope (in the museum), was piously buried, to judge from the freshness of the fragments found on site. The temple was then restored or rebuilt on the same foundations, and probably adorned with a new pedimental group of (once more) Theseus fighting Amazons, now in Rome (see **box**).

Pedimental group of Theseus and the Amazons

In 1937-8 excavations at the temple of Apollo Medicus Sosianus in Rome (late C1 BC) unearthed ancient Greek statuary once decorating the temple pediment. The figures, now displayed in the Capitoline Museum, show Athena surrounded by fighting Greeks (led by Herakles and Theseus) and Amazons. Following a theory of Italian archaeologist Eugenio La Rocca, it seems likely that the group had originally been brought from Eretria to Rome as part of the art-plunder of 198 BC, having formerly adorned the restored temple of Apollo Daphnephoros, where (on grounds of style) they would have been installed c.450 BC. A cast of one of the Amazons is displayed in the museum portico.

Lefkandi (Figs. 139-140)

Take the turn signed Παραλια Λευκαντι in the centre of Vasiliko, on the Chalkis–Eretria road. After 1.3 km. bear right and then turn right after a further 200 m. at the sign for the Αρχαιολογικος Χωρος. The 'Heroon', covered by a conspicuous corrugated-iron roof, is almost immediately on your left. For Xeropolis, take the road which drops to the seafront, then turn left and follow the coast until you reach the sign for the Archaeological Site. Xeropolis is the prominent headland crowned by olives.

Special Features

The excavations at Lefkandi, and in particular the discovery of the monumental yet enigmatic 'Heroon', have completely transformed the perception of Early Iron Age Greece as isolated and impoverished.

History

Xeropolis, literally the dry or deserted city, may lack water but is flanked by bays and is well placed to control the fertile Lelantine plain. It is therefore curious that there is no evidence of settlement on the hill until late in the Early Helladic period. The earliest pottery has a quite distinctive character and it is possible that the first settlers came from, or alternatively had trade connections with, the eastern Aegean or western Turkey. This taste for the exotic would be seen again later. By the Middle Helladic period Xeropolis was a town of some size and presumably importance. It is not certain whether this was also true of the Mycenaean settlement which eventually underwent a radical transformation in the C12 BC, in the aftermath of the destructions which affected other sites in the region and may have resulted in an influx of refugees. Despite a major fire, occupation continued at least until the end of the C12.

Most of the evidence for Early Iron Age Lefkandi comes from the cemeteries, approximately 500 m. north-west of Xeropolis.

Submycenaean and Protogeometric graves in the Skoubris cemetery date from the C11 BC but it is the Toumba cemetery which has produced the most remarkable finds. Early in the C10 a massive stone and mudbrick structure was built either as the residence or the tomb of a local chieftain and his wife. After a short space of time this structure, the 'Heroon', was partially dismantled, covered by an earth mound, and then became the focal point of a cemetery. At a time when most of Greece was impoverished and isolated, the wealth buried in these graves is almost incredible (see the display in the museum in ERETRIA). Moreover, it is clear that Lefkandi had close trade contacts not only with ATHENS and other settlements on the east coast of Greece but also with Cyprus and the Near East. This level of prosperity was maintained until the end of the C9 when the cemeteries went out of use. Settlement continued on Xeropolis but ended abruptly around 700 BC. Lefkandi may well have been a casualty of the conflict between CHALKIS and Eretria over control of the Lelantine plain.

Description

The **Heroon** has been fenced off and is not accessible at present but can be viewed from the road. Trial excavations in 1980 uncovered the central section of the structure. Unfortunately this was then bulldozed by the owner of the plot and completely destroyed. The eastern and western ends were excavated in 1981–3 and cement blocks have been used to restore the walls which were lost. The 'Heroon' faces east and measures at least 47 m. in length and 10 m. in width. The west end is not preserved but there was apparently an apse and the side walls also curve slightly. The walls were constructed of stone and mudbrick, plastered on the inside. Except at the east end there was a portico of timber posts set 1.80 m. from the outer face of the walls. Posts were also positioned against the inner face of the walls and down the centre of the interior to support the roof which was thatched with reeds or rushes. The 'Heroon' has a shallow porch and five rooms, the most important of which was clearly the central room. It was here that the excavators discovered two pits cut in the floor of the room. The north pit contained the skeletons of four horses. In the south pit a woman of 25–30 had been buried with an extraordinary array of gold jewellery—beads, rings, a pendant and an elaborate pectoral. Beside her was a bronze krater, sealed by a bowl, in which the cremated remains of a man of 30–45 had been wrapped in a linen robe or shroud. A sword, a spear and a razor had been placed by the krater which was evidently a C12 BC heirloom or an antique imported from Cyprus. It seems likely that the couple were buried early in the C10. A short time later the 'Heroon' was partially dismantled, filled with earth and made into an enormous tumulus 4 m. high, 25 m. wide and 50 m. in length. Soon there was a shaft grave cemetery east of the tumulus.

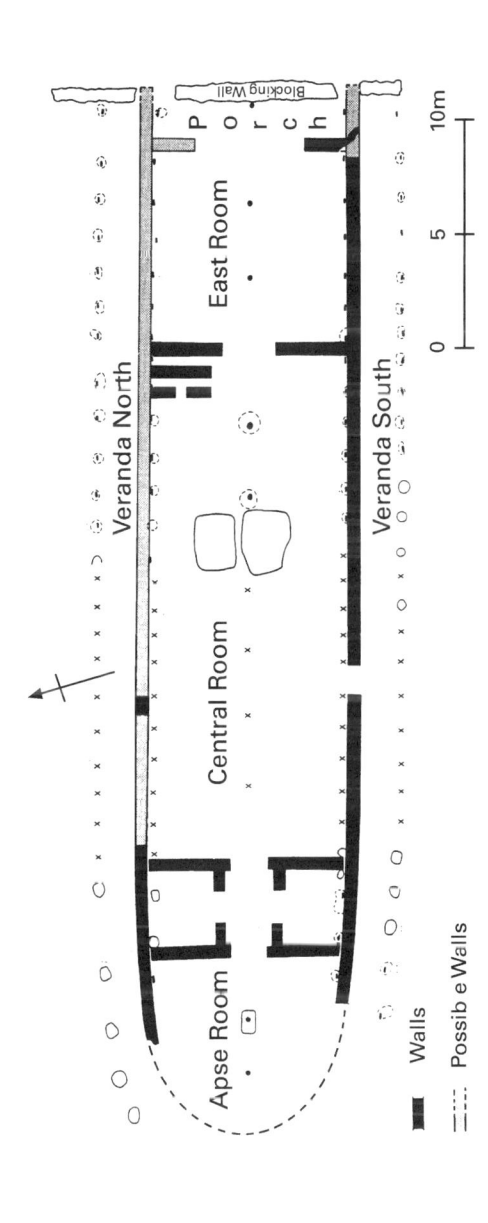

▲ Fig. 139. Plan of the 'Heroon', Lefkandi

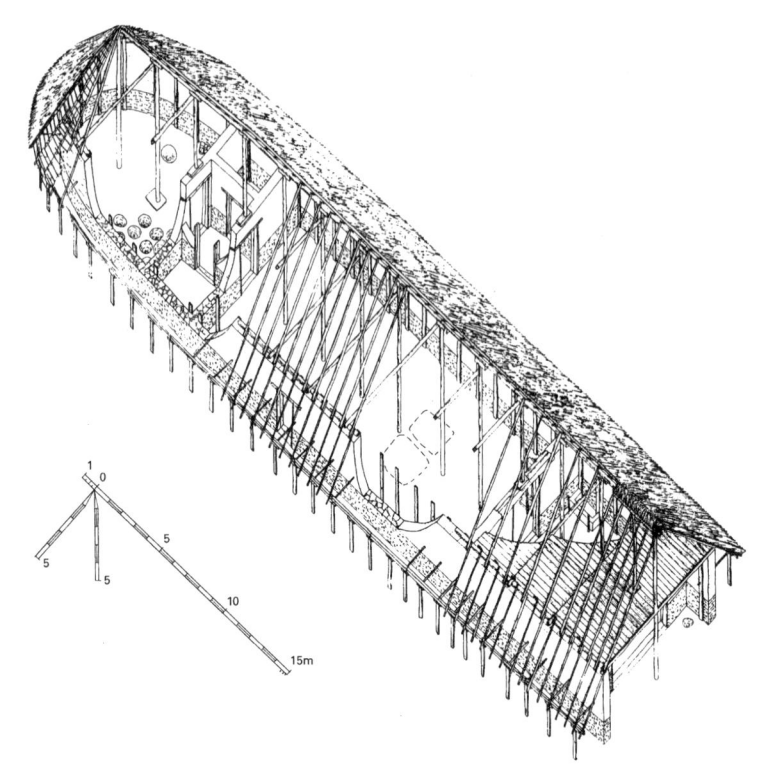

▲ Fig. 140. Reconstruction of the 'Heroon' at Lefkandi (after M. R. Popham *et al.*, *Lefkandi II: The Protogeometric Building at Toumba. Part 2: The Excavation, Architecture and Finds* (London 1993) pl. 28)

It is possible that the 'Heroon' was built as a palace for the ruler of Lefkandi and when he died it became his tomb. If the woman, presumably his wife, died at the same time, she may have been sacrificed or committed suicide, although it is not out of the question that she was buried later. An alternative theory is that the burials took place first and then the 'Heroon' was constructed. Such a mark of respect would certainly imply that the dead man had been accorded the status of a hero by the community. Indeed his treatment provides a blueprint for some of the funerals described by Homer in the *Iliad* and the *Odyssey*. The 'Heroon' is also architecturally precocious since it had formerly been assumed that structures of this size and complexity were not built before the late C8 BC when the earliest temples, such as the temple of Apollo at Eretria, were reconstructed on a more monumental scale. The 'Heroon' anticipates these developments by two centuries or more.

Xeropolis is best approached from the harbour at the west end of the headland. Trial trenches revealed that much of the summit had been eroded. Nevertheless, it is clear that occupation spread across the whole of this extensive site. The trenches which were opened up at the northeast end of the site can still be seen. The Geometric and Protogeometric levels were poorly preserved but three Late Helladic IIIC, that is C12 BC, architectural phases were identified. The pottery on display in the museum in Eretria comes from these levels. One of the trenches was excavated down to the bedrock, 8.50 m. from the surface, and indicated that the site was first occupied late in the Early Helladic II period, *c.*2400 BC. Despite the fact that this trench is so narrow, less than 3 m. wide lower down, it produced an extremely important sequence of Early and Middle Helladic pottery deposits.

Akarnania and Aitolia

Akarnania is bordered by the Ambrakian Gulf and the Acheloos River. Aitolia lies east of the river and north of the Corinthian Gulf. Much of the region is 'rough and mountainous' (Diodorus 18.24.2), particularly eastern Aitolia. If you take the road between THERMON and Nafpaktos, you will see how rugged the landscape is and understand why pastoralism was so important in the past. The terrain also provided perfect cover for bandits. Nevertheless, there is fertile land on the coast around KALYDON and PLEURON, as well as in the Acheloos valley. Because of the mountains Aitolia was rather isolated but this is less true of Ambrakia. Ships could sail quite a distance up the Acheloos, which is one of the largest rivers in Greece, and dock at OINIADAI.

Few prehistoric sites have been identified in this region. There is a Mycenaean settlement under the sanctuary of Apollo at Thermon and a number of tholos tombs have been excavated at Agios Ilias. In historic times the region, like Epeiros, hosted two states organized around 'peoples' (*ethne*), respectively the Akarnanians and Aitolians, uneasy neighbours. Urban development was quicker in Akarnania, where fortified cities, such as Oiniadai and STRATOS, already existed in the later C5 BC. The Aitolians at this time, 'although numerous and warlike, yet dwelt in unwalled villages scattered far apart' (Thucydides). By the C3 the sanctuary of Thermon, their central place, had become a town. Athenians claimed that the largest Aitolian tribe 'speak, as is said, a language exceedingly difficult to understand, and eat their flesh raw' (Thucydides 3.94.3–5). This reputation for barbarism was fanned by Aitolian brigandage, in the C3 practised on the high seas as well. All the more shockingly to other Greeks, Aitolia by now had evolved into a federal state of great power, with an extended membership across much of central Greece, and control of DELPHI, which an Aitolian feat-of-arms had saved from marauding Gauls (280/79 BC). Thermon now reached its greatest development, and the Aitolians built themselves new walled cities, of which Pleuron is the most dramatic. A misjudged relationship with Rome led to war between the two, ending (189) in an Aitolian defeat and drastic loss of territory and power. Akarnania and Aitolia were both depopulated by the creation of NIKOPOLIS, with geomorphological consequences observed by Pausanias (8.24.11): 'The reason the Echinades islands have not been joined to the mainland by the action of the Acheloos is that the Aitolian people have been rooted out and their whole land devastated. Since Aitolia has been left uncultivated, the Acheloos has not deposited mud on the Echinades in the same way'. In imperial times the river formed the frontier between the provinces of Achaia and Epeiros.

Stratos (Figs. 141–142)

If you are coming on the main road from Andirrio, turn right at the sign for Stratos a few km. beyond Agrinion. This takes you through the modern village and then climbs through a breach in the ancient city-walls, ending at the guard's hut.

Special Features

The site is just off the main road and was historically important as the Akarnanian capital. Its remains include a Doric temple which is well worth seeing.

History

In the C5 BC Stratos was the largest city in Akarnania, according to Thucydides. By 391, if not earlier, it was also the seat of the Akarnanian confederacy. The city occupied a strategic site on the Acheloos, in ancient times navigable from here to the sea. To the east it overlooked the region's border with Aitolia, to the west the fertile Akarnanian plain. It enters history in 426 BC, when, already fortified, it was unsuccessfully besieged by the Spartans in the Peloponnesian War. Stratos was the 'best fortified and biggest' Akarnanian city in 314 BC, when the Macedonian ruler Cassander built up its population with transfers from nearby villages in an attempt to contain the neighbouring Aitolians, Macedon's enemies. The enlarged Stratos flourished as never before; major new works included the temple of Zeus. The city fell into Aitolian hands *c.*250 BC. In the late C1 BC Stratos was absorbed into the vast hinterland of NIKOPOLIS. The city survived as a dependency of its giant neighbour, and there have been some Roman finds.

Description

The city is spread over four hills overlooking the Acheloos to the east. The road in the vicinity of the guard's hut provides an excellent vantage point for viewing the wall-circuit, the theatre, the agora, and, due west on a promontory, the temple of Zeus. The road itself follows the traces of a defensive **cross-wall** [1] or *diateichisma* running south from the akropolis and dividing the city into two wards.

The wall-circuit (4 km. long) in its present form probably reflects an enlargement under Cassander. The visible stretches of trapezoidal pseudo-isodomic masonry would suit this dating. Defence of the west ward (where all the main public buildings have been found) was probably the point of the cross-wall, with the ward to its east less populous and more vulnerable to capture in a surprise attack.

The **theatre** [2] is on the east side of the road, its main entrance for visitors through a gap in the fence near the guard's hut. Thought to date

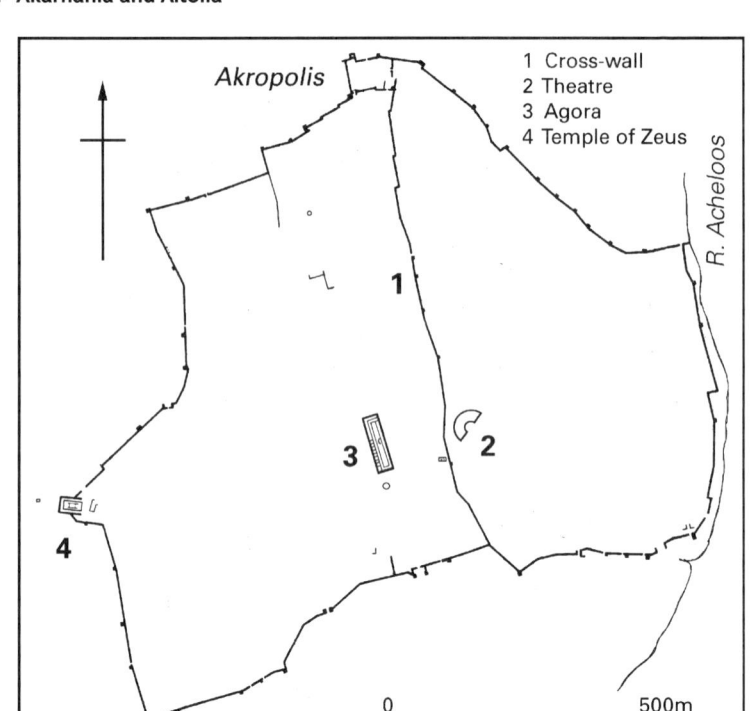

▲ Fig. 141. Plan of Stratos

to the age of Cassander, it is partly cut into the natural rock. Thrones are preserved from the front row of seats, as well as the full circle of the orchestra, with the stage-building behind. Significantly, there are no signs of Roman 'modernization'.

The planned **agora** [3] is the fenced site on the other side of the road, reached (a slight scramble) by an open gate just below the church. The rectangular plaza is framed (west and east) by long stoas and supported (west side) by subterranean chambers typical of Hellenistic stoa-architecture. Recent excavations showed that this agora was divided by a thoroughfare from an upper agora to the east. Blocks from honorific bases can be seen along the east side. The circular foundation on the west has so far defied interpretation.

To reach the **Temple of Zeus** [4], take the climbing asphalt side-street at the west end of the village, just before the Texaco garage on the main Antirrion road. This bears right and then left before passing under a concrete irrigation canal. You will see a fairly well preserved stretch of the city-wall on your right. Where the asphalt road ends, a path leads to the temple (fenced but left open) above you.

▲ Fig. 142. The Temple of Zeus at Stratos

The site was deliberately chosen for its commanding position surveying the city's farmland to the west. The cult was identified by an inscription (C2 BC), recording the liberation of a slave in the form of a fictitious sale to Zeus, the chief deity of the Akarnanians. Supported on an artificial platform, the limestone temple, dated to c.320 BC on architectural style, shows an interesting mix of orders in the manner pioneered for Greek temples by Iktinos, architect of the Parthenon. Triglyph-blocks and capitals from the outer Doric colonnade are lying about. But you can also spot dentil-blocks from the entablature of an internal colonnade, Ionic or Corinthian. An inscribed list found on the site records the names of donors of funds, perhaps for the building works. But the money must have run out, as the unfinished fluting of the column drums shows that the temple was left incomplete. Finds of Roman imperial coins suggest that the sanctuary still functioned in the late C2 AD.

Oiniadai (Fig. 143)

From Andirrio, turn left shortly after Mesolongi at the junction for Aitoliko/Neochori (Αιτωλικό/Νεοχώρι). Beyond Aitoliko, take the left turn at the fork signed (in both directions!) Ancient Iniades. You cross the River Acheloos just before the village of Neochori, from where the way to the ancient site is well signed.

Special Features

Oiniadai, an important Akarnanian city, is a drive of c.18 km. from the main Antirrion road. We include it mainly because the site offers an unusual chance to view (from a distance) substantial ancient shipsheds.

History

Oiniadai owed its importance to its natural setting, much altered since ancient times. Now *c.*7 km. inland, the ancient city was a port on the mouth of the Corinthian Gulf, with open sea reached from the Acheloos delta, which 'surrounded it with water' (Thucydides 2.102.2), almost like an island. It enters history *c.*454 BC, when an Athenian expedition under Perikles failed to capture the already fortified city. From 424 an ally of ATHENS, it served in 394 as a station for Athenian triremes patrolling the gulf. The Aitolians captured it *c.*330 and exiled its citizens. Regaining independence, the city became an important member of the Akarnanian league, its citizens holding top federal posts in the C3 BC. The city reverted to Aitolian control *c.*260 BC, then was captured by Philip V of Macedon in 219. Appreciating Oiniadai's strategic potential, the king strengthened its fortifications with building stone floated down the Acheloos. Although of no importance under Roman rule, a settlement survived at Oiniadai into the C3 AD.

Description

Crossing the marshy alluvial plain created by the Acheloos since Classical times, you reach the site on a low hill to your left, marked by a fine stretch of the city-wall. The circuit totalled over 5 km., consisting of a curtain in polygonal style, perhaps as old as the C5 BC, with eleven towers of trapezoidal masonry which may be later. The harbour-fortifications, entered by an arched **gate** [1] and overlooked by an imposing corner tower, were built by Philip V, as were the towers of the akropolis.

An asphalt road (becoming a dirt track for the last 100 m. or so) climbs past the guard's hut in the direction of the small **theatre** [2], which is fenced and possibly not accessible. Excavations uncovered traces of 27 rows of seats, along with the kerb of the orchestra and remains of a colonnaded stage-building (proskenion), with sockets in the intercolumniations for the attachment of painted scenery panels. The theatre goes back to the C4 BC, although the stone proskenion and sill of the orchestra were part of a later rebuilding (C3 BC). There are traces of scrappy further alterations, perhaps for a simple Roman stage-building (C1 BC).

A group of inscriptions (C3–C2 BC) on the first three rows of seats in the west part of the auditorium records the freeing of slaves belonging to citizens of Oiniadai. Presumably these manumissions took place in the theatre before a citizen-audience. The most prominent text (first row,

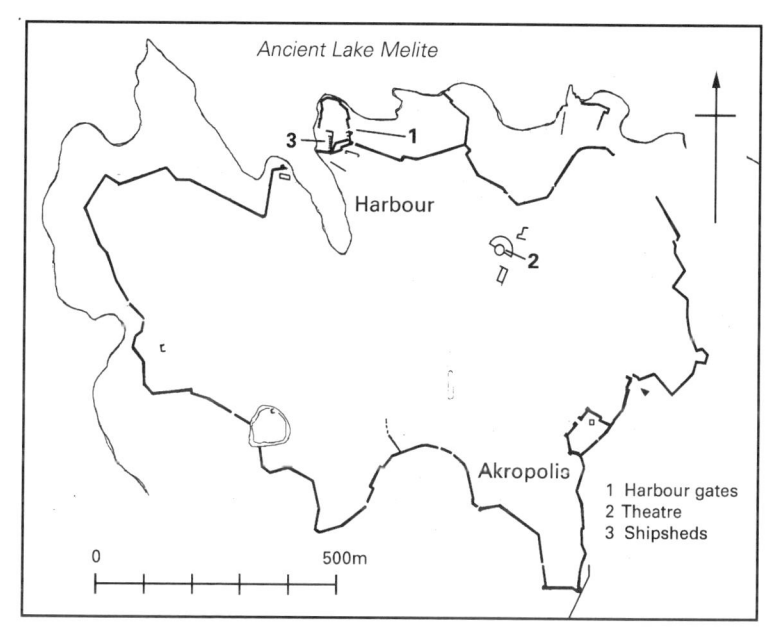

▲ Fig. 143. Plan of Oiniadai

extending over four seats) records the freeing of two couples belonging to the same master: 'Andronikos set free Onasimos, Phyllo, Onasikles and Philista'.

The **shipsheds** [3] are in the ancient harbour on the north side of Oiniadai. To visit them (fenced), return to the guard's hut, turning left onto the old road, which takes you up to the gated entrance. Should this be locked, you can still see the sheds from a distance by walking on around the fence. The main features are six rock-cut ramps for sliding ships in and out of the water, and the colonnades between the sheds, supporting the tiled roof. The complex was fortified by Philip V, who 'surrounded the harbour and shipsheds with a wall' (Polybius 4.65.11). By the C1 AD the area was being used for burials.

Pleuron (Figs. 144–145) ★

Because of the traffic on the main road, the site is best approached from the east, that is from the direction of Andirrio. Approximately 2 km. after the junction signed Αστακός, there is a sharp left turn and you should take the narrow and rather concealed road which branches off to the right, opposite a roadside shrine, before a second sharp left turn. As yet there is no sign. An asphalt road climbs up to the site which is just over 1 km. from the main road.

Special Features

The site has superb fortifications, an extraordinary cistern, and a fine view.

History

Pleuron is one of the Aitolian cities listed by Homer (*Iliad* 2.638) but originally occupied a different site. The inhabitants opted for a more secure location on Mt Arakynthos after their city had been attacked by Demetrios II of Macedon *c.*230 BC. Traces of Old Pleuron have been identified on Gyphtokastro and Petrovouni, the two hills approximately 1.5 km. south-east. There was further disruption when Augustus founded NIKOPOLIS in about 30 BC. Strabo (10.2.3) comments that: 'the cities of the Aitolians are KALYDON and Pleuron, which are now reduced, though in early times they were an ornament to Greece'.

Description

The site is quite accessible but does require some agility in places. Once you have negotiated the main gate, turn left and follow the path which leads to the **theatre**. This is tiny and could only have accommodated a few hundred spectators, which suggests that the permanent population of Pleuron did not match the size of the site. The auditorium is an exact semi-circle, whereas in most Greek theatres it exceeds 180°. The fortification wall must have formed the skene and the actors presumably made their entrances and exits through the door in the tower. The stone sill in front of the wall supported a columned stage-building (proskenion), so there will not have been much room in the orchestra for productions which required choruses.

From the theatre there is an excellent view of the **fortifications** which must have been built soon after the city was founded in the late C3 BC. Cognoscenti will recognize that the masonry style is pseudo-isodomic trapezoidal. The akropolis was included in the circuit and separately fortified, so that it could be used as a last line of defence, if the lower city were captured. None of the 36 towers is particularly massive, possibly because it was felt that siege engines would not be a threat on such an inaccessible site. Stone staircases ensured that the defenders could easily reach the battlements. There were seven gates protected by towers.

The **cistern** can be reached by a path which starts above the auditorium of the theatre. Pleuron is built on limestone which is permeable and so the water supply must have been a problem. Nevertheless the sheer size of this cistern seems quite extraordinary—it must have had a capacity of approximately 2500 cubic metres or 55,000 gallons. The interior is divided into compartments by ashlar walls, presumably so

Akarnania and Aitolia 349

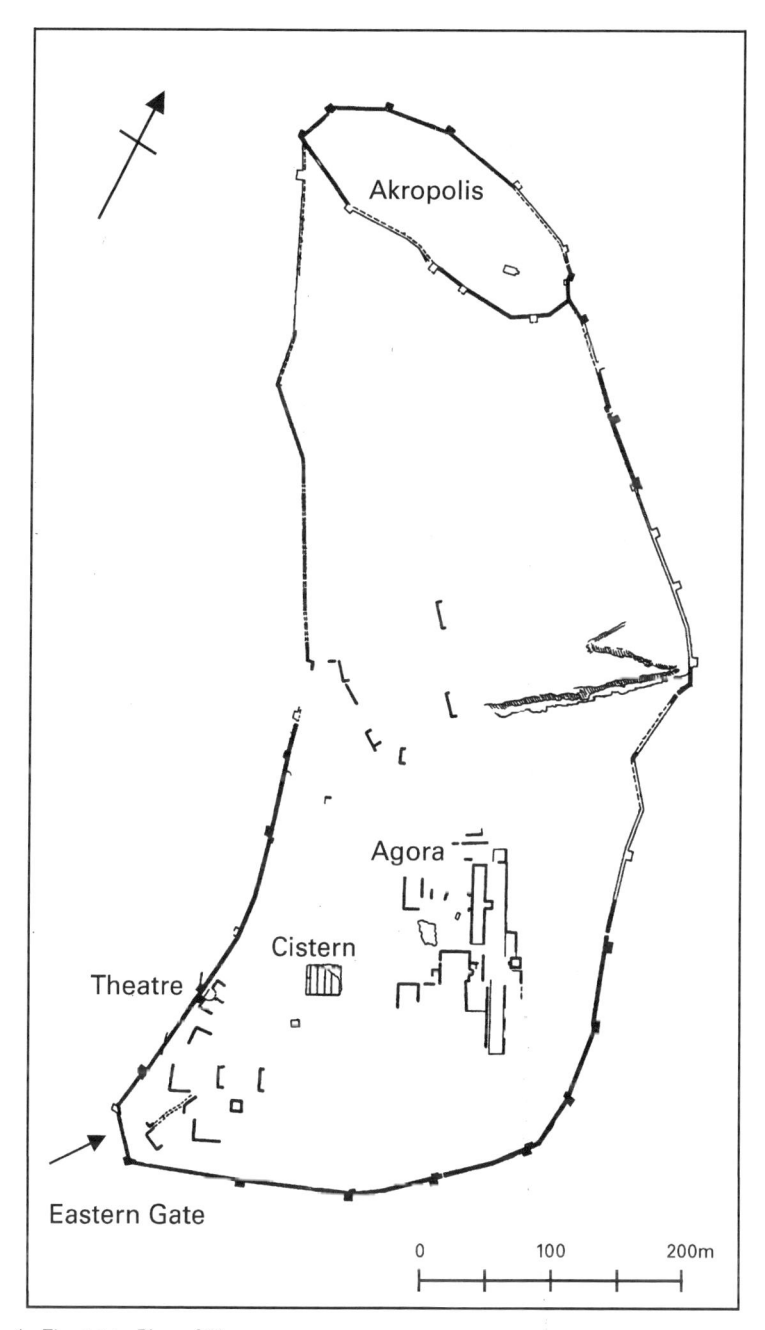

▲ Fig. 144. Plan of Pleuron

▲ Fig. 145. Cistern at Pleuron

that it could be roofed. The triangular apertures in the partition walls would have kept the water at a uniform level. The cistern was positioned so that rainwater could easily be channelled down the slope.

Beyond the cistern is the **agora**. A stoa closes off the eastern side of the square. The stone for this and the other civic facilities may have been quarried from the cistern. Just east of the stoa there is a terrace 145 m. in length, perhaps the xystos of a gymnasium.

The steep climb up to the **akropolis** is only for the inordinately enthusiastic. A ruined church occupies the site of a temple, almost certainly of Athena. In the *Thebaid* (2.727–31) by Statius, Tydeus promises the goddess:

If I return to warlike Pleuron, I will raise to thee upon the heights in the midst of the city a temple rich with the sheen of gold. Thence will you look with delight upon the storms of the Ionian main and the place where the turbid Acheloos, bursting through the barrier Echinades, lashes the deep with his tawny billows.

(translation by W.J. Woodhouse)

The best-preserved stretch of the fortifications is east of the agora and provides a convenient route back to the entrance of the site.

Kalydon (Figs. 146–147)

The site, signed Αρχαια Καλυδονα, is 7 km. east of Mesolongi on the road between Agrinion and Andirrio.

Special Features

Kalydon, conveniently situated beside the main road, is the site of the sanctuary of Artemis Laphria, whose cult involved particularly macabre sacrifices, and of an impressive heroon.

History

The city of Kalydon is best known as the scene of the mythical boar hunt. Oineus, king of Kalydon, had failed to sacrifice to Artemis and so she sent a huge boar which rampaged around the countryside. The bravest hunters were summoned and those who answered the call included Kastor and Polydeukes, Theseus, Meleager, and the virgin huntress Atalanta. The boar was eventually slain, although not before the heroes had suffered a number of mostly self-inflicted casualties. Homer lists 'lovely Kalydon' as one of the five cities in Aitolia (*Iliad* 2.640) but it is seldom mentioned by Greek historians. Augustus moved most of the inhabitants to NIKOPOLIS in about 30 BC and Kalydon never recovered.

Description

The track which runs from the entrance first passes rows of stone benches set at right angles. This was evidently the **council-house** (bouleuterion) of the Kalydonians. Further on there is a sign for the **heroon** [1] which was built for Leon, an eminent citizen of Kalydon c.100 BC. Rooms open off three sides of the peristyle court in the centre of the heroon, an arrangement which is reminiscent of grand Hellenistic houses. It seems likely that the stone benches in the north-west room were couches on which privileged participants in the cult reclined as they feasted. The centre room was apparently the main focus of cult-activity and had busts of deities—Zeus, Herakles, Eros, and Aphrodite—set in medallions around the walls. Under the exedra at the back of this room, but entered by the flight of steps on the north side of the heroon, there is a barrel-vaulted chamber tomb with ornate stone couches. Presumably Leon, who is commemorated in an inscription as the new Herakles, was buried here.

Beyond the heroon there is a ruined church built on the foundations of a **temple**, possibly of Dionysos [2]. This lay just south of one of the **city gates** [3]. The circuit-wall, which dates from the early C3 BC, is not particularly well preserved.

A **sacred way** [4] led from the gate to the **Sanctuary of Artemis Laphria**, past a **stoa** [5] which was built in the Hellenistic period. There were two temples in the sanctuary, of **Artemis** [6] and **Apollo** [7]. Both were certainly in existence by the C7 and must have been redecorated in the C6 BC. The brightly painted terracotta revetments—on display in the National Archaeological Museum in ATHENS—include metopes,

352 Akarnania and Aitolia

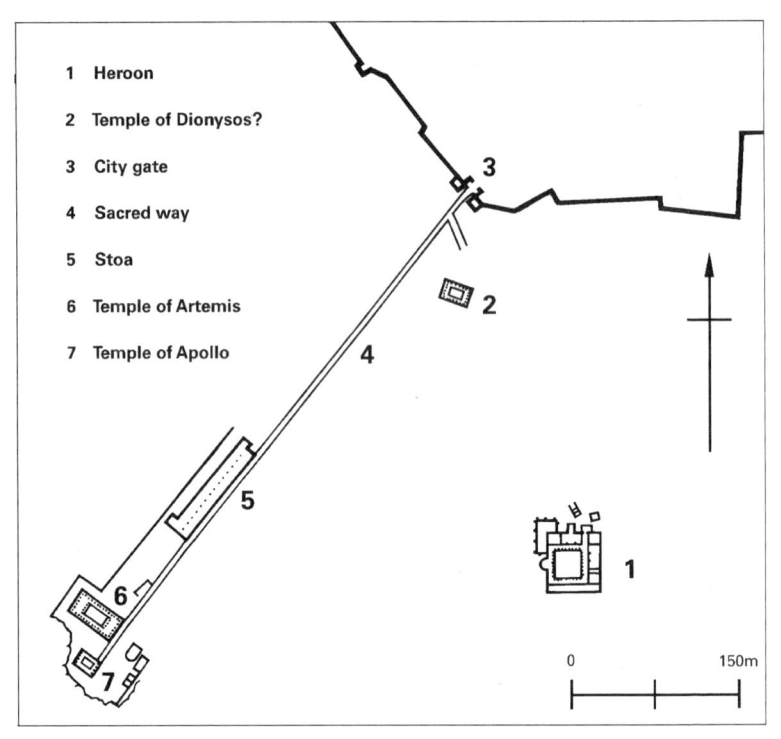

1 Heroon
2 Temple of Dionysos?
3 City gate
4 Sacred way
5 Stoa
6 Temple of Artemis
7 Temple of Apollo

▲ Fig. 146. Plan of Kalydon

akroteria, and antefixes. Like the revetments from THERMON, their style is Corinthian and it seems that they were in fact made in CORINTH. Letters had been incised on some of the metopes, presumably so that the builders could put them in the right order.

Early in the C4 BC the **Temple of Artemis** was rebuilt, a development which may have been prompted by the creation of the Aitolian Confederacy after 370 BC. A massive platform was constructed for the temple which had a peristyle of six by thirteen Doric columns. In the cella Ionic columns framed the gold and ivory cult-statue of Artemis by Menaichmos and Soidas which depicted the goddess as an Amazonian huntress. Later the cult was transferred to the Roman colony at PATRAS and the statue moved to the sanctuary of Artemis there. Pausanias (7.18) provides a graphic account of the bizarre sacrifice which he witnessed at Patrai:

They stand green logs, each thirty feet long, in a circle round the altar, and the driest logs are piled on to the altar inside the circle. When the time of the festival comes they make the approach to the altar smoother by laying down earth on the altar steps. Then first of all they walk in a procession of the greatest grandeur

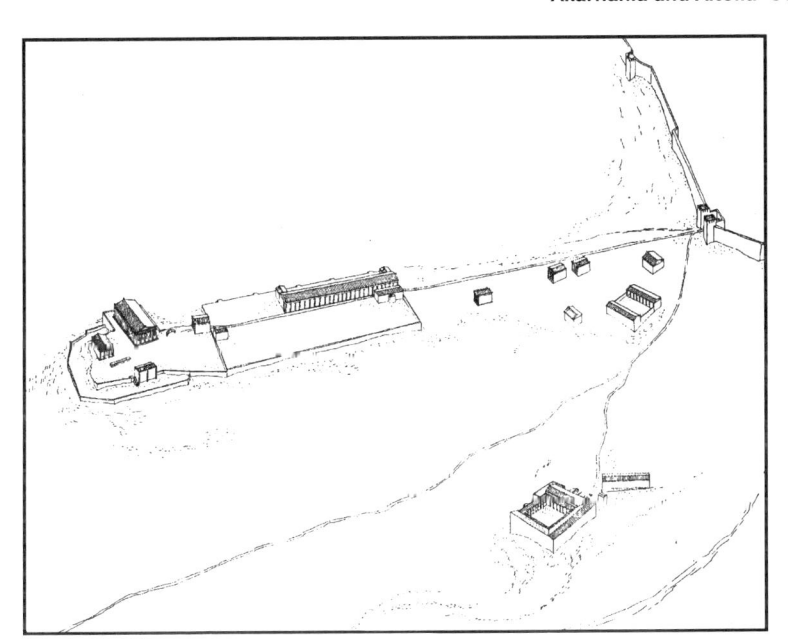

▲ Fig. 147. Reconstruction of the Sanctuary of Artemis at Kalydon (after E. Dyggve *et al.*, *Das Laphrion, der Tempelbezirk von Kalydon* (Copenhagen 1948) pl. 35).

to Artemis, and the virgin priestess rides last in the procession in a chariot drawn by yoked deer. The ritual law is to perform the sacrifice the next day. The whole city as a body prides itself over this festival, and so do the individuals just as much. They throw gamebirds alive onto the altar and all the other victims in the same way, even wild boars and deer and gazelles, and some of them throw on wolf-cubs and bear-cubs and other fully grown beasts, and they heap the altar with fruit from orchard trees. After this they set fire to the logs. At this point I saw a bear and other beasts forced out by the first leap of the flames or escaping at full strength but those who threw them in bring them back again to the funeral fire. They have no record of anyone being injured by the animals.

Thermon (Fig. 148)

The turn for Thermon, signed Panaitolio/Thermo, is just south of Agrinion on the Andirrio–Artu road. In the village square there is a sign for the Μουσείο *and then another at the left fork to the site.*

Special Features

The site is of great interest historically, as the principal centre of the Aitolians, and archaeologically, for the early development of the Greek temple. Because excavations are in progress, some of the most important features have been covered over or can only be viewed from a distance.

History

There was a settlement at Thermon in the Mycenaean period. Evidence of cult-activity in the Early Iron Age comes from Megaron B which was succeeded by the C7 BC temple of Apollo Thermios, one of the earliest Doric temples in Greece. There were also temples of Apollo Lyseios and Artemis at Thermon which was evidently one of the principal Aitolian religious centres in the Archaic period.

The Aitolian Confederacy, founded soon after 370 BC, met in the sanctuary each year for a festival and fair at which the magistrates of the federation were elected. When the Aitolians became a major political power in the C3, Thermon benefited. The stoas which were built in the Hellenistic period underline the prestige of the sanctuary at this time, when it was evidently the focus of a considerable settlement. In 218 BC Philip V of Macedon invaded Aitolia. Polybius (5.8–9) gives us a detailed description of his attack on Thermon:

He reached Thermon late in the evening, and encamping there, sent out his men to sack the surrounding villages and at the same time to loot the houses in Thermon itself, which were not only full of corn and other provisions, but more richly furnished than any in Aitolia. For as it is here that they hold every year a splendid fair and festival, as well as the election of their magistrates, they kept the most precious of their possessions stored up in this place to be used for the proper reception of their guests and for the various needs of the festive season. They also thought that it was the safest place in which to store them, as no enemy had ever dared to invade this district, and it was indeed the natural citadel of all Aitolia. Consequently, as it had enjoyed peace from time immemorial, the houses in the vicinity of the temple and around about were full of valuables. That night the army bivouacked on the spot laden with booty of every description, and next day they selected the richest and most portable portion of the household goods, made a heap of the rest in front of their tents and set fire to it. Similarly as regards the suits of armour dedicated in the porticoes they took down and carried off the most precious, exchanged some for their own, then collected the rest and made a bonfire of them. These were more than fifteen thousand in number. Up to this point all that had been done was right and fair in accordance with the rules of war, but what shall I say of that which followed? For mindful of what the Aitolians had done at DION and DODONA they burnt the stoas and destroyed the rest of the rich and artistic votive offerings, some of which were most elaborate and expensive works. And not only did they damage the roofs of these buildings by the fire, but razed them to the ground. They also threw down the statues numbering not less than two thousand and destroyed many of them, sparing however, such as represented gods or bore inscribed dedications to gods.

Philip returned in 206 BC and then in 189 BC the Romans made the Aitolians their subject allies. The confederacy never recovered and inevitably this had serious repercussions for Thermon which declined in importance.

Description

Finds from the site in the **museum** include an impressive selection of Mycenaean pottery which indicates that Thermon was certainly not isolated at this time but had a network of trade contacts. Most of the terracotta revetments come from the temple of Apollo which was built *c.*630 BC and then refurbished in the C6. The revetments protected the timber which was used extensively in these early temples. The painted metopes—the finest can be seen in the National Archaeological Museum in ATHENS—depict a number of different legends and anticipate architectural sculpture. They were locally made but may have been inspired by the decoration on Corinthian temples. Also on display in the museum are bronzes, terracotta votives, and pottery from the sanctuary. The statue base in the form of a pile of shields is particularly important, since it is likely to commemorate the Aitolian victory over the Gauls in 279 BC.

Thermon is one of the few fortified sanctuaries in Greece. The Aitolians were evidently and, as it transpired, quite justifiably concerned that their assets might be seized. The **fortifications** were built on three sides of the sanctuary. The main gate was in the south-west corner and there was a second gate on the north side of the temenos.

Because of the excavations, the northern end of the site is inaccessible at present but can be viewed from the path. The rectangular structure by the gate has tentatively been identified as a **Temple of Artemis**. The Mycenaean houses, although built of stone, have curved walls which recollect mudbrick architecture. **Megaron A** has a deep porch, a main room, and a small room at the back. It may have still been visible when **Megaron B** was constructed, possibly in the C10, since this is on the same alignment and also has three rooms. The theory that Megaron B had wooden columns and was the first peristyle temple has been refuted by the recent excavations. It may not even have been a conventional temple, although there is evidence of cult activity in the form of sacrificial deposits.

Megaron B was destroyed some time before the **Temple of Apollo** was built *c.*630 BC. Nevertheless it can be no coincidence that this has more or less the same alignment, especially as the temple also faces south rather than east. The temple had a peristyle of five by fifteen wooden columns and there was also a row of columns in the cella and the opisthodomos. The terracotta revetments confirm that this was one of the first Doric temples. It was rebuilt in the C3, possibly after Philip had

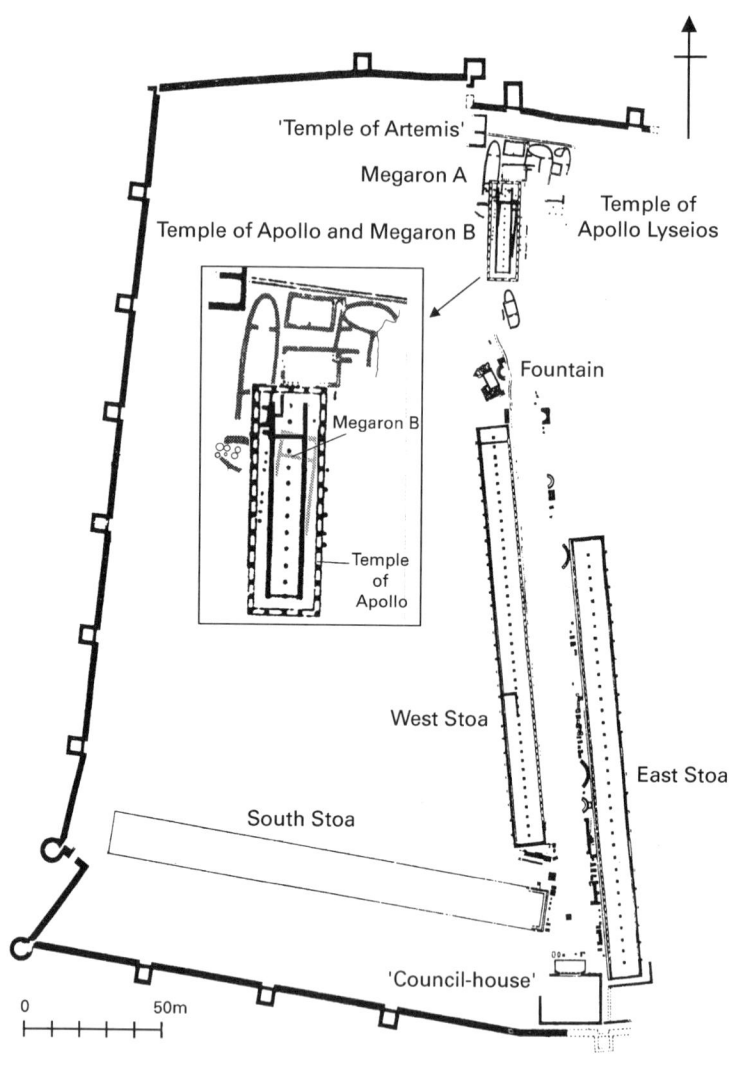

▲ Fig. 148. Plan of Thermon

sacked Thermon. A late C7 date has been proposed for the less well-preserved **Temple of Apollo Lyseios** which also had terracotta revetments.

South of the museum there is a **fountain** which still functions. You then pass a number of semi-circular statue bases, which were presumably plundered by Philip. In the Hellenistic period two enormous **stoas** were built at the southern end of the sanctuary, the west 165 m. in length and the east 173 m. The east stoa was destroyed, no doubt in

218 BC, and then rebuilt. It has stone benches and may have been used for public assemblies. The monuments set up in front of the stoa included the trophy which commemorated the victory over the Gauls. The structure south of the stoas, and inaccessible at present, could be the council-house in which the delegates of the confederacy met. West of this there is another stoa which has only been partially excavated.

Thessaly and Environs

In his account of the Persian invasion of Greece, Herodotus (7.129) observes:

It is said that in the remote past Thessaly was a lake—a not unreasonable supposition, as the whole country is enclosed by lofty hills. To the east is the great barrier of Pelion and Ossa, two mountains whose bases form a continuous chain. Then there is the range of Olympos on the north, Pindos on the west, and Othrys on the south. In the centre of this ring of mountains lies the low plain of Thessaly. A number of rivers pour their waters into it, the best known being the Peneios, Apidanos, Onochonos, Enipeos, and Pamisos. All these flow down from the mountains, unite into a single stream, and find their way to the sea through one narrow gorge. The story is that ages ago, before the gorge existed and while there was as yet no outlet for the water, these rivers made Thessaly an inland sea. The natives of Thessaly have a tradition that the gorge which forms the outlet for the water was created by Poseidon, and the story is a reasonable one, if one believes that it is Poseidon who shakes the earth and that chasms caused by earthquake are attributable to him. It certainly appeared to me that the cleft in the mountains had been caused by an earthquake.

(after De Selincourt)

Herodotus is not renowned as a geologist but his analysis of the sequence of events is essentially correct, except that the Vale of Tempe, the gorge through which the Peneios reaches the sea, was formed by erosion rather than an earthquake. In antiquity there were still two lakes in the plain and the Peneios frequently overflowed until dykes were built. The Thessalians then had a copious supply of water which they could use for irrigation. The rich alluvial soil was excellent for cereals and the rivers and lakes provided pasture for cattle and horses.

There is evidence of human activity in Thessaly 300,000–400,000 years ago. Gravel beds exposed by the Peneios have produced stone tools apparently of Lower Palaeolithic date. In the Middle Palaeolithic period, around 50,000 BC, Neanderthals hunted along the river but except for the Theopetra Cave, which is just south of Kalambaka, Upper Palaeolithic sites have proved more elusive. It is therefore likely that the first Neolithic farmers arrived and settled in Thessaly, even if we cannot be sure where they came from. On some sites there is an Aceramic Neolithic phase when pottery was not yet in use. This is soon succeeded by the Early Neolithic period (6500–5800 BC) which sees an increase in the number of settlements. Conditions in Thessaly must have been perfect for the type of agriculture which these communities had introduced because almost 300 Neolithic sites have been identified. Middle

Neolithic (5800–5300 BC) settlements can be quite extensive and at a site such as SESKLO this has implications for their social structure. By the Late Neolithic period (5300–4500 BC) these divisions in society may have become fixed, if DIMINI is typical. Possibly there was some pressure on resources at this time, since there were certainly more sites. The Final Neolithic period (4500–3200 BC) is a transitional phase in that copper is used occasionally but most implements were still made of stone. In the Bronze Age (3200–1000 BC) Thessaly appears rather isolated. Only sites on the coast, such as Pefkakia (see DEMETRIAS), benefited from the development of maritime trade. The main Mycenaean settlements were also in eastern Thessaly, particularly Dimini and VOLOS which have both been identified as the site of Iolkos.

The inhabitants of historic Thessaly constituted a distinct Greek 'people' (*ethnos*) speaking their own dialect of Aiolic Greek. They were relative newcomers with warrior-traditions, who by Classical times had reduced the previous inhabitants of the two plains, known as *penestai*, to servitude, and dominated the peoples of the surrounding mountains. By 600 BC they had won control of the Amphictyony, the inter-state organization controlling DELPHI, and they retained their preponderance of Amphictyonic votes into Roman times. In the C5 BC three rival cities, Larisa, Pherai, and Pharsalos, ruled by aristocratic houses like the Daochos family (see Delphi museum), came to dominate the region. By *c.*350 Philip II of Macedon achieved control of Thessaly, retained by his successors until 196 BC, and cemented by the foundation of Demetrias. Thessaly under Roman rule was a prosperous but provincial backwater with a reputation for witches. By the C4 AD Thessaly was a separate province, its capital Larisa. Prosperity in early Christian times is on show at PHTHIOTIC THEBES. The region's wealth was its land. The Thessalians were famous horse breeders, and their cavalry was second to none in Greece. They were also exporters of grain, as shown by an inscription from Larisa recording a huge shipment (430,000 'baskets') of wheat to Rome (*c.*135–131 BC).

Volos (Fig. 149)

History

Excavations in the older part of Volos, known as Palaia, at the western end of the town, have revealed traces of a substantial prehistoric settlement. There is a Mycenaean cist grave cemetery in the suburb of Nea Ionia and a tholos tomb was discovered at Kapakli, north-west of Palaia, after the owner of the land had been visited by the Virgin Mary in a dream—she told him that there was a church under his house. Quite understandably it has been assumed that Volos was the principal Mycenaean site in eastern Thessaly and therefore the location of Iolkos, from which Jason and the Argonauts set sail for Colchis. However, we now know that there was also an extensive Mycenaean settlement at DIMINI and some believe that this must have been the site of Iolkos. Volos (ancient Pagasai?) was not a particularly important Classical city and in 293 BC Demetrios moved the inhabitants to DEMETRIAS.

Description

There is not much of ancient Volos preserved but the **Archaeological Museum** should certainly be visited. This is on Odos Athanasaki, just beyond the hospital, at the eastern end of the city.

The displays in the Entrance Hall (**room 1**) focus on recent excavations in Thessaly. In the centre of the room there is a Classical stone sarcophagus from VELESTINO and in the cases around the walls, finds from the Neolithic site at Petromagoula Volos, grave offerings from Velestino, Almyros, and Nea Ionia, and votives from the sanctuaries at Prodromos, Kedros, and Kallithea.

Room 2 contains Mycenaean, Protogeometric, and Geometric pottery from Volos and other Thessalian sites but more particularly some of the painted grave stelai from Demetrias (see **box**).

In **room 3A** there is a display of Palaeolithic finds which come from Pleistocene deposits exposed by the Peneios; also stone and bone tools of

▼ Fig. 149. Plan of Volos Museum

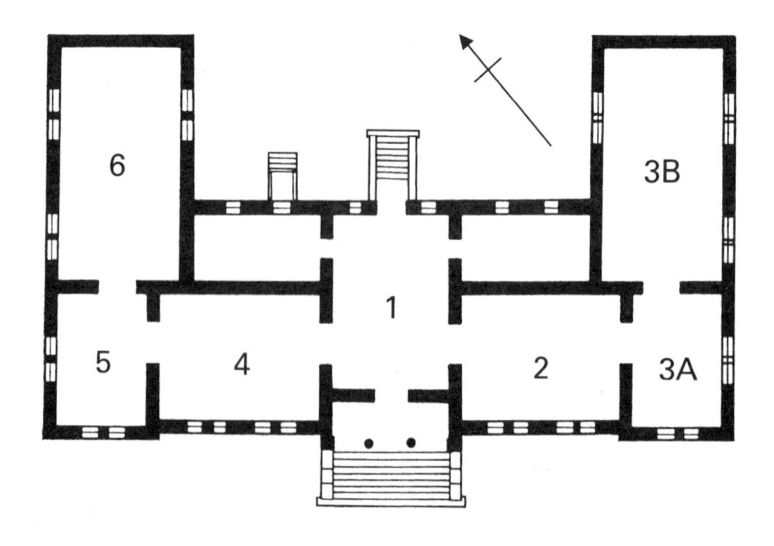

The grave stelai from Demetrias

These marble gravestones, most of which date from the C3 BC, were preserved because they had been used to build the fortifications of Demetrias. Although they were damaged in the process, their painted decoration is still quite fresh. Had they been left in situ, the colours would certainly have faded. The inscriptions record the names of the deceased and it is remarkable that quite a number were foreigners. We find men and women from Epeiros, from the northern Aegean (THESSALONIKI and AMPHIPOLIS), from Crete, and even from Askalon in the Near East. Like so many harbour towns in this period, Demetrias was evidently a cosmopolitan community. In some cases the inscriptions also tell us how the person concerned had died. One of the most poignant of these epitaphs is on the stele of Hediste:

A painful thread for Hediste did the Fates weave from their spindles when, as a young wife, she came to the throes of childbirth. Ah wretched one! For it was not fated that she should cradle the infant in her arms, nor moisten the lips of her new-born child at her breast. One light looks upon both and Fortune has brought both to a single tomb, making no distinction when she came upon them.

(after Pollitt)

Hediste lies on the bed in which she has just died. Her husband sits at the foot of the bed and stares at her, his expression a mixture of grief and incomprehension. The nurse in the next room holds the dead infant. A girl peers through the door behind. Although the painter is not particularly accomplished, the depth of the composition draws us in, so that we also experience the sense of loss.

On some of the stelai we see the dead person accompanied by a servant or child. This is a familiar scene on Classical grave stelai and also the relatives who pay their last respects. Nevertheless, even if the iconography is not especially innovative, the stelai do offer us an opportunity to study the techniques used by painters in a period when the art of illusion was still being mastered.

the Aceramic Neolithic period from various sites in Thessaly, Classical grave stelai, votive reliefs, and bronzes.

The archaeology of Neolithic Thessaly is explained in **room 3B**. On the wall by the entrance there is a reconstruction of a section through one of the sites. Excellent displays cover the architecture, agriculture, production of stone and bone tools, textiles, pottery, and figurines. The Middle Neolithic pottery is particularly impressive. The vivid designs in red and white may have been inspired by textiles. It seems that some types of pottery were made specifically for exchange, presumably by specialists. Because they might tell us about Neolithic religious beliefs, the figurines have provoked much speculation. The assumption that they represent deities and were worshipped is now thought less likely, since broken figurines were thrown away. Nevertheless, from the contexts in which they have been found, it would appear that the figurines were regarded as talismans which protected domestic activities such as cooking and weaving. They may also have been used in initiation ceremonies.

Room 4, left of the Entrance Hall, contains more of the painted stelai from Demetrias and a model of the site; also Classical, Hellenistic, and Roman glass, pottery, figurines, and fine gold jewellery. There is more gold jewellery in **room 5** and other grave offerings. **Room 6** has reconstructions of Middle Helladic, Mycenaean, Geometric, Classical, and Hellenistic graves. We see how the dead were buried and the way in which the grave offerings stress particular aspects of their personality. Social distinctions may also be expressed through the offerings or architectural refinements. As societies change so does the treatment of the dead, yet some elements of the ritual remain constant. Note that perfumed oil is included amongst the offerings in most of these graves.

Dimini (Figs. 150–151)

Take the road from Volos to Larisa. On the outskirts of Volos there is a turn on the left for Dimini. In the village follow the road signed Archaeological Site of Dimini.

Special Features

Dimini is an attractive site and well known as an important Late Neolithic settlement. Recent excavations have revealed that there was also an extensive Mycenaean town and it has been argued that this was the site of Iolkos.

History

Although Dimini is now some distance from the sea, when the site was first occupied in the Late Neolithic period (4800–4500 BC), the coastline was much closer. It is thought that the clearance of woodland on the slopes around the plain caused soil erosion and consequently a major phase of alluvial deposition in the fourth millennium. The Greek archaeologist Tsountas excavated Dimini in 1903 and discovered the Late Neolithic settlement. This had apparently been protected by a complex system of stone walls. There was a large megaron on the summit of the mound and traces of other structures lower down. Further excavations between 1974–6 raised doubts about the assumption that the site was fortified. The enclosure walls would not have deterred a determined attacker and it seems more likely that they were designed to divide the settlement into separate sectors. As the same range of facilities can be identified in each of these sectors, in particular storerooms and kitchens, it is believed that they were occupied by separate households. We do not see this emphasis on privacy in Middle Neolithic settlements, such as SESKLO, and the implication is that social divisions had become more pronounced. This would explain why the megaron was built in such a prominent position. Nevertheless, it is clear that these households would have been dependent on one another, so we should not interpret their separation as evidence of hostility.

There is an impressive Mycenaean tholos tomb on the north side of the site. Dimini must have been an important centre at this time but VOLOS is usually identified as Iolkos, home of Jason and his wife, Medea. However, recent excavations at Dimini have revealed an extensive Mycenaean settlement on the south-eastern side of the mound and it has been claimed that this was Iolkos. It seems unlikely that the question will be resolved until more of Mycenaean Volos has been excavated. The discovery of Linear B tablets would provide the level of proof which we need, since they have only been found in Mycenaean palaces.

Description

There is a plan of the site and information about the recent excavations on the display boards by the entrance. The path which leads to the summit of the mound passes through a narrow corridor and then two of the **enclosure walls**. It is clear that access could be carefully controlled. Across the **central court** is a spacious **megaron**, almost certainly of Late Neolithic date, although it may have been extended in the Early Helladic period. This has an open porch and two interior rooms. Stone was used for the lower courses of the walls and provided a base for the mudbrick superstructure. We assume that the megaron had a pitched roof of thatch or clay which would have kept the rain off the walls. Those who lived in the other sectors of the site did not have as much space for their activities but enjoyed the same degree of privacy. Rooms where food was stored and prepared can be seen just behind the megaron.

A number of Middle Helladic slab-lined **cist graves** can be seen and also traces of a **Mycenaean structure**, which may have been a megaron, at the southern end of the court. It is assumed that the mound was the focal point of the Mycenaean settlement and so it is significant that one of the **tholos tombs** should have been built in such a central location. The tomb can be reached by the path which runs around the western side of the site. Most of the contents were removed before the tomb was excavated, possibly when the vault collapsed. The date of construction is therefore uncertain but the C14 or C13 BC seems likely. A low wall closes off the end of the stone-lined dromos which was filled in after each funeral. The entrance of the tomb had also been blocked. Presumably it was thought that these measures would keep the dead in their place and

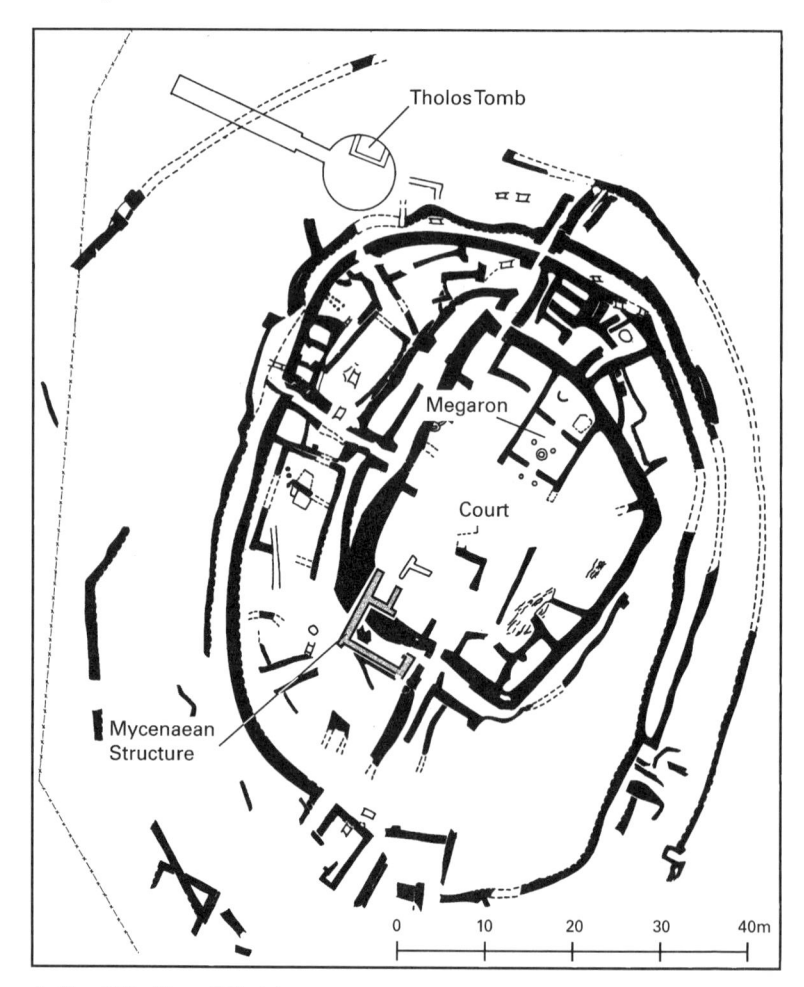

▲ Fig. 150. Plan of Dimini

deter thieves. In the chamber there is a curious stone structure which may have been used as an ossuary. The Mycenaeans usually cut pits in the floor of the tomb for this purpose but possibly the bedrock was rather hard. The tholos must have been built for the rulers of Dimini who evidently felt that their authority would be enhanced if they were buried in the settlement. Excavations on the eastern side of the site have revealed just how extensive this is. Most Mycenaean settlements seem rather disorganized but here we see wide streets and orderly rows of houses. The site was finally abandoned early in the C12, another victim of those troubled times.

▲ Fig. 151. Neolithic megaron at Dimini

Sesklo (Figs. 152–153)

Continue along the road from Volos to Larisa and take the left turn for Sesklo. There are signs for the Archaeological Site of Sesklo in the village. Note that the site may be closed on Mondays.

Special Features

Sesklo is one of the most important Neolithic sites in Greece and is attractively situated in open countryside at the western end of the Volos plain.

History

The site was excavated by Tsountas early this century and then more recently by Theocharis who demonstrated that Sesklo was first occupied at the start of the Neolithic period, around the middle of the seventh millennium. The settlers were farmers who will have been attracted by the rich agricultural land on the hills around the site. The earliest levels have not been extensively explored but it would seem that the settlement expanded in the Early Neolithic period (6500–5800 BC). Middle Neolithic (5800–5300 BC) houses have been excavated quite a distance west of the mound and it is reckoned that the site covered 20–25 acres at this time. The population must therefore have numbered several hundred, which may not be impressive by our standards but does have implications for the way in which community affairs were organized. While there need not have been a ruler, some form of central authority must have existed, if only so that disputes could be resolved by arbitration. This marks quite an advance in terms of social complexity. At the end of the Middle Neolithic period Sesklo was destroyed by fire. Since the site then lay deserted for several centuries, this destruction may not have been an accident, although the assumption that invaders were responsible is now considered less likely. In the Late Neolithic period (4800–4500 BC) the site was reoccupied but on a much reduced scale. A large megaron was built on the summit of the mound and the fact that this is separated from the rest of the settlement by stone walls presumably indicates a different and more authoritarian style of leadership. We know less about the later history of the site because these levels have been eroded but settlement evidently continued until the second millennium BC.

Description

The stone bench on top of the mound provides a convenient vantage point from which the attractions of this location for Neolithic settlers can be readily appreciated. The land around the site is not particularly flat but this would have kept the soil well drained, an advantage for farmers whose tools were made of stone and bone. The seasonal streams which run off the hills ensured that there was water. Unfortunately one of these streams has also eroded much of the eastern side of the site.

Beside the stone bench is the **Late Neolithic megaron**. This consists of an open porch and two interior rooms. At the back there is a storeroom. Stone was used for the lower courses of the walls and mudbrick for the superstructure. The roof was presumably pitched and may have been of thatch or clay. In the same central location but at a lower level there is a **Middle Neolithic megaron**. Although not as large as its successor, this also has a porch and two interior rooms. A number of other Middle Neolithic structures have been excavated, in particular the '**pottery workshop**' which is protected by a plastic roof. This has a different plan and it is thought that the buttresses in the inner room supported an upper floor which would have been reached by a ladder. In the Middle and Late Neolithic period **walls** were built around the summit of the mound and sections of these can be seen on the eastern and southern sides of the site. At first it was assumed that they were defensive, although this interpretation of their purpose has recently been questioned. They may simply have reinforced the sides of this artificial tell which would otherwise have collapsed. Nevertheless they do act as barriers which control access and this was clearly an important consideration for the Neolithic settlers who differentiated between public and private space.

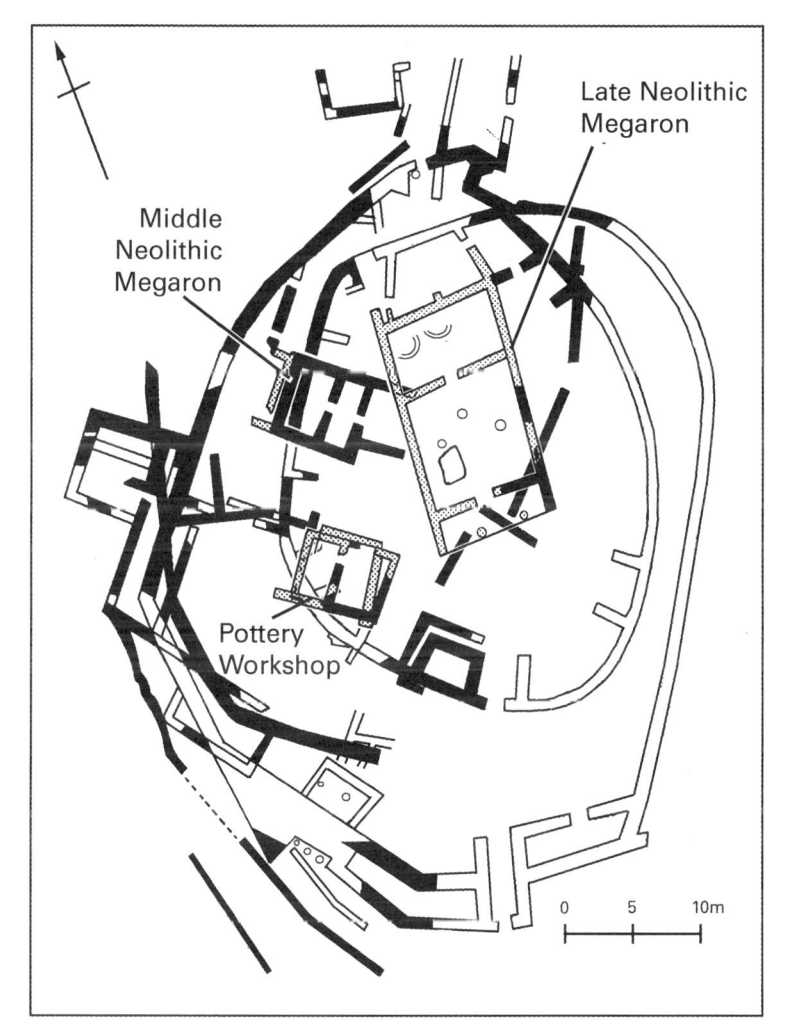

▲ Fig. 152. Plan of Sesklo

On the slope west of the site, just south of the road, excavation of the Middle Neolithic '**town**' is still in progress.

Velestino (ancient Pherai)

Special Features

Pherai is included because this was once the most important centre of Classical Thessaly. The modern town of Velestino has plans to make the traces of the ancient city more accessible in the future.

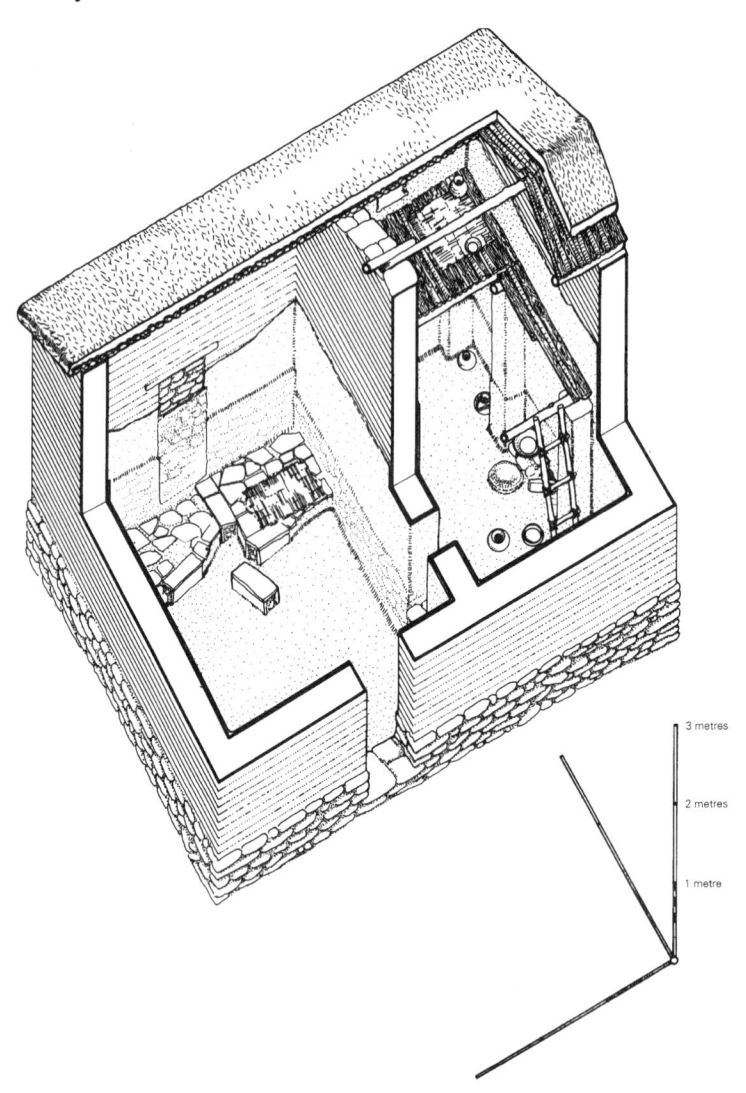

▲ Fig. 153. Reconstruction of the pottery workshop at Sesklo (after D. Theocharis, *Neolithic Greece* (Athens 1973) fig. 184)

History

Pherai owed its ancient importance to its fertile territory, its commanding position near the main north–south land route through Thessaly, and control of Pagasai, the chief Thessalian port. The city's heyday fell under its tyrants Lykophron (c.406–390 BC) and his probable son Jason, who aimed at domination of all Thessaly before his assassination in 358

BC. The Macedonian kings were the chief cause of Pherai's political decline. Philip II took control of Pagasai and its revenues in 353 BC and imposed a Macedonian garrison on Pherai (344 BC). Then came the foundation of DEMETRIAS, eclipsing Pherai as south-east Thessaly's chief centre. Pherai remained a prosperous minor city in Hellenistic and Roman imperial times.

Description

Once in Velestino, turn right on the gently climbing main street at the sign marked Chloi. At the T-junction turn right, and then fork left by the tree-lined reservoir. After a few hundred metres you will see on your left the site of a **temple** in a fenced area surrounded by pine trees and signed ΕΡΕΙΠΙΑ ΝΑΟΥ ΘΑΥΛΙΟΥ ΔΙΟΣ (Ruins of the Temple of Zeus Thaulios). Excavated in the 1920s, the remains consist of foundations and fragments of the marble platform for a colonnaded Doric temple, replacing a C6 BC predecessor on the same site. Identification of the deity as Zeus Thaulios is uncertain.

As you return towards Velestino, you can see clearly on the hill to your left (the ancient akropolis) traces of the **city-wall**, perhaps built under Jason. Before you pass the wall, a track down to your left leads to a field where the remains of a Hellenistic **stoa** (now roofed) have been uncovered. It perhaps formed part of the agora. In the town excavations have been carried out at a number of sites, which there are plans to link in due course by means of a paved pedestrian path.

Demetrias (Fig. 154)

The site sits astride the main road into Volos from the south, just outside the modern town.

Special Features

Ancient Demetrias was one of the 'fetters' which secured Macedonian domination of Hellenistic Greece. The remains, although modest, offer glimpses of the ancient city's importance.

History

Demetrias was laid out as a planned Greek city *c.*290 BC by Demetrios I, the Macedonian king, as a means of dominating Thessaly. He populated it by the enforced union of seven or so local communities, and was buried there. The heavy fortifications, the two harbours, and the royal palace suggest the city's strategic and political importance for the Macedonian kings. It was said of Philip V that 'the Thessalians and Magnesians could never enjoy liberty while he held Demetrias' (Polybius

18.11.5–6). As well as a vital naval base for the Macedonian war-fleet, it was also a commercial entrepôt, succeeding Pagasai as one of the two principal ports of Thessaly, with a cosmopolitan population to match (see VOLOS museum). Macedonian control finally ended in 167 BC with the Roman defeat of the last Antigonid, king Perseus, when the walls were slighted. Demetrias now declined in standing and population, but remained the regional centre of southern Thessaly, and was important enough to be given an aqueduct, its most notable Roman monument. By AD 431 it was the seat of a bishopric. Of the two known basilicas, the larger [**9**] was begun *c.*400 and partly funded by a woman of senatorial rank, Damokratia. It made heavy use of earlier stonework, including two massive bases for equestrian statues, probably of Antigonid kings. Justinian refortified the city, which survived into medieval times.

Description

The poorly preserved **theatre** [**1**] is visible on the north side of the main road, at the foot of a spur of the akropolis. There were alterations in the Roman period, and it is thought to have remained in use until the C4 AD. On top of the ridge above the theatre are scanty remains tentatively identified as the monumental tomb and cult precinct, or **heroon** [**2**], of Demetrios, the city's founder.

Just east of the theatre the main road passes between two of the 76 surviving piers of an **aqueduct** [**3**] of mortared rubble, the date uncertain, but hardly before the C2 AD. The source was probably a spring near modern Makrinitsa in Pelion.

Several hundred metres further west, the main road breaches the early Hellenistic **city-wall** [**4**] (signed). What you see is the stone socle for a superstructure of unbaked mudbrick, preserved in places for up to 3.5 m. The total circuit, one of the largest in Greece, measured 7.8 km., and enclosed *c.*262 ha. of land, of which about 60% is thought to have been built up in Hellenistic times. The walls included a fortified akropolis north-west of the theatre and an outer breastwork (*proteichisma*) with ditch. In the south-west circuit three towers, including the one (no. 61) just to the east of the main road, show signs of rushed enlargement, making use of hundreds of painted gravestones from nearby extra-mural cemeteries, now in Volos museum. These works are attributed to the Seleukid king Antiochos III, who held Demetrias in 192/1 BC during his ill-fated invasion of Greece.

Heading in the direction of Volos, shortly after the theatre take the turn on the right signed Pefkakia for the Pefkakia promontory. On the way you pass the northern **harbour** [**5**] of Demetrias, where traces of an ancient mole have been observed.

Pefkakia [**6**] was first occupied in the Final Neolithic period (4500–

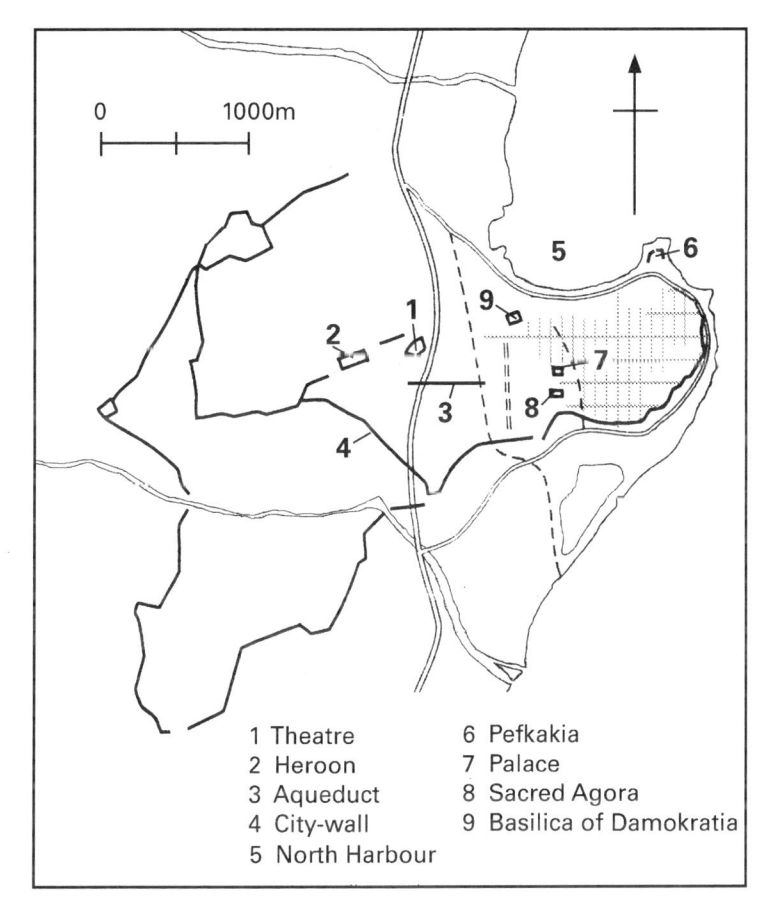

▲ Fig. 154. Plan of Demetrias

1 Theatre
2 Heroon
3 Aqueduct
4 City-wall
5 North Harbour
6 Pefkakia
7 Palace
8 Sacred Agora
9 Basilica of Damokratia

3200 BC) and the coastal location of the site was soon exploited. The imported pottery indicates a network of contacts which reached beyond Thessaly and extended even further in the Bronze Age. It was recognized that Pefkakia could provide a link between sites in northern, central, and southern Greece. The German excavators therefore concentrated on the stratigraphy of the site and cut off one end of the mound so that the sequence of levels could be studied in detail. This extraordinary trench is visible from the road and shows quite clearly how these artificial mounds grew higher as the mudbrick houses disintegrated and were rebuilt. The slab-lined Middle Helladic cist graves near the top of the section date from the time when this part of the settlement was used as a cemetery.

Above Pefkakia, on a pine-clad hill approached by a dirt track from the harbour, lie the substantial remains of a Hellenistic complex provisionally identified as a fortified royal **palace** [7] or *basileion* (in 1997 under excavation and not open to visitors). Commanding fine views, the palace dates to the reign of Philip V but overlies a predecessor. Its three colonnaded courtyards cover around 20,000 m². The best-preserved, on the east looking out to sea, features defensive corner-towers supported on massive masonry socles and rooms with off-centre doorways, probably dining rooms for royal feasts.

To its south the palace overlooked a partly excavated plaza (inaccessible) set into the city-grid, identified as the **sacred agora** [8] of inscriptions, with scant remains of a small colonnaded temple of 'Iolkan' Artemis.

Nea Anchialos (ancient Phthiotic Thebes)

The excavations are mainly contained in three large plots on the north side of the Volos road as it passes through the centre of the small town of Nea Anchialos.

Special Features

The importance of the site rests with its early Christian remains which include three major churches (C4–C6 AD) with their annexes.

History

The site of the Classical city of Phthiotic Thebes is the distinctive flat-topped hill visible, along with a stretch of the ancient circuit-wall, from the Volos road *c*.3 km. west of Nea Anchialos. Since the late C4 BC Thebes had been the chief city of Achaia Phthiotis, a Thessalian border region with its own federal identity in pre-Roman times. In 217 BC, when the city was Aitolian, Philip V of Macedon captured it and renamed it 'Philip's City' (Philippopolis), having sold the population into slavery. In Roman times the old city was gradually abandoned in favour of the more convenient location of Pyrasos, its dependent port. Nea Anchialos, occupying the ancient site, still has a small harbour, as well as a beach. Inscriptions show that the port had been renamed Thebes by the C3 AD at the latest; tombstones of men from Nikomedia (modern Iznik) and Antioch in Syria, the former a shipowner (*naukleros*), suggest its flourishing commerce in Roman times, as one of the two chief harbours of southern Thessaly. What the visitor sees today are the imposing remains of this transposed Thebes in the C4–C6 AD, when it was one of Thessaly's two main Christian centres, with a bishop attested as early as 325. As many as nine basilicas have been found so far. The city, or rather its nucleus, was enclosed by a defensive wall of rubble and limestone mortar, visible by the baptistery. There is evidence of catastrophic fire damage to the churches, linked to the incursions of Slavs, settled locally by the end of the C7 AD, after which the site seems to have been abandoned.

Description

The main area contains the lavish **basilica A** (end of C5 AD), a three-aisled church with narthex and a colonnaded forecourt flanked by towers (excavated 1924–8, one column re-erected in 1981). Notable are the finely carved capitals with lion-heads and paws gripping goats. A baptistery, its font set into the floor, occupied a room on the north side of the courtyard; in its counterpart on the south side, a storeroom, were found fragments of large jars (pithoi) stamped '(belonging to the church) of Thebes'. To the south of the basilica runs a paved street. In the south corner of the site can be seen the hypocausts of a bath-building, thought to belong to the church on analogy with early Christian Rome. At the north-east corner of the church are more storerooms with large jars (pithoi) set into the floor. A building on site (inaccessible) houses finds.

South of the main area, walking away from Volos on the main road, is **basilica G** (C6 AD), also called after bishop Peter, the otherwise unknown donor of building works named in an inscription set into the fine mosaic floor (motifs of animals and flora). Its vast size, careful construction, and lavish decoration make this one of the more important early Christian churches in Greece. The lifting of the mosaic floor uncovered traces of the terracotta paving of a predecessor (C5 AD) and, below that, of the mosaic floor and colonnaded nave of a still-earlier basilica (c. AD 300–350), in turn resting on Roman imperial remains. The portico flanking the south side of the main church has been re-erected.

Just to the south of this area, and thought to be contemporary with the first version of basilica G, is a **baptistery**, its earliest phase dated c. AD 350. Inside the square building a circular colonnade enclosed an octagonal font. There was a fine floor of coloured marbles. To the south a furnace room was added, to heat the baptismal water. In a third phase, improvements to the drainage were part-funded by a local couple, as shown by an inscription, 'Aristion and Rufina (gave this) for the church', found on the marble cover of a sump.

Returning north along the road in the Volos direction and passing the basilica A site you come to a further fenced area. At the far end, visible from the main road, is **basilica B** (C5–C6 AD), inferior in the quality of construction and decoration to its neighbours. An inscribed plaque from the site is dated to 'the term of the most holy bishop Elpidius', probably the Theban bishop of this name who championed the disputed election of the archbishop of Larisa in 538.

Lamia

History

Ancient Lamia was the Malian capital but we do not hear much about the city until 323 BC when it was besieged by the Greek forces which had marched against the Macedonian viceroy Antipater after the death of Alexander. This conflict, known as the Lamian War, ended disastrously for the Greek coalition which was defeated at the battle of Krannon in 322 BC.

Description

The recently opened **Archaeological Museum** is signed from the centre of the town. It occupies C19 barracks on the kastro, which has a superb view of the Spercheios valley. The kastro has been fortified since at least the C5 BC and stretches of the Classical fortifications can still be seen, although most of the masonry is clearly much later.

In the entrance hall of the museum there are grave stelai and inscriptions. Upstairs the room on the left has a series of thematic displays, based on finds from sites in Phthiotis, which covers the Neolithic, Early Bronze Age, Middle Bronze Age, Mycenaean, and Geometric periods (it should be noted that the information on the display boards is only in Greek). There are also dedications from local sanctuaries, in particular the sanctuary of Artemis and Apollo at Kalapodi, in the territory of ancient Hyampolis in Phokis. Architectural elements from Kalapodi include a limestone votive bench on which a tiny bronze kouros and other offerings were found in situ.

There is a display of sculpture on the landing and in the second room Classical, Hellenistic, and Roman pottery, terracotta figurines, lamps, jewellery, and glass. Also a mosaic of the Three Graces and reconstructions of different grave types. Inscriptions around the outside of the museum include a Roman boundary settlement in Latin, on which a number of familiar toponyms, such as 'Spercheius' and 'Pelion', can be read.

Epeiros

Epeiros, literally the mainland, extended from what is now southern Albania down to the Ambrakian Gulf. It had the best pasture and consequently the finest cattle in Greece. There was so much pasture and also timber because Epeiros is wetter than the rest of Greece and summer storms reduce the risk of drought. The storms do cause erosion but one effect of this is that sediment has blocked the swallow holes, or *katabothroi*, in the limestone bedrock and so lakes have formed which supply water for agriculture. However, the Epeirotes could not make the most of these resources. The harbours on the west coast were inaccessible and the Pindos range cut off Thessaly. Journeys across Epeiros were not much easier and this increased the sense of isolation.

For southern Greeks Epeiros before the C4 BC was a backwoods area, notable chiefly for its remote oracles at DODONA and the NEKYOMANTEION. Its tribally organized population, which spoke a west Greek dialect, came relatively late to city life, as at KASSOPE, founded in the C4. A group of tribes in the Dodona area, the Molossians, emerged as a powerful state in the earlier C4 BC, its army led by hereditary kings claiming descent from Achilles. One of them, Alexander I (342–330/29 BC), maternal uncle of his greater namesake, created a unified Epeirote alliance, paving the way for the spectacular if evanescent career of the most famous of Molossian kings, Pyrrhos (319–272 BC), who twice defeated Roman armies in Italy (280 and 279). Ancient Ambrakia, where he established his capital, is buried beneath modern Arta, and his impact on the region's archaeology is better appreciated at Dodona. After the fall of the monarchy (c.232 BC), the Epeirote alliance was transformed into a league with a federal citizenship, its religious showcase at Dodona. The Molossians sided with Perseus of Macedon against Rome, with devastating consequences, including mass enslavement of 150,000 Epeirotes. Parts of Epeiros never recovered. In the C1 BC the region's resources attracted Roman businessmen. According to Strabo (late C1 BC), 'desolation prevails in most parts, while the parts that are inhabited survive only in villages and ruins' (7.7.9). Against this picture of rural decline must be set the thriving Augustan foundation of NIKOPOLIS, still the regional centre in late antiquity.

Ioannina ★

History

Ioannina is not an ancient city and only became important in the C13 AD when it was fortified by the Byzantines. In 1788 Ali Pasha seized the fortress, made it his base and soon controlled most of north-western

Greece. Ali, 'the Lion of Ioannina', was a ruthless and unscrupulous but undoubtedly colourful character. When Byron visited Epeiros in 1809, the pasha showered him with 'almonds and sugared sherbet, fruit and sweetmeats, twenty times a day'. His reign of terror ended in 1822 when he was captured and executed by the Turks.

Description

There is an excellent **Archaeological Museum** on the kastro. The first room on the right contains Palaeolithic artefacts from British excavations in Epeiros (see **box**), pottery and fine bronzes from Late Bronze Age tombs, Geometric–Classical grave offerings from the cemetery at Vitsa, north of Ioannina, which include two superb bronze jugs, and finds from the NEKYOMANTEION of Ephyra. In an alcove there are votives from the sanctuary of Zeus at DODONA. Note in particular the inscribed lead oracular tablets (see p. 382) and a rare fragment of a bronze Macedonian shield. This was found in the bouleuterion at Dodona. The embossed bows, the circles and stars are typical of the type of decoration found on Macedonian shields. Punched with the inscription ΒΑ[ΣΙ]ΛΕΥΣ, 'King', it belongs to a dedication of captured arms by 'King [Pyrrhos]' following his victory over Antigonos II, the Macedonian king, in 274 BC. This type of rimless, bowl-like shield, used by the Macedonian infantry, is depicted on Alexander's coinage and elsewhere, but this is one of only two actual shields so far found. The restored door of the council-house at Dodona is also in this room.

Inscriptions from Dodona, capitals from KASSOPE, and finds from tombs at Mikalitsi, just north of Preveza, line the corridor and the next room on the right. Further down the corridor there is an informative display of grave offerings from the recently excavated cemetery at Liatovouni near Konitsa. In the room opposite are Archaic and Classical finds from the cemetery on the site of the University of Ioannina, tools and weapons from Dodona, Roman sarcophagi from the mausoleum at Ladochori on the coast south of Igoumenitsa, and a helmet of Phrygian or Thracian type from Vitsa.

Dodona (Figs. 155–156) ★

Take the Ioannina–Arta road and turn right after 7 km. The site is a further 15 km. from the turn.

Special Features

The remains of ancient Greece's oldest oracle include an impressive theatre, and occupy a setting of great natural beauty in a scenic mountain valley.

Palaeolithic Epeiros

The earliest settlers in Greece experienced climatic conditions quite unlike the present. The onset of the last glacial cycle, approximately 130,000 years ago, had a number of effects. Temperatures were of course much lower, particularly at the glacial maximum when ice sheets covered the Pindos mountains. Because so much moisture was trapped in the ice, there was increased aridity, although the rate of evaporation decreased and consequently the water level in lakes was higher, by 6 m. in the case of Lake Ioannina. However, the sea-level dropped by as much as 100 m. and this created land bridges, for instance between Epeiros and the Ionian Islands, and exposed broad coastal plains around the continental margins. These will have attracted the settlers who moved south when the ice sheets advanced. Unfortunately the subsequent rise in the sea-level has drowned the plains and whatever evidence of their activities the settlers may have left behind. This may be one of the reasons why the archaeological record for the Palaeolithic period in Greece is incomplete.

It is only recently that interest in the Greek Palaeolithic has intensified and Epeiros is the region which led this development. Between 1962 and 1967 Higgs directed a series of surveys and excavations, in particular at the sites of Kokkinopilos, Asprochaliko, and Kastritsa. The recent British excavations at Klithi have continued this tradition, if not the austerity for which the earlier projects became notorious.

The earliest evidence which we have for the presence of humans in Greece is the skull of an archaic form of *Homo sapiens* from the Petralona Cave in Macedonia. The skull cannot be dated precisely but it may be 350,000 years old. Lower Palaeolithic stone tools from Epeiros include an Acheulean handaxe which was found at the site of Kokkinopilos. The geological context suggests a date around 200,000 BP (the term BP = before present rather than BC is used for these early dates). It is thought that the settlers had base camps on the coastal plains, which have since been submerged, but came inland in the spring or summer when the snow melted and formed lakes. The water attracted animals which they hunted, although scavenged might be a more accurate description of the way in which they procured most of their food.

The Middle Palaeolithic period (100,000–35,000 BP) is characterized by flake stone tools, scrapers, and points, of Mousterian type. It is likely that these tools were made by Neanderthals, *Homo sapiens neanderthalensis*, although there is now evidence that anatomically modern humans, *Homo sapiens sapiens*, were already in the Near East by 100,000 BP. The Neanderthals have been caricatured as primitive creatures but they were remarkably successful. Most of their sites in Greece were beside rivers or lakes. The rock shelter at Asprochaliko was chosen because deer and ibex followed the River Louros when they migrated between their summer and winter pastures. The herds would have been especially vulnerable as they passed through the narrow Louros Gorge.

The Ioannina–Arta road also takes this route and the scenery in the gorge is spectacular.

The fate of the Neanderthals is still unclear but the most likely explanation is that they became extinct and were replaced by anatomically modern humans. Most Upper Palaeolithic sites date from the period after 25,000 BP. The stone-tool industry is known as the Gravettian and typically consists of small blades which were mounted on wooden, bone, or antler shafts and used as spears or arrows. Some of the sites in Epeiros were at high altitudes and can only have been occupied in the summer months once the snow had melted. Klithi, a rock shelter on the Voidomatis north of Ioannina, has extremely rich Upper Palaeolithic deposits—approximately 160,000 specimens of flint and bone per cubic metre. Yet it is thought that the group which hunted ibex from the rock shelter numbered only 5–10. The territory over which this group ranged each year must have been enormous because the cold climate limited the size of the herds. Epeiros was certainly not overcrowded at this time but the situation changed when the ice sheets finally retreated and the climate became warmer and wetter.

History

Ancient Dodona lay on the north-west margins of the Greek world in the part of Epeiros later occupied by the tribes of the Molossians. The surrounding area, known as Hellopia, was productive 'of much cornland and of good meadows, rich in flocks and shambling cattle' (Hesiod fragment 134), and unusually well-watered, which may account for the local epithet of Zeus, 'Naios', probably with the sense of 'flowing'. The local community of Dodonians were organized into a 'city' by the C4 BC. According to Herodotus (mid-C5 BC) Zeus's sanctuary here, shared with a consort, the otherwise little-known Dione, was the oldest Greek oracle. The original focus of the cult was a talking oak, known to Homer, who mentions priestly interpreters called Selloi, who 'sleep on the ground with unwashed feet'—probably observing ritual taboos. When Herodotus visited, the interpreters were no longer men but a trio of local priestesses. Other forms of divination, some of them perhaps complementary, now appear. Oracular 'doves' (possibly wood-pigeons) are mentioned by Sophocles, and inspired frenzy on the Delphian model by Plato (C4 BC). Herodotus implies divination by casting lots, and the same method is attested in about 371 BC. Finally later tradition (C1 AD on), rightly or not, claimed the use in prophecy of the echoing bronze tripod-cauldrons for which Dodona was famous. On the archaeological side, remarkable evidence comes from lead tablets (some 150) scratched with questions for the oracle (in IOANNINA museum—see **box**). They show that the clientele came mainly from central and northern Greece, although colonial south Italy and Sicily are also represented, and that consultation was

> ### Oracular tablets from Dodona
>
> Some of the Dodona lead tablets (C6–C3 BC) are on display (with English translations) in the Ioannina museum. The few that follow exemplify their chiefly personal character:
>
> > 'Timodamos asks Zeus whether he should engage in trade by land and sea with money from his silver mine. The answer is positive: he should stay in the city and engage in trade there.'
> > 'Am I her children's father?'
> > 'Eurydamos asks about the drinking cup.'
> > 'Ias Pistos stolen the wool from the mattress?'

more on private concerns—travel, family, possessions, and livelihood—than (as at DELPHI) state or panhellenic affairs.

The site's history as a sanctuary can be traced archaeologically to the C8 BC, when finds include parts of iron and bronze votive tripod-cauldrons. Generally the sanctuary has proved rich in metal finds, including bronze statuettes (see National Archaeological Museum in ATHENS), but not in stone sculpture. This is partly because Dodona remained unimpressive architecturally, indeed without a temple, until the emergence of an increasingly powerful Molossian state during the C4 BC, when the akropolis and sanctuary were fortified and the first shrines built. Dodona's heyday fell under the Molossian king Pyrrhos (319–272 BC), leader of a powerful Epeirote alliance, who transformed the sanctuary into the allied religious and political centre. He used it to display spoils from his military victories (see Ioannina museum), and endowed it with a festival, the Naia, featuring chariot races, athletic and dramatic contests, erecting monumental buildings to match, notably the huge theatre. Around 232 BC the monarchy was overthrown, and the Molossians joined a new league of Epeirote tribes, for which Dodona also served as a federal centre and showplace. The place was partly restored, with a new stone stadium, after a sack by the Aitolians (219 BC), but laid waste again by the Romans (167 BC), and never recovered its former importance. The latest-known consultation of the oracle falls in the early C1 BC, although the place carried on under Roman rule as a festival-centre, with the Naia still being celebrated as a local event as late as AD 241/2, when the president of the games was a worthy from NIKOPOLIS. The arrival of Christian worship is attested by a basilican church (C5 AD), rebuilt in the C6.

Description

Although Homer calls Dodona 'wintry', its woodland setting on the

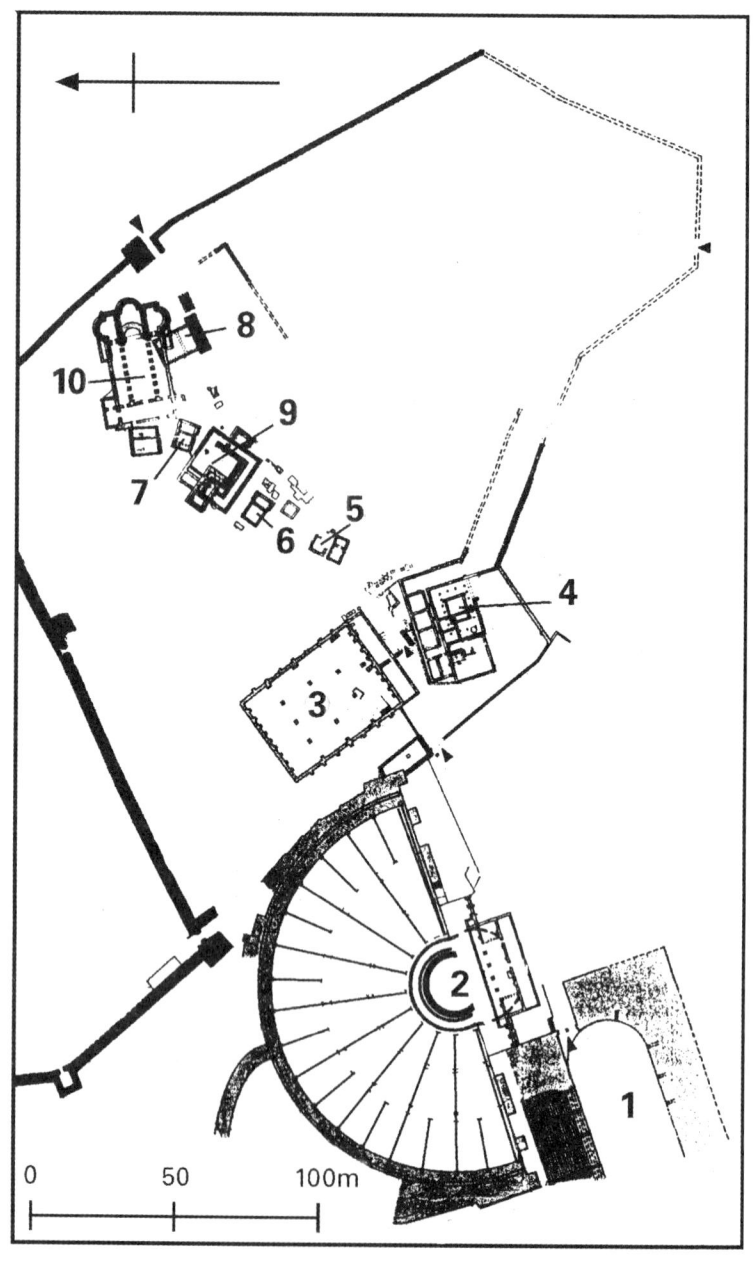

▲ Fig. 155. Plan of Dodona. Key: 1 Stadium 2 Theatre 3 Council-house 4 Prytaneion 5 Temple of Aphrodite 6 Temple of Themis 7 Temple of Dione 8 Temple of Herakles 9 Sacred House 10 Church

▲ Fig. 156. The theatre at Dodona

floor of a mountain valley will strike most modern visitors as delightful, especially in spring when wild flowers abound.

Beneath the west retaining wall of the theatre you pass the 22–23 surviving rows of the stone seating of the **stadium** [1], at the end with the turning post, resting on artificial banks. Dating to the late C3 BC, it served the athletic contests at the Naia.

The scale of the hoped-for turn-out at the Naia is suggested by the **theatre** [2], attributed to Pyrrhos and one of Greece's largest, with a seating capacity of 17,000. The retaining walls, strengthened (unusually) by towers, are particularly fine. The dramatic contests of the Naia took place here. A raised stone stage-building (proskenion) replaced a wooden predecessor in the rebuilding following the Aitolian sack of 219 BC. Apparently under Augustus, the stage-buildings were swept away, along with the first two rows of seats, in favour of a circular walled arena for Roman-style wild-beast shows. If the date is right, this change happened much earlier here than in theatres elsewhere in Greece, and may reflect the Romanizing influence of Nikopolis to the south.

Next to the theatre is a rare example in Greece of a relatively well-preserved **council-house** [3] or *bouleuterion*, identified by the large stone altar inside, dedicated (?215–210 BC) to 'Zeus who counsels (*bouleus*)' by Charops son of Machatas, leader of the pro-Roman party in Epeiros. The building is a large rectangular hall on sloping ground, fronted by a Doric colonnade, the roof supported by tall Ionic columns. The construction is fairly simple, with upper walls of baked mudbrick;

the seats on the sloping ground were presumably wooden. Fittings included the elegant cast-bronze door furniture now displayed in Ioannina museum. The building dates from the time of Pyrrhos and must originally have served the council (otherwise unattested) of the Epeirote alliance. After *c*.232 BC it was used by the council of the Epeirote League, which set up the row of six statue bases found in 1965 just outside and still in place. Three of them honoured Epeirote commanders of around 230 BC. Fragments of fine bronze statues of armoured males, one equestrian, were found nearby (now in Ioannina museum) and suggest the former attractiveness of this part of the sanctuary.

Hellenistic Dodona's overtly political role did not end here. The jumbled ruins south of the council-house (in 1997 still being excavated) have been identified as a **prytaneion** [**4**] or building for official entertainment. They are dated late C4 BC – early C3 BC, and take the form of a colonnaded courtyard, on the north side of which a suite of three nine-couch dining rooms was added *c*.200 BC, along with an Ionic portico to the east. The building was patched up after 167 BC and remained in some kind of use as late as the C4 AD.

Further on, five **temples** occupy a levelled terrace. All are small, with no continuous colonnade, just a porch. The first two after the council-house are dated to the reign of Pyrrhos and their deities tentatively identified as respectively **Aphrodite** [**5**] and **Themis** [**6**], both known from inscriptions to have had cults here. On the east side of the sanctuary of Zeus is the temple identified as that of **Dione** ([**7**]—mid-C4 BC), rebuilt after the Aitolian raid on an adjacent site in the Ionic order. Remains claimed as a shrine of **Herakles** [**8**], dated to the time of Pyrrhos, project to the south beneath the basilican **church** [**10**] (C5–C6 AD).

By far the most interesting structure on the terrace is the shrine of Zeus, or, as Polybius (mid-C2 BC) called it, the **Sacred House** (*hiera oikia*—**9**]). As at OLYMPIA, Zeus for a long time had done perfectly well without a built shrine. Instead, the ritual focus was the sacred oak. In the earlier C4 BC a small shrine with a porch was built here, with a rectangular enclosure wall added some decades later. Under Pyrrhos a more monumental effect was achieved by enclosing the temple with Ionic colonnades. After the Aitolian sack the damaged shrine and colonnades were rebuilt on a larger scale, their odd relationship probably reflecting the need to leave space for the sacred oak in the east side of the court, where a huge hole was excavated at the end of antiquity, taken to mark the site (and the end) of the oak.

Nekyomanteion of Ephyra (Fig. 157) ★

The site is just off the Igoumenitsa–Preveza road and is clearly signed.

Special Features

The Nekyomanteion, a sanctuary of Hades and Persephone, the god and goddess of the underworld, was renowned as an oracle of the dead (*necromanteion*) and offers us a glimpse of the arcane rituals prescribed for those who wished to solicit advice from beyond the grave.

History

Herodotus (5.92) mentions the Nekyomanteion in an anecdote about Periander, who was tyrant of CORINTH *c.*627–587 BC:

> Once, on a single day, he stripped every single woman in the town naked, on account of his wife Melissa—but let me explain: Periander had mislaid something which a friend had left in his charge, so he sent to the oracle of the dead, amongst the Thesproti on the River Acheron, to ask where he had put it. The ghost of Melissa appeared and said that she would not tell, either by word or sign, for she was cold and naked, the clothes which had been buried with her having been no use at all, since they had not been burnt. Then, as evidence for her husband that she spoke the truth, she added that Periander had put his loaves into a cold oven. The messengers reported what they had seen and heard, and Periander, convinced by the token of the cold oven and the loaves (because he had slept with her after she was dead), immediately issued a proclamation to the effect that every woman in Corinth should come to the temple of Hera. The women obeyed, crowding to the temple in their best clothes as if they were off to a festival, and Periander, who had hidden some of his guards for the purpose, had them all stripped—every one of them, mistresses and maids alike—and their clothes collected into a pit and burnt, while he prayed to the spirit of his wife Melissa. After this he sent to the oracle again, and Melissa's ghost told him where he had put whatever it was that his friend had left with him.

To consult the ghost of Teiresias, the blind Theban prophet, Odysseus sailed across the ocean 'to a wild coast . . . where the Periphlegethon and Kokytos, which is a branch of the waters of the Styx, unite around a pinnacle of rock to pour their thundering streams into Acheron' (*Odyssey* 10.509–15). Pausanias (1.17) claims that 'Homer must have . . . taken the names of the rivers from rivers in Thesprotia' and it is quite likely that the account in the *Odyssey* (10.516–40 and 11.23–50) was either based on or inspired some of the practices at the Nekyomanteion. Circe tells Odysseus that he must:

> dig a trench about a cubit long and a cubit in breadth. Around this trench pour offerings to all the dead, first with honey mixed with milk, then with sweet wine, and lastly with water. Over all this sprinkle barley and then begin your prayers to the helpless ghosts of the dead. Promise them that once you are in Ithaka you will sacrifice in your palace a barren heifer, the best that you have, and will heap the pyre with treasures and make Teiresias a separate offering of the finest jet-black sheep to be found in your flock. When you have finished your invocations

to the glorious fellowship of the dead, sacrifice a young lamb and a black ewe, holding their heads down towards the Erebos while you turn your own aside, as though about to recross the River of Ocean. Then the souls of the dead and departed will come in their multitudes and you must bid your men make haste to flay the sheep that are lying there slaughtered by your blade, and burn them up while they pray to the gods, to mighty Hades and august Persephone. Sit still yourself meanwhile, with your drawn sword in your hand, and do not let any of the helpless ghosts come near the blood till you have had speech with Teiresias.

On the akropolis of Ephyra, which is 600 m. north of the Nekyomanteion, a Mycenaean tumulus cemetery has recently been excavated. There were also Mycenaean graves under the Nekyomanteion but few other finds which antedate the construction of the sanctuary early in the C3 BC. This was evidently one of the sites which the Romans destroyed in 167 BC and was eventually taken over by St John the Baptist whose church and monastery were built on the ruins.

Description

The complex of rooms on the west side of the sanctuary was added in the late C3 BC. We enter the sanctuary proper through the gate of the monastery and follow a **corridor** [1], flanked by three **rooms** [2–4] in which supplicants may have stayed while they prepared themselves spiritually and physically. In the next stretch of the **corridor** [5] there were pits full of ash and burnt bones, presumably the remains of animal sacrifices. The **labyrinth** [6] would have disoriented the supplicants before they reached the main cult rooms. Notice the immense walls, 3.30 m. thick, in superb polygonal masonry, a style which may have been chosen because it looked appropriately archaic.

The pithoi in the **storerooms** [7–9 and 11–13] contained wheat, barley, and broadbeans, carbonized and consequently preserved by the fire which destroyed the sanctuary. The presence of millstones and querns implies that some of this food was consumed as part of the special diet which the supplicants were given. The broadbeans, if eaten raw, would apparently have induced mild hallucinations. Under the **central room** [10] there is an eery barrel-vaulted crypt which is cut out of the rock and must have been entered through the roof. The Greeks commonly equated caves with the entrance to Hades and it may well have been here that the anxious supplicants waited at the climax of the ceremony, if this is in fact the Nekyomanteion and not a fortified Hellenistic farmhouse, as some believe.

Kassope (Figs. 158–160) ★

The site is off the Igoumenitsa–Arta road. Take the turn for Kanalaki/Paramythia and then go right up the road signed Ancient Kassopi. As this road climbs there is a spectacular view of the Ambrakian Gulf.

Epeiros 385

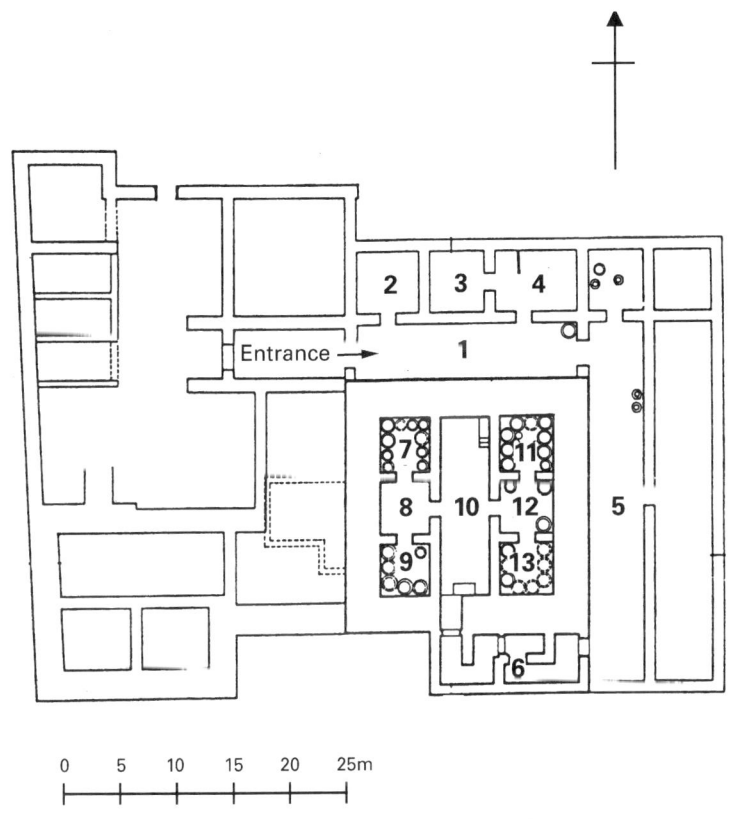

▲ Fig. 157. Plan of the Nekyomanteion of Ephyra. Key: 1 Corridor 2–4 Rooms 5 Corridor 6 Labyrinth 7–9 Storerooms 10 Central room 11–13 Storerooms

Special Features

Kassope is a particularly clear example of a systematically planned Hellenistic city. You can stroll along the streets and admire the architecture. The site is shaded by pine trees and the view is quite superb.

History

Kassope was the city of the Kassopaians who had originally lived in separate villages but must have decided that a synoikism (political union) would be advantageous. The site which they chose was easily defensible and may already have had a sanctuary of Aphrodite, their patron deity. In the middle of the C4 BC the city was laid out on a typical Hippodamian grid plan and fortified. Kassope flourished, especially in the later C3 when the civic centre was rebuilt. Soon after 200 BC the city was absorbed into the Epeirote League and presumably fought against

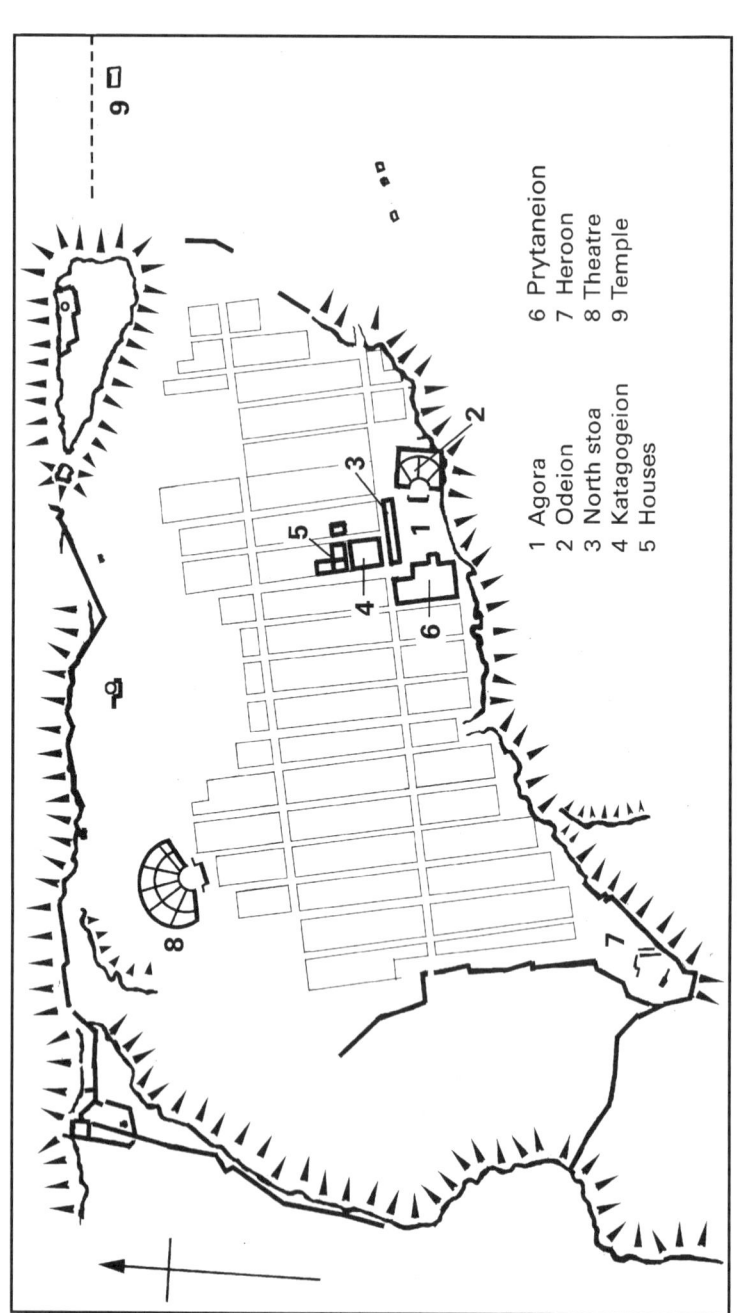

▲ Fig. 158. Plan of Kassope

1 Agora
2 Odeion
3 North stoa
4 Katagogeion
5 Houses
6 Prytaneion
7 Heroon
8 Theatre
9 Temple

the Romans at the battle of Pydna in 168 BC but was not sacked by Aemilius Paulus. The reorganization of Epeiros by the Romans in 148 BC initiated another period of prosperity which ended abruptly when NIKOPOLIS was founded in c.30 BC. The Kassopaians left their homes or at least the shells of their homes, since they took the wooden fixtures and even the roof tiles when they moved.

Description

The main street runs west from the site entrance and crosses the **agora** [**1**]. On the east side of the square there is a small theatre which was originally identified as an **odeion** [**2**] but its chief function may in fact have been political. It could seat 2000 which suggests that the Kassopaian citizen-assembly met here.

The **north stoa** [**3**] was built at the end of the C3 BC when the agora at Kassope was remodelled. The bases in front of the stoa were for honorific statues of prominent citizens dedicated ΤΟΙΣ ΘΕΟΙΣ ΚΑΙ ΤΗΙ ΠΟΛΕΙ—'to the gods and the city'.

Behind the stoa is the so-called **katagogeion** [**4**] which also dates from the last quarter of the C3 BC. Fine polygonal masonry was used for the lower courses of the walls and brick for the superstructure. The peristyle court in the centre has octagonal Doric columns. There are stone bases, possibly for tables, and brick hearths in the rooms around the court. A katagogeion is a hostelry in which guests of the city would have been accommodated but it seems likely that this was actually a covered market.

There were approximately 500 **houses** [**5**] at Kassope. A number have recently been excavated in the blocks around the katagogeion. They were constructed in the C4 BC and then modified periodically. There is usually a paved court just inside the front door. The andron, which would have been equipped with seven couches, opens off the court and also the oikos, the largest room in the house, which has a brick hearth. The rooms on the first floor were reached by a staircase from the oikos. Evidence of industrial activity has been noted in some of the houses.

On the west side of the agora there is a stone altar inscribed ΔΙΟΣ ΣΩΤΗΡΟΣ—'Zeus the Saviour'. The plastered court behind this, enclosed by a parapet, may have been used for meetings. The west stoa was added in the C2 BC and provided an impressive facade for the **prytaneion** [**6**] in which city officials conferred, ate, and entertained. One of the rooms entered from the court in the centre of the prytaneion is an andron and the sacred flame burned on the hearth in the adjacent room. Follow the main street west of the agora and you will eventually reach one of the best-preserved sections of the C4 **fortification wall**, built of polygonal masonry like so much of Kassope. On the edge of the city, in an isolated position, is a barrel-vaulted tomb. This must have been a

388 **Epeiros**

▲ Fig. 159. The agora at Kassope

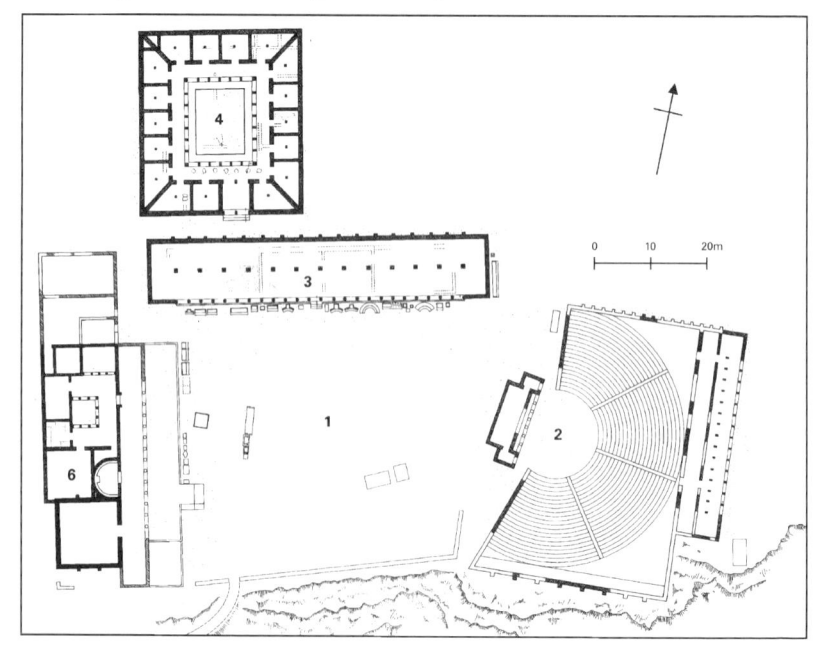

▼ Fig. 160. Plan of the agora at Kassope

heroon [**7**], possibly the tomb in which the founder of Kassope was buried. It is reckoned that the **theatre** [**8**] could hold 6000—the audience would certainly have enjoyed the view, if not the climb. As there is no trace of her sanctuary in the city, Aphrodite may have occupied the modest **temple** [**9**] 300 m. from the east gate.

When you leave the site you will be struck by the marble monument on the ridge opposite. This commemorates the Souliot women and children who threw themselves off the summit in 1803 to avoid being captured by Ali Pasha.

Nikopolis (Fig. 101)

The city sprawls over a considerable area which as yet lacks an ancient focus, since its civic centre has not been excavated. The signs for Nikopolis direct you to the museum and adjacent structures. By the entrance is a helpful site map.

Special Features

Nikopolis, a vast city conjured up from nothing by the emperor Augustus, is the best site to appreciate the Roman conqueror's transforming hand on ancient Greece's landscape. The site is large and sprawling, and a fair amount of walking is needed to visit all the major ruins.

History

Nikopolis lies on the northern of two peninsulas the tips of which, like pincers, create the sea entrance to the Ambrakian Gulf with its excellent anchorages. The southern peninsula, called Actium, gave its name to the sea battle just outside the gulf in which Octavian (Augustus) defeated the fleet of Mark Antony and Cleopatra (31 BC). In a tradition going back to Alexander the Great, Octavian commemorated his achievement by founding a 'victory city' on the site of his army camp (*c*.30 BC). This was organized as a double community embracing both a Roman colony of (presumably) legionary veterans and businessmen, and a 'free' city of Greek provincials (Pliny, *Natural History* 4.5), the latter brought in from a huge surrounding area (Akarnania, Aitolia, part of Epeiros), not always willingly, since many Aitolians fled east. Artworks and whole buildings from nearby cities like KASSOPE, now degraded to villages, seem to have been appropriated as well. To endow his new city with cultural prestige, Augustus also transferred the old games for Apollo from Actium to a site just outside Nikopolis and upgraded them to a four-yearly panhellenic festival of Olympian stature. The new games were a great success, attracting contestants from all over the eastern Mediterranean until well into the C3 AD. Initial building works, for which king Herod the Great, a client of Augustus, is said to have footed most of the bill, included grandiose amenities for these games, as well as a city-wall. A maritime station with two harbours, possessor of a vast territory (estimated at *c.*4000 km.²) and, after the creation of the province of Epeirus, an important administrative centre, Nikopolis prospered, and was the chief Roman city in north-west Greece. It was visited by Hadrian (AD 128), who probably conversed there with the Stoic philosopher Epictetus, the city's most famous resident, and may have sponsored major new public works, such as the nymphaia (fountain houses). In late antiquity the city became the seat of a metropolitan bishop. Its continuing importance in this period is shown by its impressive new walls (late C5 – early C6 AD) and by its five basilican churches. The city was sacked by Vandals (474/5) and Ostrogoths (551), but, helped no doubt by its walls, survived the Slav incursions and still existed in the C9.

Description

The small **museum** [1] contains a collection (two rooms) of mainly Roman antiquities from Nikopolis and its environs. A marble head identified as Marcus Agrippa, Octavian's henchman, is notable. An Ionic capital (C2 BC) and a Corinthian capital (early Hellenistic) may have belonged to older buildings reassembled in Nikopolis.

Behind the building is a motley collection of ancient stonework. A base (Greek inscription) from the early C1 AD for a statue of Dikaia, 'the first woman after the foundation of the city to serve as priestess of the Goddess in the Kelkaion', is interesting for its references to the new city's Greek council (*boule*) and citizen assembly (*demos*) and to its chief goddess, Artemis Kelkaia, whose sanctuary (the 'Kelkaion') awaits discovery.

Nearby are the remains of a substantial three-aisled **basilica A** [1], dated *c.*525–50. Its chief feature (which may be covered over) is a group of mosaic pavements (mainly designs based on flora and fauna), rated the best of their kind in the Balkans. Two mosaic inscriptions identify the church's founder as an otherwise unknown bishop of Nikopolis called Dometios. Beyond the church are the (overgrown in 1997) remains of a large building identified as the **bishop's palace** [2].

To reach the late antique wall, the odeion, and the nymphaia (fountain houses) from the museum, walk about 100 m. down the main road (Arta direction) and at the bend to the right take the dirt track on your left. The fine stretch of **city-wall** [3] visible before you is the inner face of the west side of the Byzantine circuit. This, with a total length of about 2 km., enclosed only a small part of the Augustan city. On its north and east sides it incorporated the Augustan walls, but here as on the south, new walls were built of rubble and mortar faced with alternating courses of brick and semi-hewn stone, a style also found at THESSALONIKI. The west gate ahead is the single most interesting feature. It was flanked by two horseshoe-shaped towers, their unusually large size comparing

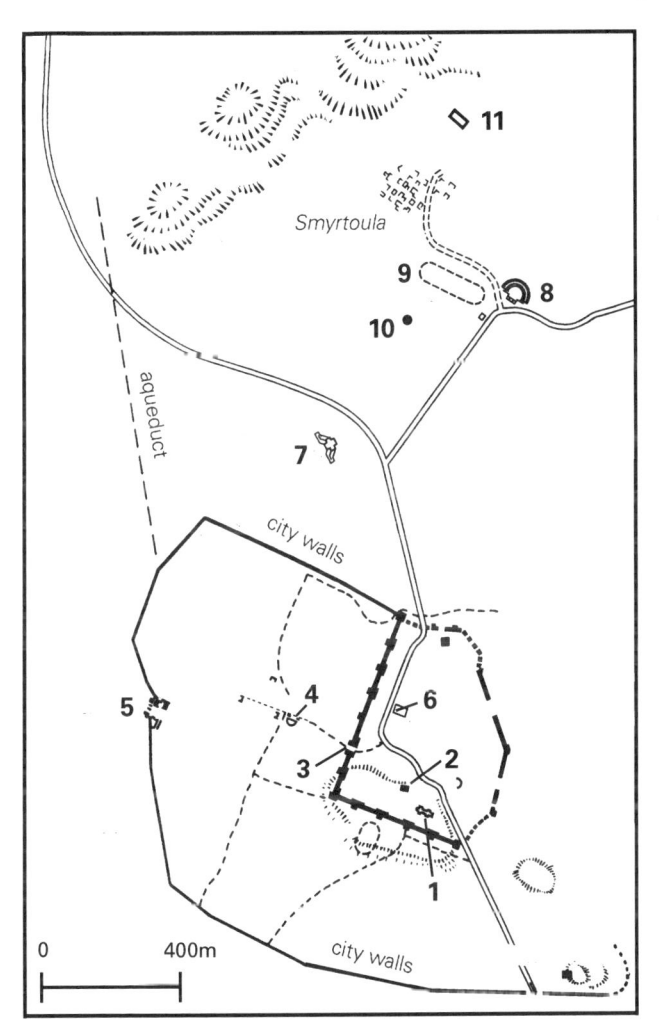

▲ Fig. 161. Plan of Nikopolis. Key. 1 Museum and basilica A 2 Palace 3 Byzantine city-wall 4 Odeion 5 Nymphaia 6 Basilica B 7 Baths 8 Theatre 9 Stadium 10 Gymnasium 11 Campsite memorial

favourably with those of Constantinople. The gateway could be closed by a boltable door and had a portcullis behind. The quality of these fortifications suggests the role of Nikopolis as a major regional centre in late antiquity.

Passing through the gate you come to (left) the impressive **odeion** ([**4**]—the main gate may be closed but the further side-gate may be open). Dated to the later C1 AD, it was rebuilt in the C2 and was once roofed.

Just beyond the odeion the track forks. Head left and then take the first right for the pair of elaborate fountain houses or **nymphaia** [5]. They were both supplied by branches of an aqueduct, some of the piers visible, bringing water from springs 70 km. to the north-east. The two fountains face each other across the street immediately inside the main west entrance to the city, and were meant to serve, and impress, visitors newly arrived along the paved road from the city's nearby port on the Ionian sea at Komaros (modern Mytika). Preserved to a height of nearly 9 m., they may originally have been higher. The build is rubble concrete faced entirely with brick, in turn originally coated with multi-coloured marble plaques. Although the dating awaits clarification, there are archaeological and historical grounds for seeing in this costly project the hand of Hadrian.

To reach the baths take the Igoumenitsa fork on the main road (heading north). On the way you pass on the right **basilica B** [6]. It may be locked but can be glimpsed from the road. Larger than basilica A, this church also occupies a more central position within the Byzantine circuit. Its architecture dates to the mid-C5 AD. An annexe room which seems to be of later date has a pavement inscription naming the room's donor as Bishop Alkison of Nikopolis, a well-known ecclesiastical figure who died in 516. The substantial but unexcavated remains of public **baths** [7] are about 100 m. along the Igoumenitsa road (on the left, fenced but visible). In planning and technique they are very like some of the buildings in Hadrian's huge villa at Tivoli in Italy and probably are also to be dated to the early C2 AD.

To reach Octavian's campsite memorial and nearby monuments, continue on the Arta road beyond the Igoumenitsa fork and shortly after take the left turn signed Monument of Augustus. The road passes between the theatre (right) and stadium (left).

This area lay to the north of the Augustan city-wall in a suburb (*proasteion*) given over to the cult and festival of Actian Apollo. According to Strabo (7.7.6) the god's 'well-equipped precinct' here was in two parts: a sacred grove with the amenities for the festival (Strabo mentions the stadium and a gymnasium), and a sacred hill (see below) overlooking the grove.

The vast and largely unexcavated **theatre** [8], built from mortared rubble faced with brick in a technique similar to that of the adjacent stadium, evidently belonged to this same programme. It is largely missing its stone seating, although the stage building (which in its present form preserves later alterations) is preserved to some height. You can still see the slots for attaching the awning at the top of the auditorium.

Just across from it, on the other side of the road to the memorial, is the **stadium** [9]. Partially cleaned in 1990 but now overgrown, its original shape is still clearly discernible. To its west are substantial remains identified as the Augustan **gymnasium** [10], which yielded two inscriptions for victorious Nikopolitan athletes.

To reach the **campsite memorial** [11] on the hill above, continue to the village of Smirtoula. Turn right (no sign in 1997) onto the side road just below the church and continue several hundred metres before turning left onto a concrete path climbing steeply to the site (in 1997 closed for restoration).

This extraordinary monument marked the site of Octavian's tent. Prominently sited on Apollo's hill overlooking the city to the south, it was inspired by the Roman tradition of rostra or speaker's platforms adorned with the prows of captured ships. Here a massive stone podium was built with a line of sockets (23 preserved from a total of about 34) for attaching a display of immense rams from the huge ships of Antony's fleet. On the platform above there are remains of a pi-shaped stoa, perhaps housing more displays of spoils. Over the rams a monumental Latin inscription (letters a foot high) ran across the entire length of the podium, reconstructed as follows:

Imperator Caesar, son of the divine Julius, following the victory in the war which he waged on behalf of the republic in this region, when he was consul for the fifth time and commander-in-chief for the seventh time, after peace had been restored on land and sea, consecrated to Neptune and Mars the camp from which he set forth to attack the enemy now ornamented with naval spoils.

(after W.M. Murray and P.M. Petsas)

Macedonia

Macedonia, which is separated from Thessaly by Mt Olympos, originally consisted of the lower valleys of the Aliakmon and Axios rivers but eventually stretched as far east as the Strymon and also included the Chalkidike peninsula. The climate is more European than Mediterranean, since there is often rain in the summer months and the winters can be bitterly cold. The Macedonian plain is extremely fertile but was not as extensive in antiquity. The alluvium deposited by the Aliakmon and Axios has filled in the northern end of the Thermaic Gulf and consequently PELLA, which was once on the coast, is now 20 km. inland. There is excellent pasture in the mountains and Macedonian timber was much in demand for ship construction. Mineral resources included gold, silver, and iron ore.

In the Neolithic period, Macedonia was the contact zone between Greece and the Balkans and this is also the case in the Bronze Age. The prehistoric settlements often take the form of *toumbas*, prominent artificial mounds which rose in height as the mudbrick houses were demolished and rebuilt. There is Mycenaean pottery, especially from the coastal sites in central Macedonia. The Early Iron Age sees the appearance of tumulus cemeteries, notably at VERGINA.

In historic times Macedonia was named for the Makedones, a tribal people originally confined to the mountains above DION. Led by hereditary warrior-kings claiming Greek descent from the mythical Temenos of ARGOS, the Macedonians from c.650 BC gradually overran the Macedonian plain and surrounding regions in a series of land-grabs, creating new lowland capitals at Aigai (Vergina) and then (c.400 BC) Pella. This territorial expansion culminated on a grand scale under the two greatest Temenid kings, Philip II (360–336 BC), who created a Balkan empire, and his son and successor, Alexander the Great (336–323 BC), who conquered Persia. In 316 BC Macedonia was seized by Cassander (316 BC), who proclaimed himself 'king of the Macedonians' c.305 BC. After years of neglect during Alexander's absence abroad, the region now enjoyed an economic boom, fuelled by loot brought home from the wars in Asia. Excavation is revealing the ostentation and luxury of wealthy Macedonians of this time, as in the palatial houses of Pella, in monumental tombs (see LEFKADIA), and in the jewellery and precious plate from Derveni now displayed in the THESSALONIKI museum. Cassander's death (297 BC) led to dynastic instability and the installation of a new dynasty, temporarily under Demetrios I (294–287 BC) and permanently from c. 277/6 BC with the accession of his son Antigonos II (died 239 BC), who was followed by three further generations of Antigonid kings, ending with Perseus, deposed by Rome in 167 BC (see p. 411).

Under the Temenids the Macedonians converted from semi-nomadism to a settled life based on agriculture and cities. This change was probably gradual, although later writers telescoped it into a sudden one under Philip II, who certainly hastened it by internal resettlement and the creation of new cities, notably PHILIPPI. Temenid kings from Alexander I (*c.*498–454 BC) on had pursued Greek cultural interests, especially Archelaos (413–399 BC), a patron of Greek artists and writers. Even so, hostile Athenians in the C4 BC could call the Macedonians barbarians. This was not just because they spoke a Greek patois (as scholars nowadays tend to see the ancient Macedonian language), but also because Macedonian warrior-society seemed politically backward (most city-states had long dispensed with kings) and culturally boorish, as exemplified by the antics of the royal court (see p. 439). But archaeological finds modify this picture, showing a love of superb Greek craftsmanship in C4 BC Macedonia, as well as the innovative architecture which produced the Greek-style 'Macedonian' tomb (see p. 139). In Hellenistic times the kings went on founding new cities, notably Thessalonike, which joined older ones as centres of the Greek way of life for ordinary Macedonians, exemplified by the superb gymnasium at AMPHIPOLIS (see also VEROIA). By the late C1 BC, the Greek geographer Strabo was in no doubt that Macedonia was part of 'Hellas'.

In 146 BC Rome turned Macedonia into its first Balkan province, shortly after linked to the Adriatic by a Roman trunk-road, the via Egnatia. Ceaseless military action against barbarian neighbours made the province a 'seed-bed of triumphs' for its governors until the creation of a new province of Moesia (roughly modern Serbia) to the north (C1 AD). Macedonia received Italian colonists in the C1 BC (Dion, Pella, Philippi), creating Latin enclaves, their western character especially marked at Philippi. Under the pax Romana city life flourished, especially in the C2–C3, when public works are attested in many Macedonian cities. In AD 214 the Alexander-mad emperor Caracalla armed Macedonians in the manner of Alexander's infantry for his eastern war, fanning Macedonian nostalgia for the old kings. In the mid-C3 AD Macedonia was exposed to Gothic incursions; cities now rebuilt their walls. By 400 the empire's military crisis had transformed Thessalonike into a major army-base and imperial centre. From the early C4 on a vigorous Christianity manifested itself in the construction of churches, among them an early basilica (*c.* AD 340) at Philippi, and the church of St George, with outstanding mosaics, in Thessalonike. Continuing insecurity prompted massive new walls at Thessalonike (late C4) and reduced cities like Dion and Amphipolis to small fortified nuclei.

Thessaloniki

The sites are mainly clustered in a compact area in the centre of the city and can easily be toured on foot.

Macedonia

Special Features

A visit to Thessaloniki is a must, if only for the spectacular finds in the archaeological museum. In addition there are noteworthy traces of the Roman and early Christian city, including an imperial palace and important early churches.

History

Thessalonike (the ancient spelling) was founded by the future king Cassander *c.*316 BC on an already settled site, probably ancient Therme. Named after his wife, Philip II's daughter, it quickly became the most important port of Macedonia. Down to a major fire in 1917 the streets of old Thessaloniki preserved a much earlier grid-plan, now thought to go back to Cassander, who probably also built the first city-wall. A royal residence, the Hellenistic city had normal civic institutions, including a gymnasium. Under Roman rule the strategic location of Thessalonike, now on the via Egnatia, made it the seat of Macedonia's Roman officials and host to Italian businessmen and a major community of Jews, with at least two synagogues by the early C3. The city now became the most populous in the province, 'the mother of all Macedonia' as a Greek poet put it, and culturally a blend of Roman and Greek, as shown by its entertainments. An inscription records three days of gladiatorial and wild-beast shows in April, AD 141. But the city also celebrated world-class Greek games, the Pythia, well into the C3 AD. The C2 and early C3 were marked by lavish expenditure on public works, including a new agora. By this date the present east–west Odos Egnatias had become the chief thoroughfare, as it still is. In the disturbances of the mid-C3 AD the city was twice besieged by the Goths (AD 254 and 268). A new circuit-wall was hastily thrown up at this time. The city's proximity to the troubled Danube frontier now gave it a new role as a strategic rear base for the military command of the Balkans. It became an imperial capital under Galerius (see **box**), who built a lavish palace-complex, later occupied by Theodosius I (379–395) during campaigns against the Goths. In his reign a massive new city-wall was built, complementing earlier harbour-works under Constantine I. In 441/2 the city became the seat of the praetorian prefect of Illyricum, one of the eastern empire's highest officials, a promotion ushering in the first great period of church-building, although the city was already a bastion of Christianity, first brought to the city by Paul (*c.* AD 50), with archbishops attested from AD 325. The city survived repeated sieges by the Avars and Slavs and other 'barbarians' from the C6 on. By *c.*650 it was an isolated imperial stronghold surrounded by Slav settlements, but still linked by sea with Constantinople.

Galerius

Galerius was one of the breed of tough army officers pitched into the top job by the military crisis of the Roman empire. An uneducated peasant from the Danube frontier, he was already a high-ranking soldier by the time he caught the eye of the soldier-emperor Diocletian, who made him Caesar (AD 293) and married him to his daughter. In 297 Galerius contributed to the military recovery by winning a major victory on the eastern frontier against the Sassanian Persians, marching as far as their capital at Ctesiphon (southern Iraq). He became eastern emperor in 306. Three years earlier, Diocletian started the last persecution of the Christians, prompted, the Christians later said, by Galerius, although other influences were certainly at work. Galerius kept up the repression in his half of the empire, only calling it off when in huge pain on his death bed at Serdica, modern Sofia (311). His portrait on an arch in the museum shows how he wished subjects to see him: a crop-haired, ill-shaven, bruiser.

Description

The **palace of Galerius** is not accessible to visitors because restoration is under way, but is clearly visible from the street. There are information panels on the north side of the site. The chief visible features of a much larger complex still covered by modern buildings are a group of rooms and wide corridors, some with mosaic floors (covered over), organized around a colonnaded courtyard, and a handsome octagonal building with a lavish floor of coloured marble. This structure is later, perhaps an addition by Theodosius I, and its function is disputed; possibly it was a throne room. The monumental scale of these ruins hints at the grandeur of what once was a vast and lavish palace-quarter attributed in the first instance to Galerius *c.*300, and embracing his arch and rotunda to the north and a circus or hippodrome for chariot-racing and imperial appearances to the east.

The **arch of Galerius** has recently been conserved. The relief panels, its most noteworthy feature and the most important example of Roman imperial art from this period, are perfectly visible from close-up. The structure was originally four-fronted, with a domed central space, and marked an important cross-roads, the two main facades spanning the Roman city's principal street (today Odos Egnatias). On the arch's north side there was access to the rotunda (below), on the south side to the palace, entered through a huge vestibule. Only the arch's west side survives, of brick-faced rubble clad in marble. The relief panels on the two extant piers, belonging to the same tradition of Roman military narrative as Trajan's Column (Rome), show Galerius's victorious campaigns against the Sassanian Persians (AD 298), the enemy's 'Phrygian' caps and barbarian trousers, and camels and elephants, evoking this eastern context. The scenes are notable for the way in which they present the victory as a joint achievement of the four co-rulers (tetrarchs) of the empire, as on the east side of the south pier (with the best-preserved sculpture) showing, second tier, Galerius in military dress, flanking an altar along with Diocletian, his senior emperor.

On its north side the arch is axially aligned to a domed **rotunda** in brick, now the church of Ayios Georgios, recently reopened after conservation. Probably begun as the emperor's mausoleum, it was unfinished at his death. The dome was only completed when the building was converted into a church. This seems to have happened in the early C6, when the dome acquired its superb mosaic decoration. Best-preserved is the lowest zone, showing saints against a golden background of fantasy-architecture.

From the rotunda we suggest that you walk west along Odos Philippou until you reach an impressive **Roman agora**, discovered in 1963. This large site is not yet accessible to visitors as reconstruction work is in progress, but it can mostly be viewed from outside. The complex dates from the C2 and early C3 AD and must either have superseded or complemented an older agora not yet found. It comprises a marble-paved open square enclosed by a double-colonnade, well preserved in the south-east corner only. Below the south side runs a vaulted underground corridor (*cryptoporticus*). An odeion forms part of the complex to the east. The drop of 1.60 m. from the front row of seats to the orchestra below has been taken to show that it was later adapted for gladiatorial combats. To the south, in an area now occupied by public gardens, there was a lower square, partly flanked by the stoa from which came the so-called Las Incantadas figures (see museum).

Just north of the agora, which it would once have overlooked, is the **church of Ayios Dimitrios** (St Demetrios), the city's patron saint, martyred in the persecution of Christians under Galerius. The present structure is a more or less faithful reconstruction of a building destroyed by fire in 1917, the original fabric of which went back at least to 620, when an earlier church suffered a fire. It is disputed how drastic the reconstruction following this fire was, since decorative details such as the marble cladding, the capitals, and the form of the columns would suit a date *c.*510–520, implying that the damage of 620 was limited to the roof. At any rate, the five-aisled basilican plan goes back to this original structure, built sometime *c.*450–520. It was constructed over vast Roman baths, the alleged site of the saint's martyrdom, and part of their ground floor was incorporated into the basilica's crypt. This, filled in under the Ottomans and only rediscovered in 1917, evolved into a cult centre of St Demetrios, its focus a basin of holy water supplied from a well. Alleged traces of a pre-basilican church in the substructures of the baths are disputed.

A short distance south-east of Ayios Dimitrios is the other great basilican church of early-Christian Thessaloniki, the **Panayia Acheiropoietos** ('Virgin Not Made by Human Hands', its medieval name, referring to a miraculous icon, now lost). Built over Roman baths, its architecture is normally assigned to the C5, as are the fine acanthus-capitals of the nave. Some soffits of the arcades preserve early Christian mosaics, although whether they formed part of the original decor is disputed.

Just to the south is the domed church of **Ayia Sophia**, beneath which have been found the remains of a five-aisled **basilica** over twice the size of its successor. This earlier church, tentatively dated *c*.475–525, is the largest known in the early Christian city, and should probably be identified as the cathedral of the archbishops. The present church belongs to the C7–C8, but its exact date is disputed.

Higher up stretches of the **city-wall** can be seen. These are mainly medieval or later, but follow the line of an early Christian circuit, its construction commemorated by a brick inscription built into the so-called Hormisdas tower in the east wall: 'Hormisdas perfected this city with invulnerable walls' (*IG* 10.2, no. 43). If Hormisdas is the prefect of Illyricum of that name, as is nowadays believed, his work on the wall dates to *c*.448. This wall seems to have followed a circuit of the C3 AD, hastily put up in the period of the Gothic raids, its predecessor in turn a scantily attested Hellenistic wall.

The **Archaeological Museum** is at the east end of the city near the site of the International Fair. Generally the display is well labelled in Greek and English.

Room 1 has a Roman copy of a Hellenistic head of Alexander the Great, purchased in 1996 from a sale in Vienna. There are impressive fragments of an Ionic temple (*c*.500 BC) from the earlier settlement on the site, presumably Therme. **Rooms 2–3** house sculpture of all periods, including a full-length Augustus. **Room 4** offers a history of Thessalonike, with an excellent display on the Roman agora and the demolished two-storey portico once known as Las Incantadas ('The Idols') from its sculptural figures, now in the Louvre. A statue base from the C2–C3 AD inscribed 'Queen Thessalonike, daughter of Philip' suggests nostalgia for the old royal family in Roman times. A small arch, from the palace of Galerius, preserves his portrait. **Rooms 5–6** have more sculpture of the Roman period, and a model of the Roman agora. **Room 7** reconstructs the facade of a rich 'Macedonian' built tomb of *c*.300 BC from modern Ayia Paraskevi (south of ancient Potidaia). **Room 8** has material from the cemetery at Sindos (see **box**). **Room 9** contains C4 BC rich finds from the tombs at Derveni (see **box**), 12 km. north-west of the city. In **rooms 10–11** there are prehistoric and Archaic finds from sites in the region (closed in 1997).

Sindos

In the inner rooms of the museum there is a display of Archaic and Classical grave offerings from the cemetery at Sindos, west of Thessaloniki. The dead had been buried in pit graves, cist graves, and stone sarcophagi. The closest settlement site is at Nea Anchialos, which may be ancient Chalastra. Quite a number of the graves had been robbed but those which were intact contained some spectacular offerings: gold masks, exquisite jewellery, helmets, swords and spears, bronze and silver vessels. There is imported Athenian and Corinthian pottery and model furniture made of iron and bronze.

Funerals were clearly treated as an occasion for conspicuous consumption. The offerings catered for the needs of the dead in the afterlife but also reflected their social status and this is why women and children were buried in some of the richest graves. In certain respects Sindos is reminiscent of Thracian cemeteries, yet there is Greek influence as well. This community was culturally eclectic, truly macédoine.

The Derveni krater

Drinking vessels in precious metals are a striking feature of Macedonian burials of the later C4 and early C3 BC, especially at Vergina and Derveni. Their superb craftsmanship adds a touch of refinement to the image of Macedonian drinking parties, notorious among southern Greeks for excess.

The most magnificent of all these vessels is the gilded-bronze krater from Derveni (probably 325–300 BC). The embossed scenes depict the myth of Dionysos: his dismemberment, 'resurrection', and marriage to Ariadne. Since Dionysos loomed large in Greek afterlife beliefs, some experts believe that the piece was a funerary commission. But an inscription in silver on the rim suggests otherwise. It records the name of the original owner, one Astioun(eos), and the piece's place of manufacture: 'from Larisa', in Thessaly. The krater was evidently a lavish item of drinking equipment which came to Macedonia either as a gift or, more likely, as booty. Dionysos was also the god of wine, and the krater, a bowl for diluting wine with water, was the traditional centrepiece of the Greek drinking party.

Olynthos (Figs. 162–163)

The site is reached via the modern village of the same name which is just off the Thessaloniki road.

Special Features

The ruins of Olynthos, set in rolling farmland, provide a rare chance to walk the residential streets of a Classical Greek city. The site offers the best evidence there is for Greek houses of the late C5 – early C4 BC.

History

Olynthos was the most important of the Greek colonies on the fertile three-pronged peninsula called the Chalkidike, where it occupied a central position. Originally an indigenous settlement, it became a Greek city c.479 BC, when it was repopulated with other Chalkidic Greeks. In 432/1 BC it was made the capital of a powerful federation formed by the Chalkidic colonies in revolt from Athenian control. Olynthos eventually succumbed to the expansionism of Philip II, who destroyed the city and enslaved the population (348 BC) after a siege. Three-barbed bronze arrow-heads from his catapults, inscribed 'belonging to Philip', were found by the excavators, although in the end the city fell through treachery. Philip's action in effect sealed the (badly fire damaged) remains of Classical Olynthos from obliteration, since the city was never refounded.

Description

The old American excavations, formerly covered over, have been revealed again and consolidated by Greek archaeologists. Excellent plans are now dotted round the site.

Olynthos occupies an akropolis-site, spread over two hills. The most interesting excavations are on the **north hill**, where the Olynthians laid out a large area of new housing on a regular plan near the end of the C5 BC, probably to accommodate migrants from neighbouring cities. This urban extension, which spread onto the plain to the east, was planned in rectangular blocks traversed from north to south by 'avenues' (A–E). Each block is made up of two south-facing rows of five houses, separated by a narrow alley for drainage. With no gardens or trees, the overall effect must have been more barracks than housing estate. Over a hundred houses have been excavated. Although they are similar, no two are identical. This is partly because households adapted interiors to their evolving needs, including letting or selling the house, as inscriptions show.

The houses had mudbrick walls (destroyed) on stone footings. Great quantities of broken roof-tiles can be seen, especially on the main north–south 'avenue D'. The typical house-plan emphasizes privacy. A single entrance from the street leads into an open court, with a portico or veranda (the so-called *pastas*) on the north side giving access to the main rooms, and other rooms leading off the court. A number of houses have stone bases for wooden staircases to a vanished upper storey.

Objects indicating how individual rooms were used are relatively rare. This is partly because houses would have been stripped of their

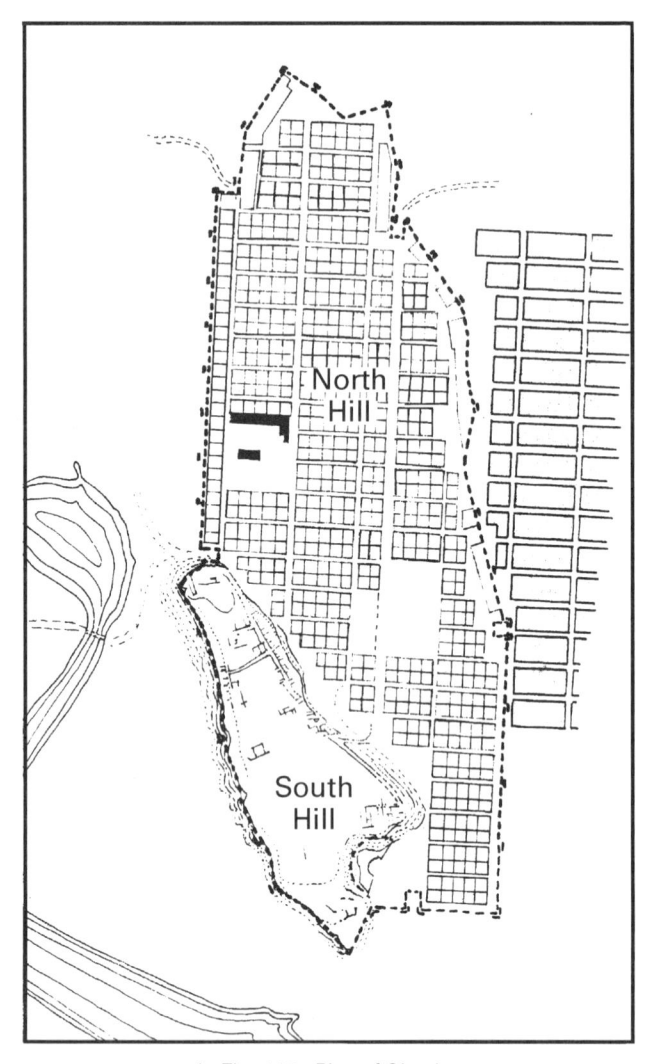

▲ Fig. 162. Plan of Olynthos

more valuable contents in 348 BC. But room-functions were probably fairly flexible anyway. It was the women who spent most time at home, and where they performed their chores could depend on a variety of factors such as the weather and season, and the presence or not of visitors. Clay weights for portable wooden looms, the chief evidence for women's activities, were usually found throughout the house (see **box**).

Apart from bathrooms (see **box**), some houses (for example A vi 6) have a room with a stone-curbed hearth and an associated air-vent

Baths

How clean were the Olynthians? There are very few natural wells or springs on the site, and most residents relied on a public water supply. An underground aqueduct delivered a strong head of water from (it seems) a source about 8 km. away to a (poorly preserved) public fountain on the north hill (on avenue B, opposite block B iii). Heavy use of this amenity is shown by the remains of 631 water-vessels found here. Only a few houses had their own cisterns for collecting rainwater from the roof. About one third had bathrooms (rooms with waterproof floors), sometimes preserving fired-clay baths, not for immersion, but for washing in a sitting position with heated water. The norm was a portable washbasin (marble or fired clay). Three houses produced signs of a fixed (clay) latrine, perhaps originally with a wooden seat; portable clay latrines would have been more common. Clay pipes discharged household waste (including, in one case, human sewage from a fixed latrine) into the drainage alleys between the two rows of houses in every block. But there was almost no effort to control waste issuing from these alleys onto the streets, which generally were unpaved, except for stretches of cobbles.

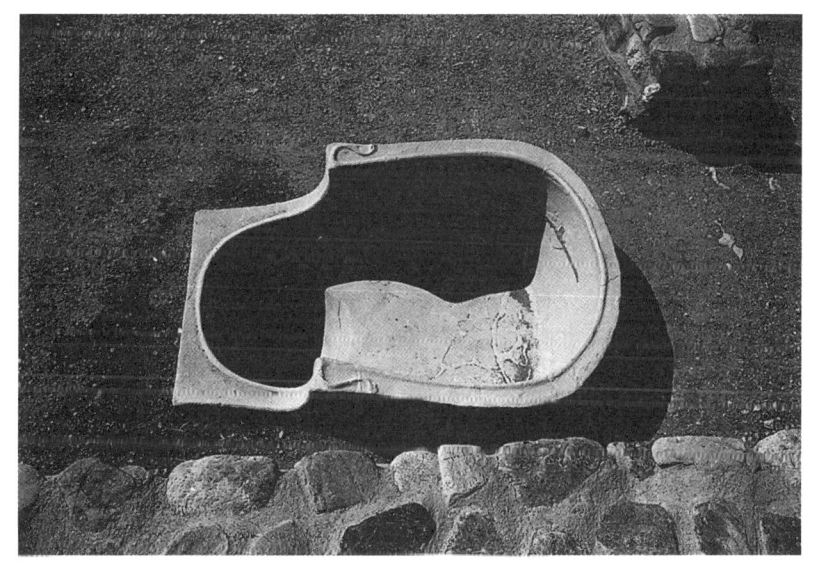

▲ Fig. 163. Terracotta bathtub at Olynthos

(flue), presumably where cooking took place. The other readily identifiable space is the 'room of the men' or andron, where male householders received other (male) guests for meals and drinking. These rooms are easily distinguished by a raised sill around the walls for dining couches, and an off-centre door. Where a house has a mosaic floor, it is usually here.

Some mosaics are exposed, others are protected by plastic. Made from pebbles, these are the first large group of mosaics known from Classical Greece. A particularly fine example in the andron of house A vi 3 shows the hero Bellerophon, wearing the Macedonian sun-hat or *petasos* and mounted on his horse Pegasos, spearing the monstrous Chimaira, shown with a lion's body and head, a snake's tail, and a goat's head sticking up from its back.

The **south hill**, where the old town was, has scrappy remains of smaller, unplanned buildings.

Loomweights

Olynthos has produced 793 clay weights for looms, as well as spindle whorls and spools, also used in making cloth. Found in almost every room of every house, they reflect the importance of domestic wool-working in Olynthos. All this spinning and weaving was women's work, the domain of wives, daughters, and household-slaves. In Greek thinking the virtuous wife was one who worked hard at home on the contents of her wool-basket, her model Homer's mythical Penelope, who passed the years of her husband Odysseus's absence patiently plying her loom. Rare finds of textiles from ancient Greece give glimpses of the remarkably skilful products of these hours of labour by ancient Greek women.

Torone (Fig. 164) ★

Follow the road down the western side of Sithonia. Take the turn signed Toroni, go through the town until you reach the sea. The site is on the low promontory at the southern end of the bay, a gentle stroll along the fine sandy beach.

Special Features

Torone is an attractive site, if not one of the better preserved, and the Sithonia peninsula is quieter and more scenic than Kassandra.

History

The Lekythos promontory was first occupied in the third millennium BC. The pottery from the prehistoric levels includes some of the earliest Mycenaean sherds in Macedonia and this suggests that Torone was already one of the main ports on the trade route which follows the north coast of the Aegean. A rich Early Iron Age cemetery of the C11–C10 BC has been excavated south of the Lekythos and in due course the settlement also expanded inland. It was inevitable that the Athenians should have taken an interest in a coastal site of such strategic importance. For much of the C5 Torone was under their control but in 423 BC it was seized by the Spartan general Brasidas, an episode which is described in detail by Thucydides (see below). Philip annexed the city in 349 BC and it must have been the Macedonians who fortified the akropolis in the late C4 BC. Torone prospered as maritime trade between THESSALONIKI and Constantinople intensified in the C5–6 AD and a number of early Christian churches were built. The Byzantine and Ottoman fortifications on the Lekythos emphasize just how vital secure harbours will have been whenever voyages were regularly made by sea around the treacherous coast of Chalkidike.

Description

Although the site is fenced, access is not restricted. The fortification walls on the promontory date from the Late Byzantine and Ottoman periods but incorporate granite and limestone blocks which must be earlier. Most of the structures inside are Byzantine or Ottoman. Classical/Hellenistic masonry can be glimpsed in some of the deeper trenches, stratified above prehistoric levels. The recent excavations have confirmed that there was a Doric temple of Athena on the Lekythos. This is mentioned by Thucydides (4.110–16) in his account of the Spartan attack on Torone in 423 BC. After he had captured AMPHIPOLIS, the Spartan general Brasidas marched against Torone. Sympathizers opened the gates and the Spartans were soon in control of most of the city except for the Lekythos where the Athenian garrison took refuge. Thucydides tells us that:

As soon as the truce was over Brasidas made his attack. The Athenian defences consisted of a badly constructed wall and some houses with parapets. For one day they beat off the attack. On the next day the Spartans brought up against them an engine from which they meant to throw down fire on the wooden part of the fortifications. Their troops were already drawing up close to the point where it seemed to them that the engine would be most effective and where the fortifications could be most easily stormed. To meet this threat the Athenians had erected a wooden tower on top of a house and they carried into this a number of great jars and casks of water and large stones. A number of men also went up into the tower but the weight was too heavy for the house to bear and it suddenly collapsed with a loud crash. This caused more vexation than alarm among the Athenians who were close to the scene of the action and saw what had happened, but those who were farther off, and particularly those who were some distance away, thought that the fortifications had already been stormed at this point, and at once fled to the sea and their ships. Brasidas saw them leaving the parapet and realized what was happening. He charged forward with his army and took the place immediately, killing those whom he found inside ... Brasidas, when he was on the point of making the assault, had

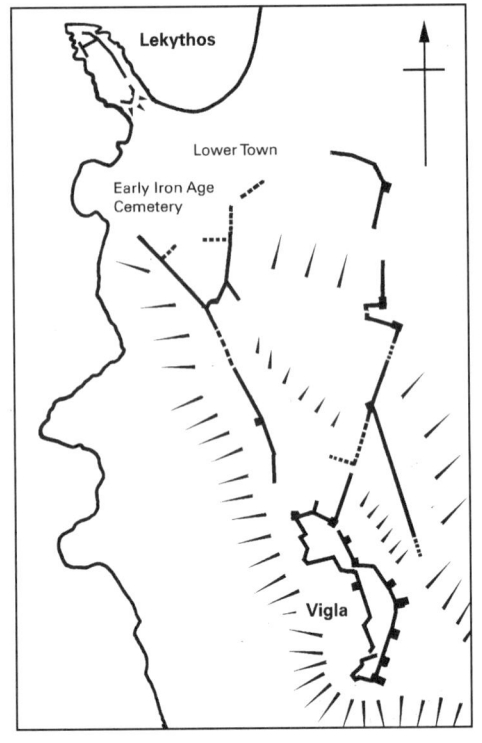

▲ Fig. 164. Plan of Torone

proclaimed that he would give thirty silver minai to the man who first scaled the wall. Now there is a temple of Athena on the Lekythos and Brasidas, considering that the capture was due to divine help rather than human means, gave the thirty minai to the goddess for her temple, dismantled the fortifications, cleared the ground, and consecrated it to the goddess.

The city was evidently quite extensive in the Classical period since houses have been excavated on the promontory south of the Lekythos, as well as on the slopes of Vigla, the hill which overlooks the site. The fortifications on the summit of Vigla were built early in the Hellenistic period and the circuit also enclosed the lower town.

The most impressive of the early Christian basilicas at Torone is the church of Ayios Athanasios. Take the left turn just before the promontory—the basilica is by the roadside shrine about 100 m. from the turn. It was evidently built as a three-aisled basilica and later became a single-aisled church.

Amphipolis (Figs. 165–166)

Amphipolis is just off the main Thessaloniki–Kavala road. The site is well signed.

Special Features

One of the best-preserved gymnasia in Greece, unique remains of a wooden bridge, and the Lion of Amphipolis are the chief attractions of this extensive site, which commands fine views in all directions. There is also an excellent museum.

History

In 437–436 BC the Athenians founded Amphipolis as a Greek colony. It took its name ('On Both Sides City') from its position on a low plateau flanked on two sides by the River Strymon to the west. The region's fertility, its timber and the gold of Mt Pangaion to the east, had attracted Greek interest since Archaic times. Athenian claims went back to *c*.476 BC, when the general Kimon seized Eion at the mouth of the river, later the colony's port. The colony was on a strategic junction (the Greeks formerly knew the place as Nine Roads), commanding routes up the river valley and along the coast. It was also a frontier town, its relations with the indigenous Thracians marked by a mix of exploitation and hostility; this, as much as anything, explains its *c*.9 km. of heavy fortifications. Amphipolis saw action in the Peloponnesian War, described by the Athenian general and historian Thucydides, who failed to prevent the city's capture by the Spartans (424 BC). ATHENS persisted for nearly 70 years in trying to recapture this cherished colony, finally giving up when it fell to Philip II (357 BC). Thereafter it was an autonomous city under Macedonian rule until its surrender to the Romans (168 BC). Under Macedon Amphipolis prospered, as shown by the impressive gymnasium and rich tombs. In the Roman empire it remained important as a station on the via Egnatia and a regional centre. Its main gate in this period (D), probably linked directly with the great Roman road, has been found at the city's south extremity, flanked by bases for statues of Augustus (30 BC–AD 14), who gave the city coveted 'free' status, and a Roman governor, Lucius Calpurnius Piso (the governor of 15 BC), 'patron and benefactor' of the city. The city had its own community of resident Romans, including slavers (see **box**), who were important enough for Hadrian to address by letter. The late antique city, its nucleus defended by a new fortification wall, was the seat of a bishopric first attested in AD 553. The cluster of fine churches on the akropolis attests the wealth and continuing importance of Amphipolis up to the time of the Slav incursions, when it was destroyed and abandoned (C8–C9 AD).

> ## Slave trade
>
> The gravestone (C1 AD) of Aulus Kapreilius Timotheus, on display in the museum, is highly unusual in celebrating an occupation which most ancient Greeks viewed with a certain contempt. In the Greek epitaph Timotheus is called a 'slave-trader' (*somatenporos*), and the form of his name shows that he was an ex-slave himself, no doubt of a Roman in the same line of business. A sculptured panel depicts a chain-gang of eight slaves, two women and children (unchained), and a man leading them, possibly Timotheus himself. The findspot implies that Amphipolis was, among other things, a slaving centre. The city was well-sited in this respect, as the Strymon valley gave access to the 'barbarian' peoples of the interior, notably the Thracians, a source of supply from early times, who fell into the hands of the likes of Timotheus through either trade with local chieftains, or local sales of Roman prisoners of war.

Description

The visible remains of the site are scattered over a considerable area. The order in which we describe the site is: gymnasium, churches, Hellenistic house, museum, Classical city-wall and bridge, lion monument.

As you approach Amphipolis on the Drama road, a vaulted **'Macedonian' tomb** [**165.1**] of C3 BC date is signed. Near the road, it is usually closed.

To walk to the C4 BC gymnasium (Fig. 166), take the dirt track roughly opposite the blue sign which indicates that it is 200 m. to the Amphipolis turn, and fork left at once. Walk uphill for *c.*500 m. until you reach the site (fenced but main features clearly visible). The gymnasium was where the Amphipolitan ephebes, citizen-males in their late-teens, received training in athletics and military exercises (finds of spear- and arrow-heads and sling-bullets are displayed in the museum). The complex was originally approached by a monumental **stairway** [**166.1**] giving onto the main building [**166.2**] or **palaistra**, a colonnaded courtyard surrounded by rooms, one of them a **bathroom** [**166.5**] with marble wash-basins; other rooms displayed sculpture and a long (139 lines) inscription publishing a law of 24/3 BC regulating the conduct of the ephebes. Bounding the complex on the north is a **covered running track** or xystos [**166.3**] in the form of a Doric colonnade, matched on its open south side by a parallel good-weather [**166.4**] **running track** (a rare feature otherwise found only at DELPHI). The finds suggest a date for the complex in the second half of the C4 BC. Important alterations (a new entrance to the main building on its north side) were still being made in the early C1 AD, when the complex was destroyed by fire and not rebuilt.

The five churches (C5–C6 AD) on the summit of the akropolis can be

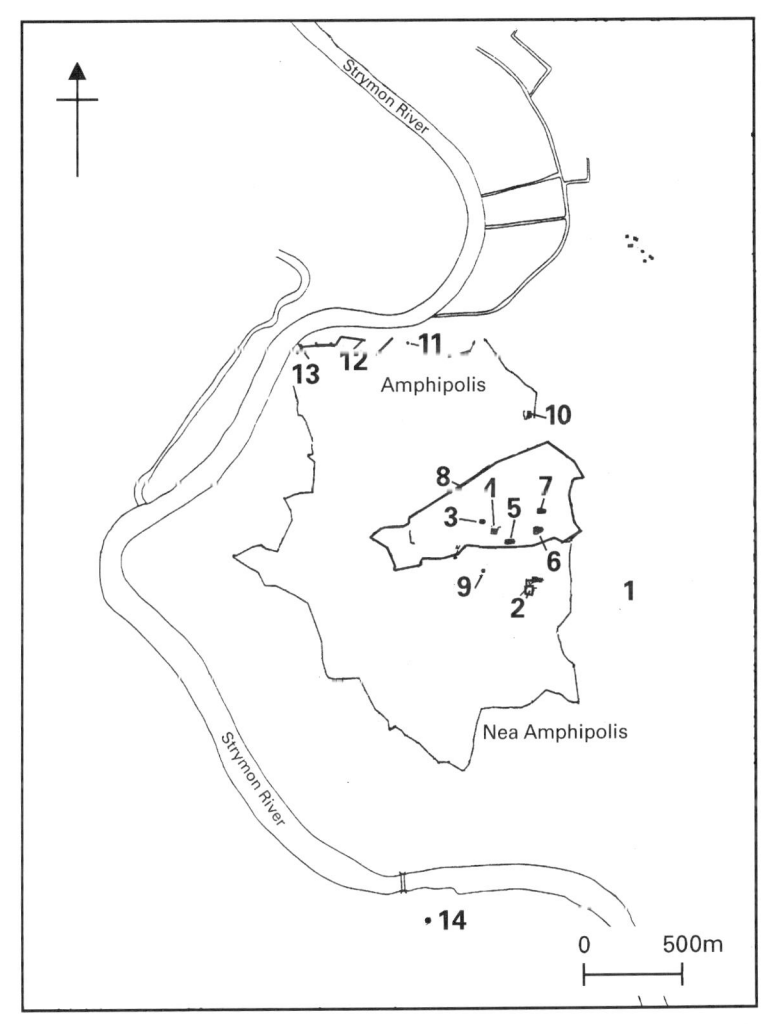

▲ Fig. 165. Plan of Amphipolis. Key: 1 'Macedonian' tomb 2 Gymnasium 3 Basilica G 4 Basilica A 5 Basilica D 6 Basilica E 7 Basilica B 8 Fortification wall 9 Hellenistic house 10 Museum 11 Byzantine tower 12 City wall 13 Bridge 14 Lion monument

reached from here. Alternatively, go first to the museum (left turn at the blue sign for Amphipolis). Continue past the museum until you reach a further left turn signed Αρχαιολογικη Χωρα, which leads (700 m.) to the entrance of the (fenced) site. The churches shelter behind a late antique **fortification wall** [**165.8**] built largely with earlier architectural stonework and equipped with two main gates, as well as an inner wall on the west side. The importance of this part of the city in early Christian

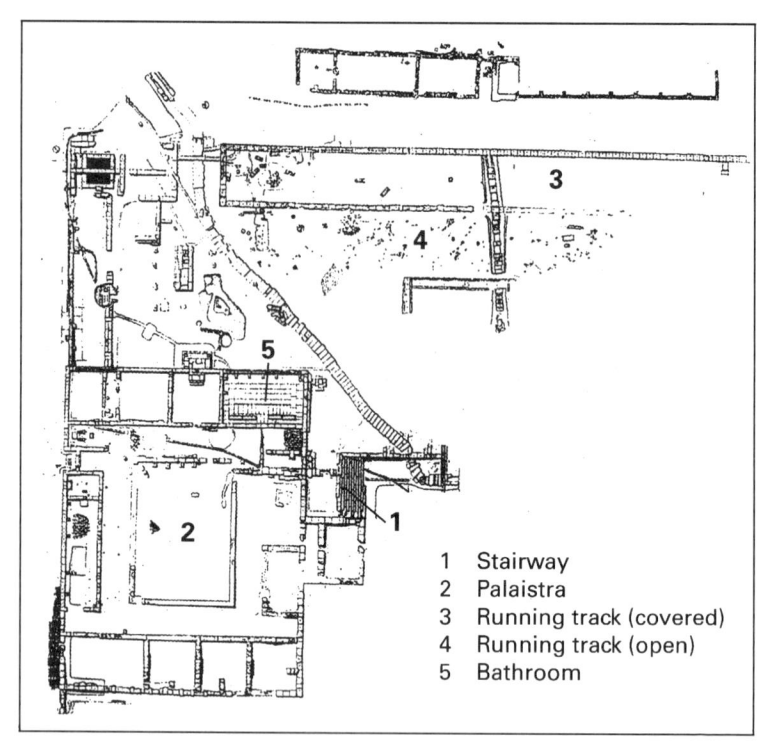

▲ Fig. 166. Plan of the gymnasium at Amphipolis

1	Stairway
2	Palaistra
3	Running track (covered)
4	Running track (open)
5	Bathroom

times is underlined by the discovery of a vast open cistern to the east of basilica A, comparable in scale to the cisterns of Constantinople, with an estimated storage capacity of 2200 cubic metres, supplied by the run-off from nearby buildings.

The group of churches were expensively finished structures making heavy use of marble and mosaics. From west to east, the first **basilica** you see is **G** [**165.3**], with fine mosaics in the nave based on fish and birds. In its latest phase the church's outbuildings were being used by squatters, who divided the east colonnade of the outer courtyard into small rooms, in which crude hearths and handmade pottery were found. The splendid floor-mosaics of **basilica A** [**165.4**], again featuring fish, birds, and animals, are now under a protective roof. **Basilica D** [**165.5**] had a double-storeyed colonnade framing the open court to the west of the narthex, an unusual feature paralleled in Bethlehem. The remarkable church to the east [**165.6**] (**basilica E**), dated C5 AD, departs from the basilican plan to take the form of an internal two-storey colonnade in the shape of a hexagon, partly inscribed within a curving outer wall. It too featured a double-storeyed (Ionic) portico framing the courtyard to the west. The decor includes fine marble floors, and Corinthian capitals incorporating the foreparts of rams. The church was partly destroyed, and then abandoned, in the C7. To the north and east is **basilica B** [165.7], on the north-east point of the akropolis, with mosaics in the north aisles featuring water-birds and partridges in roundels.

A fine **Hellenistic house** ([165.9]—C2 BC; enclosed and, in 1997, shut) can also be reached by the downhill dirt track continuing the approach road to the summit from the village. Two rooms have been found, arranged around a colonnaded court with a simple pebble floor. One has well-preserved wall-paintings, featuring a frieze of brightly coloured panels above a dado imitating multi-coloured marble. The other has white plaster incised in red and black to imitate masonry. Fragments of richly moulded architectural plaster were found, fallen from the ceiling.

The **museum** [165.10], recently opened, has an excellent display (English captions and information panels) on the site's history and archaeology (see box below).

To visit the bridge and the Classical city-wall return to the Drama road, turn left and then take the first left. You will soon see on the left a ruined **Byzantine tower** ([165.11]—C14 AD). 300 m. further on you reach a fenced area on the right. From its double gate a good stretch of **city-wall** [165.12] is visible, Classical or early Hellenistic.

Follow the fence round to the right for some way until you reach a shed (locked but interior can be glimpsed) enclosing over a thousand fossilized wooden piles for the C5 BC **bridge** [165.13] across the River Strymon behind you, those set into a higher level belonging to later repairs (including Roman). As well as iron nails, iron tools were found here, perhaps used in the construction. These are the only known remains of a wooden bridge from ancient Greece.

Victory monument

Just outside the entrance to the museum a Greek inscription set up by Macedon's last native ruler evokes the final loss of Macedonian independence to Rome. The first four lines read:

'King Perseus (ΒΑΣΙΛΕΥΣ ΠΕΡΣΕΥΣ), son of King Philip (set up this offering) from the (spoils of the) military campaigns in Thrace, for Artemis Tauropolos.'

The stone belonged to a victory-monument set up by Perseus to celebrate his annexation of a neighbouring Thracian kingdom to the east which had been raiding the Amphipolis area. Its king, however, was a Roman ally, and Rome made his expulsion by Perseus on this occasion one of its pretexts for declaring war on Macedon in 171 BC. Defeated at the battle of Pydna (168 BC), Perseus was captured and paraded in chains in the triumph of the general Aemilius Paulus at Rome. He died a prisoner in Italy, and Macedon became a Roman protectorate.

To visit the **lion monument** [**165.14**], return to the Drama road until you reach the sign for Nigrita. Turn right, cross after a short distance the old Strymon bridge, bear left and the monument is on your right. It re-erects on a modern pedestal (1936–7) made up of ancient blocks, a lion originally crowning a much larger funerary monument (*c.*300 BC). Fragments suggest that this comprised a square chamber topped by a pyramidal roof—a unique design for a Macedonian tomb, but one known from C4 BC Asia Minor. Scholarly speculation that the deceased was Laomedon, a Companion of Alexander with Amphipolitan ties, is just that.

Kavala ★

History

Kavala, ancient Neapolis, was a colony founded by THASOS in the C7 BC. The site was chosen because it commands the route which runs along the coast and there is also an excellent harbour. In due course Neapolis became the port for PHILIPPI. Few traces of the ancient city can be seen. The splendid aqueduct, which looks as though it should be Roman, was in fact built by Suleiman the Magnificent in the C16 and will have supplied water for Turkish baths; the use of a Roman architectural prototype seems particularly appropriate.

Kavala was the birthplace of Mehmet Ali (1769–1849) who became pasha of Egypt in 1805. The house where he was born, in the citadel/Φρούριο, has been restored and can be visited. Opposite the house there is an equestrian statue of the pasha. Mehmet Ali founded the Imaret which is on the western side of the castle and overlooks the harbour. It was built as an almshouse and, although dilapidated, is still an extremely fine example of Ottoman architecture. The courtyard has been refurbished as a café and offers glimpses of the interior.

Description

The **Archaeological Museum** is on Odos Vasileos Pavlou at the western end of the harbour. In the entrance hall there is Hellenistic and Roman sculpture from AMPHIPOLIS. The first room has finds from the excavations in the sanctuary of the Parthenos on the Castle. She was the patron deity of Neapolis and may have been a Hellenized version of the Thracian goddess Artemis Tauropolos or Bendis. The Ionic capitals come from an early C5 BC temple built of Thasian marble. This room also contains finds from prehistoric sites in eastern Macedonia, in particular Dikili Tash.

Grave offerings from the Hellenistic cemetery at Amphipolis can be seen in the second room. The jewellery, which includes gold wreaths and diadems, is especially impressive. Two funerary couches from the chamber of Macedonian tomb 1 at Amphipolis have delicately painted decoration. One of the offerings in this tomb was a mirror of polished silver. In the room on the first floor of the museum there is a display of finds from classical sites around Kavala.

Philippi (Figs. 167–169)

To reach the site, follow the Drama road (on the line of the via Egnatia) out of Kavala for about 8 km. The visible remains cover a reasonably compact area on either side of the main road as it leaves the modern village of Krenides.

Special Features

The visitor to Philippi will see a well-preserved Roman forum and important early Christian basilicas, and can pace the ancient via Egnatia, one of the great highways of the Roman empire.

History

The city occupies the site of Krenides ('Little Springs'), a mainland colony of THASOS occupied by Philip II in 356 BC, who renamed it Philippi and settled it with poor Macedonians. The marshy plain to the west, providing the colonists with their agricultural plots once Philip had drained it, is clearly visible from the site. Of the Macedonian city, the chief remains are parts of the theatre and wall-circuit and an intramural 'Macedonian' tomb. The Roman city was one of the chief stations on the via Egnatia, running for *c.*70 km. through its territory. Philippi's name achieved world fame in 42 BC when Mark Antony and the future Augustus won a decisive victory over Caesar's assassins on the flat land to the south and west. Antony refounded the city as a Roman veteran-colony. More western settlers arrived after 30 BC, and more again in the later C1 AD, attracted by a stake in the colony's chief asset, its rural land. In the C1–C2 AD Philippi was a thoroughly Roman place, its civic inscriptions exclusively in Latin, its citizens worshipping the Roman gods Jupiter, Neptune, and Mercury. The visible remains are above all those of this prosperous Roman colony and its Christian successor.

On a visit in AD 42 or 49 the apostle Paul founded Europe's first Christian group at Philippi, when he spent a night in the local prison. It grew rapidly, producing martyrs by the early C2 AD. After 311 Philippi became a richly endowed Christian centre and place of pilgrimage. A 'basilica of Paul', as it is described in the inscription from its mosaic floor, paid for by the local bishop, already existed *c.* AD 350. Four grander basilicas followed in the C5–C6. Urban decline is attested in the C7, although Philippi still existed as an imperial fortress in the C10.

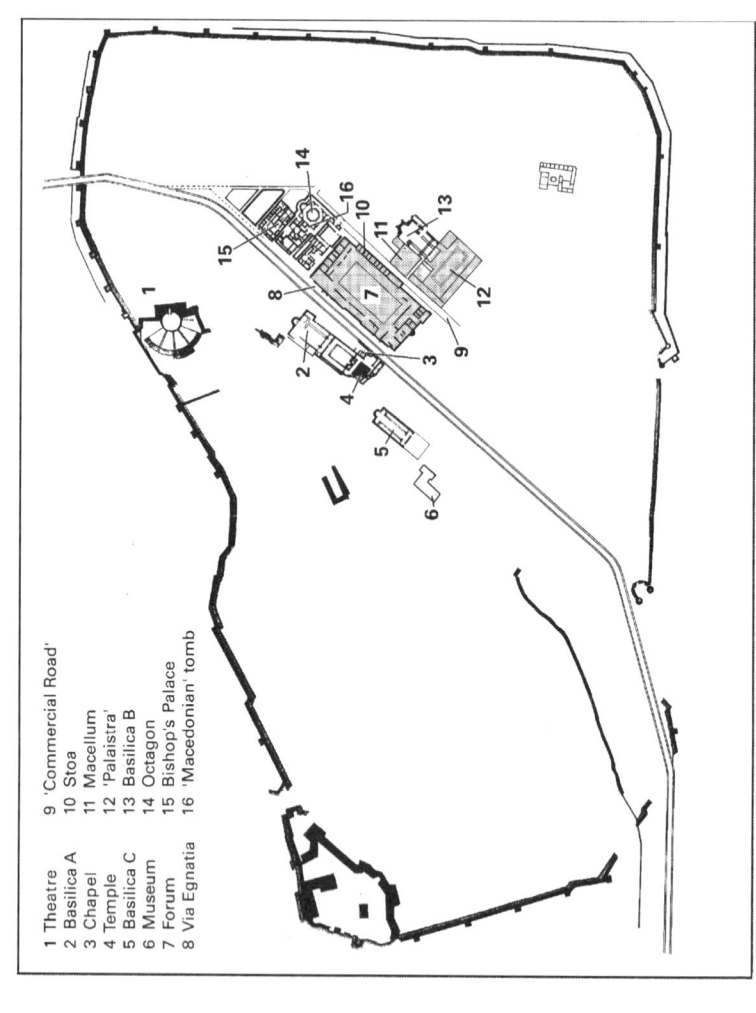

▲ Fig. 167. Plan of Philippi

1 Theatre
2 Basilica A
3 Chapel
4 Temple
5 Basilica C
6 Museum
7 Forum
8 Via Egnatia
9 'Commercial Road'
10 Stoa
11 Macellum
12 'Palaistra'
13 Basilica B
14 Octagon
15 Bishop's Palace
16 'Macedonian' tomb

Description

We suggest you start at the ancient **theatre** [**1**], on the slopes of the akropolis. It was built under Philip II, and parts date back to his reign (mainly the two side-walls retaining the seats). In colonial times (C2–C3) the theatre was remodelled and extra seating added to the rear. There are remains of a two-storey decorative stage-building (scaenae frons) in the Roman manner, which would have backed a deep Roman stage. Here mime-artists (*mimi*) are known from an inscription to have performed comic sketches in Latin. A tombstone records a different type of show put on here too: the deceased, a local benefactor, had once paid for a programme of seven pairs of gladiators and four wild-beast hunts, and for the sprinkling of saffron perfume to mask the smells. Eventually the taste for such shows led to the building of a circular arena, enclosed by a protective barrier over 2 m. high, with an underground passage allowing the sudden appearance of animals from below (C3 AD). Pottery and coins attest the theatre's continued use down to *c*.400.

From the arena a well-defined path continues to **basilica A** [**2**], dated *c*. AD 500 and built on a terrace overlooking the forum to the south. The lost splendour of the three-aisled church is evoked by marble sculpture (parapets and acanthus-leaf capitals, now in the museum), floors and wall-cladding of coloured marble, and frescoed plasterwork. The **chapel** [**3**] with traces of frescoes, just to the right of the stepped approach, was built in the C10–C11 AD over a Roman cistern by then claimed as the prison of St Paul. It remains an object of modern veneration.

The church's approach from the south reuses an imposing flight of earlier steps, leading into the first of two colonnaded forecourts. Its central water-cistern adapted the substructure of a demolished **temple** [**4**], probably C2 AD, once overlooking the forum. Fragments were found here of an important inscription (now in the museum) recording decisions by Alexander the Great about Philippi's rural territory, with references to its marshes and timber.

Continue on the same side of the road on a paved path to **basilica C** [**5**], of similar dimensions to basilica A, and notable for finds of large amounts of coloured glass fragments, probably from stained glass in the windows of the apse.

Just beyond is the **museum** ([**6**]—closed in 1997 for renovations). The courtyard contains an important collection of inscribed monuments, many with Latin texts from the Roman colonial period. The museum mainly houses architectural marbles and other finds from the Christian buildings, Roman sculpture and inscriptions, and Neolithic pottery from the nearby site of Megalo Lithari.

The impressive **forum** [**7**] of the Roman colony, its administrative and social centre, is reached from basilica A by crossing the Drama road.

It is set into a grid plan and bounded by two parallel ancient streets, both paved and rutted, the one to the north being the **via Egnatia** [8], at first the main thoroughfare of the colony. The other, the so-called **commercial road** [9], became the main artery for wheeled traffic from the C2, after a monumental remodelling under Marcus Aurelius (AD 161–180) of a smaller forum first laid out at the colony's foundation. A survivor of the earlier forum can be seen in front of the north-west temple: the inscribed base for an honorific statue of the colonist Lucius Tatinius Cnosus, with the names of the disgraced emperor Domitian (AD 81–96) later chiselled out.

The forum comprises a marble-paved square (100 by 50 m.) enclosed on three sides by stepped colonnades masking a range of public buildings. Above the north side, on the other side of the via Egnatia, was an upper terrace with monumental buildings linked to the forum, their remains obscured by the building of basilica A (above). South of the via, the forum's north side is framed by a centrally placed speaker's platform for official use, as at colonial CORINTH; two small temple-like monuments; and the basins of two symmetrically-placed public fountains. The one on the west preserves remains of the marble backing wall, with a Latin inscription naming the donor, one Decimius Bassus, and the fountain's cost (30,000 sesterces). In the north-west and north-east corners stood two identical temples in the Corinthian order, with Latin inscriptions from their facades dating them to after AD 161. The roofline of the north-west temple was adorned with statues of Athena and Victories, now in the museum. A Latin inscription shows that behind the east colonnade there was a four-room public library, where Latin works may have outnumbered Greek. The forum was maintained as late as the C5–C6 AD, when the shoddily built south colonnade was put up.

More public buildings lay to the south of the forum, fitted into the same grid-plan. Backed against the forum wall, a two-storey shopping **stoa** ([10]—Doric and Ionic orders) overlooked the commercial road. Facing it was a vast Corinthian colonnade, giving access to a **market** [11] or *macellum* (as a Latin inscription found nearby records). To the west is a massive building identified as a **palaistra** [12]. Dated to the later C2 AD, it features a colonnaded exercise court, a small lecture-hall, and a splendid 42-seater latrine, one of the best-preserved in Greece.

Market and palaistra were partly demolished to make way for **basilica B** [13], an ambitious white elephant dated to *c.*550. The lumps of fallen masonry in the apse come from an architecturally daring dome over the sanctuary, which collapsed before the three-aisled church was completed, prompting its abandonment. Acanthus-leaf capitals (finished and unfinished), destined to crown (reused) columns of coloured marble, and use of dressed stone, are further pointers to the lavishness of the project.

▲ Fig. 168. Basilica B at Philippi

To the south a fenced area of recent excavations, of great interest for the Hellenistic and Christian city, can be viewed by returning to the car park along the main road. The chief features are the so-called **Octagon** [14], a substantial church featuring an internal, octagonal, colonnade and an adjacent **bishop's palace** [15]. The church, dated *c.*400 in its first phase, supersedes and partly overlies an earlier basilica on the site, dedicated to St Paul, as recorded in an inscription in its richly decorated mosaic floor (*c.*350); on present evidence this was Philippi's earliest church.

Of considerable interest is the fact that the church overlay a (C2 BC) barrel-vaulted **'Macedonian' tomb** [16]. The deceased was found in a stone-lined cist with the name of a member of a known local family, 'Euephenes, son of Exekestos', inscribed on the lid. This tomb had some kind of superstructure and in Roman times was the focus of a hero-cult.

▲ Fig. 169. Latin inscription from Philippi mentioning colonial freedmen.

Its presence was respected by the first church of St Paul in a way which suggests that the Christian cult in some sense had absorbed its pagan predecessor.

The 'Octagon' was twice altered, the final phase (c.500–525) including construction of an imposing facade approached at right-angles from the via Egnatia by means of a colonnaded way. The church by now was part of a much larger ecclesiastical complex of the kind also found at NEA ANCHIALOS. Immediately to the north was a baptistery and beyond that a bath-building. The block to the east is filled by a large and sumptuously decorated building (wall-paintings and mosaics), identified as the **bishop's palace** [15].

Thasos (Figs. 170–172) ★

There is a ferry service from Kavala to Prino, on the north-west coast of the island. Hydrofoils run between Kavala and Limenas in the summer. Limenas is also served by ferries from Keramoti, 44 km. east of Kavala.

Special Features

Thasos is an extremely attractive island, rugged and still quite densely forested. The main town, Limenas or Thasos, is on the site of the ancient city.

History

Colonists from Paros settled on the island early in the C7 BC. They were led by Telesikles, the father of Archilochos who described Thasos in one of his poems as 'like the spine of a donkey, wreathed in unkempt forest, not a beautiful or lovely place'. The Parians must have been more interested in the mineral resources of the island which were first exploited in the Palaeolithic period. Colonies on the Thracian coast also brought the mines of Mt Pangaion under their control. In 465 BC Thasos was attacked by ATHENS. After a two-year siege the Thasians surrendered. The fortifications, which had been constructed early in the C5, were demolished, the Thasians' fleet was seized and also their territory on the mainland. The island was impoverished and did not recover until the C4 when the fortifications were rebuilt and the agora was replanned. Although revenue from the mines had decreased, local wines were widely exported. The numerous kiln sites in which transport amphorae were produced underline the scale of the wine trade. Thasian marble and timber were also in demand. The island was treated well by the Romans and benefited from the traffic between Constantinople and THESSALONIKI under the later empire.

420 **Macedonia**

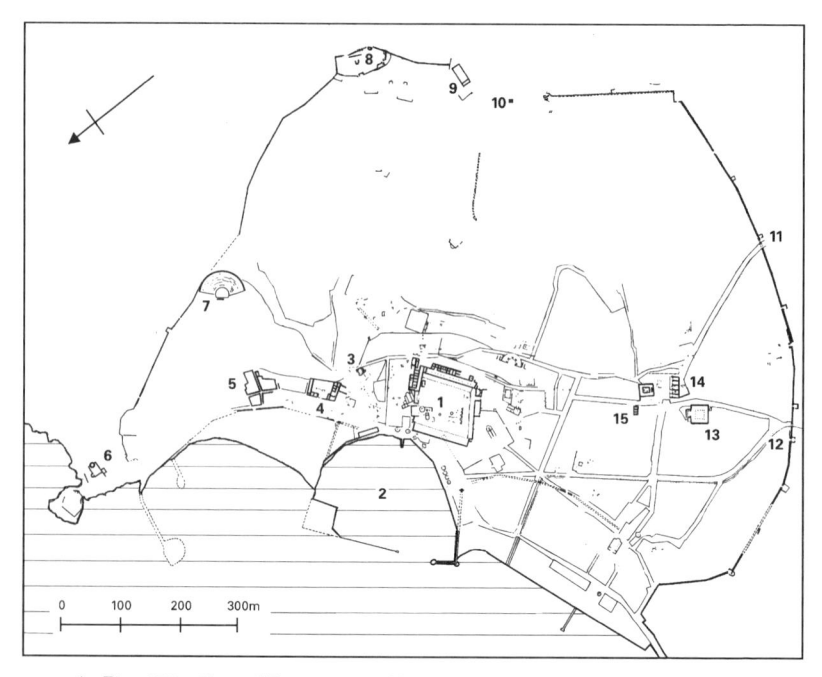

▲ Fig. 170. Plan of Thasos town. Key: 1 Agora 2 Closed harbour 3 Sanctuary of Dionysos 4 Sanctuary of Poseidon 5 Dimitriadis quarter 6 Sanctuary 7 Theatre 8 Medieval fortress 9 Sanctuary of Athena 10 Shrine of Pan 11 Gate of the Silen 12 Gate of Zeus and Hera 13 Monument of Thersilochos 14 Sanctuary of Herakles 15 Arch of Caracalla

Description

As the **museum** is closed for renovation, we begin our tour of the monuments of Thasos in the adjacent **agora** ([1]separate plan, Fig. 171) which is one of the best-preserved agora complexes in Greece. The main entrance from the ancient harbour was through a Doric **propylon** [**171.1**] in the western corner of the square. The **north-west stoa** [**171.2**] was built early in the C3 BC and closed off one side of the agora. It had a portico of 35 Doric columns but there was no interior colonnade and the roof must have been supported on massive timbers. The **peristyle court** [**171.3**] behind the stoa (not on the plan) is Roman. Gods and heroes had shrines in the centre of the agora which was as much a focus for sacred as secular activities. The **Sanctuary of Theagenes** [**171.4**] was built in honour of one of the most famous Greek athletes who won the pankration—the most brutal of the contact sports—at the Olympics in 480 and 476 BC, as well as numerous other prizes. Pausanias (6.11) relates several anecdotes about him:

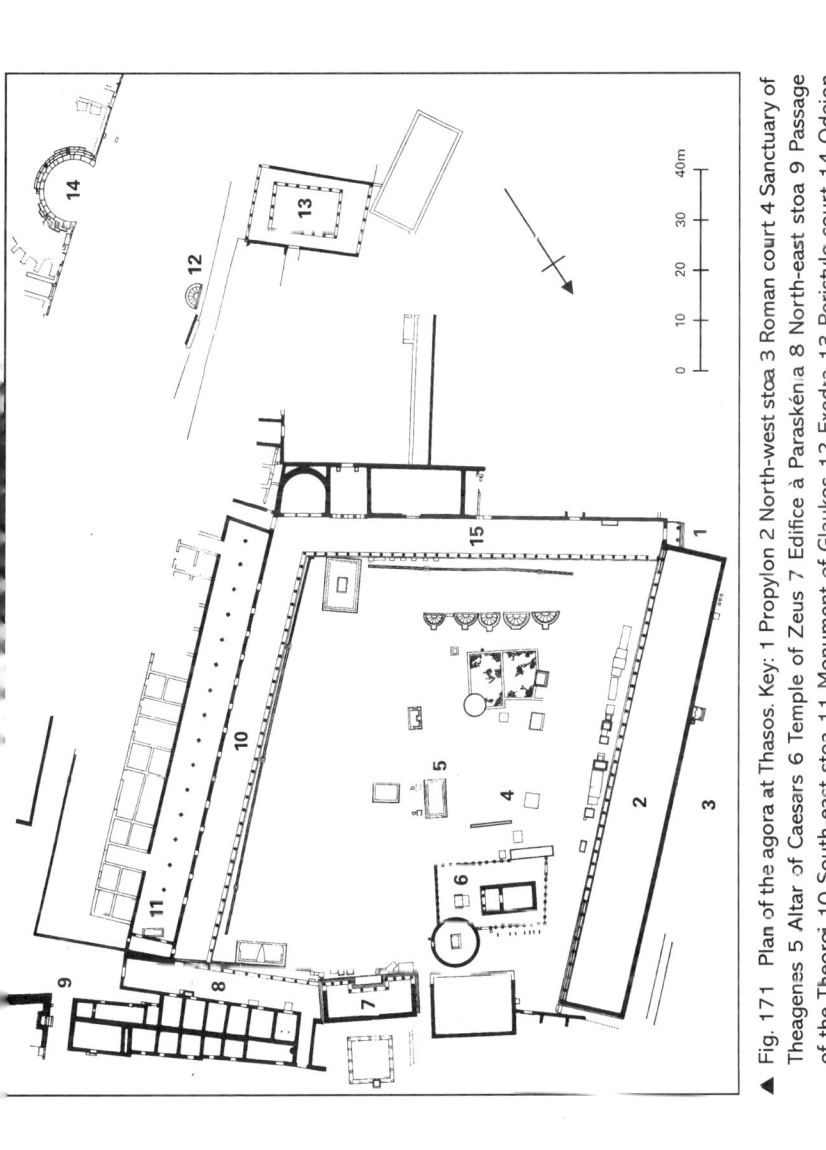

▲ Fig. 171 Plan of the agora at Thasos. Key: 1 Propylon 2 North-west stoa 3 Roman court 4 Sanctuary of Theagenes 5 Altar of Caesars 6 Temple of Zeus 7 Edifice à Paraskénia 8 North-east stoa 9 Passage of the Theoroi 10 South-east stoa 11 Monument of Glaukos 12 Exedra 13 Peristyle court 14 Odeion 15 South-west stoa

They say that when the boy was nine years old he was on his way home from school one day and pulled up a bronze statue that he liked of some god that was dedicated in the agora and carried it home with him over one shoulder. The people were furious at this behaviour, but there was some distinguished citizen of advanced age who would not let them put the boy to death, but ordered him to carry the statue back to the agora from his house. The boy did this and became famous for his strength, and what he had done was gossiped about all over Greece … When he died, someone who hated him in his lifetime came every night to Theagenes' statue to flog the bronze as if he were beating up Theagenes himself: the statue fell on him and put an end to his impertinence, but as he was killed his sons prosecuted the statue for murder, and the Thasians took the opinion of Drakon, who rules in the Athenian murder laws that even inanimate objects which fall on a man and kill him must be taken outside the boundaries, and so they drowned Theagenes' statue in the sea.

The statue, which was subsequently recovered from the sea, must have stood on the circular marble base to which an iron ring was attached so that sacrificial victims could not escape their grim fate. The **altar of Gaius and Lucius Caesar** [171.5] honoured the grandsons and erstwhile heirs of Augustus. In the corner of the square there was a **temple of Zeus Agoraios** [171.6]. Lists of officials were inscribed on the walls of the **Edifice à Paraskénia** [171.7], which recalls the Stoa of Zeus in the agora at Athens. A rich benefactor built the shops behind the adjacent **north-east stoa** [171.8].

Beyond the stoa is the **passage of the Theoroi** [171.9], who supervised the religious affairs of the city and had their names recorded here. The passage leads to an area in which a massive circular well of the C5 BC and an early Christian house have been excavated. The **south-east stoa** [171.10] was built in the C1 AD. The portico of 31 Doric columns provided an attractive facade for a spacious gallery at the northern end of which is the C7 funerary **monument of Glaukos** [171.11]. He was one of the colonists from Paros and is mentioned in a number of poems by Archilochos. South-east of the agora a section of the main street has been uncovered. This passes an **exedra** [171.12] and then a **peristyle court** [171.13] of the C2 AD which was once paved with 100 marble flagstones. A path leads to the **odeion** [171.14] which is also Roman and has three rows of marble seats still in situ. The **south-west stoa** [171.15], built in the C1 AD, completes the circuit of the agora.

When you leave the agora, make your way down to the harbour—the **closed harbour** [2] of the ancient city—turn right and then take the first road on the right. In order to follow the tour of the walls you should immediately turn left by the Patrikos Taverna, but you may wish to go straight ahead to the **Sanctuary of Dionysos** [3]. The temple has not been excavated but there is a fine choregic monument of the C3 BC. Nine statues occupied the semi-circular base with Dionysos in the centre, flanked by personifications of theatrical art forms, such as Tragedy and Comedy. The road which leads to the walls first passes the **Sanctuary of Poseidon** [4], conveniently situated beside the two harbours. Next on the right is the **Dimitriadis quarter** [5], four blocks of the ancient city which were laid out in the C6 BC and then developed and redeveloped over a period of nine centuries. On the left is a section of the fortifications and one of the harbour gates. Eventually you will reach a vantage point above the **sanctuary** [6], a church built on the ruins of an early Christian basilica which occupies the site of an Archaic sanctuary. There is a fine view of the island of Thasopoula.

Now turn right and follow the footpath which runs outside the **fortifications**, constructed early in the C5, destroyed by the Athenians and then rebuilt in the C4 BC. Blocks of gneiss were used for the inner face but the outer face is of marble, an extravagance even if it was quarried locally. The **theatre** [7] is closed for reconstruction but can be seen quite well from the fence. The proskenion is Hellenistic but the skene dates from the C2 AD when the orchestra was converted into an arena for animal combats and gladiatorial displays. The stone seats were also installed at this time.

The footpath is now marked by a line of lamps. On the akropolis there was a sanctuary of Pythian Apollo. This was dismantled and the masonry reused in the construction of the **medieval fortress** [8] in the C13 AD. The Genoese rebuilt the fortress in the C15 and were also responsible for the church and the cistern in the interior. The path continues across the summit of the akropolis to the **Sanctuary of Athena** [9] who was worshipped as 'Poliouchos', guardian of the city, so it was appropriate that she could see and be seen by her devotees. The temple, which was built in the early C5 BC and replaced a C6 predecessor, had a porch, cella, and opisthodomos but no peristyle. The altar was evidently at the western end of the temple. The path resumes and passes a rock-cut **shrine of Pan** [10] who is depicted with his pipes.

From the top of the ridge there is a steep flight of steps. The path runs outside the walls as far as the gate of Parmenon and then descends through fields and houses. You can follow the line of the fortifications again from the **gate of the Silen** [11]. A number of the gates have sculptured reliefs and this is one of the best preserved. Silens or satyrs were the companions of Dionysos and shared his enthusiasm for wine, so Thasos must have been one of their favourite haunts. This silen has his kantharos ready and certainly seems well pleased. The footpath, marked by a sign and by lamps, resumes along the outside of the walls, constructed in fine ashlar masonry. The **gate of Zeus and Hera** [12] has a relief of Hera and Iris, the messenger goddess. On the other side of the gate there was a relief of Zeus and Hermes. Now follow the road which runs into the town. On the left and currently used as a depot for sarcophagi is the **monument of Thersilochos** [13]. Just beyond this is

▲ Fig. 172. The Gate of the Silen at Thasos

the **Sanctuary of Herakles** [14]. At the southern end of the site there is a temple of the C6 BC incorporated in the row of five rooms where officials dined when the Herakleia, the great festival of Herakles, was celebrated. The altar is in the centre of the sanctuary, across a paved court which also served the C5 temple of Herakles. Finally you pass the **arch of Caracalla** [15], four massive piers which supported three arches. The inscription honours the emperor Caracalla who visited Thasos in AD 213–217 but it appears that the arch had been constructed some time before and was simply rededicated.

Aliki (Figs. 173–175) ★

If you would like an excursion on Thasos, we recommend that you take the road which runs around the eastern side of the island, through woods of plane and pine trees, to Aliki which is approximately 32 km. from Thasos town. As the road passes above Aliki, there is a dirt track, marked by a yellow sign. Follow this and you will come to the Archaeological Area of Alyki on your left.

Description

A stone path takes you past an enormous Roman sarcophagus. This has an inscription on one side and there is an incised graffito of a merchant ship on the end. Continue along the path and you will reach the **sanctuary**. This consists of two structures which differ in size but have the same layout—a portico of five columns and two rooms. As there is an altar in one of the rooms, the structures were presumably temples. The north temple dates from the middle of the C6 BC and originally had an Ionic portico which was partially replaced by Doric columns at the end of the Archaic period. Of particular interest are the erotic and mainly pederastic graffiti carved on the threshold of the porch (see **box**). On the large base (*IG* 12.8.581—C2 AD) two shipowners, one the president of a merchants' association (*archikerdemporos*), have had inscribed a prayer for 'fair sailing' (*euplea*) for 'the lucky *Herakles* of Thessalonike', perhaps a vessel carrying Aliki marble. The south temple was built *c.*500 BC and had Doric columns. The cave in the rocks on the edge of the sanctuary was also a focus for cult activity.

Above the sanctuary you will find its spiritual successors, two early Christian **basilicas** and their associated cemetery. Although Thasian marble was readily available for the construction of the basilicas, the stone for some of the columns was evidently imported and it would seem that Aliki was still a wealthy community in the C6 AD.

The source of this wealth will become apparent if you follow the network of paths which runs the length of the wooded headland. Keep to the seaward side and you will soon see the **quarries** from which marble was extracted throughout antiquity. The Romans were certainly keen customers. Seneca, in 'O tempora, O mores' mode,

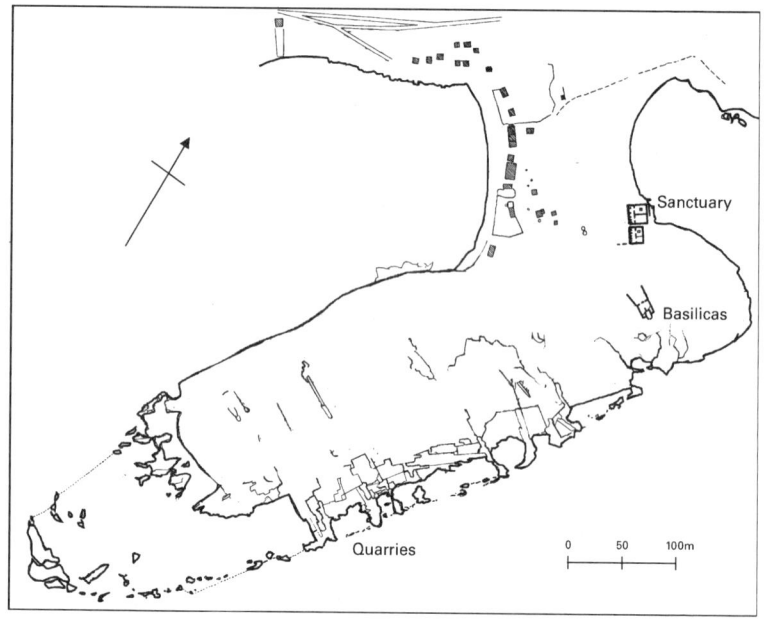

▲ Fig. 173. Plan of Aliki

ΣΙΜΟΣ
ΚΑΛΟΣ
ΓΚΑΡΔΙ

▲ Fig. 174. Inscription from the sanctuary at Aliki

comments (*Ad Lucilium Epistulae Morales* 86.6): 'we think ourselves poor . . . if our pools are not lined with Thasian marble'. The techniques used to remove the blocks of stone can best be appreciated in the series of artificial 'bays' along the shoreline, the tool marks still clearly visible. The far end of the headland has been quarried flat and it would have been relatively easy to load the blocks of marble onto ships.

If, at the end of your tour, you feel in need of revitalization, you can swim in the crystal-clear waters of the bay. There is also a convenient row of tavernas along the sandy beach.

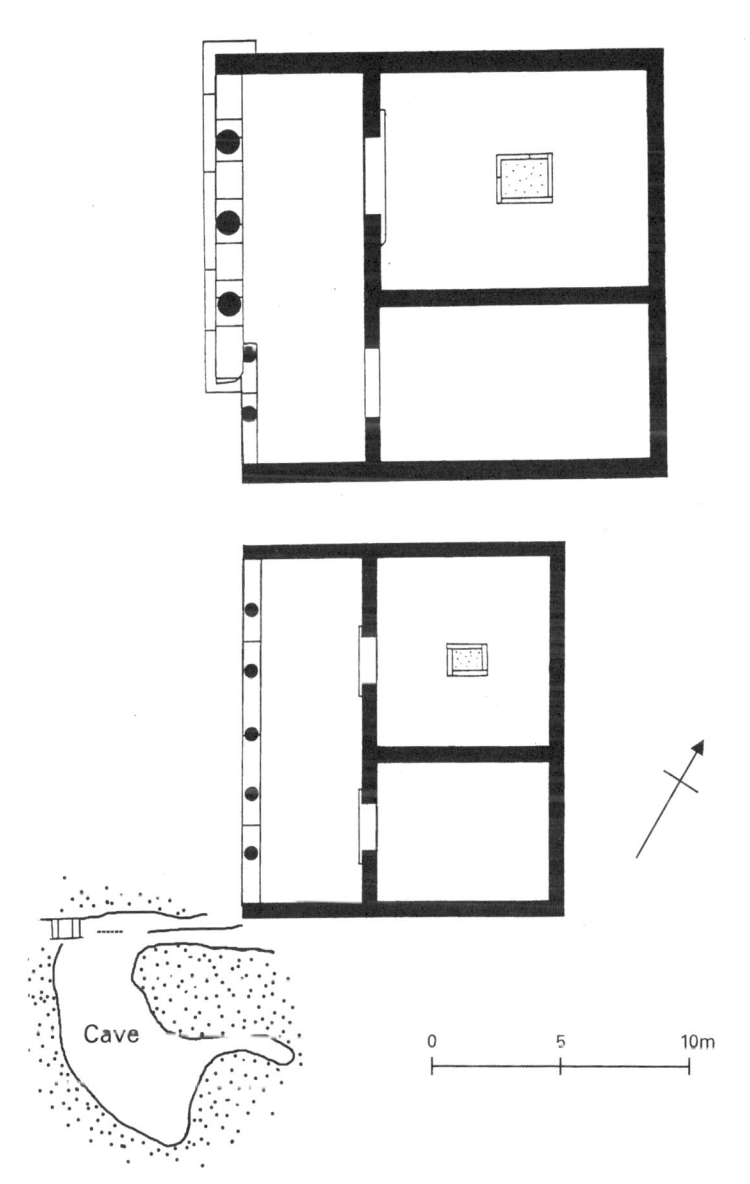

▲ Fig. 175. Plan of the sanctuary at Aliki

> ### Erotic graffiti
>
> Most of the graffiti in the porch are of a common type, acclaiming the beauty of a young man or, less often, woman, in the form of a name followed by ΚΑΛΟΣ or (feminine) ΚΑΛΗ: 'so-and-so (is) beautiful'. Two of them give the admired person's home town (both also ports). The 'truly beautiful' Nikoboule lived in Ephesos, the 'handsome' Simos in Kardia which is on the Sea of Marmara. Another appears to deliver an insult: 'Dorymenes is happy, he's being screwed' (*Dorumenes chairei pugizetai*). The idle but well-travelled hands perhaps belong to mariners or quarry workers.

Pella (Fig. 176)

The site is on the main road between Thessaloniki and Edessa.

Special Features

In Roman times the ruins of Pella were a byword for the demise of Macedonian greatness but it is still possible to gain an impression of the stupendous scale and luxury of this royal capital, much of which was paid for ultimately by the spoils of conquest.

History

Pella is mentioned by Herodotus (7.123) and Thucydides (2.99.4) but was an insignificant city until Archelaos moved the Macedonian capital here in the late C5 BC. He built a splendid palace which was mocked by Aelian (*Varia Historia* 14.17):

Socrates used to say that Archelaos spent 40,000 drachmas on his palace, hiring Zeuxis of Herakleia to decorate it, but nothing on himself. Consequently people arrived from far away, eager to see the palace, but Archelaos himself could not induce anyone to come to Macedonia unless he had bribed them.

Nevertheless Archelaos entertained some illustrious guests, in particular Euripides who wrote the *Bacchae* here. By the C4 Pella had become 'the greatest city in Macedonia'. This is where Alexander was born in 356 BC and the city also flourished under Antigonos Gonatas in the C3.

After he had defeated the Macedonian forces at the battle of Pydna in 168 BC, Aemilius Paulus encamped just outside Pella. Livy (44.46) tells us that 'he examined the site of the city on every side and noted that it had not been chosen as the capital without good reason. It was situated on a hill which sloped to the south-west and was surrounded by marshes'. These have since been drained but were formed when the bay of THESSALONIKI silted up. Under the Romans Pella was refounded as a minor colony, overshadowed by Thessalonike, and may have been devastated by an earthquake in the C1. Dio of Prusa (*33rd Oration, First Tarsic* 26) remarks in rhetorical vein that:

when the good things of the Persians came into the possession [of the Macedonians], the bad things followed in their train. Accordingly both sceptre and royal purple and Median cookery and their race itself came to an end, so that today, if you should pass through Pella, you would see no sign of a city at all, apart from the presence of a mass of pottery on the site.

Description

We suggest that you start in the **museum** [1]. The cases on the right in the first room contain finds from the Neolithic and Early Bronze Age settlement at Mandalo, which is north-east of Pella, and other prehistoric sites in the region. Part of the painted plaster decoration from one of the Hellenistic houses at Pella has been restored—as is often the case in this period, it imitates blocks or panels of coloured stone. There is an aerial photograph of the site and a plan of the ancient city. The coin hoards, metal attachments from doors and beds, figurines, and pottery in the cases in the recess come from the houses. On display in the second room there is 'West Slope' pottery, which was made locally and sold in the agora, also terracotta moulds for relief bowls and figurines. Dedications from sanctuaries and cemeteries include a Classical grave stele, a marble statue of Alexander as Pan, and gold jewellery. Some of the remarkable mosaics from Hellenistic houses at Pella can be seen in the third room. Like the mosaics at OLYNTHOS, they were made of pebbles in a limited range of colours. The technique is simple and yet extremely effective. Dionysos perched on his familiar panther is an elegant figure. Musculature is defined quite precisely by rows of grey pebbles. The dramatic Lion Hunt mosaic is much bolder in this respect and utilizes strips of lead for details, such as the faces and hair of the two hunters who may be Alexander and his friend Krateros—a dedication at DELPHI commemorated the fact that Krateros saved Alexander from a lion in 332 BC.

The plan of the ancient city is laid out on a grid in the typical manner of Greek planned settlements (see OLYNTHOS). The streets intersect at right angles and form rectangular blocks. The main street, 15 m. wide, ran through the centre of the agora which occupies ten blocks. South of the agora, across the road from the museum, several houses have been excavated. On the left is the **House of the Abduction of Helen** [2]. The eponymous mosaic is in the centre room on the north side of the court. On this occasion it is Theseus who has seized Helen. She stretches out her arms in desperation to her friend Dianeira but Theseus

430 Macedonia

1 Museum
2 House of the Abduction of Helen
3 House of Dionysos
4 Agora
5 Sanctuary of Aphrodite and Cybele
6 Palace

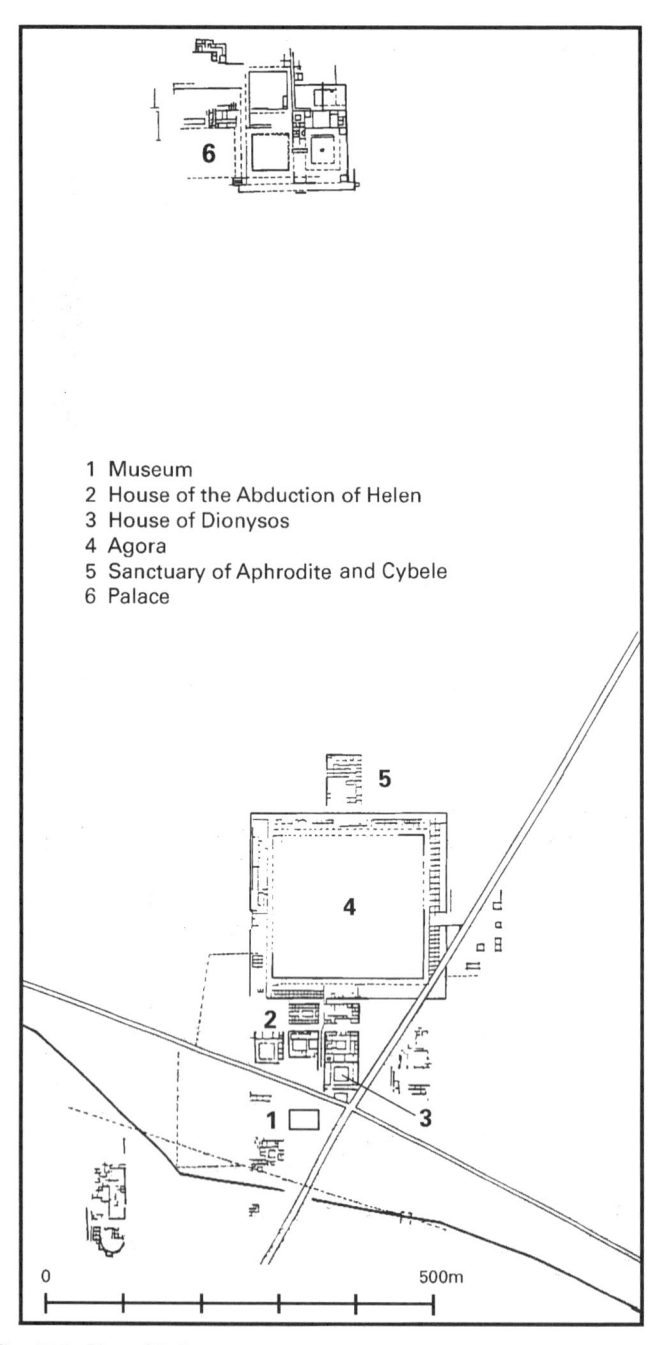

Fig. 176. Plan of Pella

has his chariot ready for a quick escape. The mosaic in the next room is better preserved. The Stag Hunt, signed by one Gnosis, is a more ambitious composition than the Lion Hunt and has a particularly splendid acanthus border. There is a mosaic in situ in one of the rooms on the east side of the court. This depicts the battle between the Greeks and the Amazons.

The **House of Dionysos** [3], built in the last quarter of the C4 BC, is an impressive reminder of the extravagant lifestyle which some of the citizens of Pella could once afford. Guests were evidently entertained in the rooms around the larger of the two peristyle courts which have mosaic floors. The Dionysos and Lion Hunt mosaics came from adjacent androns on the west side of the court. Some of the Ionic columns in the north court have been restored. It would seem that this end of the house was the more private women's quarters.

The **agora** [4] stretches north of the houses. Walk around the perimeter and you will appreciate the sheer scale of Pella. This was a royal capital, comparable with cities such as Pergamon and Alexandria. The rooms on the east side of the agora were occupied by craftsmen who made terracotta figurines and pottery. The wells in these rooms were full of industrial waste and there is a kiln in the north-east corner of the square. City officials had offices at the north end of the agora and perfume was sold in some of the shops on the west side. North of the agora is the **Sanctuary of Aphrodite and Cybele** [5]. The temple is in the centre of the complex which contains storerooms and a cistern.

The **palace** [6] is situated on the brow of the hill and dominates the city below. The site is fenced and may not be open. Take the road opposite the museum, turn left at the sign ΑΝΑΚΤΟΡΟ ΠΕΛΛΑΣ, left again at the sign for the palace, and finally left once more at another sign. The palace consisted of a series of enormous peristyle courts around which suites of public and private rooms were arranged. It is difficult to appreciate that this was once one of the great royal palaces of Hellenistic Greece but, even if the remains do not appear particularly impressive, the size of the complex certainly is.

Lefkadia (Fig. 177)

Just beyond the turn to the village of Lefkadia, if you have come from Edessa, there is a road on the left which is signed To The Two Macedonian Tombs. Follow this until you cross the railway line and you will soon see the ochre-coloured shed which protects the Tomb of the Judgement.

Special Features

The painted decoration on the 'Macedonian' tombs at Lefkadia is superb and exceptionally important because so few paintings of such high quality have survived.

History

It is thought that Lefkadia may have been the site of ancient Mieza. Aristotle taught Alexander here, in a sanctuary of the nymphs. Plutarch (*Alexander* 7) tells us that:

> Philip, seeing that his son could not be made to do anything by force, used always to manage him by persuasion, and never gave him orders. As he did not altogether care to entrust his education to the teachers whom he had obtained, but thought that it would be too difficult a task for them, since Alexander required, as Sophocles says of a ship, 'stout ropes to check him and stout oars to guide', he sent for Aristotle, the most renowned philosopher of the age, to be his son's tutor, and paid him a handsome reward for doing so. For Alexander and Aristotle he appointed the temple and grove of the nymphs near the city of Mieza, as a schoolhouse and domicile. And there to this day are shown the stone seat where Aristotle sat, and the shady avenues where he used to walk. It is thought that Alexander was taught by him not only his doctrines of morals and politics, but also those more abstruse mysteries which are only communicated orally and are kept concealed from the vulgar.

A C4 BC stoa at Isvoria, just below Naousa, has been tentatively identified as the nymphaion in which Aristotle met his pupils. The centre of Mieza was presumably between Kopanos and Lefkadia where a Hellenistic theatre has been excavated.

Description

The **Tomb of the Judgement** [1] was closed for restoration in 1997 but should reopen in due course. It was built in the last quarter of the C4 BC and has a massive painted facade, 8.60 m. high. Behind this there is an antechamber and the barrel-vaulted chamber. Like most 'Macedonian' tombs (see p. 438) it was covered by an earth tumulus but had nevertheless been looted. The decoration in the antechamber and the chamber is relatively simple, whereas the facade, finished in stucco on poros limestone, is extremely ornate. The door is flanked by engaged Doric columns and there is a figure painted in each of the four panels. The warrior on the left must be the dead man, although he is not identified. Hermes, who escorted the souls of the dead to Hades, beckons to him from the next panel. Aiakos and Rhadamanthys, two of the judges of the underworld, contemplate their verdict. Above the columns there is an architrave and a Doric frieze of metopes and triglyphs. The Lapiths and Centaurs on the metopes have been cleverly painted so that they seem carved. Each of the figures is blocked out by black or violet washes in a *trompe-l'oeil* technique which mimics relief sculpture. The next frieze is continuous, Ionic rather than Doric. A battle between Greeks and orientals, presumably Macedonians and Persians, is depicted. In this case the figures were modelled in stucco and then painted. The upper section of

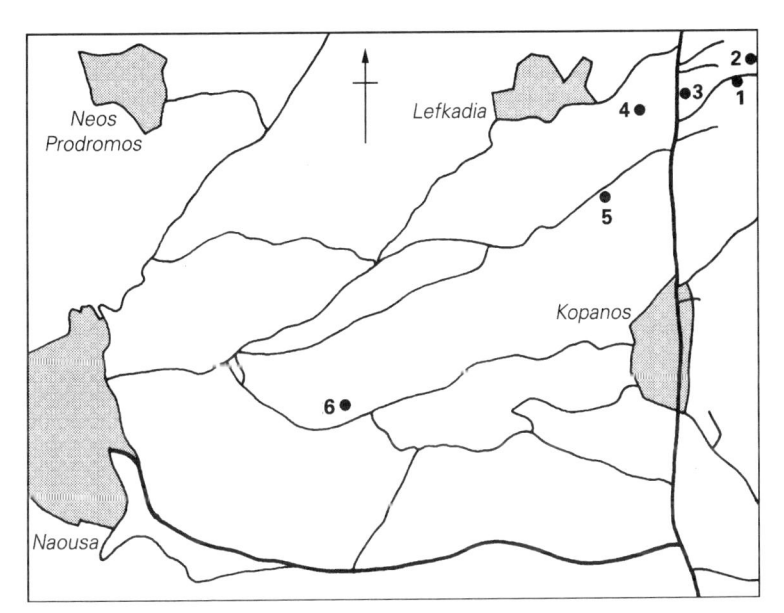

▲ Fig. 177. Plan of the area around Lefkadia. Key: 1 Tomb of the Judgement 2 Tomb of the Palmettes 3 Kinch tomb 4 Tomb of Lyson and Kallikles 5 Theatre at Belovina 6 Nymphaion at Isvoria

the facade consists of seven false doors separated by Ionic columns and a pediment, once painted. In certain respects the facade resembles a temple and so the tomb might have been conceived as a heroon. Alternatively it could be the facade of a sumptuous residence.

The second tomb, known as the **Tomb of the Palmettes** [**2**], will be opened for you by the guard and certainly merits a visit. It was built in the first half of the C3 BC and had evidently been robbed in antiquity. The tomb is entered through a central door framed by Ionic half-columns. Above the columns there is a narrow architrave, a frieze of painted palmettes and a row of dentils. A man and a woman recline, as at a banquet, in the pediment. Palmettes crown the apex and corners of the pediment. There is the most wonderful frieze of palmettes and water-lilies painted on the ceiling of the antechamber. Pausias, a C4 painter, apparently specialized in this type of composition. The splendid marble doors which sealed the chamber have fallen on the floor. The painted decoration in the chamber is more austere. A bench on the left faces the stone chest in which the cremated remains of the dead were interred.

When you return to the main road, there is a third tomb approximately 200 m. on the right. This is the so called **Kinch tomb** [**3**] which is also dated 300–250 BC. It may not be open but you can see the Doric facade from the fence. A battle scene was painted on the walls of the chamber.

The fourth tomb, of **Lyson and Kallikles** [4], is 500 m. down the dirt road on the left, just before the turn for Lefkadia. It is kept locked. Four generations of the same family were buried in the tomb in the C2 BC. Their ashes were placed in niches in the chamber. Each of the niches has an inscription which records the name of the dead person. The swords, shields, helmets and armour painted on the walls suggest a military family.

Veroia

Beroia (the ancient spelling) was the second city of Macedonia. St Paul came here in AD 49–50, after he fled from THESSALONIKI. Some traces of the ancient city can be seen, in particular a paved Roman road which runs along one of the main streets, Odos Mitropoleos, and has recently been landscaped.

The **Archaeological Museum**, on Odos Anixeos, has a plan of Veroia which marks the ancient sites. There have been quite a number of rescue excavations in the centre of the city which often result in the discovery of graves and one of the cases contains fine Classical and Hellenistic funerary offerings. In the second room there is Hellenistic sculpture from Veroia and VERGINA, also inscriptions which include the C2 BC Law for the Gymnasiarchs, the only known document of its type. It lays down the duties of the magistrate in charge of the city gymnasium and the youths who trained there. The job was no sinecure, and we learn that the incumbent was liable to both physical assault in office and, out of it, prosecution for misconduct. Some of the Roman sculpture in the third room is impressive and there is more sculpture in the garden of the museum.

Vergina (ancient Aigai) (Figs. 178–179)

The sites which we describe—palace, theatre, Macedonian tomb, and the great tumulus with its royal tombs—are either in or near the modern village of Vergina. As you enter the village from the main road the royal tombs are signed almost immediately. But we recommend that you first pass through the village to the palace (signed ANAKTORO/Palace), with its splendid view, which will give you a good feel for the terrain.

Special Features

The Royal Mound in Vergina is Greece's answer to the Tomb of Tutankhamun. The spetacular finds from the 'Tomb of Philip II' are on display here.

History

Since the discovery of unlooted royal tombs in 1977 and 1978, the modern village of Vergina has been securely identified with the ancient city of Aigai, burial-place of the Macedonian kings, named from the goats (*aiges*) which still abound here. The site is scenically located on rising ground below the Pierian mountains, looking out onto the modern plain, in ancient times a marshy inlet of the sea. Although Aigai declined in administrative importance after the foundation of PELLA *c*.400 BC, it remained a royal centre. In 336 BC Philip II was assassinated in the theatre here while celebrating his daughter's wedding 'with lavish musical competitions and brilliant banquets for friends and foreign guests' (Diodorus Siculus 16.91.5). Aigai's continuing importance is shown by the building of a new royal palace here, probably *c*.300 BC. In 274 BC some of the royal tombs were plundered by the Gauls, 'a people with an insatiable appetite for treasure, who dug up the tombs of the kings buried there, snatching the treasure and insolently scattering the bones' (Plutarch, *Pyrrhos* 25.6). The Romans damaged the city in 168 BC after their defeat of King Perseus.

Description

The **palace** is built on a terrace above the ancient city and the plain. It is of exceptional interest as Greece's only well-preserved royal palace, as well as being one of the largest buildings known from ancient Greece (105 by 89 m.). The date is not settled, but the roof-tiles and other architectural elements seem to favour construction *c*.300 BC, under King Cassander.

The modern visitor, like the ancient, enters through a monumental two-storey porch 10 m. wide, flanked by Doric colonnades, and possibly used for giving audiences. The main palace consists of a large colonnaded courtyard, originally perhaps a garden, surrounded by rooms on all four sides. The north range gave onto a large terrace enclosed by balustrades, overlooking the theatre. A smaller colonnaded courtyard to the west was added later, perhaps as a service area (or are these the women's quarters?). The palace was mainly built in mudbrick resting on a course of large blocks (orthostates) of local stone, with marble reserved for the thresholds.

At least nine of the rooms off the courtyard can be identified as banqueting rooms by the presence of drains, off-centre doorways, and raised bands around the walls for the couches of the reclining diners. Two of these dining rooms on the south side, one with an elaborate pebble mosaic, now covered up, were linked by a shared vestibule, and seem to have been of special importance. On one calculation, these rooms together could seat as many as 278 guests, making the palace in essence a gigantic dispenser of royal hospitality (as in 336 BC, although Philip presumably used an earlier palace, yet to be found).

On the east side, the floor of the circular room or tholos yielded an inscribed dedication 'For Ancestral Herakles', the heroic forefather

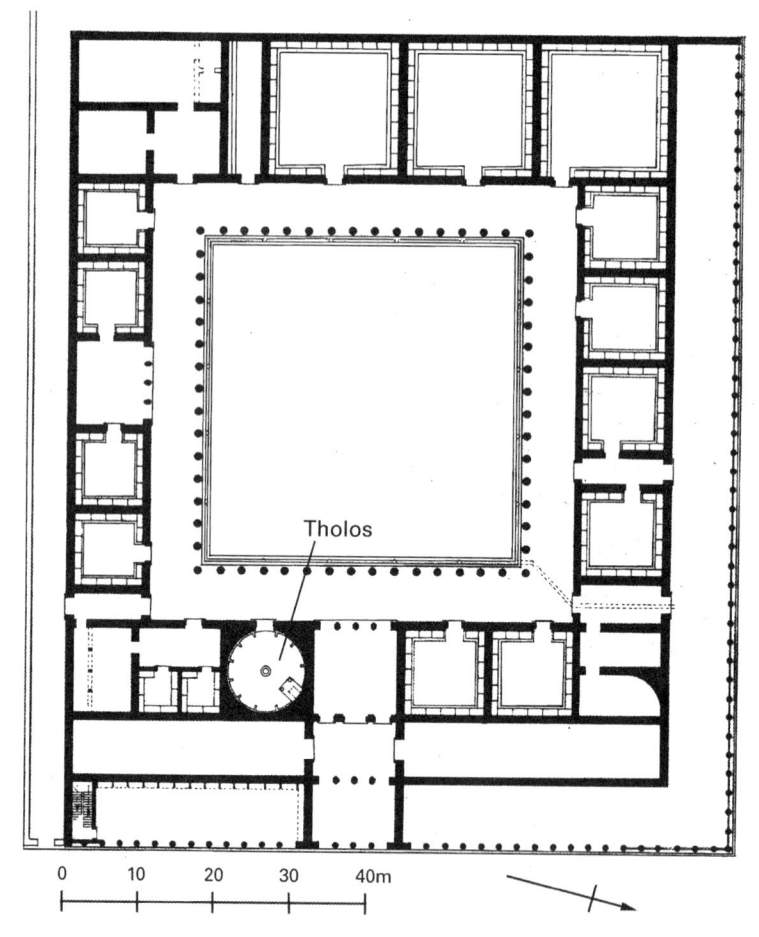

▲ Fig. 178. Plan of the palace at Vergina

of the Macedonian kings. The room is variously interpreted as a throne-room, dining area for seated guests, or shrine.

The small **theatre** below is reached by the dirt path to the left of the modern site entrance. Dated to the C4 BC, it makes a single architectural unit with the later palace above. Only the first row of stone seats remains visible. Presumably it is the theatre in which Philip II was dramatically assassinated (336 BC) by a courtier with a grudge—in full view of the astounded audience (see **box**).

Returning to the village, the '**Macedonian tomb**' (also known as 'Romaios' Tomb', from its Greek excavator) is worth a visit. It was robbed in antiquity and so is hard to date: c.300–250 BC may be about right. It comprises a paved passage descending to a tomb built of lime-

▲ Fig. 179. Macedonian tomb at Vergina

stone blocks. The temple-like facade is coated in stucco, with a painted floral frieze. Once closed with marble doors, the vaulted interior features a marble throne and footstool. Another **'Macedonian' tomb** nearby to the east (closed to the public), firmly dated to the 340s BC, has produced a similar throne, here preserving a superbly painted back. The occupant of this earlier tomb, a female, may have been Eurydike, Philip II's mother.

The climax is the visit to the great tumulus, covering three **royal tombs** of C4 BC date, including the two usually identified as those of Philip II and his grandson, Alexander IV (died 310 BC). Their discovery in 1977 and 1978 by Greek archaeologist Manolis Andronikos caused an international sensation. The excavations stripped away most of the huge ancient mound covering them, once over 12 m. high. This has since been recreated, and the visitor descends beneath it into a large underground hall equipped with information panels and helpful models. The spectacular finds from both tombs are now on display in the hall. The hall incorporates Tomb 1, the so-called 'Tomb of Persephone' (about 350 BC), viewable from its outside only. This tomb, a rectangular chamber roofed with stone slabs, had been robbed in ancient times. The jumbled bone-remains suggested a triple burial of a male adult, usually identified as Amyntas III (died 370/69 BC), an adult female, and a newly born baby. The tomb is remarkable for its superb wall-painting of the god Hades abducting the goddess Persephone in his chariot, a rare example of C4 BC Greek wall-painting of the highest artistry.

> ### 'Macedonian' tombs
>
> A new type of tomb suddenly appeared in Macedonia c.350–300 BC, ahead of other Greek architecture in its design. About fifty of these so-called 'Macedonian' tombs are now known. They are all underground, their centrepiece a burial chamber roofed with a stone barrel vault, the walls held in place by an earth mound heaped over the whole structure. The more elaborate ones, as at Vergina and LEFKADIA, have temple-like facades rendered in painted plaster, with a central marble door. In some later ones there are stone couches set along the wall (as in the THESSALONIKI and KAVALA museums). These tombs were the first Greek structures to put to use the revolutionary idea of the barrel vault. Their design reflects the need felt by Macedon's kings, followed by the military elite, for a type of monumental burial in keeping both with the traditional regional preference for underground tombs (perhaps a safeguard against barbarian raiders), and with their elevated status. The dining couches, probably symbolic, recall the depiction of dead 'heroes' in Greek art as banqueters, and suggest a posthumous hero-cult for the deceased.

Two dimly lit stairways allow close-up inspection (behind glass) of the impressive facades of the two remaining tombs, both of the monumental 'Macedonian' type (see **box**). Tomb 2, the so-called Tomb of Philip, comprises a vaulted chamber divided into two rooms connected by a marble door. In the innermost room was found a large gold casket containing the cremated bones of a middle-aged male, usually identified as Philip II (see **box**), accompanied by rich grave offerings, mainly gold and silver drinking equipment and arms and armour. The outer room housed a second burial, another cremation in a (smaller) gold casket, this time of a young woman, usually assumed to be Cleopatra, Philip's last wife.

The identity of the occupant of Tomb 2 is controversial, but the case for Philip II is based on compelling forensic evidence. Philip died aged 46, and the skeletal remains are those of a male in the 35–55 age-range. Examination of the cremated skull by a British team, including two surgeon specialists, revealed an old injury, serious enough to have blinded the right eye. This matches one of Philip's known battle wounds, an eye lost to an enemy arrow eighteen years before his death.

The architectural facade, which is all the visitor can see, has well-preserved architectural paintwork. But it is mainly remarkable for the painted frieze running across its whole width above the band of Doric triglyphs and metopes. The pitted surface reveals a hunting scene, its focus the killing of a lion (right of centre), which is about to be speared by an intent young rider in pink, approaching from the left. The

The assassination of Philip II

'The theatre had filled up when Philip himself appeared wearing a white cloak.' With these words the Greek historian Diodorus Siculus introduced his tabloid account of Philip's murder at Aigai in 336 BC.

The murderer, one Pausanias, was a handsome bodyguard of the king and his one-time lover. A while back, thinking himself spurned by Philip in favour of another man, Pausanias had mocked his rival as effeminate and an easy lay, provoking him to the extreme course of proving his manly honour by a glorious death in battle. The rival was fittingly avenged by an influential friend, a kinsman of Philip, who got the aristocratic Pausanias senselessly drunk and then handed his body over to menial mule-drivers for gang rape. Recovered, the outraged Pausanias sought redress from Philip. But the king was unwilling to act against his kinsman. Pausanias now nursed a bitter grievance against the royal lover who had failed to avenge him.

Finally came that day in the theatre at Aigai. Concealing a dagger in his clothes, 'he rushed up, stabbed the king right through the ribs and stretched him out dead.' Pausanias was promptly killed on the spot by the bodyguards.

excavator identified this figure as Alexander, who, like all Macedonian royalty, was an avid follower of the chase.

Tomb 3, also unlooted, is another two-roomed barrel vault with an architectural facade decorated with a pair of shields. In the innermost room the cremated bones of a young male were found inside a silver storage-jar dressed with a gold wreath. The grave offerings included silver plate and a pair of gilded greaves. The occupant is usually identified as the boy-king Alexander IV, Alexander's posthumous son by Roxane, his Iranian wife, murdered with his mother in 311 or 310 BC by Cassander, effective ruler of Macedonia at that time.

Dion (Figs. 180–182) ★

Dion is 6 km. off the Katerini–Larisa road.

Special Features

Excellent views of Mt Olympos can be had from this site, which is attractively laid out as an archaeological park with streams and trees. The museum is well worth a visit.

History

Dion commanded a rich agricultural plain and was a port, linked to the sea (then *c.*1 km. away) by a navigable river, the Baphyras. It derived its

> ### The Aitolian sack
>
> Skopas raised a general levy of the Aitolians, and after a march through Thessaly invaded Macedonia. He destroyed the grain crop throughout Pieria (the region around Dion), collected a great deal of plunder, then marched for Dion. The inhabitants having fled the place, he entered and destroyed the walls, the houses and the gymnasium. In addition he set fire to the colonnades around the sacred precinct of Zeus, and broke up all the other dedications which by their beauty or utility served those who came for the festivals. He also overturned all the statues of the kings. In this way, immediately on going to war and as his first deed, he not only declared war on men but on the gods.
>
> (Polybius 4.62.1–5)

name from the god Zeus (or Dis), whose throne was held to be the nearby Mt Olympos. Its sanctuary of Olympian Zeus was the 'national' shrine of the Macedonians, put on the map by Archelaos, who founded (*c.*400 BC) a Macedonian version of the Olympian games here, a festival of athletic and dramatic contests in honour of Zeus and the Nine Muses still celebrated in the C2 BC. Here the kings also celebrated their military victories and made dedications, such as the (lost) statue set up by Cassander (see below, museum). The most famous, a bronze group of Alexander the Great and 25 cavalrymen, erected to commemorate the victory at the Granikos (334 BC), was removed as booty to Rome (146 BC), where it was still on display in the early C5 AD. Under Cassander Dion received a regular city-plan and a defensive wall. In 219 BC the city and sanctuary were sacked by the Aitolian general Skopas, a sacrilege described by the C2 BC Greek historian Polybius (see **box**).

In 43 or 42 BC Dion became a Roman colony, receiving more Italian settlers under Augustus. The colony's language was Latin, although assimilation led in time to the reassertion of Dion's Greek character. The Roman city prospered to judge from its new public and private works. In the mid-C3 AD the destructive incursions of the Goths into Macedonia prompted a rebuilding of the city-wall, incorporating much reused stonework. Sometime after AD 364–367 new inner walls created a fortress, within which stood the main church of Christian Dion, seat of a bishopric first attested in AD 343. The city was plundered *c.* AD 472 and again in the C6 AD.

Description

Once in the modern village of Dion, it makes sense to start with a visit to the excellent **Archaeological Museum**. Notable finds include, on the ground floor, statues found in the Roman baths, such as the medical

> ### Footprints
>
> The inscribed slabs carved with footprints now in the museum were found in situ on the steps of the temple of Isis. Similar dedications of footprints were common in ancient shrines and usually meant one of two things. Sometimes they represent divine footprints and mark an appearance of the deity to the faithful. Elsewhere (as probably here) they were mementoes of where devotees had stood and adored the goddess. Two of these slabs were set up 'by order' of the goddess, who had probably appeared to the dedicators (one of them her priest) during ritual sleep in her sanctuary.

god Asklepios and his family (bathing was a form of therapy), and a superb portrait (early C3 AD) of a local worthy, Herennianus. Finds from the sanctuary of Isis include, as well as votive feet (see **box**), the headless cult-statue of Isis-Tyche on a three-times reused base, with an earlier Latin inscription (late C1 BC or early C1 AD) for a colonist, Herennia Prima, and the original dedication to Olympian Zeus by Cassander, 'King of the Macedonians' (*c.*300 BC). The cult-statue of Aphrodite 'worshipped at the feet of Mt Olympos' is a repair and rededication of an older statue (C2 BC) by a wealthy freed slave, Anthestia Jucunda, as a gift 'to the colonists'.

Upstairs is the important find of a unique water organ or *hydraulis* (C1 BC), its bronze pipes 'played' by means of pressurized air pumped through water into the box below. The instrument, invented by an Alexandrian engineer, Ktesibios (C3 BC), was popular in Roman times (it accompanied gladiators). Finds from the 'Villa of Dionysos' include a group of four seated 'philosophers', so called from their hand-held scrolls. One head sports the philosopher's long beard; the remaining two were reworked in the style of the early C3 AD and may be portraits.

The basement is arranged as an interactive study area for school parties. There are informative sections on the sanitation and water supply of Roman Dion, as well as a model of the 'Villa of Dionysos'.

The entrance to the **site** is several hundred metres away near the Greek **theatre** ([1]—C4 BC, with unusual brick seating on an artificial mound). Signed footpaths guide you round the site, which is generously provided with viewing platforms.

The features of interest stressed here are the sanctuary of Isis, the paved streets of the city, the Roman baths and latrine, the city wall, the 'Villa of Dionysos' and the Hellenistic 'shield monument'.

The tour begins with various monuments outside the south line of the city-wall. The path to the sanctuary of Isis transects (not signed) a

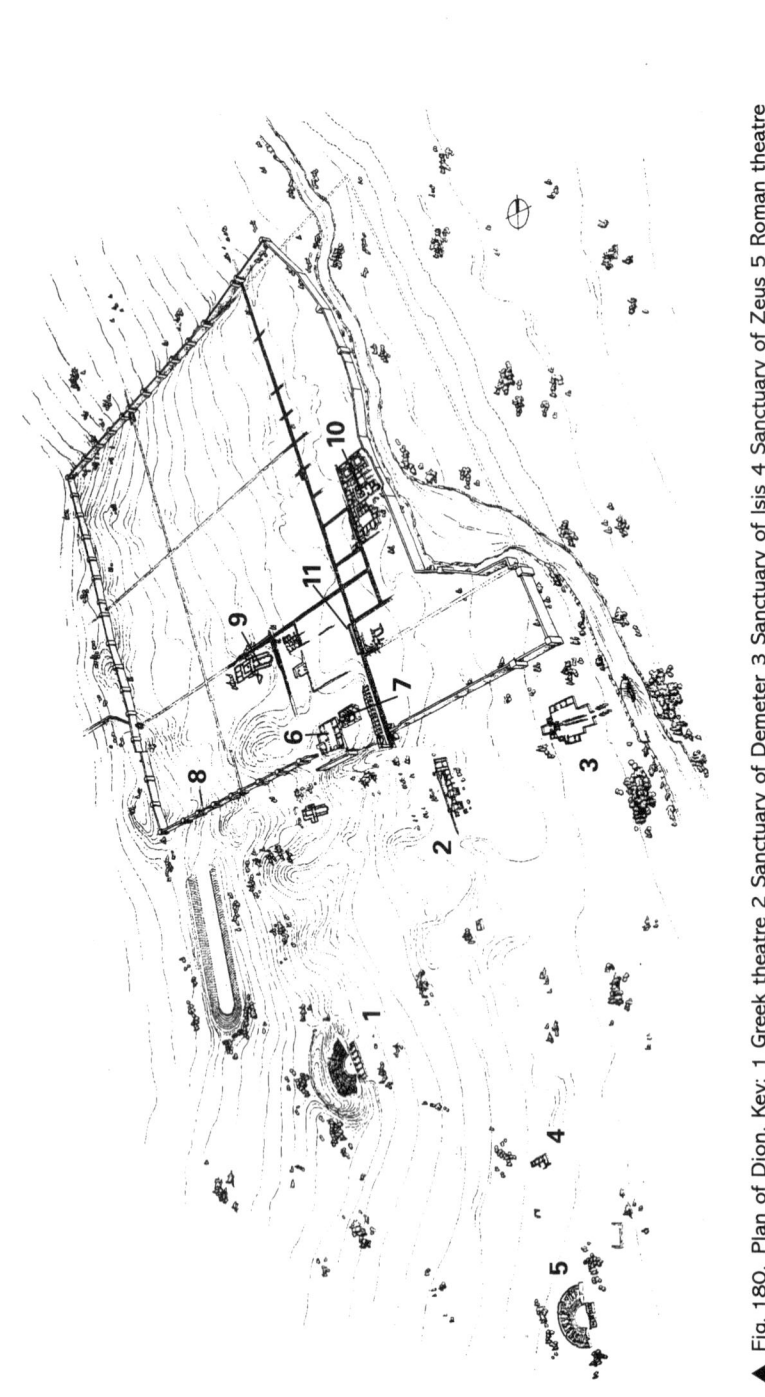

▲ Fig. 180. Plan of Dion. Key: 1 Greek theatre 2 Sanctuary of Demeter 3 Sanctuary of Isis 4 Sanctuary of Zeus 5 Roman theatre 6 Baths 7 Odeion 8 Walls 9 Church 10 'Villa of Dionysos' 11 Shield monument

modest but long-lived **Sanctuary of Demeter** ([2]—finds range from the C6 BC to the C4 AD). The chief remains are the masonry foundations of a pair of small Doric shrines with porches but no colonnade (late C4 BC) and the head of a cult-statue of Demeter (in the museum).

Crossing a bridge over the River Chelopotomas (the ancient Baphyras, here in a modern channel), you reach a **Sanctuary of Isis** [3], witness to Dion's flourishing paganism in the C2 AD, when it was built from scratch on a site previously devoted to Artemis. Isis was worshipped here as 'Lochias', presiding over childbirth, sharing her shrine with Aphrodite, goddess of femaleness, here with the homely epithet 'worshipped at the feet of Mt Olympos' (Hypolympidia). Inscriptions and statues show that women were prominent among the devotees. The sanctuary, with an Egyptianizing plan, is a walled enclosure with a row of four temples at the west end, approached by an axially aligned processional way leading from the main entrance to the monumental altar. The biggest temple, dedicated to Isis, has an unusual plan, its Ionic portico screening a flight of steps which led up to the holy of holies. The shrine immediately to the south belonged to Aphrodite, its apsidal neighbour (a later addition) to Isis as Tyche (Fortune); the shrine to the north produced a statue of Eros. Replicas of some of the statues have been set up in their findspots.

Returning on the same path, signs lead you to the **Sanctuary of Olympian Zeus** [4]. The remains are unimpressive, although finds of inscribed copies of state documents, including two royal letters, show how important the shrine once was. Nearby to the south is a Roman **theatre** ([5]—C2 AD).

Returning from the sanctuary, the footpath continues across the road into the walled city, where it becomes the main street (paved). With one important exception, the remains are essentially those of a Roman and late-antique city. Walking down the main thoroughfare, you turn left for the Roman **bath-complex** [6] after passing communal **latrines**, drained by the run-off from the baths. These public baths or therms (c. AD 200) are among the best examples in Greece of this typically Roman amenity. The baths themselves featured communal cold, tepid, and hot water pools, the heat delivered by hot air circulating under a raised floor or hypocaust and in wall cavities. Sculpture, some of it religious, decorated the rooms. Off the open court was a small **odeion** [7] or roofed theatre.

Beyond the baths to the west, a good stretch is visible of the **city-wall** [8], first built c.300 BC, with later repairs. A path leads to the main basilican **church** [9] of Dion. Begun in the later C4 AD, the church was destroyed before completion and then rebuilt. Remains of the baptistery (with a font) and its possible short-lived predecessor, a triconch room to the south, have been found.

Returning to the main street, turn left for the '**Villa of Dionysos**'

▲ Fig. 181. Latrines at Dion

[10]. This richly appointed complex (C2 AD), named for the subject of a splendid mosaic floor, extends over two or more city-blocks, although the two courtyards to the north were later made into a separate residence by blocking off a connecting door. The remainder forms a huge unit of well over 40 rooms, including shops on the street-front, a bath-complex and latrine to the south, and a large dining room ($c.$100 m.^{2}) with an outstanding mosaic floor (now under cover), depicting Dionysos in a chariot pulled by panthers and flanked by human sea-horses. A shrine of Dionysos and a library have also been identified. Along with other mosaics, marble veneers, and the quantity of sculpture, including the 'philosophers' group, this is one of the richest houses of the Roman period found anywhere in Greece. Whether privately owned, or the property of a religious association, is hard to say.

Return by the main street for the exit, you pass a Hellenistic **shield monument** [11], in the form of a facade carved in lifesize relief with

▲ Fig. 182. The monument with shields and cuirasses at Dion

alternating hoplite-shields and corslets, shown as if pierced by weapons. The wall is dated after 200 BC and seems to commemorate captured armour from a particular victory, perhaps of Philip V or Perseus. Behind this facade is the partly excavated **agora**.

Chronology

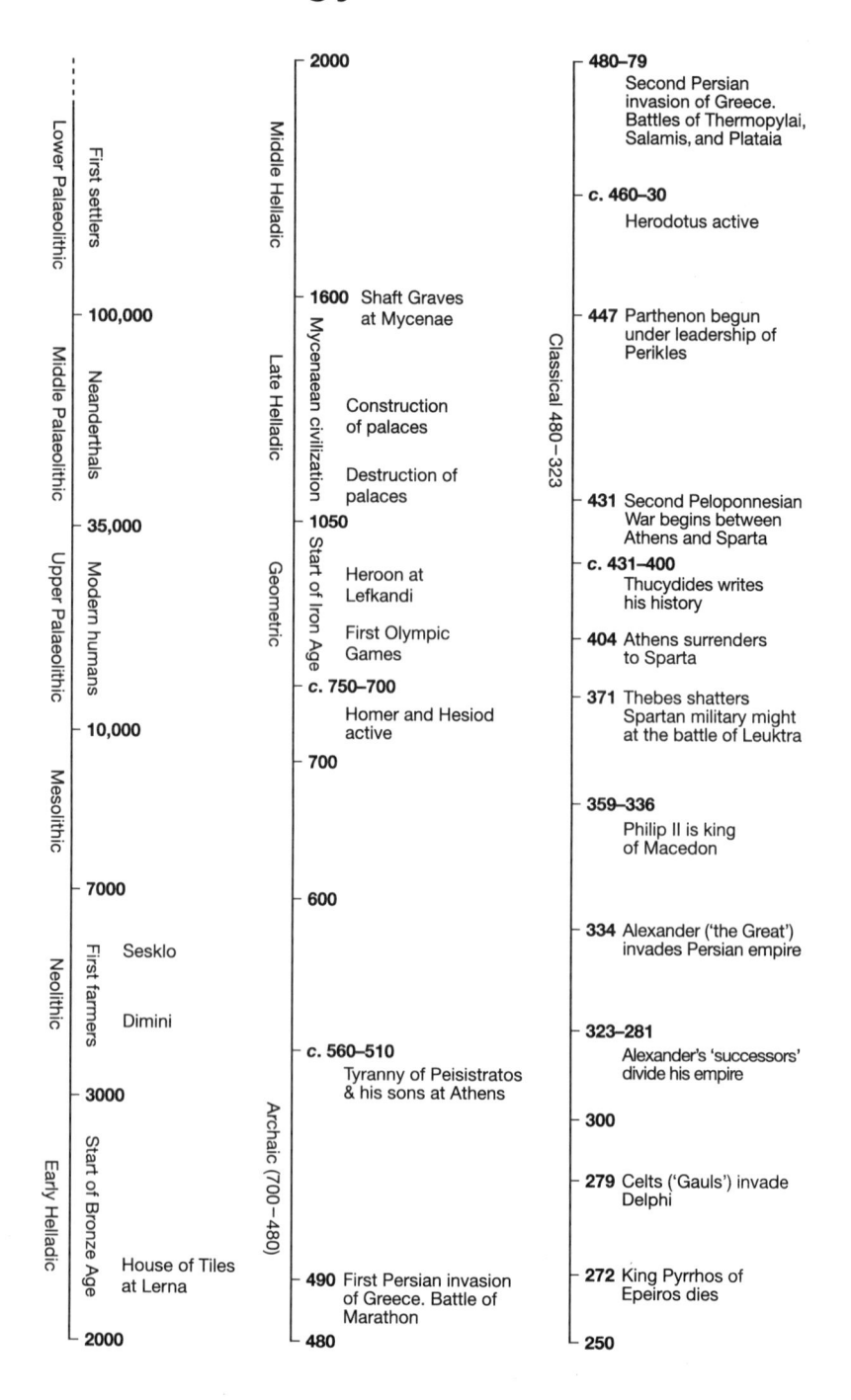

Palaeolithic/Prehistoric	Helladic/Greek periods	Historical events

Lower Palaeolithic — First settlers

— 100,000

Middle Palaeolithic — Neanderthals

— 35,000

Upper Palaeolithic — Modern humans

— 10,000

Mesolithic

— 7000

Neolithic — First farmers — Sesklo — Dimini

— 3000

Early Helladic — Start of Bronze Age — House of Tiles at Lerna

— 2000

Middle Helladic — 2000

Late Helladic / Mycenaean civilization
- 1600 Shaft Graves at Mycenae
- Construction of palaces
- Destruction of palaces
- 1050

Geometric / Start of Iron Age
- Heroon at Lefkandi
- First Olympic Games
- c. 750–700 Homer and Hesiod active
- 700

Archaic (700–480)
- 600
- c. 560–510 Tyranny of Peisistratos & his sons at Athens
- 490 First Persian invasion of Greece. Battle of Marathon
- 480

Classical 480–323
- 480–79 Second Persian invasion of Greece. Battles of Thermopylai, Salamis, and Plataia
- c. 460–30 Herodotus active
- 447 Parthenon begun under leadership of Perikles
- 431 Second Peloponnesian War begins between Athens and Sparta
- c. 431–400 Thucydides writes his history
- 404 Athens surrenders to Sparta
- 371 Thebes shatters Spartan military might at the battle of Leuktra
- 359–336 Philip II is king of Macedon
- 334 Alexander ('the Great') invades Persian empire
- 323–281 Alexander's 'successors' divide his empire
- 300
- 279 Celts ('Gauls') invade Delphi
- 272 King Pyrrhos of Epeiros dies
- 250

Chronology

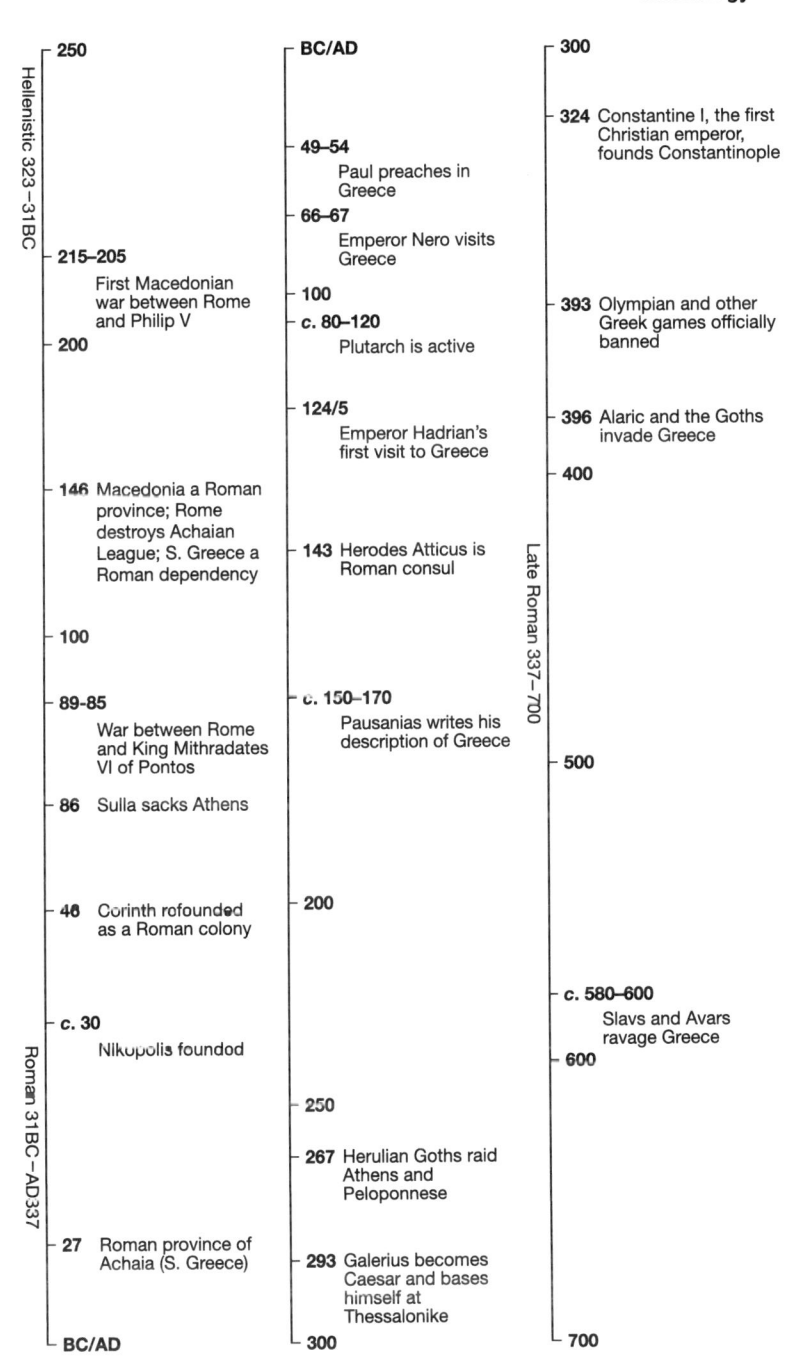

Hellenistic 323–31 BC

- 250
- 215–205 First Macedonian war between Rome and Philip V
- 200
- 146 Macedonia a Roman province; Rome destroys Achaian League; S. Greece a Roman dependency
- 100
- 89–85 War between Rome and King Mithradates VI of Pontos
- 86 Sulla sacks Athens
- 46 Corinth refounded as a Roman colony
- c. 30 Nikopolis founded

Roman 31BC–AD337

- 27 Roman province of Achaia (S. Greece)
- BC/AD

- BC/AD
- 49–54 Paul preaches in Greece
- 66–67 Emperor Nero visits Greece
- 100
- c. 80–120 Plutarch is active
- 124/5 Emperor Hadrian's first visit to Greece
- 143 Herodes Atticus is Roman consul
- c. 150–170 Pausanias writes his description of Greece
- 200
- 250
- 267 Herulian Goths raid Athens and Peloponnese
- 293 Galerius becomes Caesar and bases himself at Thessalonike
- 300

- 300
- 324 Constantine I, the first Christian emperor, founds Constantinople

Late Roman 337–700

- 393 Olympian and other Greek games officially banned
- 396 Alaric and the Goths invade Greece
- 400
- 500
- c. 580–600 Slavs and Avars ravage Greece
- 600
- 700

Glossary

abaton, sacred area, literally 'not to be stepped on'
adyton, innermost sanctuary in a temple
agora, place of assembly, market place
akropolis, 'high city' or citadel
akroterion, sculptural ornament placed on the apex and finials of a pediment
amphora, storage jar
andron, dining room
antefix, terracotta ornament covering the tile ends of a roof
architrave, lower element in the superstructure of a monumental facade
aryballos, small pottery container, usually for perfumed oil
ashlar, see Masonry Styles (p. 20)
basilica, large covered hall in Roman architecture, later adapted for churches (p. 34)
bouleuterion, purpose-built meeting place of the boule or council
caryatid, architectural support in the form of a standing maiden
cavea, auditorium of a Greek theatre
cella, main inner chamber of a Greek temple
choregic monument, commemoration of the winning production of a *choregos* (producer) in a musical or dramatic festival
cist grave, slab-lined earth or rock-cut grave
Cyclopean, see Masonry Styles (p. 20)
Daedalic, Orientalizing style in early Archaic (C7 BC) Greek art, named from Daidalos, a mythical craftsman
deme, administrative district of Athens, mostly based on villages
diazoma, horizontal gangway in a Greek theatre
dromos, monumental entrance passage to a tholos tomb, in Classical times a running track
ekklesiasterion, meeting place of the assembly
ephebe, youth undergoing paramilitary training based on the gymnasium
exedra, rectilinear or circular seating area
forum, Roman equivalent of the agora
herm, four-sided pillar topped by a portrait head, with a phallus on the front
heroon, tomb of an individual worshipped posthumously as a hero or demigod
hypocaust, system of wood-fired underfloor heating used in Greek and Roman baths
hypostyle, structure supported by internal columns
isodomic, see Masonry Styles (p. 20)
kore, a type of Archaic standing statue depicting a maiden
kosmete, Athenian official in charge of the gymnasium
kouros, nude male counterpart of the kore
krater, large open vessel for serving wine
kylix, stemmed drinking cup
larnax, clay coffin

lekythos, type of clay oil flask favoured in funerary ritual, a marble version could serve as a grave marker
Linear B, earliest known form of Greek script, found on Mycenaean sites
'Macedonian' tomb, see p. 438
megaron, building plan where a shallow porch fronts one or more rooms set one behind another
metope, square panel, sometimes with relief sculpture, in the frieze course of a Doric building
nymphaion, richly decorated fountain house, characteristic of Roman imperial times
odeion, roofed concert or lecture hall
oikema/oikos, house or chamber
opisthodomos, rear porch of a Greek temple
opus reticulatum, concrete construction faced with pyramid-shaped cubes
orchestra, circular dancing floor, usually part of a Greek theatre
palaistra, peristyle building used for athletic and other educational activities
paraskenion, in a theatre, the side wings of the proskenion
peplos, type of Greek female dress
peribolos tomb, group of burials set within a raised masonry platform
peristyle, the colonnade of a temple, also an enclosed, colonnaded court surrounded by rooms
pithos, large storage jar
podium temple, rectangular temple on a raised platform, approached frontally by steps
polis, Greek city-state
polygonal, see Masonry Styles (p. 20)
poros, type of limestone
propylaia/propylon, monumental gateway
proskenion, colonnaded facade fronting the skene of a Greek theatre, its roof serving as a stage
prostyle, columns set in front of a porch
prytaneion, public building containing the community's sacred hearth and dining rooms for officials and guests
pseudo-isodomic, see Masonry Styles (p. 20)
rostra, speaker's platform in a Roman forum
shaft grave, rectangular shaft with burials on the floor
skene, literally a tent, stage building of a Greek theatre
skyphos, beaker-like drinking vessel
spolia, see Masonry Styles (p. 20)
stele, upright stone slab, commonly used as a gravestone or for public inscriptions
stoa, see Stoas (p. 27)
strigil, curved metal implement used in male ablutions for removing dust and oil from the skin
stylobate, upper foundation on which the columns rest
temenos, sacred enclosure
tholos tomb, circular, corbel-vaulted tomb
trapezoidal, see Masonry Styles (p. 20)

triglyph, ornamental slab with vertical grooves in the frieze course of a Doric building

xystos, type of stoa housing a covered running track

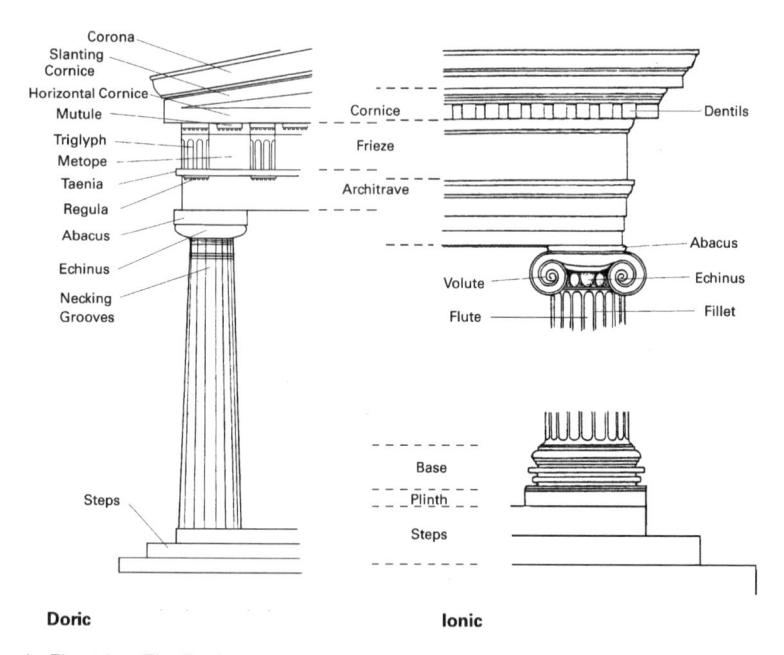

▲ Fig. 184. The Doric and Ionic architectural orders

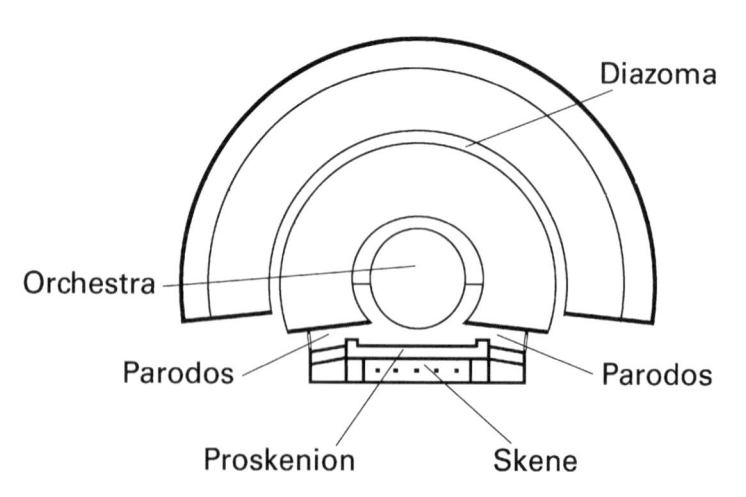

▲ Fig. 185. Plan of a Classical theatre

Select Bibliography

General

Hornblower, S. and Spawforth, A., *The Oxford Classical Dictionary* (Oxford University Press, 1996)
Hornblower, S. and Spawforth, A., *The Oxford Companion to Classical Civilization* (Oxford University Press, 1998)

Prehistoric Greece

Coldstream, J. N., *Geometric Greece* (Methuen, 1979)
Demakopoulou, K. (ed.), *The Mycenaean World* (Greek Ministry of Culture, 1988)
Dickinson, O., *The Aegean Bronze Age* (Cambridge University Press, 1994)
Hood, S., *The Arts in Prehistoric Greece* (Yale University Press, 1994)
Hurwit, J. M., *The Art and Culture of Early Greece* (Cornell University Press, 1985)
Papathanassopoulos, G. A., *Neolithic Culture in Greece* (Goulandris Foundation, 1996)
Preziosi, D. and Hitchcock, L. A., *Aegean Art and Architecture* (Oxford University Press, 1999)
Taylour, W., *The Mycenaeans* (Thames and Hudson, 1983)
Warren, P., *The Aegean Civilizations* (Phaidon, 1989)

History and Society

Cartledge, P. A. (ed.), *The Cambridge Illustrated History of Ancient Greece* (Cambridge University Press, 1998)

Alcock, S., *Graecia Capta: the Landscapes of Roman Greece* (Cambridge University Press, 1993)
Austin, M. M. and Vidal-Naquet, P., *Economic and Social History of Ancient Greece: an Introduction* (Cambridge University Press, 1977)
Bruit Zaidman, L., *Religion in the Ancient Greek City* (Cambridge University Press, 1992)
Cameron, A., *The Later Roman Empire, AD 284–430* (Fontana, 1993)
Davies, J. K., *Democracy and Classical Greece*, 2nd ed. (Fontana, 1993)
Easterling, P. and Muir, J. V. (eds.), *Greek Religion and Society* (Cambridge University Press, 1985)
Murray, O., *Early Greece*, 2nd ed. (Fontana, 1993)
Osborne, R., *Greece in the Making* (Routledge, 1996)
Shipley, G., *The Greek World after Alexander, 328–30 BC* (Routledge, 2000)
Vernant, J. P. (ed.), *The Greeks* (Chicago University Press, 1995)
Walbank, F. W., *The Hellenistic World* (Fontana, 1992)

Greek Architecture, Art, and Archaeology

Coulton, J. J., *Ancient Greek Architects at Work* (Oxbow, 1988)
Lawrence, A. W., *Greek Architecture*, revised by R. A. Tomlinson (Yale University Press, 1996)

Bérard, C., *A City of Images: Iconography and Society in Ancient Greece* (Princeton University Press, 1989)
Boardman, J., *Greek Art* (Thames and Hudson, 1996)
Boardman, J., *The Oxford History of Classical Art* (Oxford University Press, 1993)
Osborne, R., *Archaic and Classical Greek Art* (Oxford University Press, 1998)
Pollitt, J. J., *Art in the Hellenistic Age* (Cambridge University Press, 1986)
Richter, G., *A Handbook of Greek Art* (Phaidon, 1996)
Robertson, M., *A Shorter History of Greek Art* (Cambridge University Press, 1981)

Camp, J. M., *The Athenian Agora* (Thames and Hudson, 1992)
Garland, R., *The Greek Way of Death* (Duckworth, 1985)
Hurwit, J., *The Athenian Acropolis* (Cambridge University Press, 1998)
Osborne, R., *Classical Landscape with Figures* (Philip, 1987)
Snodgrass, A. M., *Archaic Greece* (Dent, 1980)
Stillwell, R. (ed.), *Princeton Encyclopedia of Classical Sites* (Princeton University Press, 1976)
Tomlinson, R. A., *Greek Sanctuaries* (Elek, 1976)
Travlos, J., *A Pictorial Dictionary of Ancient Athens* (Hacker, 1980)
Wycherley, R. E., *The Stones of Athens* (Princeton University Press, 1978)

Ancient Texts

The following translations are all available in the Penguin Classics series:

Herodotus, *Histories*
Hesiod, *Works and Days*
Homer, *Iliad* and *Odyssey*
Pausanias, *Description of Greece* (2 vols.)
Plutarch, *The Rise and Fall of Athens* and *The Age of Alexander* (selections from the *Parallel Lives*)
Polybius, *The Rise of the Roman Empire* (selections from the *Histories*)
Thucydides, *History of the Peloponnesian War*
Xenophon, *History of My Times* (*Hellenika*)

The Loeb Classical Library, published in pocket-book format by Harvard University Press, offers a full range of translated Greek and Latin authors.

Crawford, M. H. and Whitehead, D., *Archaic and Classical Greece* (Cambridge University Press, 1983) and **Austin, M. M.,** *The Hellenistic World from Alexander to the Roman Conquest* (Cambridge University Press, 1981) are selections of translated ancient sources, including inscriptions.

Epigraphy

Cook, B. F., *Greek Inscriptions* (British Museum, 1987)
Woodhead, A. G. F., *The Study of Greek Inscriptions*, rev. ed. (Cambridge University Press, 1981)

Epigraphic abbreviations used in the text

BÉ = *Bulletin épigraphique*, in *Revue des Études grecques*
IG = *Inscriptiones Graecae*
IVO = W. Dittenberger and K. Purgold, *Die Inschriften von Olympia* (Berlin, 1896)
SEG = *Supplementum Epigraphicum Graecum*

Illustrations—Acknowledgements

All photographs are the authors' originals

Reproduced from books (by kind permission)

11 from J. Camp, *The Athenian Agora* (1st edn., 1986), fig. 5, reconstruction by W. B. Dinsmoor Jnr.; **13** from J. Camp, *The Athenian Agora*, fig. 167, reconstruction by John Travlos; **14** from J. Camp, *The Athenian Agora*, fig. 171, reconstruction by W. B. Dinsmoor Jnr.; **23** from W. H. Plommer, 'Three Attic Temples', *Annual of the British School at Athens*, 45 (1950), p. 8; **29** from H. Mussche, *Thorikos: A Guide to the Excavations* (Brussels, 1974), 60–1, fig. 81; **35** from N. D. Papachatzis, *Pausaniou Ellados Periegesis, I: Attika* 1974; **39** from W. Wrede, Athenische Mitteilungen 49 (1924), fig. 11; **49** from H. Walter and F. Felten, *Alt-Agina III.1: die vorgeschichtliche Stadt* (Mainz, 1981) 19, fig. 14; **51** courtesy of the American excavations at Corinth; **57** from O. Broneer, *Isthmia II. Topography and Architecture* (American School of Classical Studies at Athens, 1973), pl. 73; **68** from E. Dodwell, *Views and Descriptions of Cyclopian Remains in Greece and Italy* (1934) pl. 10; **70** from A. J. B. Wace, *Annual of the British School at Athens*, 25 (1921–23) pl. 56; **87** from T. Apostolides in N. D. Papachatzis, *Pausaniou Ellados Periegesis, IV, Korinthiaka kai Lakonika* (1976); **101** from A. Stewart, *Greek Sculpture: An Exploration* (Yale University Press, 1990) fig. 541; **110** from A. Mallwitz, 'Cella und Adyton des Apollontempels in Basai', *Athenische Mitteilungen* 77 (Deutsches Archaeologisches Institut, 1962) 167, fig. 2; **121** from R. Bol, *Olympische Forschungen*, Bd XV, *Das Statuenprogram des Herodes-Atticus-Nymphäums* (1984); **127** from G. Daux and E. Hansen, *Le trésor de Siphnos* (Ecole Française d'Athènes, 1987), 225, fig. 133; **140** from M. R. Popham *et al.*, *Lefkandi II: The Protogeometric Building at Toumba. Part 2: The Excavation, Architecture and Finds* (British School at Athens Supplementary Volume 23, London, 1993) pl. 8; **147** from E. Dyggve *et al.*, *Das Laphrion, der Tempelbezirk von Kalydon* (Copenhagen, 1948), pl. 35; **153** from D. Theocharis, *Neolithic Greece* (National Bank of Greece, 1973) fig. 184.

Index

Sites in capitals are featured in the text. Numbers in bold indicate the main entry for a site or region.

abaton 64, 209–10, 214, 278
Achaia, Achaian 14, 43, 150, 158, 187, **284**, 296–7, 342
Achaian League 13, 133, 150, 173, 187, 213, 247, 253, 259, 261, 265, 284, 294, 298, 330
Achaia Phthiotis 372
Acheloos 3, 14, 342–3, 346, 350
Acheron 383
Acheulean 377
Achilles 6, 17, 40, 218, 255, 321, 375
ACROCORINTH 24, 42, 149, **157–9**
Actium 14, 256, 296, 389
Adrastos 175
Adriatic 15, 395
Aegisthus 185
Aelian 428
Aeneas 218
Aeschylus 35, 61, 315
Africa 292
African plate 1
Agamemnon 40, 110, 174, 180, 187, 219, 241
Agathon 84
Agetos 226
Agias 314
Agios Ilias 342
agora 25–8, 31, 34–5, 43, 60, 65–76, 79–80, 93, 96, 99, 105, 151, 173, 187–8, 191–3, 212, 222, 248–9, 256, 259, 261, 267, 271, 274, 294–6, 298, 300, 304, 324–5, 332, 343–4, 350, 369, 372, 387, 396–9, 419–22, 429, 431, 445; *see also* forum
Agorakritos 122–3
Agrileza 98–9, 109–10
Agrippa, Marcus 48, 66, 70, 126, 285, 390
Aiakos 147, 432
Aigai 12, 394, 435, 439; *see also* Vergina
AIGEIRA 88, 284, **298–300**
AIGINA 30, 96, **142–8**; Aphaia 30, 87, 96, 143–5, **146–8**; Kolonna 9, 18, 21, **144–6**, 217
Aigion 310
Aigospotamoi 305
AIGOSTHENA 19, **133–6**
Ai Khanoum 13
Aitolia, Aitolian 14, 27, 31, 33, 43, 263, 278, 294, 298, 304, **342**, 343, 346, 348, 351, 353–5, 372, 379, 382, 389, 440
Aitolian League 13, 352, 354
Akarnania, Akarnanian 14, **342**, 343, 345, 389
Akarnanian League 343, 346
Akraiphia 327
Akrotiri 89
Akte 95
Alaric 16, 46, 66, 137, 150, 187, 221, 255
Albania 375
Alea 255–6
Alepotrypa Cave 9, 219, 222, 233–4; *see also* Diros
Alexander I of Epeiros 375
Alexander I of Macedonia 395
Alexander III the Great 12–13, 34, 47, 56, 91, 119, 281, 293, 310, 316, 319–21, 374, 376, 389, 394–5, 399, 415, 428, 429, 432, 439–40

Alexander IV 437, 439
Alexandria 93, 431
Aliakmon 2–3, 394
ALIKI **425–7**; *see also* Thasos
Ali Pasha 375, 389
ALIPHEIRA 19, 253, 271, **277–80**
Alkamenes 61
Alkison 392
Alkmaionid 84, 304, 309
Almyros 360
Alpheios 3, 253, 265, 285, 291
altar 28–34 and *passim*
Amasis Painter 89
Amazons 50, 56, 88, 94, 218, 273, 332, 336–7, 431
Ambrakia, Ambrakian 342, 375, 389
Amenhotep III 198
Ampharete 41, 80
Amphiaraos 123–4, 126, 128
AMPHIAREION 27, 33, 35–6, 42, **123–7**
Amphictyony 302
AMPHIPOLIS 17, 20, 28, 361, 395, 405, **407–12**
Amphitrite 162
AMYKLAI 219–21, **230–1**
Amymone 192
Amyntas III 437
Anaphlystos 113
Anavysos 41, 87, 113
Andreas 289
Andronikos of Kyrrhos 74
Andronikos, Manolis 437
Antigonids 13, 370, 394
Antigonos II Gonatas 119, 376, 394, 428
Antigonos III 13, 259
Antinoös 88, 118, 136, 141, 259, 314, 331
Antioch 372
Antiochos III 335, 370
Antiochos IV Epiphanes 78, 255–6
Antiochos Epiphanes Philopappus 60, 269
Antiope 332, 336
Antipater 46, 374
Antoninus 206, 210–12
Antony, Mark 296, 320, 389, 393, 413
Anytos 269
Apelles 173
Aphaia, *see* Aigina
Aphrodite 28, 31, 64, 66, 88, 158, 163, 165, 191, 214, 351, 382, 385, 389, 431, 441, 443
Apidanos 358
Apollo 27–8, 31, 44, 78, 87, 89, 93–5, 142, 144–5, 151, 153, 155, 177, 195, 205, 207, 210–12, 221, 225, 230, 249, 264, 270–1, 273, 287, 295, 304–5, 309–10, 314, 327, 332, 335–7, 340, 342, 351, 354–6, 374, 389, 392–3, 423
Apuleius 163, 301
aqueduct 24, 141, 187, 191, 218, 233, 292, 296, 328, 370, 392, 405, 412; *see also* water supply
Arakynthos 348
Aratos 13, 158, 173
Archaic 34, 39, 41, 46–7, 53, 57, 71, 79–80, 87, 90,

94, 104, 111, 117, 143–4, 146, 148, 150, 163, 167, 171, 173, 177, 184, 193–5, 212, 220, 226, 247, 249, 253–6, 261, 269, 271, 274, 278, 284, 286, 294, 300–1, 310, 314, 316, 323, 327–8, 331, 334–6, 354, 376, 399–400, 407, 423, 425
Archelaos 319, 395, 428, 440
Archilochos 419, 422
Areios 263
Ares 28, 31, 41, 58, 66, 70, 98
ARGIVE HERAION 11, 27, 87, 89, 174, 190, **194–7**
Argolid 1, 10, **174**, 194, 237, 244, 254, 323
Argonauts 360
ARGOS, Argive 3, 17, 21, 24, 28, 35, 42, 44, 123, 174–5, 180, **187–94**, 195, 197–8, 200, 205, 209, 215, 302, 304, 305, 310
Ariadne 400
Arimaspian 336
Aristides 136
Aristion 41, 87
Aristodikos 87
Ariston 225–6
Aristonautes 88
Aristophanes 35, 167
Aristotle 5, 25, 27, 171, 432
Arkadia, Arkadian 174, **253**, 254, 258, 263–5, 267–8, 271, 274, 280, 282, 305, 310
Arkadian League 12, 25, 255, 278, 283
Arrachion 274
Arrhephoroi 53
Arsinoe 126, 248
Arsinoe II 291
Arta 375
Artemis 31, 50, 86, 89, 93, 95, 100, 110–11, 113–14, 138, 146, 173, 207, 220–1, 223, 249–50, 261, 263–4, 268, 296, 300, 316, 351, 353–4, 355, 372, 374, 390, 411–12, 441, 443
Asea 255
ASINE 198, **199**
Askalon 361
Asklepieion 32, 34, 64, 205, 213–14, 248–9
Asklepios 24, 42, 64, 88, 141, 163, 174, 190, 205–7, 209, 213–14, 229, 249, 255–6, 278, 281, 323, 441
Asopos 173, 317
Asprochaliko 377
Astarte 86
ASTROS **217–18**; see also Loukou
Atalanta 255, 351
Athena 17, 28, 31, 42, 47–8, 50, 52–4, 56–7, 68, 71, 74, 76, 87, 90, 93–6, 100, 109, 177, 180, 193, 223, 254–6, 271, 278–80, 302, 311, 327–8, 332, 334, 336, 350, 405–6, 416, 423
Athenaeus 141, 230
ATHENS, Athenian 3, 6, 10–13, 15–17, 19–25, 27–8, 31, 35–6, 38–9, 41–2, 45, **46–91**, 96, 101, 109–11, 114–15, 117, 119, 122–4, 128, 131, 133, 136, 138–41, 143, 147, 199, 205, 212–13, 220, 238, 252, 286–7, 291, 296, 304–5, 314, 316–17, 330–2, 334–5, 338, 342, 346, 395, 400–1, 404–6, 419, 422–3; Agora 23, 25, 27, 34, 43, 60, **65–72**, 79–80, 96, 99, 109; Akropolis 17, 30, 32–4, 42, 45, **47–58**, 90, 111, 139; Arch of Hadrian **77**, 138; Areiopagos **58**; Church of Theotokos Gorgoeipikoos and Ayios Eleftherios **76**; Epigraphic Museum 26, 47, **90**; Hill of the Muses **60–1**; Kerameikos 19, 37, 39, 41, **79–84**, 86, 119; Library of Hadrian **73–4**; National Archaeological Museum 40–1, **84–90**, 96, 121, 141, 144, 179, 195, 198, 206, 217, 231, 268, 299, 314, 321, 351, 355, 379; Numismatic Museum **90**; Olympieion **76–9**; Panathenaic Stadium **78–9**; Pnyx 25, **58–60**, 70; Roman Agora **74–6**; South Slope of the Akropolis **61–5**
athletics 34–5, 79, 114, 175, 250, 285, 287, 297, 311, 379, 408, 440; see also gymnasium, palaistra, stadium, xystos
Atreus 10, 43, 179–80, 185–6, 323
Attalids 13; see also Pergamon
Attalos I 47, 304, 311
Attalos II 47, 71
Attika 1, 3–4, 19, 38, **45**, 46, 53, 93, 101, 105, 110, 114–15, 119, 123, 131, 159, 212, 302, 304, 317
Auge 256
Augustus 14–15, 19, 48, 54, 66, 70–1, 74, 78, 88, 120, 150–1, 153–5, 165, 210, 220, 233, 250, 252–3, 256, 259, 284–5, 291–2, 296, 348, 351, 375, 381, 389–90, 392, 399, 407, 413, 440
Aulis 316
Aurelius, Marcus 118, 136, 139–40, 416
Avars 17, 187, 241, 396
Axios 2–3, 394
Ayia Sophia 399
Ayios Athanasios 406
Ayios Dimitrios 398
Ayios Georgios 398

Babylon 13
Baebia, Cornelia 153
Balkans 13–15, 17, 34, 390, 394–6
Baphyras 439, 443
baptistery 34, 135, 176, 372–3, 419, 443
basilica 34, 64, 82, 111, 133, 135, 150, 153, 165–6, 175–6, 194, 206, 210, 223, 248, 255–6, 294, 206, 210, 223, 248, 255–6, 294, 304, 309, 370, 372–3, 379, 382, 390, 392, 395, 398, 406, 410, 413, 415–16, 423, 425, 443
BASSAI 177, 264, **270–4**
Bassus, Decimius 416
bath, bathing 15, 17, 22, 24, 28, 33–4, 77, 82, 110, 124, 126–7, 147, 163, 173, 175–7, 188, 190, 192, 197, 199, 202, 207, 209, 211–12, 214, 218, 223, 239, 244, 250, 265, 280–2, 287, 291, 294, 296, 313, 334–5, 373, 392, 398, 402–3, 408, 412, 419, 440–1, 443–4; see also water supply
Bathykles 230
Bellerophon 159, 404
Bendis 412
Berbati 198
Berlin 292
Beroia see Veroia
Bethlehem 410
Bithynion 259, 314
Biton 194, 197, 314
Black Sea 6, 94
Blegen, Carl 241–2
Bogazköy 9
Boiotia 3–4, 7, 10, 41, 123, 131, 133, 199, 301–2, 315–21, 323, 327, 329, 331
Boreas 4
bouleuterion, see council-house
boundary stone 32, 70, 82, 84
Boutes 52
Brasidas 405–6
BRAURON 27, 30, 32–3, 39, 45, 50, 93, **110–14**
Brexiza 118
bridge 27, 42, 111, 127, 296, 307, 330–1, 334, 407–8, 411
British Museum 54, 180, 273
Britomartis 146
Brutus, Marcus Junius 126
Bulgaria, Bulgarian 321

Byron, Lord 96, 376
Byzantine 230–2, 330, 375, 390, 392, 405
Byzantion 292

Caesar, Gaius Julius 15, 74, 150, 320, 413
Caesar, Gaius, heir of Augustus 422
Caesar, Lucius, heir of Augustus 422
Capitoline Museum 337
Caracalla 221, 395, 425
Carpus, Gellius 217
Carthage 14
Caskey, John 215
Cassander 13, 133, 343, 394, 396, 435, 439–41
cemetery 36–42 and *passim*
Centaurs 56, 99, 273, 287, 432
Cerealis, Gaius 153
Ceres 140
Certus, Curtius 328
Chairestratos 121
CHAIRONEIA 12, 19, 38–9, 46, 94, 301, 304, **319–20**
Chalastra 400
Chalkidike 394, 401, 405
CHALKIS 13, 42, 301, **330–1**, 334, 338
Charon 36–7, 82
Charops 381
Chelopotamos 443
Chilon 221
Chimaira 404
Chios, Chian 309
CHORA **244–5**
choregic monument 64–5, 127, 422
Christian 16–17, 34, 48, 58, 64, 76, 122, 133, 135–6, 143, 150–1, 153–4, 157, 163, 175–6, 187, 206, 213–14, 255–6, 286, 294, 296, 304, 359, 372–3, 379, 395–8, 405–6, 409, 413, 415, 418–19, 422–3, 425, 440
Chryseis 195
church 16–17, 32, 34, 48, 52, 54, 58, 68, 74, 76, 111, 135, 137, 153, 165, 176, 187, 194, 206, 210, 214, 218, 221, 248, 286, 289, 321, 350–1, 359, 372–3, 379, 382, 384, 390, 392, 395–8, 405, 406–10, 415–16, 419, 440, 443
Cicero, Marcus Tullius 41
Circe 383
cistern 23–4, 105, 109–10, 141, 170, 184, 193, 197, 202, 210–11, 230, 236, 248, 269, 328, 348, 350, 403, 410, 415, 423, 431; *see also* water supply
Classical 5, 7, 21–2, 24, 27, 30, 34, 39, 41, 43, 46–8, 57, 64, 68, 76, 80, 87, 94, 96–7, 104, 117, 145, 148, 150, 161, 173, 177, 195, 207, 218, 226, 230, 232, 238, 240–1, 253, 255–6, 271, 274, 285, 294, 297, 300, 304, 314, 316, 321, 328, 331–2, 359–62, 367, 372, 374, 376, 400–1, 404–6, 408, 411, 429, 434
Claudius 150
Cleopatra, queen of Egypt 296, 389
Cleopatra, wife of Philip II 438
Cloatii 233
clock 74, 127
Clytemnestra 185
Cnosus, Lucius Tatinius 416
Colchis 360
Colosseum 78
Commodus 153, 218
Concord/Homonoia 261, 317
Constantine I 16–17, 88, 309, 396
Constantinople 16–17, 50, 291, 309, 391, 396, 405, 410, 419
Corcyra 84, 304

CORINTH, Corinthian 10–19, 23–5, 27–8, 34, 42, 80, 89, 144, **149–57**, 159, 163, 165–6, 168, 170, 173, 175, 195, 199, 296, 302, 309, 352, 355, 383, 400, 416; *see also* Acrocorinth
Corinthian Gulf 133, 149, 296, 298, 342, 346
Cossutius, Decimus 78
Costoboci 136
council-house (bouleuterion) 25, 27, 66, 153, 173, 259, 261, 265, 285, 289, 305, 351, 357, 376, 381–2, 387
Crete, Cretan 9, 29, 89, 93, 142, 146, 179, 231, 246, 316, 361
Croesus 302, 309–10
Ctesiphon 397
Cybele 431
Cyclades, Cycladic 1, 45, 86, 89, 115, 117, 142, 179, 301, 305, 331
Cyclops, Cyclopes 7, 20, 180, 199
Cyprus, Cypriot 3, 12, 253, 338
Cyrene 292, 309
Cyrus 26

Damokratia 370
Damonon 221
Damophon 88, 249–50, 268
Danaos 192
Danube 16, 396–7
Daochos II 311, 314, 359
Daphni 93
Darius I 115
Dekeleia 101, 109
Delian League 332
Delos 86, 95, 114
DELPHI 11–12, 24, 27–8, 30, 32–3, 35–6, 42, 53, 57, 171, 175, 177, 193, 254, 285, 301, **302–14**, 320, 327, 336, 342, 359, 379, 408, 429
Demeter 28, 31, 64, 72, 87, 104, 136, 140–1, 268, 277, 291, 443
Demetria 84
DEMETRIAS 13–14, 41, 359–62, **369–72**
Demetrios I Poliorketes 133, 168, 173, 360, 369–70, 394
Demetrios II 348
Demetrios of Phaleron 80, 84, 88
Demosthenes 12, 22
DENDRA 39, 86, 198, **202–4**
Derveni 394, 399–400
Despoina 88, 254, 268–70
Dexileos 80, 84
Diana 296
Dianeira 429
Dido 218
Dikaia 390
Dikili Tash 412
DIMINI 9, 18, 20, 39, 85, 359–60, **362–4**
dining room 23, 32, 111, 170–1, 287, 294, 329, 332, 336, 372, 382, 435, 444
Dio of Prusa (Chrysostom) 61, 126, 429
Diocletian 88, 397–8
Diodorus Siculus 342, 435, 439
DIOLKOS 11, 149, **166–7**
Diomedes 174
DION 15–16, 34, 354, 394–5, **439–45**
Dione 378, 382
Dionysia 63
Dionysios the Areopagite 58
Dionysos 26, 28, 31, 35, 61, 65, 101, 131, 188, 238, 261, 286, 315, 320, 323, 335, 351, 400, 422–3, 429, 431, 441, 443, 444
Dioskouroi 190, 221, 239, 273; *see also* Kastor, Polydeukes

Dipylon Master 89
DIROS 233–4; *see also* Alepotrypa Cave
Divari 239
DODONA 13, 32, 35–6, 88, 354, 375, **376–82**
Dokimion 74
Dometios 390
Domitian 266, 304, 416
Dorian 10
drains 68, 70, 170, 192, 209, 214, 244, 401, 403, 435; *see also* sanitation
Drakon 422

Early Cycladic 86
Early Helladic 5, 9, 18, 21, 29, 45, 85, 101, 115, 117, 119, 144, 174, 187, 198–9, 214–15, 217, 229–30, 284, 293–4, 301, 315–16, 331, 337, 341, 363, 374
Early Iron Age 301, 337, 354, 394, 404
Echinades 342, 350
Egypt, Egyptian, Egyptianizing 10–13, 34, 86, 88, 118, 179, 198–9, 218, 321, 412
Eileithyia 311
Eion 407
Electra 317
ELEUSIS, Eleusinian 17, 19, 33, 38, 43, 45, 72, 82, 87, **136–41**, 268, 314
ELEUTHERAI 19, 61, **131–3**, 135
Elgin, Lord 54, 180
ELIS, Eleian 3, 25, 27, 274, 276, 278, 284–6, 289–92, **294–5**
Elpidius 373
Elpinikos 335
Endoios 57
Enipeos 358
Epaminondas 237, 247, 249, 301, 316, 327
Epeiros, Epeirote 2, 7–8, 13–14, 342, 361, **375**, 376–9, 381, 387, 389–90
Epeirote League 382, 385
Ephesos 77
Ephyra 384; *see also* Nekyomanteion
Epictetus 390
Epidamnos 292
EPIDAUROS 17, 20, 32–3, 35–6, 42, 88, 124, 174, **205–12**
EPIDAUROS LIMERA 220, **231–2**
Epigone 15, 253, 259
Epikrates 109
Erastus 157
Erebos 384
Erechtheus 52
ERETRIA 11, 19, 22, 115, 301, 330, **331–7**, 338
Eridanos 79–80, 82
Eros 351, 443
Eteokles 315
Etruscan 11
Euboia 38, 115, 119, 301–2, 330–2
Eudocia 70
Eudokimos 223
Euephenes 418
Eukleides 88, 299
Eumenes II 48, 64, 309–10; *see also* Pergamon
Eumolpos 137
Eupatrids 58
Euphrosynos 253
Eupolemos 195
Eurasian plate 1
Euripides 35, 61, 138, 154, 163, 237, 428
Euripos 42, 330–1
Eurotas 3, 219, 225–6
Eurydike 437
Eurykles 223

Eutresis 316
Eva 217–18
Exekias 89

Fates 361
First Sacred War 302
Flamininus, Titus Quinctius 159, 233, 332
Flavian 88
fortifications 17–20 and *passim*
Fortune 153, 249, 361; *see also* Tyche
forum 28, 34, 151, 153–4, 165, 413, 415–16; *see also* agora
fountain 15, 24, 71, 76–7, 82, 138, 153–4, 157, 171, 173, 192, 211, 213, 218, 222, 248, 256, 265, 269, 274, 282, 292, 311, 327, 356, 390, 392, 403, 416; *see also* nymphaion, water supply
Franchthi Cave 2
Franks, Frankish 241, 263

Galerius 16, 23, 396–8
Gallio, Junius 154
Ganymede 286
Gauls 304, 310, 342, 355, 357, 435
Ge 64
Gela 292, 314
Gelon 309
Genoa, Genoese 423
Geometric 10, 37, 65, 71, 79–80, 86, 89, 101, 113, 117, 138, 140, 144, 146, 168, 174, 187–8, 199, 202, 205, 210, 219, 238, 247, 253, 255, 263, 284, 286, 297, 331, 341, 360, 362, 374, 376
GLA 10, 301, 316, 321, **323–6**
Glauke 157
Glaukos 422
Gnosis 431
GORTYS 24, 253, 265, **280–3**
Goths 16, 137, 395–6, 399, 440
Graces 33, 374
graffiti 159, 177, 425, 428; *see also* inscriptions
Granikos 56, 440
grave 36–42 and *passim*
Gravettian 378
gymnasium 25, 28, 88, 111, 173, 223, 252, 287, 294, 300, 313, 335, 350, 392–3, 395–6, 407–8, 434, 440
Gyphtokastro 131, 317
GYTHEION 219–20, **233**

Hadeia 126
Hades 31, 42, 136, 140, 236, 383–4, 432, 437
Hadrian, Hadrianic 14–15, 23–4, 46, 48, 64, 68, 70, 73, 76–8, 88, 118, 133, 136, 138–9, 141, 151, 153, 157, 161, 187, 190, 195, 213, 218, 255, 259, 289, 304, 314, 390, 392, 407
Halai 316
Halikarnassos 94
harbour 2, 42, 45, 58, 91, 95, 138, 145, 149, 163, 165–6, 168, 170, 174, 212, 219, 232–3, 235, 237–8, 240, 242, 301, 330, 332, 346–7, 361, 369–70, 372, 375, 390, 396, 405, 412, 420, 422–3
Hediste 361
Hegeso 84, 87
Helen of Troy 219, 221, 225–6, 229, 429
Heliaia 25, 71
Helike 284
Helios 154, 309
Helisson 173, 265
Hellenikon 218
Hellenistic 5, 19–20, 24–5, 27, 34, 39, 42, 46–7, 54, 56, 63–4, 66, 80, 82, 87–8, 93–4, 111, 140,

143, 145, 150, 153, 162, 168, 173, 175, 177, 182, 184–5, 194, 199, 209–10, 213–14, 218, 226, 230, 233, 235, 239–40, 246–7, 249, 253, 261, 263, 265, 280–1, 285, 287, 294, 297–300, 304, 309, 311, 316, 323, 330–2, 344, 351, 354, 356, 362, 369–71, 374, 382, 385, 390, 395–6, 399, 405–6, 408, 411–13, 418, 423, 429, 431–2, 434, 441
Hellespont 27, 90, 307
Hellopia 378
Helos 219
Hephaistos 6, 28, 31, 52, 68, 99
Hera 30–1, 35, 84, 87, 89, 168, 171, 180, 194–5, 263, 290, 292, 336, 383, 423
Heraclides Creticus 123
Herakleides 42
Herakles 28, 31, 57, 68, 94, 118, 144, 175, 188, 214, 218, 249, 256, 287, 295, 305, 315, 337, 351, 382, 425, 435
Herennianus 441
Hermes 28, 30–1, 87, 252, 286, 432
Herod the Great 389
Herodes Atticus 15, 23–4, 39, 46, 64, 78–9, 88, 115, 117–18, 150, 155–6, 162, 167, 174, 217–18, 254, 285–6, 292, 296, 331
Herodotus 26, 38, 109, 115, 117, 143, 194, 254–5, 290, 302, 304, 305, 327, 329–30, 358, 378, 383, 428
heroon 40, 175, 177, 301, 332, 334, 337–8, 340, 351, 389, 433
Heruli, Herulian 16, 46, 48, 66, 70, 74, 82, 145, 221
Hesiod 4, 6, 42, 378
Hestia 31
Hiero 309
Higgs, Eric 377
Himerios 58
Hipparchos 327
Hippias 46, 115
Hippodamia 287, 293
Hippodamos, Hippodamian 93, 385
hippodrome 35, 175, 291, 295, 397
Hippokrates 24
Hippolytos 212–14
Hittite 9
Homer 10, 17–18, 34–5, 42, 96, 174, 180, 187, 205, 219, 226, 229, 261, 340, 348, 351, 378–9, 383, 404
Hormisdas 399
hostel 175–6, 207, 387
house 20–3 and *passim*; *see also* palace, villa
Hyakinthos 230–1
Hyampolis 374
Hydra 37, 214
Hygieia 88, 104, 255–6, 311
Hymettos 45
Hypatodoros 280
Hypereides 109
Hyperesia 298

Iakchos 141
Iamidai 285, 287
Ibrahim Pasha 238
Iktinos 56, 140, 271, 274, 345
Ilissos 88
Illyricum 396, 399
imperial cult 34, 36, 68, 76, 150, 190, 250, 323,
Inachos 174
inscriptions 26 and *passim*; *see also* graffiti
IOANNINA **375–6**, 377–9, 382
Iolkos 359, 362–3
Ionia, Ionian 11, 115, 377

Ionomaos 287
Iphigeneia 30, 110, 113, 300
Iran 11
Iris 423
Isis 34, 64, 118, 163, 165, 441, 443
ISTHMIA, Isthmian 16, 32, 35–6, 149, 153, **159–62**, 165, 175, 192, 209
Isthmus of Corinth 11, 42, 149, 167–8
Isokrates 136
Italy, Italian 3, 9–10, 15, 90–1, 94, 118, 150, 165, 285, 292, 294, 296, 330, 375, 378, 395–6, 411
Ithaka 383
Ithomi 247, 252

Jason, hero 360, 363
Jason, tyrant of Pherai 368–9
Jews 154, 396
Jocasta 315
John the Baptist 384
Jucunda, Anthestia 441
Julian 58
Julio-Claudian 88
Jupiter 151, 413
Justinian 16, 151, 318–19, 330, 370

Kabeiroi 316
Kadmos 315
KALAMATA 237, **238**
Kalapodi 374
Kallidromos 329
Kallikles 434
Kallikrates 50
Kallithea 94, 360
KALYDON 27, 39, 296, 342, 348, **350–3**
Kalydonian boar 255–6, 351
Kantharos 91
Karia, Karian 327
Karyai 53
Karystos 3, 73, 301
Kassandra 404
KASSOPE 14, 19, 22, 25, 39, 375–6, **384–9**
Kastor 190, 221, 351
Kastritsa 377
Katara Pass 2
KAVALA **412–13**, 438
Kazarma 198
Kedros 360
KENCHREAI 2, 149, **163–5**
Kephisos 192, 301
Kerykes 84
Kimon 138, 407
Kissos 239
Kithairon 131, 133, 317
Kladeos 285, 287
Kleinias 173
Kleisthenes, Athenian statesman 45–6
Kleisthenes, Sikyonian tyrant 171, 305, 314
Kleitor 263–4
Klenies 177
Kleobis 194, 197, 314
Kleomenes III 13, 265
Kleonai 175
Klithi 377–8
Klytiadai 285
Knidos, Knidian 305, 311
Knossos 9
Kokkinopilos 377
Kokytos 383
Kolonna, *see* Aigina
Komaros 392
Kommagene 60

Konon 95
Kopais 3, 301, 321, 323–4
Korallion 84
Kore 72, 136 see also Persephone
Koroni 237–8
Koropissos 78
KORYPHASION 238, **240–1**
Kotys 209–10
Koukounara 239
Krana 233
Krannon 374
Krateros 310, 429
Krenides 413
Krisa 301
Kroisos 41
Krokeai 219, 330
Kronos 78, 285, 292
Ktesibios 441
Kybele 93
Kynaitha 263
Kynortion 205, 210
Kynouria 217
Kyprianon 219
Kypselos 150
Kyriakos 289
Kythera 93, 219

Lachares 47
Ladochori 376
Laios 315
Lakedaimon, Lakedaimonians, see Sparta, Spartan
Lakonia 2, 174, **219–20**, 226, 233, 235, 237, 254, 256
Lakrates 82
LAMIA **373–4**
Lamian War 46, 374
Laomedon 412
Lapiths 56, 99, 273, 432
Larisa 4, 16, 359, 373, 400
Las Incantadas 398–9
Late Helladic 9, 115, 146, 149, 198, 341; see also Mycenaean
latrine 17, 24, 74, 403, 416, 441, 444; see also sanitation
LAURION 3, 24, 45, 101, **103–7**, 110
Leake, William 240
Lebadeia 301
LECHAION 149–50, **165–6**
LEFKADIA 40, 394, **431–4**, 438
LEFKANDI 10, 40, 301, 331–2, **337–41**
Lelantine 330, 338
Leochares 310
Leon 351
Leonidas 222, 329
Leonides 289
LEPREON 19, **274–7**, 284
LERNA 9, 18, 21, 142, 174, 188, **214–17**
lesche 177, 311
Leukippos 273
Leuktra 12, 133, 220, 259, 316
Liatovouni 376
library 23, 72–4, 287, 416, 444
Linear B 10, 29, 86, 179, 185, 198, 204, 237–8, 241–2, 244–5, 315–16, 363
Lithares 316
Livia 120, 233
Livy 42, 256, 332, 428
LOUKOU 23, 174, **217–18**, 254; see also Astros
Louros 377
Lousios 280–1

LOUSOI **263–5**
Louvre 399
Lycia, Lycian 36
Lydos 89
Lykophron 368
LYKOSOURA 24, 32–3, 60, 88, 253–4, **268–70**
Lykourgos, Athenian statesman 46, 61
Lykourgos, Spartan legislator 220, 225
Lysanias 84
Lysikrates 35, 65
Lysimachides 84
Lysippos 154, 173, 188, 310, 314
Lyson 434

Macedonia, Macedonian 1, 3, 12–17, 19, 23, 25, 39–40, 43, 66, 91, 94, 96, 100, 119, 150, 158, 165, 173, 213, 247, 259, 265, 278–9, 291, 294, 301, 304, 309–10, 316, 332, 343, 369–70, 374, 376, **394–5**, 396, 400, 405, 407, 411–13, 428, 432, 434–8, 440
'Macedonian' tomb 332, 399, 408, 431, 438
Magnesia, Magnesian 369
Maior Antoninus Pythodorus, Sextus Julius 210
Makareos 84
Malea 219, 222
Maleatas 205
Malia, Malian 373
Mamaea, Julia 88
Mandalo 429
Mani 219, 222, 233–5
Manika 301, 331
MANTINEIA 19, 27, 253–5, **258–60**, 314, 316
MARATHON 11, 23, 38–9, 45, 47, 55, 57, 66, 88, **114–19**, 120–1, 123, 286, 305, 317
Mardonios 327
Mars 70, 393
Marsyas 218
Massalia 311
Matapan 235
Mausoleum 94
Medea 157, 363
Megakles 120
Megala Pefka 105
Megalo Lithari 415
MEGALOPOLIS 12, 25, 27–8, 229, 247, 252–3, 261, **264–7**, 268, 271, 278, 281
Megara, Megarian 133, 292
Mehmet Ali 412
Mela, Pomponius 101
Melampous 133
Meleager 141, 351
Melissa 383
Melos 1, 3, 87–8
Memnon 118
Menaichmos 352
Menander 36
Menedemos 332
MENELAION 9, 21, 219, **225–9**, 230
Menelaos 96, 218–19, 225–6, 229
Mercury 413
Merenda 11, 113
Meriones 198
MESSENE 12, 14, 19, 28, 32, 34, 39–40, 237, **246–52**
Messenia, Messenian 2–3, 10, 12, 205, 219, **237**, 239–41, 244–5, 247–8, 250, 261, 276, 286, 301, 316, 323
Metaponton 292
Meter 68, 292
Methana 1
METHONI 237, **240**

Middle Helladic 9, 21, 29, 39, 85, 101, 104, 115, 117–18, 142, 144, 146, 174, 178–9, 187, 198–9, 204, 210, 217, 226, 240, 294, 316, 321, 332, 337, 341, 362–3, 371, 374
MIDEA 10, 174, 179, 198, 200, **202–5**
Mieza 431
Mikalitsi 376
Miltiades 115, 286
mines 3, 45, 101, 104–5, 109–10, 305, 379, 419
Minoan 9, 29, 86, 89, 93, 146, 215, 219, 242, 246, 317, 325
Minos 146
Minyas 10, 321, 323
Mithradates VI 14, 46, 93, 95, 316, 319, 332
Mnaseas 206
Mnesikles 48, 50, 52
Mnesistrate 111
Modon 240
Moesia 395
Molossian 375, 378–9
Monemvasia 231–2
Moschato 94
Mounychia 91, 94
Mousterian 377
Mucianus, Licinius 44
Mummius, Lucius 150
Munich 147–8
Muses 212, 214, 249, 295, 440
MYCENAE 9, 10, 18, 20–1, 23, 29, 39–40, 43, 84–6, 91, 142, 174, **178–87**, 195, 198–200, 204, 229, 241–2, 315, 323, 324
Mycenaean 3, 5, 9, 12, 18, 21, 29–30, 37–42, 45, 47, 50, 65, 71, 85–6, 89, 93, 101, 104, 114, 117–18, 136, 140, 143–4, 146, 149, 159, 174, 179, 186, 187, 195, 198–9, 202, 204, 210–11, 215, 219, 222, 225–6, 229–32, 237–42, 244–5, 253–4, 284, 296–8, 300–2, 315–17, 321, 323–5, 330–1, 337, 342, 354–5, 359–60, 362–4, 374, 384, 394, 404
Myrrhine 87
Myrrhinous 11, 113
mysteries 33, 72, 136–7, 159, 206–7, 268–9, 432

Nabis 220
NAFPLION 29, 182, **197–9**, 200, 202, 204
Naia 379
Naples 126
Naukratis 143
Naupaktos 286, 342
Navarino 237–8, 241
Naxos, Naxian 3, 305, 314
NEA ANCHIALOS 17, 34, **372–3**, 419; see also Phthiotic Thebes
Nea Makri 115, 117, 119
Neanderthal 358, 377–8
Neapolis, Lakonia 219
Neapolis, Macedonia 412
Near East 11, 338
NEKYOMANTEION OF EPHYRA 33, 375–6, **382–4**
Neleus 241
NEMEA 33, 35, **174–8**, 187, 190, 191
Nemesis 99, 119–20, 122–3
Neolithic 5, 8–9, 18, 20–1, 29, 47, 65, 85, 115, 117, 142, 144, 150, 198, 214–15, 219, 233–4, 241, 253, 324, 358, 360, 362–3, 365–7, 370, 374, 394, 415, 429
Neptune 393, 413
Nereus 57
Nero 15, 56, 159, 167, 195, 285–6, 289, 291, 304, 316
Nestor 241, 244–5

Nestorios 137
Nestos 3
Nichoria 237–8
Nikandre 86
Nikeratos 39, 94
Nikias, Athenian general 109
Nikias, *choregos* 48, 65
Nikomedia 88, 372
Nikon 126
NIKOPOLIS 14, 16, 19, 24, 36, 342–3, 348, 351, 375, 379, 381, 387, **389–93**
Nisyros 1
nymphaion 24, 192, 209, 218, 286, 292, 390, 392, 432; see also fountain
Nymphs 64, 173

Octavia 151
Octavian 389, 392–3; see also Augustus
odeion 36, 63–4, 70–1, 157, 191, 296, 387, 390–2, 398, 422, 443
Odysseus 7, 155, 187, 198, 383, 404
Oedipus 315
Oineus 350
OINIADAI 342, **345–7**
Oinomaos 287
OLYMPIA 10–11, 14–15, 17, 19–20, 23–4, 27–8, 32–5, 43, 56–7, 88, 175, 177, **284–94**, 382
Olympos 30–1, 57, 358, 394, 439–41
OLYNTHOS 22, 24, **400–3**, 429
Onochonos 358
Opheltes 175, 177
Ophis 259
oracle 11, 33, 42, 123, 133, 154, 168, 177, 193, 236, 254, 285, 301–3, 304, 310, 314, 327, 375–6, 378–9, 383
ORCHOMENOS (Arkadia) 253, **261–3**
ORCHOMENOS (Boiotia) 10, 39, 301, 315–16, **321–3**, 324
Oropos, Oropian 123–4, 126
Orthagorid 171
Ossa 358
Ostrogoths 390
Othrys 358
Ottoman 15, 158, 398, 405, 412

Pagasai 368–70
palace 3, 5, 9–10, 18, 21, 23, 25, 29, 45, 47, 66, 70, 86, 88, 174, 179, 182, 184–5, 199–200, 202, 204, 215, 219, 226, 229, 237–8, 241–2, 244–5, 298, 301, 305, 315–17, 321, 325, 340, 363, 369, 372, 383, 390, 396–7, 399, 419, 428, 431, 433, 435–6; see also villa
Palaeolithic 8, 20, 198, 331, 358, 360, 376–8, 419
Palaimon 159, 161
Palaiokastro 253–4
Palaiopyrgi 231
palaistra 28, 111, 192, 197, 207, 287, 313, 408, 416; see also athletics
Paleochoria 239
Pamisos 237, 358
Pamphile 84
Pan 64, 88, 115, 117, 253, 423, 429
Panachaikon 284, 296
Panakton 131
Panama 167
Panathenaia, Panathenaic 35, 47–8, 57–8, 76, 78, 82, 90, 334
Panayia Acheiropoietos 399
Panchares 94
Pandrosos 53
Pangaion 407, 419

Index

Panhellenion 16, 46, 136, 138
Pantainos 71, 74
Parmenon 423
Parnon 219
Paros 3, 148, 419, 422
Parthia, Parthian 56, 154
PATRAS 15, 36, 284, **296–7**, 352
Patroklos 218
Paul 16, 58, 150, 154, 157, 163, 396, 413, 415, 418–19, 434
Paulus, Lucius Aemilius 42–3, 309, 387, 411, 428
Pausanias 25, 42–3, 48–50, 52, 56–7, 60–1, 63–4, 66, 68, 70–4, 78–9, 88, 96, 101, 109, 122–4, 126, 131, 133, 138, 142, 154–5, 157, 161–3, 165, 173, 175, 180, 186, 193, 195, 198, 199, 206, 209–10, 213–14, 218, 220–3, 229, 231–2, 236, 240, 248–9, 252, 254–6, 259, 261, 263–6, 268–71, 274, 276–8, 280–1, 284–7, 289, 291–6, 298–300, 302, 304–5, 310, 316, 319, 321, 342, 352, 383, 420, 439
Pausias 173, 433
PEFKAKIA 359, **370–1**
Pegasos 159, 404
Peirene 151, 154–5, 159
Peirithoos 287
Peisistratos, Peisistratid 46, 50, 52, 77, 115, 136, 138, 140, 304, 327
Pelion 358, 374
PELLA 12, 22–3, 25, 28, 39, 394–5, **428–31**, 435
PELLANA 219, **229–30**
Pelopidas 301
Peloponnese 2, 4, 9, 11, 13–14, 133, 149, 159, 170, 177, 187, 212, 219–20, 232, 234, 241, 253–5, 263, 268, 284–7, 291, 294, 296, 302
Peloponnesian War 12, 19, 47, 50, 121, 220, 255, 286, 343, 407
Pelops 287, 292–3
Peneios 3, 294–5, 358
Penelope 155, 404
Pentelikon 3, 45, 148
Penthesileia 218
PERACHORA 23, 32–3, 89, 149, **167–71**
Perati 114
Pergamon 13, 46, 64, 431; see also Attalos, Eumenes
Periander 11, 150, 167, 383
Perikles 12, 39, 46–7, 54, 91, 138, 346
Periphlegethon 383
PERISTERIA 9, 39, 237, 244, **245–6**
Perseia 43
Persephone 31, 87, 136, 138, 383–4, 437; see also Kore
Perseus, hero 141
Perseus, Macedonian king 14, 309, 370, 375, 394, 411, 435, 445
Persia, Persians 3, 11–12, 19, 27, 46–8, 52, 55–7, 65, 95–6, 114–15, 117–18, 136, 138, 143, 147, 180, 212, 222, 226, 286, 302–3, 307, 309–11, 315, 317, 321, 329, 332, 334, 336, 358, 394, 429, 432
Peter, bishop of Phthiotic Thebes 373
Petralona Cave 8, 377
Petromagoula 360
Phaidra 212, 214
Phaidros 63
Phaithon 154
Pharsalos 314, 359
Pheidias 50, 54–5, 61, 87, 94, 123, 285–7, 290
Pheidippides 117
Pheidon 187
Pherai 359, 368–9; see also Velestino

PHIGALEIA 253, 271, **274**
Philinus, Gnaeus Babbius 151
Philip II 12, 131, 175, 187, 267, 285, 293, 304, 316–19, 321, 330, 359, 369, 394–6, 401, 405, 407, 413, 415, 432, 434–9
Philip V 13–14, 119, 276, 278–9, 346–7, 354–6, 369, 372, 445
PHILIPPI 15–17, 24, 28, 34, 395, 412, **413–19**
Philon 94, 140
Philopappos, Gaius Julius Antiochus 40, 60–1
Philopoimen 13, 265, 281
Philostratus 64, 78, 115, 157
Philoxenos 84
Phoenician 96
Phokis, Phokian 301, 304, 309
Phrasikleia 41, 87
Phrontis 96, 100
Phrygia, Phrygian 73
Phthiotic Thebes 359, 372–3; see also Nea Anchialos
Phthiotis 374
Phylakos 311
PHYLE 19, 45, **127–31**
Pieria 435, 440
Pindar 327
Pindos 2, 358, 375, 377
PIRAEUS 12, 19, 39, **91–5**, 143
Pisa 284, 289–90
Piso, Lucius Calpurnius 407
Pitsa 89
PLATAIA, Plataians 11, 19, 38–9, 115, 117–18, 180, 212, 255, 274, 301, 304, 309, 316, **317–19**, 321
Plato 37, 378
PLEURON 14, 19, 23, 342, **347–50**
Pliny the Elder 213, 389
Plutarch 37, 48, 55, 60, 80, 155, 212, 219, 314, 318–19, 320, 327, 432, 435
Polemo 141
Polemokrates 218
Polla, Pompeia 231
Polybius 230, 263, 265, 278–80, 298, 347, 354, 369, 382, 440
Polydeukes 190, 221, 351
Polydeukion 39, 88, 113, 115, 118, 218, 254, 331; see also Herodes Atticus
Polygnotos 49, 311
Polykleitos 88, 195, 206, 209, 297
Polynikes 315
Polyphemos 141, 187
Polyxenos 94
Polyzalos 314
Portunus 159; see also Palaimon
Poseidon 1, 29–31, 52–3, 56, 87–8, 96–7, 99, 161–3, 165, 235–6, 254, 423
Posidippos 317
Potnia 30
Praxiteles 50, 88, 286
Prima, Herennia 441
Priscus Juventianus, Publius Licinius 161
prison 68, 72, 240, 413, 415
Prodromos 360
Proitos 263, 265
Prokonnesos 34
Proserpina 140; see also Kore, Persephone
Protoattic 89, 141, 144
Protogeometric 79–80, 89, 101, 144, 199, 338, 341, 360
Prusias II 309
prytaneion 25, 294, 382, 387
Psamathous 235
PTOION 301, 316, **326–9**

Ptolemies 13
Ptolemy II 291
Ptolemy IV 126
Ptolis 259
Puaux, René 240
Pulcher, Appius Claudius 126, 140
Pulcher, Claudius 140
Punjab 13
Pydna 309, 387, 411, 428
PYLOS **238–40**
PYLOS PALACE 9–10, 18, 21, 29–30, 39, 86, 179, 200, 219, 226, 229, 237, **241–5**, 315
Pyrasos 372
Pyrrhos 13, 375–6, 379, 382
Pythia, Pythian 302, 305, 310, 396
Python 305

quarry 3, 34, 177, 219, 235, 299, 330, 425

Regilla 64, 118, 151, 155, 286, 292
Remus 68
Rex, Marcius 140
Rhadamanthys 432
RHAMNOUS 12, 19, 45, 88, 99, **119–23**
Rhea 78, 292
Rheneia 144
Rhitsona 316
Rhodes, Rhodian 93, 126
roads 39, 65, 80, 82, 94, 131, 138, 151, 154, 162, 165, 229–30, 296, 302, 319, 329, 335, 392, 395, 407, 416, 434; *see also* Via Egnatia
Roma 48, 54
Rome, Roman 5, 13–17, 20, 22–4, 26, 33–4, 36, 38, 42–4, 46, 48, 61, 66, 68, 70, 76–8, 80, 87–8, 91, 94–5, 115, 124, 128, 136, 138–41, 146–7, 150–1, 153–4, 158–9, 161, 165–6, 168, 173–4, 187–8, 190, 197, 205, 207, 209, 211–12, 214, 217–18, 220–3, 226, 233, 235, 238–9, 247–8, 250, 252–4, 265–7, 282, 284–5, 287, 289, 291–2, 294–7, 301, 304, 309–11, 314, 316, 319–21, 323, 328, 330–2, 335–7, 342–6, 355, 359, 362, 369–70, 372–6, 379, 381, 384, 387, 389–90, 393–9, 407–8, 411–13, 415, 419–20, 422, 425, 428–9, 434–5, 440–1, 443, 444
Romulus 68
Routsi 244
Roxane 439

St John the Baptist 384
Sakai 117
Sakovouni 253
Salamis 3, 11, 87, 96, 143, 147, 212, 304
Samos 78, 84, 336
sanctuary 28–34 and *passim*
sanitation 24, 441; *see also* drains, water supply
Sarakatsani 7
Sarmatia, Sarmatian 136
Saronic Gulf 93, 142, 159, 205, 212
Sassanian 397
Schliemann, Heinrich 91, 180, 226, 241, 321, 323
Schliemann, Sophie 85
Scythia, Scythians 117
Sea Peoples 10
Seleukids 13
Seleukos I 60
Selinous 292
Selymbria 84
Semitic 10
Seneca the Younger 425
Serapis 190
Serdica 397

SESKLO 5, 8–9, 18, 20, 85, 359, 363, **365–7**
Severan 88
shipshed 12, 94–6, 100, 165, 346–7
Sibyl 305
Sicily 285, 292, 330, 378
SIKYON 25, 27–8, 42, 89, 149, 159, **171–3**, 292, 298, 305, 314
Silen 423
Simonides 330
Sindos 40, 399, **400**
Siphnos, Siphnian 3, 305, 314
Sirmium 118
Sithonia 404
Skopas, Aitolian general 440
Skopas, Parian sculptor 255–6, 281
slave, slavery 12, 87, 104, 109, 150–1, 158, 168, 309, 345–6, 372, 375, 401, 404, 407–8, 441
Slavs 17, 46, 66, 187, 241, 286, 302, 372, 390, 396, 407
Society of Travellers 273
Socrates 68, 428
Soidas 352
Solon 37, 46, 136, 140
Sophocles 35, 61, 163, 315, 378, 432
Soros 118–19
Sosikrates 84
Sospes, Antonius 155
Sostratos 143
Souliot 389
SOUNION 12, 50, 71, 86–7, **96–9**
Soureza 110
Spain 9
SPARTA, Spartan 1–3, 6, 11–13, 16–17, 19–20, 27–8, 30, 42, 46, 80, 82, 88–9, 95, 101, 109, 117, 128, 133, 150, 168, 171, 174, 187, 212–13, 219, **220–5**, 229–30, 232–3, 235, 237–8, 247, 253–5, 259, 261, 265, 268, 274, 280, 294, 304–5, 310, 316–17, 329, 343, 405, 407
speaker's platform 14, 60, 63, 153, 393, 416
Spercheios 3, 329, 374
Sphakteria 238
stadium 28, 35–6, 78–9, 126, 161–2, 173, 175, 177, 207, 214, 250, 291, 311, 370, 392; *see also* athletics
Statius 350
stoa 27 and *passim*
Stoics 27
Strabo 158, 165, 168, 187, 237–8, 285, 324, 332, 348, 375, 392, 395
STRATOS 3, 14, 342, **343–5**
Strymon 3, 394, 407, 411
Styx 36, 383
Submycenaean 79–80, 199–200, 294, 338
Suleiman the Magnificent 412
Sulla, Lucius Cornelius 46, 78, 82, 93–4, 126, 128, 205, 285, 304, 316, 319
Sybaris 292
Syracuse 292
Syria, Syrian 15, 163, 332

TAINARON 220, **234–6**, 271
Tanagra 37, 44, 317
Taygetos 1–2, 219, 225, 229
TEGEA 88, 177, 253, **254–8**, 270
Teiresias 383–4
Telemachos of Epidauros 64
Telemachos, son of Odysseus 219
Telephos 255–6
Telesikles 419
Temenos, Temenid 394–5
Tempe 358

temple 28–34 and *passim*
Tetrarchs 88
Thasopoula 423
THASOS 7, 19, 27–8, 412–13, **419–27**; *see also* Aliki
Theagenes 420, 422
theatre 35–6 and *passim*
THEBES, Thebans 10, 12, 14–15, 18, 37, 39, 41, 128, 131, 159, 173, 220, 249, 283, 301, **315–17**, 319, 321, 323, 325, 327
Themis 64, 88, 119–20, 123, 382
Themison 163
Themistokles 77, 82, 91, 95, 109, 143
Theocharis, Dimitrios 365
Theodoros 311
Theodosius I 17, 396–7
Theodosius II 70
Theogenes 117
Theoitas 146, 148
Theopetra Cave 358
Theophrastus 6
Theoroi 422
Thera 1, 89
Therapne 225–6
Thermaic Gulf 394
Therme 396, 399
THERMON 13, 27, 31, 33, 89, 342, 352, **353–7**
THERMOPYLAI 2, 180, 319, **329–30**
Thersilochos 423
Theseus 45, 68, 77, 99, 212, 287, 305, 332, 336–7, 351, 429
Thespiai 301, 316, 329
Thesproti 383
Thessalonike, queen 396, 399
THESSALONIKI 2, 16, 23, 38, 40, 361, 390, **395–400**, 405, 419, 425, 429, 434, 438
Thessaly, Thessalian 2–3, 5, 7, 14, 19, 25, 205, 310, **358–9**, 360–1, 367–72, 375, 394, 440
Thirty Tyrants 60
tholos 66, 68, 70, 171, 206–7, 209, 282, 311, 314, 435
tholos tomb 9, 39–40, 86, 104, 115, 118, 179, 185–6, 198, 202, 204, 219, 230–1, 237, 239–41, 244–5, 321, 323, 342, 359, 363–4
THORIKOS 45, 61, **101–4**, 109
Thrace, Thracian 1, 7, 90, 400, 407–8, 411–12, 419
Thrasyboulos 128
Thrasykles 64
Thrasyllos 64
Thrasymedes 209, 240
Thucydides 39, 45, 56, 77, 79, 119, 220, 235, 238, 342–3, 346, 405, 407, 428
Thyreatis 217
Tiberius 233, 250, 285
Timotheus 163
Timotheus, Aulus Kapreilius 408
TIRYNS 9–10, 18, 20–1, 23, 29, 86, 174, 179, 195, 198, **199–202**, 204, 242, 310, 315, 321
Titus 286, 332
Tivoli 218, 289, 392
tomb 36–42 and *passim*; *see also* 'Macedonian' tomb, tholos tomb
TORONE **404–7**
Tourliditsa 239
Tragana 244

treasury 10, 33, 43, 52, 54, 57, 86, 177, 179–80, 184, 186, 285–6, 292, 302, 305, 309, 311, 321, 323
Triphylia 274
TRIPOLIS 218, **253–4**, 261
Triptolemos 72, 87, 136
Triton 44, 57, 70, 74, 162
Tritopatres 84
TROIZEN 174, **212–14**
Troy, Trojan 40, 43, 50, 56, 85, 88, 91, 147, 180, 187, 195, 244, 321
Tsepi 115, 117, 119
Tsopani-Rachi 239
Tsoungiza 175–6
Tsountas, Christos 231, 362, 365
Turkey, Turkish 8, 11, 52, 54, 240, 412
Turner, William 96
Tyche 300, 441, 443; *see also* Fortune
Tydeus 350
Tyrtaios 237

Valens, Gaius Valerius 150
Valerian 78, 141
Vandals 390
VAPHEIO 9, 39, 86, 219, 229, **231**
Velatouri 101, 104
VELESTINO 360, **367–9**; *see also* Pherai
Venice, Venetian 54, 240, 309
Venus 153
VERGINA 12, 23, 40, 394, 400, **434–8**, 438
VEROIA 395, **434**
Verus, Lucius 154
Vespasian 223
Via Egnatia 15, 395–6, 407, 413, 416, 419
Victorinus 151
Victory 286, 416
villa 23, 45, 72, 174, 217–18, 254, 289, 292, 433, 441, 444
Virgin Mary 48, 359
Vitruvius 22, 56, 58, 78
Vitsa 376
Vlachopoulo 239
Vlachs 7
Vlichada 233
VOIDOKOILIA 39, 239, **240–1**
Voidomatis 378
Volimidia 244
VOLOS 39, 41, **359–61**, 363, 370

water supply 3–4, 18, 23–4, 28, 33, 105, 109, 170, 184, 191–2, 202, 215, 234, 237, 253, 281, 285, 292, 327, 348, 358, 366, 375, 392, 398, 403, 412, 441; *see also* aqueduct, bath, cistern, fountain, nymphaion, sanitation

Xenophon 128, 133, 168
Xerxes I 11, 63, 117, 329
xystos 287, 350; *see also* athletics

Zarax 44
Zea 91, 94–5
Zeno 27
Zeus 28, 30–1, 42–3, 56, 60, 66, 70, 78, 88, 123, 175–7, 195, 259, 284–7, 290–2, 299–300, 317, 331, 343–5, 351, 369, 376, 378, 381–2, 387, 422–3, 440–1, 443
Zeuxis 428